THE CHOSEN INSTRUMENT

MARYLIN BENDER

and

SELIG ALTSCHUL

Pan Am

Juan Trippe

The Rise and Fall
of an
American Entrepreneur

SIMON AND SCHUSTER
NEW YORK

Copyright © 1982 by Marylin Bender and Selig Altschul
All rights reserved
including the right of reproduction
in whole or in part in any form
Published by Simon and Schuster
A Division of Gulf & Western Corporation
Simon & Schuster Building
Rockefeller Center
1230 Avenue of the Americas
New York, New York 10020
SIMON AND SCHUSTER and colophon
are trademarks of Simon & Schuster
Designed by Edith Fowler
Manufactured in the United States of America

10 9 8 7 6 5 4 3 2 1

Library of Congress Cataloging in Publication Data

Bender, Marylin.
  Chosen instrument.

  Bibliography: p.
  Includes index.
  1. Pan American World Airways, inc.—History.
2. Trippe, J. T. (Juan Terry), 1899–   . 3. Business-
men—United States—Biography. I. Altschul, Selig.
II. Title.
HE9803.P36B46   387.7'065'73   81–21427
ISBN 0–671–22464–6   AACR2

TO JAMES ALTSCHUL

Contents

Prologue

November 10, 1943. A cold, windy day in Washington, auguring an early wartime winter. President Franklin Delano Roosevelt called a meeting at 2 P.M. in the Oval Office. The session was to be fairly brief because he intended to go to the airport within the hour to welcome Secretary of State Cordell Hull back from Moscow, where he had conferred with the foreign ministers of the U.S.S.R., Great Britain and China. The press was speculating that the President might soon hold a rendezvous with Prime Minister Winston Churchill and Premier Joseph Stalin.

The President was looking jaunty; his mood was hopeful. The war was then at midpoint, although all he could have known for sure was that the turning had been reached against the Axis Powers. Two days earlier, U.S. Army troops had landed on Bougainville, the last Japanese base in the Solomon Islands, loosening a barrier for the advance toward Tokyo through the Pacific.

The Battle of the Atlantic was won, the German submarine menace contained. The Mediterranean was open to the ships of the Allies, and the continent of Africa lay under their control. Italy had surrendered in September, and while Nazi forces were putting up ferocious resistance north of Naples, American planes were raining bombs on Cologne and Düsseldorf. The Red Army had just recaptured Kiev, capital of the Soviet Ukraine. "Victory is near," announced Stalin, displaying his new marshal's uniform. "The complete ousting of the Fascist invader is at hand."

It was taken for granted that an Anglo-American invasion of Western Europe would be mounted in the spring. The war had reached a stage, said Lord Halifax, the British Ambassador to Washington, "where anything may happen." *The New York Times* cautioned that "the hardest job is still ahead."

Still, it was not too early to be talking of peace and to be shaping the postwar world. At Moscow, the foreign ministers had declared the need for a United Nations Organization to replace the impotent League of Nations.

The President had called the meeting to discuss policy for international civil aviation, a matter that would have "a greater influence on American foreign interests and American foreign policy than any other non-political consideration." Assistant Secretary of State Adolph A. Berle, Jr., said so in a memorandum to Hull, and none of those present quarreled with that view. Sea power had been the determining factor since the founding of the nation. Air power would be the decisive element for the rest of the twentieth century.

During the past two years reports had been issued by several executive departments, and lobbyists for special interests had maneuvered for the White House's attention, but no official policy had been set. "This air business," Berle commented, "is getting to be almost as much of a war as the European war."

Adolph Berle was a small, abrasive man of giant intellect. A former law professor and a member of Roosevelt's "Brains Trust" at the onset of the New Deal, he had been, since 1941, the State Department's aviation guru. He was dissatisfied with the department's handling of aviation, both in respect to Pan American Airways, the airline that had a monopoly of foreign routes, and as regarded the British, the main competitor of the United States for commercial air supremacy after the war. He believed that the "dunderheads" at State had left the U.S. flank uncovered while the number one ally proceeded to apportion the air lanes to its advantage. Berle prevailed on Hull, who got the President to agree, to let him assemble an Interdepartmental Advisory Committee on Aviation. Some of its members were gathered around the President's desk.

Robert A. Lovett, Assistant Secretary of War for Air, was a former Yale football hero (Phi Beta Kappa and Skull and Bones), a naval aviator in the First World War, a partner in the Wall Street investment-banking firm of Brown Brothers, Harriman and, for the last three years, a public servant.

L. Welch Pogue, chairman of the Civil Aeronautics Board, the agency Congress had created in 1938 to regulate the chaotic air transport industry, was a lawyer who never let anyone forget he was just a country boy from Iowa.

Edward R. Stettinius, Jr., Under Secretary of State, was Acting Secretary in Hull's absence. Prematurely silver-haired and tirelessly affable, this former chairman of the United States Steel Corporation had answered the President's call in 1940, signing on as Director of Priorities in the Office of Production Management. His presence was helpful in negating constant charges that Roosevelt was the enemy of Big Business. Later, after his appointment as Lend-Lease Administrator, Stettinius' prestige had strengthened the controversial program for supplying Britain, China and the U.S.S.R. before the United States entered the war.

Harry L. Hopkins, Special Assistant to the President and his intimate friend, sat apart from the others in a corner of the room. He listened attentively in glowering silence, uttering not a word during the entire meeting.

It began promptly. The President said he had talked about aviation with Prime Minister Churchill when they met at Quebec in August to plan a unified command for the China-Burma-India theater of war. He was going to talk about it again the next time he saw the Prime Minister. Roosevelt acknowledged that the subject was fraught with problems. He had given it considerable thought and had prepared a memorandum of his conclusions.

He began to read it aloud. The Axis Powers would not be allowed any aviation industry whatsoever after they were defeated. No airlines, domestic or foreign. Transportation within Germany, Italy and Japan would be handled by an airline to be formed by the United Nations. International traffic to those areas would be carried by the airlines of Allied and neutral nations.

As for internal aviation in other than conquered states, "each country should own and control its own domestic air service," Roosevelt said. Before the war, the Germans had dominated the air routes of South America, posing a security threat to the United States until steps were taken in late 1940 to banish them. The sole international airline of the United States, Pan American Airways had secretly owned the airline in Colombia and overtly operated the Chinese airline in partnership with the Nationalist Government.

"American international aviation—" the President was saying as the telephone rang on his desk. He listened, and after he hung up, turned to Stettinius. "Ed, you have to get that poor old man out of the air," he said.

A four-engine C-54 was bringing Cordell Hull from San Juan, where he had broken his circuitous journey from Moscow across the South Atlantic and rested overnight. The plane was circling over Washington while those "dunderheads" at State were trying to round up the press corps so that Hull's arrival would be properly noticed. "Now, Ed, that old man is tired, so would you please go out there and see what you can do to land that plane and bring him down," Roosevelt directed the Acting Secretary. Hull was 72 and far from robust. He had traveled 26,000 miles on this, his first excursion by air, and he suffered from claustrophobia.

As soon as Stettinius was on the other side of the door, the President adopted a confidential tone. The scope of U.S. international aviation was too great to be trusted to any one company or pool of companies, he said. "Certain companies—I'm going to speak frankly: Pan American—want all the business. They've done a good job in the war, and maybe that entitles them to a senior place. But Juan Trippe cannot have it all."

He went on to explore suggestions for giving Pan American competition. That was the American way, to have the airlines privately owned and competing for the public's favor. Let the best one win. The government regulated the industry to see that competition did not get out of hand. The Europeans did it differently. Each country chose one airline which it owned, in whole or in part, and made it the instrument of national aviation policy, as Trippe, the president of Pan American Airways, relentlessly called to everyone's attention. Roosevelt was saying he disagreed with that when Stettinius returned. The President went on to the next point: should the U.S. Government own an interest in American overseas airlines?

He had shifted topics smoothly, but the significance was not lost on any man in the room. The President had taken advantage of Stettinius' brief absence to ventilate his feelings about Juan Trippe. Whether he did it out of consideration for Ed's feelings or because he suspected Stettinius might repeat his remarks his listeners could only surmise. Stettinius always went to great pains to disqualify himself from anything to do with Pan American Airways, reiterating that Juan Trippe was his brother-in-law.

The Under Secretary of State made no pretense at hiding the warmth of their personal relationship. The Stettiniuses were a close-knit family. The brothers and sisters and their spouses enjoyed each other's company. The Trippes' youngest child was Ed Stettinius' namesake.

Had he heard them, Stettinius would not have been surprised by the President's comments. He was fully aware of the animosity in Washington toward Pan American Airways and Juan Trippe. "They have the impression you're the Big Bad Wolf," Ed told his brother-in-law.

According to one canard, Trippe had changed his name from John to Juan to win operating rights from South American governments. Truer to the mark was the charge that he exploited his old school ties. Trippe was an archetype of the loyal Old Blue, and Pan American Airways was known as the Yale airline because he had drawn so many alumni into its executive ranks and its board of directors. The Administration was replete with sons of Eli, from Secretary of War Henry L. Stimson, Assistant Secretary of War Lovett and his classmate, Assistant Secretary of the Navy for Air Artemus L. Gates, down to the senior bureaucrats heeding the watch cry, "For God, for Country, and for Yale!"

"Juan Trippe is the most fascinating Yale gangster I ever met," Roosevelt said to one of Trippe's numerous adversaries, in a moment of pique at his maneuvering against the President in Congress, adding that, "In government and in war, you have to use scoundrels."

Roosevelt was, of course, a Harvard man, and he had taken abuse form Yale, a citadel of isolationism that had fostered the America First movement and produced some of his most vociferous critics, such as Republican Senator Robert A. Taft of Ohio and publisher Henry R. Luce. After Luce's candidate, Wendell Willkie, failed in his challenge to Roosevelt's bid for a third term, the founder of *Time* and *Life* proclaimed "the American Century," an imperialistic creed by which corporations like Time/Life and Pan American Airways were to disseminate the free-enterprise system about the globe.

In her maiden speech in the House of Representatives in February, Clare Boothe Luce, the publisher's wife, lashed out against an "open skies" policy for the world's airlines after the war. "Globaloney," she called it, trying to force the Administration not to make it the cornerstone of international aviation policy. Suspicion was rampant that Trippe had much to do with the composition of her speech.

Open versus closed skies, freedom of the air versus the "sovereignty of American skies" that Clare Luce propounded: the debate was fundamental to the struggle to create a common law of aviation, threatening a repetition of the battle waged for hundreds of years to secure freedom of navigation on the seas. Would nationalism restrict rights to the air lanes and access to the airports of various countries, or would open competition be the rule of the skies?

The battle made for strange alliances and permutations of economic philosophies. New Dealers like Berle argued for the widest distribution of commercial air rights and the least regulation of international airlines. Those champions of free enterprise, like the Luces, who regularly attacked Roosevelt for intervening in the economy demanded government protection of the airspace above the United States against the carriers of other nations. As a corollary to this, they espoused a single American airline for foreign service, an imperial instrument of trade.

That was the situation before Pearl Harbor. Only one airline carried the American flag abroad: Pan American Airways, symbol of U.S. economic power all around the world, more pervasive than the Standard Oil tanker. South American Indians who had never seen an automobile recognized the thunderbird with the Stars and Stripes painted on its tail. Chinese coolies on the wharves of Hong Kong waved to the silver-and-blue flying boats skimming across the harbor.

Pan American Airways camouflaged certain preparations the Roosevelt Administration made for war—island bases in the Pacific, airfields covertly built in South America, an airlift of supplies to the British in North Africa. Pan American Airways transported the President in January to Casablanca, where he and Churchill agreed to exact unconditional surrender from the enemies. The airline carried exiled sovereigns and heads of state, military advisers, diplomats and spymasters on their secret missions.

There had been talk of the government's taking over Pan American, but it flickered out. Pan American was more useful with an ambiguous status. Not until many years after the war when official documents were declassified and memoirs published would the nature and extent of Pan American Airways' and Juan Trippe's service to the nation be revealed.

Yet Adolph Berle said, "I do not trust Pan American any farther than I can see it."

Secretary of the Interior Harold L. Ickes maintained, "Trippe is an unscrupulous person who cajoles and buys his way." According to Ickes, the President described Trippe to him as "a man of all-yielding suavity who can be depended upon to pursue his own ruthless way."

Why were there such misgivings about so patriotic a man and his company? Was it the means Trippe had used to acquire the monopoly of the nation's overseas air routes—acting as master politician at home and *éminence grise* of the State Department abroad, the unconfirmed foreign minister of U.S. civil aviation? Or was it the way he had fought to preserve the monopoly, "moving heaven and earth," Berle said, to stamp out competition?

In one decade, Pan American Airways had connected the Americas and bridged the oceans from the air. It had paced the transition from the era of the barnstormer in leather and goggles to that of the scientific cockpit team, and pushed airplane technology from wooden contraptions with muslin-covered wings to sleek metal machines powered by mighty engines.

Trippe was a zealot whose religious faith was commercial air routes, a visionary who saw the future ahead of others and claimed it for Pan American Airways in perpetuity. He was referred to as a robber baron and a buccaneer, albeit a gentleman of the species. His opponents railed at his seductive politeness; strong men were mortified at having been disarmed by the foe's brown eyes and sweetly diabolic smile.

His most disturbing characteristic was his deviousness. "If the front door was open, he would go in by the side window," said an airline chieftain who happened to be his sole supporter.

Every man in the President's office that afternoon had stories to tell about Trippe. Pogue believed that Trippe was trying to undermine the Civil Aeronautics Board one way or another because it was under a mandate to see that he had competition. Recently, Pogue had dined at the F Street Club where he was seated next to General George C. Marshall and heard Trippe's self-serving message pouring from the lips of the Army Chief of Staff. How had Trippe managed something like that when the War Department was fed up with his shenanigans?

Lovett's acquaintance with Trippe went way back, as such things did in the Establishment, to the Hill School and Yale. Several of Lovett's classmates and flying comrades had dealings with Trippe, as large investors and directors of Pan American Airways or as government officials like himself. All were troubled by Trippe's lack of forthrightness. A controversy was bubbling beneath the surface in the War and State Departments over Pan American's handling of the secret airport-development program in Latin America. For reasons of security and sensitive relations with friendly states, the matter had to be kept quiet for the time being. Lovett thought Trippe had outwitted Secretary of War Stimson when the contract was drawn.

Harry Hopkins had been Secretary of Commerce when he first met Trippe as a member of the Business Council, the powerful group of industrialists who had volunteered to give the Administration the benefit of their thinking. Disgruntled persons were forever coming to Hopkins with tales of Trippe's alleged machinations; the President's Special Assistant brushed them aside, saying sharply that he wanted to hear no more on that subject. Yet he said to Ed Stettinius, "I have never liked the idea of Pan American having a world monopoly of our airlines."

Trippe's monopoly. That was something to be settled once and for all before the war was over. The President had obviously made up his mind. Every man in the room was sure that Juan Trippe had made up his mind too.

Part I

INCORPORATING A DREAM

1

A Respectable Beginning

Liverpool, January 1870. Beneath a shield of grime, the dreary city on the Mersey bustled with expectations, a gateway between the Old World and the New, and a haven for migrants with empty stomachs from across the Irish Sea. In the pub of the Washington Hotel, an 18-year-old barmaid held court. Catherine Louise Flynn, answering to the call of Kitty, was a dainty lass with hair of gold, a saucy smile and a bantering way with the patrons, who constituted a motley assortment of local citizens of standing and rogues from far and wide. Two dapper Americans seemed particularly taken with her flirty chatter. They introduced themselves as Henry J. Raymond, a merchant, and Charles H. Wells, "a man of independent fortune."

"Raymond" was an alias for Adam Worth, a rapscallion of inordinate gall and a puckish sense of humor. He had borrowed the name of no less a pillar of society than the publisher of *The New York Times*, regarding it, perhaps, as loose currency inasmuch as the eminent Henry Jarvis Raymond had suddenly died that year after suffering a heart attack while paying a visit to a young actress. "Wells's" legal name was Charles W. Bullard; his underworld sobriquet, "Piano Charley." Had he not been such an accomplished thief, he might have earned a livelihood as a musician.

Both men were wanted for robbing the Boylston National Bank in Boston, a crime perpetrated with imagination and strategic planning. Posing as "William A. Judson," Bullard had bought out a barbershop in a building adjacent to the bank and set up a sham business in wine bitters. During a period of several weeks, Bullard, Worth and three accomplices had gradually dug through the common wall into the bank. Under cover of a stormy night, they entered, blew open the iron safe and escaped with more than $400,000 in cash and bonds. They fled to New York, and by the time the police picked up their trail, they were on a ship bound for England.

Worth was more intelligent and stable than Bullard, his reputation glossier. The chief of detectives of the New York Police considered him "The Prince of Safemen"; a superintendent of Scotland Yard dubbed him the "Napoleon of Crime." He would gross over $4 million in a lifelong career of chicanery, be arrested only twice and spend less than seven years behind bars.

Bullard was the more cultivated scoundrel. Fluent in French and German besides being musically gifted, he was also more careless and less fortunate. He was to become familiar with the interiors of numerous jails on both sides of the Atlantic and languish for nearly two decades in a Belgian prison.

The black sheep of an old New York family that claimed descent from an aide of George Washington, Bullard had run through a legacy from his father and turned to crime to support his gentleman's habits. With several bank and train robberies to his credit, he established his fame as a daring bandit when he and two associates relieved a messenger of the Merchants Union Express Company of $100,000 en route from Buffalo to New York by train. The police caught up with Bullard in Toronto and had him extradited to a jail in White Plains, New York, where friends burrowed through the wall to retrieve him.

No ordinary felons, Worth and Bullard employed a cerebral approach to crime, eschewing bloodshed and any methods more brutal than a tap on the head to render a bank guard temporarily ineffectual. They were gentlemen crooks. Stealing was simply the most convenient means of gratifying their expensive appetites.

It is not surprising that two such smoothies would turn the head of a winsome barmaid, since she had ambitions of elevating herself beyond her humble station. The curly-haired and moody Bullard had the romantic advantage over his short and rather wistful partner. He swept Kitty Flynn off her feet, and six weeks after they met, they were married in a grand ceremony and reception at the hotel. Worth was best man. Mr. and Mrs. Charles Wells, so called, spent a lingering honeymoon in Paris, where they set up housekeeping in a style of champagne and roses. Worth, the self-styled merchant, moved his headquarters to London, establishing himself as a purchaser of stolen goods.

Parisian gaiety was interrupted in July by the Franco–Prussian War. Kitty and Charley hopped back to Liverpool, where he opened a

wine cellar. Their first child, Lucy Adeline, was born in October. A
year or so later, the siege of the Commune ended and, the Third
Republic in working order, they returned to the French capital. Had it
been the next century of the airplane, society columnists would have
called them jet-setters.

The 1870s were one of the golden ages of American expatriatism
that followed on the nation's great wars. The Civil War had released a
furious energy for building and acquisition. The Western frontier was
pushed back, railroads laid across the continent, mineral resources
tapped, and a country of farmers began to be transformed into one of
manufacturers. The new spirit of materialism was matched by a crumbling morality in government and business; acts of economic aggression and banditry were sanctioned and even admired.

Some of the newly wealthy moved across the Atlantic, questing
after European pleasures and refinements, and for marriage partners.
Segments of Boston and New York society and pampered stragglers
from west of the Hudson set up colonies on the Continent, where they
mingled with Russians and other cosmopolitan exiles. Some bought
their way into the native aristocracy.

Not all Americans abroad were industrialists, dollar princesses,
artists and dilettantes such as inhabited the novels of Henry James.
Some of the most captivating riders on the London–Paris–Rome expatriate circuit were burglars, forgers, confidence men and gamblers,
who knew exactly which crimes could be chased by extradition across
an ocean. The long arm of United States law could not reach bank
robbers on the banks of the Thames or the Seine.

Kitty always maintained that she had been an innocent girl de-
ceived by a cad; and she may indeed have been a Liverpudlian Daisy
Miller corrupted by a handsome Yankee. Surely, her suspicions about
her "millionaire" husband and his friends must have been aroused
when he and Worth announced that they were going to open a night
spot in Paris. They selected quarters near the Grand Hotel in the Rue
Scribe—and furnished the American Bar as a small mirrored palace of
mahogany and crystal. A well-stocked wine cellar, a dining room
catered by a first-class chef and a reading room containing a file of
American publications for homesick browsers occupied the first floor. A
flight above was the profit center, a gambling salon where the popular
game of faro was dealt to a glittering clientele of tourists and businessmen.

If Kitty had any qualms about the venture, they did not inhibit
her from acting as hostess of the American Bar, which immediately
became one of the most frequented nesting places for wanderers from
the United States. Kitty had an ear for accents and inflections, and

easily mimicked the social graces. Charley tutored her in the art of masquerade. To William Pinkerton, a private detective from America who turned up at the restaurant on the trail of Worth and Bullard, Kitty appeared as "a beautiful woman and a brilliant conversationalist who dressed in the height of fashion. Her company was sought by almost all the patrons of the house . . ."

The thriving business lasted for about a year and a half. Though Bullard and Worth were beyond the clutches of American police, their extravagant habits and the capital expenses of their trade had them constantly in need of large sums of cash. The palms of the Paris police had to be greased. On one occasion, they stole a bag of gems from a diamond merchant while he was trying his luck at their faro table, using the classic ruse of switching it for another parcel stuffed with paper. Though they managed to evade prosecution for the theft, the publicity forced the police to close down their establishment. The partners moved to London. In August 1877, Kitty gave birth in Brighton to a second daughter, Katherine Louise. Bullard, by then, had vanished.

Shortly after Louise was born, Kitty sailed for New York in pursuit of her errant spouse, only to find that Charley had been arrested and taken to Boston to stand trial for the Boylston Bank robbery. He pleaded guilty and was sentenced to twenty years in prison. Impatient as usual, he escaped from the Concord Jail in 1878 and headed for Canada and thence for Belgium, where he was again incarcerated for bank robbery. To complete her disillusionment, Kitty learned that Charley had a wife and children in the United States.

She had managed to save a few hundred dollars, the jewelry Charley had bestowed upon her and art objects salvaged from the American Bar. With this hoard, Kitty opened a boardinghouse in Brooklyn, calling herself Mrs. Kate Flynn.

It was a proper way for a recently bereaved widow to support herself and her daughters. She could rent furnished rooms on the upper floors to single "gentlemen" and let out the parlor rooms for card parties, small dances, lovers' trysts and private dinners for businessmen. A glib sophisticate like the widow Flynn could develop a fashionable clientele and a reputation as an influence peddler and go-between in financial deals hatched within her walls. For every stock subscription she pushed she collected a broker's commission, sub rosa, in cash.

Into Kate's parlor there entered one day exactly the kind of man she thought she had married in Liverpool. Juan Pedro Terry, blue-eyed, dark-haired and 30, was a genuine nabob. His father, Tomaso Terry, a Venezuelan of Irish extraction, had left his native land in the 1830s for Cuba, where, through various acts of business prudence and political agility, he had become the largest sugar planter in the area of

Cienfuegos and one of the wealthiest men in the Americas. He and his devoutly Catholic wife, Teresa, and their dozen children were sybarites of the first order. Though the source of their wealth was Cuban, they had assumed United States citizenship, but generally preferred habitats in France and Italy. The Terrys owned houses in New York and a mansion in Paris on the Rue de la Boétie, in prime expatriate territory off the Faubourg Saint-Honoré, and dwelt also in several castles of the Loire Valley, including, for a while, the magnificent Château de Chenonceau.

Most of the children took advances against their shares of Tomaso's estate; Juan siphoned off nearly $1.8 million, part of which he invested astutely in New York. According to a newspaper report, he was distinguished "for his business ability, although he is also fond of a life of luxury and pleasure."

Kate Flynn was unusually experienced in the latter regard, and that may explain how she was able to stage one of the most brilliant matrimonial coups of the year 1881. She and Juan Terry were wed in a judge's chambers at the Jefferson Market Courthouse in Manhattan.

Kate's checkered history, once it leaked out, did not compromise her social standing. There was a certain novelty to the case of "the beautiful barmaid and the bigamous burglar," as the newspapers reveled in recounting it. It set Kate apart from other parvenus scrambling for entry into New York society, which had not yet been limited to four hundred families by Ward McAllister.

The 1880s were years of social ferment from which emerged many of the institutions that defined the structure of the American upper class—restrictive institutions such as the country club and the boarding school for boys patterned after the British public schools of Eton and Harrow, and genealogical societies like the Sons of the American Revolution. But during the early eighties anything was still possible—if not in Boston, then certainly in New York, where yesterday's barmaid could qualify as a social leader.

Though apparently he did not adopt them legally, Juan Terry permitted Kate's daughters to use his name and saw that they were properly educated, with private lessons in the arts and sojourns in schools in New York and on the Continent in keeping with their rich-gypsy existence.

The Juan Terrys were living in Paris, Kate pregnant with their first child, when Tomaso died there on July 5, 1886, leaving a fortune estimated at $50 million to be divided, subject to the amounts already advanced, among his eight surviving children. Less than half the estate was based in the United States. Deducting what he had already drawn, Juan should have inherited about $6 million. Whatever the sum, he did not live to either waste or magnify it. On October 17, he died in Menton. His will, written a month before his death to dispose of what had accrued to him from his father, bequeathed one-fifth of his estate to Kate. The rest was placed in trust for their unborn child to be invested in first-class securities, preferably U.S. Government bonds, so that Kate would have the use of it during the child's minority. There was no mention in the will of Lucy Adeline or Katherine Louise.

A few months after Juan Terry's death, Kate gave birth in Paris to a baby girl whom she had christened Juanita Teresa Terry. Now a bona fide widow and a wealthy one at that, Kate moved back and forth across the Atlantic. She kept her brood together under the Terry banner, maintaining a close relationship with her brothers-in-law Emilio and Francisco Terry, executors of their father's estate. Her daughters were together in Paris when Kate died of Bright's disease in New York on March 13, 1894.

She had been a tormented woman, squandering money on finery and whims. What she did with the considerable fortune Juan Terry left remains a mystery, for when her estate was accounted for, there was less than $5,000 to be divided between Lucy Adeline and Katherine Louise. In her will, Kate left nothing to 8-year-old Juanita, pointing out that "she is already well provided for."

When the three orphans arrived in New York in response to a cable from their mother's physician, Lucy took charge of Kate's affairs. The Surrogate appointed her Juanita's guardian. At 23, Lucy was strong-willed and determined to erase her quirky heritage. She longed for respectability. Her first administrative act was to have Kate interred in a Terry Family mausoleum in Green-Wood Cemetery, an elaborately rural graveyard in Brooklyn of which *The New York Times* noted, "It is the ambition of the New Yorker to live upon the Fifth Avenue, to take his airings in the Park, and to sleep with his fathers in Green-Wood."

Kate's ancestors slept by the Mersey and in the ould sod of Ireland; her husband, in France. Her daughter made sure she would lie amidst New York's oldest families. As it happened, some of those taking eternal repose behind the imposing Gothic Revival gates were more notorious than blue-blooded, such as Boss Tweed and another Irish adventuress with a Spanish-sounding name, Lola Montez. In death, as in her incredible life, the company Kate kept was exceedingly diverse.

Kate's daughters lived together in a splendid town house in sight of the Hudson River at Seventy-eighth Street and Riverside Drive. It belonged to Juan Terry's brother Emilio, who divided his time mostly between Cuba and France. A year and a half after her mother's death, Lucy Adeline married Charles White Trippe, a strikingly handsome civil engineer of 23. His family was neither particularly wealthy nor recently notable, but it was eminently respectable and, by American standards, old.

Charles traced his ancestors back to the Norman Conquest. The Trippes of Canterbury served God and the King by producing a line of clergymen and soldiers.

In 1663, a Lieutenant Henry Trippe, who had fought in Flanders under the Prince of Orange, crossed the Atlantic and settled down to grow tobacco in Dorchester County on the Eastern Shore of Maryland. The family influence in that rural and maritime province is commemorated by a minor stream, Trippe Creek.

The most valiant member of the clan was a Lieutenant John Trippe, wounded off Tripoli in 1805 during the war against the Barbary pirates. For this and other acts of gallantry, he was rewarded with the Congressional Medal of Honor, and a century later, a series of U.S. Navy destroyers was named after him.

According to a family chronicle, the Trippes of Maryland enlarged their holdings of tobacco and slaves for three generations until a Joseph Ennalls Trippe edged his way northward and settled in East Orange, New Jersey, in 1853. His son Frederick established himself in Manhattan as a wholesaler of pharmaceuticals and chemical supplies. He was a conscientious businessman, commuting into the city six days a week during the summers from Sea Bright, New Jersey, where he installed his family in a cottage by the ocean. At noon on a sultry Saturday in August 1891, Frederick Trippe perished in his drugstore when the building at 72 Park Place was rocked by an explosion. Fire turned the structure into an inferno. The cause of the disaster, in which a hundred persons died, was never established; one theory held that chemicals stored in a vault in the basement of Trippe's store had been ignited by seepage from a subterranean steam valve.

The second of Frederick's three sons, Charles White Trippe, was 19 and a student at Columbia University when his father died. After he graduated three years later from the School of Mines, he joined the engineering corps of the Chicago World's Fair and then went west on railroad surveying expeditions.

He and Lucy Terry were married on November 24, 1895, in the fashionable Episcopal Church of the Heavenly Rest. In the bridal register of the church and on the marriage license, Lucy gave her father's name as Charles Wells. It was the only occasion in her adult life when she acknowledged, on official documents at least, a father other than Juan Terry.

Mixed marriages were not strictly regulated by the Roman Catholic Church until Pius X issued his papal decree *Ne Temere* in 1907. The code of canon law, promulgated in 1918, required promises of Catholic upbringing for the offspring of such unions, as well as a prudent attempt to convert the non-Catholic spouse. When Lucy and Charles were married, the United States was considered by the Vatican to be missionary territory, exempt from canon law. Catholics wed in Protestant churches and offices of justices of the peace with impunity, and reared their children in a spirit of compromise. Daughters took the faith of their mothers, sons that of their fathers, so that brothers and sisters were frequently of different religious persuasions.

If the Catholic partner was well-to-do and socially striving, as Lucy was, the marriage rite was likely to be Episcopalian. For to be Catholic, especially Irish Catholic, was to suffer exclusion from the inner circles of social, economic and intellectual power. Caught between concern for their salvation in the next world and their earthly aspirations, Irish-Americans who were "putting on airs and graces," as a parish priest put it, either claimed Protestant ancestry or became the first generation of renegades. Some tried to keep a foot in both churches.

Although newspaper editors, just eighteen months before, had noted Kate Terry's death with sensational recollections of the beautiful barmaid's caprices, they treated her daughter's marriage as a solemn social event. Emilio Terry, at whose house the reception was held, was alluded to as the bride's uncle. No references whatsoever were made to her parents.

Lucy and Charles made their home in the Terry house with Louise and Juanita. Charles took a job as a sanitary engineer with the New York City Board of Health. Nine months after the wedding their first son was born, Charles White Trippe, Jr.

On June 27, 1899, Lucy presented Charles with a second son. She had been positive she was bearing a daughter, whom she would name after her 13-year-old half-sister, Juanita. Unprepared to be contradicted, she called the baby Juan Terry Trippe, tying him to the man who was not really his grandfather. It was a distinctive name, one that gave the child a false air of Latin American ancestry. He would always hate it.

Juan Trippe was born at Sea Bright, New Jersey, where the family was spending the summer. On August 23, Louise's twenty-second birthday, Lucy rented a horse and surrey from a local stable to take her

sisters and children on an afternoon excursion, to be capped by a party
at their cottage.

Louise took the reins; Juanita and Charles Junior sat beside her.
Lucy climbed into the back seat with Louise Faure, a French nurse,
who held 2-month-old Juan. They drove for three hours, setting out
through the woods and returning by the ocean road. A quarter of a
mile from the cottage, the road took an abrupt turn across the tracks of
the Central Railroad of New Jersey. The view beyond the crossing was
obscured by a clump of trees. At a few minutes before 6 P.M., as the
surrey drew near, the northbound express sped past, followed by a
freight train. Louise half-turned toward Lucy, remarking that the horse
was placid, as the stable owner advertised, and apparently accustomed
to the noise of railroads. As soon as the caboose had passed, Louise
whipped the animal to proceed. The horse moved a few yards, then
balked on the second track. With their first unobstructed view, the
sisters saw the southbound express bearing down upon them.

They screamed for one long moment of terror, and Louise flailed
at the horse. Seconds later, the locomotive tore into the surrey, drag-
ging the front section several hundred feet up the track before the
three occupants were flung into a ditch. The rear seat was thrown to
the side at the point of collision.

Guests poured from a nearby hotel to gaze upon a charnel scene.
The horse had been ground to pieces. The bodies of Juanita and 3-year-
old Charles lay lifeless; Louise gasped her last breaths beside them.
Lucy fainted from the pain of fractured ribs. Mademoiselle Faure had
a cut over one eye, and infant Juan was slightly bruised. He had clung
instinctively to his nurse, and in her embrace he had been saved.

The funeral for the three victims was held the following Monday
afternoon at their home in New York. Lucy lay upstairs in her bed as a
priest from the Holy Trinity Roman Catholic Chapel, where the sisters
had worshiped, intoned the prayers for the dead, first in Latin, then in
English, over the coffins draped in white satin. The next morning, the
half-sisters and their nephew were united with Kate in Green-Wood
Cemetery.

Six weeks later, when she was up and about once more, Lucy had
Juan baptized at Holy Trinity.

Juanita died an intestate minor, giving rise to complex questions
about the sugar heiress' estate. Lucy Trippe, her sole survivor, was only
a half-sister, whom Juan Terry had deliberately excluded from the will
through which Juanita had inherited her fortune.

The estate law of New York State had recently been amended.
Though barred from taking any real property of a half-sibling's, Lucy

could take her personal property as though she had been her full-blooded sister. The legacy amounted to $191,343.96 in United States Government bonds.

Juanita's estate may have represented a mere sliver of the Terry millions, and one can only speculate whether it had dwindled through intent of the Terry family or through her mother's recklessness. Nevertheless, it was a substantial inheritance for that day. It came into Lucy's hands as the dividend of a hideous loss. Within minutes, her flesh-and-blood ties to a troubled and enigmatic past had been eradicated. There was no longer any witness to contradict memories she might choose to alter. She had no kin save Trippes; her money was Terry wealth she had never been intended to possess. Death, in tragic and senseless guise, had conferred a dowry, making Lucy an independent woman of means.

Thirteen months after the accident, Lucy and Charles had a daughter, whom they named Katherine Louise but called Louise in memory of her aunt.

Though the children were so close in age and outward appearance —in the fashion of the day, their mother dressed them in brother-and-sister outfits—Louise grew up in the shadow of Juan. He was the favorite, the only son, taking the place of the firstborn, the focus of his parents' proud expectations.

Juan was a husky boy, possessed of Charles Trippe's dark hair and patrician features and what Louise termed "our father's Maryland charm." Maryland was a badge of distinction, indicating Southern gentility, that the New York Trippes cherished, although in fact they seldom set foot in the ancestral state. As for the charm, Juan had an actor's knack of being engaging, of fixing his brown, almond-shaped eyes on one person he wished to impress and playing to the hilt the part that was certain to please. Most of the time, however, the boy was exceptionally quiet and self-contained, inhabiting a world of his own, impenetrable by outsiders.

Charles Trippe changed careers, shifting into a field with more cachet than civil engineering: the potentially lucrative occupation of investment banking. He started with the firm of Schuyler, Chadwick and Stout in 1901, not long after Juanita's estate was settled, and five years later formed Trippe & Company, buying a seat on the New York Stock Exchange, as a gentleman could do with the fruits of his own success or his wife's money.

He was an attentive father who supervised every detail of his son's education and training for life. Charles placed a high premium on intelligence, which Juan demonstrated in flashes. He emphasized the pragmatic rather than the scholarly side of learning. To be prepared and faithful—PARATUS ET FIDELIS—was the motto on the Trippe family coat of arms. If one had mastered this subject or that skill, one might get the jump on a lazier fellow. Sports were important, because they marked a gentleman's standing. Connections were made and bonds forged more often on the playing fields than in the classroom.

Lucy was a dynamic and aggressive woman, unusually capable of administering her own affairs—a trait not especially admired in high society, where mental independence for wives and daughters was discouraged almost as the Chinese bound the feet of wellborn females. One of the few socially permissible ways a married woman of her position could assert a head for figures was in real-estate investments. Lucy's strategy was to choose properties in relatively undeveloped (and consequently undervalued) areas. In 1902 she bought forty-five acres in Greenwich, Connecticut, which in future decades would become the corporate bedroom of New York City, the residence of senior executives and industrial-empire builders. At the turn of the century, it was countryside. On one part of the property the Trippes built a house, where they lived for the next five years; they called it Chadeline.

The Greenwich property became the weekend abode of the Trippes, in the English style adopted by the American gentry, after Juan reached school age. The *New York Social Register* listed their address as 1038 Fifth Avenue, near Eighty-fifth Street, until Lucy bought a row of three brick houses on East Seventy-eighth Street between Lexington and Third Avenues. The family occupied number 163. The area was frontier territory to which New York socialites would sooner or later migrate.

Lucy operated on the hunches of a gambler. According to her daughter, "She had E.S.P. about things." Later, she extended this extrasensory perception to the stock market. "She would choose to buy a stock because she just knew it was going to be good," Louise once recalled. She described her mother as an executive, an organizer, a figure of authority. But though she could channel her business instincts into investments, there was no other outlet for the managerial drive of a woman of Lucy Trippe's station and social ambitions save her family. So she became a household boss, running and organizing the lives of her husband and children. "Juan Trippe got a great deal of his executive ability from his mother," his sister said.

There is a passage in Henry James's *Portrait of a Lady* that seems to fit the Trippe family. In a musing about Ralph Touchett's parents, James wrote: "His father ministered most to his sense of the sweetness of filial dependence. His father, as he had often said to himself, was the more motherly; his mother, on the other hand, was paternal, and even, according to the slang of the day, gubernatorial." Mrs. Touchett looked after her own investments, even though her husband was a banker.

Juan was enrolled at the Bovée School, a private elementary school on East Forty-ninth Street. One of his classmates was Cornelius Vanderbilt Whitney, the only son of Harry Payne Whitney, a prominent financier-sportsman (or capitalist, as men of that ilk were identified), and Gertrude Vanderbilt Whitney, granddaughter of Commodore Cornelius Vanderbilt, the first and greatest of the railroad barons.

Young Whitney was heir to a Niagara of millions—not only Vanderbilt railroad dollars but also Whitney dollars from trolley cars, tobacco and oil.

Unlike Juan, whose parents doted on him, the Whitney princeling was in the charge of nurses and servants. His mother and father were usually traveling from one abode to another or from one diversion to the next and paid him intermittent heed. Harry Whitney had his racehorses, and Gertrude Whitney, a bountiful patroness of American artists, was occupied with her sculpture and writing.

Everyone called the blond, blue-eyed Whitney boy "Sonny," a moniker that clung to him all his life and that he tried in vain to shuck off. Hanging on to the tags of childhood and school is more than an Anglo-American upper-class crotchet. The nicknames signal common antecedents in a ruling caste. The taint of immaturity in Whitney's nickname undermined his fervent desire to be taken seriously as a grown man.

While most boys their age were absorbed with model railroad sets, aspiring to be locomotive engineers, they could not avoid being aware of strange new flying machines.

In 1903, two bicycle-shop proprietors, Wilbur and Orville Wright, outfitted a glider with a lightweight engine and two propellers mounted in the rear. On the morning of December 17, they succeeded in lifting the biplane with the muslin-covered wings off the sands of Kitty Hawk, North Carolina, under its own power. This first controlled flight of an airplane attracted scant notice, but during the next five years the brothers staged exhibitions in the United States and France, prompting a host of imitators, most of them foolhardy aviators in circus-y contraptions. With abundant newspaper coverage of their exploits, these birdmen, many of whom suffered bodily injury or loss of life, captured the imaginations of children born into the new century.

In the summer of 1909, two Frenchmen, Louis Blériot and Hubert Latham, made separate attempts to fly across the English Channel in single-wing airplanes of their own design that were radical departures from the biplanes used by the Wrights and others. Latham was the first to try, from a chalk cliff on the French side of the Channel at Sangatte.

"Start the motor," the heroic sportsman commanded his aides from a saddle above the wing. "See you in Dover," he cried as his monoplane, the *Antoinette,* ran along the ground and rose with the grace of a white bird over the sparkling waters. Onlookers roared their cheers into the dawn. Halfway across, the eight-cylinder motor failed. The plane fell gently as a wounded bird into the water, and Latham, nonchalantly smoking a cigarette as he awaited rescue, was picked up by a torpedo boat of the French Navy. A week later, Blériot accomplished the feat in a flight that lasted 17 minutes.

Ten-year-old Juan Trippe constructed an outsize model of Latham's *Antoinette* and managed to get it to fly in Central Park, powered by twisted rubber bands. In September of that year, his father took him to the Statue of Liberty to watch an airplane competition on Governor's Island between taciturn rivals, Wilbur Wright and Glenn Curtiss. Wright accused Curtiss of stealing his design for the control mechanism of the airplane. Curtiss' machine was caught in crosscurrents of wind, and he was unable to keep it in the air more than 45 seconds. Wright soared aloft three times, and in his first flight over water he crossed the mile of Bedloe's Island, where he overtook a sea gull and circled Miss Liberty before sweeping around in a figure-8 to his starting point. "New Yorkers had seen balloons but never the captain of a real aeroplane lift himself into the air high enough for millions to see and applaud him," *The New York Times* reported.

At 14, Juan was sent away to boarding school. His father chose the Hill School in Pottstown, Pennsylvania, near Philadelphia. "The Hill," run by a Presbyterian minister, prepared the sons of the affluent for admission to leading Eastern colleges and universities with somewhat less intellectual rigor and social prestige than the New England academies such as St. Paul's, Andover and Groton, where Sonny Whitney was set in his father's footsteps.

Juan, nicknamed Tripe and Trippy by his classmates, did not cover himself with scholar's laurels at the Hill. A failing mark in German nearly kept him from graduating. He joined a debating society, made the football team his junior year, and went out for track and tennis.

His photograph in the Class of 1917 yearbook shows a youth with a stiff-necked expression, no doubt induced by his high, starched white collar. His dark hair was slicked back from a high forehead; a nose straight as a plumbline ended in flaring nostrils above a wide, thin-lipped mouth. There is no hint of the radiant smile that could break out as erratically as blazing sunshine after a summer rainstorm, a smile that would forever unnerve his opponents and seduce the dubious. Allowing for the artificiality of school portraits, there is nevertheless a whiff of patrician mystery about this Juan T. Trippe, an air of a Black Prince, who, as one of the directors of Pan Am said many years later, "always kept his own counsel."

After summering in East Hampton, near the tip of Long Island, where the Trippes had been renting accommodations since the season of 1914, testing the exclusive and tranquil seaside village before deciding to buy property there, Juan marched off to higher education at Yale.

2

Those Bright College Years

Bright college years, with pleasure rife,
The shortest, gladdest years of life,
How swiftly are ye gliding by.
Oh, why doth time so quickly fly?
The seasons come, the seasons go,
The earth is green, or white with snow;
But time and change shall nought avail
To break the friendships formed at Yale.

In after years, should troubles rise
To cloud the blue of sunny skies,
How bright will seem, through mem'ry's haze,
Those happy golden by-gone days!
So let us strive that ever we
May let those words our watch-cry be,
Where'er upon life's sea we sail:
"For God, for Country, and for Yale!"

New Haven, in the fall of 1917, was a thriving Connecticut town noted for the manufacture of firearms, hardware, and leaders of American business and statecraft. Abutting the New England green and its outcropping of three Protestant churches was the Gothic enclave of Yale University, named after an East India merchant in London who had furnished the means, two centuries before, to sustain a college founded by Puritans. The symbols of capitalism and imperial mission endured. The twenty-seventh President of the United States, the stoutly conservative William Howard Taft, sire of dollar diplomacy, was ensconced within, taking a respite from public life to teach law. The Whiffenpoofs, Yale's gentlemen songsters, raised their voices to words appropriated from Rudyard Kipling.

Throughout most of the nineteenth century, Yale College had grown into a center of religious teaching, classical studies and science. From the late 1880s until the First World War, it tilted toward an elitism of athletics and social snobbery, renowned more as a football factory and male finishing school than as a temple of academe. Its Socrates was Walter Camp, sometimes called the father of football, the coach who selected the first All American eleven. His protégé Amos Alonzo Stagg, of the Class of 1888, went west to proselytize the pigskin cause from the University of Chicago. Aside from a literary renaissance that blossomed around 1909 and lasted for a decade, scholarship was in decline. In colleges everywhere, but nowhere else so much as at Yale, the gentleman's grade, just above passing, was a mark of honor. Several of Yale's pedagogical giants like Josiah Willard Gibbs, the mathematical physicist, Arthur Martin Wheeler, the history department's champion of Napoleon, and William Graham Sumner, cardinal of economic conservatism, had died; others moved into administrative positions.

But Sumner's oligarchic principles still prevailed. Syllogisms of class superiority could be constructed from his concepts of folkways, mores and ethnocentrism, and few of the already privileged youth who were admitted to Yale graduated without reinforcing their assumptions about their natural fitness for success. If most Yale men were once motivated to become clergymen, judges and teachers, by 1917 they were looking to careers in business, the bigger the business the better. And it was at Yale, where the sons of industrialists, financiers and corporate lawyers set the social standards of the campus, that those careers would begin.

Yale's archrival, Harvard College, boasted of its scholars and Presidents of the United States. Yale had only Taft to its credit in the White House, but it sent legions to all other levels of the American Establishment, from bank presidents to Secretaries of State. From the tables down at Mory's, Yale men filed to the corridors of power and the revolving doors between business and government. For decades to come, Yale would head the list of alma maters of top corporate executives, and the tradition of Nathan Hale, Class of 1773, would be carried, after the Second World War, into the Central Intelligence Agency.

Henry Seidel Canby, an alumnus who taught English at Yale in Trippe's time, wrote that the ideals inculcated there were adaptations of general idealism (even of Christianity) to the needs of an industrialized get-rich-quick country. It educated specifically for the harsh competitions of capitalism, for the successful and often unscrupulous pursuit by the individual of power for himself, for class superiority, and for a success measured by the secure possession of the fruits of prosperity.

It was a perfect education, Canby concluded, for a young man who desired

the wealth, the position, the individual power that was being worshipped just then in America—and wanted to get them quickly, easily, and with no public dishonesty. If indeed, without straining the term to the breaking-point, you can call a training for a career of this sort a true education!

This training was made available to a narrow elite. The student body was male, white, predominantly Anglo-Saxon and Protestant (the largest denomination being Episcopalian), as well as largely Republican. To read the names of the undergraduates in their navy-blue class books is to call the roll of the nation's basic industries and financial conglomerations. Du Pont, Rockefeller, Whitney, Weyerhaeuser, Heffelfinger, Auchincloss; fortunes made in chemicals, oil, transportation, grain, mining. Less celebrated names were attached to other major enterprises: Patterson of American Machine and Foundry, Knox of the F. W. Woolworth Company, Jennings of Standard Oil, Hochschild of American Metals.

Except for a few sons of investment bankers and department-store merchants of German background, like Lehman and Gimbel, or a livestock dealer's son from Kentucky, who bore the sobriquet "Jew," the slim minority of Jewish students were the offspring of emigrants from the tyrannies of Tsarist Russia, scraping out livelihoods as butchers, laborers and shopkeepers in New Haven and nearby towns. Barred from the fraternities, secret societies and committees that determined undergraduate social life, they lived apart and amused themselves away from the mainstream of student activity. Since industry and banking were no less restricted than the campus, most of them took their precious Yale degrees into the professions of law and medicine, or the retail trades of their fathers.

As for any racial strain other than fair Caucasian, so blond and blue-eyed was the student pigmentation that the nickname "nig" or "nigger" was conferred on those with dark hair and sallow complexions. Juan Trippe's coloring, in conjunction with his Hispanic given name, seemed exotic enough to evoke comment. He was tagged

"Wang," a play on the pronunciation of Juan. "He was supposed to have Cuban connections," one of his roommates remembered, "but we never tracked them down." The environment was uncompromisingly Anglophile; the bourgeoisie of the Eastern Seaboard turned to one Mother Country for standards of taste and acceptability. Trippe never quite disowned the man whose conspicuous name he carried, but he stressed his English origins. The biography in his class book states that his mother had lived in London and New York before her marriage.

Yale was not a place where shoeshine boys learned how to become millionaires, but rather, a safe haven for plutocrats to send their sons in the certainty they would not be contaminated by subversive ideas. Next to Kipling, an author much favored by students was Owen Johnson of the Class of 1900, whose best-selling *Stover at Yale* had been published five years before Trippe arrived and probably was the most pertinent manual he could have read.

In a telling passage, Dink Stover, a freshman, is counseled by LeBaron, an upperclassman:

> "Now, Stover, you're going to have a chance at something big on the football side; but that is not all. You might make captain of the eleven and miss out on a senior election. You're going to be judged by your friends, and it is just as easy to know the right crowd as the wrong."
> "What do you mean by the right crowd," said Stover, conscious of just a little antagonism. "The right crowd," said LeBaron, a little perplexed to define so simple a thing. "Why the crowd that is doing things working for Yale; the crowd."
> "That the class ahead picks out to lead us," said Stover abruptly.
> "Yes," said LeBaron frankly, "and it won't be a bad judgment. Money alone won't land a man on it, and there'll be some in it who work their way through college. On the whole, it's about the crowd you'll want to know all through life."

And then LeBaron reaches the kernel of Yale wisdom:

> "You may think the world begins outside of college. It doesn't; it begins right here. You want to make the friends that will help you along, here and outside. Don't lose sight of your opportunities, and be careful how you choose."

For reasons no more predictable than weather, institutions of learning, like vineyards, have good, mediocre and extraordinary years. There would always be self-congratulatory speculation among Old Blues as to why the classes of 1918, 1919 and 1920 produced such crops of outstanding graduates, men of literary and intellectual distinction and other men who, for better or worse, affected vital aspects of American life.

One of those was Henry R. Luce, son of a Presbyterian missionary in China, who would draw from his experience on the *Yale Daily News* to found *Time*, the weekly newsmagazine, with his classmate Briton Hadden. As would be the case with Trippe, Luce would be backed by wealthier friends he met at Yale.

Though they came to know each other slightly in New Haven—initially, both were scheduled to graduate in 1920—Luce and Trippe moved through separate and distant worlds. For reasons only sons of Eli perceived, Trippe's world was one of the slightly second-class citizens. The clue was in the letter "S" after his class year, signifying the Sheffield Scientific School.

Luce was a student at Yale College, familiarly called "Ac," the four-year undergraduate track for a classical education in the arts and sciences leading to the degree of Bachelor of Arts. A year older than Trippe, he started in the fall of 1916 and was already a sophomore when Juan enrolled at "Sheff" with the Class of 1920, intending to study mechanical engineering. The name of the school was misleading, inasmuch as Yale's true scientists pursued their studies through the College. Sheff was a three-year route for engineers and those unable to meet the College's entrance requirement of four years of Latin. Many of them had no other aim than to use the Sheff degree of Bachelor of Philosophy as a business passport.

The most popular program at Sheff was the Select Course (for selected studies in science and literature), which comprised modern rather than ancient languages, history, literature, philosophy and such vocational subjects as business finance and industrial management. Yale College men ridiculed the Select Course as a "gut," or "gentleman's," course, regarding it, with some justification, as evidence of academic slippage.

While their condescension seldom spilled into open hostility, the men of Ac treated the men of Sheff as strangers, allowing them to play on college sports teams but freezing them out of significant positions on the publications and the Prom Committee.

"Sheffield is much more than a section of a university—it is really a way of thinking about things, a point of view," Professor Canby explained. "Sheff-town" was geographically discrete, "a little country with clear boundaries and landmarked provinces within it." Situated to the northeast of the Old Campus in a territory bounded by Wall, Temple, College and Grove Streets, Sheff lay only a couple of blocks physically removed from Ac. Spiritually, it was another universe.

Each school had its own customs and clubs, fostering distinct loyalties. Sheff, for example, did not have compulsory chapel. Most of the Jewish students were to be found in Sheff. Its eight fraternities were identified by the names of their residence halls rather than by their Greek letters. Delta Psi was St. Anthony, housed in a new dormitory that was a gift of Frederick W. Vanderbilt; Delta Phi was St. Elmo. Phi Gamma Delta took its name, Vernon Hall, from its house at Grove and Temple Streets.

Nonfraternity men, such as sons of machinists and railway ticket clerks who were there on scholarships, Jews, and the occasional Arabs, Armenians and Orientals sponsored by Christian missionary funds, found more austere lodgings scattered around the area and partook of little more than the crumbs from Sheff's abundant extracurricular fare. Even at Prom and Commencement, they held their functions at Byers Hall, a student club open to all, "where they made up for glamour with expensive orchestras, dinners and costly favors in gold and silver for the girls." So a Sheff professor, Loomis Havemeyer, observed of these outcasts with condescension unbecoming a sage.

During his first few months at Sheff, Juan roomed in a freshman dormitory, Vanderbilt-Sheffield Hall. Starting out on Stover's path, he made the freshman football team, playing right guard. He was a solidly built 18-year-old, just under 6 feet tall, with an awkward muscularity that boded a lifetime struggle against fat.

"This class generally admits that the desire for learning was one of the lesser incentives that led them to enter upon a college career . . ." wrote the historian of 1920S, and Trippe was no iconoclast in that regard. Respect for the gentleman's C prevailed. Studying was an occupation for greasy grinds and meatballs. There was, moreover, a distraction from the world at large, summoning the students out of the ivy-covered cloister. In April 1917, the United States had declared war on Imperial Germany, and many of their older brothers, cousins and friends had rushed off to join the crusade for liberty and peace, to "make the world safe for democracy," as President Woodrow Wilson had asked.

Such impatience for a chance to die before they could vote would be incomprehensible to their grandsons. These young men were still under schoolbook influences of medieval chivalry; the bearing of arms was perceived as the definitive act of patriotism and manhood. And Yale had a proud tradition of volunteering in the service of the country. The war, as the 1920 Class Book noted in its section on athletics, was "the real game."

Three years before Juan arrived in New Haven, England's public schools and universities had emptied into the battlefields of Flanders and France with a grisly toll of casualties. Across the Atlantic in the New England prep schools and universities, fervor to emulate the English cousins was epidemic.

Ever since the Kaiser's army overran Belgium in the summer of 1914, Americans had debated the issues of pacifism versus preparedness. While President Wilson slowly came around to the belief that armed readiness would not compromise his bias for diplomacy as the most effective weapon for ending the conflict, the East Coast campuses were hotbeds of pro-Ally partisanship. Arthur Twining Hadley, the President of Yale, took the lead in espousing military training as a proper component of a college education. The Yale Artillery Battalion, organized in 1915 and the nucleus of the university's Reserve Officers Training Program, was said to be the best equipped of any outside Fort Sill, Oklahoma. By the fall of 1917, the trainees could practice with four 75-millimeter cannon donated by the French Government to the newly constructed Yale armory.

Seafarers had the option of joining the Yale Naval Training Unit; they took a referendum to decide whether to drill on the green in white or blue uniforms. Most students who were physically fit and normally patriotic were pressed to affiliate with one of the reserve units or obtain their parents' permission to enlist. Freshmen like Juan Trippe fretted over what they should do.

One band of Yale College men was already in combat in the skies over France or training other pilots. Setting an example of capitalist enterprise paving the way for government action, they had formed the Yale Naval Aviation Unit, embryo of the United States Naval Air Reserve.

Frederick Trubee Davison, son of Henry Pomeroy Davison, a partner in J. P. Morgan & Company, was the unit's galvanizing spirit.

In the summer of 1915, at the end of his freshman year, 19-year-old Trubee accompanied his father on a trip to London and Paris, where the elder Davison represented Morgan's in arranging loans and obtaining supplies for the Allies. The firm was to reap $30 million from acting as agent for the governments of Britain and France; that nice piece of business would be cited as war profiteering in a Senate investigation of the 1930s that drummed up isolationist sentiment for resisting involvement in the next war.

While they were in Paris, a call went out for a volunteer corps of American aviators to affiliate with the French Army as the Lafayette Escadrille. The airplane had already proved its usefulness in reconnaissance. By the following summer, it would become a combat weapon in a new kind of warfare. Bombing raids, dogfights over the trenches and formation flying, a technique perfected by the German Captain Manfred von Richthofen, who led his pursuit squadron in V-shaped swarms against Allied fighter pilots—all these bolstered the ground forces from the skies.

Trubee met some of the Escadrille pilots and listened to their tales. Upon returning to New Haven in September, he poured his enthusiasm at what he had seen and heard "about the excitement of air power" into the ears of a classmate, Robert A. Lovett, only son of a Texas lawyer who was chief executive of the Union Pacific Railroad System. Trubee and Bob talked to a dozen or more friends about forming their own flying group. But talk was all it amounted to for nearly a year.

Then in June 1916, President Wilson called up the National Guard to patrol the Mexican boundary while General John J. Pershing led an expedition in pursuit of Francisco "Pancho" Villa, the bandit rebel who had staged a raid across the border into Columbus, New Mexico, in which seventeen Americans were killed.

Toward the war in Europe, however, the President maintained a wavering neutrality, trying to act as mediator between the adversaries while avoiding entanglement in their causes. He was gearing up for a reelection campaign in which the Democratic Party would flaunt the slogan "He kept us out of war."

The U.S. military machine was not cranked up for battle, although Congress passed a National Defense Act that month to expand the armed forces; a year later, it got around to conscription. Neither the Army nor the Navy had more than a token number of men who knew how to fly. The legislation authorized an increase in the size of the Aviation Section of the Army Signal Corps from 60 to 148 officers over a five-year period. Aeronautics was lodged in the Signal Corps because military leaders regarded the airplane as merely a communications aid for the Army.

As soon as the militia was called up, Trubee set out to obtain his parents' consent to take flying lessons. Through a family friend, John Hays Hammond, Jr., an inventor of several systems in the field of wireless energy and a member of the Aero Club of America, he obtained a letter to Secretary of the Navy Josephus Daniels introducing him as the son of a Morgan partner and "one of 12 well-to-do young men who wish to prepare themselves to be of service to their country in case of trouble and are learning to fly."

Hammond and Admiral Richard E. Peary proposed an Aerial Coast Patrol, consisting of a chain of seaplane stations every 50 or 100 miles along the coast to be the first line of Atlantic defense. The Yale undergraduates would form a unit as a nucleus for the service.

Trubee's father told him to "mobilize recruits" at the Davison estate at Locust Valley, Long Island. For Trubee and eleven of his friends, "the summer of 1916 was like a jolly house party." Since the Navy had no training planes to spare, Trubee's parents bought two Curtiss F-boats, and the unit started lessons at nearby Port Washington, where Rodman Wanamaker, of the Philadelphia merchant clan, had established a flying school.

In September, "Trubee's crowd" was due back at Yale. Their training planes were transferred to the Navy submarine base in New London. New members were enrolled, enlarging the complement to 28. Among them were Trubee's younger brother, Harry, and his freshman roommate, David S. Ingalls of Cleveland, a nephew of President Taft; Kenneth MacLeish, son of a founder of Carson Pirie Scott, the Chicago department store; and William A. Rockefeller, a nephew of John D. Trubee organized the Yale Aero Club, while Bob Lovett advised other would-be fliers on the formation of two additional Yale aviation units.

Trubee's crowd went into winter training at Palm Beach, with J. P. Morgan & Co. underwriting their considerable expenses. Father Davison and his friends put up $300,000.

Feudal customs of chivalry were being adapted to the twentieth century. Knights of the Middle Ages supplied their own weapons, armor, horses, grooms and provisions when they set out for battle. Davison spared no expense to ensure his sons' proper outfitting for the fray. If, in the modern idiom, war was the ultimate sport, he was only behaving in the same way as another Yale father, Edward H. Harriman, the railroad baron, who saw to it that the varsity crew had the finest coaches and shells.

In January 1917, Congress passed an appropriations bill for a Naval Reserve Flying Corps. The United States was being drawn into the conflict as the Germans announced an unrestricted submarine campaign. On February 3, Wilson broke off relations with Imperial Germany, and seven weeks later the Navy Department at last invited the Yale units to enlist and be absorbed within the reserve. They could hardly wait for war to be declared on April 6.

In final training that summer, Trubee crashed into Long Island Sound during solo flight practice. His back was broken, his dream of aerial knighthood shattered; he would be lame for the rest of his life.

In August and September, the first unit dispersed. The ensigns, with gold wings on their chests, were ordered to naval air stations in the United States, England and France, three of them never to return.

Its much-decorated living heroes were Dave Ingalls, who became the naval ace of the war at 19 after downing six German planes, and Artemus (Di) Gates, who rescued two British fliers from a crash off Ostend and later escaped after being taken prisoner by the enemy. After they put their medals away, they would reminisce about their horseplay: Di and Dave shooting water pistols at each other at close range in the sky and blasting their machine guns at a safe distance. War was such great sport.

Initially, the unit was the only source of officers, apart from the regular Navy, for the embryonic Naval Air Service. Later, it provided the first Assistant Secretaries for Air: Trubee Davison in the War Department under Presidents Coolidge and Hoover, Dave Ingalls in the Navy Department in the same period. Gates and Lovett would fill the same posts during the Second World War, Gates going on to become Under Secretary of the Navy and Lovett rising to Secretary of Defense in the Truman Administration.

The unit also stands as a testimonial to socioeconomic-class solidarity. The members roomed together at Yale (some of them having known each other before at Groton and St. Paul's), and were tapped for Skull and Bones, the secret society that is supposed to bind its members in eternal brotherhood. Several in the unit would put up money for a nonflying Bonesman, Harry Luce, to publish his newsmagazine, as some would rally to another venture of nonunit Yale men, Pan American Airways.

Unit men would marry their roommates' sisters and settle in Locust Valley or in Greenwich, an afternoon's sail across the Sound. Di Gates took Alice Davison as his bride; Archie McIlwaine, who went into investment banking after the war at Dillon, Read, wed Curtis and Bartow Read's sister Caroline. Trubee allied with the daughter of his prep-school headmaster, the Reverend Endicott Peabody of Groton. The cohesiveness of the old school tie was transmitted to a second generation when Trubee's son Endicott Peabody Davison married Jane Ingalls, Dave's daughter.

Juan Trippe did not share in the glory of the unit, a strictly Ac affair launched before he arrived at Yale. But his passion to go to war in a flying machine was nonetheless acute. As soon as he set foot in New Haven, he signed up for the ROTC, a prerequisite for playing football that season, and attained the rank of corporal in Battery F. One late-November afternoon after the Yale freshman team scored a victory against Harvard, he and seven teammates vowed to enlist in the Marine Corps as flying cadets.

He failed the physical examination because his vision did not meet the 20/20 standard. Charles Trippe pulled strings. He had organized the Wall Street Squadron for Home Defense, and through George Woolsey, a partner in Trippe & Company, he wangled an appointment with Assistant Secretary of the Navy Franklin D. Roosevelt. Roosevelt hinted broadly that if Trippe's son could somehow overcome his deficiency, another test might be arranged. Juan committed the bottom line of an eye chart to memory—in his 70s, he would still be able to recite it: AEPHTIY—and passed his second medical screening.

In March 1918, just as his election to St. Anthony was announced, he was assigned to the naval aviation detachment at the Massachusetts Institute of Technology in Cambridge, Massachusetts, for ground-school instruction, the Marine Corps lacking facilities for such training. By July, he was learning to fly in Miami. Subsequently, he was stationed at Bay Shore, Long Island, where he made his first solo flight in a Curtiss "Jenny," and at Hampton Roads, Virginia. On September 11 he was commissioned an ensign in the U.S. Naval Air Reserve and assigned as a radio instructor to Pensacola, Florida. His father had insisted he master Morse Code before he entered the service so that he would be prepared for such an opportunity. With additional training, Juan qualified as a night bomber pilot, and late in October he was ordered to Dunkirk. The Armistice was declared on November 11 while he was en route to New York to ship out for France. Thus, peace postponed Juan Trippe's first chance at being enshrined in the pantheon of aviation heroes.

In February of 1919, he returned to New Haven. "The war is over. Yale men have done their share . . ." exulted the *Yale Daily News*. Eight thousand students, alumni and faculty had been in service; 167 Yale men had died. The newspaper reported that the "happy customs" suspended during the war, such as the torchlight parade and the annual Freshman–Sophomore Rush, would be renewed. Dave Ingalls, nemesis of the Boche, was unanimously elected captain of the Yale hockey team.

During the war, the Yale Corporation, the university's ruling body, had examined the rather anomalous relationship between the College and Sheffield and concluded that the curriculum needed reconstruction. Sheffield was to be turned into a professional school for the applied sciences. Henceforth, all Yale undergraduates had to meet uniform entrance requirements and spend freshman year together before electing to concentrate on liberal arts or engineering. The Select Course would expire with the Class of 1921, and thereafter, the bachelor's degree could be acquired in a four-year program of study.

Trippe considered transferring to Ac, but in the end he seized this last chance at the easier route to a Yale degree. He switched from engineering to the Select Course, which, in the context of his year's absence, enabled him to graduate in 1921. His first semester back in academe was a season of jostling for opportunities. Stover's formula remained in force. Competition was fiercer than ever.

Yale's prewar literary flowering was in late bloom. Luminaries like John Galsworthy, Amy Lowell and Horace Walpole descended upon New Haven to lecture at the invitation of Professor William Lyon Phelps, the effervescent Billy. Lofty reputations were in the making by students. Harry Luce and Brit Hadden enrolled in Canby's famous course in advanced writing with their classmates Thornton Wilder, a budding novelist and playwright, and Walter Millis, a future military historian. Stephen Vincent Benét, a senior in the class, had already had two books of verse published.

Luce and Hadden took command of the *Yale Daily News*—Luce as managing editor, his most competitive friend as chairman. Both had returned from Army service as chagrined as Trippe at having been deprived of overseas duty. Luce, a prodigious grind who hankered after social honors as well, was elected to Phi Beta Kappa in his junior year and tapped for Skull and Bones. He also served on the board of the *Yale Literary Magazine*, the hallowed *"Lit."*

One expression of the academic-reform movement intended to eliminate the strained relations between Ac and Sheff was a fusion of social and extracurricular institutions. The *Yale Courant* and the *Sheffield Monthly* were merged into the *Graphic*, an illustrated fortnightly containing short stories, verse, drama reviews and "an intimate glimpse of Yale men of the times."

Juan made his debut as a writer in the fifth issue of the *Graphic* in May 1919 with an unsigned article about a transatlantic flight being attempted by pilots representing most of the world powers. The U.S. entry was a flying boat built by the Curtiss Company with four Liberty engines. The "huge" size of the craft (it weighed over 30 tons fully loaded and had a capacity for carrying 70 barrels of gasoline) and the likelihood of its staying aloft even if two of its motors conked out were reassuring to the author:

> If our big naval sea plane is the first to get across, and needless to say, all Americans hope she will be, her pilots will have doubly distinguished themselves, for they will have been not only the first to fly across the Atlantic Ocean but also the first to demonstrate that a flight across the Atlantic Ocean is a perfectly safe and

sane commercial proposition and not a gigantic game in which the prospective transatlantic pilot or passenger has big odds against his safe arrival in the U.S.

Thus wrote Trippe, already a propagandist for U.S. air supremacy.

An American was indeed the first to accomplish the feat. One of the three giant flying boats entered in the race, the seaplane NC-4, under the command of Lieutenant Albert C. Read, left Newfoundland on May 16 and after flying 15 hours and 17 minutes, reached Horta in the Azores. During the next two weeks, the air machine swept into the harbor of Lisbon, touched down at Ferrol on the extreme northwest tip of Spain and continued on to Plymouth, England. On June 2, two Englishmen, Captain John Alcock and Lieutenant Arthur W. Brown, made the first nonstop crossing of the Atlantic, flying from Newfoundland to Ireland in one day. The two trails, blazed within half a month of each other, became the commercial air lanes of the Atlantic that Pan American Airways opened twenty years later.

Trippe was elected to the editorial board of the *Graphic* in June, and in the next academic year he contributed signed articles on topics as diverse as baseball and E. H. Sothern, whom he interviewed when the Shakespearean actor was playing in New Haven with his wife and leading lady, Julia Marlowe. Juan had a perceptive eye for detail, and a straightforward writing style except when he waved the flag for country and for Yale.

In the spring of 1920, he became editor-in-chief of the *Graphic*, with Worthington C. Miner as managing editor and Samuel P. Insull, Jr., son of the Chicago utilities wheeler-dealer, as assignment editor. Julius Fleischmann, Jr., of the Cincinnati family of yeast manufacturers, was elected treasurer, and Samuel F. Pryor, Jr., of Greenwich, son of the president of the Remington Arms Company, took over as business manager.

Pryor had spent his childhood in St. Louis before going to Taft, a Connecticut boarding school, to prepare for Yale College. He had enlisted in the Navy during his freshman year and served on a destroyer in European waters. Upon returning to New Haven in February 1919, he shifted to the Select Course at Sheff "so I could catch up with my friends and graduate in 1921."

Short and wiry, he compensated for his bantam size with a plenitude of energy and bonhomie. In class annals, he is recorded as the hardest worker and the most thorough gentleman. Pryor seemed to be in the thick of everything, usually acting as a loyal lieutenant. One of those he served was Edward Patrick Francis Eagan, son of a director of the Santa Fe Railway and an outstanding scholar and athlete. As captain of the boxing team, of which Pryor was a welterweight member, Eagan made the sport of pugilism fashionable at Yale. He represented the United States at the Olympic Games in the summer of 1920 and won the world championship as an amateur lightweight boxer.

Sam's other master was Juan Trippe. When copy for the *Graphic* arrived late at the printer's because of Trippe's finicky editing, Pryor mollified the journeymen. Trippe produced thirty extra pages of editorial material for one issue. "There's no way to pay for them," Sam protested. Juan looked up at the ceiling, and said, coldly, "*You* are going to pay for them." Pryor went forth to solicit his father's friends, and the *Graphic* was fattened by advertisements for the Remington Arms Company, the Baldwin Locomotive Works, the American Coal Mining Company, the Packard Motor Car Company, the General Electric Company and Quaker Oats. "Trippe never talked to anyone when he was running the *Graphic*," Sam Pryor recalled years later. "No one but me, and he only talked to me because I had to get the money."

Though the magazine's quotient of levity was slim and its literary standards modest, circulation doubled. Its reverence for business anticipated Calvin Coolidge. When the Yale Corporation chose a nonalumnus, James R. Angell of the Carnegie Foundation, to succeed Arthur Twining Hadley, who was retiring, the *Graphic* editorial commented approvingly. The office of the President of Yale ought to be filled by a "man gifted not only with the highest educational and intellectual talent but also with marked executive and administrative ability." A fund raiser or an advertising salesman might have written the tribute to the outgoing President:

> President Hadley has realized that with the demands of modern life there are more things to teach and more need for increased contact between the university and the business world.

Trippe's attention was not concentrated solely on the *Graphic*. Athletics continued to be very important to him. He made the university football team in the fall of 1919 and assumed his old position as guard. One of his teammates was Harry Davison. Juan was also on the golf squad, and he went out for crew, that most gentlemanly of sports.

There he encountered his classmate from the Bovée School, Sonny Whitney. Their paths would not often cross at Yale, for Sonny was in Ac, and as he once said when asked about Juan Trippe, "You hardly spoke to people at Sheff."

Soon after he registered at Yale in the fall of 1917, Whitney had packed up and gone to Washington to enlist as an aviation cadet in the Army Signal Corps. He had met his Waterloo at the color-identification test—a setback soon remedied by his cousin Evie, the daughter of

Representative James W. Wadsworth, Jr., from upstate New York. She borrowed a chart from a friend and coached Sonny so that he could pass on a second attempt. Whitney trained at several airfields in Texas, was commissioned a second lieutenant, and became an instructor in acrobatic and combat flying. His parents did everything they could to delay his being sent overseas; Gertrude Whitney and her daughter Flora moved to Fort Worth for a month and a half to "cultivate" his commanding officers. The war ended as he was about to ship out for France with a squadron of pursuit pilots.

After Whitney was discharged with the rank of captain in the reserve, he returned to the status of a Yale freshman. Studies were secondary to his extracurricular activities, which were divided between athletics and the arts. He played the piano, sang and acted in plays put on by the Elizabethan Club. One of his poems was published in the *Lit.*

But his efforts to be taken as someone other than a harebrained playboy were marred by well-publicized scrapes. His mother bemoaned the "fatal blue eyes that are continually getting him in messes." During his sophomore year, as he was driving back from a weekend in New York in the dawn of a Monday morning, his Stutz Bearcat collided with a horse-drawn wagon on the Boston Post Road. The friend seated beside him was killed when a portion of the windshield crushed his skull. Whitney was arrested for driving without a license, then released to have his cuts and bruises treated at Stamford Hospital.

By eerie coincidence, that accident in the fall of 1919 presaged a scene in F. Scott Fitzgerald's *This Side of Paradise*, which would be published the following spring and achieve instant best-sellerdom. In the novel, Princeton students who have "sallied to New York in quest of adventure" meet death on the road after midnight as one of their automobiles overturns on a curve. Images of his bloodstained friend lying under the lamppost haunt the hero intermittently the next day, but he thrusts them away as he is caught up in the social whirl.

In his junior year, Whitney achieved a peculiar notoriety by being named defendant in a $1-million breach-of-promise and paternity suit brought by a former dancer in the *Ziegfeld Follies*. For the better part of the next decade, she persisted in pressing the suit in numerous courts, only to be beaten back by batteries of Whitney lawyers, including the eminent Wall Street advocate John W. Davis, later an unsuccessful candidate for the vice presidency on the Democratic ticket. The scandal put enough of a blot on Whitney's career at Yale so that he was never tapped for a secret society.

Though camaraderie did not come easy to him, Trippe assiduously developed a correct social life. The nucleus of it was his fraternity, Delta Psi. Supposedly, one's loyalties lay first with the fraternity, then with Sheff and last with the university. "Wang wasn't very talkative, but he was very active," recalled Marshall J. Root, Jr., of Geneva, New York, one of his roommates for a year at St. Anthony. "He was an ambitious guy, in a quiet way. But he was persistent."

The reticence Root observed in Juan was manifested at times in a painful inability to speak that resulted in a derisive nickname, "Mummy," after he was called to discourse at a fraternity rite and could only stammer an apology. Some ascribed the fit of muteness to being shy, an attribute offered throughout his life to excuse what many interpreted as coldheartedness. Those closest to him by blood or marriage believed he was not really shy but self-absorbed. "He simply knew when to keep his mouth shut," said his sister.

The longer-lasting relationships he formed through St. Anthony were with another football player, Walton Scully, and his roommate, Alan M. Scaife, both from Pittsburgh, and with two former Navy aviators, Warner Atkins, son of a Cincinnati banker, and Thomas R. Symington of Baltimore, whose family was in railway supplies. Symington had attended the Hill School with Trippe; at Yale the leading prep schools had alumni clubs, and Juan and Tom belonged to the Hill Club.

As Dink Stover, graduate of another New Jersey boarding school, Lawrenceville, discovered, not all schools were equal in New Haven. In Stover's fictional time, Andover was the ruling clique; in Trippe's era, Groton. "You haven't the fellows ahead pulling for you, the way the other crowds have," LeBaron explained to Stover. The handicap could be overcome by dint of personality and striving for excellence outside the classroom.

Pryor, Symington, Scaife and Trippe were among a handful picked for the Aurelian Honor Society, a nonsecret organization which took its name from the virtuous Stoic, the Roman Emperor Marcus Aurelius. Election to the Aurelian indicated recognition of ability and future promise "as demonstrated by other tests than those of scholarship."

Juan was a member of the Y.M.C.A. Cabinet, a Sheff-dominated exercise in noblesse oblige. Ed Eagan was president and Sam Pryor the treasurer. Sheff men coached the poor boys of New Haven in sports and taught English, woodworking and citizenship to adult immigrants.

Like other Eastern colleges of its rank, Yale was a luxurious monastery from which respite was granted during the weekends. Girls descended upon New Haven for the fraternity dances such as the St.

Anthony German, a cotillion with much changing of partners under the benevolent surveillance of chaperones. Trippe attended the Germans, though he did not go to the Junior Prom, the Everest of college social life, held on a Friday evening in late February.

On many weekends, Yale men flocked by automobile and railroad train to the women's colleges in Northampton and Poughkeepsie and to debutante parties in New York and Philadelphia. Most of the sisters and cousins of Juan's friends ended their formal education at boarding schools in New England and the South like Ethel Walker, Miss Porter's, and St. Timothy's or private day schools such as Chapin and Spence in New York, where Louise Trippe was enrolled. They were then presented to society, a euphemism for being placed on the marriage market; the Yale fraternities and secret societies furnished eligible partners.

During the war, the Eighteenth Amendment, banning the manufacture and sale of intoxicating liquors, was ushered through Congress by Representative Andrew Volstead, a Republican from Minnesota, and as the veterans trooped back to the campus it became the self-defeating law of the land. Prohibition spawned the hip flask, the speakeasy, the poisonous contraband beverage and the manly elegance of inebriety. As Canby observed, ". . . the gift of being amusing, especially when tight" was one of the things that counted in a college career, along with good looks and political sagacity. The respected student tippler matured into the hard-drinking country-clubman and corporate executive. "Juan loved his martinis and his golf," said his associates at Pan Am when they were scratching for evidence of warmth and good-fellowship his conduct otherwise belied.

The Prohibition mentality was part of the raging success of *This Side of Paradise* when it was published during his junior year. The novel captured the snobbery, the boredom and the restlessness that composed one mood of the postwar generation of college youth. There was another side, more innocent and optimistic, which carried on what the Great War had briefly interrupted: a belief in the realization of the American Dream. The formula was modified somewhat, a little less religion, a great deal more science and a dollop of cynicism overlying the morality. But the impossible would be achieved. Trippe and his friends were supremely confident of that.

Flying was Juan's governing interest. He aligned himself with fifty returning aviators, most with records more distinguished than his, to reconstitute the Aero Club that Trubee Davison had organized before they went off to war. Trippe was elected secretary at the first meeting of the Yale Aeronautical Society, as it was renamed in January 1920—

the only one of the officers and directors who had not seen combat. Two aces, Sumner Sewall of Maine and Dave Ingalls, were chosen president and vice president, respectively.

Trippe also succeeded to the post of secretary of the Intercollegiate Flying Association, a group that united a dozen college aero clubs in the cause of advancing the "sport of sports" by sponsoring air races. Fifty-six fliers from twelve colleges competed in a meet held in May at Mineola, Long Island, before a crowd of 1,500 spectators. The feature event was a 25-mile cross-country race in Curtiss training planes with Hispano-Suiza 8-cylinder, 150-horsepower engines that had a maximum cruising speed of 90 miles an hour.

The race was close. The Yale plane, piloted by Trippe and George W. Horne, finished 10 seconds ahead of the University of Pennsylvania's entry.

Five weeks later, Juan celebrated his 21st birthday. Scarcely a month after his coming of age, his father died at their summer home in East Hampton. Charles Trippe was 47, a victim of typhoid fever, mysteriously contracted and initially misdiagnosed as malaria. Immobilized by his death, Lucy placed the responsibilities of the head of the family on her son's sturdy shoulders. Juan arranged for his father's funeral and took a hand in the settlement of his affairs. Charles Trippe died without a will, leaving an estate of $30,000. Buffeted in a postwar economic slump, Trippe & Company was piling up losses, and a year later the firm was bankrupt. Its plight was an embarrassment. A failing business stained a family escutcheon. Gentlemen were supposed to pay their debts.

Lucy Trippe's frugality, a trait her son imitated, became more pronounced. How much was due to financial straits (for she was still a woman of property and a smart investor), how much to feelings of emotional deprivation and how much to the ascetic tendency of the Protestant ethic prevailing in the old New York society she so admired can only be speculated. Yet Juan could wheedle from his mother almost anything necessary to maintain social standing. It was obvious to everyone that he was the apple of her eye.

Whatever physical vanity Lucy might have had seemed to wither in the shock of Charles's death, and she slipped into the mode of a dowdy gray-haired lady, an imperious grande dame of 50. She complained regularly about her health, and was convinced she had suffered more serious injuries in the accident at the railroad crossing than had been detected at the time.

In September, Trippe threw himself into a busy senior year at Yale. His aspirations to be a champion athlete were dashed when he injured his back in a football game and had to drop off the team and the crew squad as well. But his ardor for both sports never cooled, and he talked a good game and a swift race ever after. His curriculum vitae, issued by the public-relations department of Pan American Airways when he was at the height of his power, always contained references to his athletic career at Yale along with his club memberships and the numerous honors awarded to him by foreign governments. By his press release is an American business leader known. A corporate shibboleth holds that team sports inculcate the competitiveness, co-operative spirit and leadership necessary for the hard climb to the summit.

As Trippe and his associates handed over the reins to the next editorial board in the spring of 1921, the *Graphic* reveled in its "sound financial condition," an accomplishment that would be one of his fondest souvenirs of Yale. The magazine lasted for only a few issues under new management.

And so his "bright college years" wound to a conclusion. Trippe had followed LeBaron's advice to Stover. He may not have been the biggest man on campus, but he was part of a crowd that mattered, someone they could count on to get things done. He had maneuvered from the periphery to the center of the action. And he had made connections, "friendships formed at Yale" that would soon prove invaluable.

Trippe demonstrated "a contagious energy and reckless love of success," as the Harvard philosopher George Santayana defined the Yale spirit. The precise shape his success would take was unclear, as it usually is at 21, going on 22. Juan took a most conventional first step toward a livelihood after graduation, progressing from college gentleman to gentleman broker. He let himself be recruited by the Wall Street firm of Lee, Higginson & Company. The senior partner who hired him for the métier of bond salesman was a Yale man.

3

Was There
an Aviation Business?

The development of international air transport begins
with a myth and has its climax in a technological miracle. All airmen
recognize themselves as descendants of Icarus and Daedalus, who escaped from Crete on wings made of feathers and wax. According to
ancient legend, Icarus flew too close to the sun and plummeted to
death in the sea as his wings melted. Daedalus made it home free to
Sicily. Curiously, the son who failed is more celebrated in aviation lore
than the father who succeeded with his invention.

On July 20, 1969, two American astronauts, Neil A. Armstrong and
Edwin E. Aldrin, Jr., set foot on the moon. Their voyage represented a
triumph of imagination and cognitive process, an impossible dream
fulfilled by painstaking scientific labor.

In between Icarus and Armstrong, the first to walk on lunar soil,
lie millennia of wishful thinking, tedious advances in knowledge, and
the slow accretion of capability to move people and things through the
skies. All along there was the touching faith that as distances were
shortened, human beings would be brought nearer to one another in
peace and understanding.

Why were they so bent on flying? Freud analyzed the yearning to
emulate the bird as a disguise for infantile erotic wishes. Bird was
symbol for phallus; flight represented the sexual act the child longed to
perform. One can explain abiding desire in countless ways. Apart from
Freud, flight is a quest for freedom. To fly is to break away from the
earth, to be supremely powerful. Those who play God in modern times
—kings, presidents and corporate emperors—descend from the heav-

ens in jet airplanes and helicopters. Flying is a total experience because it embraces opposites: ascent and descent, soaring and falling, confidence and fear, success and failure.

Though the urge to fly had always been compelling, it had remained in the realm of fantasy, except for widely spaced and seemingly unrelated leaps toward enlightenment. The Chinese invented the kite a thousand years before Christ and the rocket in A.D. 1000; Leonardo da Vinci, genius of the Italian Renaissance, filled his sketchbooks with designs for flying machines, everything from ornithopters with flapping wings to helicopters that went straight up and down in the air. In the late 1800s, Frenchmen proved it was feasible to travel by hydrogen-filled balloon. The nineteenth century was a ferment of flight experimentation, from the science fiction of Jules Verne to the manned gliders of George Cayley and Otto Lilienthal.

The first practical application of airborne transport was born of military necessity. Felix Nadar photographed Paris from the gondola of a tethered balloon in 1858, and when the city was under Prussian siege twelve years later, his balloons were launched for reconnaissance and to take officials, supplies and letters to the provinces beyond enemy lines. Homing pigeons carried the return mail to the capital. Four million letters were delivered by balloon and bird.

The airmail service ceased with the French defeat, and the next advance in lighter-than-air equipment was made with Count Ferdinand von Zeppelin's rigid balloon. In 1911, Zeppelin airships were placed in commercial service to transport thousands of passengers safely between German cities until just before the outbreak of the First World War. Thereafter, the company was assumed by the German Navy and the dirigibles used for bombing runs over England.

Sending up a machine that was heavier than air hinged on finding a source of power. A contest evolved between French and American inventors, struggling independently and unaware of what others were doing. First to succeed were the Wright brothers when their biplane, powered by a small engine, sustained flight for 12 seconds above the Outer Banks of North Carolina in 1903.

Alberto Santos-Dumont, a Brazilian residing in France, got aloft briefly in 1906 in a contraption styled after a box kite; the pilot operated the controls from a standing position. In a monoplane of later design, the *Demoiselle*, made of bamboo and propelled by a two-cylinder engine, he situated the pilot under the single high wing framed by metal struts, with his feet stretched in front of him.

The decade between the first manned flights and the Great War was a frenetic period for aeronauts, who assembled their inventions from bicycle parts, piano wire and glue for attaching linen coverings to the wooden wings. Their progress was demonstrated in races, exhibitions and prize competitions on both sides of the Atlantic which the public perceived as sensational entertainment. Newspapers recorded the antics of loony aviators who frightened spectators on the hard benches of the grandstands, making them scream with panicky delight as they looped, dived and frequently killed themselves in the execution of aerial stunts. The reckless birdmen did little to instill confidence in aviation, though the punishment to which they put their machines undoubtedly forced designers to solve problems of aeronautical stress.

The tragedy of aviation, a joyful adventure embarked upon with naive hope, is that its advancement has been accelerated by war. Between 1914 and 1917, the airplane was used as a reconnaissance tool by mostly unarmed pilots. In the last year of World War I, aerial combat developed rapidly. Aircraft weaponry was largely the accomplishment of European engineers; the sole innovation from the American arsenal was the sturdy Liberty engine, which was not produced until 1918. U.S. aircraft production, directed by automobile manufacturers, was marred by major scandals of graft and excess profits. Although $1.5 billion was appropriated for the program, not one American plane did it yield for active service. The widespread cancellation of contracts after the Armistice caused a glut of military aircraft that discouraged new design and retarded the U.S. aviation industry.

As soon as the war ended, Europeans proceeded with alacrity to develop postal and passenger services. Before the peace treaty was signed, domestic airmail routes were opened in France and Germany, and passengers were transported between London and Paris. By 1920, KLM Royal Dutch Airlines inaugurated service between Amsterdam and London. Numerous airlines were organized with private capital in England and France and then consolidated into single units, generously subsidized by their governments. The Europeans regarded commercial aviation as an adjunct to military strength. At a French aircraft exhibition in 1923, visitors to Le Bourget were shown how easily bomb racks and gun mounts could be fitted into the transport planes.

Air service was not to be confined to the homelands. Though the airplane was incapable of transocean flight, aerial expertise could be exported to overseas territories where vast, impenetrable terrains and a dearth of communications and transport facilities made the new technology welcome.

In 1919, Pierre Latécoère, a French aircraft manufacturer, founded an airline with a corps of former military pilots. They started by flying mail from Toulouse to French Morocco, then continued to

Dakar, in West Africa, always with the dream of crossing the Atlantic to South America. The Line, as they referred to it, was held together by its general manager, Didier Daurat, a lonely, unbending man. He drove the pilots into the skies and across hostile mountains and desert, in peril of falling into the clutches of vengeful Moorish tribesmen. One of his more careless and poetic pilots, Antoine de Saint-Exupéry, later immortalized Daurat in a novel, *Night Flight*.

The French also initiated commercial air services in French Guiana and the Levant, the Belgians in the Congo, the British in Australia, and the Germans in Austria, Hungary, the Baltic States, Persia and South America.

In the United States, civil aviation was off to a sluggish start. Mail delivery by air won popular interest and government support before passenger service. Private capital was not attracted by what seemed to be the unlimited risks in aviation. There was a tradition for the Post Office to aid the development of new transportation systems by way of discharging its responsibility for swift transmission of letters and packages. From Pony Express and steamboat to railroad and airline was a logical progression.

In 1917, Congress voted an appropriation of $100,000 to the Post Office Department for an experimental air service, until then handicapped by a lack of landing fields and qualified pilots.

The Army furnished the pilots and five training planes of the new Curtiss JN-4 model, a biplane with a squat-nosed, clattering engine and two open cockpits that was affectionately nicknamed the "Jenny." A Washington–Philadelphia–New York route was inaugurated on May 15, 1918, in a climate of chagrin. As President Woodrow Wilson and his Cabinet waited patiently in a polo field near the Tidal Basin for the northbound plane to start, someone discovered that the gasoline tank was empty. Once that condition was remedied, the pilot took off and immediately lost his way. The southbound flight from the New York depot, the infield of a racetrack on Long Island, fulfilled the hopes of the Postmaster General and transported the mail to Washington in 3 hours 20 minutes.

The service was reasonably efficient and free of mishap during the summer months of good weather, but could not cover its costs because the expected users did not materialize.

Nevertheless, the Post Office was undaunted, and realizing that the Army could not carry mail as a sideline indefinitely, it took on the operation of a civilian aerial postal service.

In May 1919, service was begun from Chicago to New York, and in September 1920, the first transcontinental airmail flight scheduled. A newspaper editorial writer labeled it "a homicidal insanity"; of the initial 40 pilots hired by the Post Office Department, 31 were killed flying the mail during the next six years.

Crossing the varied and rugged terrains of the continent in the primitive aircraft of the day was a courtship of death, with the odds stacked against the pilot's surviving to recount his exploits to his grandchildren. Landing fields were few, the equipment outmoded. The Post Office was saddled with the DH-4, an adaptation of the British De Havilland reconnaissance plane of wartime, powered by a Liberty engine. It soon became known as the "flaming coffin": the fuel tank, placed between the cockpit and the engine, tended to explode on crash landings.

With the government taking the initiative for the carriage of the mail through the air, the transport of passengers was left to the exploitation of promoters. Most of them were veterans operating air-taxi services with war-surplus aircraft. The mortality rate for these fly-by-day ventures was high. One of the few attempts at a sound commercial operation was made by Inglis M. Uppercu, a New York distributor of Cadillac automobiles who had manufactured seaplanes for the Navy during the war. Starting in 1920, with a fleet of six converted coastal-patrol flying boats, Uppercu's Aeromarine Airways carried mail and passengers up the Hudson River between New York and Albany, to several New England ports and along the Great Lakes from Chicago to Montreal.

In the winter of 1920–21, Aeromarine began the first regularly scheduled overseas air service, between Key West, Florida, and Havana. Newspapers referred to it as the High Ball Express. Devil-may-care tourists paid a $75 fare (reduced the following year to $50) to flee the rigors of a Northern climate and of the Eighteenth Amendment.

Harry Bruno, the airline's irrepressible publicity man, took it upon himself to promote the outlandish belief that flying was safe. His basic ploy was to shame adult males out of their fears by arranging for infants, children, octogenarians and Miss America of 1921 to go for rides in the planes. Bruno had photographers on hand as they landed, visibly sound in mind and body. But his tricks could not overcome weak traffic and faulty equipment, and Aeromarine sputtered to a halt in 1923.

It was a time for airmen to chafe at the bit. The nation's railroads had been built and consolidated; the robber barons had pocketed their fortunes. Henry Ford had bred America's unshakable love affair with the automobile with his Model T, scaled to the lowest possible denominator of efficient production and selling price.

The only frontier remaining was the sky. A generation of young aviators knew the future of flying. "We were born to the air, and we could visualize," Sonny Whitney said. But what were they to do with their visions? At the conclusion of the war to end all wars, the military leaders of the United States reconfirmed their faith in tanks and warships. Airplanes that had been rushed off the drawing boards turned obsolete in the factories. Manufacturers and promoters milled about, in search of an industry to expand. Everyone was waiting for a signal to cross into the frontier.

As Juan Trippe began his apprenticeship at Lee, Higginson & Company, Wall Street seemed like an extension of the campus in New Haven. He was surrounded by Yale men and their Ivy League cousins. The securities business in the early 1920s was hardly a strenuous endeavor. The young salesmen peddled bonds to their families and friends from midmorning until midafternoon, when they departed for the golf links and other serious pastimes.

Not all of Juan's crowd was in The Street. Some of his classmates scattered to jobs in other hospitable businesses such as steel, oil and sugar; some took what their parents agreed were well-earned vacations. Sam Pryor and Tom Symington traveled around the world for a year before deciding whether to settle into family businesses.

After Sonny Whitney graduated in 1922, his father dispatched him to Nevada to learn the mining business from the pits up. Mining was one of Harry Whitney's numerous interests. A year's experience toiling underground in the Comstock mine as an ore sampler gave Sonny a certain empathy for the workingman. "I grew up from the bottom in my business career and I will always thank my father from the bottom of my heart for that," he once told an interviewer. "Later, if a worker came to me and said conditions are terrible, I knew what he meant."

By comparison with many of his friends, Juan was in moderate circumstances. After Charles Trippe's negligible estate was settled, Lucy Trippe sold her row of houses on East Seventy-eighth Street and moved to an apartment in a brownstone building at 55 East Seventy-sixth Street, one of the first residential cooperatives in the city. As the Twenties roared on, she parted with some of her Greenwich property, by then greatly appreciated. Juan Trippe "didn't have any money," his friends said. The statement was preposterous, except in the context of the plutocratic company he preferred to keep. Almost everyone had more money than he had. Still, he kept up appearances and did all the important social things such as playing in golf competitions and joining the right clubs: the Society of Colonial Wars, the Yale and St. Anthony clubs, Apawamis in Westchester for golf, and one of the oldest and sniffiest, the Union Club. On weekends, he flew a secondhand seaplane with leaky pontoons and performed aerial pranks, such as buzzing the yacht of a railroad tycoon and slicing off the tip of its mainmast.

There was a brotherhood of young Wall Streeters who flew their own planes. Trippe became chummy with John A. Hambleton, scion of a Baltimore investment banking family whose roots ran back for nine generations into the Eastern Shore of Maryland, where they entwined with those of the Trippes. The families had been partners for a time in the firm of Hambleton and Trippe.

John Hambleton, two years older than Juan, was one of the golden youths of their generation. More than his sandy-haired, blue-eyed Anglo-Saxon looks and lithe body, his sunny personality drew friends as bees to a honeypot. In his presence women fluttered; men worshiped him for his athletic ability, his physical courage, his keen sense of adventure and fun, and his modesty. "Johnny was about as attractive as a young man can be. He was a perfect friend," said David K. E. Bruce, his boyhood pal. The gods had smiled on them both. Bruce was a Southern aristocrat, a brilliant student, later a wealthy man by marriage and his own wits, and one of the nation's finest public servants.

Hambleton's earliest passion was for flying. At St. Paul's he dreamed of aviation, and read all he could about flying an airplane before he had actually seen one. He and David Bruce spent the summer of 1916, before entering college, at the military training camp for officers at Plattsburgh, New York, where Hambleton lamented that flying instruction was not offered. "One day," John confided to David, "I'm going to start a civil-aviation company."

Hambleton entered Harvard that fall and left after one semester. Without waiting for the United States to declare war against Germany, he enlisted in February 1917 in the Aviation Section of the Army Signal Corps. He was assigned to a Curtiss Flying School in Virginia and commissioned a lieutenant in July; by October, he was on a ship sailing toward France. The spring of 1918 found him at the Saint-Mihiel front with the 95th Aero Squadron. Later, he took part in the decisive battles at Château-Thierry and in the Meuse-Argonne offensive for which Colonel Billy Mitchell planned the first massed air attack, striking ahead of the American forces on the ground.

A cool, courageous pilot, nonchalant about his wounds, John Hambleton came home from the war a major, decorated with the Croix de Guerre and the Distinguished Service Cross with Oak Leaf Cluster. Rather than return to Harvard, he joined Hambleton & Company, which was headed by his older brother, T. Edward Hambleton. The firm had an office in New York. John Hambleton had enough resources at his fingertips to be considered a very rich young man. But investment banking was an accessory to his main interest, the development of aviation. For him, the elements of patriotism, commerce and sport were fused in the airplane.

Maintaining his status as an officer in the Air Service Reserve, he helped organize the Flying Club of Baltimore and the Air Corps of the Maryland National Guard. As a sportsman, he used his old Avro in simulated fox hunting. He enjoyed taking off in the single-engine war-training plane with Bruce as his passenger, barely clearing the ground and cruising across Baltimore County until he spotted a fence to swoop down and fly over. No one who flew with Hambleton was ever afraid because he was such a skilled and confident pilot. He vowed never to go up in a plane unless he was at the controls.

So much for sport. John envisioned aviation as business on a grand scale. With Bruce and a few other friends as partners, he organized the Federal Aviation Corporation, intending to invest in a range of promising aeronautical enterprises from dirigibles to parachutes.

He was constantly discussing ways and means of operating an airline. Should it be a domestic airline or one that would operate in foreign countries with ownership reserved for Americans? He and a friend from the war prepared a map of southern Arabia for a test project in the business of aerial exploration, one that never got off the ground. Hambleton was "on fire with the idea that man would eventually span the oceans by air," the friend remembered. John believed he had a great role to play in the future of civil aviation.

Juan Trippe spent nearly two years in Wall Street, the slowest and dullest years of his life. In the spring of 1923, he announced that he was fed up with the paper work and was going into the aviation business. Youth was no deterrent to grandiose schemes. In March, Harry Luce and Brit Hadden published the first issue of *Time*, the weekly newsmagazine. They had canvassed their Yale classmates for capital—with scant success until Harry Davison bought some stock and introduced them to partners at J. P. Morgan. Another Bones brother, David Ingalls, had married the daughter of William L. Harkness, a founder of the Standard Oil Company. Dave showed the prospectus to his wife, Louise, and she and her mother subscribed.

To judge from the way Juan went about his business, his training in The Street was not wasted. He typed up letterheads for J. Terry Trippe, using the address of his mother's apartment, where he lived, or 50 Vanderbilt Avenue, without identifying it as the Yale Club. Since the spring of 1922, he had been poring over advertisements in aeronautical journals looking for sales of surplus aircraft and engines. Finally, he spotted an auction of Navy training planes and entered a bid for seven at $500 each, planning to resell a few and keep the rest for a charter and air-taxi service. A single-motor seaplane could accommodate a pilot and one thrill-bent passenger in its open cockpits. He removed the 90-horsepower Curtiss OX-5 engine and substituted a Hispano-Suiza engine with 220 horsepower so that the biplane could carry two passengers, and double the $5 revenue from each trip.

He raised capital by selling stock in Long Island Airways, which he duly incorporated under the laws of New York State. Juan subscribed to 300 shares of common stock at $5 a share and solicited another $3,500 from relatives and friends who were as crazy about flying as he was, and had wealthy parents. The father of S. Davis Robins, a Princeton contemporary, upbraided him for leading his son away from the family business of manufacturing conveyor machinery into the path of foolhardy temptation.

Juan elected himself unsalaried president and general manager, a title that did not preclude his acting in other capacities, such as pilot and maintenance man, or sweeping out the hangar. A barge moored in New York Harbor near the Statue of Liberty served as his passenger depot. The base of operations was a former naval air station rented for $100 a month at Rockaway Beach in Queens. The area was then desolate swampland, with the Manhattan skyline for a backdrop.

During its two summer seasons in operation, Long Island Airways transported socialites to their oceanside summer retreats. Trippe made round-trip package deals with hotels in Atlantic City and tried, unsuccessfully, to interest local railroads in train-plane service to island resorts.

Most ventures run by former war aviators were more like flying circuses than transport businesses. The second generation of birdmen were gypsy pilots, roaming the countryside and beaches in their war-surplus crates, hawking rides at "$5 for five minutes" and scaring the bathers with their aerial acrobatics. A few enterprising souls chartered their seaplanes to bootleggers in the rum-running trade off the Atlantic coastline.

Trippe was an airman in banker's clothing, driving a secondhand custom-bodied Pierce Arrow. He looked with disdain upon the gypsy birdmen, but he rented his planes to other pilots for stunt flying and sightseeing.

He chartered one plane and pilot to the United Fruit Company for an airmail service in Honduras. Once he flew a plane for a movie company that wanted to film a chase down lower Broadway and out to the harbor. Trippe received a summons for coming in low over the sidewalks so that the cameraman could record the scene; the case was dismissed for lack of an ordinance the police could charge him with violating.

Long Island Airways operated in the red (its president was haled into court by a pilot suing for $470 in back wages), but it provided Juan with an education in a business that was not yet an industry. A coherent economic formula for airlines was still to be developed. Anarchy governed. If principles were to be applied, were they those of the sea and shipping or of the land and the railroad? The plane operated in the air, but to whom did the air belong? Who, if anyone, should regulate the service the plane performed?

Trippe compiled information about operating costs and yields and learned to calculate break-even points—granted, on a scale that bore as much relation to the airlines of the future as a Mom-and-Pop candy store has to Macy's. And he accumulated on-the-line experience far greater than most visionaries or promoters had.

He was not in the least abashed about knocking at the portals of the powerful to talk about his minuscule enterprise. He used his contacts, principally his Yale badge, for introduction to friends' fathers and uncles who were heads of railroad and shipping companies. He buttonholed W. Averell Harriman, Yale '13, a venture capitalist on a wide-gauge track, but still involved in parts of his father's empire such as the Union Pacific Railroad. "I'd like to show you my figures," Juan said boldly, but with deference, producing a photograph of one of his planes. "I hope you'll let me look at yours." From contacts at United Fruit, he learned not to count on a profit from a southbound cargo operation without a contract in hand to haul, say, bananas on the return voyage. Older men respond to a younger man who is at once shy and aggressive, respectful of their eminence, asking nothing except a chance to talk figures and economic theory.

It was becoming evident to Trippe that a transportation company had to have a franchise, a right granted and protected by the government to operate between given points. Preferably, the right should be exclusive. In order to attract private capital with which to buy the newest and best equipment to draw customers, the carrier had to be permitted to charge a rate that would ensure a profitable return. What Trippe was heading toward was the semimonopolistic system of regulated competition such as prevailed for the nation's railroads, shipping and utilities, a system of quasi-public capitalism.

Aviation may have been in a preadolescent state, but it did not lack forums and stages on which a young man could make himself visible. Very little happened in the aeronautical world to which J. Terry Trippe of Long Island Airways, Inc., did not gain admission and wiggle himself toward the forefront. He testified at a hearing of a congressional subcommittee on commercial aviation held at the Waldorf-Astoria in New York. The legislators were wrestling with the dilemma of a peacetime air force, which the U.S. military establishment was cool about supporting. They heard arguments that commercial aviation should be encouraged with government aid so that it could convert to national defense in case of war. "Subsidy" being the dirtiest word in the American capitalist lexicon, the support would have to be camouflaged. Amid a host of big guns from banking and aircraft manufacturing, Trippe appeared to report that he knew of "one hundred possible buyers of aviation equipment who are being held back because there are no suitable landing facilities around New York." That Mr. Trippe was 25 years old and his company practically broke did not stop Godfrey Lowell Cabot of Boston, president of the National Aeronautic Association, and other eminences from applauding him.

In the summer of 1924, Trippe affiliated with two older men of substance and experience in a so-called economic and management consulting service, the object being to seek out opportunities in aviation and cut themselves in on the action, taking payment in stock. Leroy L. Odell was an engineer and Major Lorillard Spencer an organizer of the Atlantic Aircraft Company, formed to manufacture Fokker planes in the United States.

Anthony H. G. Fokker, unavoidably nicknamed the Flying Dutchman, was one of those inventors who suffer for being in the avant-garde. At 18 he had designed his first airplane, but was unable to obtain financing in his native Holland. The British, French and Belgian Governments also spurned his talents, and so in 1913 he had gone to work in Germany, where he designed some of the best combat aircraft used in the war. His DR-1 triplane was flown by Manfred von Richthofen, the German Ace of Aces, and even after the Red Baron's death, his Tango Circus Squadron flew in V-shaped formation in scarlet-nosed DR-7s, Fokker's highly maneuverable, fast-climbing biplane. He also invented a device that synchronized machine guns mounted on the front of airplanes with the propellers, enabling the pilots to fire continuously.

After the Armistice, Fokker smuggled into Holland hundreds of airplanes, engines and parts, the contents of an entire German factory, which he used as inventory to start the Fokker Manufacturing Company. American military men tested Fokker models captured from the enemy and were grudgingly impressed with the welded-steel-tube construction of his fuselages, which were slip-covered with fabric. The wings of his planes were made of laminated spruce. The Army and the Navy placed orders with his factory in Amsterdam, but because of antiforeign sentiment in the United States, the planes were not labeled as Fokkers. In May 1923, Army Lieutenants Oakley G. Kelly and John A. Macready made the first nonstop flight across the continent, from Roosevelt Field to San Diego, in 26 hours 50 minutes, in a Fokker monoplane that bore the name Air Service T-2.

To overcome the stigma of his wartime career, Fokker came to the United States in 1922 to set up a plant with American partners in Hasbrouck Heights, New Jersey, and for the next few years he was a transatlantic commuter. Trippe hoped to buy American Fokkers for Long Island Airways to start a Newport service, but he was unable to raise the money to pay for them.

Juan's social relationships were drawing him into an ever-larger web of powerful associations, in which romance played no small part. Hambleton was engaged to marry Margaret Elliott, daughter of George Blow Elliott, president and later chairman of the Atlantic Coast Railroad. Trippe's fraternity brother Alan Scaife, whom he visited occasionally in Pittsburgh, was a good friend of Richard King Mellon, nephew of Andrew W. Mellon, Secretary of the Treasury during the entire Republican decade. Richard's sister Sarah had a crush on Alan that would eventually lead to the altar.

Through the St. Anthony Club, Trippe met another fraternity brother from the University of Virginia, Edward Reilly Stettinius, Jr., son of a partner in J. P. Morgan & Company, and a cousin of David Bruce. Ed, a good-natured youth, had left the university in his senior year, short of credits required for a degree, and took a job as stockroom clerk at 44 cents an hour in a Hyatt Roller Bearing plant. Before long, he became an assistant to a vice president at General Motors Corporation. His father was a director of G.M.

The senior Stettinius was a self-made man. The son of a Lutheran wholesale grocer of Prussian-Hungarian extraction and his Irish Catholic wife, he had been educated by Jesuits at St. Louis University. By his mid-20s he had made and lost a fortune in the corn pit of the Chicago Board of Trade. He transferred his financial skills to industry with more lasting success, first as treasurer of the Sterling Boiler Company, then as a Mr. Fix-It for the ailing Diamond Match Company. He married Judith Carrington, a Richmond belle from one of the First Families of Virginia. In 1915, he was recruited by J. P. Morgan & Co.

to oversee the purchasing of supplies for the Allied governments, and after the war he joined the firm.

In the summer of 1924, Edward Stettinius, Jr., invited his Delta Psi brother Juan Trippe to his family's estate at Locust Valley for a weekend. There Juan met Stettinius' 20-year-old sister, Elizabeth, an effervescent brunette with sapphire eyes.

The spark of love was ignited on the links of the Piping Rock Club. Juan was impressed by the sharpness of Betty's driving stroke, and on the third hole he blurted out, "Do you ever come to town on Saturdays or Sundays?" She divined that this dark, stocky young man was "very, very shy." Why else would he ask such a ridiculous question; it was unimaginable that a New York debutante would leave the North Shore for Manhattan on a weekend in July or August.

Late that afternoon she presented him to her taciturn father, who was then in failing health. As Juan wooed Betty that summer on Long Island, and at the Stettinius mansion at Eighty-fifth Street and Park Avenue in the fall and winter, she noted hopefully that he was the only one of her beaux her father did not refer to as a whippersnapper. Stettinius recognized in Juan certain familiar attributes of mental agility, overindustriousness and furious ambition, but those did not make him an eligible suitor until he proved himself further.

When they met, Betty was the beneficiary of a trust that had capital assets of $333,000; Stettinius had provided well for his four children. At his death of a sudden heart attack at the age of 60, in September 1925, the bulk of his $5-million estate was bequeathed to his wife for her lifetime; the children were to inherit what remained of the principal after she died.

Though Betty would not be dependent on her husband to keep a roof over their heads, "the family"—namely, her mother and elder brother, William Carrington Stettinius—would not consent to a match "until Juan has a business." It was a formidable hurdle to his courtship, for Trippe seemed to have nothing but "crazy" flying schemes. Long Island Airways ceased to be a going concern; his investment was wiped out. Nevertheless, he maintained a tiny bank account for the company at the Bank of New York. One never knew when an empty corporate structure might be useful.

4

Mail Carrier

The U.S. Post Office Department had been asserting all along that it would turn the airmail service over to private enterprise as soon as its feasibility was demonstrated.

Safety accessories recommended by the pilots were added to the planes, with the result that fatalities and operating costs were reduced. In 1923, a lighting system was installed over the route from Chicago to Cheyenne to make night flying possible, and a year later it was extended to New York.

In 1924, Representative Melville Clyde Kelly, a Republican from Pittsburgh, offered a bill authorizing the Postmaster General to contract with private operators to carry mail by air over designated routes. Kelly was bombarded with ideas for domestic airmail legislation by J. T. Trippe, a persistent young New Yorker introduced to him by Alan Scaife, his Yale fraternity brother. The Scaifes were an old Pittsburgh family identified with metalworking, and among Kelly's more prominent constituents.

The Kelly bill sailed through Congress and was enacted on February 2, 1925. It set a minimum postage rate of 10 cents an ounce, with a proportional share of the revenues going to the operators, who were awarded three- to five-year contracts; the law was amended a year later to make weight the basis of payment.

The Air Mail Act of 1925, thereafter called the Kelly Act, was the long-awaited signal for the aviation industry, providing at last the modicum of stability to pique the interest of entrepreneurs and investors. Several thousand aspiring operators made applications to the

Postmaster General, and several well-capitalized groups were organized to bid on the routes.

One was National Air Transport, led by Clement M. Keys, a financial journalist from Ontario turned Wall Street promoter, and Howard E. Coffin of the Hudson Motor Company of Detroit, a somewhat discredited czar of aircraft production during the war. Keys bought control of the faltering Glenn Curtiss Company in 1920. He used it as a vehicle for gobbling up other aviation companies in frank emulation of James J. Hill, the Canadian speculator who had allied himself with J. P. Morgan against Edward H. Harriman in the titanic battle at the turn of the century for control of the Chicago, Burlington & Quincy Railroad. Keys visualized himself as an aeronautical successor to Hill.

Another powerful entrant upon the scene was Henry Ford, who bailed out William B. Stout, the inventor of a plane made entirely of metal, by taking over his company. Stout designed the Ford trimotor, otherwise known as the "Tin Goose," a nearly indestructible aircraft. In April 1925, Ford started a scheduled airline to move freight from his automobile company between Detroit and Chicago.

While the Kelly Act was still being lobbied, Trippe and his consulting partners, Spencer and Odell, prepared an analysis of the costs and market potential of various types of air service. By April they had drawn plans for organizing a company to transport mail, merchandise and passengers with Kelly Act contracts. Service would be introduced on a line between Boston and New York to connect with the government's night flying service to Chicago.

They expected their volume to consist mainly of express mail; an important attraction for businessmen and bankers was the opportunity to present checks for clearance a day sooner than if they were sent by rail, thereby gaining them an earlier use of the moneys collected. Connecting lines to Washington, Atlanta, Miami and Havana were to be established later on.

According to their estimates, $250,000 capital was needed for the New York–Boston line—to acquire landing fields, equip the airway with lights and weather facilities, and to buy four planes. They drew in as associates Robert G. Thach, a lawyer and former war ace from a noted political family in Alabama, and Sherman M. Fairchild, son of a partner of Thomas J. Watson in the company that became International Business Machines. Aviation, for Fairchild, was a means of getting out from under his father's shadow; he had patented an aerial camera device.

They named their company Eastern Air Transport, Inc., and incorporated it in Delaware. Spencer was president, Trippe vice president, Odell secretary and Fairchild treasurer. They were to take a total of 15 percent of the stock in promoters' fees. As they were soliciting subscribers during the summer, in anticipation of the Post Office's opening bids in September, they learned of a competitor for the New York –Boston route. Colonial Airlines, a charter service based in Naugatuck, Connecticut, had been organized by a group of New England businessmen, one of whom, John H. Trumbull, was currently occupying the Governor's Mansion in Hartford. A hasty merger was arranged, Trippe went to Washington to enter a bid, and on October 7, Colonial Air Transport was awarded the contract airmail route (CAM 1) from Boston to New York by way of Hartford.

CAM 2, covering St. Louis to Chicago, went to Robertson Aircraft Corporation, which then hired several pilots, including a 23-year-old Minnesotan, Charles Augustus Lindbergh, Jr. Keys's National Air Transport picked up the Chicago–Dallas route. Henry Ford won two routes, Detroit–Cleveland and Detroit–Chicago. A dozen routes, totaling 5,500 miles, were handed out in the first round of contract awards. Postmaster General Harry New's concept was to let the operators gain experience with these feeder lines before he opened bids on the transcontinental route.

October 1925 was a watershed in U.S. aviation history. Apart from the significance of the distribution of airmail contracts, there was the Army court-martial of Brigadier General Billy Mitchell. The leader of the American expeditionary air force in France, Mitchell was an angry prophet of air power, a martyr who deployed newspaper publicity in his war against a military establishment that was indifferent, if not downright hostile, to the airplane.

No sooner was the Armistice signed than he was warning of the threat of Japanese and German aviation capability. In June 1921, to prove his point about aerial weaponry, he staged the destruction of a captured German submarine destroyer and a heavy cruiser by a group of bomber pilots. He added further proof in July, when his fliers rained bombs on the 23,000-ton battleship *Ostfriesland*, sending the dreadnought to the bottom of the Atlantic.

Mitchell was getting nowhere with his advocacy of a separate air force. Frustrated, he pressed his attacks on the military leaders from his position as assistant chief of the Army Air Service. He persistently called attention to crashes of Army and Navy airplanes—"winged coffins," as he termed them. In September 1925, after the Navy dirigible *Shenandoah* was torn apart in a storm over Ohio, Mitchell called a press conference. He blasted the administration of national defense by the War and Navy Departments as "incompetent, criminally negligent and almost treasonable." Mitchell deliberately painted himself into a corner by attacking his superiors while still in impeccably tailored uniform. He was brought up on charges of insubordination and conduct violating the military code of discipline, found guilty and suspended for five years from rank, command and pay. President Coolidge offered to moderate his punishment if he would only behave, but Mitchell scoffed and resigned, preferring to be vindicated, as it developed, after his death in 1936.

Mitchell's charges that national security was endangered by neglect of air power gained widespread attention through the press. Simultaneously, aviation promoters were clamoring for federal regulation of commercial air operations as a means of establishing public confidence, and of avoiding the chaos that would result if each state separately asserted jurisdiction of the air above it. Free-entrepreneurs called on the government to provide the solid base they could not afford to erect for their risky businesses. In response to these different pressures, President Coolidge appointed Dwight Morrow of J. P. Morgan & Co. to head an investigation.

The Morrow Board's report, issued in December, dismissed Mitchell's contention that the nation was in danger of air attack ("protected, as the United States is, by broad oceans from possible enemies") and rejected his plea for a unified government air service. However, the board recommended immediate legislative action to encourage the development and use of civilian aircraft.

Congress embraced the board's proposals and the following May passed the Air Commerce Act. It entrusted airplane safety to the Commerce Department: to license aircraft and pilots, draw up operating regulations, and establish and maintain airways and navigation facilities. The nasty word "subsidy," was neatly sidestepped. William P. MacCracken, Jr., a lawyer and former Army pilot, was named Assistant Secretary of Commerce for Aeronautics, and Trubee Davison, the organizer of the Yale Aviation Unit, Assistant Secretary of War for Air. Edward P. Warner, a former professor of aeronautical engineering at Massachusetts Institute of Technology and a director of Colonial Air Transport, was appointed the Navy's Assistant Secretary for Aeronautics.

Billy Mitchell's court-martial, the end product of a military dispute, turned out to be a catalyst for the airline business.

Once he had the Boston–New York airmail contract, it was easy sailing for Juan to attract subscribers for stock in Colonial Air Transport. He started with wealthy air-minded friends like John Hambleton and William A. Rockefeller, a member of the Yale Aviation Unit and a neighbor of the Trippes in Greenwich. Rockefeller interested unit-brother Harry Davison. Hearing that Cornelius Vanderbilt Whitney was back in town, Juan took his proposition to his old schoolmate.

Whitney had acquitted himself respectably in his father's Western mining business and had married Marie Norton, a New York debutante. The elder Whitney wanted him "to get started in the city and take over some of my things." By the fall of 1925, Sonny was set up in an office at 120 Broadway, just off Wall Street. Harry P. Whitney was on the board of the Guaranty Trust Company (one of his fellow directors was Edward R. Stettinius, Sr.), and so, in the mornings, his son went to the bank "and learned a few things." When his father died in 1930, the bank elected Sonny a director.

"On the side, I looked for enterprises," Whitney said, and as always happens to those who have money to burn, entrepreneurs looked for him. After Whitney put himself down for stock, Trippe could approach Richard F. Hoyt, a high-powered Wall Street speculator and sportsman whom Whitney knew from Long Island. Juan's New York crowd subscribed with the understanding that the company would bid on numerous airmail contracts as they opened up, including one from Key West to Havana that had lapsed with the demise of Aeromarine Airways.

Colonial Air Transport was described in *The New York Times* of December 15, 1925, as "the first definite adventure of important financial men into the field of commercial aviation, with the avowed intention of extending their activities to all parts of the country if their efforts prove successful."

Odell acknowledged that it was a risky business. "When I have talked to any of these men," he told a reporter, "I have said that this was a gamble, a speculation, but that it offered unlimited possibilities, and that if it proved a success, we might as well be in it. We are sure it will be, but for the time being, this New England line will be a laboratory in which we will learn everything there is to know about commercial flying."

Governor Trumbull of Connecticut was elected chairman of the board and W. Irving Bullard, a Boston banker and head of that city's Chamber of Commerce, president of Colonial Air Transport. J. Terry Trippe appeared on the roster as one of four vice presidents. He was designated to run the operation, at a salary of $7,500 a year, which he was not to start drawing until the spring of 1926, when service started. He also received 600 shares of common stock, of no value until the enterprise became successful.

"Fix it so that our crowd is in control," Juan directed Thach. The lawyer came up with a device to balance power among blocs; the common stock was placed in a voting trust. There were seven trustees: Trippe, Hambleton, Rockefeller and four New Englanders. Then Governor Trumbull ceded his place to Theodore Weicker, vice president of E. R. Squibb & Sons and the father of a younger Yale friend Trippe had made in St. Anthony. Weicker was one of the larger stockholders brought in by Juan.

Much had to be done before the line could begin operating, including the purchase of equipment. In the meantime, Trippe was spending a good deal of time with Tony Fokker, who had developed a new plane, roomy enough to carry both mail and passengers. Reasoning that engine failure was the bane of aviation safety, Fokker made a quick conversion of his F-7A single-motor design by mounting three of the new 200-horsepower air-cooled radial engines manufactured by the Wright Aeronautical Company on the nose and each side of the wing. The Wright Whirlwind was a radical improvement on the heavy Liberty engine, since it did away with the bulky radiator and the need to carry water for cooling.

Fokker's craving for additional capital and an assured market for his trimotor coincided with Trippe's need to persuade Colonial's board of directors to approve the order he placed for two of the ten-passenger planes, which cost $37,500 apiece.

Trippe instructed Harry Bruno, the press agent for the Whirlwind engine, to build up public acceptance for the Fokker plane so as to pave the way for Colonial's introduction of passenger service and to influence his directors. Bruno's resourcefulness in ballyhoo seemed inexhaustible. Trial flights were staged over New York City with tea served aloft and all the amenities pointed out to the press, including a toilet that was Fokker's pride and joy. The impression was conveyed that the Fokker trimotor emblazoned with the Colonial insignia was safe and comfortable, a veritable "flying Pullman car."

In December, Trippe was a passenger on a "giant survey trip" of Florida. The rosy-cheeked Fokker, cutting a stubby figure in golf knickers and boisterous sport jackets, was photographed filming alligators through the windows of the plane and landing to a hero's welcome in several cities, where he made speeches extolling the virtues of his aircraft and its sturdy engines. Spectators were unaware that before reaching Florida the plane had been forced down by bad weather in a cotton field outside Atlanta.

The crowning event of the campaign was a flight from Miami to Havana on Christmas Day in the record-breaking time of 125 minutes. The mechanic who had been tending the Wright engines en route noticed that they were overheating during flight, and he refused to make the journey over water. Unable to secure the requisite high-test aviation gasoline at the various landing fields, Fokker had allowed the plane to be refueled with half automobile gasoline and half benzol. Over Havana, the pilot cut one of the engines and then a second, demonstrating to the crowd below (which included the new Cuban President, Gerardo Machado) that the F-7 could stay in the air with two-thirds of its power gone.

There was no publicity about the deal Trippe struck behind the scenes in Havana. Through a Yale connection, Juan hurried to see a lawyer who prepared a letter of agreement in which the Cuban Government granted Trippe landing rights at Camp Colombia, the army airport, as well as tax exemptions and other concessions. In the freebooting environment of Latin America, such rights were often granted to individuals rather than the companies, allowing the recipients to transfer them later. Machado was a businessman who had taken office in May with a popular mandate for economic reform. He granted Trippe a hearing that evening, and an official signed the letter, which Juan pocketed, leaving Havana the next day with something precious in his possession.

On the way back, two engines began knocking and overheating; the plane rattled as though convulsed and then lost altitude above the Florida Keys. The pilot landed on a coral reef near Key Largo, and he and his two passengers climbed out and jacked the plane up with an engine crank to prevent it from being carried away by the oncoming tide. A Good Samaritan appeared to row them to shore, where they hiked to a railroad track and lit a fire on the ties to stop the next train to Miami. They made arrangements to ship new engines down by boat. The plane was sold to Edsel Ford, who christened it the *Josephine* and gave it to Lieutenant Commander Richard E. Byrd for his exploratory flight to the North Pole in May 1926.

Also in December, Trippe and Hambleton laid plans to bid for mail routes in Alaska. "A territory where people pay four hundred dollars for the privilege of walking behind a dogsled for ninety days is a good prospect for an airline," Juan said. The point had been tentatively made by Ben Eielson, a former Army pilot who had migrated to Fairbanks with a Curtiss Jenny to which he added skis and made a round-trip hop in one day to a settlement 300 air miles distant, beating the dogsled schedule by five weeks.

They hired Eielson as their agent and supplied him with a ski-equipped Army-surplus DH-4, which he flew in a gypsy operation for several months, competing against the dogsled deliverers. Juan obtained permission from his directors to change the name of the dormant Eastern Air Transport to Alaskan Air Transport, Inc., preparatory to bidding in the spring of 1926.

Everything hinged on whether the Postmaster General would decide to incorporate the territory into the domestic mail system. The dogsled operators, pressing their case through the Governor of Alaska, maintained that the Star Route mail contracts covering the territory were not written to include service by air.

Hambleton asked David Bruce for an introduction to Harry New. David was living in Washington, about to enter the Foreign Service and to become betrothed to Ailsa Mellon, daughter of the Secretary of the Treasury. Juan was granted an interview by the Postmaster General, but in the end, the dogsled operators had greater influence. New ruled that he could not entertain bids from an airline. Trippe and Hambleton recognized defeat and withdrew, leaving Eielson to pioneer alone in the frozen North.

Months before Colonial Air Transport carried a single letter through the New England skies, dissension set in between its regional factions. The businessmen from Connecticut and Massachusetts were satisfied with trying to compete against the railroads of the Northeast by appealing to a market of bankers and manufacturers. The rich investors from New York were on the lookout for wider worlds to conquer.

Juan's failure to communicate his intentions, a habit that was to be the hallmark of his modus operandi, irritated the older Yankee directors, who did not enjoy being captives to the enthusiasms of their 26-year-old managing director. They were dubious about the commitments he made for three-engine equipment (two Fokkers and two Stout metal planes designed for Ford). At that stage of technology, a dichotomy existed between mail and passenger service. A single-engine high-speed aircraft resembling a fighter plane was considered by the Post Office to be ideal for expediting mail; the pilot could bail out from an open cockpit if something untoward happened. Colonial had to be in possession of ten mail planes to qualify for the contract. It owned three: two Curtiss Larks and a Fokker Universal. Passenger transport entailed larger, multiengine planes with a greater margin of safety and comfort, as well as higher operating costs. Trippe's acquisitions, together with the smaller mail planes, represented a capital investment of $250,000. Time was running out. Other successful bidders were already operating their mail routes. By June 1926, it was urgent for Trippe to get the Post Office to reconsider its ruling.

With Hambleton working his magic connection again (David Bruce had become the son-in-law of Secretary of the Treasury

Mellon), Trippe descended on Second Assistant Postmaster General W. Irving Glover. Glover, a former New Jersey politician whom New had placed in charge of airmail, was eager to go down in history as the apostle of the new service. "Businessmen will not be content to have their mail creep along on an iron horse," he declared in one of his numerous speeches. He could be cultivated by a persuasive young man seemingly backed by the great fortunes of America.

Juan found him amazingly receptive. "He went so far out of his way to be agreeable," he reported to John Hambleton, "that I came near to being embarrassed. Mr. Morrow had evidently done some yeoman work in our behalf." Just how the intervention of the head of the President's Air Board was arranged is unclear from the record, though several in Trippe's crowd (Davison, Whitney and Bruce) had access to the Morgan partner. "There was no further talk of Colonial providing ten ships, nor even five," Juan exulted to John.

Trippe seized the opportunity to broach another project he and Hambleton were pursuing—to activate the route from Key West to Havana. Glover was encouraging; "His attitude left no doubt in my mind but that he would cooperate with us to the utmost," Juan said.

This assumption was a manifestation of Juan's incorrigible optimism, a source of annoyance to the New England directors and similarly vexing to his later associates. He always came away from a meeting absolutely convinced the other party agreed with him, even in the face of evidence to the contrary. And no sooner was one part of a dream partially taking shape than he was off on another tangent. "A New York–Havana run is not out of the question with Glover in his present frame of mind," he informed John.

Colonial inaugurated regular postal and express service on July 1, 1926. The planes left Boston at 6 P.M., stopped at Hartford at 7:15 P.M. and arrived at the New York terminal, Teterboro Airport in New Jersey, at 8:15 P.M. The northbound lap was begun at 6:15 the next morning, scheduled to arrive in Boston at 9:15 A.M., in time for the second morning mail delivery.

Juan sent Betty Stettinius a letter bearing the special cancellation of the first flight, a prize for stamp collectors.

Problems mounted. The route had to be shifted from the shoreline to a northerly course to avoid the fogs that blotted out pilots' visibility. A half-hour before takeoff, they were handed reports of weather conditions at their destinations. The information was gathered from upper-air readings of balloons sent aloft at Boston and New York, and notes of surface wind velocities and cloud formation at Hartford, which were telephoned or telegraphed along the line.

Support for the service fell short of expectations. Colonial had to carry 150 to 300 pounds of mail a month to break even. Loads were running around 30 pounds. Businessmen concluded that the time saved over the rail system on such a short route (220 miles in all) did not warrant altering their mail-distribution methods.

Whether the fault lay with the conservatism of Yankee businessmen or the shortcomings of management, the fact remained that the 278-mile Chicago–St. Louis route operated by the Robertsons was showing a profit. Still, most operators were scratching to survive, resorting to tricks of padding such as mailing bricks, wet blotters and telephone directories to themselves and friends. The Post Office based remuneration on poundage as estimated by weighing sacks of mail without examining the contents. Trippe told Colonial agents to send mail and registered letters to each other in 1-pound pouches.

Criticism was falling on the managing director from all sides. To allay friction, Juan agreed to bring in an older man as an active president for the airline, replacing Bullard. The Boston banker had been a figurehead. As far as Trippe was concerned, Major General John F. O'Ryan, a reputable transportation expert, was to give Colonial a veneer of prestige and senior statesmanship, and that was all. He barely concealed his contempt for the General, and either ignored his suggestions or belittled them with remarks such as "We've already been working on that and we've found there are operating difficulties."

Juan believed an all-out effort had to be made to secure longer routes, not necessarily for Colonial but for him and his friends. He was encouraged when Dwight Morrow delivered the opinion that the Key West–Havana route with extensions to the south was "the best opportunity now existing." Trippe proposed to Hambleton that they revamp Alaskan Air Transport as a vehicle for luring new capital. He believed Colonial could be induced to sell the Fokker trimotors for "payment 50% cash, 50% stock in a new company."

Trippe and Hambleton sniffed around Washington to ascertain that a New York–Chicago route, the eastern half of a "Columbia," or transcontinental, airway, would probably be opened to competitive bidding by the Post Office early the following year.

Trippe thought Colonial's chances would be enhanced if it were linked with a proposed extension of Henry Ford's Detroit–Cleveland service to Buffalo. Aided by Bill Rockefeller and William Mayo, Ford's chief engineer, he tapped wealthy Yale alumni in Buffalo for pledges of half a million dollars, promising to raise like amounts in Cleveland, New York and Chicago.

Before the year was out, Trippe's investors put up more capital. Whitney subscribed an additional $25,000, his cousin William H.

Vanderbilt $50,000. Dave Ingalls and his Cleveland friends signed for $25,000. And Trippe scraped together $24,000, just about all he had from his father's estate.

Trippe and O'Ryan were at verbal swords' points, slashing at each other mostly in letters and memoranda. Behind Juan's back O'Ryan referred to him as his lackey. Trippe went from director to director, disparaging the General as incompetent to run an airline and incapable of devising a long-range strategy for its survival.

Was he whistling in the dark when he wrote Hambleton on December 2 that "I am going to stick, and five years from now I will turn back ten dollars for every single dollar invested, or 'bust' in the attempt"? His determination was fueled by the knowledge that "I personally persuaded Messrs. Weicker, Rockefeller, Whitney, Fairchild, Hoyt and others to invest." If they lost their money, the shame would be his.

On January 15, 1927, the Post Office opened the bidding for the New York–Chicago route and, on a technicality, threw out all the offers submitted. Shortly before the deadline for the second round of bidding, the internal feuding at Colonial reached the boiling point.

This time pricing was the thorny issue. O'Ryan, with most of the New Englanders behind him, wanted to offer the lowest possible bid to ensure winning the contract. He had made a proposal to National Air Transport for joint operation and was promised he would keep his position as president if they were awarded the contract. Trippe's group, "the conservative element" as he called them, insisted on a rate that would give Colonial "a reasonable chance to break even." They were disenchanted with the wildcat competition enveloping the domestic mail routes. The prospects of constantly trying to better the records of the efficient railroads with new planes looked bleak. Overtaking slow steamships was an entirely different matter.

"The situation is discouraging," Juan wrote to one of the directors. "We are running in the hole over $8,000 a month—less than $100,000 capital remaining. The overhead must be cut down, or we are finished." He was willing to make sacrifices, to carry on without remuneration if necessary because so many personal friends were involved in Colonial.

On March 18, a week before the closing of the bids, the seven-man executive committee voted to have Colonial's minimum price set by agreement among O'Ryan, Trippe, Odell and a fourth officer of the corporation. The next day, O'Ryan decided not to be bound. He called another meeting of the executive committee in Hartford, knowing that Trippe was in New York closing a sale of some of his mother's property and that two of his associates, Weicker and Odell, were also unable to attend. The four members present authorized O'Ryan to name his figure for the bid and gave him the assurance he sought, that he and not that impudent young Trippe was the chief executive of Colonial Air Transport.

Trippe conferred with some of his largest stockholders, Rockefeller, Whitney, Davison and Hambleton. They felt their investments endangered by the turn of events. One course of action remained for Trippe—to go to the voting trust Thach had had the foresight to set up more than a year before. There Juan was certain of a majority. Hambleton and Rockefeller were with him all the way. He had lunched with "old man Weicker" just the other day. "You can count on me," the white-bearded pharmaceutical tycoon had told him.

Since Colonial was a corporation chartered in Connecticut, the trustees could act only in that state. Greenwich was the first town beyond the New York border. Juan called a meeting of the voting trustees for 12:01 A.M. on March 24, the last day for bidding, in the Greenwich railroad station. The deed was quickly done: the trustees voted 4 to 3 to restructure the board to a more manageable number and constituted a new slate of directors favorable to Trippe's "conservative" stand on the bidding. The victorious quartet took the milk train back to New York, where, as a quorum of the board, they fixed the minimum bid at $1.68 a pound.

Juan and John Hambleton hurried to Teterboro Airport, climbed aboard a small Fokker plane and flew to Washington. Outside Glover's office at 11:30 A.M. they met O'Ryan and Governor Trumbull. The deadline was at noon. "The board has met and all of us from Boston and Hartford feel that we should withdraw our bid," Trumbull informed them. "We think Colonial should stay with the Boston–New York route. After all, the New Haven Railroad hasn't done so badly with that route."

"That board was disbanded this morning. The new board is submitting this bid," Trippe said. The only thing that made economic sense, he argued to Trumbull, was a long haul from east to west, with a southern extension from New York, the junction center for traffic feeding to and from New England. Trumbull shook his head. Trippe turned to enter Glover's office and place the bid on his desk.

The next morning, Juan received a telephone call from the legal counsel of Colonial informing him that the voting trust was illegal; it had been drawn for a term of ten years, and Connecticut law specified a maximum of seven years. Trippe met with Governor Trumbull again. "Let's put it before the stockholders," he proposed. Trumbull assented.

They tossed a coin for the place of the meeting—heads for Hartford, tails New York. Heads it was.

Trumbull called the shareholders' meeting to order in the Governor's Mansion. The vote was 52 to 48 in favor of withdrawing the bid. O'Ryan stated what Colonial's long-range policy was going to be: to stick with Boston–New York and do development work on routes to Montreal and Buffalo through separate companies.

There was nothing for Juan to do but quit. "Inasmuch as I have no confidence whatsoever in his [O'Ryan's] ability to successfully manage an air transport company I am resigning as vice president to take effect today," he wrote to a Buffalo banker on May 2. "I was responsible last September 1 for putting him in—a sad mistake," he confided in the letter, which he asked the banker to destroy on receipt. He also urged him not to invest in any Buffalo venture O'Ryan might organize. "It will almost certainly end disastrously."

Despite Juan's efforts at undermining O'Ryan, Colonial succeeded in extending its service to Albany and Buffalo, and won a foreign airmail contract between New York and Montreal before it was absorbed in 1930 into a predecessor company of American Airlines. The New York–Chicago route was awarded to National Air Transport; the western end of the transcontinental trunk line was subsequently won by Boeing Air Transport, an arm of an aircraft company organized by William E. Boeing, a Yale-educated lumber heir from Seattle.

It would always rankle Trippe, who was to devote the rest of his life to international air transport, that had it not been for the myopia of the New Englanders, he would surely have built up the nation's largest domestic air system.

In the spring of 1927, though, he was a man without a business. Moreover, when the accounts were finally settled, he lost the money he and his friends had invested in Colonial. Trippe's status was not likely to captivate the Stettinius family. He called on Betty and they walked up and down Park Avenue while he told her he had no right to see her for a year.

5

What Everyone Was Waiting For

J. T. Trippe, unemployed airline manager, drove to Roosevelt Field on Long Island in a pelting rain before dawn on Friday, May 20, to mingle with several hundred aeronautical buffs and celebrity hunters in front of a roped enclosure protecting a silver monoplane with *Spirit of St. Louis* inscribed on its nose. The bulldog edition of the New York *Daily Mirror*, which hit the streets at 9 o'clock Thursday evening, had scored a beat with the news that Charles Lindbergh was about to take off for Paris.

The 25-year-old mail pilot had been waiting around for a week for the weather to clear so that he could make his bid for the $25,000 Orteig Prize. In 1919, Raymond Orteig, the French-born owner of the Hotel Brevoort on Fifth Avenue, had offered the purse to anyone who could make a nonstop flight between New York and Paris in either direction. In June of that year, two Englishmen, Captain John Alcock and Lieutenant Arthur Brown, had flown without stopping between St. John's, Newfoundland, and Clifden, Ireland, a distance of 1,936 miles, the shortest span of the North Atlantic, to qualify for a $50,000 prize from the London *Daily Mail*. For lack of an aircraft with sufficient power to cross the 3,350 miles of open sea between New York and the French capital, Orteig's prize was still unclaimed after eight years.

Now that problem was solved, or so three contenders believed, with the advent of the Wright Whirlwind, lighter and more efficient than any engine previously on the market. Charles Levine, a blustery dealer in military parts, and his pilot, Clarence Chamberlin, were planning to set out in a Bellanca cabin plane built specifically to show what the Whirlwind could do. Lieutenant Commander Richard E. Byrd, backed by Rodman Wanamaker, was going to attempt the crossing in a Fokker trimotor with three crewmen aboard. Both planes were outfitted with radios and instruments.

The newspapers referred to Lindbergh as "the flying kid" (some called him "the flyin' fool"). Unlike his remaining competitors, he was bound for Paris with neither companion, radio nor sextant. He was going to navigate on dead reckoning in a single-engine plane stripped down to the severest minimum in order to accommodate extra fuel. His long, skinny body was wedged into a wicker seat in the cockpit, gasoline tanks filling the space around him. For nourishment, he had five delicatessen sandwiches supplied by a publicity man for Wright Aeronautical, and two canteens of water.

The omens were unfavorable for his departure. A report of partial clearing over the ocean had prompted his sudden decision to risk flight. But even as he climbed aboard, the wind shifted from east to west, giving his bloated plane an unwanted 5-mile-an-hour tail wind. He signaled the mechanics to start the motor, pulled the goggles down over his ice-blue eyes and nodded for the blocks to be kicked away. The men tugged at the wing struts to dislodge the plane from the muddy soil. The engine emitted a sluggish roar, as though complaining of weight and humidity. The *Spirit of St. Louis* felt more like an overloaded truck than an airplane, Lindbergh thought, as it lurched down the soggy field under its 2½-ton burden. Takeoff seemed hopeless. The wheels left the ground for a second; the plane trembled and bounced back twice before it lifted up and, avoiding telephone wires at the edge of the runway by 20 feet, disappeared into the misty horizon.

Harry Bruno scurried alongside the plane in a yellow roadster with a policeman seated beside him, holding a fire extinguisher. "By God, he made it!" he cried when Lindbergh was in the sky. The crowd of spectators, Trippe included, breathed a collective sigh, relieved of their concern that the overloaded plane might crash as it was being coaxed into the air. Thirty-three hours 39 minutes later, "the Lone Eagle" arrived at Le Bourget, the idol of the century.

A month after he watched Lindbergh across the rope barrier at the airfield, Trippe attended a breakfast in Lindbergh's honor given by Orteig at the Hotel Brevoort before the presentation of the prize money. Juan could do little but observe and drink his coffee, for the flier was now a hero twelve feet tall, with a lawyer and millionaire friends to guard him. A new competition had started, this one among businessmen begging for Lindbergh to endorse their products or otherwise lend his halo to their enterprises. "We've got to get to him," Sonny Whitney said, and Juan and John Hambleton agreed. Whitney was the likeliest to succeed in establishing contact, through his father's Wright connection and some of his Long Island crowd who were giving Lindbergh shelter from his admirers.

On a commercial scale, the Lindbergh flight registered the seismographic shock that aviation promoters had been hopefully awaiting. "The American people gave way to a veritable orgy of air-mindedness," said Edward Warner, the Assistant Secretary of the Navy for Aeronautics. The eighty-two cities Lindbergh was scheduled to visit on a tour of the United States in the *Spirit of St. Louis* went on an airport-building-and-improvement spree. The promotional frenzy surrounding the young Galahad of the air spurred a proliferation of new mail routes and of companies formed to bid for them; vast demand for aircraft was anticipated.

In a capitalist system, new services and new products require new sources of financing. Investor appetites must be whetted. The Lindbergh phenomenon stimulated recollections of "getting in on the ground floor" of the automobile industry and becoming rich overnight. A boom of manic proportions developed in Wall Street around the aviation business, modest as it was. With gross revenues of only $90 million, it ranked 144th among manufacturing industries—even corsets were bigger business, an analyst noted. The wheels had been greased by Secretary of the Treasury Mellon, whose program of reducing taxes on capital gains was drawing investors out of the sleepy bond market into the livelier play of common stocks.

Between March 1928 and December 1929, some $300 million in aviation securities were issued to the public, and a churning market inflated their paper value to $1 billion before it collapsed. Promoters and speculators swam together to form holding companies for stock in aircraft and air-transport enterprises. Uninhibited by government regulation or by concern for the investing public at large, the sharks devoured the smaller fish in the pond and then randomly switched allegiances, the better to prey on one another.

Aeronautical inventors and design geniuses short of capital and capacity for handling the millions of dollars in orders that began coming in were the first to be swallowed. "We feared we would be left out in the cold if we didn't have some hookup with an airline or a big group," said Grover Loening, whose amphibian plane was highly regarded by explorers and Army and Navy surveying expeditions. The Loening Aeronautical Engineering Company was taken over by Hayden, Stone & Company, aggressive investment bankers, and merged with Keystone Aircraft.

Incestuous marriages between investment trusts and the aircraft and airline companies they controlled, principally through memberships on each other's boards of directors, were patterned after the plunderers of older industries like railroads and utilities.

The hungriest shark was Clement Keys, of the grabby Curtiss Aeroplane Company. His National Air Transport walked off with the New York–Chicago airmail contract after Colonial Air Transport dropped out of the bidding. In 1928, Keys was instrumental in organizing a coast-to-coast passenger line, Transcontinental Air Transport, in partnership with the Pennsylvania Railroad, and in securing Lindbergh's help in surveying its route. With Lindbergh-induced acquisition fever running high, Keys formed a new holding company, North American Aviation, Inc., capitalized at $25 million, to absorb his past interests and initiate a new buying binge. One of his associates in that venture was General Motors, with its ties to the Du Ponts and J. P. Morgan. G.M. bought a slew of companies that manufactured aviation components such as brakes, carburetors and weather instruments, the largest of these being the Bendix Aviation Corporation. In 1929, G.M. acquired Fokker Aircraft.

Keys's fiercest rival, turned an ally in T.A.T. and North American Aviation, was Richard F. Hoyt, a partner in Hayden, Stone and chairman of the board of the Wright Aeronautical Corporation. Besides being a financier, the mild-mannered Hoyt was a yachtsman, speedboat racer, amateur pilot and womanizer. He may have been the first to appreciate the efficiency that a private plane lends to a busy man's schedule, enabling him to wedge amorous rendezvous between appointments to structure financial deals. All in all, Dick Hoyt was regarded as Wall Street's aviation oracle, a gatekeeper of its insiders' paradise, the man to see about any proposition that had to do with flying.

For months after Trippe lost his job, he and he investors tried "to straighten out the Colonial mess." Juan being persona non grata to the New Englanders, Hambleton, Whitney and Rockefeller were appointed a committee to try to amass enough shares for them to have a controlling majority or to be bought out at a price they considered fair compensation for their stock. In the end, they took losses on their investments. All that could be immediately rescued from Colonial was the two Fokker trimotors O'Ryan was willing to sell them at a bare-cost price.

In the meantime, Trippe, Hambleton and Whitney set about organizing another company with more compatible partners than the Yankee businessmen. It would be an engineering and management corporation formed by wartime pilots to furnish experienced management and, in some cases, part of the capital to develop the many new air routes they were confident the Post Office would soon be advertising for bids.

The talents of the triumvirate were well meshed. John had the winning personality and a key to the Republican Administration in Washington through the Secretary of the Treasury's son-in-law, David Bruce. Sonny could turn on his money spigots and was interested in being the "guiding light" of a great aviation enterprise. Juan was doggedly tenacious and desired nothing other than "to devote my entire time and efforts" to the venture.

They thought in regional terms, something for different groups of investors: a service out of Buffalo, another to the society resorts within a radius of New York and Baltimore, and a network of routes to the Caribbean and South America.

Operating a commercial airline over 100 miles of water between Florida and Cuba was only a plausible beginning for them. "We were flying since we were eighteen; we had great faith," Whitney said. They talked of spanning 3,000 miles of Atlantic and 5,000 miles of Pacific. One weekend Hambleton invited Juan and another friend to his country home outside Baltimore to talk about financing an airline for foreign service. John introduced an idea he had been mulling over for some time: an intercontinental polar route. It seemed almost as farfetched as that of travel to the moon until they examined a globe, and saw how distances between major capitals were abbreviated and how much less water there was to worry about if one headed north.

For all their faith and all their connections, they could not convince bankers that they had a sound business concept. Even Whitney was unable to persuade the Guaranty Trust to grant a loan. The only avenue open to them was through the equity market by selling stock to men of like faith and speculative instinct who hoped to take advantage of the fever rising in Wall Street.

That was how everyone else was doing it. Promoters scouted franchises—routes supported by airmail contracts—and formed corporations to bid on one or more routes. When several promoters converged on the same route, two or more joined forces and ganged up on their competitors.

As soon as one contract was in their pockets, the winners set their sights on the next. The certificates for the stock they sold were supposed to represent physical properties or other assets. Often, the assets consisted solely of the hope of operating an air route subsidized by government mail pay. Amid the swapping of stock certificates, book values (or the presumed worth of the corporate assets) were highly inflated. The process of fusing corporate entities and issuing new certificates was known as watering the stock, an opportunistic tradition that had attended the building of the railroads and that was to be repeated as transportation took to the skies. The sheer glamour of aviation generated great expectations of profits, and in the last of "the crazy years," as the French labeled the Twenties, expectations bred higher and higher prices for the stock.

The trio became an organizing quintet with the addition of Bill Rockefeller and Sherman Fairchild. For a while, they thought of dusting off Eastern Air Transport as their vehicle, but decided instead on a new one with a grander title, Aviation Corporation of America. It was incorporated in Delaware on June 2, 1927, and initial subscriptions for $200,000 capital were solicited from a dozen Colonial investors and other fliers. Each share of preferred stock, priced at $100, included one share of common stock as a bonus. Trippe, Hambleton, Rockefeller, Whitney and his cousin William H. Vanderbilt subscribed $25,000 apiece. Fairchild, the Yale Buffalonians Ansley Sawyer and Seymour Knox, a 5-and-10-cent-store heir, and Edward O. McDonnell of the investment firm of Grayson, M. P. Murphy & Company, who had been a training instructor for the Yale Aviation Unit, each put up $5,000. Bob Thach came in with $1,500, and Grover Loening invested $1,000.

With the exception of Thach, Loening and Trippe, the investors represented powerful industrial and financial interests. All of them, including Hambleton, were stirring other investment caldrons as well. Trippe was to be their hired hand. He would operate whatever airline was established.

It was agreed that none of the original investors should draw a salary or other compensation for his services. In lieu of remuneration, and for devoting "much time to the affairs of the company," 1,000 shares of management stock were distributed at 20 cents a share. The measure of the time and efforts contributed can be gleaned from the amounts awarded. Trippe acquired 490 shares, or almost half the total; Whitney 220 shares; Hambleton 180 shares.

Securing a contract for the idle foreign airmail route from Key West to Havana was the first priority. They learned that others were aiming at the same target.

The most active group was headed by John K. Montgomery, a former Navy pilot, and Richard B. Bevier, son-in-law of Lewis Pierson, chairman of the board of the Irving Trust Company. Montgomery was heir to a plan conceived by officers in the Army Air Service for a Caribbean line to feed into South America.

In 1925, Major Henry H. Arnold had been alarmed by intelligence reports of a small airline in Colombia, SCADTA, operated by German pilots. The head of the airline, Peter Paul von Bauer, was ambitious to extend service to Panama and Miami, via Cuba. He was seeking financing in New York, and was about to ask for authority from Washington to carry U.S. mail to Barranquilla and Bogotá. Hap Arnold sounded the tocsin in the War Department of a foreign military threat to the Canal Zone. He asked the Postmaster General, "Under the law, would you have to give him a contract?" Harry New pondered and then replied, "I think I would, unless there were an American line to perform the service."

Arnold enlisted the aid of friends, Majors Carl Spaatz and Jack Jouett, in drawing a plan for a route and a company to operate it. They appointed Montgomery, who was out of uniform and knew people in Wall Street, to drum up investor interest in a proposed Pan American Airways. During the peaceful interval of the Twenties, prospects for advancement in an Army career were sluggish, and the officers seriously considered resigning their commissions to run the airline.

Then in the fall of 1925, the Billy Mitchell affair shattered the tranquillity and tested the allegiances of American military men. Arnold and Spaatz helped Mitchell with his trial strategy and testified in his behalf. Punished with a transfer to a post in Kansas, Hap Arnold abandoned his plan to resign in order to persevere in the cause of air power. Montgomery continued on his capital-raising tour and found a financial scout in Dick Bevier, who attracted a few wealthy and very social New Yorkers, including G. Grant Mason, Jr., just out of Yale and mad about flying, and Mason's brother-in-law, S. Sloan Colt, Yale '14 and a vice president of the Farmers Loan and Trust Company. In March 1927, they incorporated Pan American Airways, Inc., and started a campaign to persuade the Postmaster General to advertise the Key West–Havana route.

Another group with less crystallized plans of the same nature was led by Richard Hoyt on behalf of Hayden, Stone and a clique of investors in Florida Airways, an airline founded by Eddie Rickenbacker, the wartime American Ace of Aces, and his companion in the 94th Aero Squadron, Major Reed M. Chambers. They had operated CAM 10, the mail route between Miami and Jacksonville, for about a year, and extended it to Atlanta until lack of volume and a dearth of passengers put Florida Airways into bankruptcy. Chambers and a brokerage salesman, Virgil Chenea, thought they might do better in the Caribbean and got Hoyt to promise backing for their Atlantic, Gulf and Caribbean Air Lines.

With three aspirants for the same contract, it was logical to merge forces, or so it seemed to the Trippe and Hoyt groups. They were social acquaintances and had been in deals together. The Montgomery-Bevier group was the stubborn outsider, convinced it could go it alone because it had a head start.

The directors of the infant Aviation Corporation of America authorized Juan Trippe to bid on any mail routes according to his best judgment and to invest in Pan American Airways if it should win the Key West–Havana contract. Montgomery and Bevier were invited to a meeting with Trippe and Hoyt to talk about consolidating, and acted cocky. They were confident that Arnold's spadework gave them the best chance of winning the contract. Montgomery had already leased an airfield in Key West and one in Havana and was negotiating a mail agreement with the Cuban Postmaster. Trippe disclosed that he had obtained landing rights and concessions from President Machado on a visit to Havana with Tony Fokker two years before. A contract from the U.S. Post Office to carry mail to Havana, or even a return agreement, was worthless without Cuban operating privileges.

"There won't be a U.S. airmail contract unless you accept our merger proposal," Hoyt added. Still they resisted. "And if you don't believe me," Hoyt said, "why don't you come on my boat and get it straight from Glover himself?" They all went cruising off the coast of Florida on Hoyt's yacht, and the Second Assistant Postmaster General indeed confirmed the threat: unless the parties got together, the route would not be advertised.

Montgomery and Bevier began to realize that they were outmatched. Trippe's group had close to a quarter of a million dollars in capital and two new Fokkers on order. As the aviation wizard of Wall Street, Hoyt seemed to have unlimited resources to tap. Moreover, he was a killer shark.

Montgomery notified the Post Office that the three groups would be getting together and asked that FAM 4, the route from Key West to Havana, be advertised. On July 19, Pan American Airways was awarded a nine-month contract for the route; its bid of 40½ cents undercut the one other candidate, Cuban-American Air Lines, Inc., of Miami which offered to carry the mail at 46 cents a pound.

Juan rented an office for Aviation Corporation of America at 50 East Forty-second Street. Sonny Whitney contributed $20,000 for expenses and to pay the salaries of the half-dozen employees Trippe began recruiting.

He hired André Priester, a Dutch friend of Tony Fokker, and gave him the title of chief engineer. Priester had managed the P.R.T. Air

Service, an offshoot of the Philadelphia Rapid Transit System, during the summer of 1926, when it transported tourists between Washington and the city's sesquicentennial exposition on Fokker trimotors. Edwin Musick, a P.R.T. pilot who had previously flown for Aeromarine, became chief pilot.

The office resembled a garret. Priester shared one room with Trippe, who worked at a rolltop desk which he locked every time he left the room. Their secretaries occupied the other room. There were no chairs for callers or desk space for other executives.

As soon as the contract was won, Montgomery, listing himself as a vice president of Pan American Airways, tried to persuade Hap Arnold to leave the Army and manage the airline. He offered him $8,000 a year plus stock, apparently in the belief he had such executive power. He and Bevier assumed their group was entitled to an equal third of the merged enterprise with "the Hambleton-Whitney outfit" and "the Hoyt crowd." Juan did not rate billing, at least in their correspondence with Arnold. The illusion persisted for about a month until Hoyt set in motion a series of rapid-fire financial maneuvers to seize their company. In October, he formed a holding company, Atlantic, Gulf & Caribbean Airways, Inc., to buy Pan American Airways from them for $10,000 cash and $45,000 in potentially more valuable stock. Shortly thereafter, he sold 52 percent of the holding company's stock to the Aviation Corporation of America for $199,500—its entire capital.

Despite the technical majority held by Trippe's crowd, Hoyt took the reins as chairman of the board of Atlantic, Gulf and Caribbean Airways, Inc. He was then 39, a good ten years older than the Yale fliers and Hambleton, and infinitely more practiced in the gambling exercise known as stock speculation. Moreover, he had misgivings about Juan Trippe. As far as Hoyt was concerned, Juan had not covered himself with glory in Colonial Air Transport. But at Whitney's insistence, Trippe was named president and general manager of the operating subsidiary, Pan American Airways, and John Hambleton a vice president. John and Sonny were made directors of Atlantic, Gulf and Caribbean, as was Bevier for a brief time before he faded away with Montgomery to try their luck at organizing another international airline.

At a board meeting on October 13, Trippe read a memorandum presenting a blueprint for the airline's development. Starting from Miami, one trunk line extended to Colón, in the Panama Canal Zone, and down the west coast of South America to Valparaiso, Chile. A second line emanating from Miami cut across Cuba to Puerto Rico and Trinidad, a stepping-stone to the east coast of South America. Trippe said they would organize a national corporation in Cuba to seek mail concessions on the island. In Central and South America, franchises and mail contracts would be secured by the purchase of interests in local companies. He suggested joint operations with the aggressive SCADTA in Colombia.

A lot of work had to be done quickly to get this bold plan started. First, there was the Key West–Havana mail contract, which would be forfeited unless exercised by October 19; Pan American Airways would lose the $25,000 bond it had posted. On the 18th, Ed Musick flew one of the Fokkers that had just been delivered down to Miami, but he could not proceed to Key West because the runways at the abandoned military airport they had leased were not ready. Workmen had been digging up rocks and filling holes until rainstorms turned the landing strips into a swamp.

So Priester in New York and the airport manager in Key West began to search by telephone up and down the eastern coastline for a seaplane that could inaugurate the service. By early afternoon, the manager learned of a Fairchild FC-2 being repaired in Miami for ferrying to the Dominican Republic. The owner was the West Indian Aerial Express Company, recently organized by Basil Rowe, a pilot backed by Dominican sugar planters. After another series of telephone exchanges with Cy Caldwell, the pilot of *La Niña* in Miami, and with Rowe in Santo Domingo, Pan American Airways chartered the amphibian for $175.

Caldwell flew it to Key West before sunset and at 8 o'clock the next morning took off on the 90-mile journey to Havana. The plane was loaded with seven bags containing 30,000 letters, most of which had arrived an hour before on the "Havana Special" of the Florida East Coast Railroad and had then been delivered by truck to the wharf, where a Coast Guard cutter completed the relay. In order to accommodate the mail, Caldwell was obliged to leave his mechanic behind on the pier.

One hour 20 minutes later, *La Niña* landed in the harbor of Havana near the landmark Morro Castle, and the Postmaster rowed out in a small boat to pick up the mail. The cablegram reporting Caldwell's departure from Key West arrived an hour later. His mission accomplished, Caldwell flew on to Barahona to deliver the plane to West Indian Aerial Express.

By October 28, two dirt runways were completed at the field in Key West, and the Fokker trimotor with PAA painted on the fuselage lumbered off in a swirl of dust at 8:30 A.M. Captain Hugh Wells was at the controls, with Ed Musick beside him and a mechanic to complete the requisite three-man crew. The Fokker carried seven bags of mail weighing 772 pounds. The Cuban Government asked the pilot to pass over Morro Castle and perform historic reverences before landing at Camp Colombia in a driving rain. The plane was christened the *General Machado* and loaded for the first official return flight.

Pan American Airways had commenced regularly scheduled service as an international air carrier. That afternoon Juan cabled this scintilla of evidence that he "had a business" to Betty Stettinius in Paris, where her family had sent her in the vain hope she would forget about Juan Trippe. "FIRST FLIGHT SUCCESSFUL," the cablegram said.

Part II

LATIN AMERICA

6

Behind the Scenes

"Ten percent of aviation is in the air, and 90 percent is on the ground," observed Clement Keys in a remark that knocked the romance out of flying and clashed with the public view of aerial knights in combat with Nature to deliver the mail and a few courageous passengers. Juan Trippe understood what Keys meant from the moment he left Lee, Higginson to make flying his business. Even celestial businesses were made on earth.

Airlines were made of planes and pilots, to be sure, and landing fields and radio stations. The less tangible elements—capital and political influence—paid for the aforementioned. Antoine de Saint-Exupéry, buffeted in his night plane between the peaks of the Andes, was actually less at the mercy of Nature than at that of bankers and politicians in Paris. Pan American Airways, the nation's first, and for a long while only, airline in foreign service, was built in Washington, D.C.

Postal contracts lured private capital into domestic air transport. Until similar support was awarded for the carriage of mail overseas, no international airline of any size and scope could be developed in the United States because overseas flying looked to investors like an even riskier proposition. Mail routes were created in the office of the Postmaster General, in the cloakrooms of Congress and in other corners of the Administration, which is why, as soon as the inaugural hoopla of Pan American Airways' mail service to Havana was finished, Juan and John Hambleton turned their attention back to Washington.

The climate could not have been more sympathetic for young fliers who looked and acted like conservative businessmen. "The business of

America is business," said the frugal Vermonter in the White House. Calvin Coolidge's predecessors may have believed America's business was freedom, justice and peace; but Silent Cal drew his faith and ethics from business, and his Administration was devoted to its promotion and protection. So much so that while other Presidents placed their private moneys in government bonds to avoid the merest suspicion of conflict of interest, Coolidge invested in industrial stocks; and during his Presidency, the stock market awakened from a long hibernation and went wild.

Herbert Hoover was completing his second term as Secretary of Commerce, a pulpit from which he preached a philosophy of "cooperative capitalism." The former mining engineer from California viewed the American economy as a collaborative effort by industrial monopoly groups, who could be trusted to regulate themselves while the Federal Government cast a benevolent surveillance over all.

Upon taking up his Cabinet post under Warren G. Harding in 1921, he noticed that no one was paying much attention to commercial aviation, "and all this in the country that had given the airplane to the world."

At his suggestion, Coolidge convened the Morrow Board, and it was his recommendation for creating a civil aviation bureau (lodged in the Commerce Department) and contracting the airmail to private carriers that the board adopted.

When Pan American Airways won the Key West–Havana contract, the annual Congressional appropriation for foreign airmail service was a scant $150,000. The system of competitive bidding with which Postmaster General Harry New opened the domestic airmail service was under attack from several quarters. As companies sprang up to bid for airmail routes and contracts were awarded in piecemeal fashion, Hoover saw an unfortunate parallel with the chaotic development of the railroads in the nineteenth century. He warned of a "permanent muddle" instead of a cohesive system.

The experience of Colonial Air Transport convinced Juan and his associates that mail subsidy from competitive bidding was insufficient for the enterprises they were planning. The lowest bidders won the contracts and often lost their airlines in a sea of red ink. The problem was aggravated by the need for expensive equipment to carry passengers as well as mail. When the airline operated beyond the borders of the United States there would be additional requirements for huge capital to create communications and landing facilities such as the Federal Government provided for the domestic lines.

An international airline would be even more dependent than a domestic carrier on mail contracts, and investors would insist on more stability, not less. The compensation formula would have to be reversed—the highest rate instead of the lowest—and the term of the contract extended.

Pressures were mounting from two directions for the government to assist in the development of an air service to Latin America. The War Department was obsessed with the potential threat to national security posed by the aerial machines of foreign nations cruising over the Panama Canal Zone. Businessmen had visions of trade bonanzas south of the border that they could not develop on equal terms with European competitors unless they had better north-south communications through postal and freight services.

Early in November 1927, Coolidge appointed an interdepartmental committee of subcabinet officers to assist in the development of commercial aviation to Central and South America. The chairman was Francis White, Assistant Secretary of State, Yale '13. Trippe and Hambleton needed no introductions to Assistant Secretary of War for Air Trubee Davison and Edward Warner, his counterpart in the Navy, nor to Dave Ingalls when he took Warner's place the following year. As for the other power centers in Washington, Hambleton counted on David Bruce to open doors.

On November 23, the interdepartmental committee made its recommendations: an increase in appropriations for the Post Office, with authority for the Postmaster to make longer-term contracts on a graduated compensation scale, and flexibility to award them to the company that in his judgment best served U.S. interests. Two routes to Latin America were proposed: one from Havana to the west coast of South America via Mexico, Central America and the Canal Zone; the other from Key West to Havana, Trinidad and Venezuela, where it might connect with the Colombian airline. These were the routes Trippe had outlined to his board of directors a month before.

The committee stressed the importance, both military and economic, of having an airline owned by U.S. citizens serving the sensitive Caribbean area. A week later, Coolidge approved the recommendations and directed the Commerce Department and the Post Office to begin working out the necessary legislation.

The next morning, John Hambleton started on his Washington rounds. His first appointment, with Secretary of the Treasury Mellon at 9 A.M., was arranged by David Bruce. Mellon showed him a report from the Gulf Oil Company, a province of the Mellon empire. John and Juan had visited Gulf headquarters in Pittsburgh with a proposition for the oil company to make an investment in Pan American Airways.

"They give you a good send-off," Andrew Mellon told John. Gulf accountants had made a thorough analysis of Pan American's financial statement and concluded that it was a going concern. The report said, however, that Gulf ought not to stray from its own field of operation.

"Why don't you see the Aluminum Company of America?" the Secretary of the Treasury suggested. Alcoa was another Mellon holding.

Richard B. Mellon joined in the discussion. He had succeeded Andrew as head of the Mellon National Bank and bought his brother's stock when he went to Treasury. R.B., who was Alan Scaife's father-in-law, said that he was very much interested in air transport.

After the meeting, John went to David's office to report what had transpired. "Go back there for lunch—I'll arrange it—and tell Andrew Mellon to introduce you to Herbert Hoover," Bruce said.

John finished out the morning at the State Department with Francis White and at the War Department with Trubee Davison, who allowed him to study an Army report of geography and weather conditions in Latin America, valuable to a prospective airline operator.

At lunch, both Mellons wanted to hear more about air transport. John mentioned that they were having a problem getting adequate supplies of aviation gasoline at Key West. "I'll take it up with William —as you know, he's the president of Gulf—as soon as he returns. He's cruising in the Caribbean now," said the Secretary of the Treasury. William L. Mellon was his nephew.

The Secretary volunteered to speak to Herbert Hoover. "It will mean more than if I just give you a letter of introduction which obviously looks as though you asked for one," he said.

John saw the Secretary of Commerce that evening. They talked about legislation for foreign airmail contracts, and Hoover invited him to return the next afternoon. It was amazing how much could be accomplished in one day in Washington when one was properly introduced.

At Hambleton's meeting with Second Assistant Postmaster General Glover, he learned that Glover and Harry New were inclined to back one solidly established American company in the international sector, because there the competition came from foreign entrepreneurs sponsored by their governments.

Everything seemed to be going swimmingly except for the modest amount of subsidy Glover proposed—roughly a dollar a mile. "If you can't do it for that, others can," he snapped.

Hambleton wrote to Trippe:

I am going to leave Glover entirely to you from now on as I don't seem to hit it off with him any too well. I can handle the State, War and Treasury Departments and, if successful this afternoon, will get along with the Commerce Department, but you are welcome to the Post Office.

And so Trippe accepted responsibility for the care of W. Irving Glover—and discharged it so competently that some years later the postal official's secretary told a Senate investigating committee, "Mr. Trippe, of course, was a friend of Mr. Glover's."

Trippe talked to Glover in the language that a New Jersey real-estate operator now a political figure in search of a higher pedestal could understand. Juan was New Jersey–born, he reminded Glover, and he had learned his real-estate lessons at his mother's knee. He was respectful to the older man—Glover was twenty years his senior—but he spoke authoritatively, a veritable expert on postal subsidy.

Trippe fixed his brown eyes on Glover as he bore in with an economic theory. Mail pay should be fixed at a rate that would enable the operator to recover his round-trip cost on the compensation for a one-way trip. Assuming the service had a wide acceptance resulting in heavy volumes of mail, the government might recoup what it paid the operator, and perhaps even more, from the payments by foreign governments for carrying their mail to the United States. Those moneys would be turned over by the carrier to the Post Office.

"We're not asking for subsidy," Trippe said, showing his dimples when he smiled. "We're giving the government a chance to make money, don't you see?" Rose-tinted glasses were required for that. If the volume of mail was low, the government would be absolving the airline of its losses and even assuring it and its stockholders a profit while the Post Office footed the bill. If not subsidy, what was it?

Juan left nothing to chance. When not camping in Glover's office, he was on Capitol Hill visiting the proud father of domestic airmail. Representative Kelly of Pittsburgh was primed to sire the foreign-airmail act. In January 1928, he introduced a bill authorizing the Postmaster General to enter into contracts with private carriers for the transport of mail to foreign countries for periods up to ten years, at fixed rates per pound or per mile but not to exceed $2 per mile.

Testifying before Congress to urge passage of the Kelly bill, Glover asserted:

> I can say, with the great strides aviation has taken in this country, that there is no concern in the United States, as rich, strong, and big as they are, that can start a line from Key West and go to Cuba and across the long stretch of air there down the coast . . . and open our markets and increase the trade in Central and South America, and do it on the proceeds they receive on the freight and express they carry without Government backing.

Glover had been to Europe on a postal survey. He reported that the French Government had appropriated millions of gold francs for a line from France to South America which placed American commercial interests in the region under a handicap. That was why a U.S. line had to be subsidized for a period. "We must stand back of whoever takes it over," he said. But he referred to one company:

> At the present time the contractor for the route between Key West and Havana is pioneering the way themselves, taking the dollar out of their own pockets. They have bought a plane and they are putting on three of their representatives and they are going over this very same route, down through Central American countries, just a tour of good will.

The most important feature of the bill was a vaguely worded provision giving the Postmaster General an escape hatch from competitive bidding. It allowed him to award contracts to "the bidders that he shall find to be the lowest responsible bidders that can satisfactorily perform the service required to the best advantage of the Government." Moreover, his decision was to be final, not subject to review except by the President and the federal courts.

The Foreign Air Mail bill was enacted on March 8 and an appropriation of $1.75 million voted two months later. The next step was to prepare for bidding on Latin American routes. Trippe asked his directors to increase the capital of their company to $1 million, and if they obtained a route to the Canal Zone, to $2 million. Whitney put himself down for $50,000 more before the Kelly bill was introduced, and subscribed an additional $100,000 after it was passed, thereby becoming the largest individual stockholder. He brought in W. Averell Harriman for $50,000.

Through Weicker Senior, Juan was introduced to Dr. William C. Beckers, a founder of the National Aniline and Chemical Company (later acquired by Allied Chemical). Trippe buttonholed Beckers as he was preparing to sail for Europe and proposed he take a $250,000 block of stock. Beckers promised to take $25,000 worth. Juan sent a letter by messenger to the millionaire chemist's cabin on the *Île de France*. In it he described the organizers of Aviation Corporation of America as "a group of gentlemen, all of whom have had much previous experience in Commercial Aviation matters," and assured Beckers that "the Administration have indicated their willingness to assist us in every way possible, and only last week the Secretaries of State, Commerce, War, Navy and the Postmaster General invited representatives of this Company to an informal meeting with the Inter-Department

Committee, designated by President Coolidge to assist us." Wouldn't he rather increase his personal subscription to $50,000? Beckers wired from the high seas: "I ACCEPT YOUR PROPOSITION. MY SON WILL ARRANGE PAYMENT."

Juan disclosed to Beckers that Pan American Airways had lost $1,000 during its first three months of operation with only mail revenue from Key West to Havana. On January 16, passenger service was inaugurated, with the blare of public-relations trumpets heralding the blessing of the United States Government upon the airline. The sixth International Conference of American States was convening in Havana —Trippe was attached to the U.S. aviation delegation, a chubby representative in a white linen suit—as the *General Machado* arrived with 4 passengers aboard who had each paid a one-way fare of $50. The second Fokker carried 3 "deadheads," or nonrevenue passengers, and 753 pounds of mail. Mrs. Calvin Coolidge christened it the *General New* in the presence of her husband, President Machado and the panjandrums of both countries. A tradition was set for First Ladies of the United States to baptize the planes of Pan American Airways.

Later in the conference Charles Lindbergh arrived, the most sought-after ambassador of commercial aviation. From July to October 1927 he had toured eighteen states in the *Spirit of St. Louis* and was credited by Postmaster General New with stimulating a 50-percent increase in airmail usage. In December, he made a breathtaking nonstop trip from Washington to Mexico City on the invitation of Dwight Morrow, who had been appointed ambassador to the unhappy neighbor nation south of the border. Lindbergh's arrival caused an epidemic of air-hero worship to break out; New immediately started negotiations with Mexican postal officials for an airmail service between the two capitals. On New Year's Day, Lindbergh set off on a six-week swing through fourteen Latin American countries and the Canal Zone.

He was warned that it was foolhardy to try to fly around the Caribbean in a land plane. The weather was too unpredictable: he would be prey to frequent rainsqualls; there were few places where he could land without mishap to the wheels of his plane. He arranged his schedule around daylight flying and carried a large fuel reserve, the same margin of safety with which he had started across the Atlantic.

The Lindbergh Circle, as airmen dubbed the 9,000-mile trail he blazed, was the dramatic spur for an air link between the northern and southern continents of the Western Hemisphere—a route to be woven through Mexico and Central America by a privately owned, U.S. Government–approved transport company.

He flew into Havana brimming with enthusiasm for the commercial opportunities and tourist attractions of the region. "This territory is waiting for airlines," he declared. Juan and John Hambleton had just announced that Pan American Airways was about to make a survey of the Caribbean. They tried to pin Lindbergh to a formal relationship with the airline, but he was noncommittal. Hambleton wrote him a thank-you letter from Baltimore: "We appreciate greatly all the help you gave us in Havana and I can assure you it was very great help indeed."

A week after the Foreign Air Mail bill was passed, Lindbergh was on the scene in Washington. He called on the Postmaster General, addressing Harry New as "my old boss" in reference to his past career as an airmail pilot. He was accompanied by Trippe and Hambleton, Assistant Secretary of Commerce William MacCracken and Ford's chief engineer, William Mayo. They discussed airmail service between the United States and the Western Hemisphere lands to the south.

On March 30, the Postmaster General began advertising foreign airmail routes. They were closely patterned after the Lindbergh Circle and the imitative Pan American Airways survey that followed in his tracks. The first to be put up for bidding was the Key West–Havana route, due to expire in July and readvertised under the more generous terms of the new legislation. It was awarded to Pan American Airways for five years at the maximum $2 a mile. Pan American immediately applied to have its U.S. terminus changed from Key West to Miami, more than doubling the length of the route to Cuba and the revenue accruing to the airline.

The next two routes advertised offered annual mail payments totaling $2.5 million a year. FAM 5 covered service from Miami to the Canal Zone, a distance of 2,074 miles, with a possible extension along the north coast of South America to Paramaribo, Dutch Guiana. Bidders had thirty-two days in which to submit their proposals. One individual protested that the time limit was too short for him to make the necessary arrangements with foreign countries, and asked for a thirty-day extension. It was denied; the contract was awarded to the only other interested party, Pan American Airways, at the maximum $2 a mile.

The advertisement specified that payment for the return trip from Cristóbal to the United States was to be based on "direct distance." Trippe wanted that changed at the signing of the contract, a simple matter to arrange for someone who had *carte blanche* in Glover's domain. A bureaucrat was called in by the director of the international postal service and told, "Fix it so it says 'direct distance by the most practicable route.' " He noticed Mr. J. T. Trippe seated at a corner of the director's desk making himself at home. The change cost the Post Office an additional $1,874 for each return trip.

There were two bidders for FAM 6, a 1,930-mile route to Puerto Rico and Trinidad via Cuba, Haiti and the Dominican Republic—Pan American Airways and West Indian Aerial Express, the airline whose loan of the Fairchild plane had saved the day the previous fall. The Dominican-based company, headed by Basil Rowe, had been operating over 700 miles of the proposed route for several months, after investing $92,000 to develop the service, and it had a strong endorsement from the Governor of Puerto Rico.

Rowe and his operations manager, Roscoe Dunten, went in search of Wall Street financing as soon as the route was advertised, and obtained commitments from Sherman Fairchild and Lehman Brothers, the investment bankers. Fairchild insisted on submitting a bid no lower than Pan American's, at the maximum $2 a mile—suspicious behavior for a director of both companies. Trippe then offered to buy out his competitor for $105,000 in Aviation Corporation of America stock. Rowe and Dunten turned him down, confident that they stood the better chance of winning the contract.

What they did not know was that Irving Glover was taking a personal interest in the matter. He let Juan examine their bid and its supporting evidence so that he could amend his application. Trippe informed Glover that he had made overtures toward taking over West Indian Aerial Express, "somewhat strengthening the situation in Puerto Rico."

"Some months ago, Pan American established the policy of inviting in responsible American interests who could be helpful or were interested in developing transportation in the Caribbean and South America," Trippe said. "We're perfectly willing to have the Fairchild interests join in our enterprise."

Glover acted relieved to have everything simplified. "I appreciate your telling me," he said. "I'll award the Puerto Rican contract not later than Friday."

Juan wired Richard Hoyt, from Washington:

ALL DEPARTMENTS OFFICIALLY ON RECORD FAVORING PAN AMERICAN ACCOUNT PAST RECORD DEVELOPMENT AND PREPARATORY WORK DESCRIBED TRANSMITTAL LETTER AND ABILITY CARRY OUT PENDING CONTRACTS AND LATER SOUTH AMERICAN EXTENSIONS STOP AMBASSADOR JUDAH HAS OFFICIALLY STATED HERE TO STATE DEPARTMENT AND POST OFFICE HIS OPINION NONE BUT PANAMERICAN COULD OPERATE CUBA STOP YOUR CONFIDENTIAL INFORMATION QUOTE GLOVER

TOLD ME UNOFFICIALLY TODAY GENERAL NEW AND HIMSELF FAVORED
US STOP . . .

To George Mixter of Stone and Webster, an ally of Hoyt's who
had been tapped to take a big block of stock, he sent this message:

PRACTICALLY ASSURED PUERTO RICAN TEN YEAR CONTRACT TWO DOL-
LAR ROUND TRIP BASIS FRIDAY THIS WEEK OR BEFORE IN ADDITION TO
PANAMA ROUTE HOPE YOU CAN PERSUADE ROCKEFELLER WEBSTER
AND STONE TAKE UP RIGHTS BEFORE EXPIRATION IF NOT ALREADY IN
FOR PERSONALLY CONFIDENT STOCK WILL SHORTLY APPRECIATE CON-
SIDERABLY STOP HAVE BORROWED CONSIDERABLE SUM TO TAKE UP MY
WHOLE ALLOTMENT SIXTY EIGHT THOUSAND MYSELF.

Three days after Trippe's telegrams were sent, the Postmaster
General awarded the contract for FAM 6 to Pan American Airways, on
the premise that the company had already demonstrated on another
route that it could perform satisfactory service.

"While we had been developing an airline in the West Indies,"
Basil Rowe figured out, "our competitors had been busy on the much
more important job of developing a lobby in Washington." He accepted defeat with good grace, and in the takeover received a job as a
pilot with Pan American Airways and a packet of Aviation Corporation
of the Americas shares, though nowhere near as many as Fairchild and
Lehman. Trippe reduced his price to $75,000 in stock for all the assets
of West Indian Aerial Express, including planes, landing fields and
concessions in Haiti and the Dominican Republic.

It was Dunten who discovered an oversight in the Foreign Air
Mail Act: the $2-a-mile subsidy applied only to outgoing trips; no
provision was made for payments to bring mail back from foreign
countries. A campaign to redress the imbalance was swiftly mounted.
Congressman Kelly introduced an amendment to the law, and Juan
asked Lindbergh to help. He wrote him:

Dear Slim—I am asking Mr. Nagle [P. E. Nagle, a Washington
representative of Pan American] to deliver to you a suggested
draft of a letter which may voice your feelings on the necessity of
passing Congressman Kelly's new amendment. He would like to
have a letter from you on this matter to assist him in securing
"unanimous consent" in the House to bring this bill before that
body next Monday morning. I do not think either I, or P.A.A.,
should appear in any way in this matter for obvious reasons.

Lindbergh did as he was directed. He called on Kelly at his office
and offered him a letter which the Congressman from Pittsburgh read
from the floor of the House.

The amendment was passed on March 2, 1929; it provided for the payment of $2 a mile each way, plus $1 per 1,000 miles for each pound in excess of the specified load. Lindbergh accepted nothing for his work except an annual airline pass that Juan sent him.

Before selling stock to the public, a company must present an alluring facade. It needs a "concept" to titillate the sophisticated investors who supply the capital in the initial stage of corporate development, and then a good "story" to spread, with the cooperation of newspaper and magazine editors, in advance of the public offering, from which the insiders take out their profits.

As soon as the foreign-airmail legislation was enacted, and Aviation Corporation of America was hunting for another million or so in capital, Trippe retained Doremus & Company, an advertising and public-relations firm specializing in financial promotion for blue-chip corporations. Doremus assigned William I. Van Dusen to the account. A slicker press agent than Harry Bruno, Van Dusen was only too willing to conceal truth or distort it at a client's behest.

He learned that Trippe had firm ideas about selling his company "as an American institution created to represent the United States on the airways of the world." Van Dusen agreed that national pride was a salable commodity, both to the public and to the government officials whose support was crucial to the enterprise. The impression would be created that the airline was quasi-governmental, an instrument of national policy.

Trippe disputed Van Dusen on the matter of names. He wanted to erase "Pan American Airways"; he preferred "Aviation Corporation of the Americas." Van Dusen filled the gaps in Juan's Sheff education and instructed him in the Greek meaning of the word "pan": all or every— the airline of all the Americas, and of every American traveling abroad.

"You should use your name: Juan," he insisted. "It's a *simpático* line with Latin America." "Absolutely not," said Trippe.

" 'J. Terry Trippe' might sound okay for a Park Avenue doctor, but not for the president of a South American airline," Van Dusen shot back. He was baffled by Trippe's anger. Why should he not use his name when it was such an asset? Juan looked Spanish to him, and he was doing business with Spanish-speaking countries. Trippe informed him that he did not speak a word of Spanish and that his forebears were English. "So why were you named Juan?" Van Dusen asked. Trippe mumbled something about an ancestor who had married a woman from Venezuela. Van Dusen grasped at a straw and thereafter fed reporters tips about Trippe's Venezuelan aunt. The saga of Juan Terry and the beautiful barmaid reposed in peace.

But why did he hate his name? Van Dusen kept wondering—until one day Trippe let it slip: "Because nobody can pronounce it. In New Haven, they made fun of it. They called me Wang."

Van Dusen won only half that battle. "J. Terry Trippe" was retired, and in his place for the next dozen years, the president of Pan American Airways was J. T. Trippe.

During this period of hyperactivity, Juan was able to conclude his courtship of Betty Stettinius. He was almost 29, seven years out of Yale and at the hub of a conglomeration of wealth and industrial power. Her family still had reservations about him, but undeniably, he "had a business." A risky business, to be sure, but some of their friends thought it was "a good thing" and wanted a piece of it. In January 1928, shortly after Pan American Airways inaugurated passenger service to Havana, Mrs. Edward Stettinius, Sr., announced her younger daughter's engagement to Juan Terry Trippe.

It was a love match, all right. What did she see in him? the family had wondered for nearly four years. She saw a beautiful young bear of a man, "so serious and full of zeal," self-centered and humorless, a man of destiny. He was never observed looking at another girl. Why should he, when his "Betts" was the perfect companion for a lifetime?

In marriage as in his business alliances, Trippe displayed an uncanny knack for acquiring essential assets he lacked. Everyone remarked on his choice of "a better half." Betty filled the voids in his character. Her sparkle brightened his opaque personality; her warmth and sensitivity melted hearts frozen by his callous disregard. Juan ignored anyone who was not useful to him at a given moment. He forgot names. Betty seemed genuinely interested in human beings, be they cooks or bankers. She had total recall of the significant minutiae of their existences, from rheumatic knees to grandchildren's math scores. In contrast to Juan's haughty patrician, she appeared the fun-loving democrat. "It's not who your ancestors were but who you are," she said to her prospective mother-in-law as Lucy Trippe exalted the Trippe genealogy.

The wedding took place on June 16 at the Stettinius estate in Locust Valley. The ceremony was performed in the drawing room at 4 in the afternoon by a Jesuit priest from St. Ignatius Loyola Church in New York, Lucy Trippe's parish.

Juan had Warner Atkins, a Yale fraternity brother, as his best man. A Yale contingent marched as ushers—Alan Scaife, Walton Scully, Theodore Weicker, Jr., and Cornelius V. Whitney—along with John Hambleton and Edward Stettinius, Jr. After the ceremony, which was witnessed by relatives and close friends (the custom in a mixed marriage which could not be held before the altar of a Roman Catholic church), the wedding party moved to the terrace to greet the eight hundred guests who arrived by private yacht and chartered motorbus from the city. Among the notables were General John J. Pershing, commander-in-chief of the American Expeditionary Force in the Great War, John W. Davis and a covey of Morgan partners.

The bride and groom left in a shower of rice for a honeymoon in New York over what remained of the weekend. Juan's business affairs were too pressing to allow for a proper wedding trip to Europe. He had booked passage on the S.S. *Rotterdam* for a sailing in October, when they could take in the Berlin air show and he could get some business done in London and Paris as well.

In December 1927, Pan American Airways and its parent company, Aviation Corporation of America, moved to larger quarters, a suite of four rooms on the twenty-third floor of 100 East Forty-second Street, directly across from Grand Central Station.

Trippe occupied the largest room, an unapproachable figure bent into his rolltop desk. To talk to visitors or the staff, he swung his chair around and confronted them across a flat-topped table spread with maps and drawings. A large globe stood alongside, on which he took quick measurements with a piece of string.

His secretary, Sally Swaggerty, a motherly Southerner, was listed on the corporate roster as E. S. Swaggerty, assistant secretary and assistant treasurer. Marie Blaske, a spectacled Bronx matron, took dictation from André Priester. Althea Lister, a spirited 19-year-old from Brooklyn, rotated as girl Friday.

Juan accepted directives from Dick Hoyt over the telephone or went downtown to his office at 25 Broad Street, where he was wheeling, dealing and assembling paper empires. John Hambleton appeared two or three days a week looking tweedy, his wing-tip shoes unshined and the laces half-looped. He warmed the office with his smile. Though based in Baltimore at Hambleton & Company, he was devoting increasing time to Pan American Airways, mostly on Washington matters and flying to survey routes. Sonny Whitney dropped by, walking bouncily on the soles of his feet. Hambleton and Whitney chatted with the staff in a relaxed and friendly manner. Direct conversation with employees was a measure of last resort for Trippe. Encountering them by chance in an elevator, he looked to the side or stared blankly. The man in charge of freight, who sat in a cubbyhole 30 feet away from Juan's office, tried in vain to force him to answer his good-mornings.

Trippe's frigidity engendered exhaustive theorizing among the employees. Was he a snob? The freight man, a Basque who had lived in Mexico, was positive Trippe disliked Latins. Was he a vague genius, like the proverbial absent-minded professor? Or was he hoarding politeness for bankers and Washington officials?

He could be just as indifferent to his mother. Lucy Trippe visited the office regularly, expecting him to take her to lunch. While she waited, she held court among the secretaries, who minded her poodle when she went out. On one occasion as Lucy was gabbing and the hands of the clock were moving toward 2, the secretaries afraid to knock at Trippe's closed door, he telephoned from Hoyt's office. He had ducked out, unnoticed, via the men's room. "Is my mother still there?" he inquired. "Tell her I'm having lunch with Dick Hoyt."

The office operated at a grueling pace. The staff was small and there was so much to be done: letters written, schedules mapped, manuals composed, equipment bought and bids submitted to the Post Office in Washington. The workweek stretched to include evenings and weekends, without overtime pay, supper money or an appreciative word from Trippe. Praise was not his only stinginess. He smoked the cheapest cigars and always left the taxi fare for his companion to pay. A dime was his all-purpose tip except for the nickel he gave every third day to the bootblack for a 10-cent shoeshine.

Juan started dictating to a secretary at 11 A.M. and continued to 5 P.M. without a break, asking her to transcribe the day's work before she went home. At midnight she departed on her hour's subway journey to an outer borough.

Sometimes they worked until it was time for Trippe to catch the midnight train to Washington. Gerry Lister and James Eaton, the traffic manager, "walked" him to Pennsylvania Station: down in the elevator and across to Grand Central to take the shuttle to the West Side Subway, which transported them to the railroad depot. En route, they went over the schedules to be filed the next morning at the Post Office.

The employees knew they were overworked and underpaid, but it never occurred to them to look for other jobs. "We were building an airline that was going to be bigger and better than any other," Gerry said.

The day before the Christmas holiday in 1928, Trippe authorized a celebration for the New York office and sent out for ham sandwiches and Coca-Cola. Bonuses of a half-month's salary were distributed. Trippe's was $750—not until July, after FAM 5 and 6 were won, had he begun to draw an annual salary of $18,000.

They were toasting the season when Juan started speaking to no one in particular. He sat on the edge of a table gazing out the window. "We are going down the west coast of South America and up the east coast," he said haltingly. "Then we will be going across the Atlantic and after that, across the Pacific. We are going around the world." Seven pairs of eyes regarded him "as if he had ten heads," Gerry said. What he was saying sounded so improbable, and so personal. Ordinarily he hardly recognized them, and now he was sharing his dream.

In the spring of 1928, the market for aviation stocks began to sizzle. Assured of winning the first long-term contracts for foreign airmail, and anticipating that additional routes would soon be advertised by the Postmaster General, Trippe and his associates judged the time was right to go public.

Hoyt guided them in watering the stock. The first step was to fuse the interests of the organizing groups into a larger company with a simpler structure. On June 23, the Aviation Corporation of the Americas was created, pluralizing the name affixed to a dream just a year before. It acquired all the assets of the Aviation Corporation of America and of Atlantic, Gulf & Caribbean Airways, Inc., absorbing in the process the entire stock of the operating company, Pan American Airways, Inc. Hoyt was chairman of the new entity, Whitney president, and Trippe and Hambleton vice presidents. Juan remained head of the subsidiary Pan American Airways, Inc. (keeping the name as Van Dusen had urged), and John a vice president. Forty-five thousand shares were issued to the stockholders of the dissolved companies; Trippe's group took 56.4 percent and Hoyt's contingent the remainder. The stockholders were required to subscribe to an additional 90,000 shares at $15 a share in order to pump in $1,350,000 of new capital. They did so eagerly, believing their stock was "hot," and as Juan told Beckers, he borrowed to the hilt to take up his allotment.

Another million dollars was raised by a broadening of the circle of investors. With help from the Commerce Department, Dick Hoyt compiled a solicitation list of more than a hundred individuals and companies interested in trade with Latin America. About one-third of these shares was taken by North American Aviation, a $25-million holding company Clement Keys formed with Hoyt's help to absorb the companies he had devoured and to initiate a new buying binge. Smaller amounts of stock were snapped up by individuals. Juan let his Yale comrades and other friends "in on the good thing": Sumner Sewall (50 shares), Harry Davison and Alan Scaife (100 shares each), Scaife's brother-in-law Richard King Mellon (1,000 shares), Lucy Trippe (100 shares).

There was more to come. A year before, Juan and the other organizers of Aviation Corporation of America had received management stock at 20 cents a share. Now they were given warrants to subscribe to additional stock in the new company at $15 a share at any time within the next five years. According to the distribution formula, Trippe, holding 490 shares of old management stock at a cost of $98, emerged with a call on 37,301.25 new shares at $15 a share. Whitney and Hambleton had proportionately smaller numbers of warrants; Hoyt pointedly wound up with the lion's share in his group.

These warrants constituted the reward to the promoters, costing them practically nothing and offering a tremendous potential for profit while creating fresh capital. Initially, Aviation Corporation of the Americas was an insider's deal. The new subscriptions and the issuance of the warrants broadened the pool of shareholders and gave rise to a public market for the stock. It traded first in the over-the-counter market, and early in 1929 was listed on the New York Curb Exchange. One day in March 1929, the stock sold for $89 a share, its highest price before the crash in October. At that peak moment the company was operating at a loss of $300,000 a year, an indication of the frenzy in the market. Juan had a huge paper profit, though he cashed in on the boom only to the extent of selling 5 percent of his stock and warrants.

Even if only on paper, Juan Trippe was a millionaire before his 30th birthday.

7

The Mexican Company

Between the two world wars, the airplane was the universal vehicle of hope. Stock speculators, politicians, empire builders and seekers after heaven on earth invested the wondrous flying machine with boundless expectations. Idealists declared it "a servant of mankind," and by the same token perceived the commercial airline as a transforming agent for economic and social justice, "a constructive force for human betterment."

Nowhere was air service more welcome than in the Latin half of the Western Hemisphere—a giant land mass, 6,000 miles long from the Rio Grande to Cape Horn, 3,000 impenetrable miles from Brazil's Atlantic bulge to where the Andes descended toward the Pacific at Peru. Latin America had the sparsest population of any continent except Australia: 128 million persons clustered along its seacoasts and in widely separated cities. Its topography was cruel. Jagged mountains, swollen rivers and dense jungles foreclosed communication and economic development. Before the airplane, the western coast of South America was walled off from the rest of the continent by the 4,000-mile Andean range.

The steamship was the principal mode of transportation to South America from the outside, as well as between countries on the continent and within the immense region of the Amazon. Travel by highway and railroad was fragmentary, and in many areas the mule was the carrier of passengers and freight.

Latin America, *terra incognita*, beckoned to restless heroes after the European battlefields had been returned to pasture and factories.

The airplane was the celestial chariot for adventurers and entrepreneurs. Antoine de Saint-Exupéry, the French pilot-troubadour,
encapsulates his experiences flying the mail for the Aéropostale Company in his small poetic novel *Night Flight*. The pilot Fabien crashes in
a storm over the Andes, faithfully obeying the edict of Rivière, the
unyielding manager of the line, for whom the duty to carry the mail is
"a dark sense . . . greater than that of love."

Rivière, a character modeled after Didier Daurat, the general
manager of the company, also gave an economic rationale: "For us it is
a question of life or death, since we lose, each night, the advance
gained, during the day, on the railroads and the ships."

Latin America was a natural frontier for air imperialism, in that it
offered virgin opportunities for exploitation and few native sources of
capital. Governments were generally weak and unstable, and the fringe
of wealthy oligarchs uninterested in financing such risky ventures as air
transport. Franchises were readily granted to outsiders willing to
chance harsh geography and volatile politics. Regardless of the source
of political authority, distant king or local military chief, the economies
of the Latin American nations were controlled by aliens. European
capital—French, Dutch, English, German as well as Spanish and
Portuguese—developed the natural resources and built the rudimentary transportation systems. Immigrants established the commercial
services, shops and smaller banks and industries. Frequent intervention
by outsiders to protect their financial interests was sanctioned by international law. Though the southern part of the hemisphere was more or
less left as a European sphere of influence, the United States became
an imperial power in the Caribbean and Central America following the
war with Spain, begun under President William McKinley in 1898 to
liberate Cuba. By declaring the right to intervene to protect life, property and individual liberty, the Platt Amendment to an Army appropriation act in 1901 made Cuba a protectorate of the United States.

Before World War I, Latin America looked to Europe for cultural
affinity and trade. After the outbreak of hostilities, American bankers
and manufacturers benefited from the military distractions of their
competitors and enlarged their footholds in the region. Though the
Europeans acted to regain their former positions after the war, capital
from the United States continued to trickle southward. By the end of
1928, Americans had invested $5.6 billion in Latin America and were
doing $2 billion a year in business.

The Commerce Department under Herbert Hoover was the
"world's most formidable engine of foreign trade conquest," opening
offices abroad and coaching businessmen in the intricacies of operating

overseas. As early as 1924, he proposed an airmail and passenger service to Central America to assist U.S. entrepreneurs.

The airplane made the old slogan "Trade follows the flag" more apt than ever, not only by facilitating the sale and distribution of a country's products but by establishing a national presence wherever it touched down. "The West Indies look upon the United States as the flying nation," a British official observed enviously in the Thirties. "Pan American Airways have got a footing there and that injures our prestige."

Commercial air service created markets for aircraft. Almost before the ink was dry on the peace covenant, Europeans moved into the Latin American backyard of the United States to find employment for their aviators and customers for their planes.

The limitations imposed by the Treaty of Versailles on their military manufacturing made the Germans particularly venturesome. Few were as candid about their commercial motives as Hermann Goering, commander of the Flying Circus after Von Richthofen's death. In 1922, Goering told Eddie Rickenbacker:

> Our whole future is in the air. It is by air power that we are going to recapture the German Empire. To accomplish this we will do three things. First we will teach gliding as a sport to all our young men. Then we will build up a fleet of commercial planes, each easily converted to military operation. Finally we will create the skeleton of a military air force. When the time comes, we will put all three together—and the German Empire will be reborn. We must win through the air.

The following year, Goering joined in an abortive "beer-hall putsch" organized in Munich by Adolf Hitler, the leader of the Nazi Party.

Germans entrenched themselves in South America in local airline operations, directed wholly or in part from the homeland and supported by hospitable colonies of immigrants. The first was Sociedad Colombo-Alemana de Transportes Aéreos (SCADTA), organized by former military pilots who established, starting in 1921, regularly scheduled mail and passenger service in Colombia. Operating Junkers hydroplanes, SCADTA made the 600-mile journey between the seaport of Barranquilla and the mountain capital of Bogotá in 8 hours, competing against a steamboat that took 6 to 10 days on the Magdalena River, longer in the dry season.

Germans living in La Paz obtained a subsidy from the Bolivian government for Lloyd Aéreo Boliviano (LAB) to begin operations in 1925, financed by Junkers aircraft interests. Sindicato Condor, successor to a German aerial-survey company, was incorporated as a Brazilian unit in 1927 to fly the 900-mile stretch between Rio de Janeiro and Rio Grande do Sul.

The Italians set up flying schools, sold naval planes in South and Central America, and announced daring plans for a transatlantic service between Rome and South America with super-seaplanes powered by Isolta-Fraschini engines. Most of their accomplishment was in expeditions "for the glory of Fascist Italy," such as the crossing of the South Atlantic in February 1927 by Francesco de Pinedo, a swashbuckling marchese who piloted a twin-engine Savoia-Marchetti flying boat from Dakar to Pernambuco, hopping from island to island across the ocean.

The French effort to connect Europe with South America also began with aviation schools and sales of military aircraft to the countries on the east coast of the continent. In 1924, the Latécoère company obtained rights to operate between Buenos Aires and Rio de Janeiro, and three years later for an extension to Natal, at the Brazilian bulge. Pierre Latécoère ran out of money to finance his dreams and sold out to Marcel Bouilloux-Lafont, a banker with extensive holdings in Argentina. He renamed the line Compagnie Générale Aéropostale and, aided by subsidy from the French Government, poured more than $1 million into airports and communications systems to support a mail service along the 2,900-mile coastline between Buenos Aires and Natal. In March 1928, it was fused into a steamship-air service. French naval cruisers picked up the mail at Natal and carried it to Dakar, where it was put aboard Aéropostale planes and relayed to Toulouse. American businessmen complained vociferously to Washington about the advantage this new 8-day schedule between Buenos Aires and Paris conferred on French traders. It took 20 days for a letter to reach the Argentine capital from New York.

In April, the French speeded up service further by introducing night flying from Rio de Janeiro to Buenos Aires. Jean Mermoz, the fearless chief pilot for the line, managed without radio or weather forecasts. "Hovering in the pitch-black night Mermoz would land by the faint glimmer of three gasoline flares," his brother-pilot Saint-Exupéry reported.

The United States was at first indifferent to what was happening in the skies above Latin America. The War Department discouraged sales of surplus military aircraft to foreigners, the entering wedge used by Europeans for commercial business, until reports from State Department emissaries in the field began suggesting that such economic penetration of the hemisphere, particularly by the recent German enemy, could also pose a threat to the Panama Canal. The Morrow

Board recommendation of export sales of aircraft as a basis of military preparedness was welcomed by an Administration dedicated to reducing the national debt. This stimulated additional proposals for a U.S. commercial airline as a countervailing force to European imperialism in the region.

After the ecstatic reception given to Lindbergh in Mexico City in December 1927 it was virtually certain that the U.S. Postmaster General would actively push to open air service to Mexico. Relations between the two countries hung in delicate balance after years of U.S. interference in Mexican revolutions and dissension over American claims to oil and mineral deposits and land. Dwight Morrow's mission as Ambassador to Mexico was beginning to bear conciliatory fruit.

Whitney volunteered to negotiate operating rights for Pan American Airways. "I have entrée to the Mexican Government," he said.

As a result of a deal that represented his first successful solo as a businessman, Sonny was on terms of backslapping cordiality with General Alvaro Obregón, a former President of Mexico who was due for reelection in 1928.

In 1924, Whitney had bought on the open market his father's shares in a dormant irrigation project in the state of Sonora for $3,150 and proceeded to spur development of the 150,000 acres. With the cooperation of Obregón, a substantial landowner in the area, the irrigation project went forward along with plans for an Obregón City complete with commodities mills, packing plants, warehouses and railroad yards. In 1926, Sonny sold more than half his acreage, by then fertile farmland, to the Mexican Government for $500,000, which he plowed straightway into aviation.

Before Whitney set out in February 1928 on behalf of Pan American, Sherman Fairchild mentioned his interest in Compañía Mexicana de Aviación, an air taxi service organized in Tampico by George L. Rihl (pronounced as in tile), a banker from Philadelphia. Mostly it delivered payrolls of gold dollars to oil drilling sites in the outlying districts, keeping them beyond the reach of the bandits who roamed the countryside terrorizing prospectors.

Rihl hit on the idea of augmenting revenues with aerial survey work and sold 20 percent of the stock to Fairchild, who supplied an airplane equipped with his patented camera and a pilot to fly it. The little airline then obtained an exclusive contract from the Mexican Government to carry mail between Tampico and Mexico City.

At Fairchild's nudging, Whitney made an agreement with Rihl whereby the president of Compañía Mexicana was to try to secure a ten-year mail and passenger concession between Mexico City and the Texas border at Brownsville, a route then being operated by the military. Without telling him of his arrangement with Whitney, Rihl had his right-hand man, Erwin Balluder, a longtime resident of German ancestry, hack through the political underbrush, and the franchise was transferred from the army to Compañía Mexicana. "We did underhanded things," Balluder gloated later. "We got the Mexican postmaster to say that only a Mexican company could have the mail rights. Though it had American capital, Compañía Mexicana had been organized in Mexico."

It was also the only airline operating in that country, and now it blocked the path of any U.S. carrier that had to fly through Mexican airspace to reach the Canal Zone. FAM 5, the Caribbean route to the Canal Zone awarded in July, called for an intermediate stop on the Yucatán peninsula. FAM 8, the land route from Brownsville to Cristóbal through Mexico and Central America that was next on the U.S. Postmaster General's list, could not be performed without landings in Tampico and Mexico City.

On January 2, 1929, Harry New wired the Director General of Posts to inquire whether he considered the Mexican aviation company a satisfactory contractor. Three days later, an affirmative reply received, he advertised FAM 8 for a twenty-one-day period. On January 16, the Aviation Corporation of the Americas bought Compañía Mexicana for $150,000 in stock plus warrants for the two controlling stockholders. Rihl was also given a contract to direct Mexican operations as a vice president for Pan American Airways at a salary of $15,000 a year.

On January 30, New telegraphed to the Director General of Posts the names of seven bidders who had responded to his advertisement, announcing that he would award the contract to the lowest qualified bidder acceptable to the Mexican Administration. The reply from Mexico City said that bidders must make arrangements with Compañía Mexicana, the only company authorized to transport mail in Mexico.

On February 1, Irving Glover wired Rihl asking him to choose the bidder for whom his company was willing to act as a subcontractor to perform the contract. None except Pan American Airways, Rihl wired back.

On February 16, the U.S. Post Office awarded the contract for FAM 8 to Pan American Airways—the highest bidder, at $2 a mile.

Trippe had a pat answer for antitrust investigators and other critics who subsequently questioned the remarkable coincidences in the awarding of FAM 8 and other mail contracts which combined to give Pan American Airways a monopoly of the Latin American routes. He blandly said, "The purchase of this Mexican company could have been arranged by any other American company interested in providing service to Mexico." Not likely in Harry New's twenty-one-day bidding period.

In authorizing Pan American to subcontract the carriage of U.S. mail to Compañía Mexicana, the U.S. Post Office set a precedent for the purchase of other national subsidiaries. Pan American reimbursed the Mexican company for the use of its airports, benefiting from the exemptions it enjoyed from import taxes on airplanes, parts and fuel, and the expropriation rights that facilitated development of ground facilities. The Mexican company acted as a feeder line for Pan American throughout Mexico.

Daily round-trip service between Brownsville and Mexico City was inaugurated in a shower of publicity on March 10, 1929, by Charles Lindbergh. Piloting a brand-new Ford trimotor that carried mail and eight passengers, he completed the 470-mile trip over what The Associated Press called "revolt-ridden Mexico" in 5 hours 18 minutes. His fiancée, Anne Morrow, the Ambassador's shy and literary daughter, was waiting for him at the airport in Mexico City, where hundreds of onlookers were disappointed to observe the young couple exchanging only smiles before driving off to the U.S. Embassy.

Lindbergh was at last formally affiliated with Pan American Airways after being wooed separately and in force by Trippe, Hambleton, Whitney and Hoyt. The young Galahad, already a prisoner of fame, had weighed a variety of offers—to lecture, to endorse cigarettes and to act in a movie to be produced by William Randolph Hearst. The newspaper publisher had charged into the film business in order to advance the career of his mistress, Marion Davies.

But in the last analysis, Lindbergh knew that he was more interested in the development of aviation than in anything else. Though "from a financial standpoint, it was not the most desirable thing to do," as he later told a Senate committee, he sold his services to two noncompeting airlines, one domestic, one international. In May 1928, he signed a contract with Transcontinental Air Transport to become chairman of its technical committee. Clement Keys offered him a yearly stipend of $10,000 and $250,000 in cash to pay for 25,000 shares of T.A.T. stock at $10 a share, with an option on 25,000 additional shares. The stock was issued in a street name after Keys advised him that registering it in his own name "would excite a lot of attention" when he sold it. Within the next five years, Lindbergh made a profit of $195,653.75 on the stock.

He laid out a coast-to-coast route for T.A.T. (which counted the

Pennsylvania Railroad among its principal investors), a two-day service by rail and plane. Passengers left New York at night by train; boarded a Ford trimotor in Columbus, Ohio, the next morning for a flight to Waynoka, Oklahoma; proceeded overnight by Santa Fe Railway Pullman to Clovis, New Mexico, and on the second morning out, completed the journey to Los Angeles by plane.

During the summer, Lindbergh paid several visits to Trippe's office at 100 East Forty-second Street to talk about joining Pan American. He left by the freight elevator after word of his presence spread through the building. Later, when he called at Betty and Juan's apartment at 1111 Park Avenue, he disguised himself with a hat, eyeglasses and a dark mustache. During one of the sessions in the office, Juan said, "Slim, why don't you have a lawyer work it out?" In January 1929, Trippe and Lindbergh's lawyer, Colonel Henry Breckinridge, drew an agreement whereby Charles was to be paid $10,000 a year for the next four years to act as Pan American Airways' technical adviser— the job and title he preferred, but which gave no outward recognition of the priceless public-relations function he performed.

Lindbergh also received a piece of the action—warrants for 40,000 shares of Aviation Corporation of the Americas at $15 and $30 a share. Over the next five years, he exercised some of the warrants and sold the rest, turning a profit of $150,884.50 on these transactions. He kept 9,500 shares of stock. Despite these substantial returns, Lindbergh told a Senate committee in later years, somewhat disingenuously, "I have invested materially more money in the industry than I have received from it." He added, "I have never sold a warrant except to reinvest in the company." The bulk of his profits from Pan American, $132,500 worth, resulted from selling warrants on 26,500 shares at $5 a warrant to C. V. Whitney, to obtain funds to exercise another 7,400 warrants at $15 and $30 a share.

Still, Lindbergh probably gave more than he got. In the company's formative stage, when it was essential to instill public confidence in the new mode of transportation, the linkage of the popular idol with Pan American Airways was akin to a papal benediction for the airline. The most imaginative press agent could not have contrived a campaign or paid for an endorsement that would have been as helpful as the torrents of publicity generated by a single activity of Lindbergh in behalf of Pan American.

During the three years following the signing of the contract, Lindbergh undertook several route surveys and four inaugural flights for mail and passenger service to Latin America. More accurately, perhaps, he was the starring player for these dramatic events. A week before he was to open the mail route from Miami to the Canal Zone on February 4, 1929, it was realized that no one really knew what conditions prevailed at some of the intermediate landing sites. John Hambleton, who had undertaken the responsibility early on for getting the routes into operation, made an inspection flight, saw that temporary ramps were built and took care of necessities. His trip was under a press blackout so as not to detract from the main event. Lindbergh, meanwhile, was charming Miami by taking seven planeloads of municipal fathers and winter visitors on flights over the city, while a crowd of fifty thousand persons clogged the roads leading to the airport with their automobiles. When Lindbergh took off from the new Pan American Airways terminal on his 27th birthday, Hambleton was aboard the Sikorsky amphibian as copilot on the inaugural mail flight.

8

Going 50-50

One fine morning in October 1927, shortly after the first
Pan American Airways plane had taken off for Havana from Key West,
a tall man with an exuberant head of curly black hair appeared in Dick
Hoyt's office. "I have an idea for starting an airline," he said. "Look at
this."

Harold R. Harris was an Army test pilot on extended leave. He
had joined Huff Daland, a small aircraft manufacturer in upstate New
York which had developed a method for dusting crops from the air.
Harris and Collett E. Woolman, an entomologist with a formula for
annihilating the boll weevil, had dusted vegetable crops in Mexico for
Huff Daland, and then moved on to the cotton fields of Peru.

While they were there, Harris had talked to bankers and businessmen who felt hampered by their dependence on the steamship and
were impatient for someone to start an international air service. When
the 1927 crop-dusting season was over, Harris had taken a trip around
South America, looking for new markets for Huff Daland but also
exploring the possibilities of airmail routes. He traveled by steamer
down the coast of Peru and by rail to La Paz, continued by train across
the Argentine to Buenos Aires, took a boat to Montevideo and another
steamer to São Paulo, where he caught a train to Rio de Janeiro, and
then sailed for the United States.

The trip lasted four months, and when Harris arrived in New York
in October, he learned that his employer had been taken over by
Hayden, Stone and renamed Keystone Aviation. Harris went around to
see his new boss, Richard Hoyt. He showed him a map outlining a

complete land route to South America from Texas through Mexico and Central America, down the west coast of the continent and across the Andes to Buenos Aires.

Hoyt studied it, then made a telephone call. "Come down here, Trippe," he said. "There's someone here who is two years ahead of us."

Harris' plan came to grips with the reality of aviation technology. The farthest an airplane could fly with a useful payload was 600 miles. Pilots had no radio, meteorological services or aerial maps to guide them, a deficiency that made flying over water especially risky. On a map of the Western Hemisphere, the southern half of the Americas appears to be flung eastward into the Atlantic almost in an S-curve. When a ruler or a piece of string is placed between New York and Buenos Aires, the straightest, shortest route is seen to follow along the Pacific coast of South America to Chile and over the mountains to Argentina. Harris told Hoyt and Trippe that except along the northern stretch between Ecuador and Panama, there were numerous landing fields on the Pacific side. Indeed, said Clement Keys when Hoyt mentioned it to him, "No big mountains, no big oceans, no big jungles, and a nice traffic center every thousand miles." The west coast was the main line to South America.

"Work it out with Harris and Priester," Hoyt told Juan. In the meantime, they agreed, concessions had to be obtained from west-coast governments so that when the U.S. Postmaster General saw fit to open the route to bidding, Pan American could offer proof of ability to perform.

Woolman and Harris were assigned to the task in Peru and Ecuador, and by the time Woolman, a formidable salesman of the Louisiana-farm-boy school of persuasion, had succeeded, a newborn corporate shell, Peruvian Airways, was ready to receive the concession. Harris became chief pilot, mechanic, general manager and vice president. Woolman returned to the United States to operate a mail route between Dallas and Atlanta that grew into Delta Airlines.

Hoyt opened a dialogue with W. R. Grace & Co., the grandee of Latin American colonizers. He wanted Pan American to join with leading steamship companies in each region—United Fruit in Central America, the Grace Line in South America—believing, as he said to Robert H. Patchin, a Grace vice president, that "one large company could do the job better than a number of separate and smaller concerns."

W. R. Grace was one of the most adept international trading companies, with roots planted deep into the soil of Peru seventy-five years before by William Russell Grace, an Irish immigrant of titanic energies. He had sired eleven children and a business empire straddling three continents and found time to serve two terms as Mayor of the City of New York.

By 1928, W. R. Grace was a diversified enterprise dealing, as the family liked to say, "in everything from pins to locomotives." W.R.'s son Joseph P. Grace was running the company with Stewart Iglehart, his best friend from college days at Columbia University, where they had been classmates of Charles Trippe. Grace was a trading firm, a merchant banker in London, a commercial banker in New York and Lima, a manufacturer of agricultural machinery and of fertilizer. Grace owned textile mills and sugar plantations in Peru, rubber plantations in Brazil, chain stores in Chile. It built railroads in the Andes and operated a shipping service to carry mail from New York to Valparaiso and transport Chilean copper, Bolivian tin, Ecuador's bananas and Colombia's coffee northward. Grace's "Santa" ships took wealthy Yankee tourists on winter cruises in southern waters. If the east coast of South America was predominantly European in terms of industrial and transport development, the west coast was U.S.-dominated by virtue of the Guggenheims in mining, Standard Oil and W. R. Grace.

A company as jealous of its markets as Grace could not have avoided being interested in aviation. It had commissioned studies of airmail transport and had exploratory discussions with the U.S. Post Office Department.

On August 31, 1928, the veteran South American trader and the novice airline stepped gingerly into partnership. Grace and the Aviation Corporation of the Americas each put up $25,000 to form a corporation to study the costs of operating a route from the Panama Canal to Chile and the advisability of asking the Postmaster General to advertise for a mail contract. The company bought the Peruvian franchise from Huff Daland Dusters and deposited it in Peruvian Airways; a few months later, similar steps were taken with a concession obtained by a Chilean national company.

Trippe, meanwhile, was busy at the Post Office in Washington. In mid-January, Harry New informed him that an appropriation was available for a 4,551-mile route from Cristóbal to Santiago with an option to extend over the Andes to Buenos Aires and Montevideo.

New felt he needed a capstone to his career, for he was uncertain of reappointment. The efficient Quaker of the Commerce Department had been elected President in November and let it be known that he was not going to reveal his Cabinet choices until the eve of his inauguration in March. New was a popular and relatively colorful figure in the drab Coolidge Administration, instantly recognized by his broad-brimmed black slouch hats, two-inch heels and Hoosier drawl. But he was 70, the Post Office was the most political seat in the Cabinet and Hoover had been critical of his handling of the competitive bidding for the domestic contracts. If he was to leave Washington, Harry New wanted to go with a grand finale to his airmail program.

The sooner bids were called for FAM 9 the better, he said, because it looked as though there might be strong competition for the route.

Trippe was concerned about one point: he had not yet secured landing rights in Colombia, and that might delay the opening of service. "Don't worry," said Irving Glover. "The Post Office has given you postponements on your Caribbean contract. You won't be held in default on this one."

On January 25, the partners increased their equity to a total of $1 million to create a new corporation, Pan American–Grace Airways, Inc., expressly to bid on the route. The Postmaster General advertised FAM 9 for bids on January 31, and five were received. Only one was lower than Pan American–Grace's $1.80: American International Airways bid $1.44. Its organizers were John Montgomery and Richard Bevier, backed again by Bevier's father-in-law, Lewis Pierson, whose Irving Trust Company did a thriving business with South America.

Had they known of a conversation between the American President-elect and Harold Harris a month before in Guayaquil, they might not have bothered to bid. Hoover was on a preinaugural journey to Central and South America to signal the desire of the United States to be a "good neighbor." He made it a point to discuss aviation rights with every President he met and elicit support for a U.S. commercial air service. Harris flew to meet the battleship *Maryland*, as it steamed into Guayaquil with Hoover aboard, to deliver a letter of welcome from the President of Peru. "You go right ahead with your plans," Hoover told him. "We'll make sure you get your airline."

On March 2, New awarded the contract to Pan American–Grace, and gave a much fuller explanation than usual as to why he had rejected the lowest bidder. He conceded the financial ability and integrity of the competing parties; his decision was based on "other very material considerations."

"This is the most important airmail contract that has yet been awarded," said New, and its importance dictated a showing of "proven and recognized capacity for performing the service contemplated." Pan American–Grace had filed evidence of extensive preparations to operate the route. He referred to the national subsidiary companies through which it had obtained the necessary foreign franchises. In short, New admired the way Pan American had locked up the field in advance of the bidding. "And in addition to this," he said, "it will have the benefit of all the facilities of the Grace Line of steamers now operating by sea along the whole line of the route." The lowest bidder had no facilities, no organization and no operating personnel already in the field. Bevier had admitted to the Postmaster General that his stockholders had subscribed conditionally—they would put up the money if his company were awarded the contract.

In final rebuttal of charges certain to be leveled that he had played favorites with Pan American Airways on every foreign airmail contract he had awarded, the retiring Postmaster General maintained that he had had no alternative to choosing Pan American–Grace over the lower bidder because "failure on this route would be a serious blow to the prestige of American aeronautical enterprise."

He signed the contract on March 4, his last day in office. Hoover had decided not to invite New into his Cabinet after all. Warmed by the belief he had carved himself an honorable niche in postal history, Harry New sped into the revolving door between government and industry and emerged on the board of directors of a new aviation holding company formed by W. A. Harriman and Lehman Brothers.

Montgomery and Bevier filed a protest. A hearing was held before New's successor, Postmaster General Walter F. Brown, who upheld the award to Pan American–Grace after a ruling by the Attorney General. The Foreign Air Mail Act of 1928, with its latitude for the postal official to use his judgment in awarding route contracts, was working out just as Trippe and his friends had intended.

The partnership of Pan American Airways and W. R. Grace was flawed from the beginning. Fifty–fifty may be an ideal basis for a union of man and woman, but in a corporate merger it is unworkable. "They were sure there would be no profits for a long time and so the deal was put together on the basis that they would share the losses," Harold Harris recalled later. "Actually, no one was prepared to give up one percent, so fifty–fifty was the best compromise in the first instance."

The partnership agreement, which left more to misunderstanding than was committed to paper, divided the continent into two spheres of influence. Pan American–Grace, or Panagra, would keep the west coast, donated by its parent, Grace, and Pan American Airways would take Mexico, Central America and the east coast of South America. The east/west division implied that the west coast of Colombia went to

Panagra and the north, or Caribbean, coast and the interior belonged to Pan American Airways.

At the outset, the marriage seemed exquisitely logical. Grace had the South American connections and personnel experienced in Latin ways. Pan American had the technical knowledge to get the airline off the ground and navigating safely through the turbulent skies.

In the original exchange of letters that served as the nuptial agreement, it was stated that "Grace would attend to the business on the Coast and Pan American would attend to the operations."

John D. MacGregor, a former oil-company representative who spoke excellent Spanish and had lived in Mexico and Colombia, was named vice president and general manager of the airline. He was based in New York. Harold Harris was put in charge of operations and stationed in Lima. Panagra did without a president, at Juan Trippe's insistence. He wished to establish the impression that it was a division of Pan American Airways rather than an independent airline. Trippe treated Panagra as an unwanted child of a marriage of convenience. "You don't expect that I would be as much interested where I have only fifty percent as where I may have a hundred percent in the operating company," he said to Grace vice president Patchin.

In a 50–50 arrangement, neither side has control but each has the power to block. The board of directors was composed of three members from each side, pledged to refrain from exerting influence when conflicts of interest arose. In such instances, they might attend a meeting in order to constitute a quorum, but would not vote.

Panagra's was a long, skinny network linking Panama, Colombia, Ecuador, Peru, Bolivia, Chile and Argentina. The mail was carried over it by winged "pony express." At Cristóbal, the postal sacks were transferred from the Pan American Airways flying boat that brought them from Miami to a Panagra amphibian for relay to northern Peru, where they were loaded aboard a land plane and sent south to Lima and Santiago. On October 12, 1929, a Panagra Ford trimotor scaled the wall of the Andes to inaugurate commercial service between Santiago and Buenos Aires, an 8½-hour flight of symbolic importance in the economic development of the continent.

The 795-mile journey had taken José de San Martín four months to complete in 1817 when he led an army from the Argentine pampas over the Andean passes to secure Chile's independence from Spain. Since the time of the Liberator, travelers had had to choose between brutal monthlong sails around Cape Horn or through the Straits of Magellan and a two-day train ride on a single-track railroad often interrupted by tempests of snow and landslides.

The aerial voyage was a sight-seeing trip of fear and wonder. The air was so violent that the plane might be tossed from 13,000 to 22,000 feet in a matter of moments. Entering Uspallata Pass, the slash in the Cordillera where San Martín had begun his climb, the two-engine aircraft was enveloped in a universe of ice, of crystal gardens overhung with tints of violets and sapphire and of mountains turbaned in drifting snow. The steward identified the peaks by name and height: Aconcagua, at 23,080 feet the highest in the Western Hemisphere; the Christ of the Andes standing 30 feet tall on the boundary of Argentina and Chile, a monument to peace, holding the cross above his head with his left hand, his right raised in benediction. In a stone hut a few yards distant, Panagra's radio and weather operator kept watch over climatic conditions in the pass, with only a boy servant to keep him company in his one-room abode during the six months of winter. Supplies of food and fuel were trekked to him by truck and burro from Santiago, a hundred miles away.

The plane carried a cylinder of oxygen with individual tubes placed next to each seat for passengers, their ears stuffed with cotton against the din of the engines, to relieve their headaches and the vertigo brought on by high altitudes.

9

Imperial Diplomacy

As an early bird, Pan American Airways swallowed the air routes of Latin America. By taking a partner such as Grace, by acquiring concessions through the purchase of national companies like Compañía Mexicana and by dispatching agents through the continent to lock up operating rights and contracts to carry mail back from foreign countries to the United States—all before the bids were opened —Pan American had offered the Postmaster General an ironclad excuse for deciding in its favor.

None of this could have happened without a special relationship with the State Department—a remarkable relationship between a private enterprise and a government agency, one that gradually took on emotional characteristics, of love and hate, seduction and manipulation, cooperation and rivalry. At times it was unclear who was calling the tune, Pan American Airways or the department, or whether, indeed, the company had become the nation's foreign ministry for international aviation.

The legal framework for airline operation was still incomplete as Pan American began knocking at the gates of Latin America. A few basic principles were established after the First World War when the proven military efficacy of the airplane alerted governments to potential menace in the skies. These were embodied in the International Convention for Air Navigation of the Paris Peace Conference in 1919.

The air over the high seas was acknowledged to be free. Every nation claimed exclusive sovereignty over the airspace above its territory and adjacent waters, and reserved the right to permit or deny admission to regularly scheduled foreign aircraft. Though the United States signed the convention, it was not bound by the provisions, inasmuch as the Senate refused to ratify the Treaty of Versailles. The United States, Mexico and the Central American republics were signatories to the Pan American Convention on Commercial Aviation which issued from the Havana conference in January 1928 and which stated the principles in somewhat vaguer language. Earlier, the Air Commerce Act of 1926 had affirmed the sovereignty of the United States over its airspace and given the authority to grant landing rights to foreign aircraft to the Secretary of Commerce.

In both the Paris and the Havana conventions, nations jealously guarded the rights to internal traffic from outsiders. Some Latin American countries willingly extended such privileges, known as cabotage, to foreigners in the absence of native companies able to perform the services, but many withdrew them as soon as national airlines were organized.

Although governments alone were the source of operating concessions for external carriers, the United States was not engaged in intergovernmental negotiations to establish international air service. Since an airplane capable of navigating the oceans with a payload had not yet been invented, European nations were not asking permission for their carriers to serve the United States, and the accessible Latin American countries, with one exception, had no airlines on whose behalf they wished to demand reciprocity. So the State Department tolerated private individuals and companies making their own deals with Latin American governments, in competition with each other and with freebooters of other nationalities. The department stood ready to assist its citizens, but as one of several critics observed, "During this epoch, only one American company appears to have enjoyed the advantages of American nationality."

As a consequence, the Latin American airways were secured in political ambiguity and confusion as to whether the Yankee imperialist or the good neighbor was approaching from the skies.

Juan Trippe took the position that the State Department should undertake a diplomatic initiative with Latin American governments on behalf of his airline. His requests were invariably couched as urgent directives and accompanied by vigorous flag waving. "On behalf of Pan American Airways," he typically ended his notes to Assistant Secretary of State Francis White, chairman of the interdepartmental committee on aviation, "I wish to take this opportunity to thank you for the assistance and sympathetic cooperation extended to this

Company—a 100% American owned Corporation—now interested in extending service to Central and South America."

Soliciting White's intervention in obtaining the domestic mail concession in Cuba for Pan American, he wrote, "I understand that certain German interests are in there." The vague conspiratorial tone left the impression that he had secret sources of intelligence. Could the Assistant Secretary have the American Embassy in Havana put in a good word for Pan American?

White fired off a message, adding:

> We are most anxious here to have American aviation as prominent as possible in the Caribbean region and for that reason this Department did everything possible to favor the bill that was enacted by Congress at its last session authorizing the Post Office Department to give subventions for the carrying of air mail in the Caribbean region. The Pan American Airways is a hundred per cent American owned and managed company and for that reason we would be glad to see it, rather than Germans, have the contract in Cuba.

White's cooperation was boundless; he was to be Pan American's chief door opener as well as surrogate, ordering the Foreign Service officers in Latin America to act as errand boys for the airline. This Baltimore-born, Yale-educated career diplomat apparently believed, as firmly as the founders of Pan American Airways, that their business coincided with the public interest, and that it was proper for the State Department to be a private company's sponsor. All Trippe and Hambleton had to do was to ask for favors; White sent telegrams, signed by himself or invoking the name of Secretary of State Frank B. Kellogg, to the envoys in the field, exhorting cooperation with the airline's agents and demanding full reports on problems they encountered. The Pan American representatives freely used the State Department telegraph system to communicate with Washington and with Trippe in New York. Expenses were charged to the airline's account.

The amount of assistance was extraordinary. "We have been moving heaven and earth to help Pan American Airways," Stokeley W. Morgan, chief of the division of Latin American Affairs, acknowledged in a memorandum of January 1929. "This company is in an exceptional position in that the Department is very seriously and vitally interested in the success of its undertaking." During a period of a year and a half, starting in February 1928, while the foreign-airmail legislation was still being lobbied in Congress, close to sixty messages of varying length and firmness were sent from Washington to State Department officials in Latin America in behalf of Pan American Airways.

At first the legation staffs understood that they were under standing instructions to assist all credentialed Americans impartially, but it soon became evident that the department's efforts "to promote American aviation in Latin America" excepted them from that rule. If anything, one indignant memorandum writer in Washington declared, some instructions were "designed to frustrate the efforts of competing American interests to obtain air mail contracts or to hold what they had."

The agents of Pan American went for broke in bargaining for foreign concessions. They asked for exclusive rights to carry mail and passengers between the Latin American country and the Canal Zone or the United States, a franchise for commercial air service within the country as well, and numerous collateral or derivative privileges: exemption from customs duties on airplane fuel, spare parts and supplies, and from personal taxes; the waiving of landing fees; the use of national waters and airports for its seaplanes and land planes and, where they did not exist, the right to expropriate private properties to build airports.

They asked for free use of the national radio and telegraph facilities on an exclusive or at least a priority basis, arguing that since the facilities were limited, Pan American Airways would be hindered in its operations if another airline were to share the privilege. Sometimes they sought permission for Pan American to build its own radio stations, hotels, restaurants and auxiliary transportation systems. Bob Thach drew the contracts to run for twenty-five or thirty years with renewal options.

Little or no monetary subsidy was requested, although tax incentives are usually construed as subsidy. The airline offered to render the service of carrying the mail at a price per pound that matched what it hoped to get from the U.S. Post Office for the outbound trip.

The contract with the foreign country could be assigned to another company. In Ecuador, an ample concession was granted to Harold Harris, who promptly transferred it to Pan American–Grace Airways. Because Ecuador and Peru were not the friendliest of neighbors, Harris had been advised to make no use of his Peruvian Airways calling cards and instead negotiate personally when he went to Quito. He ingratiated himself with President Isidro Ayora by flying him and his son to Guayaquil and back. "That put him on the right side of the balance sheet," Harris said.

The contracts aroused the suspicion among Latin Americans that imperialistic Yankees were trying a new trick to exert control over them, by violating the sovereignty of their airspaces. Public sentiment was at times vehement. Most countries were reluctant to grant exclusive privileges to foreigners; the Germans skirted the problem of xenophobia by setting up national companies.

The monopolistic features in the Pan American contracts did not pass muster in Washington either. Asked for an opinion on a concession Pan American sought from the Government of Guatemala, the Solicitor of the State Department said of the provision for exclusive mail rights:

> . . . the Department has consistently refused to take any action on behalf of persons or firms having concessions with foreign countries which are monopolistic. In the event that Guatemala should undertake to grant a similar concession to another company, especially if it happens to be an American company, the Department will take the position that it cannot make any representation on behalf of the Pan American Airways.
>
> Broadly speaking, the United States should not support American interests in seeking in foreign countries rights the granting of which to European interests would be held objectionable from the viewpoint of our economic policy. The United States would be charged with inconsistency . . .

In half a dozen countries legislative opposition forced Pan American Airways to back down on its monopolistic demands, but its representatives were unfazed by nationalist outrage. "Anything goes" would seem to have been their motto.

Expediency was the moral imperative of the Pan American Airways empire builders, and they made no apologies for the means they used or the company they kept. That Pan American was hated and feared for its Latin American activities or that it reputedly wielded sinister influence was their mark of achievement. "I was a friend of all those dictators," said Erwin Balluder. He was chummy with the dreaded butcher of the Dominican Republic, Rafael L. Trujillo, and with Gustavo Rojas Pinilla, the corrupt Colombian general. "We didn't work through the embassies," Balluder boasted. "We worked directly with governments. We actually reached such good understanding with some of those governments and their leaders that we aroused the envy of our own missions in those countries."

Frequently, Balluder worked in tandem with David E. Grant, a New York lawyer who was Pan American's counsel for Latin American affairs. Having been raised in New Mexico, Grant was fluent in Spanish, and he possessed raconteurial gifts that endeared him to democrats and dictators alike. It took more than Grant's droll stories and Balluder's tolerant attitude toward sadistic leaders to achieve results. Pan

American chose influential natives and experienced foreign residents as local agents, "people who knew people in the government," as Balluder said. In Guatemala, Pan American's man was the son of the country's railroad builder; in Mexico, a former postal official; in Honduras, the brother-in-law of a highly placed general.

Following Hoyt's dictum, Pan American rode on the coattails of the United Fruit Company, colonizer of the banana republics and pioneer, for forty years, in monopolistic concessions. The company operated radio stations and transport systems within Central America, and its ships carried mail under U.S. postal contracts. Acting under instructions from Boston headquarters cued by Trippe in New York, the Fruit Company's satraps supplied introductions for Pan American representatives on the scene, and in Honduras and Nicaragua did the spadework on air rights, withdrawing in favor of Pan American as the contracts were ready to be signed. The companies came to an agreement whereby United Fruit was to continue limited air operations and give Pan American a monopoly of its passenger business.

The pairing of Pan American Airways with the hated United Fruit Company inflamed Central American sensitivities, and attempts were made to disavow the connection. When MacGregor telegraphed that newspapers in Honduras were whipping up opposition to the Pan American contract by alleging a link with the Fruit Company, John Hambleton telephoned Francis White to assure him that "there is no connection whatsoever with United Fruit Company" and asked that the U.S. legation in Tegucigalpa make that assurance known. White complied at once, and a week later reinforced his instructions:

> PAA feel that some of the hostile press reports in Honduras may have been inspired by the German aviation interest in Colombia. As they have been hostile to American interests in the past, this is not unlikely. Please report. Department, of course, is most desirous that this service should be in the hands of a reliable American company rather than in the hands of foreign interest.

A few days before Hambleton's telephone call, *The New York Times* had reported that Pan American Airways was laying plans to develop air services in the Caribbean in association with United Fruit and with the Radio Corporation of America, which jointly held certain radio patents. The story had undoubtedly been picked up by the Honduran press. Subsequently, an editorial writer for the newspaper *El Cronista* took the denials to be equivalent to a "public confession that the United Fruit Company is a pernicious organization which has occasioned deep, grave and frequent injuries to Honduras. If this were not so, what importance would it attach to denying that Pan American Airways has connections with the United Fruit Company?" Intimidated by the newspaper campaign, the Honduran Congress rejected the contract, and it took nearly two years for one to be approved. During that period, the American consul in Tegucigalpa reported, it was a matter of common knowledge that a United Fruit subsidiary, Tropical Radio Telegraph Company, had been engaged to install and operate the radio stations Pan American was to be allowed to build under the contract.

Guatemala lay midway on the Central American sky route to the Canal Zone. Pan American's contriving for air rights in that vital area began in March 1928, two months before the Postmaster General advertised FAM 5. John MacGregor arrived in Guatemala City proffering the one-sided agreement to the Minister of the Interior and the President of the Guatemalan Republic.

Arthur H. Geissler, the U.S. Minister, went out of his way to secure a cordial reception for MacGregor. Geissler had been urging his superiors in Washington since 1922 to get an American-owned air service going to Central America. Despite the minister's effusive intercession in MacGregor's behalf, the terms of the Pan American contract, particularly the exclusive mail rights and the tax exemptions, stirred a political hornet's nest, and the Guatemalan Cabinet resigned over the issue. The nonpolitical gnomes of the State Department registered their misgivings; the economic adviser recommended against assisting Pan American unless the contract was modified.

On orders from New York, MacGregor pushed on to El Salvador, Honduras and Nicaragua, encountering ill will everywhere.

In May 1929, George Rihl appeared, newly invested with the title of vice president in charge of Mexican operations for Pan American Airways. The legation was expecting him. Francis White had sent the usual instructions to give him "all possible assistance," with an additional reminder that Pan American Airways was the possessor of six U.S. airmail contracts.

Rihl was pursuing a more ambitious objective than MacGregor— namely, a Guatemalan concession for "Pan American Airways and its affiliates." This would allow Pan American to enter Guatemala from the east on FAM 5, the Caribbean route to the Canal Zone, and Compañía Mexicana to fly in from Mexico City with the U.S. mail from Brownsville, and to continue from Guatemala City to San Salvador. Rihl discovered that the Minister of the Interior had just awarded an airmail contract to another American company. Latin American Airways was backed by Claude Ryan and other aircraft-manufacturing interests who aspired to build an airline system from the west coast of the United States to South America. They had just obtained rights to operate between Mexico City and Tía Juana, continuing on to Los Angeles, and with the Guatemalan concession they hoped to add a Mexico City–El Salvador leg.

Rihl was relying on the Mexican Embassy for assistance. He had been spreading the word in Mexico City that Compañía Mexicana was going to carry the Mexican flag through Guatemala and the rest of Central America. Mexico had tried throughout the nineteenth century to assert suzerainty over the other nations of the region. Apparently, Rihl did not figure on his strategy of catering to Mexican national pride backfiring in Guatemala.

Geissler was taken aback by his brazen approach. "Money will finally decide whether the Mexican Aviation Company will be permitted to fly in Guatemala," Rihl declared, and the U.S. Minister promptly reported to the State Department:

> Mr. Rihl indicated that he is prepared to resort to corruption, notwithstanding the fact that it has been made clear to him that the Legation would frown on such procedure. I doubt that he will succeed if he makes that attempt.

Rihl rattled on to Geissler and to Stanley Hawks, the legation secretary, whom he impressed as being "of the promoter type," about dispensing bribery and payoffs, indicating that it was his standard business practice in Mexico. He said, quite casually, that he had been given an indirect opportunity to "buy" the Guatemalan Minister of the Interior but had not yet paid out any money. "But it will finally get down to a question of money," he said. "I haven't settled the fee with my lawyer here yet because it will have to include the contribution to the minister."

Geissler remarked with a sour smile, "You seem to think that all public officials are either crooks or fools."

"No, not all of them," Rihl answered, chuckling. "Not quite all of them."

If he could not accomplish what he had come for quickly enough, he would put a spoke in his competitor's wheel from the other side of the border. "I'm sure I can get the Mexican Government to deny them the contract to carry the mail from Mexico City to Guatemala and to give it to Compañía Mexicana," he said.

A few days later, the Minister of the Interior announced that he was going to allow Pan American Airways to fly from the northeast coast to the capital and on to San Salvador, and Latin American Airways to come in from the direction of Mexico City, to the west. As for Compañía Mexicana, no Mexican airline was going to operate in his country.

Geissler thought that this decision was eminently reasonable and fair to both American companies, and made it easier for the legation to be evenhanded in extending assistance. Rihl was cheerfully obstinate. "It won't do," he said. "I'm going to New York for further talks." Before leaving, he told Geissler, "All that Pan American is trying to do is carry out the wishes of the Postmaster General to have a two-day mail service from Texas to the Canal Zone."

Confused and exasperated, Geissler asked the State Department for instructions. The Republican guard had changed in Washington. The new Secretary of State, Henry L. Stimson, was perplexed by the competition between the two American airlines in Guatemala. On June 21, he asked Postmaster General Walter Brown for an expression of his views on the matter. Stimson noted:

> . . . it has not been the practice of this Department to extend assistance in obtaining business to foreign corporations even though their stock is controlled by American interests . . .
> This Department is very reluctant to extend diplomatic assistance to one American company against the other, particularly where the interests of different sections of the United States appear to be involved, as in the present case where one company appears to be endeavoring to establish a route from the western part of the United States into Central America, and the other from Texas. It would be unfortunate on the other hand if the rivalry between the two companies resulted in the failure of either to obtain permission to enter Guatemala and El Salvador.

On June 25, Brown replied:

> Since the Pan American Airways has a contract for this Department under which service may be extended, it is requested diplomatic assistance be rendered that company in preference to any other company including Latin American Airways.

Brown was new on the job too—the Ohio lawyer had been rewarded for delivering his home state to Hoover in the November election—but he learned quickly, and he had the benefit of the President's explicit guidance on improving the efficiency of the postal service.

Years later when Brown was quizzed by a Senate committee about his motives for interceding with the State Department in behalf of Pan American, he explained:

> Well, we had a contract with Pan American, and we were trying very hard to help them get enough revenue so they could return postage to us and make the company self-sustaining. It seemed as though one company with a contract was enough for us to support at the time . . . whatever we did in the matter we did with a view to making Pan American self-sustaining so the burden on our Government would be very small, so the postage would be sufficient to pay the $2.

But why did the Post Office repeatedly intervene when the opposition in the Latin American parliaments to Pan American was so fierce? Said Brown:

> I think the State Department finally reached the conclusion the United States Government was in partnership with the Pan American in a mail service to South America in which they took the mail from our country down and brought the mail from the other countries back, and they were very anxious to get a complete service and justify the expenditure, and I suppose the State Department did just what I did, tried to make a success of it.
>
> I think when we started—some of it comes back to my mind now—when we started the conversations with the State Department, they were not aware that we had a contract, had made a contract with Pan American for this service, and they thought they were asked to choose between two companies that were on the same footing, but when they finally reached the conclusion the Government itself had an interest in Pan American, then I think they exerted themselves in every proper way.

On July 12, Geissler received his marching orders from Washington: the legation should support "in every proper way American companies which have been awarded contracts by the United States Post Office Department, in efforts to obtain privileges necessary for carrying mails to Guatemala in accordance with [those] contracts . . . and in rendering diplomatic assistance where concessions are involved to carry out the contracts it is desired that those contractors be given preference."

In August, another envoy of Pan American Airways strode into the muddled scene. Wilbur L. Morrison, traffic manager for Compañía Mexicana, was a tall, heavyset Texan with a rough tongue and a memory bank that stored the addresses of the bordellos of Central America. The Guatemalan manager of the United Fruit Company telephoned Hawks at the legation to say that he had been instructed by his head office to give Morrison all the help necessary to obtain a mail contract.

Morrison's behavior was peculiar, Hawks thought. He spent most of his time at the Mexican Embassy or in the company of a local newspaperman who boasted of his political influence. Morrison snubbed the Minister of the Interior by calling on every other member of the Cabinet but him.

Latin American Airways, which had been reorganized as Pickwick Airways, lodged a protest through a native lawyer, claiming it had prior rights to the Guatemalan mail contract and that it was improper for the U.S. Legation to help a Mexican company usurp the right of a U.S. company such as Pickwick to carry U.S. mail into the country.

The Minister of the Interior agreed. He had learned that Compañía Mexicana would be paid $2 a mile by the U.S. Post Office and understood that this would surely be a lethal blow to Pickwick's operations from the west coast. "You tell the State Department," he said to Geissler, "that I believe that sort of subsidized competition is illicit, that it will result in the establishment of a monopoly in Guatemala and I do not believe that the Government of the United States would favor such a thing if it fully understood the circumstances."

He notified the Mexican Government that Compañía Mexicana was not welcome in Guatemala.

In complete accord with the Minister of the Interior, Geissler wrote to Washington:

> It seems undesirable that a foreign company other than one incorporated in the United States operate an air transport line in Central America and even less that the Government of the United States facilitate it.

Then he sat back to wait for further instructions.

There was a tone of embarrassment in the State Department's response. It had been informed that the reason Pan American Airways was insisting on Compañía Mexicana as the carrier, even over the objections of the Guatemalan Government, was the impracticality of changing planes at the border if it was to meet the stipulation by the Post Office for two-day service. Therefore, would Geissler get permission from the Guatemalan Government for the Mexican company to bring in the U.S. mail.

Before Geissler could perform the disagreeable chore, a Compañía Mexicana plane arrived and disgorged sacks of mail. A former provincial governor of Mexico, now a vice president of the airline, was aboard with a retinue of Mexican newspaper correspondents. "We're bringing mail into Guatemala whether a permit to do so has been granted or not," he said.

The Minister of the Interior was livid. "If Pan American uses such methods as coercing Guatemala with the aid of Mexicans now, what will it do after it has a monopoly?" he asked Geissler.

The next day, the Pickwick Airways representative was invited to a meeting at a hotel with Morrison and the secretary of the Mexican Embassy and threatened with revocation of his airline's license to fly over Mexican territory.

Morrison interjected, "We don't mean any unfair competition to you."

A week later, the Minister of the Interior granted Compañía Mexicana a provisional license to carry mail to Guatemala City from Mexico, a one-way permit that was not to be taken as abrogating the privileges given to Pickwick Airways.

Geissler and the old hands at the State Department were chagrined, and there were signs at the higher levels—Francis White excepted—of concern about Pan American Airways' overstepping the bounds of propriety.

Recently, Trippe had written to Hoover, forwarding a letter from the President of Nicaragua to the President of the United States that had been carried by the pilot of the first regularly scheduled airmail plane en route from Santiago. Secretary of State Stimson asked Hoover's secretary to send his reply through the Nicaraguan Minister of Foreign Affairs, the normal diplomatic channel for exchanges between heads of government. Stimson said:

> Exceptions may sometimes be warranted . . . but if the practice is extended to commercial aviation companies each request will lead to others and ultimately give rise to a feeling of unfair discrimination. The competition between the various American aviation interests throughout is already very keen and bitter and in such a situation it seems best for this government to maintain a strictly impartial position.

10

Tour de Force

In the imagination of his unsuccessful competitors, Juan Trippe took Latin America by tour de force of personal diplomacy. Some grumbled that he traded on Spanish ancestry to win favors from Latin American governments. Others alleged he had changed his name from John to Juan for that purpose.

Nothing could have been further from the truth. Trippe effected what David Bruce called "his imperial vision" from New York and Washington. Most airmen are by nature nomadic; Juan was not particularly fond of traveling, least of all to Latin America, a region for which he seemed to have an aversion. He made one major diplomatic journey to Latin America in September 1929, announcing himself, contrary to Van Dusen's advice, as J. T. Trippe.

He and Betty were accompanying Charles Lindbergh on a 7,000-mile tour of the Caribbean. Pan American's technical adviser was to open FAM 6 carrying the first U.S. airmail from Miami to Paramaribo, Dutch Guiana, in four days, a demonstration of the two-week advantage the airplane had over the steamship schedule.

The expedition was mounted with the fanfare of a royal honeymoon. Lindbergh had married Anne Morrow in May, and now the Eagle, no longer lone, flew with his bride, a copilot, a radio operator and the Trippes. They made an appealing foursome of the sort featured in the rotogravure sections of Sunday newspapers, looking like socialites embarking on a ship's cruise rather than a promotion tour for commercial air service. The tousled aviator wore a suit of businessman's gray instead of the expected leather jacket and breeches, and carried his helmet rolled up in one hand. His slip of a wife, in pastel dress, brimmed hat, delicate stockings and shoes, brushed aside helping hands as she jumped out of the plane at each destination. The Lindberghs were the magnet for worshipful mobs that hailed them as though they had descended from heaven. In their shadow followed the Trippes. Juan, a dark, chubby figure in a white Panama suit and brown-and-white saddle shoes, paid courtesy calls on sixteen governments in twenty days. Betty was the smiling extrovert of the group, always knowing just what to say to put a native official at ease, or to charm an American consul.

The trip was exhausting. They rose every morning at 4 or 5, took off two hours later and touched down every few hours to refuel and to deliver and pick up mail. They stopped before dark to stay the night. Always, there were the adoring crowds, with the inquisitive leers that Anne quickly grew to fear and despise; and always there was the press.

Scarcely a moment went unrecorded. The young matrons, daughters of J. P. Morgan partners, confided their impressions to their diaries and the mothers they left behind. "It was such fun to see Betty Trippe this morning and compare notes on cramped baggage space, short-notice trips and photographers," Anne Lindbergh wrote to Elisabeth Morrow as they passed over the Florida Keys and pointed toward Havana. "I am so glad they are along. She is now writing reams on a small pad to her mother."

The Boswell of the flight was the radio operator, William W. Ehmer. Copies of his log, filled in ebullient detail, were distributed to the press after doctoring by a publicity man for Pan American Airways at Miami. "A combination of Rudyard Kipling and a public relations counsel," an editorial writer termed Ehmer's prose, while conceding that "the most blasé would still have thrilled at the idea of a plane passing down in a single day over the whole romantic and remote geography of the Lesser Antilles."

The allusion was to Ehmer's log for the third day, which *The New York Times* published in nearly one and a half columns of agate type. "Slipping over endless tiny islands, like jade gems in turquoise settings, under sparkling clear skies" was the passage singled out for scorn. Ehmer noted each luminescent change of color in the tropical sea over which the Sikorsky S-38 cruised at 90 miles an hour; the lush green hills; the volcanic peaks and coral reefs; the whitewashed steeples of the island churches and courthouses; the tranquil skies and the pockets of bumpiness entered without warning and from which they exited just as suddenly. "Mrs. Lindbergh served lunch unperturbed, like the good sailor she is," the radio operator observed approvingly. Much of the time, she read from a hoard of novels and literary criticism, "settled comfortably in lounge chair . . . as if home on front porch 4,000 miles away in Miami."

He marveled at being able to maintain constant contact with Miami and with land stations throughout the West Indies. Everywhere they were greeted by cheering, flag-waving multitudes and officials welcoming them with speeches and floral bouquets. The ritual became familiar—and for the Lindberghs, tiresome. A band struck up the national anthem and, occasionally, "Lucky Lindy." Lindbergh delivered a sack of mail to the Postmaster General, and then came what Anne described to her mother as "the triumphal home-from-the-wars ride through the streets."

At Port of Spain, the mail load was again fatter than anticipated, so Lindbergh ordered a paring of unnecessary weight. Even their coats and the welcoming flowers were left on the shore.

At Georgetown, Lindbergh slipped the amphibian into the choppy waters of a harbor crammed with ships dressed as for the arrival of a king, their whistles shrieking. In Paramaribo, an oasis of Dutch solidity on the northeast coast of South America, the travelers were mobbed by a dancing, torch-bearing crowd. Juan found himself riding alone into the center of town in a car festooned with colored lanterns after Lindbergh refused to get into the vehicle.

The mission of opening a new airmail line was completed at Paramaribo. The party rested a day and a half and then took off, to retrace the flight path to Port of Spain, carrying the first northbound mail from Dutch Guiana to Trinidad, where it was transferred to a regular mail plane. From there on, the trip was billed as a survey of the western Caribbean for future passenger service.

Between Port of Spain and Maracay, Venezuela, the daredevil still lurking in the canonized aeronaut asserted himself. When Lindbergh had barnstormed through the Midwest in 1922, he had walked on the wing of a plane as it looped through the air, secured by invisible wire cables. Now he turned over the controls to Charles Lorber, the copilot, and climbed out over the bow of the amphibian to take photographs from an altitude of 1,500 feet. He positioned himself in the compartment that held the anchor and clicked away, unperturbed by the propeller whirring a few feet behind him.

Returning to the controls, he responded to a radio message from General Juan Vicente Gómez asking him to circle over Caracas and give a salute from the air. The Venezuelan dictator, acting as Minister of War while one of his toadies, Juan Bautista Pérez, occupied the

Presidency, was on hand to welcome the party at Maracay. Lindbergh kept General Gómez waiting for twenty minutes on the field while he went about his usual routine of letting the engines cool before putting the plane to rest for the night. The strongman, a former cattle farmer, was captivated. "He is a good man, he looks after his beast," he remarked. When Lindbergh was at last ready to meet him, the 70-year-old Gómez reached up and pulled Charles's head down to his stubby level to kiss him on both cheeks. Then he grasped the flier's hands and exclaimed, "What a stick of a man!"

One of the cruelest and most corrupt of Latin American despots, Gómez had been opposed to granting concessions supposedly because the airplane provided a nearly foolproof means of escape for dissidents and riflers of the national treasury. Yet his consent was essential if Pan American were to open service between Maracaibo and Port of Spain, thus making it possible to fly a ring around the Caribbean.

The Lindberghs and Trippes stayed at the home of Preston Buford McGoodwin, the Pan American agent in Caracas. McGoodwin, the former U.S. Minister to Venezuela, was one of the first of a string of Foreign Service officers hired into "the other State Department," as Pan American came to be called. The next day, while Betty and Anne rested and went sight-seeing, Charles and Juan were taken by Mc-Goodwin to meet President Pérez and his Cabinet. They discussed plans for a survey of a Venezuelan air route, edging on claims staked by Aéropostale. The following morning at 8, Gómez received them at his palace and Juan left behind a draft agreement for the Venezuelan Government to examine.

Unrestrained crowds flanking the runway at Barranquilla prevented a landing. Lindbergh tossed notes from the plane begging them to disperse and circled for almost an hour, to no avail. Surmising that he was running out of gas (the plane had no fuel gauge), he climbed to leave the area of the airport—at which point the twin engines went dead.

His passengers surrendered to the feeling of absolute calm that attends moments of great crisis. Lindbergh headed for the nearest uncluttered stretch, warning them to "hold tight" as he came down on "the sweetest little lake" his wife had ever seen. He had spotted it while they were mesmerized by the crowds. The landing was smooth and the passengers graceful under pressure. The men laughed; the women giggled. The radio operator took out a cigarette, and Betty Trippe bowed to Lindbergh as he was popping nuts into his mouth. "Thank you *very* much," she said.

Native farmers rescued them from the lake in a boat and then drove them into town by automobile. Trippe made one attempt at overcoming the language barrier. "Aéroplano field?" he inquired. Lindbergh corrected him: *"El campo de aviación."*

The 450 miles from Barranquilla to Cristóbal was covered in 4 hours with a stop at Cartagena. Two thousand persons waited for hours in drizzling rain at France Airfield to catch a glimpse of Lindbergh and his bride. For three days, they submitted to an ordeal of luncheons, teas, dinners, balls, receptions and more speeches. "The Trippes have been such fun, and wear so well," Anne Lindbergh told her diary. "I think they are remarkable. The more I see of them, the more I think it. They both have a wonderful sense of humor and are such a reassuring comfort in hot moments."

Lindbergh and Trippe racked up fourteen-hour workdays, wedging meetings on business and technical matters between festivities. As the transfer station for the lines to South America, the Panamanian Isthmus was the vital spot in the Pan American Airways system. Tempers were frayed over the question of the airfield Pan American was to use. The War Department insisted the airline operate from a protected base inside the Canal Zone; Panamanians saw this as a restraint on their commercial development, for the Pan American planes bearing the mail would be followed by planes with businessmen and tourists. In Managua, they were welcomed in a tropical downpour by the commander of the U.S. Marine Corps detachment while Nicaraguan officials waited at the American Legation in the city. Nicaragua had looked like easy going for Pan American Airways fifteen months before, when John MacGregor had had the contract accepted by the President almost at once. But the legislature had then begun hacking at the monopolistic provisions, and what was finally approved in the spring of 1929 was a nonexclusive agreement for ten years.

Yet that was more than had been achieved in El Salvador, a hotbed of anti-Yanqui feeling. Lindbergh landed at San Salvador for just long enough for his presence to have a thawing effect on the Minister of War, in whose grasp aviation rights were held.

They pushed on to Guatemala City, arriving in the late afternoon. Charles and Anne rushed to offer condolences to the family of a slain Guatemalan aviator and place a wreath on his tomb. As Geissler was escorting Lindbergh to pay respects to the President and his Cabinet, he turned to Juan. "You may come along," the minister said. Juan accepted, hanging back unnoticed on the periphery of Lindy-worshipers at the Presidential palace. That evening at a dinner in Lindbergh's honor at the Legation, Geissler lectured Trippe on the history of relations between Mexico and Guatemala and why the heavy-handedness about Compañía Mexicana stirred so much emotion. "I suppose," he said, "your people in the Mexican company told you that the Guatemalan Government would be more disposed to grant an aviation contract to them than to an American concern."

"They did," Trippe mumbled, "and I have concluded that was a mistake."

"There is serious talk of organizing a Guatemalan aviation service to fly between Central America and Key West, and it has the support of the Minister of the Interior," Geissler warned. Moreover, there was a plan afoot to levy a heavy tax on foreign-subsidized companies which could be annoying to Compañía Mexicana. "It would be easier to defeat the project if Pan American Airways were operating between here and the Mexican border instead of the Mexican company," he said.

The next morning before boarding the plane, Juan said to him, "On thinking it over, I believe you may be right."

Trippe realized that Pan American was not going to operate in Guatemala without a compromise. By spring, the Guatemalan assembly approved a nonexclusive twenty-year contract for Pan American Airways to operate in Guatemala. The mail from Brownsville was transferred from Compañía Mexicana to a Pan American plane at the western border with Mexico and flown to Guatemala City and on to San Salvador. Another Pan American plane, coming from the Caribbean, landed at Puerto Barrios, in northeastern Guatemala, and flew on to the Canal Zone via San Salvador. Within a year, Pickwick Airways was bankrupt, another competitor for Pan American Airways eliminated.

Concessions in other Central American republics were wrapped up by the middle of 1930, also after Pan American gave up insisting on exclusive rights. On the U.S. side, however, the monopoly conferred by the Post Office on Pan American Airways was strengthened, to the dismay of State Department officials—Francis White excepted. As far as they could see, the Department was hostage to a program that violated its declared policy of "vigorously opposing monopolistic or exclusive concessions which would close the door upon American competitive effort" in foreign countries.

Juan may have learned something about the limits of Yankee imperialism in Latin America during his Lindbergh-led tour, one of the few occasions on which he practiced open diplomacy. His preferred method of negotiating international agreements was the secret covenant secretly arrived at—as in Colombia.

A country of severe physical contrasts, of fertile valleys and high-lands separated by mountains and jungles from the sea, Colombia was the one Latin American republic with an efficient and expansionist airline, SCADTA.

Its director, Peter Paul von Bauer, was the youngest son of a landed Austrian family, intelligent, imaginative and intent on making his fortune as a New World pioneer. Under his administration, SCADTA was shortly paying dividends to shareholders. Its main sources of revenue were aerial surveying and a concession to operate a national air postal service. SCADTA maintained its own post offices, set its own rates, issued stamps and kept the proceeds from the sales. Von Bauer represented Colombia at international postal conferences. The airline was the nation's pride, and its director, though an alien, was regarded as one of its most distinguished citizens.

Almost from the outset, von Bauer envisioned a Caribbean network extending from Colombia through neighboring Panama to Key West. In 1925, he and his brother, Viktor, an Austrian consular official in Cuba, made a pilgrimage to Wall Street and Washington to promote his dream.

The War Department shuddered at the prospect of German-owned aircraft flying near the Canal Zone and put a brake on his plans. Though von Bauer lined up mail concessions in Central America, Post-master General Harry New, hearing the alarm bell rung by Major Henry Arnold, denied him a U.S. postal contract and let it be known that he would look with favor upon a U.S.-owned international airline.

The Air Commerce Act of 1926 provided that foreign aircraft, even of nonmilitary character, had to have permission from the State Department to fly through the airspaces of the United States, including that of the Canal Zone, and then only if reciprocal privileges were accorded American civil planes would it be granted.

In Colombia, public sentiment toward the United States was intermittently hostile. Combustible memories of Theodore Roosevelt's role in abetting the revolution of 1903 in which Panama declared its independence from Colombia, a prelude to the United States' completing the construction of the canal across the isthmus, were inflamed by the rebuffs to von Bauer.

In November 1927, Enrique Olaya Herrera, the Colombian Minister to the United States, asked the State Department to discuss the matter of his country's civil planes flying in and around the Canal Zone. At that time the War Department had not yet drawn up regulations for aerial operations in the zone, and White put Olaya off, saying that until that was done, there was nothing for them to talk about.

Later in the month, the report of the interdepartmental committee alluded to a possible tie-up between a U.S. airline and SCADTA. In December, Trippe, Hambleton and Hoyt chatted with von Bauer about various approaches to joint operations; Hayden, Stone had been one of the oases where von Bauer had stopped at on his Wall Street expeditions. In order to expand, von Bauer needed new planes and means of financing them. SCADTA operated German equipment—Dornier-Wal seaplanes and obsolete Junkers models. Von Bauer paid for them with stock, with the result that Deutsche Luft Hansa, the government enterprise that absorbed German aircraft companies, and through them controlled overseas airline ventures, became the dominant investor in SCADTA.

On his belated honeymoon in October 1928, Juan met with von Bauer and Luft Hansa officials in Berlin. Betty found the director of SCADTA a Viennese charmer, "with all his bowing and hand-kissing." Francis White had alerted the embassy that Trippe was coming to transact "the establishment and operation of commercial air service in Latin America." Pan American had an option to extend to Venezuela from the Canal Zone by way of Colombia on the FAM 5 contract and was laying the groundwork for bidding on the route to the west coast of South America, which also necessitated a stop in Colombia. SCADTA blocked both routes.

Von Bauer had been making a nuisance of himself, as far as White was concerned. The Assistant Secretary of State was positive the Austrian had "egged on" Olaya at the Havana conference in January to insert provisions in the Pan American Convention that would weaken U.S. sovereignty over Canal Zone airspace. White threatened that the United States would not sign the convention, and Olaya backed down. Everywhere Harold Harris and C. E. Woolman turned in Peru, Ecuador and Bolivia, there was SCADTA vying for the same concessions.

Harassment was a game two could play. That summer, a new airline was chartered in Colombia, Sociedad Anónima Colombo-Americana de Aviación, with native and American stockholders—among the latter Sherman Fairchild, Graham Grosvenor and H. Case Willcox, associates in West Indian Aerial Express, which Pan American was then taking over. Trippe assigned Willcox to go after Colombian mail contracts.

But by December, nothing was accomplished, and Juan was casting nervous glances at the calendar. Pan American Airways was scheduled to open the mail route to the Canal Zone in about a month and wanted to make a survey for the extension at the same time. Would the State Department help Pan American get permission to land and refuel in Colombia? Trippe asked Francis White. He enclosed a memorandum, prepared in consultation with Elihu Root, Jr., outside counsel for Pan American Airways. Root, the son of the eminent statesman-jurist, was the first of several lawyers of distinction Trippe engaged to help him find a legal means to his visionary ends. He used Bob Thach, the vice president and general attorney, for the meaner tasks of politicking.

The memorandum was in fact a draft of an international air agreement by which Pan American received ample permission to operate in Colombia, including the right to discharge passengers and cargo, and in return, like privileges were accorded to SCADTA in the Canal Zone.

Until then, Francis White had shared the apprehension of the War Department about admitting this Teutonic airline to the airspace above the canal, but other factors were now compelling. The Post Office was soon to open bids for FAM 9, which meant, White said, "Colombia controls our extension to the south and we control their extension to the north." The good neighbor was unlikely to lower the barriers to its airspaces without a corresponding favor. Moreover, the War Department was shortly to announce rules for civil aircraft operating in the Canal Zone so that Pan American Airways might start the mail service. Once that was done, how could the United States ban Colombian commercial planes without provoking retaliation and a diplomatic imbroglio?

A solution to the security threat was suggested to White by Pan American's acquisition of Compañía Mexicana. "If von Bauer will sell out to an American company, a big thorn will be removed in the development of our airlines to South America," he said.

Late in January, White sent Olaya a draft of a reciprocal aviation agreement for their two countries, almost word for word Trippe's memorandum. A week passed, and Juan's level of anxiety rose. The Postmaster General was advertising FAM 9, and without operating rights in Colombia, Pan American would not be able to offer satisfactory evidence of ability to perform. On February 8, he implored White for help in persuading Colombia to allow Pan American Airways flights to land three times a week.

On February 23 in Washington, five days before the Post Office closed the bidding, Secretary of State Kellogg and Minister Olaya signed an exchange of notes that was hailed as this country's first bilateral air treaty. The Kellogg–Olaya Pact was the impressive title given to one single-spaced typewritten page and a paragraph running on to a second, allowing full commercial rights to the airlines of the United States and Colombia.

The agreement gave the commercial aircraft of the United States permission to land along the Atlantic and Pacific coasts of Colombia, and planes of Colombian registry to do the same at the Atlantic and Pacific ports of the United States, including the Panama Canal Zone. There was no mention of frequencies or of duration of the protocol, except for termination on ninety days' notice.

The gate to South America swung open for Pan American Airways, and to the north for SCADTA. Von Bauer lost no time. In April, SCADTA formally inaugurated service to Balboa in the Canal Zone and negotiated a provisional concession to operate in Panama. The War Department exerted pressure, and the final contract was highly restricted as to permissible air lanes and denied permission to construct radio stations on the ground. In South America, von Bauer seemed to be hatching a scheme for a continental system. He was causing mischief in Peru, trying to get Harold Harris' concession annulled, and he was negotiating with other Americans, notably John Montgomery, Curtiss Aeroplane and Elmer Faucett.

Clearly, he was shopping for a merger partner, and Trippe was a candidate. "I have these choices," he told Juan. "Either you buy me out or I shall have to sell out to Luft Hansa." There was a third possibility not uttered—bankruptcy; but that could involve a period of attrition. Trippe was in a hurry, although as more and more adversaries were to discover, he could not be rushed in driving a hard bargain. First he tried to avoid giving cash, then to pay as little as possible in stock, and finally to obtain control. He already saw the flaw in the 50–50 deal with Grace, although he could say that that was the fault of Hoyt, who had been breathing down his neck.

Peter Paul von Bauer was a mean trader in his own right. He wanted to be saved and he wanted to keep control. And so they met, no one would ever know how many times, during the rest of that year. Juan visited von Bauer in Barranquilla in June, and shortly afterward, Willcox resigned. Trippe was restraining every move he made to get the Colombian-chartered airline off the ground. "I've decided my principal is using me as a stalking horse," Willcox complained to a friend at the legation in Bogotá. "He intends to negotiate rather than compete with SCADTA." Willcox was mistaken if he thought he was the only Pan American employee with whom the president was not being aboveboard. Juan habitually kept the staff uninformed, and occasionally misled them.

In December, Bob Thach paid a visit to Barranquilla, and a month later, Henry Friendly, a young associate at Root, Clark, Buckner, Howland & Ballantine, was ordered to go uptown to see Trippe about drawing up an agreement. Friendly recalled noticing a young man, "quite large and swarthy-looking," waiting in an office at the firm about a year before when the associate was learning how to fill out a bid for a foreign airmail route. "Oh, that's Mr. Trippe, the president of the company," he was told.

Now Trippe was telling Friendly he had to do all the work on this agreement in his office, and not take a shred of paper back to his law firm. He was being very mysterious. It was a "gentlemen's agreement," a convoluted one, to take place in stages.

In essence, in February 1930 Aviation Corporation of the Americas bought 84.4 percent of SCADTA stock from von Bauer, his brother and their associates for $1,142,000, a little less than half in cash, the rest in stock. Since the shares were in bearer certificates, it was impossible to ascertain the identity of the owners; Luft Hansa was understood to represent an important segment. The SCADTA stock was placed in escrow with the Commercial National Bank and Trust Company of New York, of which Hoyt was a founder and director—a further obstacle to tracing the change of ownership. It was agreed that von Bauer would vote the shares at the annual stockholders' meeting under Trippe's instructions. For his part, von Bauer promised to withdraw SCADTA from international service and to make preferential traffic agreements with Pan American to the exclusion of the German lines with which it had been cooperating elsewhere in Latin America.

Von Bauer extracted the vow of secrecy from Trippe by convincing him that anti-American feeling was running so high in Colombia that his career and the viability of the airline would be endangered if Pan American's ownership were revealed.

Juan divulged the outline of the arrangement to Francis White and high officials of the Post Office Department, who believed he would "Americanize" SCADTA forthwith. Within Pan American Airways, only one person other than Henry Friendly knew the full story. "He telephoned me in Mexico City, because he was afraid I'd put my foot in it," said Erwin Balluder.

Trippe wrote the press release stating that Pan American Airways had acquired "a substantial interest" in SCADTA "in pursuance of the program sponsored by President Hoover that American enterprises in South America should expand with successful business enterprises already operating there." Stockholders were given the same information. No securities law existed then to compel greater candor. Newspapers in the United States reported "a reciprocal operation agreement," and in Colombia the press approvingly noted "a consolidation with purchase of a part interest by a powerful commercial aviation company" that would furnish SCADTA with luxurious new planes.

Among those left in the dark was Pan American's partner, W. R. Grace. Had Grace management been aware that Trippe was planning to buy the airline that controlled Colombian rights, they would surely have demanded a proportionate share of the stock. As it was, when they found out, they considered his action a breach of their agreement reserving the west coast of the continent to Panagra. In territorial disputes, Trippe sided with SCADTA against Panagra, usually by entangling the 50–50 board of directors in what a Grace director remembered as "a very long and metaphysical discussion as to whether Medellín or even Cali was east coast or west coast."

Trippe was notably solicitous of Peter Paul von Bauer. During the year it took for the deal to be completed, the price of Aviation Corporation of the Americas stock declined considerably. An adjustment was arranged to make von Bauer whole, but not his associates. On the face of it, Juan grossly overpaid for SCADTA's 1,700-mile route system and fleet of aging aircraft. In justification, he was buying the passkey to South America for Pan American Airways.

The veiled nature of the agreement enabled von Bauer to maintain the fiction that SCADTA was a Colombian airline and to preserve his German relationships. He ran it with a free hand for nearly a decade, while Juan sidestepped his promise to the U.S. Government to de-Germanize SCADTA even after the Nazis came to power in 1933.

11

Fight for Control

On March 2, 1929, the Saturday on which Harry New awarded FAM 9 to Pan American Airways, the stock of Aviation Corporation of the Americas gained 26 points on the New York Curb Exchange. Shortly after the market opened on Monday morning, as New was signing the contract and Herbert Hoover was on his way to take up residence in the White House, the price of the shares shot up another 5 points to 89⅞, an all-time high for an airline with slightly more than a year's experience operating a single route 250 miles long.

During the last nine months, however, Pan American Airways had steadily been acquiring additional routes, and New's final gift in office enlarged its system to 12,000 miles. Moreover, Pan American Airways was the sole international air carrier of the United States.

Empire building of such remarkable speed and intensity sharpened appetites. The airline hungered for capital to construct facilities and buy planes to operate the routes. With every new contract won, speculators in Wall Street snapped up its shares, driving the price to abnormal levels. While Juan Trippe was expending every ounce of energy to build his business, the sharks were maneuvering to control it.

The first half of 1929 witnessed massive consolidations of aviation trusts and holding companies which further fueled the speculative madness in the stock market. On March 1, the investment-banking firms of W. A. Harriman and his Yale classmate Robert Lehman underwrote a $35-million trust, Aviation Corporation of Delaware. David Bruce was treasurer and one of seventy directors. David was branching out from under the Mellon umbrella as a protégé of Harriman. Another director was Sherman Fairchild, who had recently combined his Fairchild Aerial Camera Company with a Maryland plane manufacturer to form Fairchild Aircraft Corporation, and sold Aviation Corporation of Delaware a big chunk of its stock.

Harriman was a seminal investor in Pan American Airways, having been brought aboard by C. V. Whitney in January 1928. Now Harriman's new trust was buying shares in the open market, and Dick Hoyt was worried. He and his Hayden, Stone group had 100,000 shares, or one-fifth, of the outstanding stock of Aviation Corporation of the Americas. The Harriman-Lehman-Fairchild group owned 90,000 shares. The rest of the stock was widely scattered. Hoyt felt uneasy about his margin of control and his iron grip on the board of directors.

What could he do to protect himself? The railroad robber barons used to frustrate antagonists by watering stock; they simply printed certificates representing thousands of new shares for themselves. Hoyt doubted that the board of directors would accommodate him in a similar manner, and even if they increased the number of capital shares, the Harriman group would ask for a block to match his.

Hoyt had another reason for wanting to lay his hands on additional stock. Ever the speculator, he was caught in a squeeze from selling Aviation Corporation of the Americas short. As an insider, he had realized that the market valuation of the stock was wildly inflated. Pan American Airways was just getting started, and was operating at a loss with scant hope of immediate profits. The market was reacting to ballyhoo, counting on earnings he knew were in the distant future.

Positive that the price had to drop sharply, he had taken a short position, selling stock borrowed from brokers with the intention of buying it back at much lower prices to make a killing. For an insider to act on his pessimism by short selling without disclosure to the public is unethical conduct, but in 1929, with no Securities and Exchange Commission to act as watchdog, the practice was common.

In January and February, Aviation Corporation of the Americas stock began to climb from the low 30s. When it reached $42 a share, Hoyt went short 20,000 shares. At that price, the market was according the company a value three times the worth registered on its books. Instead of falling, as fundamental analysis told him it should, the price of the stock soared, propelled by aviation euphoria and Harry New's confidence in the company. At the peak price of nearly $90 a share, Dick Hoyt had a paper loss of $100,000. The next day, the stock began to slide, but not far enough, and after every decline, it bounced back. On March 26, the stock markets were hit by a convulsive wave of selling brought on by a sharp rise in the rate banks were charging for loans to buy stock on margin. By the end of the week, the banks reconsidered, credit was loosened and the markets rallied. Aviation Corporation of the Americas stock traded around $65 a share.

In the parlance of Wall Street, Hoyt was "sweating." He may have recalled an aphorism attributed to Daniel Drew, a notorious speculator and short seller who battled on the side of Jay Gould against Commodore Cornelius Vanderbilt for control of the Erie Railroad: "He who sells what isn't his'n must buy it back or go to pris'n."

Desperate for an ally, Hoyt turned to Frederick B. Rentschler, president of United Aircraft & Transport Corporation, another recently agglomerated darling of the market. Into it were packed the Pratt & Whitney Aircraft Company, an engine maker Rentschler organized in 1925; the military-aircraft manufacturing companies of Chance Vought and William Boeing; the latter's Boeing Air Transport and Pacific Air Transport; and two propulsion companies, Hamilton Propeller and Standard Steel Propellers. The National City Company, holding company for the bank of the same name, shepherded the complex amalgamation. Gordon Rentschler, Frederick's brother, was an officer of the bank, soon to be named president. Between October 1928, when National City arranged a private placement of Boeing stock to a preferred list of investors, and January 1929, when Boeing paper and Pratt & Whitney paper were traded for shares in United Aircraft & Transport, the stock for which Rentschler had paid $253 three and a half years before was worth over $21 million, and by May $35 million. Other fortunate insiders, including the officers and directors of the bank and their friends, more than doubled their money.

In April, Hoyt proposed to Rentschler that United Aircraft & Transport invest in Aviation Corporation of the Americas. "Foreign companies are operating in South America, and if Pan American does not get in there with the wholehearted support of the whole industry, the foreign companies will get the better of us there," he said. Moreover, Pan American Airways was going to be buying a great deal of equipment, both land planes and seaplanes. It was already a customer for Pratt & Whitney engines and could be a bigger one. When Rentschler discussed the proposal with Bill Boeing, the Seattle manufacturer's ears perked up. "We are bending our efforts here toward the development of a flying boat," he said.

For United Aircraft & Transport to buy stock in the nation's only international airline would give Pratt & Whitney and Boeing a competitive edge in the engine and aircraft markets. Pan American would receive an infusion of capital, and Hoyt, by a secret agreement with Rentschler, would have the stock he needed to cover his short sales.

On April 16, the board of directors of Aviation Corporation of the Americas authorized an increase in the capital stock of the corporation to 1 million shares, and sold 50,000 shares of the new issue to United Aircraft & Transport at $57.50 a share, reaping $2.875 million in sorely needed cash for Pan American Airways. The previous day, the stock had closed at $62.75, which meant that United Aircraft & Transport could show an instant book profit of $262,500.

A month later, it sold half its recently acquired shares at $59.50 a share, realizing a $50,000 profit in the transaction. Hoyt and Hayden, Stone purchased 10,000 of those shares directly; Trippe, Hambleton and Whitney took the rest in 5,000-share lots apiece, which they promised to make available to Hoyt. He was now insulated from further debilitating losses if the market should continue to work against him.

Two months later, Hoyt showed Fred Rentschler who had the largest muscles in aviation. For some time, he and Clement Keys had been talking about solidifying their loose alliance. On June 27, they combined Curtiss Aeroplane, Wright Aeronautical and Hayden, Stone's Keystone Aircraft into the Curtiss-Wright Corporation, the largest holding company in American aviation with $70 million in assets.

From then on, the struggle among the Goliaths escalated. On the board of Aviation Corporation of the Americas they were warily balanced. The executive committee was composed of Hoyt, Rentschler, Graham Grosvenor, an associate of Sherman Fairchild representing Aviation Corporation of Delaware, Whitney and Trippe.

Juan's position was once more in possible jeopardy. Of fifteen directors besides himself, only one, C. V. Whitney, was a chosen ally. At least three, Fairchild, Hoyt and Patchin of W. R. Grace, were outspokenly dubious about his operating style. He treated these supremely powerful directors no differently than the Yankee businessmen at Colonial, a little more politely but still without communicating what he was up to. "He was a man who kept his own counsel, a very secretive man," said David Bruce, who took Harriman's seat on the board the following year.

Trippe used the board to his advantage. To the outside world, he portrayed himself as the creature of his directors, simply carrying out their commands—even though in fact he had not yet informed them of what they were directing him to do. Their mighty presence enabled him to assert in the annual report to shareholders that Pan American Airways was "a community effort on the part of the American aviation industry throughout the country to operate in the international field." The message was tailored to please Herbert Hoover, and to intimidate prospective competitors.

Juan Trippe, John Hambleton and C. V. Whitney—a triumvirate of gentleman fliers sharing a dream, making it into a business and guarding it against sharks who might very well take it away from them unless they were vigilant.

The three-sided relationship was in fine working order. They agreed that Pan American Airways was Juan's to run, although John did much more than he took credit for, including keeping Trippe in rein. Juan respected Hambleton, stood in awe of him, listened to him as to an older brother. When John said, "Juan, you are wrong about that," Trippe accepted his word.

Business was not the only cement for their friendship. They had good times together as couples—Johnny and Peg, Juan and Betty. Their wives got along extremely well. In a restaurant in Havana, both recognized at the same instant the man at the next table with the telltale stitching on his cheek. It was Scarface himself, the gangster king Al Capone. Peg and Betty exchanged glances and waited to giggle together afterward. Were the speakeasies in Chicago running dry? They hoped he was traveling on Pan American Airways.

With Sonny, it was different. He was the grasshopper, darting into and out of the business, but always there to lend the weight of his money and name. He defended Juan to the directors. "I agree with him; let him have what he's asking for," he said. Whitney regarded Juan as a steward for one of his enterprises, a good man if a little peculiar. You gave a good steward guidance and then you let him alone. If Trippe ignored some of Whitney's suggestions, Sonny failed to notice. His attention span was limited. They seldom met away from the office. As it had been at Ac and Sheff, "our paths didn't cross," Whitney said. His pals played polo, chased pretty girls and experimented with sensual pleasures. Adultery was socially acceptable. He found Trippe dismayingly straitlaced. His bluest language was "Oh, gosh" and "Darn," and all he talked about was business, football and golf. Juan seemed immune to lust. He neither sent nor received sexual signals.

The Trippes disapproved of Whitney's carryings-on. "He had that quality of very rich people, that you couldn't get close to, as though they thought they were royalty," Betty said. She understood gradations of money: old and new, rich and very rich. The men she looked up to worked very hard. "My father died from overwork," she said. Sonny could never convince his friends that he worked. "He sings, he plays the piano, he has imagination, but he is a charming dilettante," said David Bruce.

On June 8, 1929, John Hambleton flew from New York to Miami on a business matter for Pan American Airways as a passenger in a small private plane. It was one of the few times he violated his precept of not surrendering the controls to any pilot other than his equal, like Charles Lindbergh. Hambleton asked to stop in Wilmington, North Carolina, so he could see his wife, who was visiting her family there. Peg was pregnant with their second child.

It was a glorious afternoon, with perfect visibility for miles around. As Peg waited on the landing field, the yellow aircraft appeared in the cloudless sky. She watched it bank for a landing at an altitude of about 300 feet, suddenly dive—and fall to earth about a mile from the airport. John and the pilot were killed instantly as the fuselage closed into the wing, accordion fashion. No cause for the accident was determined, except that possibly the plane had become trapped in an air pocket and forced into a nose dive.

The aviation community was appalled by Hambleton's death and the manner in which he had died. "Someday we shall build airplanes that cannot be stalled," Billy Mitchell, his former commanding officer, wrote in a tribute in the Baltimore Sun.

Whitney expressed his grief in an aeronautical magazine, revealing as much about himself as he honored his friend. "Recently there passed from our midst a young man in the very prime of life," he wrote. Hambleton had been 31.

> He died in the pursuit of the work to which he had given the past ten years of his life. He died at a moment when his ambitions and dreams were approaching fulfillment. We meet many people who drift through their span of years aimlessly—who give us an impression of futility—who are dissatisfied with their lot or accept their luck as if they believed the world owed it to them.
>
> This young man was none of these. He was what most of us wish we could be, modest, sincere, loyal to his friends, decent in his ways, balanced in his actions and, in short, what has been described as a very perfect gentleman. It is a pity that this young man could not have lived longer so that many more people might have benefited from personal contact with him . . .

Juan mourned privately, but his pain was evident. "Johnny's elimination was a great blow to Juan," David Bruce said. Trippe always spoke reverently of John Hambleton; theirs was the one friendship that never faded in his erratic memory.

In the Biblical legend of Jonathan and David, the tragic death of the nobler prince ensured the succession of the more fallible survivor. With one of the founding triumvirate gone, and a second physically and emotionally unable to stay put for a sustained period of time, it appeared that Pan American Airways was to be Trippe's airline.

12

The Science of Adventure

Juan called a meeting of the staff in Pan American Airways' little office at the Sevilla-Biltmore Hotel in Havana one afternoon in July 1928. He announced that they were going to be flying mail and passengers around the Caribbean and to the mainland of South America.

"Impossible," said André Priester, the chief engineer. The airline fleet consisted of two Fokker trimotors fitted, at his insistence, with emergency exits, but their range was only 100 miles. A Sikorsky S-36 amphibian leased for survey purposes had been returned to the manufacturer.

James M. Eaton, the traffic manager, agreed with Priester. Where was the market? he wanted to know. Customers were not exactly beating down the doors demanding long-distance transportation over water. The marketing strategy of Pan American Airways stressed relief from the Volstead Act: at a bargain fare of $100 round trip, including 30 pounds of baggage, a thirsty U.S. citizen could save two days traveling from Miami to Havana by airplane instead of steamship—"48 hours to bathe in Bacardi rum." Peg Hambleton's father, head of the Atlantic Coast Line Railroad, arranged for a Pan American ticket salesman, Vic Chenea, to solicit business aboard the Florida trains. At Key West, he hired Cuban boys to take the passengers' trunks over on the ferry while they rode the Fokkers. In Havana, Chenea worked the La Floridita bar, sweet-talking inebriated patrons into a free ride to the airport, exacting payment for the plane fare on the way out.

And now Trippe said they were going to South America. He drew from his pocket a scrap of paper covered with unintelligible jottings. The Post Office had just awarded them routes to Puerto Rico and the Canal Zone, he said. The contracts had options for various extensions, and preparations must be made for fulfilling them. Bob Thach, the company attorney, pointed out that permissions would have to be obtained from foreign governments—a drawn-out process, uncertain at best. Agents were already in the field trying to sew up landing rights and mail concessions, Trippe responded. He unfolded a scenario of European invasion; French and German operators were already on the wing in Latin America, and it was incumbent on Americans to overcome their lead.

Juan's technique of persuasion owed much to Walter Camp, and was also a forerunner of political methods of thought alteration that would be known as brainwashing. The meeting started at 2 P.M. Hours ticked by as he delineated his routes in the sky. He zigged, he zagged, and he kept talking. The more exasperated and profane his listeners became, the more sweetly patient was Trippe. Every obstacle they raised was a boon. If the planes were too small to support a sufficient payload, that was good, since traffic was light. He let them in on a secret: new S-38 amphibians had been ordered for delivery in the fall, and though they might not accommodate more passengers than the Fokkers, they could land almost anywhere.

By 10 P.M., having tasted neither food nor drink for eight hours, the staff was worn to acceptance. Priester had a watch fob in the shape of a pistol. He put it to his forehead and moaned, "What this company needs is blimps." On that note, they adjourned for dinner and to prepare for service to the Caribbean.

Thus it would always be. Trippe doggedly enunciated the dream, a guarded vision suddenly revealed as dogma, and it was for those who heard him to swallow their doubts and make the dream reality. Juan gave them no alternative, entertained no possibility of failure.

"Trippe visualized success," a Pan American executive once said, explaining his idiosyncratic management style. "It never crossed his mind that if we were going to open a route, that it just wouldn't go off like clockwork. He didn't worry. It wasn't a problem—not for him, not for anyone. He figured, 'I'll get it set up and tell the guys to do it.' "

Trippe's was not a private vision, by any means. Most fliers understood the airplane's potential and perceived its eventual global reach; but not all of them followed timetables as accelerated as his. Within three years of its founding, Pan American Airways became the world's largest international air carrier, outpacing its own successes. As soon as the Postmaster General gave the signal, Trippe ordered his men to fulfill the promises he had made. Every route award was anticipated with a greasing of political wheels and orders for planes. But everything else remained to be done—surveying the route, building ground facilities, conquering the unknown. Before one challenge was fully mastered, Trippe presented another.

If the passionate adventure of blithe young men were to be converted into a business, flying had to acquire scientific discipline. If the sport of gentlemen were to become transportation for the masses, risk had to be eliminated, safety and reliability sold with every ticket.

The son of an engineer who had left the profession for Wall Street, Juan had abandoned engineering for a less taxing route to a college degree. Yet he had tremendous respect for the applied science and an intuitive grasp of its principles. He recruited a team of dedicated technical men, the foremost being Lindbergh, whose poor marks in high school had kept him from studying aeronautical engineering at a university. Another was André Priester, the chief engineer. Priester was a product of a Dutch colonial upbringing and all that that implied in autocratic behavior and international shrewdness. He was born in Java, the son of a provincial bureaucrat, and upon reaching high school age was sent to Holland for an engineering education. After serving in the war as an artillery officer, he took flying lessons, but never made a solo flight. In 1919, he joined KLM as assistant to the manager of the Amsterdam airport. Promotion opportunities in Dutch enterprises were slow to ripen, and by 1925, when he was 34, he and his wife were disposed to look for greener pastures in America.

His boyhood friend Tony Fokker steered him to Philadelphia Rapid Transit, which needed someone to run its model airline. When the season of operation ended, Priester took a job in the Ford factory in Detroit, a siege in purgatory while he waited for a call from another airline. In the summer of 1927, he received a telegram from Trippe, whom he remembered meeting in Fokker's factory in Hasbrouck Heights, summoning him to work for Aviation Corporation of America. Desperate to leave Detroit, he succumbed to Juan's enthusiasm for what sounded to Priester like ephemeral schemes.

Juan gave him jurisdiction over the mechanical phase of operations, a responsibility that grew to embrace planes, personnel, and surveillance of aircraft and engine manufacturers. Priester reported directly to Trippe, who interfered only to the extent of setting those "impossible" goals for him to fulfill.

Priester took it upon himself to become the technical conscience of the airline, and thus protector of the lives of its passengers and crews. Safety was the holiest word in his vocabulary. Long before there was a

Federal Aviation Agency, he created an in-house equivalent for Pan American Airways and served as its de facto chairman. During the first eight years of operation, Pan American had three fatal accidents, in which four persons were killed—an impressive record for a pioneer in a new technology. Another gauge, schedule efficiency, is less a matter of life and death than of commercial dependability. In its first decade, Pan American's score as kept by the U.S. Post Office Department surpassed 99 percent, an indication that practically all scheduled flights reached their destinations, though not necessarily on time.

Priester taught operational integrity by manual. The first edition he composed, published in 1929, consisted of thirty-six pages clipped together between black covers like a schoolboy's composition book. It expounded stringent rules for inspection and maintenance of aircraft under a heading "SAFETY FIRST," and for the conduct of the flight crews, whom he was molding into an elite corps of aeronauts.

"Always bear in mind the comfort of your passengers," the manual instructed them. "Handle your aircraft and regulate your flight as to accomplish maximum comfort for them and to inspire their confidence in yourself, your aircraft and in air transportation."

"Bumby [*sic*] air is psychologically disturbing to passengers and should be avoided whenever practicable," another section noted, going on to suggest how to do this:

a. by flying above clouds when they are broken sufficiently to permit glimpses of land and water.
b. by not flying in clouds.
c. by flying at high altitudes when smooth air can be found.
d. by flying over the water when air is rough over land, provided a too great deviation from the regular course, or too great increase of time required for the flight does not result.

We give rain squalls and local disturbances a wide berth when practicable.

On the wall of his office was an axiom attributed to an English flier: "THE AIR LIKE THE SEA IS NOT INHERENTLY DANGEROUS BUT IT IS TERRIBLY UNFORGIVING OF INCAPACITY OR NEGLECT." He had it typed at the bottom of memoranda as well. Rigorous discipline would redound to a safe operation, Priester believed, and in the long run that would be the most effective sales argument for overcoming the primeval instinct that told the public not to board airplanes.

Priester was not an ivory-tower engineer. He was sensitive to the commercial value of projecting a seductive image. In one memorandum, he directed employees to consider themselves actors on a stage. If the costumes are not eye-catching, if the scenery contains one jarring element, if the performance of the cast is pallid, the audience will be dissatisfied and not return for a second viewing. He equated costumes with uniforms, scenery with ground and air facilities, actors with flight and ground crews. Not even grease monkeys were exempt from his dicta. He fired an airplane mechanic whom he spotted in a photograph with soiled white overalls, and a steward who refused to pick up newspapers and magazines strewn on the floor of a plane after it landed in Miami, saying that cleaning was not part of his job.

Priester's unyielding perfectionism gave rise to apocryphal legend. In one account, he noticed an automobile, rather the worse for wear, on the field at an airport in Brazil. After inspecting it inside and out, running a finger over the hood and peering underneath, he administered a verbal drubbing to the field manager, who stuttered the apology that it was his personal car, not Pan American's. Priester was adamant. Attitudes about one's person or property, he believed, carried over to one's work.

In the first two frenzied years of Pan American's growth, Priester achieved a goal that he afterward constantly refined: a standard of operation consistent in every detail. An engine could be overhauled in Brownsville exactly as it was in Miami. The field manager in San Salvador was as thorough in his supervision as his counterpart in Cozumel. As Trippe asserted in his first executive memo, "All airports are Pan American airports. All pilots are Pan American pilots." Such a uniform standard could anticipate mechanical failure and human error and devise corrective measures to minimize damage.

The standard for flight dispatch was based on satisfactory weather conditions at points of departure and destination and the mutual judgment of pilots and airport managers, neither of whom could have his doubts overruled by the other.

Delayed schedules for whatever reason are costly to an airline and annoying to passengers. Pan American managers complained that Priester's concept of "safety first" bordered on the fanatic. Yet he was conscious of costs in other respects. Forty years before an Arab oil embargo made it crucial, he campaigned for fuel economy, even to printing a reminder on his Christmas cards.

Priester was the prototype of the tough, unreasonable operations boss of airline literature and film—Saint-Exupéry's Rivière with a Dutch accent and an obsession about safety, a thundering Zeus packaged in pint size. With his large, balding head atop a slight body and his guttural speech—a staccato of transposed *v*s and *w*s, and Low Country *o*s as round and hard as cannonballs—he was an irresistible subject for mimicry. He commanded respect and obedience by conviction and example. Having drafted the regulations forbidding smoking on duty, he never opened a package of cigarettes in his office, and abstained from alcoholic beverages until the repeal of Prohibition. His silences were as intimidating as his rages; in either event, his hazel eyes seemed to turn yellow.

Juan Trippe was the remote president unseen by most employees in operations. Priester was the stern, just father, the moral authority who gave flesh to their ideals. Most of them joined Pan American as though they were entering the military or the Church, and they pledged an allegiance to the airline such as few business institutions receive from their personnel. Trippe was casual about salaries. He could be stingy and unpunctual about payments. Priester hounded him, aware that discipline is a two-way street. The chief engineer was also the organizing force behind the employee pension plan. When his assistant, John C. Leslie, a young engineer trained at M.I.T., was moving to a new job, he asked Priester for advice. "Always be fair," he said.

Pilots flying the U.S. airmail across the continent navigated by the seat of their pants. If visibility was poor, they came down as low as they could and searched for a railroad track along which to fly until they came to a sign that told them where they were. At night there were beacons on the ground, though no ground-to-air communication by radio range, because the plane was too small to carry anything but the pilot, the mail and gasoline. Radios were too bulky to be taken aboard.

Charles Lindbergh found his way to France over the Atlantic without a radio; as long as his compass was working, he said, it would have been almost impossible to miss the coastline of an entire continent. Even if he had been hundreds of miles off course, he still could have reached Paris nonstop. But regularly scheduled airline service over unexplored terrain and island-specked seas was a totally different matter. Without guidance, pilots were jeopardizing passengers' lives and their own.

Aviation and communications grew up together, industries of the twentieth century. Guglielmo Marconi sent his first wireless-telegraph message across the North Atlantic in 1901. After the First World War, the United States Government, realizing that most of the radio stations in the country were under the control of Europeans, effected the formation of the Radio Corporation of America, which absorbed the Marconi Wireless Company, whose primary activity was in communications with vessels at sea. In the flurry of interest caused by Charles Lindbergh's preparations for his transatlantic flight, the plans department of

R.C.A. decided the company ought to be getting into the aviation business.

Hugo C. Leuteritz, a staff engineer trained by the Navy, was told to develop transmitters for various types of aircraft. When his $25,000 budget proposal for an aviation radio system was turned down by David Sarnoff, the general manager, Leuteritz went ahead and designed a 100-watt transmitter for a telephone-telegraph system in a commercial transport plane.

In July 1927, Leuteritz received a call from André Priester, asking him to meet him at Teterboro Airport. Priester led him to a Fokker, which Leuteritz recalled had been ordered by Colonial Air Transport, and asked him how he would propose to equip it with a radio. The plane had no electricity, so Leuteritz showed Priester that a storage battery and a wind-driven generator could be attached to the Whirlwind engines, with a one-blade propeller mounted on the strut.

Leuteritz was given no clue as to where his massive contraption might be used. A few weeks later, Priester called him again and told him that a Mr. Trippe, whom Leuteritz had met at Colonial, wanted to see him. He directed him to an office with an unmarked door in a building on lower Broadway. Among the men assembled there were Trippe, Hambleton, Hoyt, Bevier, Grosvenor and Tony Fokker. Later, he would learn that except for Fokker, they were the directors of a new airline. Trippe asked Leuteritz to talk to them about the value of communication in aviation. "Where are you planning to operate?" the engineer inquired. "We can't tell you that," Trippe said. After his lecture was finished, Leuteritz left and heard no more for almost a year.

In May 1928, Priester telephoned him again. "We are now operating between Key West and Havana. Won't you come down here, please?" Priester was concerned about safety. Pilots were taking off in clear weather and soon encountering the dread Caribbean squalls, which sent them chasing around clouds and cut off visual reference, their only guide. Forecasts from the U.S. Weather Bureau in Key West and the Jesuit Observatory in Havana proved contradictory, as the pilots, to their dismay, discovered in midair. Without navigation aids, they were as likely to wind up at Matanzas as at Havana. "Something must be done," they were begging Priester. "You need navigation badly," Leuteritz told Priester after a few days in Key West. The chief engineer suggested he rig up his 100-watt transmitter and a receiver in one of the Fokkers and conduct experiments.

For more than a month Leuteritz flew back and forth between Key West and Havana, taking measurements on the ground and sending and receiving by telegraph and voice from the Fokker to the Navy station at Key West, which then telephoned the message to the Pan American operations shed at Meacham Field. On the morning of August 15, he boarded the *General Machado* with 2 passengers. One was bundled into the plane by his brother-in-law after a drunken week's revel at the Sevilla-Biltmore. The pilot was violating Priester's rule about not accepting intoxicated customers.

The weather had been stormy for several days, and the sea was rough. After takeoff from Havana the wind blew the plane off course, and they flew for two hours sighting only whitecaps. Thinking he was east of the Florida Keys, the pilot decided to head northwest, not realizing he was over the Gulf of Mexico about 90 miles west of Tampa. He spotted a tanker and Leuteritz began broadcasting by voice for help, unaware that he was being picked up in Hialeah; his receiver had stopped functioning.

The flight mechanic shot flares from a pistol to attract attention from the tanker, and the pilot stripped off his shirt and attached a note asking the skipper to head in the direction of land. He circled over the ship to drop the message, and as the plane banked, its fuel tank went dry and the engines quit. The pilot brought the plane down on the water and issued instructions to ditch. The crew, an injured Leuteritz and the drunken passenger were rescued by lifeboat sent from the tanker while the Fokker kept afloat on its plywood wings. The other passenger, stone sober and jittery, vanished and was presumed drowned.

The Fokker disintegrated as the tanker crew was attempting to hoist it aboard by rope, thereby reducing Pan American Airways' fleet by half. Leuteritz was hospitalized for treatment of a fractured pelvis and shoulder. "We better do something about navigation," he said to Priester as soon as he was released.

Because the radiotelephone system was too cumbersome and pilots would be communicating with non–English-speaking countries, a change to radiotelegraph was imperative. In a dry-goods store near the La Concha Hotel in Key West, Leuteritz bought a ¼-inch rubber panel and dry cells, and put them together with vacuum tubes, sockets, wires and a telegraph key to rig up a low-frequency, battery-operated transmitter weighing about 10 pounds. It was subject to vibration from the plane and tossing about during storms. He went back to the store and bought women's garter elastic with which to hang the radio from the four corners of a frame. The invention tended to give out after an hour or so in the air, but he kept tinkering with it until he produced a set with a 150-mile range. A radio operator skilled in Morse code was added to the flight crew.

Now Leuteritz had to help the pilot find out where he was. The direction finders used on ships were too heavy for aircraft. Leuteritz designed one for the ground. In a shack at a corner of Meacham Field, he set up a loop device—a 4-foot-square wooden frame wrapped with wire—and placed it above a stand to which he nailed an inverted pie tin. He calibrated it by having an airplane fly over specified points about Key West. The pilot read his compass and signaled to the radio operator on the ground, who reported back his readings of the plane's movements. Transmitting in telegraph code (a dot was five miles east, a dash five miles west) and by communicating with the shore and with ships of the United Fruit Company and the Grace Line, the pilot established his position by triangulation. From such makeshift beginnings, international air navigation was born.

Every day, Leuteritz plotted airplane positions. At first, the pilots balked at taking directions from someone on the ground—giving up their authority in the cockpit, they thought—and Priester was skeptical about radio navigation until he dropped by to watch one afternoon. He observed that a "know-it-all" pilot, ignoring Leuteritz' signals, was going to hit the coast of Cuba 50 miles east of Havana. "He can't be that far," Priester said. "Wait and see," Leuteritz replied. The pilot landed half an hour late. When he returned to Key West, Priester criticized him for flying off course. "I was on the mark," he said. Priester made Leuteritz show his chart. "This is navigation," the radio engineer said, "and it's for your good." The pilot had to agree.

Leuteritz was still in the employ of R.C.A., and in October he was called back to New York and then sent to the aviation show in Berlin. When he returned to his office after Thanksgiving, his secretary reported that André Priester had been telephoning every day. "Mr. Trippe wants to see you," he told Leuteritz. They made a date for the three of them to meet at the Hotel Commodore Grill.

"I want you to come with Pan American to head up communications," Trippe said over martinis. "You have only two airplanes and a ninety-mile route," replied Leuteritz, mentioning that he was 31 years old and had a wife to support. "We'll be flying around the world," Trippe declared—with unwarranted confidence, it seemed to Leuteritz. For though Lindbergh had flown the Atlantic, there were no prospects, as far as he knew, for planes big enough to carry passengers. It was just a gamble. "I want you and André wants you," Trippe said with a smile, showing the dimple in his right cheek. His dark eyes fixed on Leuteritz as though he were trying to hypnotize him.

"I know where I am now. I don't know where I'll be if I go with you," Leuteritz said uneasily. "I would have to give some notice."

"Do it by the first of the year," said Trippe.

That evening, Hugo and his wife, Alice, figured out how far their savings would stretch if he were to take the gamble and Pan American Airways failed. "I think I'll take the chance," Hugo said. The next morning he went to see the chief engineer at R.C.A. "Mr. Trippe has talked to me," his boss greeted Leuteritz. Hugo found himself repeating what he had said the day before: "I know it's a gamble." "If you think it's worthwhile, go ahead," the chief engineer urged him. "If you're not pleased at the end of the year, you can come back here."

Leuteritz phoned Trippe and said, "It's a deal." Trippe directed him to start the day after the New Year.

"Who do I report to?"

"Directly to me."

"Not to Priester?"

"No, to me."

From then on, he was in a race to keep up with Trippe's plans. Domestic airlines had the direct help of the U.S. Government, almost $60 million worth, in constructing ground facilities and navigational systems to support the air routes, as well as in the services of the U.S. Weather Bureau. Pan American had to build its communications system, airports and meteorological stations from scratch, adapting maritime practice to the needs of aerial transport.

There was no room for another desk in the small office at 100 East Forty-second Street, so Leuteritz camped in a chair next to Priester's and for a week and a half worked up a budget on a pad of paper. He took it in to Trippe and said, "Here's the budget. What about expenses?" Juan answered, "I'll tell the controller in Key West you have an open account."

For the Lindbergh tour around the Caribbean, Leuteritz perfected the airborne radio so that contact was assured with the ground and with other planes. A pilot who had just come through a violent storm could warn another pilot who was heading toward the turbulence. Meanwhile, the radio station at an airport advised about landing conditions, so that a pilot bouncing around in black clouds as he headed south over Cuba could be notified by the station at Santiago de Cuba of unlimited ceiling there and that a detour over the coast might be preferable to the straightforward approach into the Sierra Maestra. Direction finders were installed at Miami, Port au Prince, Cozumel and other points in the route network until research made it possible to put a loop-type direction finder with amplifier and receivers aboard all aircraft.

Tropical weather forecasting did not exist in Latin America, so Pan American developed forecasting techniques using methods of upper-air analysis. With records collected from various stations, the operations department determined the flight level where the most favorable winds obtained, and its meteorologists predicted the development of hurricanes. All weather information was passed on to the United States Weather Bureau without charge.

Static conditions and excessive humidity in the tropics wreaked havoc with the radio equipment and the engines. Particularly from May to November, static reduced the range of the radio. A plane that sat overnight on a Caribbean airfield would not function in the morning because of the quantity of moisture absorbed. Leuteritz bought an electric hair dryer and blew it over the engine. He cured the problem of moisture's penetrating the gasoline barrels by having the fuel filtered through chamois cloth. Since he was having to invent communications systems for over-water flying, Pan American set up a subsidiary to manufacture radio and navigational equipment, some of which was sold to other airlines.

A chain of 93 radio and weather stations, some placed in remote mountain passes, was built to support Pan American's Latin American system, the largest private radio network in the world. The cooperation of twenty-seven countries had to be obtained—no small political achievement. Many nations hoarded their communications rights. Leuteritz and David Grant, the Latin American legal expert, negotiated agreements whereby the airline installed its equipment to be operated by natives under local-government control. By the end of 1930, more than $7 million was spent to construct the radio stations and 160 land and marine bases.

Brownsville, the operations base for the area encompassing Mexico and Central America, became the training center for blind flying, a procedure tested by Lieutenant Jimmy Doolittle of the Army Air Corps in September 1929.

Doolittle flew in a training plane with his cockpit hooded in canvas so that his vision was totally blocked. The pilot in the second cockpit kept his hands in his lap. Doolittle took off from Mitchel Field on Long Island, flew over a 15-mile course and landed, guided only by instruments: a sensitive barometric altimeter, an airspeed indicator, a radio direction finder, and a newly invented combination gyroscope and artificial horizon. A short-range radio beacon installed at the field cast a beam in two directions for 20 miles. Two short reeds on his instrument panel oscillated to the right and the left, the vibrations becoming more intense as he approached the radio transmitter. When Doolittle passed overhead, it showed his exact position, so that he could calculate his descent without looking out the window.

Blind flying was a necessity if service along the 200-mile stretch from Tampico to Mexico City was to be maintained on a regularly scheduled basis. From the Gulf coast to the plateau of the Mexican capital, pilots encountered cloud-shrouded mountains, pockets of turbulent air and thunderstorms. They flew for hours at a time with no reference except wiggling instruments and cool nerves.

When they first began to grope their way around the mountains of Central America, the pilots relied on maps clipped from geography textbooks. But elevations marked in meters on old Spanish documents had been copied as feet, they discovered when they emerged from clouds into mountains charted as several thousand feet lower. So they made their own maps and gave the topography caustic names like Hogsback Mountain, and Perkins' Plop for a lake on which an amphibian landed with its wheels down.

While breakthroughs were being made in aerial navigation, other Pan American engineering teams under the direction of L. L. Odell, Trippe's former consulting partner, were laying down airports and emergency landing fields. The airport at San Juan was rolled out over a marshy meadow. On the 800-mile stretch between British Honduras and Panama, space was claimed from the jungle by machete.

First, an airplane surveyed the area from the air. When the site was selected, the pilot took a reading on his position from the sun and then threw sacks of white flour out of the plane to seep through the matted vegetation to the jungle floor. Engineers set out from the nearest village with construction crews, traveling on foot, by burro trail and by canoe. Indian bearers, who had never seen an automobile or a railroad train, much less an airplane, were pressed into reluctant service with trinkets and sheer duress. Food and supplies were conveyed to the site by plane and dropped from the sky.

One particularly difficult assignment was the building of the airport at Uyuni, Bolivia, 12,000 feet above sea level, as part of the route extension from Peru to Argentina. As the deadline for activating the concession approached, available manpower was commandeered to fight in the Chaco War against neighboring Paraguay. Harold Harris in Lima heard nothing from the airport engineer to whom he had given the assignment until twenty-four hours before the deadline expired, when suddenly the radio station at Uyuni began broadcasting an announcement that flight service would begin the next day.

After he returned to Lima, the engineer presented Harris with a bill for two bottles of Scotch. He had given one to the chief of police of Uyuni and told him what needed to be done. The official then drove across the pampas in a truck, lassoing male Indians, whom he herded into an area enclosed by barbed wire—the site for the airport. During the next few days, the Indians pried rocks from the ground and loaded them onto trucks, stopping only to take food from their women, who had followed them and camped outside the fence. When the surface of the field was smooth, the Indians were released and the chief of police received the second bottle of Scotch.

13

Closing the Loop

Another man had a bold vision of an airline to South America. Like Juan Trippe, he was resourceful, tenacious and dependent on Wall Street financiers. And of course, Trippe had to destroy him because he posed the last obstacle to Pan American's monopoly of the U.S. air routes of Latin America.

Ralph A. O'Neill, the son of a San Francisco banker, was a mining engineer and a much-decorated Army ace. After the war, he spent several years training squadrons for a Mexican air force. Subsequently, he canvassed South America as a sales agent for Boeing aircraft. He was three years older than Juan, looked like an athlete, and carried himself with a jutting chin and a slight chip on his shoulder.

O'Neill's reading of the map contradicted the wisdom of the due-south approach down the west coast of the continent by land plane. He detected good harbors spaced every 300 miles or so on the Atlantic shoreline and believed he could operate a safe and profitable air service from New York to Argentina with large seaplanes.

On the east coast lay the metropolises of Buenos Aires, Montevideo and Rio de Janeiro, generating more than three-fourths of South America's world trade. The French Aéropostale Company, operating a combined sea and air route to Toulouse via Natal and Dakar, offered European businessmen a two-week advantage over North Americans in corresponding with Latin American customers. Perturbed exporters and manufacturers in the United States were importuning the Post Office for an airmail service to the east coast of South America.

From his analysis of trade and shipping statistics, O'Neill was convinced that an airline could make money if it attracted 5 percent of the traffic on the Atlantic side and charged the equivalent of domestic airmail rates and first-class steamship passenger fares.

He received encouragement in Washington from William Mac-Cracken, the Assistant Secretary of Commerce for Aeronautics, and the Navy and State Departments gave him letters of introduction to the appropriate government ministries, enabling him to start negotiating for operating concessions. He had a chilly meeting with Irving Glover in February 1928, shortly before passage of the Foreign Air Mail Act. The postal official appeared pessimistic about prospects for a route to the east coast; but should one be opened, he said, "We will naturally favor the airline with the most operating experience of a similar nature."

After nearly a year, he found his backers: Major Reuben Fleet, president of the Consolidated Aircraft Company, manufacturer of an aerial patrol boat for the Navy, and James H. Rand, Jr., president of Remington Rand Company, an aviation buff and a high-roller among securities speculators. In April 1929, they incorporated the New York, Rio & Buenos Aires Line around O'Neill's concept. Fleet agreed to contribute six flying boats converted for mail and passenger use. Rand made a personal commitment of $1.5 million and undertook to find the rest of the money NYRBA might require.

They were joined by a syndicate with over a million dollars in capital led by Lewis Pierson; his son-in-law Richard Bevier and John Montgomery had just suffered their second defeat at the hands of the Trippe-Hoyt group in the bidding for the airmail route to the west coast of South America. "It was a grudge fight from the start," observed an onlooker in what was to be a vicious battle for the remainder of the continent.

Naively, O'Neill's forces took heart from the change of administration in Washington. Rand hired as general counsel and a director of NYRBA Colonel William J. Donovan, a former assistant attorney general reputed to be a warm friend of Herbert Hoover. Had Rand's intelligence sources been more perceptive, they might have realized that Juan Trippe's alliance with the Post Office was as solid as ever and even about to be strengthened. Harry New was gone, but Irving Glover stayed on as Second Assistant Postmaster General and deputy for airmail. The new Postmaster General, Walter Brown, was even more inclined than New to favor Pan American Airways, though perhaps from a different perspective.

"Competitive bidding in the airmail business is of doubtful value and is more or less of a myth," Brown is on record as saying about his predecessor's method of awarding domestic mail routes. "We would have promoters come in who had stock to sell and who hoped to get their stock sold before their losses were so great in carrying on the business that they could not sell the stock. There would be, in my judgment, very little real substantial bidding by men of experience able to carry on an industry of this kind in the present state of the art." He intended to use his legal discretion to the utmost to avoid competitive bidding in international-route awards.

A pro-Trippe environment also prevailed at the State Department. Despite the change of Secretaries—Kellogg replaced by the scrupulously unbiased Stimson—Latin America remained the fiefdom of Francis White. As O'Neill moved up and down the east coast and over to Santiago battening down additional concessions, charges that NYRBA was working in concert with French interests were floated along the State Department's communications system. White requested confirmation from Buenos Aires, Rio de Janeiro and Caracas, urging that nothing be done "to promote such foreign interests against those of other American firms."

The embassy in Buenos Aires responded that NYRBA was negotiating with Aéropostale to use its landing facilities along the east coast and in Martinique. This caused a flurry of memoranda within the Latin American Division of the State Department.

The assistant to the division chief wrote:

This raises the question of what policy is to be adopted toward NYRBA. If we support them we are helping the French against Pan American; if we don't we are helping the latter against the field, including any other American interests.

Meanwhile, John Montgomery was speaking frankly to Dana Munro, acting head of the Latin American Division. Montgomery confirmed that NYRBA had arranged to rent landing fields between Buenos Aires and Natal from Aéropostale to connect with the sea/air mail route to Europe—in accordance with U.S. Post Office regulations, he assured Munro. Munro advised White:

There has been very bitter competition, particularly in Argentina and Venezuela, between the [NYRBA] interests and the Pan American Airways, which is a purely American concern. It would be most unfortunate if the American legations in those countries were compelled to maintain a strict neutrality while a *bona fide* American company's interests were injured through support rendered to a combination of American and foreign interests by the diplomatic representatives of another country. I should think, therefore, that we would be justified in informing our missions in

Argentina, Brazil, Chile and Venezuela that the Pan American Airways, as an American concern, is entitled to all proper diplomatic assistance, but that no assistance should be rendered to the [NYRBA] company because of the probability that such assistance would be helpful to foreign as against American interests.

Could Munro have known that in September 1928, when Juan Trippe was preparing to go on his honeymoon and business trip to Europe, White had asked the embassy in Paris to assist him in talking to the Latécoère company about setting up air service in Latin America? Or that White was then urging Juan to consider buying SCADTA?

By the fall of 1929, White was almost apoplectic about NYRBA's relationships with Aéropostale, which the French Government cited as an excuse for not giving Pan American Airways rights in the French West Indies. White pressed the embassy in Paris to exert maximum effort in Pan American's behalf:

> In any conversations officials of the Embassy may have with the foreign office, they might press the proposal made in the note of June 12th to the French embassy here. If it is accepted the present difficulty will be removed, and if it is not going to be accepted, it will be well to know it so that when the next French aviator asks for permission to fly over American territory, his application can be held up and he can be told exactly why it is held up.

NYRBA's counsel, Bill Donovan, tried to allay suspicions that his client was the agent of foreign interests. He gave Irving Glover a written statement that the company was entirely American-owned and financed. Glover sent it to White with this comment:

> You, evidently, know as well as I do, that they are certainly muddying the water in South America and making it doubly difficult for the Pan American Airways and the Pan American-Grace Airways, Inc. to carry out the terms of the contract that they now have with this Government.

White forwarded Glover's letter to Secretary of State Stimson with this endorsement:

> Mr. Glover is correct in stating that the New York, Rio and Buenos Aires Line is muddying the water in South America and making it difficult for the Pan American Airways to carry out their contracts. There is evidence of active opposition and hostility by this company to the Pan American Company in Chile and also that they are trying to link up with the French Latécoère in Brazil and the German Company in Bolivia to make a combination which will exclude the Pan American Airways.

The immediate concern of Glover and White was that NYRBA might detract from the west-coast mail route that Panagra had opened in July 1929, but only as far as Santiago. O'Neill was making arrangements to carry Chilean mail over the Andes to Argentina and ultimately up the east coast to the United States. Pan American was lagging behind NYRBA in lining up nonexclusive contracts from Argentina, Uruguay and Brazil, the intention at that point being that it would fly the mail from those countries to the United States, via Panagra, on the roundabout west-coast route to the Canal Zone, where it would be transferred to Pan American Airways planes for Miami. The big difference was that Pan American was being paid by the U.S. Post Office to do this reverse hauling, while O'Neill thus far had only the revenues from the contracts he had negotiated at bargain rates with the South American postmasters.

O'Neill had the faith of innocent martyrs and old-fashioned American entrepreneurs. He believed that with thorough preparation in securing foreign concessions and with outstanding performance, he would make it impossible for the Postmaster General to award the east-coast route to anyone but him.

He was spending millions, as fast as Rand could raise them, to construct hangars, mooring buoys, repair shops and radio stations, and to purchase equipment. He was assembling a fleet of more than two dozen planes, about half consisting of Consolidated Commodores. For that era, they were gargantuan flying boats, with 65-foot hulls, 100-foot wing spans, 22-passenger capacity and 650-mile range. O'Neill was planning for a payload capacity of 100,000 pounds, 10 times that of any competitor. In retrospect, he was to admit that it was "a monumental task to load our planes, considering that everybody in the region was air-fearful."

Trippe was far more prudent. He never expended funds to develop a route until the contract, signed by the Postmaster General, was in his grasp. In the summer of 1929, Pan American Airways owned a dozen and a half planes, mostly Sikorsky S-38 amphibians and Fokker-10 land planes, none with half the capacity and range of NYRBA's Commodores. Juan took infinite pains with political preparation, however, and for this aggressive adversary he formulated a new strategy: to keep the Postmaster General from advertising the east-coast route. Let O'Neill spend himself to death, for without U.S. mail contracts he could not survive.

In August, Irving Glover came into possession of a memorandum addressed to Trippe by his representative in Rio de Janeiro. Glover forwarded it to Francis White with the notation "It seems to me that this is rather unfortunate and tends to hurt the progress of the friendly relations of the United States with the South American countries." The document reported scurrilous propaganda allegedly circulated by O'Neill in Rio to the effect that Pan American was "a favourite of the U.S. Government," that its contracts were obtained "under the guns of the U.S. Marines" and that the Postmaster General was in its employ.

O'Neill tried to put out the fire with an affidavit from the Brazilian Minister of Transportation avowing that he had said no such thing. But then White had a gossipy message from the Ambassador to Argentina that John Montgomery had told someone in Buenos Aires that the former Postmaster General had signed a contract with Pan American "10 MINUTES BEFORE GOING OUT OF OFFICE." If the report was true, it was only the mildest hyperbole. But Montgomery also "inferred" that Harry New had benefited from making the award under the deadline.

During this period, Donovan was presumed to be earning his fees as NYRBA's counsel by going horseback riding with the President at the Rapidan River Camp, his retreat in the Blue Ridge Mountains of Virginia. This was Donovan's way of "preparing the ground" for the Postmaster General to advertise the east-coast route. At a Cabinet meeting in mid-July, Hoover uttered the opinion that NYRBA ought to be given a chance to establish such a line—which fell somewhat short of the order Donovan sought.

Even that slim opportunity could be undermined by Trippe's strategic politicking. FAM 6, the Puerto Rico route awarded to Pan American, had an option for extensions to Trinidad and Paramaribo on the South American mainland, important legs of an east-coast route. The Post Office was not automatically obliged to give them to Pan American. Donovan hoped to persuade Brown to open them to bidding. Learning through his postal intelligence sources that a conference had been scheduled between Donovan and Brown, Juan pushed Glover to execute a contract for the extensions and had it rushed to New York for Trippe's signature and carried back on the midnight train by Henry Friendly, who delivered it to the Post Office at 9 A.M., an hour before Donovan's appointment.

By the fall of 1929, NYRBA was operating passenger service between Buenos Aires and Montevideo, and over the Andes to Santiago, and O'Neill was completing arrangements for a schedule to La Paz. It seemed as though he were building the airline with his bare hands, even to piloting inaugural flights. And while he was in the field in South America, operations in New York and Miami were in a snarl, due partly to John Montgomery's meddling. The worst calamity to befall O'Neill was the collapse of the stock market in October, just as

NYRBA's shares were being listed on the New York Curb Exchange. Rand, overextended in his borrowings for stock speculation, saw much of his personal fortune evaporate, and from then on he deferred to Lewis Pierson for NYRBA's financial direction.

In December, Trippe announced that Charles Lindbergh would be making an inspection tour for an extended mail route to Buenos Aires and Rio de Janeiro. O'Neill exploded with fury. Until then, relations between the operating personnel of the rival airlines had been cooperative. NYRBA used Pan American's radio facilities for a fee, and Pan American planes were serviced at NYRBA's stations. Now O'Neill cabled the employees in the field: "DISCONTINUE RENDER ANY AND ALL SERVICE AND ASSISTANCE TO PAN AMERICAN PILOTS, TAKING EFFECT IMMEDIATELY."

A Pan American plane on a survey of the east coast with George Rihl and his wife aboard was running out of fuel and touched down at a swampy outpost of NYRBA's at Montenegro, the only fuel stop on the 600-mile stretch between French Guiana and Belém, in the northernmost corner of Brazil. By the normal fellowship among fliers, the NYRBA mechanic would have accommodated the Pan American pilot; but he was afraid of losing his job and refused. The pilot took off again, ran into a tropical storm and was forced down in a mosquito-infested Amazon marsh to await rescue, four days later.

"If we can keep the contract from being advertised for eight or nine months, I believe the NYRBA will disappear or make any kind of agreement we want," Rihl advised Trippe from Rio.

NYRBA had a new chairman of the board, William MacCracken, who had left the Commerce Department on the assumption he could wield influence with his former boss at the White House and elsewhere. He had hardly begun to try when Postmaster General Brown asked Congress for appropriations to extend FAM 9, from Santiago to Buenos Aires, Montevideo and Rio de Janeiro. Brown was effectively serving notice that he wanted South American mail carried backward to the United States over the route that favored Pan American Airways and Panagra. O'Neill was incoherent with anger. "Nothing could be more impractical and ridiculous than to fly the Rio mail fifteen hundred miles south to Montevideo, a thousand miles west to Santiago and six thousand miles north to the United States," he said. It was tantamount to awarding a New York–Alaska contract via the Panama Canal.

O'Neill would not acknowledge that he had gravely miscalculated in his marketing plan and in so doing had played into Trippe's hands. He had set his rates below those of Aéropostale and Condor, and much below Pan American's. O'Neill contracted with the Argentine Government to fly mail to Miami for $10 a pound; Pan American was asking

$25 a pound, to match the charge for outbound mail from the United States. Under the provisions of the Foreign Air Mail Act and its amendment, Pan American was paid for carrying 800 pounds of U.S. mail regardless of how much was actually loaded on the plane, and it remitted to the Post Office the revenues received from foreign governments for return mail.

Juan expanded his theory that Pan American was in partnership with the Post Office so that now he was telling Brown, "NYRBA is in direct competition with the United States Government, and is bringing about a direct loss to the American Post Office Department." As Brown later told a Senate committee, "If any other company had taken the northbound mail at a lower price, the natural thing that would happen would be that Pan American would get no northbound mail, at least unless they met the price, and if they met the price, our Government would not get it."

According to this line of reasoning, O'Neill was undercutting not Pan American Airways—because as Trippe kept insisting, his airline was only a conduit for foreign mail revenues—but his own government. Brown was dedicated to running the Post Office as a businesslike proposition; but the red ink was gushing from the international airmail service, and he was convinced he could come closer to offsetting the losses by favoring Pan American over NYRBA. Thus far the losses were enormous. Initial loads at the start of the Canal Zone–Santiago service were less than 10 pounds. By September 1929, volume had doubled, but even so, the Post Office was taking in about $700 a week for a round-trip mail run that cost the government $13,356.

O'Neill maintained that NYRBA was carrying four times the volume of Pan American, and that this would increase and eventually yield much greater revenue for the Post Office. But that had yet to be demonstrated, and for the present, all Brown could see was that as long as NYRBA was in the picture, there was no chance of forcing Latin American governments to pay the $2-a-mile rate the Post Office was obligated to give the contractor. Brown was going to throttle the last chance to test the hallowed American theory of competition in the air-transport markets of South America.

In April 1930, Donovan had another horseback chat with the President and extracted a promise of fair play: the Postmaster General would advertise an east-coast route. Brown contradicted him, saying that no bids would be entertained on the route until "certain matters are settled between competing companies." Rumors of an impending merger between the companies circulated in Wall Street; O'Neill was the last to hear them.

He was busy with sundry mishaps on the weekly service NYRBA

was operating between Buenos Aires and Miami, with not one mile covered by U.S. mail subsidy. The Argentine Post Office was holding him to the letter of his contract, which stipulated a seven-day service. The Commodores were slower than the manufacturer warranted, so O'Neill improvised a costly solution. The mail left Buenos Aires on a fast, single-engine plane after midnight, overtaking the Rio-bound Commodore that had left the day before about 600 miles up the line, where the postal sacks were transferred.

In May, MacCracken, whose White House influence had produced nothing for NYRBA, told Rand that the Postmaster General had summoned him to a meeting. At Rand's urging, O'Neill hurried to Washington to accompany MacCracken to the session with Brown, only to find NYRBA's chairman having breakfast at the Mayflower Hotel with Juan Trippe and Sonny Whitney. After exchanging embarrassed hello's, MacCracken and Trippe sneaked off to the Post Office, leaving him under Whitney's surveillance.

The message that MacCracken brought back and that Bill Donovan repeated after he went on a mission to Brown was that the Postmaster General was insisting the companies merge before he offered the east-coast contract for bids.

O'Neill tried desperately to hold out, alternately hoping for business to improve and for the Hoover Administration to be turned out at the polls two years later. But NYRBA's board of directors declined to support him. The company was losing more than $250,000 a month; the investors had committed almost $6 million, and they feared further exposure. O'Neill was expendable. Rand, his principal backer, was whipped. It was up to Pierson and a new personage on the board, Joseph Ripley of National City Bank. In February, the bank exercised an option for $1.4 million in NYRBA stock for its clients. Ripley had been an associate of Fred Rentschler in the creation of United Aircraft & Transport Corp., and Rentschler was an influential director of Pan American Airways.

All that was left was for Juan to haggle over the terms of the merger. First he asked for an exchange on the basis of physical assets, to which O'Neill and Rand gladly assented, figuring that NYRBA's fleet of 32 almost entirely new aircraft and its substantial investment in ground facilities would give it a 3-to-2 advantage.

After several meetings, Juan changed course and insisted that gross income from airmail contracts must be reckoned among the assets. At a luncheon meeting at the Union League Club, Lindbergh and Ripley appeared to side with Trippe. O'Neill resisted. There were more meetings. Lindbergh proposed submitting the dispute over the merger formula to an arbitrator—his father-in-law, Dwight Morrow. He could not understand why O'Neill was livid. The suggestion was tabled.

Ripley pronounced the words of requiem. Noting that he was the only one present with investments in both airlines—an acknowledgment that in future years would have ruled him in conflict of interest—he said, "The Postmaster General has decided that there will be no U.S. airmail contract for the east coast of South America until the New York–Rio line merges with Pan American. Without the contract, the route is a losing proposition and I doubt that anybody can afford it."

So there had to be a merger; but still the question was: on what terms? Rand was deeply indebted to National City, and he was just about ready to give NYRBA away. Juan arranged for that to be done by going sailing on Long Island Sound aboard Lewis Pierson's yacht. He hammered the point that NYRBA's assets were overstated and got Pierson to agree to settle on the basis of its audited balance sheet. The company's net worth had declined to $4.1 million, of which a little more than half was chalked up to development costs. "Development costs are not solid assets," said Juan, knocking them off the bargaining table. In the end, he paid about $2 million for NYRBA with highly inflated stock of Aviation Corporation of the Americas. The mark of his persuasive powers in describing the potential of Pan American Airways is seen in the value Pierson and Ripley accepted for his stock: $65 a share. When the agreement was signed on August 19, 1930, shares of Aviation Corporation of the Americas were trading at $44 a share, and its book value was $18 a share.

O'Neill cannot be adjudged paranoid for thinking Trippe had euchred him out of his business—in a perfectly legal way, of course. Pan American Airways wound up with 32 of the most advanced planes on the market, a ready-made system of ground facilities and a local airline O'Neill had established in Brazil. Juan asked him to stay on as manager of Pan American's new east-coast division. "You can steal my house, but you can't ask me to run it for you," he said, and went off to the mining business in Bolivia. Trippe pretended to be baffled by his bitterness. "They were nice young men who thought that they would like to run an international airline," he said afterward. "But they really didn't know what it was all about."

The day after the merger agreement was signed, NYRBA petitioned the Argentine Government to cancel its mail contracts. And Postmaster General Brown advertised FAM 10 for bids. The route from Paramaribo to Rio de Janeiro was awarded to the only bidder, Pan American Airways, at the maximum $2 a mile, and immediately after the contract was signed, the route was extended to Buenos Aires.

The acquisition of NYRBA sealed Pan American Airways' monopoly of the nation's foreign air transportation. All that was needed to complete the circuit of Latin America was the Venezuelan overhang. In 1931, General Gómez granted rights to open service between Maracaibo and Port of Spain, enabling the airline to fly a ring around the Caribbean. Pan American was now the world's largest international airline, operating 21,000 miles of routes through twenty-nine countries in the Western Hemisphere. The entire domestic route system of the United States, operated by more than a dozen carriers, was 30,451 miles.

Juan felt neither desire nor obligation to inspect his new empire. *Time* noted a few years later that he had never ventured south of the Canal Zone. He was too busy, the magazine reported.

14

The Autocrat

During the bargaining over the price he was going to pay for NYRBA, Juan carefully obscured the condition of Pan American Airways. The airline was nearly broke. At the closing of the purchase agreement, it had $176,000 on hand against liabilities of $1.5 million. Just when it needed working capital to field the new operation, its credit was so weak that no bank would lend it money. Trippe and Whitney personally endorsed $900,000 in uncollateralized corporate notes.

At the end of September, a special committee of the board recommended what it said was the only means of raising capital: an inducement to warrant holders to exercise at once, instead of waiting until the expiration date, June 30, 1933. The exercise price was reduced from $15 to $12 a share, a 20-percent discount, on warrants exercised by October 15, 1930.

A little more than half the warrants outstanding were exercised during a two-week period, attracting $1,093,434 in fresh funds. As an original holder of management stock in Aviation Corporation of America, Juan held warrants on 37,301 shares of stock which had cost him virtually nothing. Acting on inside information and with exquisite timing, he rushed on the day of the announcement to exercise warrants on 15,000 shares, catching the market at $37.35 a share. His paper profit was $378,750. The news exerted downward pressure on the stock, and by the time Whitney and Hoyt's group exercised their warrants, the price had fallen 5 points.

On the last day of December 1930, Trippe issued the first of a series of executive orders that set the shape and tone of his administration for the next four decades.

Essentially, it provided for decentralized operation of the airline. Latin America was divided into five divisions; the managers were appointed by the president and general manager, J. T. Trippe, and reported directly to him. In the event of his absence or "disability," George Rihl, first vice president, was empowered to act in his stead. Since Juan had no compunction about rescinding others' orders, Rihl's power was soon realized to be hollow. Division managers had to consult the president before hiring, firing or shifting key personnel, but were given discretionary authority over local matters. In time, they exercised this freedom with considerable latitude, aware that Trippe was too busy politicking to cover every base. It gave the executives, particularly those farthest afield, an exhilarating sense of independence —"If he trusted you, he gave you a free hand," said Erwin Balluder, head of the Mexican and Canal Zone divisions—and also furnished Trippe with the ability to disclaim knowledge of questionable acts when the company's complex affairs came under Congressional scrutiny.

Parallel to the operating line of command were the staff sovereignties: financial, public relations, foreign administration, traffic and technical, all reporting directly to Trippe. He reserved the handling of relations with the U.S. Government and all "outside company" relations to himself "exclusively."

A distinguished figurehead presided over the foreign department. Evan E. Young, a former State Department officer, had served most recently as Minister to the Dominican Republic. The technical staff had the most autonomy, parceled among Priester, Leuteritz, Odell and Franklin Gledhill, Yale '23S, the general purchasing agent.

Closest to Trippe, at least on paper, were the advisers: Lindbergh for technical matters; Elihu Root, Jr., as general counsel; Robert Thach, listed as vice president special assignments, extension and development—a euphemism for Washington lobbyist—and Edward E. Wyman, assistant to the president and manager of the New York office.

Wyman was a Sheff graduate, 1918 vintage, and a Navy flier in the war. He could sign Trippe's name on routine correspondence and was the one to see or telephone during Trippe's frequent and often unexplained absences from the office. Pan American had moved to spacious quarters on the forty-second floor of the Chanin Building, at 122 East Forty-second Street. Before long, Ted Wyman became the butt of other executives' frustrations. He was no more skillful a reader of

Juan's mind than they were, and they resented his attempts at wielding authority when they knew he had none.

The elaborate paper work, and the meetings for department heads twice a week in Trippe's office, gave an outward impression of a team operation, conducted according to modern principles of professional management. In reality, Pan American Airways was an autocracy, and a rather undisciplined one except in its technical operations.

The executives waited days and weeks for appointments with Trippe, even when summoned from afar. At the end of the year, budget-preparation time, Balluder and Roscoe Dunten, chief of the Caribbean division, camped on a couch outside Trippe's office. One week stretched into another. Christmas was around the corner, and they longed to return home for the holidays. Finally, Juan was ready. "Let's go to the apartment," he said—keeping them there until 3 A.M., meticulously going over every figure, until Betty's voice floated insistently from their bedroom: "Juan, these men want to go home."

Trippe reported to a seventeen-man board of directors through an executive committee. Directors are usually reluctant to interfere with management unless forced to do so by a crisis, and from 1930 on, most of his board were preoccupied with staving off the effects of the worsening Depression in their corporate and private bailiwicks.

Though they were powerful men, most of them older and wiser than he, Trippe kept them at bay with meager information, revealing what he had already put into effect at the point where he needed their approval. The board meetings were models of gentlemen's clubbiness. According to David Bruce, Trippe was polite but authoritarian, "because he knew more than anyone." He let egotists preen. Anyone could make a comment; but if he lacked the figures to back up his opinion, Trippe did not hesitate to embarrass him. He smiled sweetly, his brown eyes took on the glow of a coal fire and he unleashed an encyclopedic mass of facts and statistics. The directors consulted their watches. They had other meetings to attend; other problems weighed upon their minds. Juan was unhurried, his sense of time imperfect. He could drag out a board meeting until midnight, exhausting the directors into consent.

No one challenged Trippe's one-man rule. Hambleton was dead, and Whitney and Hoyt were otherwise engaged. Harry Payne Whitney died in November 1930, bequeathing $20 million to his only son. His father's death obliged Sonny to make instant decisions about several matters. He took control of the Hudson Bay Mining & Smelting Company just as its huge copper- and zinc-producing mine, the Flin Flon, was about to start operations. He borrowed $1,261,000 to buy the

Whitney racing stable from the estate; Papa had chosen not to will it to him. A few days after the transfer, Equipoise, a two-year-old Whitney colt, won the Pimlico Futurity, and during the next three years, the stable was a big winner of racing purses.

Marie Whitney divorced Sonny in the fall of 1929 and married Averell Harriman five months later. Easing whatever strain there might have been at the board meetings, Harriman relinquished his seat to his aviation scout, David Bruce. David's wife's cousin Richard King Mellon, president of the Mellon National Bank of Pittsburgh, went on the board shortly after. Whitney took a new bride, Gwladys Crosby Hopkins, a blond socialite horsewoman from Philadelphia. Reporting on their wedding trip to Central America by yacht and plane, the society scribe of *The New York Times* wrote, "It was understood that Mr. Whitney, who is interested in aviation, wished to spend much of his honeymoon in the air."

Though he devoted less and less attention to how it was run, Sonny increased his investment in Pan American Airways, and in 1931 became chairman of the board of Pan American Airways Corporation, which superseded Aviation Corporation of the Americas as the holding company for the airline. He invited John Hay Whitney, a cousin with whom he was constantly being confused, to become a director. Jock, also a Yale man, polo player, racing-stable owner and connoisseur of beautiful women, was considered the more serious and intelligent of the two. His main interests at that point were modern art and movies.

Dick Hoyt remained a member of the executive committee of the board and chairman of the finance committee, but he was no longer much of a threat to Juan. He was a director of scores of companies in disparate fields, from transportation to sugar and retailing, and after the crash the value of his speculative investments was severely diminished just as he most needed money for social obligations. He had to settle $1.5 million on his first wife so that he could marry Martha Nicholson Doubleday after her divorce from Nelson Doubleday, the publisher. When Hoyt died suddenly in March 1935 at the age of 46, his affairs were revealed to be a tangled web of bankrupt companies and uncollectible promissory notes.

Trippe had no such distractions. Pan American Airways was his consuming passion. His wife was adoring, and in June 1932 they had their first child. Betty wanted to name her Juanita, but Trippe refused to perpetuate the name he so disliked. The baby was given her mother's name and called Betsy. At his daughter's birth, Juan made a decision that caused his mother anguish. He forsook Catholicism, and from then on, the family of Juan Trippe celebrated life's rituals in Episcopal churches.

The whirlwind expansion of Pan American Airways in the midst of the depressed world economy was newsworthy, and as the company took on Trippe's personal stamp, the press hailed him as a business prodigy, "the Merlin of Modern Aviation," an "Il Duce of Airways," albeit "an unseen figure." Juan preferred corporate propaganda tightly controlled at the source to personal publicity, and after halfheartedly making appointments for interviews, he invented excuses to cancel them. He did, however, have an acute sense for knowing when to elbow himself into a photograph with persons of renown.

Mystery men are irresistible to journalists, and Juan Trippe was admiringly portrayed in the magazines, particularly in *Time* and *Fortune*, organs of the opinions of Henry Luce, his Yale contemporary. In facing the challenge of reporting on the inaccessible imperialist of the air routes, writers were assisted by William Van Dusen. Articles invariably alluded to Trippe's "swarthy complexion" and his unusual name, and to the shadowy great-aunt from Venezuela. One writer was carried away to state that his success was due "to his sympathetic understanding of the Latin temperament" and his way of talking and doing business "as if he were a Latin himself."

15

To Build
the Better Machine

Juan Trippe was in perpetual quest of power—political power to secure routes, powerful aircraft to operate them. The dream of linking continents and spanning oceans was futile without planes to carry a sufficient payload of mail, cargo and passengers to warrant government support and to attract private capital. For forty years, he would try to push "the state of the art," to spur the design of larger, faster planes capable of flying over longer distances without stopping to refuel, and reducing the operating cost as calculated for each passenger and ton of cargo.

At the outset, the aircraft market offered a limited choice of equipment, and since Trippe knew Pan American was to be the only U.S. airline operating over wide stretches of water as well as jungles and mountains, he decided to commission airplanes for its special needs. It was to be a collaborative effort between Pan American engineers and aircraft manufacturers—and often a frustrating one, inasmuch as airplane design was generally more advanced than engine development.

The possibility of engine failure haunted pilots and restricted the progress of air service. Flying through fickle Caribbean skies and over the dense vegetation of Central America, pilots wondered, What if? What if the engine gave out? Would they spin into the sea? Would the plane stay afloat until rescuers appeared? If they fell into treetops, how would they climb down? If the plane crashed through branches, would they be hurt? and if not, should they look for a native settlement or head for the river they had spotted from above?

The fear of engine failure tied the pilot to the earth, a fainthearted

Icarus, for as he flew he was always casting an eye for a place to come down. Engine failure loomed large in the continuing technical debates within the Pan American Airways organization. Priester delayed the purchase of all-metal Ford trimotors for service on the mountainous inland routes of Mexico and Central America because he believed a wooden plane like Fokker's had greater buoyancy in case it was forced down in water, as had happened when the engines of the *General Machado* went dead over the Gulf of Mexico.

A seaplane or an amphibian—a flying boat with alternative landing gear "that carried its own airport on its bottom"—had a psychological advantage, according to Priester, and was the only sensible equipment for Pan American to penetrate virgin territory. The pilot could always descend on a bay or a river—as long as there was daylight and reasonably good weather; in darkness, he could not see debris in the water or detect the presence of other aircraft. Lindbergh believed that the psychological edge would vanish with reliable engines. Once passengers acknowledged that land planes could carry them over mountains in fog and storm, they would trust them over the oceans as well.

At the Berlin Air Show in the fall of 1928, Juan saw what the European aircraft industry had to offer. The Germans, particularly, held to grandiose designs, as though they actually wanted to put wings on seagoing vessels. There were exciting reports of a Dornier flying ship in production that would carry 100 passengers. Crossing the Atlantic on luxury steamships, Trippe visualized Pan American Airways operating over water with a fleet of ocean airliners. Early in 1929, he approached Igor Sikorsky with a proposal to design a transport plane to Pan American's specifications.

Inventors of flying machines were an eccentric lot. Sikorsky, a small, bald man with an obtrusive mustache, was a sweet-tempered genius, a modest gentleman of the Tsarist school. If Trippe seemed to his associates to hatch plans in a private world of his own, Sikorsky, a Slavic mystic, spoke eloquently of arriving at concepts in other levels of consciousness. He quoted from Tennyson's *Locksley Hall*, implying that he too "saw the Vision of the world, and all the wonder that would be; Saw the heavens fill with commerce, argosies of magic sails, Pilots of the purple twilight, dropping down with costly bales."

During his boyhood in Kiev, where his father was professor of psychiatry at the university, Igor's scientific appetite was fed by Leonardo da Vinci's drawings of flying machines and the science fiction of Jules Verne. At 11, he had a dream so profoundly affecting that he never forgot a single detail. He saw himself walking down a narrow, luxuriously decorated passageway bathed in a bluish light. Though it looked like a steamship corridor, with stateroom doors on either side, and he felt vibration under his feet, he knew he was in a vehicle flying through the air. Just as he opened a door into a well-appointed lounge, he woke up.

In 1913, after nearly losing his life at the age of 24 in a forced landing of a single-motor plane caused by a mosquito blocking the carburetor, he became a multiengine advocate. Sikorsky designed the first four-motor aircraft, fittingly christened the Grand. Its innovations, remarkable for that era, included an enclosed cabin with elegant furnishings, a toilet and an outside platform from which passengers viewed the underlying scene. Adapted into a bomber for the Imperial Russian forces, it was one of the most successful military weapons of the First World War.

During the Bolshevik revolution, Sikorsky departed for the United States, to scrape out a penurious existence until fellow exiles and American admirers chipped in to set up the Sikorsky Aero Engineering Corporation.

Sikorsky's trimotor S-35, designed for René Fonck's attempt at competing for the Orteig Prize, crashed on takeoff at Roosevelt Field. The S-36 was a twin-engine amphibian smaller and less powerful than the Fokker F-7 and therefore of limited use. Pan American Airways leased one for its initial surveys of the Caribbean.

After the start of passenger service to Havana, Trippe placed an order for three of Sikorsky's improved-model amphibian, the S-38. It was an ungainly bird that invited comparison with prehistoric monsters. The fuselage was shaped like the hull of a boat, with a prow resembling a duck's bill. Two 420-horsepower Wasp engines were hung above the cabin section, sheltered by a 71-foot parasol wing, the tail assembly mounted on high outriggers. Critics twitted, "There go the spare parts of a Sikorsky flying in formation."

The S-38 was fitted with valves for dumping fuel, a brand-new safety measure. In narrow harbors like Nassau's, it could taxi across the shallow water and, with its wheels pumped down, waddle across the beach to a passenger pier. The amphibian had a cruising speed of 100 miles an hour and space for seven passengers, a crew of three and a steward—a ratio of personnel to payload that guaranteed unprofitability. But it was the most efficient plane for Pan American in its beginnings, and after another nine were acquired from NYRBA, the plane served as the workhorse of the Caribbean fleet.

Air-minded celebrities like Jock Whitney, Colonel Robert McCormick, the Chicago publisher, and Martin and Osa Johnson, the filmmaking explorers, ordered S-38s (the Johnsons painted theirs with zebra stripes), and this publicized acceptance thrust Sikorsky into professional sunlight at last. In 1928, his days of scrounging for capital seemed to be over; a group of Wall Street backers reorganized his company and then sold it a year later to Frederick Rentschler's United Aircraft & Transport.

The commissioning of Sikorsky to design a transport plane for Pan American Airways was something of a family affair. Pratt & Whitney, the engine maker, and Hamilton Standard, manufacturer of the propeller, also had the same corporate parent, and Rentschler was a member of the executive committee of the customer's board of directors. Such coziness, disallowed under later standards of business propriety, represented the acme of Hooverian economic philosophy, in which groups within an industry cooperated under the tolerant eye of the Federal Government, and if monopoly was the result, they made the most of it.

The gestation process was protracted, starting in Trippe's office in the Chanin Building and ending in the sheds of the Vought-Sikorsky Division in Stratford, Connecticut, where the amphibian was tested on the nearby waters of Long Island Sound and the Housatonic River. The permanent midwives were Trippe, Sikorsky, Lindbergh and Priester, with itinerant help from Hugo Leuteritz, Frank Gledhill and Michael Gluhareff, one of Sikorsky's tight circle of Russian émigrés and a specialist in wing design. Their objective was an aircraft to serve the Caribbean and the coast of South America, and also pave the way for crossing the Atlantic.

Thinking big was Sikorsky's forte. Before long, he would be predicting thousand-ton flying boats several stories high with ballrooms, dining salons and staterooms to transport many hundreds of passengers on a single trip. But size was an added complication in the already manifold engineering problems of an amphibian—a "three-in-one machine of transportation," Igor said. It had to remove passengers from land, operate from water and fly through the air, whereas the land plane had only two mediums to conquer. At slow speed, it was like a steamship, supported by the displacement of water. As it moved faster, the striking force of the water gave it dynamic support, and when it lifted into the air, its wing carried the weight. Both the designer and the purchaser of the flying boat weighed the balance between performance and seaworthiness, trading off safety in range and engine performance against safety as related to the strength of the boat hull. A hull that could quickly get up "on the step" (the intermediate position when it skimmed the surface of the water before takeoff) sacrificed some measure of seaworthiness.

Lindbergh wanted a radically new design, a plane "cleaner" than

Sikorsky felt he could produce at that stage of experience. Sikorsky stressed high performance and the art of the possible. Priester was concerned with safety, with reliable scheduling and with getting a plane that would be economical to maintain in far-flung stations in the tropics.

Trippe stayed on the sidelines, deferring to superior technical wisdom. Now and then he interjected a pertinent question. He did know something about flying, after all. On summer weekends he piloted a Fairchild floatplane to East Hampton. Juan's main interest in aircraft purchases would always be "How soon can we get delivery?" Pan American Airways had to be first with the biggest.

Lindbergh could not conceal his disappointment when Sikorsky rolled out the drawings for the S-40 on Juan's table. There was a four-engine amphibian, an oversized son of the S-38, with the familiar struts and wires and bulbous pontoons, presenting obvious resistance to wind. "It will be like flying a forest through the air," Lindbergh said.

"You are right, Coronel," Sikorsky replied. The sounds and rhythms of the Dnieper permeated his self-taught English. He pronounced the suffix of verbs in the past tense. "But I have designéd it that way for a reason. This we know we can do. The S-38 has given us the necessary experience. This will be a bigger and better S-38. We believe this is the step we should take now. You are right about the resistance, but we think that should be another step, the one after this one, when we have gainéd more experience. Then we will build the kind of plane you suggest."

Priester sided with Sikorsky, and with time constraints compelling a decisive vote, Lindbergh put aside his misgivings about the design and recommended that Pan American place an order for two of the planes with an option to purchase a third.

Even after the order was signed, at $125,000 a plane, certain features of the design were debated. Lindbergh had a fixation about the placement of the cockpit. From studying crashes of military and mail planes, he deduced that the pilot was mortally endangered unless he was seated as far back as possible behind the engine, propeller and fuel tank.

Sikorsky reasoned that in a plane as large as the S-40, the pilot should be seated in the center section of the high wing, or in the bow of the boat hull. Striving to overcome his crash phobia, Lindbergh told himself that maximum visibility for the pilot was one of the best means of curtailing accidents. The crew compartment of the S-38 was situated below and behind the engines, and during takeoff spray struck the propellers and splashed against the windshield, blinding the pilot for several crucial seconds before the plane got up on the step. In the compromise, the cockpit of the S-40 was placed one-third of the way from the wing to the bow.

A search was mounted for springs strong enough for a 17-ton craft with 114-foot wing span supported by two-wheel landing gear. The springs used for medium-size railroad cars proved to be just right.

The S-40 was the largest airplane built in the United States. It had capacity for 40 passengers, seated four abreast in wood-paneled, comfortably upholstered compartments. Powered by four 575-horsepower Hornet engines, it cruised at 115 miles an hour, with a range of 700 miles, which could be doubled by a sharp reduction of the payload and substitution of extra tanks of gasoline. In addition to the pilot, copilot and radio operator, a fourth member of the crew attended to the engines.

Sikorsky walked through his plane on the return lap of a test flight over Long Island Sound at sunset. As he admired the walnut paneling, observed the doorway to the smoking lounge at the rear and the blue glow from the overhead lights, and felt the vibration of the engines, he realized he was inhabiting his boyhood dream.

The S-40 made its debut in the fall of 1931, dubbed "America's mightiest airplane" by *The New York Times* and christened by Mrs. Herbert Hoover on Columbus Day at the Anacostia Naval Station in Washington. In deference to the law of Prohibition, she used a bottle said to be filled with Caribbean water. The ceremonies, marked by Navy and Marine bands playing "The Stars and Stripes" and a patriotic message by Juan Trippe, were broadcast over a nationwide radio hookup.

On November 19, the plane made its maiden voyage from Miami to the Canal Zone with 32 paying passengers, piloted by Charles Lindbergh with Basil Rowe as copilot. The 660-mile leg from Kingston to Barranquilla was the longest scheduled flight over water. As a courtesy, Lindbergh ceded the controls to Sikorsky for brief intervals. As one of his associates said, "Igor flies like a professor with a textbook in his hand."

At dinner every evening during the stopovers en route, Sikorsky, Lindbergh and Rowe began planning the next step: an ocean airliner with a range of 2,500 miles and capacity for a 50-percent fuel reserve. They covered the backs of menus with sketches for a flying boat that could make the transatlantic crossing with two stops, either at Bermuda and the Azores or in Newfoundland and Ireland.

Trippe gave the first S-40 its name, the *American Clipper*—reaching back, he said, to tap his Maryland ancestry. Those swift sailing ships which had plied America's international trade in the early nineteenth century had originated in the shipyards of Baltimore. How appropriate, then, to call the first transport ship designed for international air commerce after those magnificent vessels. All Pan American airliners were thereafter designated Clippers, and the company that projected itself as America's merchant marine of the air based its traditions on maritime custom and lore. The speed of its planes was calculated in knots, or nautical miles per hour; time in bells; and a crew's tour of duty was referred to as a watch.

Priester thought of dressing the pilots as naval officers, in spanking uniforms of navy-blue serge with gold wings pinned to their breast pockets. Rank was proclaimed by stars imposed on wings: one for copilot, or first officer; two for pilot/captain; three for master ocean pilot, a super-rank created later on. Gold stripes on the sleeves and "spaghetti" on the brim of the white officers' caps were added after World War II. The title of captain implied master of the ship, or chief executive of the flying boat. As the planes grew larger, the captain was assisted by several officers with separate responsibilities for navigation, surveillance of the engines and radio operation, though their functions were interchangeable.

The naval trappings served to set distance between the airline and aviation's all too proximate, madcap history as symbolized by the khaki breeches, leather puttees, jacket and helmet of the daredevil flier. Pan American Airways' pilots were invested as engineers to whom flying was a scientific business rather than a thrilling escapade. Placing them on regular salary instead of paying them by hours logged, as had been the practice of the trade, was intended to remove some of the motivation for reckless flying. Though this was not articulated for the public, they held the lives of their passengers and crew, as well as an airplane worth many thousands (and later, millions) of dollars, in their skillful hands and thought processes. Until after the Second World War, Pan American hired most of its pilots from the U.S. Naval Aviation Corps, and they maintained the snobbery of their branch of the service, belittling Army pilots as "only having to follow the railroad tracks," whereas they were intrepid Magellans.

Some of the earliest pilots hired had started out when the airplane was little more than a gadget, and they were dauntless teen-agers; they resisted being enclosed in cockpits of steel and Plexiglas, taking directions from a panel of instruments and radio operators on the ground. As one of them lamented, for so many years he had been

feeling my way around the sky like a prowling cat, my ears tuned to the note of the wind through the flying wires, my fingertips testing the feel of the controls.

As the equipment evolved into increasingly complex machinery, the requirements for qualifying as a Pan American Airways pilot became stringent and the pilot's education never-ending. It began with a college degree, preferably in aeronautical engineering, plus a transport pilot's license and experience in military and commercial flying, and continued in training, mostly in correspondence courses administered from Miami, in engine mechanics, celestial navigation, radio, meteorology. He had to have more than a nodding acquaintance with international and maritime law, and a smattering of a foreign language. His proficiency was tested by examinations and certified by degrees; he advanced from apprentice pilot to junior pilot to flight engineer and then senior pilot. With each improvement in efficiency and power, the airplane became more complicated to operate, so that the pilot was taking courses and studying manuals during his entire career.

The noncommissioned officers of the Pan American Airways crew were the stewards, modeled in function and appearance after the personnel of luxury ocean liners. Their uniforms were black trousers and white waist-length jackets over white shirts and black neckties. Stewards distributed remedies for airsickness, served refreshments (and in the S-40, prepared hot meals in the galley of the aircraft), pointed out scenic attractions from the windows of the plane and assisted with the red tape of Customs and landing procedures.

Before repeal of the Eighteenth Amendment, they occasionally had to subdue unruly passengers who had "tanked up" on Cuban rum before leaving Havana. On the Clipper flights to South America, the steward blindfolded passengers who were crossing the Equator for the first time and led them to the lounge for an initiation ceremony presided over by Jupiter Rex, a flight engineer decked out in life jacket and sneakers with a crown on his matted wig. Before landing at Belém, he handed out certificates attesting to the passengers' newly won status as condors—aerial equivalents of the shellbacks, who crossed by sea.

One of the first stewards hired was an industrious Cuban-American, Charles B. Rebozo, whom everyone called Bebe. He quit after a few years to open a filling station, and later, as a banker in Key Biscayne, became the confidant of a future President of the United States, Richard M. Nixon.

The Pan American Clippers were a shining symbol of popular culture in America during the Thirties. In Miami, visitors flocked to the terminal at Dinner Key to watch the flying boats come in over palm-fringed Biscayne Bay. *Flying Down to Rio*, a movie in the new genre of musical extravaganza, introduced the song-and-dance team of Fred Astaire and Ginger Rogers. Armchair travelers contemplated two-week vacations to semitropical islands in the Caribbean and foreign countries to the south along the Lindbergh Circle, itineraries requiring "months of tedious travel by any other means."

The planes were vehicles for political getaway. In August 1933, the Cuban Army staged a coup d'état against the regime of Gerardo Machado. The dictator fled to Nassau in a chartered plane, while an aide dashed aboard a Pan American flying boat as it was about to depart for Miami. Rebels were at his heels, shooting at the plane as it took off. Angered by the escape, they took the manager of the Caribbean division and two other employees, none of whom spoke Spanish, into custody and marched them off, with hands bound, to an uncertain fate until the airline's Cuban traffic manager interceded.

What Trippe cared most about was the positioning of Pan American Airways as "an official institution of U.S. business." Said *Time* magazine, "It goes where foreign trade can be developed. It carries the sample case, the estimate pad, the order book, the spare part." By arrangement with Railway Express Agency, shippers could consign freight by rail and air direct from warehouse to point of destination in Latin America with a single document, the Pan American Airwaybill.

In 1931, the airline carried 820,000 pounds of mail and cargo, 45,000 passengers, and flew 12,479,000 passenger-miles. That year, it showed its first profit: $105,000 on revenues of $7.9 million, after a loss of $700,000 in its first two and a half years of operation.

During the next few years, Pan American's earnings multiplied geometrically; in 1934, it reported profits of $1.1 million on operating revenues of $9.6 million. And for much of that, Trippe had to be grateful to the Republican postal officials. Under its ten-year foreign mail contracts, Pan American kept accumulating payments at the maximum rate of $2 a mile while domestic airlines were collecting at a fraction of that rate and on a decreasing scale every year. Moreover, Pan American Airways had no competition from U.S. operators in Latin America. And this was by edict of Postmaster General Brown.

During the spring of 1930, as he was ordaining the merger of Pan American and NYRBA, Brown applied the same shotgun-marriage technique to the domestic airlines. His purpose, said the righteous autocrat of the national postal service, was "to revamp the airmail plan of the country and make it a logical one." Brown summoned the heads of the seven largest airlines to meetings in his office and coerced them into amalgamations so that only one well-financed and compliant operator bid for each major route. He excluded small independents from the "spoils conferences," at which 14,700 miles of new airmail routes were distributed almost entirely to airlines controlled by the three largest aviation holding companies. He created two additional transcontinental routes and awarded them to T.W.A. and American Airways, new giants produced by rapid mergers.

Sometime during this period, Brown said to Trippe, "You should give up the domestic field." Juan did as instructed and sold New York Airways, the resort taxi service in which the founding triumvirate had lost interest once their international airline was established.

The buyer was Eastern Air Transport, operating between New York and Washington, and a part of Clement Keys's North American Aviation. Thomas B. Doe, the president, also watched over another Keys venture, Compañía Nacional Cubana de Aviación, which had a local airmail concession from the Cuban Government. In July 1931, Captain Doe complained to Brown that Pan American was attempting to squeeze the Cuban airline out of business.

The Postmaster General wrote Doe a letter setting him straight:

I have stated frankly to the air mail operators that in the present state of the industry it did not seem the part of wisdom to invade each other's territory with competitive services and that I did not believe that money paid for postal service should be used to set up services to injure competitors. In pursuance of this policy I suggested the abandonment by the Pan American Co. of the domestic field in the United States, and as a result of that suggestion you are now negotiating with the Pan American Co. for the taking over of their Atlantic City service. Their field is the international service to Mexico, Central and South America, and the West Indies. Consistently with the policy outlined, it would seem improper for any of our domestic air mail operators to use mail pay to invade the peculiar field of the Pan American Co.

The policy was strictly Brown's. It had no force of executive order or Congressional mandate. But it was sufficient grounds for Trippe to assert ever after that Pan American Airways was the chosen instrument of the United States Government in international skies. A year later, Pan American bought Doe's Cuban company for what was considered a bargain price of $500,000.

Part III

THE OCEANS

16

Preparing to Cross an Ocean

Latin America was a laboratory for Pan American Airways and the piggy bank for Trippe's insatiable desire to fly the oceans. He and his associates would have preferred to head northeast over the Atlantic, the principal trade route for the United States. They pointed their airline south because it was virtually impossible to choose another direction, given the state of aeronautical technology, and their backer, the U.S. Government, was interested in air service as a security measure for the Panama Canal.

So it was engine power, or the lack thereof, and imperialism that dictated the course of international air transport. European colonial powers directed their airlines to "follow the flag" to the corners of their empires. Great Britain's Imperial Airways was charged with linking domains over which the sun never set. Flying over France and Italy to Cairo, Imperial cast a line toward Cape Town, in the Union of South Africa; another toward India and Australia. By 1930, KLM connected Amsterdam with Batavia, in the Dutch East Indies, then set about developing service among Holland's possessions in the Caribbean and along the northern coast of South America. Several French companies, eventually combined into one national airline, embroidered a web of Continental routes as far east as Warsaw and Istanbul, reached out to France's African colonies and across the South Atlantic to Latin America, and by 1931 touched the Orient at Saigon. Shorn of its colonies in the war, Germany created the most efficient commercial air network in Europe, and planted stakes in South America and China by sponsoring local airlines.

Almost all these strides were made by geographic expediency, hopscotching from continent to continent so that planes could come down on land as often as their anemic engine power was spent, and avoiding the great oceans. Yet the crossing of the Atlantic figured in all European aviation plans. Britain, France and the Scandinavian countries drew up routes to North America. France and other Mediterranean countries with potential launching sites in their African colonies and historic ties to South America concentrated attention on the South Atlantic.

How to transform Lindbergh's one-man feat of 1927 into a viable business of regularly scheduled public transportation: that was the challenge for airmen in the 1930s. Aircraft range was less than 1,000 miles at the turn of the decade and, pending technological breakthrough, could be extended only by the addition of fuel and reduction or elimination of the payload of passengers and mail. The hope of covering the cost of ocean flights thus dimmed.

Pan American had under serious consideration a plan to save weight by microfilming letters, and a company was formed in association with British Imperial Airways and Eastman Kodak; it failed to come to commercial fruition, although a military application, V-Mail, was used during the Second World War.

In 1933 an engineer for Du Pont, Edward A. Armstrong, put forth a concept of floating islands anchored in concrete every 500 miles across the Atlantic, where planes could land on steel piers for fuel and servicing while passengers waited in elegantly furnished marine inns. Armstrong promised a 24-hour air service between the United States and Europe if the Federal Government would advance $30 million from the Public Works Administration to construct his seadromes. The Secretary of Commerce approved a trial run, but the State Department was concerned lest the "steel stepping-stones" bear an enemy tread. With foreign allies adding demurrers about sovereignty and maintenance fees, and Trippe dismissing the man-made islands as too small for Pan American's flying boats, the project died a natural death.

Lighter-than-air ships had a zealous following, undiscouraged by the hideous disasters that periodically befell the hydrogen-filled leviathans. A spacious dirigible could transport 50 or more passengers in comfort and quiet across thousands of miles, by day and night, without pausing to refuel.

Count Ferdinand von Zeppelin's first airship was put into commercial service in Germany in 1900; as he lay dying seventeen years later, military versions were dropping bombs on English cities. Estopped by the peace treaty from manufacturing dirigibles, the Ger-

mans fidgeted while British and American promoters tried to exploit
their invention, and failed dismally. After treaty restrictions on aircraft
construction were modified, the Germans produced a super-airship, the
Graf Zeppelin, in 1928. The majestic balloon made a round-trip transatlantic voyage; circled the world the following year, crossing from
Japan to California in less than three days, and went into service as an
air shuttle across the South Atlantic.

In October 1929, a group of German and American investors (including United Aircraft & Transport, National City Company and the
Goodyear Company) formed the International Zeppelin Transport
Company to operate airships between Europe and the United States.
Prominent stockholders in Pan American Airways, such as Lehman
Brothers and W. A. Harriman, were among the organizers of the Pacific Zeppelin Transport Company, which planned a 36-hour service
between California and Hawaii in 100-passenger airships. Trippe was a
director of the company.

Though detractors asserted that the airship was too slow, too expensive to operate and dangerously susceptible to wind currents on the
ground and above, it was regarded as serious competition for the flying
boat, the equipment Pan American was committed to throughout the
Thirties. Proposed legislation to encourage the construction of airships
with government loans and mail contracts—the kind of support that
heavier-than-air machines enjoyed—never emerged from Congress,
and Trippe was suspected of being unhelpful in the lobbying process.

The French and Germans demonstrated that flying boats could
cross the shortest span of the South Atlantic, from the elbow of Africa
to the bulge of Brazil, aided by favorable easterly trade winds. In 1930,
Jean Mermoz of Aéropostale made the first transatlantic mail flight; in
1931, the Dornier DO-X, a luxurious 52-ton seaplane with twelve engines, got across after several mishaps. It continued up the coast of
South America to New York, where it was welcomed with a ticker-tape
parade led by the city's playboy mayor, James J. Walker. After returning across the North Atlantic via Newfoundland and the Azores, the
experimental plane was retired to a Berlin museum.

The next German attempt at overcoming the formidable Atlantic
distances was by catapult of mail-carrying seaplanes from the decks of
steamships several hundred miles offshore. In 1934, an overseas mail
route was inaugurated; Dornier-Wal flying boats alighted midway in
the South Atlantic beside a mother ship and, after being taken aboard
for refueling, were catapulted in the direction of Natal.

The South Atlantic was the long way round to Europe from the
United States. The North Atlantic was the puddle Pan American had to

jump. The hurdles were awesome, and not only technical but political as well. Every possible terminal on the other side, and all intermediate stepping-stones, were under foreign control. Britain, with its imperial outposts in Canada, Newfoundland and the Irish Free State, and Portugal, with its mid-Atlantic islands, held the keys to air commerce over the ocean.

In his youthful brashness, Trippe may not have realized how difficult it was going to be. Practicing aviation diplomacy in Latin America was one thing—the continent was underdeveloped and submissive to economic imperialists, and most of the countries were unable to muster their own air services. But in bidding for ocean routes as the Secretary of State of Pan American Airways, he was pitted against nations of the first rank which employed their airlines as instruments of battle for trade and security.

Juan made his first overtures in the fall of 1928, during his European honeymoon. As a very green international negotiator, properly introduced by Francis White, he tried to pry landing rights in the Caribbean colonies from the air ministries in Paris and London, which regarded such matters as properly covered by intergovernmental treaties.

He was not too successful in Paris, either with the government bureaucrats or at the offices of Latécoère, which had won operating rights in Venezuela from General Gómez, an admirer of Gallic culture.

In London, he fared better. He secured temporary permits from the British Colonial Office and was received at the headquarters of Imperial Airways by George E. Woods Humphery, the managing director. It was the beginning of a special relationship, both liked to say, an alliance of English-speaking airlines. At times the relationship would be perfidious, and often it would be subject to strain, for Imperial was entirely the creature of its government, while Pan American was a private enterprise with an ambiguous status.

Imperial was an amalgam, since 1924, of four pioneer companies, and the "chosen instrument" of Britain's will to maintain in the skies the superiority enjoyed for centuries on the seas. The airline suffered from the pernicious anemia that began to eat away at the marrow of British industry after the war. While European governments open-handedly subsidized their airlines, the British Air Ministry stifled civil aviation with "step-motherly parsimony," as a newspaper critic put it. Imperial was supposed to operate as a commercial enterprise, benefiting from a monopoly of overseas routes, yet was saddled with a mission incompatible with profit-making: its primary duty was to bind the Empire together with a system of strategic aerial arteries, otherwise known as the All-Red Route (for the color of British territory on a world map).

The airline was restricted to a "Buy British" policy for equipment, even though planes made in England were slower and less efficient than those of other nations, notably the United States. The British aircraft industry was a victim, too, of the Air Ministry's miserliness in regard to nonmilitary research and development, as well as of slothful working habits. As late as 1933, Imperial was flying biplanes and was just converting to the air-cooled engine. For several years to come it had no blind-flying instruments, deicing equipment or even spare parts and planes; a single accident could tie up an entire route.

Another handicap was the management of Imperial. The dictatorial chairman, Sir Eric Geddes, was a Scottish industrialist who had been rewarded for his wartime achievements in railroad financing and matériel transport with numerous sinecures. Neither he nor the government saw any conflict in his presiding over Imperial Airways while occupying the chairmanship of the Dunlop Rubber Company and dabbling in a dozen other enterprises. Woods Humphery had a shopkeeper's mentality. The pilots detested him. Their work schedules were long and their salaries low. While American pilots were exalted as culture heroes, Imperial's occupied positions below the stairs in British class hierarchy. The managing director treated them as flying chauffeurs.

On this first visit, Trippe raised the subject of cooperation on the Atlantic. Pan American then had a mere foothold in the Caribbean backyard of the United States, while the other airline was an imperial instrument. Though a plane to fly the ocean had not yet been built, Juan spoke as though transatlantic service were just around the corner. David knew no better; Goliath listened.

A few months later, Sir Eric Geddes visited New York, and it was his turn to suggest cooperation—on a service between New York and Bermuda, a prelude to a more extensive route across the ocean via the Azores. In May 1930, Imperial and Pan American formed a joint development corporation, and each company filed for and obtained a two-year permit from the Bermuda Government.

Subtle shifts in the balance of power were taking place. Pan American Airways was dominating the air roads of Latin America, an area in which Imperial was conspicuously absent. And Trippe had ordered a four-engine flying boat, the S-40, that might be adapted to fly the 775 miles between New York and Bermuda.

The French Aéropostale, owned by Marcel Bouilloux-Lafont, a financier with a craving for routes who had taken over the failing

Latécoère company, stole a plum from under Imperial's nose. Though Portugal was a satellite of Britain, Aéropostale, through a Portuguese affiliate, obtained exclusive landing rights for fifteen years in the Azores and the Cape Verde Islands, stepping-stones to the mid- and South Atlantic.

Aéropostale also had a concession from the French Government for a mail service by ship and plane to the United States. Upon learning of Pan American's Bermuda permit, André Bouilloux-Lafont, brother of Marcel and managing director of Aéropostale, was impatient to start trading with Trippe. He arrived in New York in October with two items on his agenda: Aéropostale's franchise in French Guiana, which the government allowed him discretion to subcontract to another airline, and the Azores concession.

Trippe was eager to conclude an agreement for landing rights in Cayenne, the last strategic outpost to be secured for his new east-coast route to South America, but he held him at exasperated arm's length on the Azores and the transatlantic mail line until his preferred ally, Woods Humphery, sailed into port in mid-November on the Cunard liner *Franconia*.

The bargaining sessions took place in Trippe's office, a rather modest setting for what newspapers were to describe as a secret tripartite conference to divide the Atlantic. Far from feeling outnumbered, Trippe acted as though he had the largest stack of chips. In the absence of bilateral government treaties for air rights, the United States was closed to foreign operators, and Woods Humphery and Bouilloux-Lafont had to come to terms with Trippe, at least for the time being. Juan played statistical bluff, asserting out of the blue that 80 percent of the eastbound mail emanated from the United States, whereas only one-fourth of the westbound mail funneled through Britain.

After a week of haggling in English (which put Bouilloux-Lafont at a disadvantage), they reached an agreement to cooperate in establishing a mail service across the midsection of the North Atlantic, via Bermuda and the Azores, with Norfolk, Virginia, as the U.S. terminal. A port that was ice-free the year round was needed for flying boats. Half the traffic was apportioned to Pan American, the rest to be shared by Imperial and Aéropostale.

Before the ink was dry, Irving Glover announced the pact, promising that the Post Office would furnish the mail. At the end of November, Postmaster General Brown posted advertisements for bids on ten-year transatlantic airmail contracts, but withdrew them three weeks later under protest from the Zeppelin crowd and a domestic airline.

In March 1931, Aéropostale capsized in a bankruptcy scandal which implicated the French Prime Minister and the Minister of Finance. Trippe was a whirlwind of activity on other fronts. In July, Pan American Airways offered the winning bid for FAM 12, the airmail route between Bangor, Maine, and Halifax, Nova Scotia, and obtained permission from the Postmaster General to sublease the domestic airmail contract between Boston and Bangor during the summer. "We're getting experience in northern flying for Europe," Juan said.

He had Frank Gledhill invite the six leading aircraft manufacturers to submit designs for a new plane: "a high speed, multi-motored flying boat having a cruising range of 2,500 miles against 30-mile headwinds, and providing accommodations for a crew of four together with at least 300 pounds of airmail."

As they moved pieces of string tautly across the turquoise and gold patches on the standing globe in Trippe's office, Pan American's technical men were drawn to the far northern portion where continents almost touched. Only 50 miles of Bering Strait divided North America from Asia, while the largest reach of water on the subarctic course to Europe was the 600-mile span between Labrador and the Danish colony of Greenland. Such distances were manageable for the planes that served the Caribbean. The Great Circle Route around the top of the world looked logical and easy.

But globe-gazing within the four walls of a Manhattan skyscraper was an unsatisfactory test of aerial experience—at least for Lindbergh, who was itching for adventure again. Late in 1930, he began preparations for a survey flight to repeat the quest of earlier English and Norwegian seafarers for a Northwest Passage to the East.

Charles funded the trip mostly from personal resources. He chose a Lockheed Sirius, a single-engine, low-wing monoplane that the manufacturer finished to his specifications; one innovation was sliding covers for the cockpits. He had used the plane in a transcontinental flight to prove a hunch that speed, performance and economy were to be found at altitudes above 12,000 feet, where bad weather could be surmounted.

Anticipating a dearth of landing fields on the Arctic road from New York to Tokyo, Lindbergh asked Lockheed to fit the plane for the survey flight with pontoons and with tanks for sufficient fuel to extend its range to almost 2,000 miles. He also had the engine changed to a 600-horsepower Wright Cyclone, the newest and most powerful, to lift the bloated bird from the lakes and coastal harbors where it would have to land. Leuteritz installed a long-range radio with telegraph transmitter and the fixed-loop direction-finding apparatus that was working wonders in the Caribbean.

Anne Lindbergh was going along as conavigator and radio operator. Smith College had nurtured her literary talent and she could quote French poets by heart, but she considered herself a dunce in mathematics and physics. For love and worship of a demanding husband, Anne conquered her incompetence by taking a crash course in Morse code and tutoring from a Pan American technician.

The Lindberghs christened the Sirius *Tingmissartoq*, the Eskimo exclamation for "one who flies like a big bird," and set out from Long Island at the end of July 1931. They followed a slanting course through Canada across Hudson Bay, tracing the Arctic shores along the Amundsen Gulf and the Beaufort Sea to the tip of Alaska at Point Barrow. From there they dipped down to Nome, a short leap from Soviet territory in Asia. Russian fur trappers and fishermen welcomed them to the miniature settlements of the Kamchatka Peninsula. Later, when curious friends sought her opinions of the strange communist system, Anne said, "It isn't 'it.' It's Them, and I like them."

Japanese sailors came to their rescue when they were forced down by fog in the Chishima Rettō, or Kuril Islands. From Japan, they crossed the Yellow Sea to China, then in the grips of a periodic calamity, the overflow of the Yangtze River. The Lindberghs offered to map the stricken areas for the National Flood Relief Commission. The Sirius was damaged as it was being lowered into the river from a British airplane carrier, and soon after that disruption to their schedule they received word of Dwight Morrow's death and hurried back to the United States by ship from Yokohama.

Lindbergh was discouraged by what he discovered on this first Arctic survey for Pan American. The ice-packed harbors, the frozen terrain, the pervasive fog and mysterious electronic obstructions that diminished the efficiency of the radio led him to discount the Great Circle Route to the Orient until the faraway time when airplanes would have the range to overfly the region.

His pessimism about a transpacific airway through the North was reinforced by political difficulties. Trippe tried to stimulate a dialogue with the Russians in the fall of 1931. He dashed off a letter addressed to the "All-Union Union of the Civil Air Fleet, Kremlin, Moscow," proposing cooperation on a commercial air service and an exchange of technical data. "We have valuable radio communications," he wrote. The letter ended with this statement: "The Pan American Airways System is a community effort on the part of the U.S. aviation industry." Officials of the Union of Soviet Socialist Republics were unwilling to discuss concessions in Siberia as long as the United States refused to recognize Lenin's successors and the government they had established by revolution fourteen years before.

Still, the lure of the Arctic and the potential, however faint, of the Northwest Passage remained irresistible. Dick Hoyt, the ubiquitous promoter, commissioned Vilhjalmur Stefansson, a polar explorer and early advocate of Arctic flight, to prepare a report on an intercontinental route through the Bering Sea. Stefansson outlined a course proceeding from the southern coast of Alaska to the Aleutian Islands, the Asiatic coast and the Japanese Islands.

Ever since he and John Hambleton had investigated a mail route in the territory, Juan had been keenly interested in Alaska. Ben Eielson succeeded in establishing a charter and mail operation, Alaskan Airways, a subsidiary of American Airways, but after he died in 1929, it floundered. The other principal mail contractor, Pacific International Airways of Alaska, was losing so much money that it served notice of imminent demise.

There was little chance that Pan American Airways might turn a quick profit in a wasteland lacking airports and weather stations, where thermometers plunged in winter to 60 degrees below zero and summertime brought hordes of ravenous mosquitoes. But somewhere down the road there was the possibility of linking up with trunk routes to the forty-eight states, and in the meantime, much could be learned about Arctic conditions. Trippe was aware of the strategic importance the Navy and War Departments placed on Alaskan air lanes.

In the fall of 1932, he bought the two airlines for $90,000. In light of the half-million dollars they had poured into development, the price was dirt cheap.

17

Babes in
the Oriental Woods

Another bargain appeared ripe for plucking: an airline in China—a potential anchor for Pan American Airways on the far side of the Pacific.

The airline was part of the distress merchandise being peddled by North American Aviation, Clement Keys's monster trust. Keys was now physically ailing and a financial cripple. He had been pummeled in the stock-market crash, and in May 1930 was beaten in a proxy fight with Fred Rentschler for control of National Air Transport. Wall Street said it was E. H. Harriman and James J. Hill all over again, except that the railroad robber barons had compromised in the end. Air baron Rentschler took N.A.T. away from Keys and attached it to his Boeing Air Transport to create one transcontinental line, United Airlines Transport. "The air between the coasts is not big enough to be divided," he said. After that, Keys's house of cards collapsed.

Thomas A. Morgan, president of Sperry Gyroscope, and a Horatio Alger character who wore a rose tattoo on his left arm, a souvenir of his apprenticeship as an electrician in the Navy, took over the running of Curtiss-Wright and North American Aviation. Determined to shuck off the weaker units, he sold the Cuban airline to Pan American. Trippe looked like a logical customer for the Chinese one as well.

In the euphoria of 1928, Keys had hit on the idea of scouring the world for markets for Curtiss airplanes, and his eye had alighted on the Orient.

Aviation had much to offer China, a territory of unbridged distances and woeful technological backwardness. A letter mailed from

Shanghai arrived two weeks later in Chongqing. The trip between Chongqing and Chengdu, the capital of Sichuan province, was made by sedan chair over 300 miles of twisting mountain paths and flatlands of stinking paddy fields. It took 10 to 15 days, during which the traveler and his bearers quaked at the prospect of being held up by bandits. The same journey, only 170 miles as the crow flies, could be completed in 2 hours by plane.

Both as a means of communication and as transport, the airplane could knit an economic and political fabric for a new nation. At the least, it could fly passengers, mail and cargo over the grasp of belligerent provincial lords. Besides hastening the peaceful expansion of Chiang Kai-shek's authority, a commercial air service might be converted to a military arm. And so, in a recurring pattern of Chinese history, the Nationalists suspended their distrust of foreign barbarians in order to satisfy their technical needs; they entertained bids from aviation promoters.

In April 1929, Keys representatives won an exclusive ten-year airmail contract to operate over three routes radiating from Shanghai, and to construct airports, aircraft factories and flying schools. The American entity held 45 percent of the stock in the China National Aviation Corporation, the majority interest being reserved for the government.

"One who has been a resident of China for many years cannot be optimistic at the prospects of the contract," the U.S. Consul in Shanghai commented prophetically. The Nationalists interfered with mail operations by commandeering planes for military use. When the American field manager at Hankow refused to hold a plane past its scheduled departure time for Chiang Kai-shek and his aides, the Generalissimo ordered him jailed. On the other side of the prevailing chaos, the warlord of Sichuan province, who did not recognize Chiang's authority, announced he would have C.N.A.C. aircraft shot down if the airline tried to establish service between Nanjing and Chongqing.

When the Japanese bombed Shanghai, the seat of C.N.A.C.'s operations, in January 1932, the operations manager, William Langhorne Bond, coolly kept the service running to Nanjing despite protests to the American Consul from the Japanese Army. A precedent was established for notifying the Japanese through diplomatic channels that C.N.A.C. was a strictly commercial organization, that its planes were flown by American and Chinese pilots under the direction of American operating personnel and that its rights as a nonmilitary entity should be respected. The procedure was given frequent airing in the years to come.

Keys had sunk nearly $700,000 into the project. Losing money at an annual rate of $250,000, C.N.A.C. needed intensive care, which Morgan was averse to giving. He suggested to Trippe that he buy out the Curtiss interest. Juan's motive was different from the Curtiss group's—they had wanted to sell planes; he was building an international airline—and so even as Morgan's representative was trying to collect payments and straighten out other matters with the Nationalist officials, Trippe sent his personal emissary to negotiate with them.

Morgan construed this as an unfriendly act. "We are put in a position of having no alternative except resistance in every way possible to your attempt to exploit this territory," he declared in a letter to Trippe.

It was all a misunderstanding, Trippe replied, and went ahead to appraise C.N.A.C. with the eye of a junk buyer. On March 31, 1933, Morgan sold out for $181,385 in Pan American Airways stock plus a two-year option to buy additional stock at a price then below the market. As he had done in buying NYRBA, Trippe placed a highly inflated value on the Pan American stock. The Chinese franchise has to be chalked up as another steal.

Trippe's representative, who had set sail for China from Seattle in January, was a new Pan American hand, hired at Lindbergh's urging. A former St. Louis banker, Harold M. Bixby had plumbed the local money pots to buy the plane for the flight to Paris. He accompanied the conquering hero on his nationwide tours, and their association remained warm and close.

Saddled with debts in the aftermath of the stock-market crash and vowing to repay them to the last cent, he seized the opportunity to start anew at the age of 42, at last in a business he passionately loved. Bixby saw the job of Far Eastern scout Trippe offered him as doing "missionary work" for the visionary plan of bridging the Pacific.

A man of the American heartland, he carried with him to China a conviction that he could do business without kowtowing or distributing cumshaw and squeeze, the bribes and kickbacks that for centuries had greased the wheels of Chinese commerce. Rude surprises awaited him. At the first board of directors meeting he attended, he learned that it had been called to decide whether or not C.N.A.C. should declare bankruptcy.

Bixby had no inkling when he left America that the normal xenophobia of the Chinese, now aggravated by the realistic fear of the encroaching Japanese, would thwart Pan American's purpose in buying the airline: namely, to secure Shanghai, the commercial center of the Far East, as an Asian terminal for a transpacific service. Were an

American company given concessions to operate an international service out of Shanghai, the most-favored-nation clauses and the Open Door policy embodied in the Nine Power Treaty of 1922 would obligate the Chinese Government to extend equal rights to airlines of other nations, of whom the most-feared was Japan. In September 1931, the Japanese Army had seized Mukden and occupied the mineral-rich, fertile northern province of Manchuria. The following January the puppet state of Manchukuo was established and a bombing attack launched against the helpless civilians of Shanghai's Chinese district.

Bixby was working against a tight deadline. The Shanghai–Canton franchise, Route Number 3, was due to expire on July 8, 1933. To save face for the government and allay its qualms about the Japanese, Bixby devised an arrangement whereby Pan American created a subsidiary, Pacific American Airways Co., incorporated in Nevada, to operate the coastal route as a subcontractor for C.N.A.C. The airplanes would bear Chinese markings with the PAA legend in small English letters beneath. To complete the subterfuge, the terminus of the transpacific service would be fixed just beyond the borders of China—say, at Hong Kong, with a connecting service to the Canton–Shanghai line. Despite the elaborate ruse, Trippe regarded the route as an American operation and hoped to nourish it with U.S. mail subsidy for the projected transpacific route.

The Chinese Minister of Communications dickered right up to the deadline over the amount of expected losses against which he would indemnify the American partner. On the crucial day, while the Minister was in Nanjing, refusing to order the release of the mail, Bixby effectively seized the franchise for Pan American. He coaxed the Postmaster in Canton, a Norwegian (most postal officials at that time were Europeans), to put two bags of letters on an S-38 leaving for Shanghai. The sacks arrived at the destination a few hours later, and the airmail contract was technically performed. It was an Oriental rerun of Pan American's opening chapter, Key West–Havana.

A provisional operating contract for the coastal route was signed early in October after Bixby had taught the Minister of Communications a lesson in propaganda warfare. In August, he made a survey flight from Hong Kong to the Philippines. He inspected possible landing sites in northern Luzon and around Manila, inquired into the procedure for asking the legislature for operating rights, granted interviews to local journalists in which he expansively described how the Philippines could fit into a transpacific service and returned on the first Hong Kong–Manila round trip ever made by air.

Back in Shanghai, Bixby announced that he was moving operations to Hong Kong. Shanghai newspapers reflected the concern of the business community about missing out on the transpacific hookup. The Minister resumed negotiating. But he also continued his objections to Americans' dominating the operation and maintained that Chinese should be trained to take over many of the jobs.

Pan American sent from Miami two Sikorsky S-38s, and flight personnel consisting of three pilots and four mechanics who could double as radio operators. The team was headed by William Grooch, a quixotic pilot who had flown with O'Neill in NYRBA.

Priester lectured Grooch on "safety-first methods of operating" and presented him with a book on *Qualities of Leadership*, a farewell gift of as much use as the ball gowns that appeared in contribution boxes for foreign missionaries. "Weather in China is about the worst anywhere," Bixby wrote to Lindbergh, and the Pan American pilots were unprepared for it. C.N.A.C. lacked even rudimentary navigation aids; its single-engine planes were unequipped with radios, and the fliers were totally dependent on visual contact with the ground.

Along the coastal route the planes were trapped in blankets of fog and buffeted by wind currents between the jagged mountains and the sea. The Yangtze River was a deceitful enemy, its muddy waters blending into the constant haze to create zero visibility in which the pilot mistook the fog beneath him for the river he wanted to follow. Newcomers learned to fly along the Yangtze's edges rather than down its middle, and to turn back as soon as they could no longer see the ground, for that meant they were lost.

Meteorological support was primitive. At each stop, pilots were given reports about the weather farther along the route, radioed from the next station by Chinese employees who read just enough English to decipher the simple code. There were three checkpoints: X, a half-mile from the radio station; Y, a mile or more distant; and Z, a landmark such as a mountain 5 miles from the observer. The pilot's decision as to whether or not to hazard a takeoff was based on a radio message indicating X visible, Y dull, Z invisible. In April 1934, an S-38 plowed into a hill and fell into the muddy waters of the bay, killing the crew and its single passenger—the second crash in dense haze in five months. The accidents impaired Pan American's vaunted reputation for technical skill and concern for safety and stiffened the Chinese Government's skepticism about the viability of the coastal route.

Nevertheless, the annual report of Pan American Airways for 1934 alluded to the "cordial and friendly relations" between the company and Chinese officials, and asserted, "Already China National Aviation Corporation is generally recognized as an outstanding example of successful Sino–American business cooperation." The statement, written by Trippe, was reality distorted; but the report to shareholders was always a showcase for his phantasmagoria.

And the hyperbole about China was mild compared with what appeared in the pages of *Time*. For Henry Luce had embarked on the greatest missionary cause of his life, the exaltation of Chiang Kai-shek as the Chinese antidote to godless Russian Communism and the welding of American opinion toward the stalwart Christian China he fervently imagined.

Luce and Trippe were neighbors now. In the summer of 1933, Pan American Airways had moved its headquarters again, to join *Time* and *Fortune* as a tenant in Walter Chrysler's new Art Deco skyscraper on Forty-second Street.

18

Setbacks

Several air roads led to Europe from North America, each with distinct physical advantages and drawbacks given the technical limitations of aeronautics.

The path Lindbergh chose in 1927 had the least total mileage, but it included nearly 2,000 miles of open water between Newfoundland and Ireland, and murky weather at either end. Five hundred fewer miles of ocean lay between Newfoundland and the Azores, the route taken in 1919 by the Navy aviators in the Curtiss flying boats. In winter, Bermuda offered an agreeable alternative to Newfoundland, but that was the roundabout way—2,070 miles from Hamilton to the Azores and another 1,050 miles to Lisbon.

The extreme northern route had the virtue of the shortest reaches of water, but it was packed in ice, and during the winter was covered in darkness for as much as twenty hours of the day. Pilots were inexperienced in night flying.

The political aspects of the subarctic were the least bothersome, however. Transamerican Airlines Corporation, one of Dick Hoyt's companies, won a seventy-five-year franchise from the Government of Iceland. Trippe bought it for $55,000 in the spring of 1932 and sent an agent to Denmark to obtain a concession anticipating regular air service 'across Greenland.

Concurrently, he went after operating rights in Newfoundland. He figured on extending the Boston–Halifax service to St. John's and from there fastening on to a transatlantic route. Newfoundland was a self-governing part of the British Empire, enjoying the same dominion status as Canada. In some respects it was similar to Latin America—a backward area in which political corruption was endemic. Successive governments had bartered away concessions for exploiting mineral, timber and other natural resources to foreign corporations for negligible returns.

Juan assigned Alan Winslow to be his negotiator in Newfoundland. He admired Winslow, who had rowed on the crew with Trubee Davison at Yale, served in the renowned 94th Aero Squadron with Eddie Rickenbacker and lost his left arm in an aerial duel. After the war, he had followed the well-grooved path from New Haven to the State Department, married the daughter of an Under Secretary, and been posted as first secretary of the embassy in Mexico and thence to Pan American Airways.

Winslow curried favor with local businessmen and retained an influential law firm in St. John's to grease the legislative wheels for a fifteen-year concession, including the right of Pan American to nominate a European carrier as its opposite number. After the proposal had gone smoothly through two hearings in the House of Assembly, Sir Eric Geddes telephoned Trippe from London. "I hear you have a wonderful franchise," he said. "Would you nominate Imperial as your opposite number?"

"That's just what I was going to do," Juan replied. "I understand the chances are a hundred to one that we'll get final approval."

Before a third hearing could be held in April 1932, a mob vented its fury over abysmal economic conditions in the Dominion by wrecking the House of Assembly and trampling on the beleaguered Prime Minister. The British Navy steamed into port to restore order.

In the fall, Trippe sent Major Robert A. Logan, a distinguished Canadian explorer, to scout for bases for transatlantic flying boats in Newfoundland; he recommended Botwood. And early in 1933, Winslow tried again. Just when it appeared he had lined up his pins for a strike, negotiations were suspended on orders from London.

The Canadian Government was alarmed at the prospect of a private U.S. company's setting up bases in its backyard without Ottawa's having anything to say about it, and had stirred anxiety in the Dominions Office in Whitehall. The British Privy Council looking into civil aviation concluded that Britain, Canada and Newfoundland should jointly assume control over a transatlantic air service.

As soon as Winslow notified him of the bad news, Juan called Geddes, who was a member of the Privy Council. "Do we not have an understanding?" he asked the autocrat of Imperial Airways. Geddes allowed that they did.

"I was going to share everything with you," Trippe said, "and you have a moral obligation to share any concessions Imperial gains with Pan American."

Responding to the gentlemen's code Trippe invoked, Sir Eric informed the Privy Council that he felt bound to honor his commitment. In July, a meeting of British and Canadian air officials was convened in St. John's, attended by Geddes and Trippe. Imperial was permitted to assign its rights by subcontract to Pan American and to a Canadian airline, subject to approval by the Newfoundland legislature.

Winslow was in Ottawa a few weeks later to consult with Canadian postal officials when he tumbled from the window of his third-floor hotel room and died of injuries sustained in the fall. The mysterious accident provided an ominous note to the muddled plot.

Late that fall, as Imperial was submitting its request to the legislature in St. John's, that body voted itself out of existence, adopting a recommendation by a royal commission that the insolvent Dominion surrender its right to self-government and revert to the status of a Crown Colony until its financial health improved.

With access to Newfoundland in doubt, Trippe dispatched an agent to Lisbon to inquire after the Azores concession held by Pan American's erstwhile associate Aéropostale. The French Government had reorganized several failing companies into one national airline, Air France, and while that was happening did nothing about exercising the franchise.

Portugal's new premier, Antonio de Oliveiro Salazar, was leading the country through the constitutional process of becoming a corporative state modeled after Mussolini's Italy. The monastic economist intended to resume the posture of huddling under Britannia's protection. The concession to the French airline was cancelled, leaving Pan American to cling to Imperial's coattails in a tedious round of new negotiations for Portuguese traffic rights.

In the summer of 1933, Lindbergh surveyed the Arctic trail to Europe. It appeared to be such a marvelous route, he thought. All those nice pieces of land strung out right where you'd want to land. Evidence from earlier explorers was conflicting. He was looking not just for adventure this time, but for a return to normality for himself and Anne, still numb from the tragedy of their firstborn's death after being kidnapped from his crib while they were having dinner in their house in Hopewell, New Jersey. Departing from Maine, they took off in the Sirius for Newfoundland and Labrador, then continued to Greenland, which Lindbergh explored on both east and west coasts up to about 70 degrees latitude before surveying the west coast of Iceland. Pan American had chartered the S.S. *Jelling* as a supply and base ship for the Sirius, and Lindbergh was supplied with reports from Stefansson, the polar explorer retained as consultant to the airline, and from two scientific expeditions it had sponsored in 1932.

A quick look at the fogbound Faeroe and Shetland Islands was enough to establish their unreliability as air bases. After investigating several possible operating sites in Norway, flitting around Scandinavia and the Baltic, the Lindberghs made a surprise visit to Leningrad and Moscow. He concluded with some disappointment that the far-northern route could be operated only during part of the summer and that its promise lay in a distant future when radio engineers, meteorologists and aircraft manufacturers would have made flying and landing in fog and storm safe operations.

They had intended to follow the mid-Atlantic route back to America from the Azores to Newfoundland, but the harbor at Horta was too small to accommodate the Sirius—laden with fuel reserves, it required a long takeoff—and the swells in the open sea were too high. Amending their plans, they lightened their gasoline load and turned south to Africa; from Bathurst they crossed the Atlantic to Natal and flew home over familiar Latin American jungles.

At least some aspects of the Atlantic and its imperfect choices were resolved. Lindbergh identified Bermuda–Azores as the most satisfactory route for the present, even though the Portuguese islands in mid-ocean did not have sufficiently sheltered waters for seaplanes. The survey convinced him of the shortcomings of flying boats for regularly scheduled transatlantic service. They could not be used in icy waters such as extended part of the year as far south as New York. There would have to be seasonal changes of air lanes and terminals. Long Island Sound might do for spring and summer, but Baltimore, Norfolk or Charleston, South Carolina, would have to be the aerial gateway to America in fall and winter.

Landing a seaplane after sunset or in bad weather was too risky, because haze and darkness diminished the radiance of beacons and flares. According to Lindbergh's analysis of the market for ocean air travel, planes would be competitive with steamships only if they flew at night, although a forced landing at sea in anything but daylight was impossibly dangerous.

Through most of the Thirties, Lindbergh and André Priester were to debate the merits of sea versus land planes. From both technical and psychological standpoints, Priester fixed on the advantage a boat hull had in keeping afloat until rescuers arrived. Because the crews will feel less safe in land planes they will be more fatigued, he said. Lindbergh, equally concerned with the security of passengers and equipment, argued that seaworthiness of an aircraft was less important than ensuring that it stayed aloft. Better to eliminate the possibility of emergency descent on water by pushing the production of infallible engines and airframes, so that planes could climb to altitudes above storms and keep flying until they reached destinations on land.

Since aeronautical technology was not advancing quite as fast as his theoretical preferences, he accepted the reality that Pan American Airways would open service over the ocean with flying boats. When he made his survey report in 1933, he assumed the ocean was the Atlantic.

19

A New Deal

Pan American Airways was the godchild of two Republican Administrations. Suddenly, in March 1933, its sponsors were gone from Washington. President Hoover, the aviation-keen engineer, had succumbed to the economic depression he had thought he could cure with mild doses of technocratic medicine. Postmaster General Brown and his assistant, Irving Glover, ordered their papers crated—inexplicably, official documents were removed with personal effects—and retired, respectively, to Toledo and Brooklyn.

Trippe could no longer call on the Yale crowd of assistant secretaries. Trubee Davison had left the War Department to run for Lieutenant Governor of New York and lost. Dave Ingalls, his Navy counterpart, had been rejected by the voters of Ohio as a candidate for Governor. Francis White had quit the State Department to salvage private investments in defaulted foreign bonds.

A legion of intellectuals led by law professors and economists from Harvard and Columbia descended on the capital to fashion the New Deal promised by the Democratic President-elect. Although he had other priorities in the grim debut of his Administration, Franklin D. Roosevelt was keenly interested in aviation. He told a group of Senators that the nation lacked a broad aviation policy. Could this mean a new deal in the offing for Pan American? Trippe had to make sure it was as good a deal or better than the Republicans meted out.

Juan was a dyed-in-the-wool member of the party of Abraham Lincoln and would remain one in the privacy of the voting booth. But with Democrats in power for the first time in his adult life, he changed his outer coloration to nonpartisan beige so that he could proclaim, a few years later, "Pan American Airways has been a friend to all administrations and a favorite of none." In truth, he was a neutral opportunist; it mattered not what political label attached to government support for his airline as long as it was forthcoming.

Pan American had a line to the Roosevelt White House from the office of its chairman, C. V. Whitney, who had offered himself as a sacrificial lamb to the Democratic Party in November 1932. Having previously cast but one vote in his life and that one for Herbert Hoover in 1928, Whitney ran on the Democratic ticket for the Congressional seat from the First District of New York, an area that took in Long Island and part of Queens. He campaigned energetically, in a speaking voice that sounded like a mouthful of marbles, and dropped his middle name in the hope that voters would not associate Cornelius Whitney with the malefactions of wealth. Though the Democrats won the nation in a landslide, the First District of New York returned the Republican incumbent to the House of Representatives.

His defeat was far from ignominious, however. He lost by only 25,000 out of 350,000 votes cast, and Roosevelt was effusively grateful. Whitney nurtured the relationship. He scribbled little notes to the President, asking for appointments and pressing the cause of Pan American. The Roosevelts had the Whitneys to lunch at Hyde Park.

At first, Juan relied on Whitney to obtain audiences for him with the President. Trippe reminded Roosevelt that he had helped an astigmatic Yale freshman get into the Navy air service sixteen years before. Then he moved closer to the White House by other means. He placed Roosevelt's former law partner Basil O'Connor on a retainer of $1,000 a month. O'Connor was relentless in his flow of memoranda to the President asking him to see Trippe or to read a report endorsing a Pan American position.

O'Connor, a fund raiser non pareil, got Trippe to serve on the Committee for the President's Birthday which solicited contributions for Roosevelt's favorite charity, the polio-treatment center at Warm Springs, Georgia. Juan bombarded the President with Pan American memorabilia such as ashtrays and first-day stamp covers commemorating the inauguration of new routes. He had messages radioed from the plane that "Pan American Airways is an American-owned company flying the American flag using American-built aircraft piloted by an American crew." Roosevelt was fishing off the northern coast of Cuba on Vincent Astor's yacht when a Pan American Airways Commodore on a regularly scheduled flight from Miami to St. Lucia landed alongside so that one of the passengers, the President's son Jimmy, could say hello to his father.

Juan commuted to Washington by train to beat a path between the White House and the pillared castle next door that housed the State Department and part of the Navy Department. He was bent on preserving the special relationships Pan American had enjoyed under the Republicans.

Late in 1933, he drafted a proposal to set up an Interdepartmental Committee on Civil International Aviation along the lines that had previously been so helpful to Pan American. It was to consist of representatives of the State, Commerce, Treasury and Post Office Departments, with an assistant secretary of state as the chairman. He believed he could bring his influence to bear more easily on such a group than on any other Roosevelt might assemble as he groped toward formulating aviation policy. The Latin American airmail contracts would be expiring during the next few years, and Trippe had to safeguard their renewal. He planted the idea for a committee with the heads of major divisions of the State Department, such as Western European Affairs and Far Eastern Affairs, and with Under Secretary of State William Phillips. They seemed receptive. Stanley K. Hornbeck, the Far East baron, had made a similar suggestion to Secretary of State Hull.

Trippe harped on these themes. First, the relationship between civil and military aviation in future wars—a relevant consideration what with Fascist tub-thumping in Europe and the growing influence of truculent Army elements in the Japanese Government. Second, with government-controlled foreign airlines like Imperial, Air France, KLM, Luft Hansa and Japan Air Transport trying to monopolize air transport in certain strategic areas and gain trade advantages to the detriment of other nations, international aviation had taken an imperial thrust.

He raised the suggestion of an American international airline's performing certain strategic services that might be "politically impossible for the Government" or for which official funding was unavailable —such as installing emergency landing fields and radio stations.

The interdepartmental-committee proposal was batted around the Executive Branch for more than a year without the President's coming to grips with it until Trippe gave Assistant Secretary of State R. Walton Moore his draft. He was cultivating Moore, a former Congressman from Virginia distantly related to the President who usually greeted him "Hello, cousin." Moore took it to Roosevelt with the admonition Trippe had given him, that if the United States Government did not pay heed, other nations would preempt the entire field of international aviation.

Juan spoke at the committee's first meeting, reminding the members that Pan American Airways was the only international airline of the United States and the only such carrier not owned wholly or in part by its government. The competitive battles of the international air lanes, he declared, would be fought with diplomatic weapons, since each nation could bar the airlines of other countries from its airspace or admit them only on reciprocal terms.

Trippe relied on Bob Thach for Congressional expertise. Bob hailed from Alabama and had an unslakable thirst for Southern whiskey. He focused on Southern Democrats holding the reins of the major committees with jurisdiction over aviation, Senators Carter Glass of Virginia, Walter George of Georgia and Josiah Bailey of North Carolina. Trippe flashed his Eastern Shore genealogy to the Marylanders, Millard Tydings and George Radcliffe.

Thach contracted for special services with glad-handers and contact men. Their bills never appeared on Pan American books. His resident jack-of-all-trades in the Washington office, William McEvoy, was a convivial bachelor who wined and dined useful politicians of second rank and planted rumors with the press corps.

Ann Archibald, the rotund widow of a Marine flier, ran the office with the iron whim of a society dowager. When the company's cash position was tight, she sprinted to the Post Office to collect mail payments. As Pan American's fortunes improved and its needs multiplied, she was promoted to lobbyist. Her technique was not to catch flies with honey, but to command government bureaucrats to do Pan American's bidding.

Congress had been digging into the inner chambers of the aviation industry, especially the cupboards containing the airmail contracts awarded by Postmaster General Brown. In January 1934, a special committee of the Senate headed by Hugo L. Black, an Alabama Democrat, opened hearings on the subject.

Black employed the courtroom-packing techniques that had served him well as a county prosecutor and as a trial lawyer for the underdogs of Birmingham. Courteously, he led the witnesses to the question trough. When they shied, he took them down another lane, and when their attention was thus diverted, he led them back again.

He made them all tell their stories, the high and the not-so-mighty men of aviation: the operators who had bent their knees to the Great God Brown and benefited from his favors, and those like the scrappy Braniff brothers, Tom and Paul, with their passenger lines in and out of Oklahoma, and C. E. Woolman, the former crop duster threading his Delta Air Service through the Southeastern states, whom Brown had barred from his spoils conferences for being too small or too independent.

Joseph Ripley of National City Bank, who had already appeared before the Senate Banking and Currency Committee which had the dukes of Wall Street in the dock, repeated how investors from the preferred lists had been cut in on the ground floor of companies like Boeing Airplane & Transport, and how it had grown into United Aircraft & Transport and enriched them.

Most of the witnesses resisted at first, as though gentlemen didn't talk about money, or because they were angry or afraid. Black wormed the information out of them—how they had cleared millions from newborn aviation securities before the crash in 1929, and from salaries and bonuses that seemed so exorbitant when enumerated in the famished environment of 1934. It all sounded so clubby: everyone taking a piece of the other fellow's action, and their exchanging seats on each other's boards.

Walter Brown descended from the Olympian heights of Toledo to which he had retired in order to defend himself from charges by his successor, James A. Farley, that he had acted illegally and made awards on the basis of "conspiracy and collusion."

During ten hours in the witness chair over two days, Brown stoutly held his ground. He maintained that he had only wanted to build a strong, efficient air system for the nation, one that would carry the mail, transport passengers and throw off enough profits to spur the development of faster, safer airplanes, all the while preserving aeronautical leadership for the United States.

Brown showed himself as not a venal man but a pillar of an economic structure the New Dealers were starting to take apart and would put back together again with a broader base and sounder ventilating and security systems.

Farley relied on the Post Office Solicitor, whose inspectors were scouring the files of the Department to confirm the evidence oozing out of the Senate hearings.

He and Black assured Roosevelt there were sufficient grounds for cancelling the domestic airmail contracts and that the Postmaster General could do so as soon as the Attorney General gave his opinion that Brown's awards were illegal because they violated the mandate for competitive bidding. Farley's assistant checked with the War Department to see if Army pilots might fly the mail temporarily.

On February 9, the President issued an executive order approving the Postmaster General's cancellation of the airmail contracts and directing the Army to fly the mail "during the emergency."

The aviation industry was outraged. On February 11, Lindbergh, whose contracts and preferential stock awards from T.A.T. and Pan American Airways had been fully itemized for the Black committee, sent a telegram to the White House. Simultaneously, he offered it to newspapers for publication the next morning. It read in part:

> THE PERSONAL AND BUSINESS LIVES OF AMERICAN CITIZENS HAVE BEEN BUILT AROUND THE RIGHT TO JUST TRIAL BEFORE CONDEMNATION. YOUR ORDER OF CANCELLATION OF ALL AIRMAIL CONTRACTS CONDEMNS THE LARGEST PORTION OF OUR COMMERCIAL AVIATION WITHOUT JUST TRIAL . . . CANCELLATION OF ALL MAIL CONTRACTS AND THE USE OF THE ARMY ON COMMERCIAL AIRLINES WILL UNNECESSARILY AND GREATLY DAMAGE ALL AMERICAN AVIATION.

Stephen Early, Roosevelt's press secretary, accused Lindbergh of discourtesy and crass publicity-seeking in releasing the telegram before the President had had a chance to read it. Shy Lindy looking for publicity? The public refused to believe it. Early's statement loosed an avalanche of mail in Lindbergh's defense, cornering the President in a popularity contest with an unbeatable rival. Roosevelt had made his first political miscalculation.

A more serious mistake was to have accepted a general's word that the Army Air Corps was competent to carry the mail. The pilots were unacquainted with the routes and were inexperienced in night flying, and military planes were not equipped for such duty. A cycle of abnormal weather set in, paralyzing the East Coast and the Midwest with blizzards, windstorms and fog. Ten Army pilots died—four actually flying the mail, the others in training or en route to their assignments. Most of the public outcry was leveled at the Postmaster General, who was depicted in a newspaper cartoon and in a broadside from Eddie Rickenbacker as a murderer. Ever the loyal lieutenant, Farley shouldered responsibility for the disaster, though he was wounded by Roosevelt's failure to come to his aid or to utter a private word of comfort.

On March 10, the President told Secretary of War George Dern that "the continuation of deaths in the Army Air Corps must stop." Service was suspended for a week until the weather improved and safety modifications were installed in the planes. When the Army fliers resumed on a curtailed schedule, two fatal accidents and dozens of forced landings occurred.

In April, Farley reopened the routes for bidding, and by May the airlines were back in the business of transporting the mail. In June, Congress enacted new domestic-airmail legislation introduced by Black and his ally Senator Kenneth McKellar of Tennessee, who reigned over the Post Office Committee. It gave a temporary reprieve to competitive bidding for one year, but placed rate-fixing power in the Interstate Commerce Commission as Brown had advocated.

Severe restrictions were imposed on aviation conglomerations, slicing the industry in two. Aircraft manufacturing and air transport were forbidden to inhabit the same corporate shelter. In order to qualify in the new round of bidding for airmail contracts, reorganizations were impetuously effected, entities were spun off, names were superficially changed and executives tainted by association with Brown in the spoils conferences were exiled. United Aircraft & Transport split into several parts: the manufacturing side into Boeing Airplane in Seattle and United Aircraft in Hartford, while the United Airlines Transport division evolved as United Air Lines. Aviation Corporation hacked off American Airways as American Airlines. General Motors, which had taken over parts of Keys's North American Aviation, quit the skies to dominate the highways; it untethered T.W.A. and Eastern Air Transport, the latter emerging as Eastern Air Lines.

The new law inhibited interlocking directorates among aviation companies, and mail contracts could not be awarded to an airline whose officers were paid more than $17,500 a year.

Pan American Airways had not participated in the spoils conferences that were solely concerned with domestic routes. But Senator Black wrung telling admissions from Walter Brown about the awarding of the Latin American airmail contracts. The former Postmaster General was forgetful of the pressure he had exerted on operators like Ralph O'Neill and on Secretary of State Stimson to clear the path for Pan American. Black jogged his memory with correspondence from Brown's files. His reaction, upon being shown the letter from Thomas Doe of Eastern Air Transport complaining of being harassed by Pan American in Cuba, was contemptuous of Doe. Said Brown:

> It was his friction with Pan American, in trying to crowd Pan American out all the time and make trouble for all of us, that I did not like. We did not have time to bother with that sort of thing.

Senators Pat McCarran of Nevada and Warren Austin of Vermont questioned him about the maximum $2 a mile Pan American was paid. Brown was as unconcerned about the profits the airline was making with the subsidy as J. P. Morgan had been about the cost of maintaining a yacht. He had never even inquired. Why should he have? he retorted. A contract was a contract, he was "old-fashioned to believe," and Pan American was performing its contract.

That Farley omitted Pan American Airways from his wholesale cancellation of the airmail contracts struck some members of Congress and the press as suspicious, especially since the alleged illegality was the absence of competitive bidding in the award process. The Post Office disclosed that the foreign-airmail contracts had been under inspection for months, and that the Postmaster General would make up his mind about them after he weighed all the evidence. A spokesman for Pan American "welcomed the inquiry." Perhaps, said Representative Hamilton Fish, Jr., an Old Guard Republican from Roosevelt's home district of Dutchess County, Farley was too busy with his political chores to notice "that the Pan American Airways, whose chairman of the board is C. V. Whitney, a prominent Democrat, and who has on his board David K. E. Bruce and Robert Lehman, other distinguished Democrats, have a monopoly of the foreign airmail service."

Noting that Farley was chairman of both the New York State and National Democratic Committees, and was "dealing in favoritism and politics every day," Fish questioned whether the Postmaster General could act as a "statesman on Monday morning and a politician and dispenser of federal patronage on Tuesday morning without getting his various capacities and aliases confused."

Fish was aiming at the right target—of all Cabinet posts, the Post Office was the most political—but he misjudged the nature of the politics involved in the Pan American contracts. The Democrats were handling a hot potato baked in a Republican oven.

Trippe answered a questionnaire from the Black committee in candid detail. He had nothing to hide in the way of unconscionable remuneration or shifty trading in the stock market. Then he and Thach met with committee members behind closed doors at the Post Office and hinted that there was enough dirt in the history of the contracts to warrant reconsidering whether it ought to be swept into public sight. Brown's testimony was only the tip of the iceberg. Countries might be provoked to cancel the concessions for transporting the U.S.-bound mail.

The State Department seconded the warning, and when the matter was discussed by the Cabinet, other cautions were raised. Americans doing business in Latin America would be upset if their communications were disrupted. According to Admiral William Standley, Chief of Naval Operations, Navy pilots were capable of operating the Pan American routes, but he said he preferred not to have them do so.

State put in additional dissuasions: not only would it be necessary to secure the consent of foreign governments for military planes to fly back and forth over their territories, albeit as mail carriers, but since Pan American had made the contracts for return mail on its own, the

Post Office would find it virtually impossible to annul those numerous agreements simultaneously.

On July 11, the President signed an executive order directing the Postmaster General to examine and report on both foreign airmail and ocean-mail contracts. Pan American was invited to present its side of the case for cancelling or modifying the contracts at a public hearing on January 3, 1935.

It became painfully apparent to Trippe in April 1934 that he had overestimated his prowess as a diplomat. Imperial notified Pan American that the British Government wanted their agreement rewritten to make any assignment of rights conditional on a reciprocal award of routes into the United States. And that was not in Juan's power to give. From further discussions on the transatlantic telephone with Geddes and Woods Humphery, he deduced that reciprocity would henceforth be the sticking point on the Atlantic, if not everywhere in the British Empire. "I can't see much future for Pan American Airways on the North Atlantic," he admitted to himself. His formula of go-it-alone diplomacy was not working with John Bull.

He had let himself be gulled into believing that Geddes was going to give him an ocean in exchange for his letting Woods Humphery see the blueprints for his planes and radio equipment. He should have paid more attention to Sir Eric's remarks at Imperial's annual shareholders' meeting in October 1933:

> As you probably know, we are working also in cooperation with Pan American Airways, which, if I may be allowed to put it this way, is the equivalent in the U.S. of the Imperial Airways in this country: that is to say, it undertakes for the U.S. Government the operation of long-distance overseas American air-transport services.

His Majesty's Government pulled the strings for Imperial, and if it viewed Pan American Airways as a similar instrument of national policy, then it would want to settle matters with the United States Government. For Great Britain, imperial prestige and economic necessity were overriding considerations. Geddes and Woods Humphery had sold their government on an Empire Air Mail Scheme whereby mail between the United Kingdom and the Commonwealth countries would be carried on the Imperial Airways network without surcharge. No place for foreigners in that scheme. U.S.-bound mail would probably be dispatched from Montreal on Canadian planes, bypassing Pan American. And regardless, the price of admission to the Atlantic for a

U.S. carrier through use of the stepping-stones of Canada, Newfoundland and Ireland would have to include equal rights for Imperial Airways and its British-made aircraft.

There was the other rub. Lindbergh had talked at length to Woods Humphery in London during his Atlantic survey trip, and he wrote Trippe, "I believe we are considerably ahead both in our planes and engines." Imperial had nothing under construction that approached the planes Pan American had on order. In 1932, the British Air Ministry had wiped out a program to develop a Vickers six-engine flying boat, leaving Imperial without any equipment capable of transocean service.

Only two aircraft manufacturers believed they could meet the challenge posed by Pan American's invitation to design an ocean flying boat. Igor Sikorsky longed to climb to the next stage of aeronautical evolution. Glenn L. Martin, an early bird of aviation with an estimable record of building giant military planes, was casting about for commercial business to feed to his plant in Baltimore during the famine in government spending.

Trippe, a stout believer in competition for everyone but himself, pitted them against each other by accepting bids from both. In November 1932, he ordered three planes from each manufacturer.

Trippe extracted the maximum publicity by calling a press conference to which reporters flocked just for the chance to question Lindbergh, who had been shunning journalists since the kidnapping ordeal. He fielded queries about the planes to Lindbergh as head of Pan American's technical committee. Seated cross-legged on Trippe's map table, Lindbergh answered with a contagious enthusiasm that leaped out of the next day's newspaper columns. He said he hoped Pan American would be flying over both oceans in five years.

The task Pan American had set for the manufacturers was to disprove the current wisdom, rooted in the aerodynamics of machines made of wood and fabric, that large airplanes were inefficient in their proportion of fuel and payload to empty weight. Long-distance flying through wild fluctuations of weather with sufficient passengers and cargo to make the trip worthwhile entailed carrying thousands of gallons of gasoline.

The solution was to make every part of the structure responsible for part of the load, which would have been impossible if the plane did not have a metal skin. Sikorsky had observed that large seabirds had stronger wings than those whose natural habitat was over land. He burdened the wings of the S-42 with an unprecedented load, 30 pounds of weight per square foot. A new flap design in the wings decreased speed for landing.

The 19-ton bird cruised at 145 miles an hour. Its four 750-horsepower Hornet engines were more reliable and less thirsty than earlier Pratt & Whitney power plants. The blades of the variable-pitch propellers manufactured by Hamilton Standard could be adjusted after takeoff to an angle permitting less fuel consumption during long flights, an innovation analogous to shifting gears on an automobile. Placed in South American service in the fall of 1934, the S-42 reduced the Miami–Buenos Aires flying time from 8 to 5 days.

Sikorsky acknowledged that the boat hull was a streamlined imitation of a whale; but most of the external bracing, the "flying forest" effect Lindbergh disliked so much, had been removed. Lindbergh still had reservations about the S-42. He warned Priester that it would require an appreciable change in flying techniques and pilot training. "I do not believe it is a dangerous plane," he declared, but it "necessitates pilots who are also engineers."

The much bigger flying boat Martin was building in Baltimore, in the secrecy attending military construction, was scheduled for delivery in the fall of 1934. Pan American had commitments of $2 million for ocean aircraft. They were expensive: the S-42 bore a $210,487 price tag; the Martin cost $417,000. Panagra's newest land plane, the Douglas DC-2, was bought for $80,000. What would Pan American do with the flying boats if not fly them over the Atlantic?

Trippe and four executives asked themselves that question as they pulled their chairs around his map table one summer morning. Priester and Leuteritz were there, along with Evan Young, head of the foreign department, and John C. Cooper, Jr., an expert in international law Juan had just hired.

There were two options. One was to renege on the planes—a dubious measure, for it would subject the company to contractual penalties and damage its credibility with the aircraft industry. The momentum of Pan American's astonishing growth and leadership would be lost.

A prudent businessman might have argued that in the face of such overwhelming uncertainty, Juan should take that option, and be content with the prosperity the company was enjoying through its monopoly of Latin American air routes.

But aviation was not a cautious man's industry. It belonged to those who risked life, limb and financial well-being, and it offered no guidelines, historical precedent or consulting sages for America's only international airline.

As usual, Trippe talked about competition. The Europeans had been gaining on the Orient. The French were in Indochina, the Dutch in Java. British Imperial Airways had pushed through, via Cairo, to Port Darwin in partnership with Australia's Qantas Airways. Europe would soon be eight days away from Asia by air. An opportunity would be lost if Pan American, with the finest equipment ever built, were not to seize it.

The northern route to the Orient was still blocked. In 1933, Juan opened a dialogue with representatives of the Japan Air Transport Company about landing rights; but the air ministry denied access to Japanese soil and waters to foreigners. Right after the Roosevelt Administration recognized the U.S.S.R. in November, the Amtorg Trading Corporation, a Soviet Government agency, made an attractive proposal to Trippe for establishing a line from Nome to Moscow, but the State Department asked him to call a halt until the countries resolved the problem of pre-Revolution debts. What we will do then, Trippe announced to the four executives, is fly from California to China through the mid-Pacific.

They stared at him in disbelief. Trippe was proposing to operate a commercial service over an 8,700-mile airway when the longest distance regularly flown over water was the 1,865 miles of South Atlantic between Dakar and Natal, and that was by French mail planes carrying no passengers. Pan American's maximum experience was on the 660-mile stretch of Caribbean sea between Kingston and Barranquilla. The Pacific was the ocean of extremes: the world's largest, deepest body of water, 9,000 miles long between the earth's polar regions, 11,000 miles wide at the Equator, its floor as far as 35,000 feet below the surface. Ferdinand Magellan had conferred its inaccurate name after a violent sailing through the strait at the southernmost tip of the Americas. He hopefully believed he had discovered a peaceful sea. Other explorers learned the boisterous nature of the Pacific. Voyagers were trapped in its doldrums, lashed by the westerly gales at Cape Horn, awed by the submarine quakes that made its northern waters seem to boil.

Thirteen aviators died during a dozen attempts to fly the Pacific, ten of them lost in a race sponsored in 1927 by James D. Dole, the "Pineapple King" of Hawaii, who aspired to reap for his ocean what Raymond Orteig's prize had won for the Atlantic.

Six months before Trippe made up his mind, six U.S. Navy flying boats crossed from San Francisco to Pearl Harbor in less than 25 hours. The mainland to Honolulu: there was a vigorous market for steamships. Juan eyed it for Pan American. We can take it; we will have the planes, he said.

20

Pacific Partners

Trippe's decision to cross the Pacific was made as the Administration in Washington was trying to get its bearings in the conduct of foreign affairs. Swept into office on a tide of economic woe, Roosevelt concentrated first on a domestic program of curative measures and reforms. But before long he had to reckon with political unrest abroad, manifested in militant nationalism and the virulently negative ideology of fascism.

Looking toward Europe, the United States was in the position of a worried cousin hoping to stay aloof from a family quarrel, for there the disorders stemmed from the 1919 peace treaty to which it was not a party. In the Pacific, America was directly involved in prickly relationships with Britain, its closest ally, and with Japan, an erstwhile partner behaving more and more as a foe.

Japan's industrial strength, developed after Admiral Matthew Perry bullied the island nation into trading acquaintance with the West in 1854, whetted an imperial appetite. Japan appropriated chunks of Asian territory as the spoils of victories, over China in 1895 and Russia in 1905. While Western colonial powers were engaged on the European battlefront in 1914, Japan pounced on the Micronesian islands of the Pacific belonging to Germany. The Paris Peace Conference endorsed the seizure by awarding the former possessions of the defeated enemy to Japan as mandated territories. Under an ambiguous form of protectorate, the trustee nation could administer the mandate as part of its own empire but was not supposed to fortify it. The League of Nations, as supervisor of the peace, was to make sure that no cheating went on in the remote and inaccessible areas.

Japan regarded these islands—the Marshalls, Carolines and Marianas, lying north of the Equator and west of the International Date Line—as a security fence. An invisible "no trespassing" sign was posted at the 180th Meridian placing the ships of other nations on notice to stay out of the northwestern Pacific.

Almost from the beginning, there was suspicion that Japan was violating the terms of the mandate and fortifying the islands. After a tour of the area late in 1923, Brigadier General Billy Mitchell informed the War Department that the islands could be used as launching pads for a Japanese sweep across the Pacific culminating in a surprise aerial attack on Pearl Harbor.

With Japan accorded the status of one of the world's five great powers by the Treaty of Versailles, President Warren G. Harding was impelled to call a conference in Washington in November 1921 to rearrange the balance of sea power and to attempt to stabilize the new rivalries in the Pacific.

The conference produced a naval arms reduction agreement fixing a ratio of 5:5:3 for the largest battleships, cruisers and aircraft carriers of the United States, Great Britain and Japan; France and Italy accepted lesser shares of 1.75 for their capital fleets. Four nations, Italy excluded, pledged to respect one another's Pacific possessions. Fortifications were prohibited in the western Pacific. The treaty contained an escape hatch: any signatory could serve two years' notice in December 1934 of intention to terminate the accord.

Parity was a burr scratching against Japanese sensibilities in the 1920s, when a relatively democratic government was dominated by business-minded civilians pushing to attain industrial equality with the West and restraining the army's taste for military interventions. In the United States during that era of making money and whoopee, the inclination to pull back behind the two ocean barriers was sufficiently strong for Congress to prevent the Navy from even filling its quotas under the treaty.

The naval race continued on the level of auxiliary vessels such as lesser cruisers, destroyers and submarines. In 1930, President Hoover prodded Britain to convene a conference in London, where Japan extracted parity with its Big Two competitors in submarines and a larger ratio in cruisers and destroyers. That agreement also was timed to expire in 1936. Reading public opinion as opposed to rearming, Roosevelt carried water on both shoulders on the touchy issue of maritime strength. While advocating naval arms limitation, the erstwhile Assistant Secretary of the Navy could not tolerate a handicapped fleet. Early in 1934, he backed legislation for new ship construction up to treaty levels.

The political climate in Japan was undergoing radical change as the spreading blight of worldwide depression choked off international markets for its most important export products, rice and silk. In 1931, army officers precipitated the Manchurian incident as a pretext for overrunning the area and setting up a puppet state. Condemned for this action by the League of Nations, Japan quit the peacekeeping body. In 1932, militant nationalists assassinated the Prime Minister and other moderate leaders, and during the next few years, coalitions of ultra-rightists and military figures eliminated the power of the legislature and assumed control of successive Japanese Cabinets.

Since 1905, the U.S. Navy had been preparing for war with Japan under the assumption that the enemy would strike first against the American military base in the Philippines, which would have to hold out until the fleet steamed across the Pacific to repel the invader. Despite numerous revisions over a quarter of a century, the concept of a supporting chain of Pacific island bases remained, although the likelihood of activating the strategy kept receding as the Navy's strength was sapped by treaty limitations and reduced Congressional appropriations.

A facility was built at Pearl Harbor in Hawaii; but the Navy's original plan to fortify Guam, which lay in the midst of the Japanese-mandated islands, was frozen by treaty compromise. At the Washington Conference, the status quo of the bases west of Hawaii was exchanged for Japan's reluctant acceptance of a tonnage ratio inferior to that of Britain and the United States. In 1923 and 1924, the Navy conducted a scientific expedition (a transparent cover for intelligence-gathering) to several clusters of islands south and west of Hawaii. Although their value as shields for Hawaii or stepping-stones to the Philippines and Australia was recognized, no encouragement for developing them was forthcoming, and from then on the strength of the U.S. Navy steadily ebbed.

The move to set the Philippine Islands free, a decisive step in the U.S. "retreat from imperialism," was seen through naval eyes as a grave threat. In January 1933, a Republican Senate and a Democratic House of Representatives overrode President Hoover's veto of the Hare-Hawes-Cutting Act, which codified the Wilson Administration's promise, seventeen years before, of eventual independence. The bill prescribed a ten-year period of transition to self-government, but allowed the United States to keep its military and naval bases. Even Manuel Quezon, the normally pro-American Filipino leader, declared that the retention of the bases made "a farce" of independence, and the insular legislature rejected the bill.

Upon taking office, Franklin Roosevelt found Quezon's objections reasonable. A new legislative package, the Tydings-McDuffie bill, withdrew all military installations from the archipelago and left the naval facilities to further negotiation. It was passed by Congress and approved by Roosevelt in March 1934, and accepted by the Filipino legislature on May 1, the thirty-sixth anniversary of Admiral George Dewey's lightning victory at Manila Bay. Convinced its Pacific strategy had been dealt a lethal blow, the demoralized Navy Department floundered to produce a substitute.

The State Department was growing wary of Japanese maritime truculence. In December 1933, Ambassador Joseph C. Grew reported from Tokyo that a Dutch diplomat believed the Japanese Navy was so eager for an incident to match the army's Manchurian excursion that it might occupy Guam. Five months later, Stanley K. Hornbeck, director of the Division of Far Eastern Affairs, asserted, "The Japanese Navy is a menace to us." The danger of war with Japan imposed a need for increasing American naval strength, he added.

Persistent rumors that the Japanese were fortifying the former German-held islands were hard to verify. Fortification is more than the visible placement of gun turrets. The construction of airfields, railroads and fuel-storage facilities and the deepening of harbors can serve offensive as well as defensive military goals. The Japanese severely restricted access to the islands, and once Japan withdrew from the League of Nations there was little the Mandates Commission could do to check up on the trusteeship.

The U.S. Navy, on the other hand, could not proceed to develop the strategic islands under American sovereignty without being judged guilty of treaty violation. If only the Navy had a Trojan horse—or perhaps, a stalking bird.

In June 1934, the State Department's Historical Adviser received a telephone call from the Navy Office of Hydrographer. Under which Department was Wake Island administered? he was asked. The historian had not the foggiest notion. Why did the mapmaker want to know? An aviation company had been inquiring about a possible air route across the Pacific with refueling points at Wake, Guam, and the Philippines.

The historian consulted his files only to discover that Wake, lying 5,000 miles off the U.S. mainland, and a minor trophy of the Spanish-American War that no one had given a thought to for thirty-five years, lacked an administrative housekeeper. He concluded that Navy and State would jointly have to decide whether to grant a landing permit.

The interested company was Pan American Airways. Juan had

sent C. H. Schildhauer, a former Navy pilot, to snoop around the Navy Department and find out as much as he could about the islands.

The trail across the mid-Pacific from San Francisco to the Orient had one advantage over the Atlantic: a sprinkling of islands under U.S. jurisdiction where aircraft could pause for servicing. There were the naval outposts at Pearl Harbor, Guam and the Philippines and two groupings of pin specks in between. Midway, 1,380 miles northwest of Honolulu, was a coral atoll on which an American flag had been planted by a Navy ship in 1867, and subsequently ignored until a cable company set up a small operating station in 1903. Wake, 1,260 miles farther west, was a barren cluster of three uninhabited islets Trippe spotted while poring over the hydrographic maps in his office.

On October 3, Trippe notified Secretary of the Navy Claude Swanson that Pan American Airways had been making preparations to start service across the Pacific, and needed suitable marine airports at Wake, Guam and possibly Midway. He asked permission to operate through the three island groups, and for a five-year lease on Wake at a rental of $100 a year, to protect the large investment the company would have to make in constructing aeronautical facilities. The matter was urgent and deserved a prompt reply, he said, "because of the competitive international air transport situation in the Far East."

He also wrote a letter to the same effect to the Postmaster General, whose reply, released to the press, was interpreted as conferring the Administration's blessing on the transpacific service. It was important, Farley wrote, "if the U.S. is to maintain its position in trade with the Far East."

Swanson conferred with his colleagues at State to ascertain whether there were any diplomatic objections to the Navy's taking administrative jurisdiction of Wake. Then he went to the White House to acquaint the President with the dilemma of island sovereignty and to suggest that a commercial airline might present a heaven-sent solution to certain problems.

Another round of naval disarmament talks had begun in London. The Japanese were insisting on parity with the two English-speaking nations, arguing that the lesser number of vessels allotted to them was overt evidence of racial discrimination. It seemed quite likely that Japan would interpret any step to develop Wake, which lay in the angle of a V formed by the Marianas and the Marshalls, as a treaty violation.

Nevertheless, the State Department responded that if it was "highly desirable" from a defense point of view for the Navy to assume control of Wake, the Secretary should go ahead, but would he please see it was done expeditiously and with the least amount of publicity before the London talks ended. Otherwise the Japanese might interpret the action as retaliation for their denouncing the treaty at the end of December.

Ambassador Grew had just been informed unofficially that the Japanese Government intended to do so. He composed a stringent dispatch to Secretary of State Cordell Hull asserting that diplomacy must be shored up with national preparedness. There was a "swashbuckling temper" in Japan, he said, that might lead to "national suicide". Unless the United States was "prepared to subscribe to a Pax Japonica," it should build up its Navy to treaty ceilings and, if the treaty expired, maintain the ratio regardless of cost as a form of war risk insurance.

Grew recommended that the United States "speak softly but carry a big stick." Almost simultaneously, Hornbeck of the Far East Division was writing a memorandum to the same effect. Hull gave both reports to the President with his concurrence. Regardless of public opinion, the conviction in the Executive Branch of government was for strengthening the Navy.

On December 13, Roosevelt signed an executive order placing not only Wake, but Johnston Island, Sand Island in the Midway group, and Kingman Reef under the administrative umbrella of the Navy. The order, which was simply listed in a monthly catalog of public documents rather than being announced by press release, noted that since "a number of requests" had been received from airlines wanting to use portions of the islands as well as some of the naval reservations in the Pacific, it would be better if they were all put under one Department.

Swanson informed Trippe that a South Seas Commercial Company had applied for permission to develop the islands for a transpacific route identical to his, and also proposed another line through American Samoa to Australia, where it would link up with the British. South Seas, which was headed by Donald Douglas, a California aircraft manufacturer, and Harold Gatty, a Tasmanian navigator, offered to build land and seaplane facilities without charge to the government and to make them available to the Navy and other airlines.

Trippe responded in sweetness and light. He promised not to interfere with the other company, and would even let it share in the staggering project of making Wake habitable. But did the Secretary realize that this inexperienced little company would not be able to organize an efficient operation? It was unnecessary for Juan to remind him of Pan American's proven success record. The Navy's files were full of encomiums about Pan American, its cooperativeness and its potential as a wartime asset. The Director of Naval Communications pointed out that Leuteritz and his technicians could install radio stations and direction finders, so valuable "for both peace and wartime," more quickly than the Navy.

Without using the incriminating word, Trippe was proposing Pan American as the Navy's surrogate. Aside from the diplomatic fury fortification of the islands would provoke, there was slight chance for the Navy to obtain funds from Congress for the project. Pan American could establish an American presence and, at least partially, develop the islands as bases using private capital or, as Trippe had in mind, by turning on other government spigots to cover the costs.

After mulling the situation over, Swanson chose Pan American over South Seas. On December 31, he granted temporary permits for the use of the naval facilities at San Diego and Pearl Harbor, and the following March, revocable leases for Midway, Wake and Guam. Within a year, Pan American was allowed to operate over Subic Bay in the Philippines.

Japanese reaction was predictably irate. Why were American air routes being thrust so far into the western Pacific, where the United States had no vital commercial interests, demanded Admiral Nobumasa Suetsugu, former commander-in-chief of the fleet, if not to threaten the islands which were "Japan's first-line of marine defense"? Under the guise of commercial enterprise, the Americans were establishing military airports extending "to the gates of Japan," a Tokyo newspaper charged. American publications observed that Pan American's Pacific route passed through the middle of the mandated island area, and that with a slight deviation from the flight plan on the approach to Guam, a pilot could spy on Japanese submarine bases. Secretary Swanson readily admitted to reporters that Pan American was to turn over the facilities if the Navy were to declare an emergency.

A partnership had already been formed—between Pan American Airways and the U.S. Navy. It would usually be referred to as an "informal working arrangement." Navy personnel repaired and maintained airline equipment, tested its planes, rode on its survey flights, and many of them, from skilled technicians to admirals, retired from the service into Pan American's employ.

After he had his leases from the Navy, Trippe was able to buy the South Seas Commercial Company for a nominal sum. He invited Donald Douglas to become a director of Pan American and hired Harold Gatty to be his negotiator in New Zealand and Australia.

In the same vein as what had been done in Latin America, Trippe tried to sell stock to the powerful interests that dominated trade between California and Hawaii. The Matson Navigation Company was one. Just as he thought he was getting somewhere, Stanley Kennedy, president of Inter-Island Airways of Hawaii, a Matson subsidiary, announced he was planning an air service between San Francisco and Honolulu in conjunction with the parent steamship line.

In his top-level associations with the press, Juan had made an admirer of Roy Howard of the Scripps-Howard chain. Howard leaped to his defense. He placed his influential Hawaiian friends on notice that Pan American had a special relationship with Washington.

"The President and at least three departments of his official family are keenly and intimately interested in the success of this venture, because of the effect that it will have on certain of our national operations," he wrote in a letter to Earl Thacker, a leading citizen of Honolulu, hinting at press reprisals if Kennedy did not back off. Howard described Juan Trippe as a selfless pioneer:

> I don't know whether the Pan-American crowd will ever make any money or not. Personally, I rather doubt if Trippe makes any, because he's at heart a pioneer, and even though he goes pioneering on a cloud, he's just as much in character as though he rode a pinto pony, wore a buckskin shirt, and carried a squirrel rifle.

Thacker circulated the message, and in June 1935, Trippe smoked peace pipes with Matson and Inter-Island. The two companies exercised options for $1 million of Pan American stock and agreed to furnish a variety of services to the airline such as weather reporting and acting as its agent in Hawaii. Wallace Alexander, Matson's chairman, took a seat on the Pan American board.

Without waiting for formal permission from the Secretary of the Navy, Juan plunged ahead with setting up Pacific island bases. He assigned L. L. Odell, Pan American's chief airport engineer, to prepare an argosy. Odell rented a warehouse on a pier in San Francisco and chartered a freighter for a voyage of 18 weeks.

On March 27, 1935, the S.S. *North Haven* steamed through the Golden Gate laden with 118 men and a $500,000 cargo. Crammed in its hold and lashed to its decks were 250,000 gallons of fuel and a million items from channel buoys, tractors, motor launches, water-storage tanks, radio navigation components, windmills and diesel power plants to sustenance for twentieth-century Robinson Crusoes such as fresh meats and vegetables packed with dry ice into refrigeration vans, cartons of candy bars, toothpicks, books, films, a movie projector and tennis nets.

The cargo also included prefabricated plywood sections, plumbing and electrical fixtures for two villages. The technicians and construction workers were selected for physical endurance, building-trade skills and eagerness to test their mettle against the forces of Nature. There was no turning back from this voyage for a spare tire, or for instructions on how to unload in a typhoon. Also on board were three naval officers assigned to survey Midway and Wake for landing sites.

The Navy was besieged with applications from young men who had read of the expedition in their newspapers and wanted to join as laborers or colonists. They were sent a form letter that disclaimed any intention of establishing additional naval bases in the Pacific and stated that the Navy Department was "in no way connected" with the commercial airline that was developing temporary facilities on the islands.

Shortly after Midway was transformed into a U.S. colony of office buildings and residential bungalows, with radio masts towering above the sand and underground tanks linked by pipeline to refueling barges, the Navy used it as a base for war games staged in the area.

In his aerie on the fifty-eighth floor of the Chrysler Building, Trippe kept tabs on the progress by shortwave radio messages relayed to him from the set in Leuteritz' office. On July 27, the *North Haven* sailed back into San Francisco Bay on schedule with half its complement of bronzed explorers; the rest remained on the islands as permanent staff.

As usual, Juan left it to Priester and Leuteritz to carry out his farfetched plan against unreasonable deadlines. "He gave you your job and it was up to you to get it done," said Hugo, uncomplaining. Did Trippe really grasp the magnitude of the job of navigating the Pacific from the air? Or was he just a reckless gambler trusting to luck? According to Leuteritz, "He understood once you explained to him in layman's language."

Meteorology for the Pacific was fragmentary and scarcely more than hearsay. Synoptic charts, those regional weather maps essential for long-distance flying, did not exist. Wind patterns above the ocean had never been charted. An old flier's tale advised that planes would be sucked into a vortex off the California coast. Not until pilots flew between Guam and Manila would there be warnings of thunderstorms 40,000 feet high, of cumulus clouds as tall as Mount Everest and visible only when the moon shone. Straying into one of those cloud towers, the plane would be caught in a high-speed elevator.

Unlike the Atlantic with its crowded shipping lanes, the Pacific was sparsely trafficked. West of Hawaii, steamship schedules were so infrequent that the captains' twice-daily reports to the U.S. Weather Bureau were of little use in airline planning. There were a few weather stations in Honolulu, Midway and the Aleutians, but reports from the Philippines and Indochina did not include upper-air data, and the Japanese weather services in the western Pacific were uncooperative. As in the Caribbean, Pan American had to create its own information-gathering network.

Airline meteorologists established techniques for predicting typhoons, and for teaching pilots to identify different types of clouds. "Don't fly through a blue-black cloud or you'll really get a ride" was one rule of thumb. The information amassed was shared with the U.S. Navy and with national weather services in the Far East. Pilots were required to complete a course in ocean meteorology as part of Priester's perpetual correspondence school, and a new certification amounting to an advanced academic degree, Master of Ocean Flying Boat, was introduced into the curriculum.

The Caribbean experience was insufficient preparation for the long-range forecasting necessary to formulate Pacific flight plans. Eight air tracks were laid down between San Francisco and Honolulu. At departure time, a track was selected according to the most favorable combination of wind and weather conditions to ensure the safest trip and the most efficient consumption of fuel. With greater accuracy in forecasting and analysis, fuel reserves could be reduced and payload increased.

Pan American's flight-time analysis added two new phrases to the vocabulary of aviation. The "point of no return" was the limit beyond which there was no turning back. A supplemental point of no return was figured in the event of failure of one engine. Once those points were determined, the payload could be calculated. The "Howgozit Curve" referred to a progress report that monitored engine performance and fuel consumption in flight. Actually, five curves were plotted against estimates made before departure: miles versus gallons, gallons versus hours of flying, hours versus miles, and two lines for "ahead" and "return" conditions on three engines.

Between Honolulu and Guam there were no aeronautical radio facilities at all—a communications void corrected by the *North Haven* expedition. Leuteritz had been experimenting for seven years to extend the range of radio navigation. His loop device was adequate for tracking a few hundred miles at most and was unreliable in darkness and bad weather. To meet the challenge of the 660-mile stretch of open water between Jamaica and Colombia, he had initiated research on a different system. The Adcock was named after an English inventor who strung an antenna between four telephone poles corresponding to the points of the compass. By attaching dipoles to the poles and transmitting at higher frequencies and shorter wavelengths, Leuteritz extended the range to between 500 and 1,000 miles. After 1931, his experiments were aimed at the Atlantic, and a constant range of 1,200 miles was achieved. A plane could be covered for double that distance by the overlapping ranges of two stations. The pilot would be guided from takeoff at New York by the direction finder installed in Long Island until he was picked up by the unit at Newfoundland, and so on to Ireland. But Trippe changed oceans, and before the equipment was fully tested on the Atlantic, Leuteritz was transferring it to the vast unknown of the Pacific.

Almost everything had to be manufactured by the Pan American Supply Company. To supplement the big direction finders on the ground, smaller units were developed for installation on the aircraft so that the radio operator could take bearings on ships and other stations within an 800-mile circle. The Pan American ground stations were manned by operators discharged from the Navy with top security clearances. The Navy processed Leuteritz' requests for technicians as expeditiously as if Pan American were a government agency. Hugo acted as liaison with the Office of Naval Intelligence and the Federal Bureau of Investigation. Among their other duties, the radio stations on Wake, Midway and Guam tracked the movements of Japanese naval vessels.

It was obvious quite soon that transpacific laurels were not to be Igor Sikorsky's. He had designed the S-42 for the Atlantic and its British-held stepping-stones, a plane to fly 1,250 miles with 32 passengers, a crew of 5 and 2,500 pounds of airmail and cargo. By reduction of the payload, its range could be extended, but not enough for profitable operation of the California–Hawaii route, a distance of 2,400 miles to which a 500-mile margin had to be added for safety.

The Martin aircraft was delayed in production, and so Trippe's theory that the Pacific could be flown had to be tested on the S-42. The first of the Sikorsky series was christened the *Brazilian Clipper* and put into service in South America. The second was returned to the factory and stripped of its elegant cabin furnishings; every inch of space was given to crew and extra fuel tanks in order to increase its range to 3,000 miles.

In February 1935, the plane was sent to Miami for endurance flights in the Caribbean. In mid-March, Captain Ed Musick and a crew of five flew a round trip between Miami and the Virgin Islands non-stop, simulating the San Francisco–Honolulu run. During 17 hours 16 minutes in the air, mostly in darkness, they computed fuel consumption against altitude and cruising speed. Fred Noonan, the navigator, took fixes on the stars—the Pacific was to be navigated with a combination of direction finder and celestial methods with dead reckoning. The DF radio beam guided Musick out over the 1,200 miles of Atlantic to the Virgin Islands and back.

Everything gleaned from experiences with the Sikorsky was referred to Priester and his engineers keeping watch at the Martin plant in Baltimore so that changes could be made to improve the performance of the bigger flying boat. Then the S-42 was ferried to Alameda, the headquarters for Pan American's new Pacific division. Trippe had hired Clarence M. Young, an aviation pioneer and former director of the Bureau of Air Commerce, to run it.

A crowd of twenty thousand gathered to watch the S-42 glide out of the fog over the Golden Gate. "GIANT SILVER CLIPPER SHIP ARRIVES FOR TRANS-PACIFIC SERVICE," proclaimed the San Francisco News. "The world map shrinks as the trans-Pacific line gets under way," a columnist wrote. From Washington, the picture looked gloomier. The Post Office Department was withholding approval for a Pacific mail subsidy inserted into an appropriations bill by Senator William Gibbs McAdoo of California. Farley and his assistant Harllee Branch said they were unsure such a service was technically feasible. The Bureau of Air Commerce had been conducting experiments with a radio compass and direction finder developed by the Army Air Corps, casting doubt on Leuteritz' equipment. An eminent government researcher told Trippe that navigational science was too primitive for safe flight across the Pacific and urged him to postpone his plans.

The first survey flight to Honolulu and back was scheduled for April 16. Juan arrived in San Francisco on the evening of the 15th in a lugubrious downpour. As soon as he reached the St. Francis Hotel, he called Hugo to his room.

Trippe was jittery. He told the engineer that certain unnamed persons in Washington were skeptical about the adequacy of the navigation equipment. For the first time, he was questioning Leuteritz. Was his system foolproof? Would his communications net hold? Hugo enumerated the checks he had made on the direction finder. He reported that the meteorologists at Alameda were forecasting clear weather.

"I'm convinced the equipment can do the job," Leuteritz said. Juan was silent for several minutes. "All right, then, let's go," he said.

The next afternoon was as bright as the weathermen predicted. The S-42 skimmed the waters of San Francisco Bay in an arc, and with its engines drawing with the power of 3,000 horses, was up to the step and in the air in half a minute. The radio-compass beams at Alameda reached out to their Hawaiian counterparts, guiding Musick toward Honolulu. He landed in 18 hours 37 minutes, bettering by six hours the record set by Navy fliers a year before. The return flight on April 22 was another story. Musick bucked head and cross winds for 2,200 miles; his cruising speed slipped below 100 miles. The plane was overdue five hours, and when it arrived at Alameda, Van Dusen filtered information to the press. *The New York Times* noted that the men looked well rested, "clean shaven and natty, in contrast to the disheveled condition of most transoceanic fliers." Musick was quoted as saying, "A fine trip without motor trouble and satisfactory in all particulars. We could do it all over again tomorrow if it were necessary. I think this flight has removed the element of chance in the trans-Pacific journey." According to the newspapers, the delay was intentional; he and the crew had been conducting experiments on three different air tracks during the 23 hours 41 minutes of "leisurely" flight.

That they were lost for part of the time and that their fuel supply was exhausted upon landing went unreported. "Not once did the plane falter in its stride or get off the course," said the *Times*. Trippe, standing by tensely in Washington, telephoned Musick to congratulate him. "The results fully justify early inauguration of through service to the Far East," he said for publication.

The S-42 brought back fourteen thousand letters from Honolulu, the first mail carried by air over the Pacific. Trippe counted on postal subsidy to help underwrite the ocean service, but an airmail contract was far in the offing. The same newspapers that printed the story of the S-42's pioneer flight on their front pages tucked another report inside. The House had voted down the $2-million appropriation for a Pacific airmail service on advice of the Post Office. Technical doubts were given as the reason, but there was another.

Pan American was still under the cloud of the Black hearings. The Postmaster General had set January 3, 1935, for a public hearing as to whether Pan American's mail contracts should be cancelled or modified. Trippe and his lawyers were sure nothing worthwhile could come out of it for the airline. Reading the pertinent statute one day, Henry Friendly noticed that it gave the contractor a right to be heard, but no authority to the Postmaster General to force him to submit to a proceeding. Friendly recommended to Elihu Root, Jr., that Pan American waive its right. Knowing the evidence amassed by the Post Office was indisputable, it was better to remain mute and to continue by other means the campaign of convincing Farley that cancellation was not in the public interest.

Farley made a preliminary finding on the basis of an investigation by Department auditors. It confirmed what Trippe's foes had maintained for years: namely, that Pan American Airways was shown favoritism by the Republican officials of the Post Office. "It appears as if it was the policy of the Post Office Department to award every air mail contract in Latin America to the Pan American Airways System, regardless of whether it was the lowest bidder or not." There was exhaustive documentation of collusive practices to throttle competition and tricks of extracting maximum subsidy through subterfuge and infractions of law. During the seven years ending December 31, 1934, Pan American Airways and Pan American Grace Airways collected $35.7 million from the Post Office. Farley concluded that the foreign airmail service cost the government too much; Pan American was being paid at a rate five to six times as high as the domestic carriers.

In order to prove his allegation that Pan American overcharged the government on most of its contracts, and to establish the degree of excessive profits, postal sleuths attempted to analyze the proper costs of operations. They were frustrated at every turn. Account books for the various mail contracts were scattered through the operating divisions in Central and South America and elsewhere, rather than being kept in a central office. Caribbean division records were held in Miami and Brownsville; Chinese accounts reposed in Shanghai, the Alaskan books in Fairbanks.

The expenses of "off air-mail operations," or internal routes in foreign countries, were lumped with expenses of the U.S. mail routes and were sent to New York headquarters in homogenized reports for divisional operations. The practice of not segregating these expenses disguised the true cost of carrying the mail.

Pan American charged foreign governments modest rates while taking the maximum from Washington. Panair do Brasil, a subsidiary, operated a difficult route in the interior of Brazil for 50 cents a mile; the U.S. Post Office paid Pan American $2 a mile for a less troublesome pattern of service.

Statistics about the costs of overhauling planes and engines, and records of passenger-miles and seat-miles flown by different types of planes—the basic data for developing cost analyses of airline operations—were secreted in nine field offices, as the investigators discovered to their consternation.

Each division manager was left to his own devices within a monthly budget and simply held accountable for expenditures beyond the allocated amount. He had full latitude as long as he followed broad policy directives from New York—and Trippe was insulated from knowledge of activities in the field that might prove embarrassing. This blind-man's-bluff system of accounting was common enough in later years among U.S. multinational corporations and Greek shipowners for tax avoidance. Trippe's motive was not to outfox the Treasury but rather to tap the public—through the postal spigot—for his private vision. Arguably, it was a vision to benefit national security and prestige; but since the government had not agreed to bear the costs, he was siphoning the money covertly.

Though they were balked in their efforts to decipher costs, the postal auditors easily spotted the bulge in profits through the artful bookkeeping. Pan American's general administrative expenses were four times as large as those of the domestic carriers. Overhead for the New York office, headquarters for an expanding world empire, was charged to the Caribbean division, the unit in which 90 percent of operations consisted of airmail contracts billed at maximum rates. This paper deception saddled the Post Office with the tab for the engineers and technicians working at headquarters on experimental designs for aircraft and radio equipment and laying plans for air routes over the oceans.

Farley believed he had it in his power to void Pan American's contracts for having been awarded by negotiation rather than competitive bidding. Already scarred from the domestic-airmail donnybrook, he flinched from exercising that option. It was pointed out to him that an interruption of service would damage trade and diplomatic relations. No other U.S. airline had the experience, the equipment and facilities, and the necessary concessions from Latin American countries to perform in Pan American's place. And there was the specter Trippe kept on twenty-four-hour call: the possibility that airlines from other nations would fill the vacuum.

The Postmaster General decided instead to chop the mail payments to Pan American by 25 percent and perhaps to make further cuts after a more thorough audit. The airline would still make "a substantial profit," he declared, and the government would save about $1.7 million a year.

During the next nine months, the Post Office dickered with Pan American over the proposed reductions. Meanwhile, Trippe was experiencing the agony Ralph O'Neill had known in South America. For the first time, he was spending a fortune to develop a route before he had the airmail contract in hand. Farley was letting him dangle. "I don't know how long my board will let me keep spending," Juan said plaintively during his rounds at the State Department. "My board is worried."

As preparations were made to survey the Honolulu–Midway segment of the route, Farley said he would recommend the appropriation to Congress. The day Musick took off from San Francisco, the Postmaster General laid his final report on the investigation before the Black committee, and his charges of favoritism and overpayment stole the headlines. In August, just before the survey of Midway–Wake was completed, Farley advertised for bids on FAM 14, a weekly airmail service from San Francisco to Canton. The announcement noted that contractors would have to make their own arrangements for foreign concessions, a provision that had always favored Pan American; the specifications for the aircraft—a multimotored seaplane capable of flying on half its engine power at 1,000 feet, and with a fuel reserve to allow for a 30-mile head wind—could have been written for the Martin flying boat.

New strings were attached to the package, however; the Postmaster General's decision had to be reviewed by a committee of the Cabinet.

On September 25, Pan American's negotiations with the Post Office were wrapped up to its unexpected satisfaction. The $2-a-mile rate was moderately reduced, and the $1-million annual saving in mail subsidy was considerably less than Farley had heralded. In his letter to the President, Farley asserted:

> The contractors have not thus far made any unreasonable profits. In fact, they have not had any considerable return on their investments. They are rendering a splendid service in the promotion of relationships between the United States and the countries they serve. They are operating in such a manner as to build up good will and increase the prestige of the United States with our neighboring Latin-American countries.

He praised the airline's employees and the service performed, predicting it would "become even more valuable as time goes on."

What had converted an adversary into a friend at court? In the interim, Pan American had transformed barren Pacific islands into air bases. Airmail service to the Orient was to begin two months hence. National-security needs were being camouflaged. The Latin American subsidies that less than a year ago had seemed to Farley to be dishonestly diverted to airline profits were now perceived by the Cabinet as a worthy application of Congressional funds the Navy could not obtain for itself.

With the President's approval, the rate reductions and changes in service patterns were declared effective as of October 1, 1935. On Monday, October 21, the day set for the bidding on FAM 14, only one airline submitted a proposal. Pan American Airways made its usual offer at the maximum $2 a mile, which the Postmaster accepted, citing the service as "a boon to domestic aviation as well as the West Coast" and expressing the hope that bids would soon be opened for the Atlantic.

Trippe was confident of the outcome. "EXPECT AWARD FOLLOWING RETURN OF PRESIDENT TO WASHINGTON THURSDAY," he advised Lindbergh. And indeed, the Secretaries of State, War, the Navy and Commerce, the Attorney General and the Postmaster General, meeting as a committee, gave their assent.

21

China Clipper

Trippe scheduled the inauguration of Pacific mail service for a month later. It was touch-and-go all the way. The Wake–Guam section of the route was surveyed in mid-October with Musick's first officer, Captain R. O. D. Sullivan, at the controls of the S-42. Musick had moved to Baltimore to test the M-130 as it came, tardily, out of Glenn L. Martin's plant.

Martin was one of the quirky inventors of U.S. aviation, the third man to fly a heavier-than-air machine of his own design. That was in 1908, and Martin went on to manufacture planes, to merge with the Wrights and to break away again, forming his own company specializing in heavy bombers.

A gangling, wavy-haired Kansan who neither drank, smoked nor uttered profanities, Martin cut an odd figure of propriety in the two-fisted environment of the military contractor. A dapper sort, he was often seen in the company of beautiful women, but it was clear that his mother supplied all the love and housekeeping needed for him to devote his life to designing and building airplanes and surviving the machinations of aviation financiers. The order from Pan American afforded Martin the entrée to the commercial field he sought to lessen his dependence on government contracts.

His M-130 was a 25½-ton flying boat powered by four 800-horse-power Wasp engines with a cruising speed of 156 miles an hour. Its structural weight was half the gross load the plane could lift, an engineering advance in making large aircraft efficient. The capacity was for 41 passengers, although on the Pacific more than half the cabin space would be taken up with extra fuel tanks.

The hull was divided into a spacious lounge, three smaller cabins convertible into sleeping compartments, dressing rooms and lavatories. The crew rested two at a time in bunks in the tail of the plane while the other five members were on duty. The M-130 had the first aerial galley furnished with refrigerator, sink and an electric grill for preparing hot meals.

Illness prevented Martin from attending the ceremony marking the delivery of the first M-130 to Pan American. Trippe presided with Lindbergh at his side; he announced that it would be named the *China Clipper* "after her famous predecessor which carried the American flag across the Pacific one hundred years ago."

He remarked on Lindbergh's role, as head of the technical committee, in the development of the plane. Juan always wanted Slim's blessing on his aircraft, and Van Dusen blithely exaggerated the hero's connection with the Pacific project. According to press accounts, Lindbergh and Trippe had fixed on the mid-Pacific route four years before, and the M-130 was the fruition of Lindy's dream of an oceangoing plane.

Lindbergh had tried to wriggle out of the publicist's mantle Trippe kept dropping over his shoulders. Through most of 1935, he was too immersed in other matters to keep in close contact with the M-130 or other phases of the airline's affairs, and he asked Trippe to discontinue his retainer. He was working with Dr. Alexis Carrel at the Rockefeller Institute for Medical Research on a perfusion pump to keep human organs alive. And he was enduring the nightmare of justice brought to bear amid a circus atmosphere. Bruno Hauptmann, a German-born carpenter, was arrested in September 1934 for Charles Junior's kidnapping. The trial began in January and lasted for six weeks in a courtroom in Flemington, New Jersey, that was besieged by reporters and publicity freaks. Anne and Charles testified, and he sat impassively through the entire proceedings. Hauptmann was convicted of murder (the child's death having resulted from the commission of a felony) and sentenced to die in the electric chair.

During the courtroom ordeal, The Associated Press reported that Lindbergh planned to survey the Pacific route for Pan American just as soon as the trial was over. His "intimate associates" were cited as sources for the story, which recounted Pan American's past achievements and warned of competition from foreign airlines rushing to the Orient. The story was Van Dusen's hokum.

Under harassment by the press and by morbid celebrity-hunters, Lindbergh's frame of mind was warping. He would sail away with Anne and little Jon, in a clandestine departure just before Christmas, to take up residence in England. As he left, he scribbled a note to Juan enclosing the last check he had received from Pan American. "Whatever time I have spent on company business during the period this check covers I have been glad to spend both because of past association and because of the interest I will always have in Pan American," he wrote.

More than just a technical feat, the spanning of the Pacific was uplifting public theater. The drama of flight provided a distraction from somber realities close at hand, such as the bleak statistic of ten million unemployed, the magazine photographs of farmers and their hollow-cheeked children crushed by dust and drought, and from afar, the rumblings of predatory Fascist dictators.

Physical courage and scientific ingenuity were pitted against the intolerant forces of Nature. The cast of characters was all-American, including the quaintly named airplane. The hero would be the pilot flying the *China Clipper* across the Pacific. With Lindbergh unavailable, the starring role was assigned to a reluctant understudy, Ed Musick, Pan American Airways' Pilot Number One.

He was a bit too old and homely for the part, a slight, round-shouldered man of 41 who looked tall only when seated in a cockpit. His face was a mask, the brown eyes forever squinting toward a horizon. The officer's cap hid a sparsity of dark hair. He tried every brand of razor on his heavy beard because Van Dusen fretted about how Musick's 5-o'clock shadow would photograph. Musick loathed the chores the public-relations man inflicted on him: circulating at aviation banquets; posing in a Santa Claus suit at Christmastime to publicize Pan American as a freight carrier; catering to the press. "It's a job," he said when coaxed for details about ocean flying. Van Dusen told him to wire good copy during the first flight to Honolulu. "I'm a pilot, not a newspaperman. I wouldn't know what to send," he protested. "Send something about sunset over the Pacific," Van Dusen said. Musick wired, "SUNSET, 6:39."

The most color the researchers for *Time* could produce about him for a cover story on the *China Clipper* was contained in a sentence: "He lives quietly with his blonde wife, Cleo, has no children, likes baseball, Buicks, apples, ham and cheese sandwiches, vacations in Manhattan."

A birdman in his youth, performing before carnival crowds, and later an itinerant pilot for short-lived airlines, Musick had been cured of his daredevil impulses by a brush with death in a freak accident. He became infinitely cautious, attentive to preparatory details, or what

Anne Lindbergh termed "the back stairs of aviation magic." Like Priester, he acquired a reputation as a testy martinet. " 'Pop' Musick is as fastidious about his planes as an old maid about her kitchen," a newsmagazine reported.

Pan American's Pilot Number One had logged 10,000 hours and more than 1 million miles in the air without an accident. And for this reason there was no quarreling with his judgment about safe procedures. On the inaugural flight of the *Brazilian Clipper* to Rio de Janeiro, he encountered a heavy fog less than an hour away from the city. A reception committee of notables was assembling. Senhora Getulio Vargas, wife of the President of Brazil, was to christen the plane. Rather than risk lives, Musick brought the flying boat down in a cove along the Atlantic coastline, where it sat until the atmospheric barrier lifted the next morning. Since the nearest village had no hotel accommodations, Trippe and the press titans aboard had dinner in the plane, played bridge and took turns napping in the berths until the haze cleared and Musick took off for Rio.

As long as the American notion of masculinity held to "the strong, silent type," as personified by the cowboy, the frontiersman and now the pilot, Van Dusen could turn the drawback of having an inarticulate hero to advantage. By implication, the public need have no concern about flying the ocean because Musick had checked everything out so thoroughly. The trip was just a routine—"clockwork precision" was the phrase that appeared in every newspaper story—and nothing more had to be said.

The four survey flights of the Pacific route were reported on the front pages of newspapers. Rationing them to an island at a time, Trippe told his Washington contacts, habituated the public to the notion that flying the Pacific was as safe, reasonable and glamorous as hurtling across the continent in one of the new streamlined stainless-steel passenger trains like the *Twentieth Century Limited* and the *Super Chief*.

The next stop on the route after Guam was Manila, but the Philippine franchise was snagged in the campaign to elect the first President of the Commonwealth. The Pan American presence was linked to the sensitive issue of the United States' retention of its naval base. The application for operating rights was put off by the insular legislature until after the voting in September.

Once the election was out of the way, Harold Bixby's Philippine and American friends went to work, and on October 16, Pan American was granted its concession. Construction began on a base adjoining the

U.S. Naval Station at Cavite, outside Manila. The U.S. Asiatic Fleet Command assisted in raising the hulks of old Spanish gunboats that posed a menace to Clipper landings in Manila Bay.

There was a rush to attend to myriad details. The U.S. Bureau of Engraving designed a special 25-cent airmail stamp, displaying a Yankee Clipper, a steamship and the *China Clipper* against a blue-and-white ground. The proofs were shown to the nation's most prominent stamp collector. Roosevelt's mother had sailed to China as a child in a Clipper ship, and he noticed that the vessel had been drawn with only two masts. The plate was hastily corrected. The *China Clipper* was ferried to Alameda on November 11, and for the next ten days, Musick and his crew rehearsed for the inaugural mail flight. The day before the departure was filled with celebrations arranged by the city and state fathers. Trippe was the nervous guest of honor at a banquet that evening. Two Japanese had been caught meddling with the direction finder—attempted sabotage according to the FBI. The doubting Thomases were still vocal; Grover Loening, a Pan American director, found fault with the M-130, and who was he to be lightly dismissed? Loening was an aircraft designer, and moreover, the Martin had never been tested in the Pacific—a sobering fact overlooked by the newspapers. The Governor of California proclaimed November 22 Pan American Airways Day. San Francisco was drenched in sunshine as a hundred thousand spectators assembled along the shores of the Golden Gate and the hills of Marin County. The event was to be broadcast on nationwide hookup by the two major radio networks and relayed to the other continents, excluding only Africa.

Another twenty thousand persons waited on Alameda's sandy shoal, where the *China Clipper* bobbed gently in its mooring, an American flag draped across its nose. At 2:45 P.M., big Jim Farley strode to the platform that had been erected for the dignitaries, wearing a slight scowl on his usually jovial countenance. In his wake were Governor Frank Merriam and the portly impresario of the spectacle that was about to unfold, Juan Trippe.

A radio announcer intoned the momentousness of the occasion, noting that the original Clipper ships had set sail from the very same bay "across the perilous Pacific." Flinging superlatives to the breeze, he paid tribute to the Post Office, to the aeronautical industry and to Pan American Airways, "the standard-bearer for America and American aviation in the international field. On the wings of these sturdy Clipper ships are pinned the hopes of America's commerce for a rightful standing in the teeming markets of the Orient."

Doffing his brown fedora, Trippe stepped before the microphone. "The first scheduled air service over a major ocean route is being started under the auspices of the American Government, by an American company operating aircraft designed and built in the United States and in charge of American captains and crews," he said. Farley read a message from that "air-minded sailor," the President. Then seven men in navy-blue uniforms marched briskly along the catwalk into the front hatch of the Clipper as the announcers called their names and rank: two pilots, a pilot-in-training, a navigator, two engineers and a radio operator. Captain Musick was the last to step aboard. A disembodied voice, in the reedy sound of shortwave radio transmission, filtered through the loudspeakers. "Manila calling San Francisco . . . Manila calling San Francisco."

The announcer responded: "This is San Francisco; go ahead . . . this is San Francisco; go ahead." The next voice was that of President Manuel Quezon, delivering his greetings. "What far-reaching facilities for our mutual commerce! For travel! For international understanding! For peace!"

It was Honolulu's turn. The Governor of the territory rejoiced that his islands would be no farther from the mainland than San Francisco was from San Diego by rail, an overnight journey. "How swiftly moves the history of the world today," Governor Joseph Poindexter marveled.

Trippe returned to the microphone, his script memorized.

TRIPPE: *China Clipper*, are you ready?

MUSICK: Pan American Airway's *China Clipper*, Captain Musick, standing by for orders, sir.

Five Pan American Airways bases in the Pacific signaled by their code letters, "Standing by for orders."

TRIPPE: Stand by all stations. (*Turning to Farley*) Postmaster General Farley, I have the honor to report, sir, that the transpacific airway is ready to inaugurate airmail service of the United States Post Office. . . .

FARLEY: Mr. Trippe, it is an honor and a privilege to hereby order the inauguration of the first scheduled service on Foreign Air Mail Route Number Fourteen . . . on this day which will forever mark a new chapter in the glorious history of our nation . . . a new era in world transportation . . . a new and binding bond that will link, for the first time in history, the peoples of the East and West.

TRIPPE: Captain Musick, you have your sailing orders. Cast off, and depart for Manila in accordance therewith.

MUSICK: Aye, aye, sir.

Ground crewmen in white coveralls stepped forward to remove

the flag and cast off the lines. A band struck up "The Star-Spangled Banner," Musick opened throttles and the *China Clipper* taxied into a harbor filled with hundreds of small craft tooting their whistles. Gaining momentum in a veil of spray, the great bird strained into the air. Encumbered by the ton of mail in its belly, it leveled off at the height of the catwalks of the San Francisco–Oakland Bay Bridge, apparently bound to hit the span head on. In a split second of choice, the old barnstormer ducked his plane underneath and emerged free and clear. The crowd released a collective hurrah that echoed from all sides of the bay. The flying boat climbed higher, casting its shadow on the *Star of New Zealand*, one of the last surviving Clipper sailing ships anchored in the bay, before disappearing into the radiant horizon.

Winging toward the largest stretch of open sea in the world, where fiery sunsets were suddenly consumed by enveloping darkness as though Jehovah had snapped off the light switch, the *China Clipper* was suspended for eight hours in a black void between layers of clouds that shut out the stars above and the sea below.

Ground stations at San Francisco, Los Angeles, Honolulu and Midway guarded the Clipper. Every half-hour, Fred Noonan, the navigator, received a radio compass bearing, and at 30-minute intervals Musick reported his position. They spoke to a U.S. Coast Guard cutter 200 miles to the northeast, to a Norwegian freighter 300 miles due north, and to a U.S. cruiser 900 miles west. Whenever Noonan sighted a hole in the cloud ceiling, he wriggled into fur coveralls and leather helmet, opened a hatch in the aft of the plane and took a celestial reading. The officers changed watch every 2 hours, taking 45-minute naps in the berths, and those not on duty breakfasted together in the lounge.

At Pearl Harbor, the crew was welcomed with leis and speeches. Mail for Hawaii was taken off and a new cargo was loaded, including crates of turkeys and the fixings for Thanksgiving dinners on Midway and Wake.

The flying boat departed at dawn to race with the sun over the chain of volcanic islands and coral reefs to Midway, the only portion of the route that offered visual relief from the monotony of sea and sky.

Symbolic checkpoints marked the desolate stretch from Midway to Wake. At 200 miles en route, they crossed the invisible frontier of the International Date Line and were catapulted into tomorrow. A Yokohama-bound Matson liner was sighted on its eleventh day out of San Francisco. Transport ships of past and future saluted each other with dipped wings and smokestack blasts. After that encounter, they flew blind in clouds as thick as cotton using dead reckoning and radio bearings, and it was Noonan's pride to strike Wake's coral pinpoint "on the nose."

On the next lap, to Guam, they spotted a cruiser and learned from the exchange of radio greetings that it was carrying Secretary of War George Dern eastward from Manila. Musick radioed an invitation from Trippe (who was back in the Chrysler Building, monitoring the flight by the shortwave radio set in Leuteritz' office) to the Secretary to inspect the island bases and to join the Pan American staff for Thanksgiving dinner at Wake Island.

Between Guam and Manila, they practiced charting the mercurial trade winds of the Eastern Hemisphere. Musick descended to 1,000 feet so that Noonan could take a drift sight, by dropping a quart jar of aluminum powder over the side. As the glass cracked on contact with the sea, the powder spread, leaving a slick on the surface of the water as a reference for measuring the drift of the aircraft and the speed and direction of the wind.

As his first official proclamation, President Quezon proclaimed a half-holiday on Friday, November 29, and two hundred thousand Manilans lined the banks of the harbor to follow the plane's progress, charted on a huge signboard with a miniature Clipper moved across its surface. Two hours before the scheduled arrival, a typhoon-warning whistle signaled that the flying boat was sighted off the west coast of Luzon.

A tumult of voices, automobile horns, and factory and boat whistles rolled out to greet the *China Clipper* as it emerged from high fleecy clouds and glided over the bay, skimming the water to a halt. Six days had elapsed since the plane's departure from Alameda, the journey completed in 59 hours 48 minutes' flying time. The crew stepped ashore to be enveloped by newspapermen begging for lively copy. Musick threw cold water on their feverish curiosity. "Without incident, an uneventful trip," he said before he was driven off to the Malacañang Palace to deliver the first transpacific airmail letter, from the President of the United States to the President of the Philippine Commonwealth.

The *North Haven* set out on a second chartered voyage to the Pacific islands in January 1936. This time the project was to build luxurious accommodations for passengers on Midway, Wake and Guam—forty-five-room inns with wide screened verandas and palm-lined gardens. The ambience of a Somerset Maugham tale of the exotic East was to be included in the $799 one-way ticket from San Francisco to Manila.

New problems undermined the chances of viability for the Pacific operation. A cycle of mischievous weather played havoc with schedules. Twice Musick had to turn back en route to Honolulu, once when he was 1,025 miles out of San Francisco, because of brutal winds that reduced the *China Clipper*'s flying speed to 85 miles an hour. The engines of the Martin flying boat tended to overheat and had to be replaced, causing further delays. In a second incident, which smacked of sabotage, the hull of the Clipper was sliced apart during takeoff by a spiked cement block lying beneath the water in its taxiing lane. During the three months following the trumpeted inaugural flight, the *China Clipper* completed only two round-trip Pacific crossings.

In addition, deficiencies in the design and construction of the S-42 were exposed in the Latin American service. On two occasions, the Sikorsky "porpoised" during landing, bouncing violently into the air after its engines stalled, then dropping back into the water, injuring both its hull and the passengers inside. Pilot error during a predawn takeoff from Trinidad in April was responsible for a third mishap in which two passengers and a steward drowned. That two of the accidents occurred in darkness seemed to bear out Lindbergh's contention that seaplanes were especially vulnerable during night flying.

The prominence of some of the passengers and the loss of lives made inevitable wide newspaper coverage for the Trinidad episode; but the fact that during the two preceding months not one Pan American Airways Clipper was in operation, and that the airline was pinched by a shortage of equipment, escaped notice. Such omissions were a triumph of public-relations skill.

The former editor of the Yale *Graphic* believed the press could be manipulated with circuses and bread. His invisible hand was behind the promotional extravaganzas such as the *China Clipper*'s maiden voyage and the aircraft christenings. He played gracious host to editors and publishers on special flights to preview new routes and equipment. Bill Van Dusen dispensed the bread to the working press in copious material about the new aviation technology and beguiling tidbits about the pilots and the inaccessible president of Pan American Airways. He also churned out glowing articles about the airline under his own by-line without disclosing that the author was an employee.

The *China Clipper* was a magnet for publicity. Trippe authorized Van Dusen to strike a deal with Warner Brothers for a movie about the Pacific flight, reserving the right to censor technical material and the story line relating to the winning of airmail contracts. The scenario was a fairly literal dramatization of the history of Pan American Airways. To Van Dusen's astonishment, Trippe approved it "without batting an eye." The villains of the film were the weather and time, conspiring to keep the pilot from reaching the coast of China before the airline's landing permit expired. The tyrannical chief of the cinematic airline was a visionary who sacrificed personal relationships to further his dream of transocean crossings. The character was a composite of Trippe and Priester, with an Americanized dab of Rivière, the stony manager, in Saint-Exupéry's *Night Flight.*

The Musick-like pilot was played by Humphrey Bogart. After battling a typhoon to arrive at the destination on time, he grumbled about his boss: "I was just thinking how swell it would have been if he'd said thanks." The line invariably drew chuckles from those who worked for Trippe. His vocabulary did not include words of appreciation, even for those who executed his impossible demands.

China Clipper earned rave reviews. *The New York Times* critic regarded as "a pardonable enthusiasm" the praise for Pan American's Caribbean pioneering and the scriptwriter's assumption that a Chinese terminal for the Pacific route had been secured, when in fact, the negotiations were still going on.

Although FAM 14 was advertised as a route between San Francisco and Canton, the *China Clipper* flew as far as Manila and turned around. East of the Philippines, Trippe's plan to connect the mainlands of America and Asia bogged down in international politics.

Bixby had done much to straighten out the mess Trippe purchased in China; by 1935, C.N.A.C. showed a small profit and was operating without drawing funds from New York. His achievement was all the more striking considering the tenuousness of his support lines. As Pan American's Far Eastern representative, he had to pierce Oriental sensibilities while implementing the will of an inscrutable Yale man far away. "Maybe you could help inculcate the Heathen Chinee with Juan Trippe's Christian ethics," he joked in a letter to Lindbergh inviting him to visit China. Bixby had returned to the United States in 1934 to have his mission clarified. After spending four months in the New York office, he had Trippe's ear for ten minutes. Juan was preoccupied with the transpacific project and with the threat of cancellation of the airmail contracts.

So Bixby went back to China and did as he thought best. The one thing he could not accomplish was to make the Nationalist Government yield on letting Pan American operate an international service into and out of its cities. More than ever, the Chinese were fearful that the Japanese would claim equal rights.

Trippe then selected Hong Kong for his Asian terminal, intending for C.N.A.C. to fly a connecting service between the British Crown

Colony and Canton. He counted on help from his friends at Imperial Airways.

"We are using all the influence we possess to get the Government of Hong Kong to permit the service from Shanghai to Canton to be extended to Hong Kong," Woods Humphery assured him. In return, he expected Trippe to pry from the Chinese permission for Imperial to fly across South China between Hong Kong and Hanoi, the capital of French Indochina, as well as operating rights for a coastal route from Hong Kong to Shanghai. Trippe agreed to try.

Woods Humphery offered to defer operations for the coastal route for two years, "since it is the only route on which you can hope to recoup the money already sunk in your operation in China," but he emphasized its importance to the British. "Although I have no authority for saying so, I cannot help feeling that if we secure this permission you would be much more likely to get the full term authorization to operate via Newfoundland . . ."

Without admitting it, Woods Humphery was willing to postpone Far Eastern plans for the same reason Imperial was shilly-shallying on the Atlantic. Though by 1934, Imperial Airways had extended its routes to India, Burma, Malaya and Australia, with another major trunk running from Cairo to South Africa, it lagged behind Pan American in its equipment. With the exception of KLM, the progressive Dutch airline, all the European carriers were limping along with antiquated aircraft.

As Bixby described the situation to Lindbergh in a letter, quoting a British friend:

Everyone—even British—fly to Europe via KLM. If there are no seats and we must go, then we travel on Imperial. Only French officials who have passes on Air France and are too poor to buy tickets on KLM or Imperial—and can't wait for a boat— ever ride on the French line. That statement is undoubtedly too strong but it does describe the situation fairly well.

Trippe put out feelers in London and had Bixby do the same in Hong Kong. They learned that the British would ask for reciprocity in the Philippines if he were to make a formal application for operating rights in Hong Kong. Trippe knew that that request would surely be denied. Moreover, it was becoming clear that the Air Ministry in London saw the Crown Colony as a chess pawn in the battle for supremacy over the Atlantic air lanes and as such, too valuable to be surrendered without intergovernmental negotiation.

From the Chinese perspective, the British stood in the same light

as other foreigners, and Trippe surmised he could not deliver on that
score either. He directed Bixby to make secret overtures to the Portuguese colonial government in Macao. The oldest foreign port on the
southeast coast of China, 40 miles west of Hong Kong, Macao had
been settled by Portuguese traders in 1557 and had thrived in the era
of sailing ships. Its harbor was shallow, and with the advent of large
ocean steamers, the colony had been eclipsed by Hong Kong.

Macao was not half as attractive a gateway as Hong Kong or
Canton, but its harbor could be adequately reclaimed for flying boats,
and an adjacent area was available as an airport for land planes. Bixby
and his Pan American engineers were greeted as saviors, and after
Richard Long, Trippe's emissary to Portugal, prepared the way for
authorization from Lisbon, the Macao officials cooperated with alacrity
and enthusiasm. A five-year contract was approved giving Pan American exclusive rights to carry mail between Macao and Manila, to connect with the Pacific service to North America.

Work went forward on construction of a radio station, a direction
finder and docking facilities as though Macao were to become the
terminus of Pan American's Pacific service. Local authorities initiated a
housecleaning program, replastering and painting hundreds of properties in readiness for the first Clipper flight. Bixby pointed out to well-
placed friends in Hong Kong's financial community how self-defeating
it was for the British to refuse operating privileges to foreign airlines
like Pan American and C.N.A.C. unless equivalent rights were tendered. It was "obviously unfair to expect to exchange rights at the
small colony of Hong Kong for rights over the vast territory of China,"
he said. "It was like trading a button for an overcoat." He suggested
that if, as a result of granting rights to the British, the Chinese had to
give them to other neighbors as well, the Japanese would probably
build an airport near Hong Kong on Chinese soil "and thus become a
very grave threat to the safety of the Colony as a strategic military
base."

Swallowing the Macao bait, the Governor of Hong Kong invited
Trippe to send the first Clipper flight beyond Manila to Hong Kong for
a courtesy call. Juan directed Bixby to decline, saying, "While we
understand that Kai-tak Airdrome is excellent for the purpose which it
is designed to serve, we fear that it would not have the proper facilities
for handling a ship such as the trans-Pacific Clipper."

Little more was necessary to instill the fear that the colony might
lose its position as the great transshipment port for the Orient and be
left out of the coming air age. The bankers and the heads of the
powerful trading companies clamored for the Air Ministry to make

Hong Kong a free international airport, open to any airline that wished to serve it, and to stop insisting on reciprocity.

London yielded to their alarm. In September, Pan American Airways and C.N.A.C. received operating permits for Kai-tak airport, and negotiations were begun on an airmail contract.

The timing was exquisite. In the United States, *China Clipper* was playing to packed movie houses. Hundreds placed their names on the waiting list for the inaugural transpacific passenger flight which was scheduled for October 21. On the fourteenth, Trippe and Whitney led a blue-ribbon tour of fifteen all the way to the Far East. Because of the heavy load of fuel required on the Alameda–Honolulu segment, only eight could ride the Clipper on the first lap. The others preceded them on the S.S. *Lurline*.

The Matson liner reached Hawaii before daybreak on the fifteenth. Betty Trippe went to the captain's bridge to listen for the drone of the Clipper's engines coming out of the east. As the horizon lightened, the plane circled above the ship, and Betty burst into tears.

After a day and night of celebration—a revelry of hula dancing and feasting on roast pig—the group departed at dawn for Midway, united for the rest of the trip on the *Philippine Clipper*. At Manila, the parties lasted two days. President Quezon gave a reception to honor the Trippes at Malacañang Palace, with dancing under the stars. En route from the Philippines, Trippe sent a message to the White House from the plane:

> FEW MINUTES WE ARE LANDING AT MACAO AND HONG KONG COMPLETING THE FIRST TRANS-PACIFIC PASSENGER FLIGHT TO ASIA FROM THE U.S. WE ARE GLAD TO INFORM YOU THAT THIS FIRST FLIGHT WAS MADE DURING YOUR ADMINISTRATION BY AN AMERICAN COMPANY WITH AIRCRAFT BUILT IN U.S. AND IN CHARGE AMERICAN CAPTAIN AND HIS FIVE FLIGHT OFFICERS.

The flying boat touched down at Macao for a three-hour orgy of flag-waving, cheers and banqueting. The charade would soon be over and the Portuguese colony would slip back into obscurity, never to be the Asian gateway for which it had primped.

The next morning in Hong Kong, the travelers transferred to C.N.A.C. for an 8-hour trip to Shanghai by way of Canton and Fuzhou in Douglas Dolphin amphibians. Trippe emerged from his shell at Shanghai to charm the Chinese officials.

The Trippes and the Whitneys visited Nanjing and Peiping and then, while Sonny and Gee retraced their way back to the United States, Juan and Betty headed westward from Hong Kong. Robert

Lord, Trippe's browbeaten secretary, accompanied them on the arduous journey. They flew, in land planes and flying boats that seemed slow and graceless compared with the Clippers, on Imperial Airways' Empire route through India, Arabia, Egypt, Greece, Italy and France. In Paris, they had a luxurious interlude at the Ritz before flying to London. There was a reunion with the Lindberghs in England. Juan and Charles inspected possible operating bases for a transatlantic service. Then the Trippes doubled back to Frankfurt, via Amsterdam and Berlin, to board the Zeppelin *Hindenburg* for the flight across the South Atlantic to Rio de Janeiro. Juan had them listed on the manifest as Mr. and Mrs. Brown. Two newspapermen and Dorothy Kilgallen, Hearst's star reporter, were in a race to circumnavigate the world by commercial aircraft, and Trippe wanted no part of that sort of publicity for their round-the-world trip.

From Rio to Miami, they flew on a Pan American Sikorsky Clipper. When they reached New York on Eastern Air Lines from Miami, it was December 4, and they had traveled 36,466 miles in almost two months.

On August 6, 1937, Juan stood before Roosevelt's desk in the Oval Office to receive the Collier Trophy, an annual award for distinguished service to aviation, for the establishment of the transpacific air route by Pan American Airways.

"You well deserve it. You have done a grand job," the President said. Juan's face lit up with that devilish smile. Some of the aviation leaders who looked on believed Glenn Martin deserved to share the honor.

22

The Atlantic

While Pan American's engineers and pilots were conquering the Pacific, Trippe's second choice of ocean, he kept plugging away at his main chance—the Atlantic.

His representative in Portugal, Richard Long, was ingratiating Pan American with the Salazar regime. Long found a businessman from the dictator's circle of acquaintances to act as the airline's agent in bargaining for landing rights.

Pan American and Imperial submitted identical proposals—since the cancellation of the Aéropostale franchise, France had been receiving the cold shoulder from the Portuguese National Air Council—but Trippe took pains to assure Assistant Secretary of State R. Walton Moore that "we aren't negotiating jointly." He tried to douse the suspicion, planted by a French air mission to Washington, that the English-speaking airlines were ganging up against the French in Portugal.

But Trippe reminded Moore that "the British hold the key to the situation to a great extent, in view of the fact that British territories such as Canada and Bermuda would have to be made use of in the proposed service." He implied that he was taking care of U.S. interests and suggested letting the French fend for themselves.

In a spirit of noblesse oblige, Juan offered to keep the State Department "fully informed" as to his plans. He was requested to do so informally, "without involving any committal or responsibility of the Department." Moore was treading cautiously. An international air policy for the United States was still to be defined, and the State Department could not risk appearing to be negotiating on behalf of Pan American.

Congress had recently amended the Air Commerce Act of 1926 to give the Bureau of Air Commerce authority to issue certificates for foreign as well as domestic service, and Trippe had promptly filed applications for the various Atlantic routes, but there was no hurry about granting them. Both Secretary of Commerce Daniel Roper and Postmaster General Farley wanted competition for the overseas routes; after the Black hearings, they could hardly have been otherwise disposed. Farley had not yet asked Congress for an appropriation for a transatlantic mail service, since no carrier was ready to perform, but he hoped to choose from more than one qualified bidder.

Meanwhile, Trippe's British partners were in trouble. The management of Imperial had taken a drubbing in the British press, along with the rest of the aviation hierarchy, for falling behind the Americans. The inferiority of British-made aircraft was at issue, particularly after an air race between London and Melbourne in October 1934. Although the winner was a De Havilland Comet specially built as a racer, the runner-up was a Douglas DC-2 on KLM's regularly scheduled flight to the East Indies. After unloading in Batavia, the pilot took off and finished the race in second place. Another American land plane, a Boeing 247, edged out a British racer for third place in the 11,000-mile race.

The Times of London commented:

> Thus it has been held by implication that if the United States can produce a Douglas air liner and a Sikorsky flying boat then Great Britain should be able to produce something better than the air liners and seaplanes which cruise at speeds between 105 and 125 miles an hour.

Imperial would do better, Sir Eric Geddes said defensively, if the British did not have to pay three to four times as much for the high-grade gasoline consumed by efficient engines as the U.S. airlines, which inhabited a paradise of cheap fuel.

Sir Francis Shelmerdine, the director of civil aviation, and Sir Donald Banks, the head of the Post Office, began calling the shots for Imperial. In December 1934, the Empire Mail Scheme received a final blessing, and the two officials won a $10-million appropriation for a fleet of twenty-eight four-engine flying boats to be manufactured by Short Brothers to span the Atlantic and operate the Empire routes in the Eastern Hemisphere, and a dozen Armstrong Whitworth land planes for the European services. The days of stepmotherly parsimony toward Imperial were evidently past.

In the course of scouting for a site for a transatlantic base, Shelmerdine was confronted by a demand from the Irish to share in the agreement between Imperial and Pan American in return for furnishing territory for the facility. He conceived a plan to set up an Atlantic Company, 51 percent owned by Britain, 24½ percent each by the Irish Free State and Canada. In November 1935, he and Banks called a conference in Ottawa with delegates from the three countries and Newfoundland, to give birth to this "chosen instrument" of His Majesty's transatlantic air service which would tie Canada into the Empire chain of communications to the Middle East, South Africa and the Orient.

They intended to bar the French and other European carriers from the North Atlantic skyway by denying them the use of their stepping-stones. Trippe feared that the Atlantic Company would choose Montreal as a North American terminal and demote Pan American to a branch service for transporting mail from New York. Geddes and Woods Humphery tried to reassure him, and language was hammered out for an agreement between the two airlines asserting "it is the intention of the parties that each side should have a square deal in the sense that this expression is interpreted by fair and reasonable-minded men."

From Ottawa, Banks and Shelmerdine sent word to Washington that the delegates wished to confer at a government-to-government level. The interdepartmental committee invited them for December 5.

A week before they were to arrive, Trippe asked Secretary of State Hull to forward to London his request for fifteen-year operating authority between the United States and Britain via Newfoundland and Bermuda. The State Department complied, and Trippe followed up with similar applications to France, Germany and Spain.

He was asked to brief the committee at a meeting called to rehearse the U.S. bargaining position. Harllee Branch of the Post Office said an exclusive arrangement with the British was out of the question inasmuch as the French, the Germans and the Dutch were also planning Atlantic routes. "Without British cooperation, no one will be operating on the North Atlantic for years," Trippe replied. He reviewed his six-year effort to prepare for a transatlantic service and the rationale for his special relationship with Imperial. The only question remaining was whether the United States was willing to give Imperial operating rights.

Trippe said the United States ought to have a larger share of the North Atlantic service than a mere shuttle operation to Montreal. Branch agreed. "We have three points to trade," he said. "The right to land in the United States, the amount of business offered by the United States and the moral obligation of Imperial to Pan American in view of the long-standing agreement."

Trippe could not have put it any better himself.

On December 4, the State Department issued a press release announcing the conference and extending an invitation to "any American air line company that desires a hearing." Pan American Airways was the only airline to respond. "Who could possibly get ready in twenty-four hours but us?" Trippe remarked with a Mephistophelean grin.

Trippe and Woods Humphery attended the sessions wedded as tightly as a pair of Siamese twins, breaking away from some of the meetings to continue their business offstage.

On December 12, the conference ended with an announcement of a reciprocal agreement between the two Atlantic nations to extend operating privileges to each other's airlines and to share the expenses for radio guidance systems. The designation of the carriers was made in the oblique manner that characterized Trippe's diplomacy.

Throughout the negotiations, the interdepartmental committee scrupulously avoided references to Pan American—it discussed rights for "a United States airline company." The British officials consistently referred to Imperial Airways. After agreement was reached on the conditions for operating a transatlantic service, the United States was asked to declare Imperial acceptable, which was done. The British director of civil aviation advised the Secretary of Commerce that he was going to recommend that his government approve Pan American Airways' application, as forwarded by the State Department, if he was informed that the choice was acceptable to the United States Government.

Nine months were to elapse before the Commerce Department pronounced Pan American acceptable, and when it did, it meant that Trippe had obtained a fifteen-year authority to operate over the Atlantic without actually being chosen by his own government. By this appearance of merely responding out of courtesy to British initiative, the director of the Bureau of Air Commerce was able to maintain with a straight face that Pan American had not been handed another monopoly.

The British authorization for two round trips a week contained a restrictive Clause H, binding the airlines to "reciprocal scheduled transatlantic service" and explicitly withholding privileges from Pan American until Imperial was ready to start. Later, Trippe insinuated that the negotiators from Commerce and State had bungled the whole affair. Not at all, they replied heatedly: the new international aviation diplomacy was practiced with complete reciprocity.

After the conference was adjourned, State transmitted Pan American's applications to the governments of France and Spain. Trippe, on his own, made an agreement with Albert Plesman, the vigorous chief of KLM, to cooperate on the North Atlantic.

During the next year and a half, transatlantic bargaining took on a vicious character. "The whole thing reminds me of an electric fan," Trippe's harassed aide Ted Wyman confided in a letter to Lindbergh. "Anyone who sticks his fingers in it is going to get them cut off."

Juan's almost total absorption with the negotiations and his constant presence in Washington kept him from devoting much attention to the operation of the airline, which, de facto, fell to Priester. Morale among the fatigued executives in the Chrysler Building sank to new depths.

Trippe turned first to completing the agreement between Pan American and Imperial, a companion piece to the bilateral government pact. He was on the telephone almost daily with Woods Humphery in London, to review the contract. A serious point was the clause providing for a pooling of service. Elihu Root told Juan it would lead to antitrust problems under the Sherman Act. Root drafted a new clause in which the parties pledged to use their "best efforts" to help each other procure the necessary government permits and to develop the service, and to "cooperate to the fullest extent." The language about a square deal was reiterated.

The contract was signed on January 25, 1936, but the problems were just beginning. French and German air officials denounced the conference as an effort to freeze their airlines out of the North Atlantic and bluntly accused Trippe of putting the U.S. Government up to the deed.

Juan telephoned Woods Humphery as the French delegation was sailing into New York. "I always make it clear to them that I have a close working relationship with Imperial," he said. He signed a contract with Air France in February 1936 for operation of a North Atlantic service between New York and Paris. It contained promises of mutual assistance in winning concessions from their governments and from Portugal. Imperial was cut in on everything because of its "close working understanding with Pan American Airways," but the agreement was exclusive with regard to French and American carriers.

The French, long accustomed to cartels, mistakenly assumed they were dealing with the chosen instrument of U.S. air policy. The Roosevelt Administration was determined not to become hostage to Trippe's secret diplomacy or permit him to exclude other American operators from the Atlantic. Subsequently, the State Department informed the French Foreign Office that the Air France–Pan American contract imposed neither legal nor moral obligations on the U.S. Government and that intergovernment agreements would have to be made first.

The Germans had been building big four-engine flying boats and by January 1936 were ready to attempt an airmail service between Berlin and New York. In weighing the German request for reciprocal landing rights, the interdepartmental committee had to consider Hitler's decision to rearm and the unleashing of his anti-Semitic campaign with the passage of the Nuremberg laws depriving German Jews of their civil rights. The United States acceded only to permits for "experimental" flights of German planes and airships, including the scheduled trips of the *Graf Zeppelin* and the *Hindenburg*. During the next two years, Lufthansa* made two dozen survey trips across the Atlantic with Dornier-Val flying boats catapulted from mother ships.

Pan American was designated the U.S. operator because Trippe was the only American responding to the interdepartmental committee's invitation to join the talks. As part of the reciprocal arrangements, Lufthansa used the Pan American base at Port Washington, Long Island, and the airlines exchanged weather information.

More than a year went by and still no British permits. Trippe was convinced Canada was playing its imperial cards to have the Atlantic terminal at Montreal rather than New York. Was there nothing Woods Humphery could do to hurry things up? he kept importuning the managing director by telephone.

The Portuguese concession was signed in Lisbon on April 4, 1937. It granted Pan American permission for twenty-five years to operate between Lisbon and North America via the Azores and between Lisbon and Britain. A similar franchise was awarded to Imperial.

The interdepartmental committee was bothered by a clause awarding exclusive rights for fifteen years to Pan American against any other American company or individual, although the provision could be nullified by agreement among the governments. The onus was placed on Washington to have the monopolistic feature excised.

On the morning of April 20, the British Ambassador and the ministers of the Irish Free State and Canada arrived at the Commerce Department to deliver to the president of Pan American Airways the long-awaited permits to use their bases and airspace for a twice-weekly Atlantic service.

Secretary of Commerce Roper pointedly used the ceremonies to quash the impression that holy water was being sprinkled on another Pan American monopoly. "The agreements are nonexclusive and any

---

* The spelling of the name had been consolidated in 1934.

company properly equipped can obtain the same operating rights," he said.

Roper's remarks were made to refute charges by an enraged Glenn L. Martin, who felt he had been badly used by Trippe. Even before the M-130 was put into service on the Pacific, Juan had had Gledhill send specifications to aircraft manufacturers for a flying boat capable of cruising 4,800 miles, loaded with 8,000 pounds of mail and cargo, and with accommodations for 50 passengers "equal to the best available in rail transport."

The letter offered a prize of $50,000 for the winning design and no reimbursement for expenses to anyone. "I believe in tying the bag of oats out front," Trippe said.

Gledhill and Priester vetoed Martin's design, a refinement of the M-130, as being too modest in passenger capacity and too expensive. Martin was bitterly disappointed. Unless he received orders for a second generation of planes from Pan American, the only commercial customer for giant flying boats, he would fail to recover his development costs on the original model.

Trippe could not be swayed by loyalty or compassion. Pan American had to be first with the newest aircraft, on which he had driven the hardest bargain. He would push manufacturers to give their utmost and it was no concern of his if they nearly went broke doing so. "Sure, Martin lost money, but he didn't have the next step," he said.

The Sikorsky design, as expected, was the most advanced of all entries and therefore could not be delivered in less than four years.

Lindbergh, whose advice Trippe sought even though he was living in England and no longer on a retainer, believed the Sikorsky was worth waiting for. Pan American could not keep its enviable lead over the world's airlines in equipment, he argued, if it took just little steps. Big strides were necessary. How could Sikorsky be expected to make quantum improvements in his planes if the intermediate orders were given to other manufacturers?

But Pan American would be needing new equipment to fly the two oceans—it was already turning away passengers on the South American flights. And so, on the advice of Gledhill and Priester, Trippe settled on the Boeing design, which Lindbergh considered mediocre, and ordered six B-314s, at an aggregate price of nearly $5 million, for delivery starting in December 1937.

He tried to pay Lindbergh for the advice he rejected and for various other counsel. He begged him to accept a retainer once more; but Lindbergh refused. He would agree only to being reimbursed for $20 to $25 worth of cables he had sent during the year.

Trippe recruited Colonel J. Carroll Cone, assistant director of the Bureau of Air Commerce, to run his Atlantic division, which was established in operating headquarters at Port Washington. Cone, a former Army flier, was a political animal of Democratic pigmentation, a protégé of Senate Majority Leader Joseph T. Robinson, from his home state of Arkansas.

Juan also hired a 27-year-old lawyer from the State Department who had worked on the British and German negotiations. James H. Smith, Jr., a product of Groton, Harvard (where he rowed crew, was elected to the Porcellian and joined the Flying Club) and Columbia Law School, was assigned to help John Cooper with the Portuguese contract. Trippe delegated responsibility for operational matters, Smith observed, but reserved absolute control over the closing of contracts. He went over the completed document as approved by the Portuguese Government with a fine-tooth comb, taking a week or more to do it, then sent it back for revisions. Smith brought it to him for approval a second time. Juan went over it again, meticulously. He thought of another contingency to be nailed down. Back and forth the document traveled, the lawyers on both sides despairing it would ever be signed. "He was always nibbling for a little more," Smith said. "He managed to close his contracts just before he lost them."

In June 1937, commercial air service between Port Washington and Hamilton, Bermuda, was inaugurated at last; Pan American operated a Sikorsky S-42B on the 775-mile route, Imperial one of its new Short flying boats. Lacking Atlantic range, the 20-ton Royal Mail Aircraft *Cavalier* was sent by ship to be assembled in Bermuda.

Simultaneous surveys of the North Atlantic began on July 3. Captain Harold E. Gray was at the controls of the Sikorsky. A tall, blond Iowan of 31, Gray had been the first pilot to earn the coveted rating of Master of Ocean Flying Boats for the Pacific. He thought of his work as science and of himself as a pilot in the Lindbergh mold.

Gray and a crew of six flew from Long Island to Shediac, New Brunswick, then on to the new British-built station at Botwood, Newfoundland. The next day, cruising eastward at 156 miles an hour above clouds and fog, they passed unseen the Imperial flying boat *Caledonia* crossing "uphill" against the west winds. In a chill morning rain, President Eamon De Valera of the Irish Free State congratulated Gray upon landing at Foynes, the base on the River Shannon, after 12 hours 27 minutes. "It was a pleasant, enjoyable trip," he said.

Van Dusen arranged for Gray to "write a report" for a newspaper service assuring readers there were "no unknown quantities about transatlantic flight." The schedules were prepared according to mathematical formula by engineers who were "pure scientists." The pilots were merely verifying the facts, "getting acquainted with the ocean."

In August Gray surveyed the mid-Atlantic route from New York to Southampton via Bermuda, the Azores, Lisbon and Marseille. But there was to be no transatlantic service for another two years.

23

South Pacific

In the early 1920s, the Navy, wary about Japanese expansion, had focused on the islands of the South Pacific as a shield for Hawaii and the Panama Canal, and as stepping-stones for an alternative route to Australia in case Guam, the linchpin of the mid-Pacific lanes, was attacked from the mandated islands. Aside from a few naval survey expeditions, nothing was done to breathe life into the plan.

Once Japan announced its intention of abrogating the naval-limitation treaty, Roosevelt felt compelled to strengthen U.S. security in the Pacific. The only question was how to do so during the two remaining years that the agreement was legally binding.

Numerous pin specks on the Pacific map presented strategic opportunities and diplomatic obstacles. Some lay relatively near the Japanese mandates. The sovereignty of others, in the vicinity of the Equator, was in dispute between the United States and Great Britain; for several years, the longtime allies engaged in a surreptitious colonizing race. A British man-of-war would sail up to an island and deposit a few seamen to tack proprietary signs on palm trees, and as they departed, a U.S. expedition would land, tear up the notices and affix its own markers.

The President urged the Navy to find a legitimate means of occupying the islands to the south and southwest of Hawaii, a suggestion the department would eagerly have complied with had funds been available. Once again, a commercial air route offered a propitious cover.

Trippe had been contemplating a spur route through the South

Pacific to Australia—a significant market for the United States, second to the entire Far East. By steamship, Australia was closer to Europe if one traveled over the Atlantic and Pacific rather than by way of the Mediterranean, the Suez Canal, the Red Sea and the Indian Ocean. He emphasized the importance for American business of maintaining that advantage in the air.

One possible track over the 7,000 miles of ocean between San Francisco and Brisbane lay via Hawaii, one of the equatorial islands such as Canton, and the British colony of Fiji. A less direct path could be plotted from Hawaii to the American-held Kingman Reef and Pago Pago to Auckland, New Zealand.

In March 1935, as the *North Haven* was setting forth to colonize the mid-Pacific islands, the Bureau of Air Commerce launched a secret expedition to the equatorial islands lying south of Hawaii on the eastern side of the International Date Line. Enlisted Army men on leave were sent from a ship to take weather readings, study the vegetation and survey the terrain for landing fields on Jarvis, Baker and Howland Islands. Howland was only 400 miles from the Japanese Micronesian chain.

In June, Juan called at the Navy and State Departments accompanied by John Cooper. His vice president and specialist in the new field of international aerial law was erudite and rather pompous, a perfect errand boy for Trippe on the diplomatic circuit.

Juan was bubbling with enthusiasm about guano, a forgotten topic into which the State Department's researchers had just been delving. Nineteenth-century clipper captains sailing back from the Orient were the first to become interested in guano, the excrement of seabirds useful as fertilizer. In 1856, Congress passed the Guano Act, which provided that a U.S. citizen who discovered the bird manure on an island not occupied by another government could take peaceful possession of the territory and thereby obtain the exclusive right to the guano and the protection of the U.S. Army and Navy.

Trippe imparted two gems of information. The Oceanic Nitrates Corporation was preparing to scout for guano on Jarvis, Baker and Howland. It was unclear whether the United States or Britain had title to the islands. Although Trippe and Cooper disavowed a connection between Oceanic and Pan American, Juan had recently chartered the nitrates company—"the little company we formed under the bridge," as he referred to it privately. Its Park Row address was a stone's throw from the Brooklyn Bridge, and his old friend Dave Robins was president of the corporate shell. Trippe demanded government assistance for the expedition as a matter of national interest, for guano prospectors could establish U.S. sovereignty over the islands "promptly and quietly." He said he had learned that the British were about to survey them for an Imperial Airways route.

Two weeks later, the yacht *Kinkajou*, chartered by Oceanic, set sail from Honolulu under the direction of a Johns Hopkins University professor, ostensibly to study fish and bird life and investigate guano deposits. Harold Gatty, just back from a mission to Australia for Trippe, was aboard. Assisted by the Navy and the Coast Guard, the *Kinkajou*, which was fitted with equipment for aeronautical and radio tests, toured the islands for three months, filing coded messages to the Pan American station at Honolulu.

When the tour was completed, Cooper reported favorable collections of bird droppings to the State Department and asked that Jarvis Island be placed under the jurisdiction of the Interior Department so that Oceanic could secure a mining license and recover its prospecting costs. Such a license would confer exclusive use of the island on Oceanic, a privilege that could be exercised to keep out Pan American's competitors.

In March 1936, the President acted. He entrusted the islands to the Interior Department, not to accommodate Trippe but because the State Department feared the Japanese would protest if the Navy were to take them over. Interior sent out several colonizing expeditions to tuck the islands under U.S. sovereignty. Oceanic's request for a license was denied, and Juan was out of the mining business as quickly as he had gone into it.

Howland was a sea-gull roost with a single attractive feature, its proximity to the Japanese outposts. The President drew funds from the Works Progress Administration (W.P.A.) to build a landing field on the island so that Amelia Earhart could touch down for refueling on her round-the-world trip.

At 39, Earhart was America's heroine of the air, the first woman to fly the Atlantic (in 1928), the first person to make a solo flight from Hawaii to the mainland (in 1935). The press referred to her as "Lady Lindy," and indeed, she bore an uncanny resemblance to Lindbergh with her cropped hair, scrubbed Anglo-Saxon wholesomeness and slim figure clad in leather jackets and trousers.

Earhart's was a private journey for which she asked and received government cooperation. What was the quid pro quo? She had planned to fly from Honolulu to Tokyo and refuel, with the Navy's aid, in the air over Midway. In December 1936, she changed her routing to Brisbane because of the promise of the landing field at Howland. Her navigator was Fred Noonan of *China Clipper* renown, who had been dismissed by Pan American because of his uncontrollable drinking habit. Earhart and Noonan left Lae, New Guinea, on July 2, 1937, supposedly bound for Howland. Navy ships tracked their progress. The last radio communication carried her worried voice announcing a diminishing supply of gas and a position some 100 miles off her island destination.

Despite an intensive search by the Navy, to which Pan American lent its radio facilities, Earhart and Noonan had vanished. Suspicions were aroused that she had been on an intelligence mission to observe and perhaps photograph the fortifications of the Micronesian islands. Clues indicating that she had deliberately flown off course, been captured and died with Noonan in Japanese hands were discovered during the Second World War and subsequently. Numerous investigations foundered on official silence in Tokyo and Washington, leaving the fate of Amelia Earhart an everlasting mystery.

The South Pacific airway was blocked by the British lion. Fulfilling the Empire Air Mail Scheme, Imperial Airways reached Australia through the Middle East, Burma and Malaya. East of Singapore, Imperial operated in partnership with Qantas Airways, the pride of Australia. From Brisbane, the empire route was to continue across the Pacific to Vancouver, link up with a Canadian air service and connect with the ephemeral Atlantic service.

The sine qua non of Pacific operations was Hawaii, which the U.S. War Department adamantly opposed opening to foreign aircraft. So tit for tat, the British denied Fiji to Pan American. The Australians were also inhospitable. Trippe was back where he'd left off on the Atlantic, stymied by reciprocity.

He dusted off his Macao ploy and sent Harold Gatty to Wellington to negotiate a postal concession. New Zealanders were apprehensive that their Dominion might be left out of the Empire Air Mail circuit. A clause in the contract provided for termination in the event a British airline was refused permission to land at a U.S. port—a patent attempt at getting Pan American to bind its government to open Hawaii. Cooper assured Secretary of State Hull that the clause was meaningless, just something the New Zealanders had inserted to keep London happy. Hull was not appeased. He instructed the consul in Wellington to tell the Prime Minister that the United States would not be bound by a private company.

A year elapsed. Short of equipment and plagued by assorted problems on the mid-Pacific, Pan American failed to exercise the concession. When Gatty requested an extension, the New Zealanders tried to hold his feet to the fire: no extension would be granted without a promise that Pan American would use its presumed influence with the U.S. Government to secure reciprocal privileges for a British airline.

This did not go down well in Washington. Once again, Pan American's unilateral negotiations with a foreign government were creating a diplomatic contretemps. Moreover, Trippe was asking the Post Office to defray the expenses of the New Zealand service by awarding a $1.4-million mail contract. With the New Zealand concession sewed up, Pan American would be the only airline in a position to bid on the San Francisco–Auckland mail route, and in the absence of competition, it would bid the maximum $2 a mile.

The committee insisted that Gatty write a sharp letter to the Prime Minister—a peculiar missive from a businessman to a head of government—declaring his lack of authority to obligate the United States. The State Department sent a communiqué to the same effect. The committee fully understood the implications of Pan American's private deal with New Zealand for the much more important transatlantic route.

The phobia of isolation and the need for an aerial connection to the outside world were overriding for New Zealand. The Prime Minister accepted the rebuff and granted the extension, reminding Gatty that Pan American's obligation was "entirely one of honour."

Hasty preparations were made to survey the route. Little was known except the temperamental nature of the weather in the South Pacific, the incubator for typhoons and hurricanes that wreaked damage on the mid-Pacific and the China Seas. With the three M-130s engaged on the San Francisco–Manila run, it was decided to outfit a Sikorsky S-42B with extra fuel tanks, name it the *Samoan Clipper* and use it to open a bare-bones mail service.

Musick was none too happy about his assignment to be the South Pacific pathfinder. He had just received the Harmon Trophy, an aviation prize previously awarded to two other fliers, Charles Lindbergh and Wiley Post, who had set records circumnavigating the globe and then been killed in a crash in Alaska. Ed was weary from tension and overwork, a chronic condition among operating personnel in the Pacific division. He had expected the route to be flown with Boeing 314s, but the larger planes had not been delivered. Pan American Airways Pilot Number One accepted his lot and wore a glummer expression than usual.

On the morning of January 11, 1938, in the course of the *Samoan Clipper*'s second scheduled trip, Musick took off before dawn from Pago Pago, heading for Auckland. Two hours 20 minutes later, the radio operator at the American Samoan station received a message from him that the number four engine had developed an oil leak. Musick was turning back, expecting to land at 8:30 A.M.

At 8:27 A.M. he reported that he was 74 miles west of Pago Pago and dumping fuel to lighten his load before landing in 10 minutes. There was no immediate concern because of the Sikorsky's vaunted ability to operate with one or more engines disabled. When the plane was overdue and its radio silent, the Navy began to search the area. The next morning, a Navy pilot spotted an oil slick 14 miles northwest of Pago Pago. He followed it until he saw the detritus bobbing on the swells of sapphire water. A navy-blue jacket with a Pan American emblem of the winged globe on a pocket. A pair of trousers with a tie clasp in one pocket. A desk drawer containing navigator's instruments, half-burned remnants of an engineering log and cargo manifests. A sprinkling of charred airplane parts gave evidence of an explosion. There was no likelihood of recovering any parts of the seven crewmen's bodies from the shark-infested waters, the naval report noted.

Musick the meticulous, whose very name was synonymous with safety and public confidence in flying, had died by fire, the element of danger he had told his friends he feared the most and prepared most diligently to avoid.

An investigation confirmed that the fuel-dumping valves, positioned under the amphibian's high wings, had been too close to the engine exhausts and that the vaporization of the escaping gasoline had induced a combustible process. The Bureau of Air Commerce disclosed that it had forbidden fuel dumping on the Sikorsky S-42 series the previous October, pending further tests, but that the order had not been applied to the *Samoan Clipper* because it carried no passengers.

With one less plane in the already shrunken Pan American fleet, service to New Zealand was suspended.

24

Threat of Competition

Grover Loening was the bristling egotist on the Pan American board of directors. A small, peevish man, he had served from the very beginning. Perhaps because he was jealous of the larger stature in the industry of the other aircraft manufacturers on the board —Donald Douglas, Sherman Fairchild and Fred Rentschler—he was the most assertive in criticizing the course on which Trippe was guiding the company.

Loening believed the Pacific operation was inherently dangerous and unprofitable. He disapproved of the drain it caused on earnings from the South American routes. "Earnings first and prestige of our system second, this is sound business. More lines on the map of the world in PAA's colors do not necessarily mean larger net earnings," he lectured Juan.

"The Atlantic run will be to Pan American what the Alleghenies are to T.W.A. and United," he said, alluding to its turbulent weather. According to Loening, Pan American management was not up to handling a transatlantic operation.

He reserved his sharpest words for Pan American's procurement program. "We are pretty incompetent technically," he said. "Our weak point is in the airplane engineering side." He cited at length the flaws in the S-42 and dismissed the M-130 as out of date. "The flying boat is a myth in forced landings in the Atlantic. It will never get up again," he said.

Finally, Loening thought Juan was dead wrong in striving to monopolize the international air routes. He predicted "a political rumpus" if he persisted. In light of both Democratic and Republican policies, "monopoly won't last," he declared.

Juan was as polite and uncommunicative with Loening as with his other directors, but he wounded his vanity by refusing to retain him as a technical consultant. In the spring of 1937, Loening told Trippe he would not stand for reelection to the board. Thereupon he became a vociferous foe, in the capacity of aviation consultant to Joseph P. Kennedy, chairman of the U.S. Maritime Commission.

After the explosive hearings on the airlines, Senator Hugo Black had turned his investigation back to the ocean-mail contracts and harvested a bumper crop of scandal: relevations of exorbitant subsidies to shippers for delivering modest cargoes of mail, and of an archaic merchant fleet that *Fortune* decried as a "disgrace even to a second-rate nation." Roosevelt ordered the Post Office to conduct a study in tandem with its airmail investigation.

In January 1935, Farley recommended cancellation of most of the contracts and revision of the formula for shipping subsidies. The President batted the problem back to Congress, and for more than a year Black dueled with the hardy shipping interests to hammer through the Merchant Marine Act of 1936. It created a five-man commission with broad powers of investigation, administration and rate-fixing. To head the agency, Roosevelt tapped Kennedy, a tough, cynical financier who had distinguished himself as the first chairman of the Securities and Exchange Commission.

With Pan American already winging across the Pacific and designated for the Atlantic, Kennedy had to consider the implications of the airplane's overtaking the steamship. Loening urged him to reach out and assert jurisdiction over the airline. This he could do by pressing for an amendment to the Merchant Marine Act enlarging the definition of a "vessel" to include oceangoing aircraft. There was "no reason for turning over the rule of the air in America's foreign air commerce to Trippe, the Whitneys, the Mellons and a few associates when the genius of our country is bound to develop particularly in the Trans-Atlantic service, an additional source of the Merchant Marine of the Air," he wrote in a confidential memorandum to the chairman framed as an indictment of Pan American Airways and Juan Trippe for the sins of monopoly.

To support his thesis that international airlines, except when they flew overland to Mexico and Canada, belonged under the same regulatory agency as shipping, Loening had to do an about-face from his position on the Pan Am board as a proponent of land planes for the Atlantic.

He prepared a report for Kennedy larded with charts and statistics to prove that a fleet of eighteen flying boats could perform service equal to that of the superliners *Normandie* and *Queen Mary* at a fraction of the construction price. He recommended government loans for aircraft in foreign trade at 75 percent of construction cost—a massive blood transfusion for manufacturing companies and an encouragement to shipping companies to establish airline subsidiaries.

In November 1937, Kennedy presented the Loening report to Congress, where it was drafted into amendments to the Merchant Marine Act. He sent word to Trippe to call on him at his house in Hyannis Port, Massachusetts. Juan flew to Cape Cod in the small seaplane he piloted in summer between Manhattan and East Hampton. Kennedy dispensed with small talk and told Trippe he wanted him to testify in Washington in support of the amendments. Juan demurred.

"I'll give you enough time to walk up to the point and back to make up your mind," Kennedy snapped.

"I don't need the time," Trippe answered. "I cannot do it."

"Well, then, you can leave," the chairman of the Maritime Commission rejoined in a cutting voice. His two eldest sons, Joseph, Jr., and John, took pity on Juan and helped turn his plane around for takeoff. As they pushed on the wings to edge the pontoon into deeper water, Rose Kennedy, his embarrassed hostess, watched from the beach. Her husband glared at the departing guest from his rocking chair on the porch.

Trippe spoke out against the legislation in a typically sly manner. He blasted the loan provision as a patent discrimination against the domestic air carriers, when in fact it was Pan American that was presented with an immediate threat from a shipping company. In March 1937, the American Export Steamship Corporation had set up a subsidiary, American Export Airlines, and asked the Department of Commerce for permission to conduct experimental flights in the Mediterranean and across the Atlantic.

American Export was one of the shipping companies roasted on Senator Black's investigatory spit. After its owner was forced to resign, William H. Coverdale, a consulting engineer, and an associate, John E. Slater, bought the plundered company for a pittance with the help of a syndicate led by Lehman Brothers and proceeded to reorganize it.

Slater hired James Eaton, Pan American's first traffic manager, to run the airline. With Loening as Kennedy's *éminence grise*, with Eaton and lesser Pan American alumni climbing aboard American Export Airlines, and with the firm of Robert Lehman, a fixture on the Pan American board, as Export's banker, Trippe felt old friends gaining upon him as new enemies.

Juan ordered land planes for the Latin American routes, the models Donald Douglas had developed for the domestic carriers: the DC-2 for T.W.A., the DC-3 for American Airlines. Then in 1936, Pan American joined three trunk airlines in commissioning an experimental four-engine plane, the DC-4.

Development of a land plane for transocean service was much more difficult. By mid-1937, Lindbergh was beseeching him not to consider a flying boat "bigger and better" than the yet-undelivered Boeing B-314. Flying boats could not land in New York or Newfoundland in winter and did not adapt well to cabin pressurization. Shifting terminals and routes back and forth from north to south by the seasons appeared ridiculous to Lindbergh. He believed that the American terminal of the transatlantic route would have to be fixed at New York during the entire year, and this mandated the use of land planes.

Priester regarded seasonal migrations as an advantage. "It is always better to operate in good-weather areas in order to have maximum safety," he asserted. Applying the caution of a man who wore a belt and suspenders, he could not be budged from his preference for seaplanes and his fixation about emergency landings on water.

In December 1937, Gledhill solicited bids from eight aircraft manufacturers for planes to transport 100 passengers and a crew of 16 at altitudes of 25,000 feet on nonstop flights of 5,000 miles. Although the type of aircraft was unspecified, the ocean planes were to have accommodations to rival the *Normandie* and the *Queen Mary*, with cocktail lounges, dining salons and staterooms.

The letters contained the customary instructions to address the bids to Lindbergh as chairman of the technical committee. Newspapers reported that Lindbergh had drawn the specifications for his "dream ship" and that it would be the country's "first line of defense against competition from Europe's powerful air transport systems on ocean trade routes."

Lindbergh had received a tentative copy before it was sent to the manufacturers, and that was all he had to do with the specifications. He wrote to complain to Juan, and later to Van Dusen, about the "false impression" which brought a tide of mail and visitors to his retreat in the English countryside. Lindbergh wanted to be part of Pan American Airways—he used the first person plural in his letters dispensing advice —but he had neither the time nor the will for substantive consultation as long as he was living on the other side of the Atlantic.

During that period, Lindbergh made several trips to Germany to inspect airfields and aircraft factories. The first visit, in July 1936, was initiated by Major Truman Smith, a military attaché in the U.S. Embassy in Berlin. Smith guessed that Nazi officials, especially Hitler's Number Two man and Air Minister, Hermann Goering, would be sufficiently awed by Lindbergh's celebrity stature to reveal information about aeronautical strength that American intelligence was unable to ferret out. Lindbergh toured aircraft plants, and Luftwaffe commanders boasted to him of their plans to build an invincible air force. He went back to England and gave chilling reports to the Minister of Defence, Members of Parliament and acquaintances in government and other high places of German aerial might, which he judged to be superior to all but that of the United States.

In October 1937, Lindbergh attended the Lilienthal Aeronautic Congress in Munich as a guest of the German Government. On this second visit, he was admitted to engine plants and test fields and shown hitherto-secret models of bombers, fighter planes and helicopters. Flying his own plane, he could count for himself the number of military airfields in plain view. He helped Major Smith prepare a report for Washington with a bell-ringing estimate of the "astounding growth of German air power" in only four years.

Great Britain was, by contrast, flabby and smug. France's aerial muscle was pronounced inferior. Germany would attain technical parity with the United States in four or five years, sooner if current rates of development were retarded by politics or conflict within the American armed forces commands.

Soon after he returned to England, he wrote to Frank Gledhill:

> With the inherent German ability in scientific development, mechanical design, and the operation of aircraft (demonstrated both in war and in commerce) it is difficult to prophesy where the present development will end. I have never seen any general programme in aviation which I believe has been as soundly laid out as the one now going on in Germany.

Juan was in the thick of the battle that had raged since the Black hearings over regulation of the airlines. The sticking point was not the need for government supervision—on that there was near-unanimous consent—but who was to be the regulator.

By 1937, a sense of urgency about the airlines permeated Capitol Hill, fed as much by a stricken industry as by the tempo of the New Deal. The ledgers of the domestic airlines were stained with red ink. Replacement programs for obsolete aircraft hung in limbo until the uncertainty could be resolved about their future after the expiration of their airmail contracts. Bankers closed their loan windows to the airlines; investors shunned their securities.

Half of the $120 million privately invested in American air transportation in the past decade was wiped out in losses and in the demise of more than eighty companies, and the prices of the remaining equities were so eroded that $35 million could have bought all the airline stocks on the market.

A craving for fresh capital transformed the wolves of aviation enterprise into a flock of sheep bleating for protection. The "cutthroat" system of competitive bidding for mail contracts was the *bête noire* of the surviving airline operators. They begged for legislation to give them permanent franchises such as the railroads and motor carriers enjoyed, and to enforce a status quo for consolidating their hard-won positions.

The freewheeling Mr. Trippe was just as eager as his domestic brethren for regulation. The ebullient publicity about aggressive Pan American Airways and its orders for new planes were a smoke screen for a precarious condition. Its ten-year airmail contracts were due to run out in a year or two, and Farley was firm in his intention to readvertise them for bidding. If this were to occur, the airline, with millions of dollars sunk into equipment and facilities, faced the grimmest alternatives. A low bidder might make away with its routes, or after doing so, hold Pan American up to extortion by saying, "How much will you offer to buy them back?" Or Pan American might defensively place the lowest bids and go broke operating the routes.

The Federal Aviation Commission, created in the aftermath of the Black hearings, recommended a separate agency to regulate civil aeronautics, but Roosevelt favored giving the responsibility, at least at the outset, to the Interstate Commerce Commission, supervisor of the railroads and buses. Bills to vest control over air carriers in the I.C.C. were introduced early in 1937 by Representative Clarence F. Lea of California, chairman of the House Committee on Interstate and Foreign Commerce, and Senator Patrick McCarran of Nevada, a maverick member of the Black committee.

Trippe was alarmed that neither bill mentioned foreign air commerce. He wrote to the President and to Joseph Eastman, chairman of the I.C.C., entreating them to understand what a mistake it was not to extend the commission's authority to international air service, an "instrument" of national prestige and defense. His real concern, unstated, was that once the domestic carriers were fortified with their certificates of franchise, they would go after Pan American's routes.

At this point, he revised his battle plans to make common cause with the domestic airlines, while concurrently seeing to it that the legislation was tailored to Pan American's advantage. He assembled a mighty force, with powerful resources, to infiltrate the capital.

Juan perceived that Colonel Edgar S. Gorrell, the soldierly president of the Air Transport Association and an eloquent pleader for the impoverished trunk lines, would be the most credible mouthpiece for his claim that the industry's only international member deserved special treatment. Henry Friendly of Elihu Root's law firm sculpted provisions for Gorrell and the association's counsel to espouse. Bob Thach, leading from his strength among the Southern conservatives on the committees, secured the Hill. Thach drew from a $100,000 reservoir of funds recorded on the Pan American books as "Account Number 47, Travel, Hotels and Incidentals." The travel was concentrated in the District of Columbia, and the incidentals covered massive telephone bills, expenditures for entertainment (itemized as sight-seeing, deck chairs and meals) and disbursals to registered lobbyists.

A weapon widely deployed was the "plain-paper memorandum." As its name indicated, it was a comprehensive statement of the Pan American case, typed on white paper without a letterhead, signature or other identifying mark. Copies of these self-serving documents flooded the offices of Congress and the Executive agencies. "It was a little naive of Trippe to think no one knew where they came from, since it was perfectly obvious," observed Jim Smith, who, as an amanuensis to John Cooper, helped Juan cover the State Department.

Another effective form of propaganda ammunition was manufactured by Van Dusen. Early in 1937 he began writing letters to reporters and other molders of public opinion. Under the salutation "Dear Señor," these chatty missives, running to three or four pages of single-space typing, recounted in encyclopedic detail the wonders of the new aircraft and the preparations for a safe crossing of the Atlantic. With one of Van Dusen's letters on his desk, a newspaperman could produce an authoritative and colorful story about international aviation without exerting himself to unearth a single fact.

"Pan American has successfully wound up official Washington on its little finger—and has a marvelous press in addition," Grover Loening lamented to Kennedy.

The first element of Trippe's strategy was to ensure that either the legislation embraced both domestic and international airlines or there would be no legislation at all. In August, the McCarran bill was talked to death in a three-day filibuster by Senator Kenneth McKellar of Tennessee, fighting for his territorial prerogative as chairman of the Post Office Committee.

To settle the rivalries among the several Executive departments that owned pieces of the aviation corpus, Roosevelt formed an interdepartmental committee of assistant secretaries of State, War, the Navy, Post Office, Commerce and Treasury. Grover Loening was named technical adviser. The Pan American forces attached themselves to the committee through Gorrell and his counsel.

"Once we have an independent agency, all our troubles will be over," said Juan, and that was what the committee recommended in the fall of 1937. The President relented and gave his blessing to the establishment of a Civil Aeronautics Authority endowed with all the powers previously dispersed among several agencies, except for routine postal functions. The most important of these were the sanctioning of operating rights, setting of mail rates and approval of passenger and freight tariffs. Loening proceeded with his plan to make an exception for international carriers and goaded Kennedy to offer amendments to the Merchant Marine Act.

Meanwhile, Lea and McCarran revised their bills for introduction at the third session of the Seventy-fifth Congress early in 1938. Trippe would boast later on that Henry Friendly had written the new law—an honor Root's associate disclaimed. The wisdom of Washington attributed the authorship to the Air Transport Association.

All previous airmail contracts were to be superseded and competitive bidding for new routes abolished; the Post Office's life-and-death power over the airlines passed to the Civil Aeronautics Authority. The certificate of public convenience and necessity became the licensing instrument for the airlines, establishing a franchise for a particular route such as a railroad had along a right-of-way, or a utility for a geographic region.

By virtue of a grandfather clause, an air carrier that had operated continuously over a route, domestic or international, from December 1, 1936, until the new law took effect had a vested right to certification as long as it was rendering adequate and efficient service.

At Trippe's insistence, an important distinction between domestic and international lines was written into the bills: the State Department was to be consulted on overseas routes. Under the former system of distributing routes with mail contracts, the Post Office had specified that contractors had to make their own arrangements for foreign. concessions—an encouragement for Trippe's private diplomacy. But in the Atlantic bargaining, Britain had insisted on negotiating with the U.S. Government. The New Zealand caper and the exclusivity provision in the Portuguese concession had solidified the growing conviction in official Washington that the State Department and not a private company must henceforth do the trading with foreign governments for air rights. Trippe was only recognizing the inevitable.

Moreover, apart from friction when he was caught dealing behind the Department's back, Trippe had excellent relations with the diplomatic service, particularly with Judge Moore, who was elevated to the rank of Counselor of the State Department, equivalent to an Under Secretary, by a special act of Congress. "Pan American Airways is the only agency to which we can look to avoid the field's being occupied by foreign agencies," Moore told the President.

Juan went a step further and demanded that the President approve overseas routes because they impinged on national defense. The President was commander-in-chief of the Army and Navy as well as custodian of the interest of the United States in foreign affairs. There was validity to the argument; but Trippe had other motives—namely, to ensure that no shred of jurisdiction over Pan American was given to the maritime board, or to unsympathetic agencies like the Commerce Department, which persisted in assailing monopoly in international routes.

It was a matter of pride, perhaps hubris. "He considered the White House his playing field," Jim Smith said. The idea that air service was so important as to merit sponsorship from the State Department and the White House was just a step removed from the designation of a single airline to act as the chosen instrument of the nation's foreign-aviation policy, a counterpart of Imperial Airways and Air France.

In one respect, he oversold his theory. Domestic-route awards could be appealed in the courts, and Trippe wanted that means of challenging potential competitors too. But having accepted that overseas operations were so delicately entwined with matters to which only the President was privy, the legislators decided that to subject his decisions to judicial overturn was to endanger national security. The fate of foreign routes was to be sealed on the President's desk.

Assistant Secretary of Commerce J. Monroe Johnson, the thorn in Trippe's flesh, predicted that the Presidential prerogative would return to haunt Pan American. The portals of the White House might not always swing open for Juan Trippe, he noted. One day, his willing couriers like Judge Moore would be gone from the scene.

Initially, the certificates of convenience and necessity were to be limited to ten years or less. Juan pointed out that I.C.C. awards to railroads and motor carriers were for unlimited periods, subject to termination only for cause. Without assurances of continuity for airline operations, private capital could not be enlisted. To a degree, he was persuasive. The grandfather clause effectively gave a lasting franchise on existing routes. However, the Civil Aeronautics Authority was permitted to award new route certificates for "such limited periods as it found required by the public convenience and necessity." A door was left ajar for future competition.

The statement in the legislation with the most far-reaching consequences for Pan American Airways was the declaration of policy on competition. As American capitalists invariably do once they have staked out the turf and trounced the first wave of contenders, the domestic airline operators were seeking protection from unbridled competition.

In a radio speech shortly after Roosevelt's reelection in November 1936 by the largest landslide in Presidential history, Robert H. Jackson, Assistant Attorney General in charge of the antitrust division, announced that the New Deal was ready "to call a halt to monopolistic practices which threaten to throw our economy out of order." Though he did not single out air transport for condemnation, he signaled the Administration's opposition to monopoly.

The policy adopted by the Administration and promulgated by Congress represented a compromise between unchecked competition and none at all. Under a system of regulated competition, several operators could vie on a single route with the government as referee, seeing that there was enough business for everyone to make a profit.

The regulatory agency was directed to consider:

competition to the extent necessary to assure the sound development of an air transportation system properly adapted to the needs of the foreign and domestic commerce of the United States, of the Postal Service and of the national defense.

On this cornerstone would be laid, almost as soon as the law was passed, applications from Pan American's competitors for route authority, as well as Pan American's demands that they be denied.

Juan was also disturbed by a provision empowering the new aviation agency to fix passenger and freight rates for American-flag airlines in international commerce. He was concerned that foreign countries might retaliate by setting rates for carriers crossing their borders at very low levels. The shipping lines which would be the airlines' competitors on the Atlantic arrived at their fares in conference with foreign operators, a mechanism Trippe wanted to copy. Pan American carried the day on that issue. The C.A.A. was denied authority over international passenger fares—a sore point with the agency for the next forty years.

Hearings on the Lea bill began in March 1938 and were followed by quibbling to reconcile it with McCarran's bill in the Senate. With Kennedy departed for England to be Ambassador to the Court of St. James's, American Export executives made a futile effort to save the Loening-inspired amendments to the Merchant Marine Act. They maintained that unless jurisdiction over airlines flying overseas was reserved for the Maritime Commission, foreign air transportation would be frozen in the hands of the first American company to inaugurate international service: namely, Pan American. But they were overwhelmed by the combined forces of the Air Transport Association and the interdepartmental committee whom Trippe had rallied.

In mid-June the Civil Aeronautics Act was voted by both houses of Congress. Juan monitored the progress with more than his usual impatience when he learned that Farley had ordered advertisements for the Latin American routes to be released on June 23. On that day, Roosevelt signed the law into being.

It created a five-member agency, appointed by the President for six-year terms with a mandate to foster a healthy economic climate for the airlines. An administrator for the technical development of civil aviation and a three-man Air Safety Board were also established within the Civil Aeronautics Authority.

On June 3, Trippe telephoned Lindbergh in England to ask whether he would accept the chairmanship of the Civil Aeronautics Authority. He said he was acting on a confidential assignment "from headquarters" to ascertain Lindbergh's availability for the post. Lindbergh declined, saying he thought it unwise to move his family back to the United States "under present circumstances." Privately, the Lone Eagle knew he would feel caged by the routine of a regular job.

It was then, and would be ever after, the practice for industry leaders to sound out persons considered sympathetic to their cause as to their willingness to be their regulators. If the response was affirmative, the industry unleashed its lobbyists on the White House. Lindbergh inferred that Trippe's cryptic reference to "headquarters" meant Roosevelt, and he wondered whether the offer was motivated by politics or by outside pressure. In October he returned to Germany for a third visit. At a stag dinner at the U.S. Embassy in Berlin for Nazi and American notables (among the latter was Igor Sikorsky), Goering presented him with a civilian medal for his service to aviation. Lindbergh did not understand what was happening—Goering swooped at him without prior warning and spoke in German—but when he showed the medal to Anne later that evening, she recognized it at once as "The Albatross."

If the President really wanted a giant to lead the Civil Aeronautics Agency, whether Lindbergh or another, he was unable to lure one. With few exceptions, throughout its history the economic regulators of the airlines were businessmen, academicians and bureaucrats, undistinguished for either brilliance or political courage.

25

Darkening Clouds

The summer of 1938 was fraught with ominous portents.
The Pacific service appeared to be Trippe's folly. Pan American
lost $504,000 operating the route in 1937, and the deficit was mounting
to $1.155 million for 1938. During those two years, the Latin American
service, which accounted for 90 percent of total revenues, yielded
profits of $1.035 million and $1.287 million. The cash benefits that
cascaded from the hemispheric monopoly were dissipated in the great
blue yonder now overhung with war clouds.

On July 7, 1937, Japanese troops on maneuvers near Peking skir-
mished with soldiers from a Chinese Army garrison at the ancient
Marco Polo Bridge. The crackle of arms fire signaled the start of an
undeclared war, or what the Japanese referred to as "the China incident." A few Cassandras believed the Second World War had begun.
By the end of the month, Peking and its seaport of Tientsin were under
Japanese control.

In August, Chiang Kai-shek gathered his forces at Shanghai, and
for three months the Japanese bombed; the Chinese hung on in a
determined, if feeble, retaliation, while Westerners observed the
carnage with passive horror in the newsreels in movie theaters and
the gory photographs in magazines.

Despite constant striving by Harold Bixby and W. L. Bond, the
operations manager of C.N.A.C., to maintain a commercial and nonmilitary character for the airline, the planes were commandeered for
rescue and attack missions by the Nationalist Government. In August,

Bixby directed that the fifteen Americans who constituted most of the pilot roster and operating management of C.N.A.C. be evacuated to Manila for the duration of the war. Chiang Kai-shek's air force seized whatever equipment had not been destroyed and shifted the airline's headquarters to Hankow.

What a pity, Bixby thought. The airline had just posted earnings of $150,000 for its last fiscal year, and under normal conditions, its profits would have more than tripled in the coming year. Given a respite of peace, Pan American could have recouped the development costs of $850,000 incurred on the now-suspended coastal route between Shanghai and Hong Kong.

He was forced into making his decision by the State Department, which nervously reiterated the policy of nonintervention in foreign wars even in cases of naked aggression. The consul in Shanghai advised Bixby that C.N.A.C. had breached neutrality law and that the American employees would be magnifying the embarrassment they had caused their government if they remained. The consul in Hong Kong, on orders from Washington, stamped the passports of C.N.A.C. pilots about to take off for Canton "not valid for travel to or in any foreign state in connection with entrance into or service in foreign military or naval forces."

W. L. Bond was in the United States on home leave while Bixby was coping with the war in Shanghai. At lunch in the Cloud Club, the businessmen's midday hangout atop the Chrysler Building, Bond pleaded with Trippe to keep C.N.A.C. running. Juan told him that Pan American could not deviate from the policies of the State Department. Planes would be shot down sooner or later, and this would create an awkward situation for the U.S. Government.

"China needs air service now more than ever," the old China hand protested. "And if Pan American doesn't go back, it will be finished in China, because the Chinese will be very upset."

Bond outlined a plan. He would resign from Pan American Airways, on whose payroll he had been carried as an assistant to Bixby, but would retain his alternative status as executive vice president and a director of C.N.A.C. From then on, he would draw his salary from the Chinese Government. Any American employee who wished to remain in China could take the same steps.

Bond returned to China to gain the consent of Madame Chiang Kai-shek, who had been appointed by her husband to oversee aviation, for preserving C.N.A.C. as a nonmilitary entity. He stressed the worthwhile connections that Pan American had in Washington and how helpful this could be to China if the partnership were maintained. But he insisted on assurances that the Americans would be allowed to operate a commercial service without interference.

Service was resumed in the spring of 1938 from new headquarters in Chongqing, which later in the year would become the Nationalist capital for the duration of the war. The eastern half of China lay under Japanese control, and a map in Pan American Airways' annual report for 1937 dramatically illustrated Trippe's now-proud assertion that a route connecting Hankow with a new overland service between Hong Kong, Canton and Chongqing was "an extremely important artery of communications." Willy-nilly, Pan American was involved in a war.

On August 24, five Japanese planes swarmed around a C.N.A.C. DC-2 as it left Hong Kong bound for Chongqing with a crew of four and fourteen passengers. Captain Hugh Woods put the plane into a dive and landed on a river in a hail of machine-gun bullets. Only the pilot, the radio operator and one passenger survived the strafing by swimming to shore.

Secretary of State Hull sent a sharp protest to the Japanese Foreign Office through Ambassador Joseph Grew in Tokyo. It firmly acknowledged Pan American's part ownership of C.N.A.C. and the State Department's responsibility for this American property.

From then on, C.N.A.C. flew into and out of Hong Kong only at night and at secret hours of departure. In October, Hankow and Canton, China's last sea portal, were swallowed by the Japanese. The air route between Hong Kong and Chongqing became China's umbilical cord to the outside world.

The Sino–Japanese conflict undermined the optimistic projections for Pacific passenger traffic and mail. The Clippers flew nearly empty westward from Hawaii. Even on the longest, most lucrative haul, between San Francisco and Honolulu, they sometimes carried as few as two passengers. The island bases had to be maintained in tip-top order, even though the Pan American flying boats touched down only once a week. When traffic demand spurted, it was turned away because of a shortage of aircraft, aggravated by the loss of one of the Martins on July 29, 1938. The radio operator of the *Hawaii Clipper*, en route from Guam to Manila, gave his position as 565 miles from the Philippine capital. Weather conditions were unexceptional. He ended with the signal "GOOD," but when the ground operator at San Francisco tried routinely to establish contact with the plane a minute later, he was rewarded with silence. The plane, with its six passengers and crew of nine, had vanished, as though an Aladdin had rubbed it out of existence.

The Navy searched with ships and submarines, and six Army

bombers crisscrossed an 80-mile area around the Clipper's last reported position. Nothing came to light except unverifiable rumors of Japanese sabotage. One of the passengers, the owner of the China Clipper restaurant in Jersey City and a fund raiser for Chinese war relief, was carrying a large amount of currency to turn over to Nationalist authorities.

Another victim was Ted Wyman. After ten years as Trippe's administrative lackey, he had finally made the break in June and joined Curtiss-Wright as vice president for export sales. He was on his first business trip to the Orient.

Meanwhile, Trippe was still trying to reach Australia. After the crash of the *Samoan Clipper* with Musick and his crew aboard, the Commerce Department closed Pago Pago as being an unduly hazardous port for seaplane operations. Pan American was forced to consider the alternative route to Australia via Canton Island and Fiji.

Juan descended upon the Navy, State and Interior Departments expounding again on the virtues of guano and calling for the seizure of Canton Island. Throughout 1937, Britain and the United States had squabbled over the island in a thoroughly unamicable manner. Neither country had an airtight claim to Canton, which had been unattended for more than seventy years. Suddenly, in March, Whitehall issued an order annexing Canton Island, presumably in the interests of security and air imperialism.

In July, a landing party from a New Zealand warship clashed with an American scientific group sponsored by the Navy and the National Geographic Society. The New Zealanders set up a radio station on Canton, ran up the Union Jack and claimed the island in the name of the King; whereupon the Yanks dug a flagpole for the Stars and Stripes and left metal replicas of the banner on stone markers. The British, in a note to the State Department, demanded their removal. An international incident was brewing.

Admiral William D. Leahy, Chief of Naval Operations and Acting Secretary of the Navy, was so keen about Canton Island, as a seaplane base of utmost strategic importance in the defense of Hawaii and the North American continent, that he urged that colonists be landed.

To reduce the strain on the Navy's budget, he favored having an airline pay for the necessary improvements such as blasting coral heads out of the lagoon and installing radio and meteorological facilities. Judge Moore agreed with him over the protests of Secretary of Commerce Roper, who was still objecting to the agreement Pan American had made with New Zealand. Secretary of State Hull, the conciliator, preferred to give diplomacy another chance. But the British refused to relinquish their claim of sovereignty over Canton.

In March 1938, the President issued an executive order claiming Canton and its sister in the Phoenix Group, Enderbury Island. The White House announced that the move had "nothing to do with war" but was motivated solely by commercial aviation needs.

The Japanese suspected an offensive action, especially when Britain began acting so civilized about the whole matter and agreed to share sovereignty of the island with the United States. But the British persisted in mingling the sovereignty question with aviation rights, wanting to trade access to Australia and New Zealand for permission to land in Hawaii.

The War, Navy, Interior and State Departments all agreed that it would be a mistake to let any foreign country have that privilege, "partly for reasons of national defense and partly because we would thereby be destroying our present monopoly of transpacific flights."

And so Secretary of the Interior Harold Ickes granted Pan American a license to use Canton Island as a base. Trippe asked for a Navy supply ship to transport Pan American engineers to the island to start building an air station. Roosevelt denied permission at first, until Juan fed the Navy a cable message he had received from an agent in New Zealand: "OUR COOK IS LEAVING BY BOAT"—a warning in code that another British expedition was setting out for Canton. Navy and State persuaded the President to change his mind.

In December, the outflanking action was completed when Pan American was allowed to establish a base at Noumea, in the French colony of New Caledonia, an alternative to British Fiji. France had higher priorities for its aviation resources than a transpacific route, and was willing to waive reciprocity on its South Seas possession. Pan American was poised to jump to either New Zealand or Australia.

But when was Pan American going to cross the Atlantic? Congress appropriated $2 million for transatlantic mail subsidy that year, and the Post Office said it was only waiting for prospective operators to demonstrate their ability to perform before advertising the route for bids.

As Van Dusen gamely heralded the "huge Atlantic Clipper series of flying boats" in his Dear Señor letters, the B-314s were running a year behind schedule at the Boeing plant.

And in the meantime, Grover Loening fulfilled his prophecy of a political rumpus over the Pan American monopoly. During the hearings on the Merchant Marine Act amendments, he made much of

Trippe's special relationship with Imperial as manifested in the Atlantic agreement which conferred exclusive rights on Pan American. "No other American airline can land in England whether we decide we want it or not," he said. Loening went on to draw a conspiracy scenario —Trippe conspiring with the British to help establish "one of the most flagrant monopolies the government has ever had grow up under its nose" and the bamboozled government permitting Pan American to walk off with the entire transatlantic commerce. Those were fighting words, and Trippe's lawyers feared the Attorney General might be listening.

Juan was on the phone to Woods Humphery, quite frantic this time, asking to change the contract. His lawyers informed him that the square-deal clause and the agreements to pool passengers and freight could subject Pan American to prosecution under the Sherman Act for attempting to restrain trade.

Woods Humphery went to bat for him with the Air Ministry. "I have not found Pan American guilty of a breach of faith so far and I have been working with them for ten years," he said. The last thing British officialdom wanted was to be implicated in a criminal proceeding on the other side of the Atlantic. The surgery was performed; the guts of the contract were removed, and by the end of 1938 the partnership was effectively dead.

But Clause H in the agreement between the governments was still alive, and it bound the two airlines to simultaneous introduction of transatlantic service. Imperial had no oceanworthy plane, only a hope on a drawing board. Not one of the touted Empire flying boats had the range to cross from Ireland to Newfoundland with a payload.

As the facts became known in Britain, Imperial Airways was caught in the crossfire of a Parliamentary investigation. Members of the House of Commons pelted the British civil-aviation community with ridicule, noting that the United States had become the predominant seller of airplanes to the international market. "We are laughed at by other countries!" shouted an M.P. Even British Airways, recently formed to serve northern Europe, bought Lockheed Electras rather than national-brand aircraft. Imperial Airways was held to the purchase of British models, however obsolete.

The management of Imperial was rebuked for contentious labor relations and for self-serving conduct. Sir Eric Geddes had died during the summer of 1937, and the brunt of the criticism fell on Woods Humphery. A committee headed by Lord Cadman produced a report in March 1938 that recommended larger subsidy for the airline and a drastic overhaul of its management structure. The managing director's powers were curtailed, and Woods Humphery resigned to save his pride.

Imperial was ordered to modernize. But it could not overcome blockages in aircraft production caused, according to caustic observers, by red tape at the Air Ministry and "the leisureliness of British workmen." The fault lay as much in aircraft engineering. The prototype of a land plane intended for transatlantic service, the four-engine De Havilland Albatross, had its back broken during a test landing.

Another idiosyncratic design was the Mayo Composite. It consisted of a four-engine flying boat, the *Mercury*, so loaded with fuel as to prevent takeoff under its own power, riding piggyback on a four-engine mother ship, the *Maia*. In July 1938, the composite lifted off the River Shannon at Foynes under the combined force of its eight engines. The *Mercury* was disengaged and flew westward, landing in Montreal in 20 hours 20 minutes with 1,000 pounds of mail—the first revenue crossing of the North Atlantic.

In August, the *Lieutenant de Vaisseau Paris*, a six-engine French flying boat that had crossed the South Atlantic in 1935, navigated from the Azores to New York without stopping. But with the amount of reserve gasoline required to accomplish this, there was little capacity left for a commercial payload. The flight amounted to a demonstration that Air France was no more prepared than Imperial to operate the transatlantic service.

Only the Germans appeared to be nearing that capability. The efficient Zeppelin service that Trippe found so threatening had been suspended after fire claimed the *Hindenburg* as it landed at Lakehurst, New Jersey, in May 1937. But the flights of the catapulted seaplanes were stepped up in the summer of 1938 to a weekly schedule, and in August a four-engine Focke-Wulf Condor flew the 3,800 miles from Berlin to New York nonstop in 24 hours 36 minutes—the fastest east–west crossing. Three days later, the land plane made the return trip safely. The Condor was too small for profitable operation—nine passengers were supposedly the most it could carry with a 2,500-mile range—but it showed that the Germans had taken the next step beyond the flying boats.

The only thing holding them back from a scheduled mail service was permission from Washington. The prospects grew dimmer after Hitler detached the Sudetenland from Czechoslovakia in September. Though the British Prime Minister, Neville Chamberlain, bought an illusion of peace at Munich, the Air Ministry harnessed resources for military preparedness, and attention was diverted from planning for Imperial's transatlantic plane.

American Export purchased a Consolidated flying boat capable of flying from New York to the Iberian peninsula nonstop with a payload of mail and obtained landing permits for France, Germany and Italy and a tentative concession in Spain.

Trippe approached John Slater with a proposition to divide European territory. Pan American kept its exclusive rights to northern Europe, Great Britain and the intermediate stops. American Export took southern Europe with exclusivity in Italy, the Balkans, the Near East and North Africa. They would split frequencies to France and Germany. Trippe ended up with the plums, Slater the little green apples.

Once the delivery date for the Boeings was fixed for January 1939, Juan's patience evaporated. Right after Thanksgiving, he startled a meeting of State Department and Civil Aeronautics Authority officials with a disclosure of intelligence gleaned from unidentified sources.

The British had lost interest in New York as a terminal for the transatlantic service, he said, and were reverting to the All-Empire scheme routed through Montreal. Instead of admitting the change of heart, they were going to resort to a dastardly trick. Imperial would apply for a permit from the C.A.A., as the law now required, and then simply not use it. That would leave Pan American tethered to the reciprocity provision, inhibited from starting across the Atlantic.

He proposed that the State Department help Pan American obtain a six-month permit from the French Government to land at Marseille with the possibility of continuing to Southampton if the British relented. Trippe knew that French traffic rights were impaled on the issue of reciprocity, and that the U.S. Government wanted to keep the gateway to France open to at least one other carrier besides Pan American. But, he argued, persuasively enough to convince the skeptics at the C.A.A. and State, a temporary permit would not interfere with an agreement France and the United States might reach later on, and it just might change the British intentions about New York.

Just before Christmas, the embassy in Paris forwarded his request for a preliminary permit; within three weeks it was granted. The embassy in London filed a blunt inquiry with the British Air Ministry. Was it ready to begin scheduled operations to the United States, and if not, would there be any objection to Pan American's going ahead with service to England?

At the end of January 1939, the State Department was informed that Imperial Airways would initiate transatlantic schedules on an experimental basis in June. If Pan American Airways wished to depart from the principle of simultaneous action and start its service sooner, His Majesty's Government would not object. Clause H was waived.

And just in the nick of time. On January 29, Frank Gledhill took delivery of the first B-314 in Seattle. The 42-ton aircraft was the last and the biggest of the Pan American flying boats, one and a half times the size of the *China Clipper* and with twice the payload. Despite attempts to streamline the plane in the current mode of aeronautical design, the B-314 looked like a potbellied flying fish with 1,500-horsepower Wright Cyclone engines tucked in its outstretched wings.

The flight deck, or working quarters for the twelve-man crew, was equal to the entire cabin space of a DC-3. Passenger accommodations approached the luxury of the stellar transcontinental railroad trains, if not quite the grandeur of the floating palaces on the oceans. There were three lounges, a dining room and thirty-five sleeping berths aligned behind the main cabins. The transatlantic fare was set at $375 one way, $675 round trip, about the same as the price of one of the better cabins on the *Normandie*.

The first two 314s were assigned to strengthen Pan American's badly depleted Pacific fleet. Captain Harold Gray, who had inherited Musick's mantle of chief pilot, ferried the third flying boat to Baltimore, pausing at Treasure Island to show it off at the San Francisco Fair. On March 3, at Anacostia in Washington, Mrs. Eleanor Roosevelt christened it the *Yankee Clipper* with a beribboned bottle said to contain the waters of the seven seas.

Pan American filed an application with the C.A.A. for a certificate of public convenience and necessity to operate a service to Great Britain and France. Reading the political tea leaves, Trippe offered to waive the exclusivity provisions of the Portuguese concession if asked by the government to do so.

During its half-year of existence, the regulatory agency had busied itself with "grandfathering," or safeguarding, established routes such as Pan American held in Latin America and the central Pacific. Now it was addressing itself to the question of a new route across the Atlantic.

Taking heed of its legislative mandate to consider competition as an element of public interest, the C.A.A. restricted Pan American to two weekly round trips out of the total of six negotiated by the interdepartmental committee three years before. "If no restriction is placed upon the number of weekly frequencies on which a given carrier may utilize such landing rights, a single air carrier might monopolize all of the existing landing rights," the C.A.A. noted.

Pan American was further confined to New York (with Baltimore an alternative in bad weather), London and Marseille as terminal points. Lisbon was listed as an intermediate point along with the

Azores (and Bermuda for climatic necessity), Shediac, Botwood and Foynes.

The certificate was awarded, after President Roosevelt approved the C.A.A.'s decision as the law required for international routes, two days before the date set for the first commercial transatlantic flight. On May 20, the twelfth anniversary of Lindbergh's Paris flight, Harllee Branch, vice chairman of the C.A.A., presented the precious piece of paper to Trippe in a ceremony at Port Washington.

Trippe made minor changes in his Pacific script. Turning to Captain Arthur E. Laporte, to whom Gray had ceded the inaugural honors, Juan asked whether the flight was in order.

"The *Yankee Clipper* is ready, sir. All stations are manned, standing by for orders, sir," the pilot said. Trippe handed him the manifest and ordered him to cast off. The crew walked down the ramp two by two, posed for photographs and disappeared into the hull of the flying boat, which was packed with 1,800 pounds of mail.

The engines awakened with the roar of a pride of lions. The *Yankee Clipper* lifted off Manhasset Bay in a noon sunshine, veered toward the New York World's Fair and passed 500 feet over the heads of the Saturday throng. The chairman of the C.A.A., presiding at the dedication of the Aviation Building, saluted the crew by radiotelephone. "Thank you, sir. We are proceeding for Europe," Laporte's voice called back as he headed out toward the Atlantic.

After eleven years of Trippe's secret diplomacy and never-say-die machinations, of frustrations and wavering hopes, Pan American Airways was operating over the North Atlantic, the first airline to span the ocean commercially.

Juan tasted gall in the cup of victory. The C.A.A. struck down his agreement with Slater as "adverse to the public interest," and American Export Airlines filed an application for a certificate to fly the same transatlantic routes as Pan American plus permission to serve Rome as well.

An hour before the departure of the *Yankee Clipper*, Sonny Whitney put his name to a twenty-year lease Juan had negotiated with Mayor Fiorello LaGuardia for a seaplane base at the new municipal airport. Whitney was signing agreements, issuing commands and running Pan American Airways. Juan Trippe was no longer chief executive. In March, an exasperated board of directors had stripped him of his powers.

26

Deposed

Ironically, *Fortune* had named him one of fifteen businessmen who were "masters in their own corporate houses." Despite the presence on the Pan American board of one Mellon and two Whitneys, said the editors, it was Juan Terry Trippe, "a man with a hell of a lot of energy and an almost psychic grasp of the future," who had made the airline.

Yale awarded him an honorary Master of Arts degree. He marched in cap and gown to the commencement ceremonies with Secretary of State Hull, H. H. Kung, the Chinese Finance Minister, and Ernest O. Lawrence, the radiation physicist, who were receiving doctorates.

Look announced that Carole Lombard, the Hollywood star, considered Juan Trippe one of the world's ten most interesting men. (Among others on her list were President Roosevelt, Manuel Quezon, Chiang Kai-shek and G. B. Shaw.) According to the actress, "His world is a world of romance, but more than that he holds a great power for both peace and preparedness."

And at that point, he was heading for a downfall.

With vision, perseverance and unflagging optimism, he had nurtured the airline into an organization of nearly 7,000 employees operating 53,548 miles of routes and grossing $16 million in revenues.

As a State Department official analyzed the situation:

Up to the spring of 1939 Trippe had been the three dimensions of his company. It is said that he wrote policy with his right hand, executed it with the left, and saw to it that neither hand knew what the other was doing.

There had been no one to stop him from overreaching; no one to check those darker qualities of his nature, the arrogance, the secretiveness, the unwillingness to take his associates into his confidence.

In the begetting of Pan American Airways, he had been one member of a triumvirate with complimentary strengths and weaknesses. But Hambleton, the stabilizer, had died, and Sonny Whitney, with his gobs of money and roving nature, could not focus on the company with consistency or depth. If Juan had a one-track mind, Sonny's was a whirligig. He played championship polo; raced horses under the blue-and-brown Whitney colors; hunted foxes in Pennsylvania, jaguars in Mexico and beautiful women everywhere, while aspiring to make his mark as an entrepreneur in his father's mold.

Concurrent with his role as chairman of the board of Pan American, he had his interests in mining and the Guaranty Bank to oversee. As a token of his esteem for the outdoors, he invested half a million dollars in Marineland, an oceanarium near St. Augustine, Florida. He was a partner in his cousin Jock Whitney's movie ventures. Their first dabbling, Pioneer Pictures, was formed to exploit the Technicolor Process. This was followed by Selznick International, a showcase for a young producer, David O. Selznick. As Pan American was preparing to cross the Atlantic, Selznick was getting ready to shoot *Gone with the Wind* and hiring Alfred Hitchcock, a Briton with an exquisite sense of the macabre, to direct the film *Rebecca*.

The seat of Whitney's business empire was a suite of offices in the New York Central Building, an ancestral edifice at 230 Park Avenue, a few blocks from Pan American headquarters in the Chrysler Building, where Trippe occupied a large office in the southeast corner of the fifty-eighth floor, the senior executive domain.

Harold Bixby described the morose environment in a letter to Lindbergh in January 1939:

Some nine months in the N.Y. office has convinced me that—
1. J.T.T. will *never* delegate authority—with the result that he is partial to "yes" men—a bad omen for me because I will not conform.
2. Paper work—the servant—has become the master in the P.A.A. organization and most personnel are so busy writing about their work that they have little time left to do it.
3. The human side of personal contacts and the inspiration of real leadership has been lost—displaced by bulletins and circulars. The executives in N.Y. write letters—instead of going over their

divisions. Evan Young, for instance, in charge of the Eastern Division, made his last trip over the line in 1934—five years ago. Even Clarence Young, Div. Mgr. of the Pacific has only made one trip over the line and that was in 1936. He has never been to Hongkong. In short, reorganization and leadership—sorely needed—will probably not be forthcoming.

The directors of Pan American were similarly unhappy with the autocratic president. Grover Loening orchestrated his dismay into a political campaign. Richard Mellon and David Bruce resigned quietly. However much David respected Juan's foresight and stick-to-it-iveness, he was bothered by what he termed "a disregard for the ultimate return to the stockholder." Bruce sold his stock at a loss when he left the board. "Pan American was a lousy investment," he said.

Earnings, weakened by the Pacific operation since 1936, plummeted to 3 cents a share for the year 1938. The directors had no choice but to pass the dividend in January 1939. The dividend was sacred to Trippe, for it was part of his circuitous reasoning for higher mail subsidy: Pan American performed vital services for the nation; therefore it behooved the government to provide the means to keep the earnings at a level to attract private capital.

The company was famished for capital. An immediate expenditure of $200,000 had to be authorized to develop a base at Noumea to comply with the French concession. An option for six advanced-model B-314As needed for the transatlantic service was to expire on October 1. The aggregate cost of exercising the option: $6 million.

Banks slammed their credit windows shut. Pan American was bloated with debt—$2.5 million in callable bank loans and $3.5 million in equipment trust certificates, the equivalent of mortgages on the first six 314s. In the cash till was only $300,000, urgently required for working capital.

Lenders and investors dislike uncertainty such as clouded Pan American's future. In October 1938, applications were filed for grandfather certificates on the Latin American and Pacific routes, and though it was unlikely they would be denied, there was no telling how generous the C.A.A. would be in setting mail rates. A member of the C.A.A. had offered to use his influence to defer the Pacific rights west of Honolulu for two years, but Trippe declined the favor and instead petitioned for an increase in the mail subsidy.

During the rate proceedings, a staff counsel for the C.A.A. acted the part of a criminal prosecutor and attempted to show that Pan American's fuzzy accounting was a cover for political disbursements. Coming on the heels of the Loening ruckus during the lobbying for the civil-aeronautics legislation, it embarrassed the directors and made them uneasy about what else the uncommunicative Mr. Trippe might be hiding from them.

Among the fifteen remaining after Mellon and Bruce left, the directors most concerned about Pan American's deteriorating financial condition were those who controlled large blocks of stock and had been in at the creation of the airline. They were Sherman Fairchild, whose confidence in Trippe had always been wanting; Robert Lehman of Lehman Brothers and Edward O. McDonnell of Grayson M. P. Murphy & Co., underwriters of Pan American securities; S. Sloan Colt, president of Bankers Trust; Fred Rentschler of United Aircraft and the Whitneys, Sonny and Jock. Sonny was the largest individual stockholder in Pan American, with 156,032 shares; Jock Whitney owned 28,200 shares. Juan had 7,056 shares in his name. He had taken profits in more than half the stock he had acquired through the exercise of warrants, and placed 10,000 shares in trust for his three children, Betsy, 6, Charles White Trippe, 4, and John Terry Trippe, born in October 1938.

In a recurrence of earlier crises in Juan's career, the worried directors formed a cabal; but this time, his defender, Sonny Whitney, was the rallying figure. As the director with the largest investment to protect, and with a great fortune behind him, he was the logical one to lend an air of soundness and stability to the shaky organization while they explored means of rescue. He was in a mood to be coaxed by his friends—particularly Jock and their polo playmate Bobby Lehman—to show that he could run the company. At that juncture in his hectic life—Sonny turned 40 in February 1939—he had a gnawing ambition to be considered an active captain of industry rather than just a lucky investor.

The coup d'état took place on March 14, and it was done swiftly and coldly, as gentlemen arrange these matters in their boardrooms. A bare quorum attended the directors' meeting: Colt, Lehman, McDonnell, Fairchild, Lyman Delano of the Atlantic Coast Line Railroad, the two Whitneys and Trippe. According to the minutes, the board voted to amend the bylaws to make the chairman of the board the chief executive officer and to have Juan Trippe "continued as president and general manager."

Afterward, Van Dusen was ordered to write a press release so that the financial community could glean from the sparse legalistic wording that Juan Trippe had been deprived of his power.

Many years later, Sonny would say that the directors chose him because he was "the most qualified" and had been responsible for getting them onto the board and for raising most of the capital for the business. "The board didn't feel it was being fully informed," he said. "They had confidence in me to keep them informed, and so they put me in charge. But it was a temporary thing. There was never any question about his operation of the company." First, last and always, Juan Trippe was his hired hand.

And Trippe, when he could finally bring himself to mention the most humiliating episode in his life, said, "It didn't change anything. He had clout through his father's bank. He needed the title for his self-esteem."

Whitney picked new directors to fill the vacancies on the board. Artemus L. Gates, the gallant Di of the Yale Aviation Unit, was president of the New York Trust Company, which had purchased one-third of the equipment notes; William S. Paley, president of the Columbia Broadcasting System, a friend and future brother-in-law of Jock Whitney.*

John M. Franklin, president of the United States Lines, took one of the seats reserved for shipping interests. In 1936, Trippe had made an agreement with the steamship company similar to his arrangement with Matson in the Pacific to act as Pan American's European passenger agent and to buy 1.5 percent of its stock.

Another transportation representative was Mark T. McKee, president of the Wisconsin and Michigan Steamship Company, a politically astute infighter in Wall Street proxy wars. Thomas Morgan, president of the Sperry Gyroscope Company, was well versed in Pan American's affairs from his association with Curtiss-Wright and North American Aviation. He bore the scars of his negotiations with Trippe for the sale of the Chinese airline.

Morgan was asked to form an internal-audit subcommittee of the board consisting of himself, Colt and Rentschler, to examine the corporate patient and prescribe a course of remedial treatment.

To emphasize the seriousness he attached to the responsibilities of chief executive, Whitney left 230 Park Avenue and took possession of Juan's office. Trippe was banished to a small office in the southwest corner of the floor, displacing the corporate secretary, with his rolltop desk, his 'brass spittoon and the standing globe that was his favorite prop for magazine photographs.

A modest redecorating program signaled Whitney's attempt at an

---

* After a round of divorces, they would wed two of the three beautiful Cushing sisters of Boston. In 1942, Jock married Betsey Cushing Roosevelt after her divorce from the President's eldest son, James. Paley and Barbara Cushing Mortimer were married in 1947.

open administration. Cheerful draperies were hung at the windows and a flat glass-topped desk placed in a catercorner position facing the door, with half a dozen chairs in a semicircle around it. One executive would always remember the revolution as "the day Whitney moved in his captain's chairs."

The walls of the reception area were covered with a photographic mural of clouds, and there, in celestial solitude, the brunette Eleanor Searle was installed. A doctor's daughter from Plymouth, Ohio, she was working to earn tuition for voice lessons. On weekends she sang in churches and synagogues. The secretaries gossiped about her dates with senior executives and Pan American directors.

Whitney seemed to relish the exercise of executive power. He held press conferences in his office, signed the most routine company announcements and made some substantive changes in assignments. He tackled the mess in Washington first, and fired Bob Thach.

Sonny held weekly meetings on Wednesdays at 9 A.M. He went around the table asking each executive to report on his phase of operations. Trippe was a silent hulk, exuding fury. The others sensed he was rating them on the degree of their cooperativeness toward Whitney, storing their grades away in the recesses of his mind, biding his time toward a day of reckoning. After one meeting, he upbraided George Rihl for being too responsive. "What am I supposed to do when the chairman asks me for information?" Rihl asked. He and Sonny were friends from the days when Rihl had sold him Compañía Mexicana.

"I'm your boss," Juan snapped.

"The hell you are," Rihl retorted.

Trippe wore a smiling mask on the outside and pretended nothing had happened. He had lunch with Lindbergh at the Cloud Club. Charles was hearing different interpretations of the takeover from his many friends in the Chrysler Building. He wrote in his diary:

> Juan continues as president but with much less influence. In many ways, I am sorry to see this, for I like Juan. I always felt he had great ability.

The first transatlantic paying passengers were booked to leave on the *Dixie Clipper* for Marseille on June 28—a gala event, with a band playing and a speech by Sonny, all to be recorded by newsreel cameramen and reported on page 1 of *The New York Times*. Betty was going on that flight with the Whitneys and would meet Juan in Paris.

Five days earlier, Juan escorted twenty officials, including Judge Moore and Presidential secretaries Stephen Early and James Rowe, aboard the *Yankee Clipper* for the first mail flight over the northern route. Early undertook to broadcast his account of the trip when they reached London. They spent three days at anchor at Shediac, the first refueling stop, waiting for fog to lift at Botwood, 600 miles to the north.

When the Clipper was en route to Foynes at last, and the stewards were serving a hot turkey dinner in the dining saloon, a radio message was brought to Juan's table congratulating him on his 40th birthday. A cake with candles blazing was placed before him, champagne corks popped and the passengers serenaded him with "Happy Birthday" and "He's a Jolly Good Fellow." In the spring of his discontent, he was the guest of honor at the first birthday party ever held 8,000 feet above the Atlantic.

During a nervous summer of vanishing peace, Pan American Airways' transatlantic service was off to a rousing start except for the usual mechanical problems with new aircraft and delays of as much as a week for the flying boats trapped in the harbor at Horta by the monstrous swells outside.

The Clippers plied the Atlantic, which had shrunk to the proportions of a pond that could be hopped over in a day, taking socialites and dress manufacturers eastward for the seasonal rituals of sport and high fashion. Westward they carried cargoes of fall designs from the Paris haute couture and the first wave of immigrants who could afford to arrive in America by air, the wealthy refugees from the Third Reich.

American Export Airlines surveyed the mid-Atlantic route three times. The *Lieutenant de Vaisseau Paris* made two crossings with a complement of French dignitaries, and Imperial Airways inaugurated twice-a-week mail service to the United States with advanced-model Empire flying boats refueled in midair.

On August 27, the Imperial flying boat *Cabot* arrived at Port Washington with newsreels of the crisis in Europe. Only the date on which Hitler would ignite the flames of war was imprecise. That afternoon, the *Lieutenant de Vaisseau Paris* slipped its moorings at the Long Island base and without serving notice took off for France. The following day, American flags were painted on the hull and the undersides of the *Yankee Clipper*'s wings—marks of neutrality in the world conflict less than one week away.

On September 12, the C.A.A. presented Pan American with a bountiful package of relief. It raised the Pacific mail rate from $2 to $3.35 a mile on the San Francisco–to–Manila segment of the route, and $7.12 a mile from Manila to Hong Kong, retroactive to April 1.

The staff counsel had offered evidence of malfeasance in open proceedings; in both the mail rate and the grandfather cases, the C.A.A. heard secret testimony from the Navy as to the national interest the Pacific routes served. Pan American had "generously" put its bases at the Navy's disposition; its navigational and weather-reporting systems were useful to the defense of the Pacific and to shielding Hawaii from enemy attack. "Pan American activities should be encouraged and expanded," advised Admiral William Leahy, Chief of Naval Operations.

The net effect of the rate increase was to reduce the annual Pacific loss from more than a million dollars to $200,000. Combined with the war-induced boom in transatlantic and Latin American traffic, it turned 1939 into the most profitable year in Pan American's history— earnings of $2 million would be reported on revenues of $20.6 million. At the end of September the option on the six Boeing 314As was exercised.

With credit exhausted, an equity issue was the only feasible method of paying for them, and since the company looked like a sickly wallflower to Wall Street, it had to be a rights offering rather than an outright sale of stock. The board authorized an increase in the company's capital stock by 525,391 shares. Stockholders and certain officers and employees were given warrants to buy stock at $12.75 a share, or about $3 below the prevailing market price. Once again, the directors were forcing current investors to put up more capital to keep their equity from being diluted. More than $6 million was raised when the program was put into effect early in 1940. The bank loans were paid off, leaving nearly $4 million in cash.

The financial dilemma had been resolved, but the operation of the company was in near chaos. It had been discovered that the keys to the Pan American Airways system were locked in Juan Trippe's head, and true to his old nickname, Mummy was not about to hand them over. Problems kept popping up for which the files yielded no answers, and there was no use asking other executives. Some of the commitments Juan had made seemed to be bound up with national security, and no one knew how to go about unraveling them, or whether, indeed, they should be let alone.

Throughout this period, one observer noted, "Juan was sitting it out like the deposed kings at Estoril," and like a monarch in exile he was still treating with other sovereigns. Trippe visited his old stamping grounds, the State and Navy Departments, and Basil O'Connor, Roosevelt's former law partner, on retainer from Pan American, importuned the President to have Trippe to lunch. The President granted him an interview without food.

The C.A.A. hearings on American Export's application for Atlantic-route certificates were scheduled for October 1, and it was inconceivable that Pan American would mount an attack on a competitor without Juan Trippe commanding the battle stations.

The directors hopefully hit on a plan to bring Juan under control by making him report regularly on everything but routine matters to the executive committee. The committee was reshuffled to represent both old and new guards: Colt; McDonnell; Graham Grosvenor, a satellite of Sherman Fairchild's; Morgan; McKee; Trippe and Whitney. Tom Morgan was designated chairman of the committee on September 28, Trippe the alternate chairman.

Two months went by, and the accounting firm retained by the audit committee produced a report confirming that Pan American suffered from eccentric management. Financial and administrative controls were inadequate; executive responsibilities were undefined. There was only one door at which the blame for this state of affairs could be laid, and behind it sat Juan Trippe guarding the secrets of the company.

Sonny Whitney was proving unequal to the task of straightening out the mess. He was tiring of the day-by-day grind of being a chief executive; his other interests beckoned; his marriage was disintegrating.

Morgan concluded that it would be futile to look for another leader. The only solution was to bring Trippe back. Colt and Rentschler, flinty pragmatists also, agreed with him. The audit committee recommended that the board restore full executive powers to Juan Trippe at a reasonably early date and let Sonny Whitney revert to the status of a goodwill ambassador for the company. Basic to their proposal were a management reorganization and the appointment of an administrative vice president to maintain the orderly operation of which Trippe was incapable.

On January 9, 1940, the executive committee adopted their recommendations, and on January 23, after a scrappy meeting that lasted late into the evening, the full board assented. Trippe was reelected president and named chief executive officer, Whitney "continued as chairman of the board."

Morgan and Colt believed a subtle public-relations campaign was required to restore the sheen to Pan American's reputation and Juan's as well, a task that called for greater sophistication than Van Dusen could muster. Besides, Trippe had marked him down as a traitor for what seemed to him excessive zeal in promoting press coverage of Whitney.

Morgan admired the wizardry of Benjamin Sonnenberg, a press

agent who had worked miracles for several gilt-edged corporate clients including Sperry Gyroscope.

Sonnenberg was a fascinating enigma in his own right—part huckster, part street-wise boy from the Lower East Side, part sensitive intellectual. A walrus-mustached dandy, he operated from his home, a mansion on Gramercy Park originally built for Stuyvesant Fish and decorated in *fin-de-siècle* opulence, and from tables at "21," the Colony, the Cub Room of the Stork Club and the zebra-striped womb of El Morocco.

A meeting with Trippe was arranged at the Union Club. Sonnenberg sized up Juan in an instant. "He has a romantic name and a swarthy complexion; that makes him a romantic figure," he said. Upon further study, he identified him as a robber baron trapped between centuries, "no longer of the nineteenth and not yet of the twentieth." He appreciated his "guts and cunning," but found his life-style inappropriately modest. Though Juan celebrated his restoration by moving to an apartment overlooking the East River at 10 Gracie Square, buying a house and seven acres in Greenwich for a weekend abode and adding to his property in East Hampton, the Trippes' style of living was more Grand Yankee than imperial. And Sonnenberg sniffed, "He has no books or pictures on his walls."

In due course, stories appeared in *Life* and *Reader's Digest* extolling Juan Trippe as a latter-day Magellan and Pan American Airways as a branch of U.S. defense. "Juan had such skill with reporters," Sonnenberg observed. "He was always showing the hand that wasn't doing anything."

Whitney hired his own press agent to put out copious press releases documenting his business acumen and claiming credit for saving the airline. Not for another year did he cede Juan's office back to its former occupant, though he used it infrequently, and mostly as a mailing address for his goodwill missions, which included asserting the status of an old friend of the President's to argue Pan American's case against American Export Airlines.

In the spring of 1941 he and Gee were divorced and he married Eleanor Searle, who had retired from the fifty-eighth-floor reception desk. The day after Pearl Harbor, he resigned from Pan American Airways, having already sold his stock at a huge profit and chalked up another killing as a venture capitalist. Sonny Whitney went off to serve his country as a major in the combat-intelligence unit of the Army Air Forces. He asked permission to wear his World War I pilot's wings on his uniform.

Jock Whitney left the board at the same time, and Paley told

Trippe he wanted to resign too, but Juan pleaded with him to stay, and he did for another year. Subsequently, during one of his recurring bouts with depression, Whitney wrote Juan an anguished letter in which he alluded to the hurt he had caused him. But they were never reconciled.

"Our paths don't cross," Sonny said many years later. "I see no point in exaggerating what happened. The company kept going, going, going."

Part IV

THE WAR YEARS

27

Cover-Up

A time bomb had started ticking just before the Whitney takeover and it continued to bedevil Trippe, his puzzled directors and the U.S. Government for more than a year afterward.

Early in March 1939, Juan was called to the War Department for a meeting with Major General Henry Arnold, chief of the Air Corps, and Brigadier General George Marshall, deputy chief of staff. They directed him, as a matter of national security, to see that the German pilots employed by SCADTA were replaced immediately.

Francis White had encouraged Trippe's secretive purchase of the airline in 1930 with the understanding that he would de-Germanize it and remove a threat to the Panama Canal. But Trippe had done nothing of the kind. On the contrary, he let Peter Paul von Bauer run SCADTA with pretty much of a free hand, and the Austrian insisted on preserving its essential Germanic character along with the fiction that he still owned it.

Juan was exceptionally attentive to von Bauer's wishes, certainly more than to those of his partners in W. R. Grace, from whom he concealed the truth about the Pan American interest in SCADTA. They accused him of trying to undermine their offspring, Panagra.

Juan's motive in favoring SCADTA was comprehensible in the context of Pan American's 84 percent, or virtual ownership, but that was the hidden factor. As he moved ever onward to buy more advanced aircraft for Pan American, he sold some of its surplus inventory of planes of SCADTA. This served both to reinvigorate the Colombian airline initially and to provide fresh capital for Pan American's purchases. As SCADTA prospered, Pan American milked it for what it was worth. From one-third to one-half of SCADTA's earnings were distributed as dividends instead of being plowed back for development, to the benefit of the principal stockholder and the eventual detriment of the Colombian company.

Though a Colombian occupied the figurehead post of president, the management of SCADTA and its pilots and technical and commercial personnel were almost exclusively Germans and Austrians. Several married native women, took out Colombian citizenship and wove themselves into the fabric of Colombian life. Colonel Herbert Boy, the representative in Bogotá, was an adviser to the Colombian Air Force. In 1933, the airline's ground facilities and its German pilots were enlisted, under his direction, to serve in the Leticia incident, a dispute between Colombia and Peru over a corridor in the upper Amazon Valley. Boy was rewarded by having a small town named after him, Puerto Boy, and the SCADTA Germans were lauded as Colombian patriots.

After Adolf Hitler was elected Chancellor of Germany and assumed dictatorial powers in March of that year, the U.S. War Department became warier than ever of the German presence in South America, particularly at the Colombian point of proximity to the Canal Zone. Juan asked von Bauer for a confidential breakdown on SCADTA employment. He reported that more than one-third were Germans, all in the higher positions. While conceding that nationalism was on the rise in the country, von Bauer said:

> I am also very doubtful if it will be possible within the next years to replace european employees by Colombians, the entire organization is to delicate a machine, and to complicated to be handled by Colombians.

Most of SCADTA's pilots were recruited from the German air-transport training school and served as reserve officers in the German Air Force. The military pay augmented their airline salaries. As the Hitler regime stepped up its militant nationalism, the younger pilots flaunted Nazi allegiance. Few stayed beyond their basic two-year tours of duty but were rotated to other German airlines in South America, then back to Germany, or otherwise incorporated in military aviation.

U.S. intelligence sources gathered increasing evidence of the strength and espionage capability of Nazi sympathizers in Latin American shipping and airline companies. Early in 1937, a Naval Intelligence report identified Colonel Boy as an anti-American, pro-Nazi troublemaker. There was also concern about SCADTA's German radio operators, the "brains" of the flying operation that had no direction finders aboard its planes.

Von Bauer's sympathies defied deciphering. He was married to a German; one of their sons managed a family farm in Germany, and the other was a German Army officer. After his contract with Pan American expired in 1935, he remained as general manager, unsalaried but drawing a bonus pegged to performance. In 1936, he asked Trippe to let him buy back a majority interest in SCADTA, at a price higher than the market value of the shares on the Bogotá Exchange.

Trippe vacillated and turned him down. Twenty years later, defending his handling of the SCADTA affair, he told a Congressional committee, "We were suspicious that Dr. von Bauer might be in the control of the German Nazis as early as in 1936." If so, his conduct is all the more confusing.

Juan made another convoluted deal with von Bauer. He gave him power of attorney to vote a majority of the SCADTA shares owned by Pan American and to sell them to Colombians if the government nationalized the company, but only under instructions. He made him pledge the Pan American stock he had received for his SCADTA shares as bond for his dubious word of honor. And he allowed him to buy 1,200 shares of SCADTA treasury stock. The arrangement shored up the facade of his ownership of the airline.

Von Bauer warned Trippe that the government might cancel SCADTA's airmail concession and lift its tax exemption if it learned it was not a Colombian company. "The government considers me tacitly as a Colombian," he said, "but I would be willing to accept or to acquire the Colombian nationality, Austrians, by the way, being allowed to have two nationalities."

Olaya Herrera, the President of Colombia at the time of the Pan American acquisition, was dead, and von Bauer deliberately misled his successor, President Alfonso López, as to the controlling interest.

Trippe continued to defer to Von Bauer's wishes in masking the deal they had made. In February 1937, he had Elihu Root, Jr., write to President Roosevelt: "If this transaction so beneficial to our country is published, the entire system built upon it will be broken down."

During a visit to Austria shortly after Hitler annexed the country, Von Bauer was summoned to the Air Ministry in Berlin and directed to reacquire the SCADTA stock originally belonging to his backer, Lufthansa, and turn it over to the German Government. He went to New York to resubmit his bid to Juan, again to no avail.

In May, the Colombian legislature passed a law, to take effect within four years, mandating majority ownership and management of domestic aviation companies by nationals.

The proper response to this expected turn of events, which was developing in other countries where Pan American did business, would have been to train natives to take over the administrative and technical jobs, but this was not done. Von Bauer continued to disparage the abilities of Colombians and to hire German pilots. He formally applied for Colombian citizenship.

In September, German troops occupied the Sudetenland. Roosevelt, having decided to elevate the status of the U.S. Mission in Bogotá, appointed Spruille Braden to be the first Ambassador to Colombia. Braden's qualifications for a diplomatic post in Latin America stemmed from a fortune made in Chilean copper. He was a Sheff graduate, five years ahead of Trippe, a man used to having his orders carried out and to saying exactly what was on his mind. Braden saw himself as a scourge of the Nazis, and with goading from General David Stone, the commanding general of the Canal Zone, made it his mission to cleanse SCADTA of its German employees.

Precisely how Pan American fitted into the picture no one at the State Department could tell him. Francis White might have enlightened him, but he was long since gone from the department, apparently without leaving a record in the files.

Just before taking up his post in Bogotá, Braden tried to elicit the facts from Trippe. He recorded their meeting at the State Department in his memoirs:

> Trippe is suave and soft-voiced, and I found him a past master at side-stepping subjects he preferred not to discuss—such as SCADTA.
> We started to discuss SCADTA and before I knew it Trippe was describing his problems in Asia. "Now, Mr. Ambassador," he asked, as sweet as molasses. "What do you think we should do in this situation?"
> "Mr. Trippe," I answered, "I'm not here to consider what you should do in Asia. We're discussing SCADTA, and that's the only subject I'm going to talk about."
> "Oh, yes, of course, Mr. Ambassador. Forgive me."

Braden learned nothing at that meeting, and Juan stood him up for a second appointment the day before the Ambassador sailed for Colombia. But Braden bullied Evan Young, a vice president of Pan American, into disclosing the full extent of the company's interest in SCADTA.

Young assured him that von Bauer was impeccably anti-Nazi. "In fact, he has some Jewish blood and that makes him all the more so," he said. That information was as dubious as the heart condition von Bauer offered as an excuse for avoiding Braden when he arrived in Colombia. Erwin Balluder, who had cognizance of SCADTA as manager of Pan American's western division and was a close friend of von Bauer's, said later, "Von Bauer was not a Jew. He was an Austrian nobleman."

Braden's haste to de-Germanize the Colombian airline was buttressed by testimony from Grant Mason, then a member of the C.A.A., to a Senate committee in February 1939. Mason asserted, "SCADTA is a menace to the defense of the Canal." Juan regarded this as treachery by a former Pan American executive. A month later, Trippe was called to Washington by Generals Arnold and Marshall.

His answer to their request to replace the German pilots was that Pan American could not afford the going rate for American pilots, which he quoted at $10,000 a year. The SCADTA Germans received about half that amount, presumably supplemented by military reserve pay.

Juan was desperate at that point. SCADTA was then a spent airline. Its mail concession was due to expire in a few years, its equipment was run-down, passengers complained that the service was poor, and it was feeling competition from another airline, SACO, started by Colombian businessmen with encouragement from the government. Von Bauer estimated that SCADTA needed an infusion of $300,000 in cash plus a loan of $500,000 to survive. Given Pan American's precarious financial condition and his own jeopardy, Trippe was in no position to authorize such commitments.

The new President of Colombia, Eduardo Santos, a former journalist, was on cordial terms with the United States, but he walked a political tightrope. Both his rivals in his own Liberal Party and his Conservative opponents adopted anti-American postures. Many of the German settlers in the country, some of the Catholic clergy and followers of the would-be Conservative strongman Laureano Gómez were Nazi sympathizers. Santos was vulnerable to attack for doing the bidding of Yanqui imperialists, which was why he was reluctant to sanction an abrupt cashiering of the Germans and a substitution of American pilots.

Von Bauer became a Colombian citizen in March 1939, duly renouncing allegiance to Austria and Germany, as required by Colombian law but of no binding effect in the Third Reich. He then gave his oath to President Santos that he personally owned 51 percent of

SCADTA stock—"a piece of sophistry," according to Braden, that made him appear in compliance with the nationalization law and entitled him to remain as managing director of the airline.

Rumors of a planned attack on the Shell Oil Company refineries in Curaçao, a major source of England's fuel supply, circulated in Bogotá in April. The Colombian Government ordered SCADTA to replace its German airport managers and radio operators with Colombians as soon as competent natives could be found, and pressed for a merger between SCADTA and its competitor SACO into one national company.

Braden fired off an agitated report to Washington about von Bauer:

> He is a shrewdly intelligent man, has a tendency to overplay his hand, that he occasionally makes conflicting statements, that he doth protest too much his innocence, loyalty to Colombia and disconnection with Germany—in short, he bears watching.

After the Nazi juggernaut rolled into Poland on September 1, the Colombian Government placed the commercial airlines operating within the country under military control and assigned army officers as copilots on the planes.

On September 5, David Grant, Pan American's Latin American legal expert, arrived in the capital—to supervise the de-Germanizing process, he said. He was under instructions from Trippe to protect von Bauer in any circumstances, and was prepared to confirm to President Santos von Bauer's account of the ownership of SCADTA. Braden intercepted the affable lawyer and administered a tongue-lashing. Grant cracked. "Trippe doesn't confide in the officers of his company," he said. As for the ownership, "the whole thing is hokus-pokus, now you see it, now you don't."

With Braden practically sticking a pistol in his ribs, Grant called on President Santos and in carefully nuanced Spanish recited the peculiar facts of the stock title. He promised that steps would be taken promptly to cleanse SCADTA of its German personnel without disrupting the organization.

Pan American sent a troubleshooter to act as assistant manager of SCADTA and make an undercover survey of the operation. Von Bauer dispatched SOS messages to a dozen of his German managers vacationing in the homeland that they were in danger of being booted out in absentia and should return to Colombia at once.

In October, George Rihl flew to Bogotá with a directive from

Trippe to negotiate a nationalization merger for $1 million cash, tantamount to recouping almost what Pan American had paid for SCADTA—a patently unrealistic objective.

Braden worked up a formula for a phased nationalization and merger of the two airlines. Pan American would remain in a dominant position until the Colombian Government, then strapped for credit, could afford to buy a substantial participation in the new airline. Rihl agreed to the proposal as part of a plan to gradually substitute Americans and Colombians for the Germans in SCADTA's technical and managerial positions.

State Department officials were now taking an active interest in what they viewed as a dangerous situation and had drawn Whitney into the discussions. He confessed he was embarrassed to be learning for the first time what had taken place in Colombia.

In a meeting Whitney and Trippe attended at the State Department, Juan repudiated the Braden plan to which Rihl had assented. "We have to move very carefully and not upset the apple cart," Juan said. He posed the problem as being SCADTA's near-obsolete equipment. American pilots would never consent to fly such aircraft, he said. It would cost $100,000 to buy new planes and radio equipment, and Pan American lacked the wherewithal. Because of certain commitments to the banks in connection with its loans, the directors could not authorize the expenditure.

On the spur of the moment, he thought of a solution: a loan from the Export-Import Bank to finance the purchase of aircraft for SCADTA. Of course, the State Department would have to push for the loan.

It did not take much perspicacity to figure out what Trippe was aiming at. In the run-down state of the airline, the price of the SCADTA stock Pan American was being forced to sell to Colombians in the nationalization process would be nowhere near what he had paid for it. New equipment, financed by the U.S. Government, would heighten the value of the stock. Or as Braden said, "Mr. Trippe, perhaps, hoped to transfer a possible loss on PAA's investment in Colombia to the United States Government."

To Juan's chagrin, Thomas Burke, chief of the State Department's Division of International Communications, insisted on laying the matter before the Pan American board. "This is most unusual," Trippe protested. Besides, many of the directors were out of town, he said. Finally, he agreed to call a meeting of the executive committee. The meeting was held on December 29, and afterward the full board accepted the committee's recommendation to authorize a $65,000 credit to SCADTA to buy radio equipment and to cover the expenses of American technicians who would supervise flight operations in Colombia.

But although he was supposedly under surveillance by the State Department and by his own directors, Trippe, as Burke noted, "reverted to form whenever an opportunity presents itself." Seemingly cooperative about minor details, he avoided letting his associates know how he was handling major matters. He tried to undercut Braden in Bogotá by telling Burke in Washington that President Santos was reluctant to see Colonel Boy and other key Germans dismissed. Santos was in fact eager to be rid of the Germans, just so long as the matter was handled in a manner that would not make his administration look like Yanqui puppets.

Burke pressed hard, convinced that Trippe was consumed with fear of having it look as though von Bauer had "outmaneuvered him," and at the same time wanted to shift the costs of a bungled venture. That he might damage relations between the two countries or endanger the defense of the Panama Canal seemed not to concern him. "I personally find no fault with Trippe for his legitimate efforts to protect the interest of his company," Burke wrote, "but I regret to state I am definitely convinced that he has gone far beyond the limits of existing business practice in this case."

During the first few months of 1940, a few American managers were introduced into the SCADTA system, and with Rihl temporizing and Braden issuing ultimatums, fifty Germans in administrative jobs were discharged. German airport managers, pilots and mechanics remained. Those who left did not go silently. Von Bauer, who had been permitted to resign, tried to stir up sympathy for himself through his lawyer, who was the President's brother-in-law. Meanwhile, Erwin Balluder, the director of Pan American's Western division and overlord of Mexican and Central American operations, was being summoned to headquarters to answer for alleged Nazi sympathies.

A Naval Intelligence report had identified Balluder, who had been naturalized as an American citizen in 1935, as being blatantly pro-German and a Jew-baiter. It cited his concentrated socializing with the German colony in Mexico City, and his vociferous criticisms of President Roosevelt and of the nations allied against Hitler in the war, which he predicted would end in a German victory. The report also mentioned a rumor of a secret airfield in a remote corner of Mexico where he was said to be assembling planes for shipment to Germans in South America. One source for the reports was a German-speaking journalist who had visited Balluder and his family at their home in Cuernavaca, and subsequently poured her suspicions into the ear of General Stone in the Canal Zone.

Erwin proclaimed his innocence to Trippe, who had regained his full powers, and Juan sent him back to Mexico City admonishing him to be more circumspect. He considered Balluder's Mexican contacts and intimate knowledge of the commercial mores of Latin America to be invaluable. He ignored suggestions from the State Department, relayed from General Stone to Braden to Washington, that he fire Balluder.

The Ambassador was waxing apoplectic over Trippe's casual attitude toward Nazi threats to U.S. security. Since the German pilots were still flying under the guidance of their compatriots at SCADTA's ground radio posts, Braden insisted that Pan American install three Adcock direction finders near the Panama border so that any plane off course would immediately be detected and the commanding general in the Canal Zone could be alerted to take precautionary measures.

After an interval of weeks, Braden cabled Under Secretary of State Sumner Welles to call Trippe on the carpet. Juan assured Welles that the first direction finder, "complete with pole," was being shipped by air express and that the other two would shortly follow. Welles wired the good news to Braden, who informed him that Trippe had pulled the wool over his eyes. Neither the hundred-ton direction finder nor the 60-foot cedar pole could possibly be shipped by air.

When the German Blitzkrieg of Holland and Belgium began on May 10, President Santos agreed with Braden that a gradual changeover in SCADTA personnel was no longer feasible, and that the eighty-four Germans still employed as flight crews and mechanics had to be eliminated immediately. Italy's declaration of war on England and France a few weeks later stiffened Santos' resolve and emboldened him to stand up to his political opponents.

Braden and Burke met with Trippe, Rihl and Tom Morgan, chairman of the Pan American executive committee, on May 14. Juan was ready to take decisive action at last. He had a plan to discharge the Germans provided Pan American was reimbursed to the tune of $250,000. He was figuring into the expenses the severance pay—one month for every year of employment. Burke promised to recommend that the C.A.A. consider the expenditure in weighing the Pan American mail subsidy.

He had no way of knowing that Basil O'Connor had slipped a plain-paper memorandum to President Roosevelt with a note: "If you'll read this you'll see how unfair the statements re Pan-Am are." The memorandum referred to the $250,000 item and said that the Pan American board regarded the problem "as a contribution to the national defense" similar to the development of the Canton Island base.

Rihl scheduled interviews at the Chrysler Building for the last Sunday in May. Two dozen men were hired. A week later, they boarded a DC-3, one of the planes to be introduced into SCADTA service with exuberant publicity. Posing as tourists, they dispersed to Colombian towns along the airline network.

On June 11, Rihl called a staff meeting for 5 P.M. at SCADTA's operational headquarters in Barranquilla, and sent a code message of instructions that were to take effect at that hour at every airport and office in the system. As military police formed a ring around the base, the German pilots and mechanics were handed envelopes containing notices of dismissal, checks for severance pay and offers of transportation to Germany or any other destination of their choice. The next morning, American crews climbed into the cockpits of the SCADTA fleet; they detected borings for bomb racks and machine guns in the interiors of the fuselages.

Some seventy-five Germans were still on the payroll as airport and office managers and chiefs of airmail and air freight, a source of concern and vexation to the U.S. Government. Scary instances of attempted sabotage were reported—tampering with engines, a bomb placed aboard a plane just before takeoff. The mountain peaks charted on the pilots' maps were shorn of a thousand feet or more.

The purge of the German employees and the severance of the airline's German banking connections were not completed until after Germany declared war on the United States on December 11, 1941. Colombia broke relations with the Axis partners the day after the Japanese attack on Pearl Harbor.

Von Bauer lived in Barranquilla for about a year after he retired from SCADTA, ostracized by both Germans and Colombians. Late in 1940, he made a donation of 100,000 pesos to the local Nazi party. The Colombian Government tried unsuccessfully to deprive him of his citizenship, and the U.S. Government blocked his assets in the United States, including his Pan American stock. He and his wife moved to Chile and, after the war, divided their time between that country and Austria. David Grant, acting as his lawyer, succeeded in having his property in Colombia and the United States restored to him.

After his death, some of his Pan American associates maintained that he had been wronged. Trippe, except in his testimony before Congress, took the tack that he had not been a Nazi after all. Balluder believed he had been persecuted by Braden and the State Department, and that he deserved to be remembered as an aviation pioneer, a good businessman and a refugee from Hitler.

The welter of evidence in government documents and personal recollections is confusing except on two points: von Bauer was an opportunist; and as negotiators and intriguers, he and Trippe were peers.

The reorganization of SCADTA into a Colombian entity went forward in stages. A new company, Aerovías Nacionales de Colombia (AVIANCA), was created to absorb SCADTA and SACO. Pan American was initially to hold a 64-percent interest, which was to be reduced to 40 percent as the Colombian Government found the means to exercise its option for 40 percent of the stock. The remaining 20 percent was to be sold to private Colombian interests. State Department officials felt that Trippe's vacillations had embarrassed the Department in its conduct of foreign affairs and needlessly raised the costs of the changeover. The reaction of Laurence Duggan, Chief of the Division of the American Republics, to Trippe's demand for full expense reimbursement was choleric:

> To me, this request is a positive affront to our mentality. Only Trippe would have the brass to make it. Instead of the Government reimbursing Pan American Airways, the Government should in equity reduce its $7,000,000 a year subsidy to Panair by the amount it saved Panair through the Scadta reorganization. What Trippe would have had to do later at a probably enormous loss has, through our efforts alone, been effected under the most favorable terms for Panair. Further, because of the danger to the Panama Canal which Trippe permitted for *ten years* after he informed the Department in 1930 he was going to rectify immediately, his administration of Panair should be thoroughly investigated. I dare say that if any German bombing of the Canal is ever attempted, the odds are 100 to 1 that those participating will be former Scadta pilots.

Trippe presented General Marshall with a bill for nearly $1.3 million for de-Germanization expenditures; the largest item was for severance compensation. The War Department allowed $922,666.06.

In his memoir, Braden justified the payment:

> Pan Am presented the government with a bill in excess of the cost of the changeover. They had had Avianca, SCADTA's successor, borrow the money. Default would have ruined Avianca and left the Colombians feeling, justifiably, that the Yankees had swindled them. I was obliged to recommend payment of Pan Am.

Another rationale appeared in the blizzard of memos on the subject. This was from Under Secretary of State's Liaison Office in September 1940:

> Mr. Welles had held no brief for Pan American Airways as such, but that he felt in the present emergency we must use the tools which were at hand and in the present case the Pan American Airways was the one company which we could use for our expansion program in South America.

The United States was preparing for its own defense and probable entry into the war. The country's only international airline was needed for a massive and secret effort to be mounted in Latin America.

The SCADTA affair illustrates the ambivalence of Pan American's position. Had it truly been a chosen instrument of the U.S. Government, a national airline by force of law instead of de facto, it would have done as the government asked and banished the German personnel. But Pan American Airways was a private company, albeit one subsidized through government mail contracts, and in this instance, the desire of its president to cover his mistakes was in conflict with the national interest.

The State Department kept urging Trippe to get rid of Balluder, and after the United States entered the war, Juan met with him in the Pan American office in Washington to pronounce sentence. "The White House says you're a security risk, I have to let you go," he said. Balluder fainted, and Trippe caught him as he sagged. When he came to, he swore that he was a loyal American citizen, that he was sure Wilbur Morrison, the general manager of Compañía Mexicana, had fingered him to the F.B.I. because he wanted his job.

Juan relented. "I can't keep you in Mexico City, because you obviously have enemies there," he said. He transferred him to the New York office to work in semiobscurity as executive assistant to vice president Evan Young and appointed Morrison to his job in Mexico City. Balluder's name was taken off the corporate executive roster, as manager of the Western division, until after the war, when it reappeared as a vice president.

His fellow executives, Morrison included, would always scoff at the notion of Balluder as a Nazi partisan. If his conversation was venomously anti-Roosevelt, and randomly anti-Semitic—he referred to his associate David Grant as "a Jew who spoke fluent Spanish"—that was common habit in the executive suites and country clubs of America, not proof of treason. Years later, Balluder learned that he had been cleared in an F.B.I. report.

ABOVE LEFT   Fall 1918. At 19, Juan Terry Trippe was commissioned an ensign in the U.S. Naval Air Reserve.

ABOVE RIGHT   After the First World War ended, he resumed his studies at Yale University and played guard on the football team in the fall 1919 season.

BELOW   On July 1, 1926, J. T. Trippe, the 27-year-old managing director of Colonial Air Transport, welcomed the arrival of the first airmail flight from Boston to New York at Hasbrouck Heights, N.J. Trippe is at far right.

ABOVE In 1927 Trippe and his wealthy friends laid plans for an overseas air service. In order to meet the performance deadline for the Key West–Havana mail contract in October, Pan American Airways chartered this Fairchild FC-2 from another carrier.
BELOW Anthony H. G. Fokker, a Dutch aircraft designer, equipped the Fokker VII with three Wright air-cooled radial engines and promoted it as a "flying Pullman car," safe enough to carry passengers as well as mail.

By 1931, Pan American Airways had become the world's largest international airline, serving Latin America from gateways in Florida and Texas.

PAN AMERICAN AIRWAYS SYSTEM
1927-1932
▪▪▪▪ Affiliated and subsidiary companies

NORTH AMERICA

El Paso

Torreón
Mazatlán
Guadalajara **Brownsville**
Tampico
Mexico City Veracruz Mérida Key West **Miami**
Nassau
Havana
Tapachula Belize
Guatemala Puerto
(city) Barrios
San Salvador Kingston
Managua Port au Prince
San José Cristóbal
Panama City San Juan
Barranquilla Maracaibo
Medellín Port of Spain
Bogotá
Guayaquil Georgetown
Paramaribo
Cayenne
Lima Manaus Belém (Pará)

SOUTH AMERICA Fortaleza
Natal
Antofagasta Recife
São Salvador
Santiago Rio de Janeiro
Mendoza
Pôrto Alegre
Buenos Aires Montevideo

PACIFIC OCEAN

ATLANTIC OCEAN

0   500   1000
Miles

ABOVE Pan American Airways established the tradition of having its planes christened by First Ladies in January 1928 when Mrs. Calvin Coolidge baptized a Fokker VII named after Postmaster General Harry New. Trippe is at far right.

BELOW Trippe (at left) and C. V. Whitney (standing) were present when Second Assistant Postmaster General W. Irving Glover opened bids for airmail routes to Puerto Rico and the Canal Zone in July 1928. Pan American Airways, the winner, then took over West Indian Aerial Express, the only other bidder, represented by T. H. Bane (at right).

ABOVE   John A. Hambleton (fourth from left) was one of the founding triumvirate of Pan American with Trippe and Whitney.

BELOW LEFT   In September 1929, Charles A. Lindbergh (second from left), technical adviser to Pan American, opened the mail route to the Caribbean. Accompanying him on the 7,000-mile tour were his wife, Anne (beside him), and Betty and Juan Trippe.

BELOW RIGHT   Lindbergh and Trippe on the tarmac in Panama during the Caribbean tour.

TWO PHOTOS: UNITED TECHNOLOGIES CORPORATION

TOP   October 1931. The Sikorsky S-40, a four-engine amphibian, was designed for the Caribbean routes.

CENTER   Attending the delivery of the Sikorsky S-42 in May 1934 were (from left to right) Captain Edwin Musick, Pan American's chief pilot, chief engineer André Priester, Charles Lindbergh, Juan Trippe, and Igor Sikorsky.

BOTTOM   The Martin M-130 flying boat, *China Clipper*, about to be loaded for the first Pacific airmail flight from San Francisco to Manila on November 22, 1935. Captain Edwin Musick is at the cockpit door, Postmaster General James A. Farley behind the mail sacks, and Juan Trippe, in profile, at right.

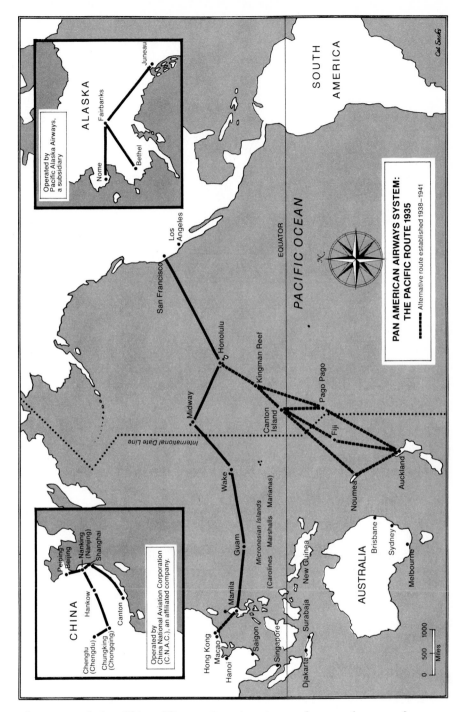

The route of the *China Clipper*. Pan American subsequently opened a second Pacific route via Honolulu to New Zealand. Insets show routes in China and Alaska flown by Pan American subsidiaries.

ABOVE August 1937. Trippe received the Collier Trophy from President Franklin D. Roosevelt for establishing the transpacific airway, as Thomas H. Beck, president of *Collier's Weekly*, the trophy's sponsor, looked on.

BELOW March 1939. Mrs. Eleanor Roosevelt (seated behind Trippe at the podium) christened the Boeing B-314 *Yankee Clipper*. It was the first flying boat with a transatlantic range.

ABOVE LEFT   Henry Luce, the publisher of *Time,* and his wife, Clare Boothe
Luce, a playwright, sailed for Europe on the *Queen Mary* in 1938. Trippe,
a Yale contemporary of Luce's, had played Cupid during their courtship.
ABOVE RIGHT   Trippe's favorite pose for photographers was before the
standing globe in his office.
BELOW   At a White House ceremony in 1946, President Harry Truman
presented the Harmon Aviation Trophy to Trippe in recognition of Pan
American's contribution to the war effort.

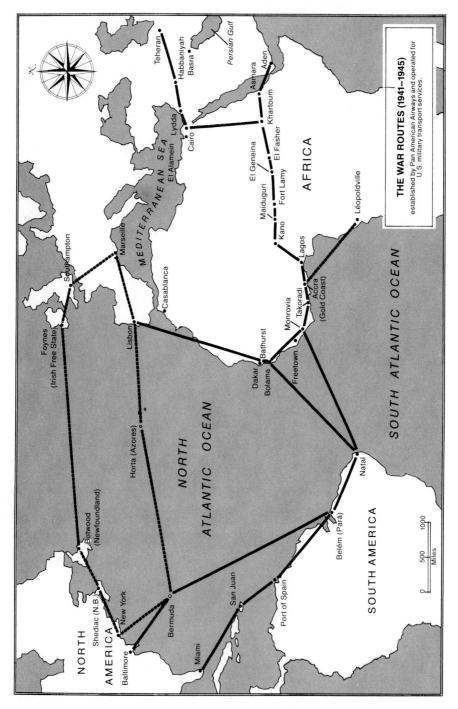

The supply route laid down by Pan American and operated by the Air Transport Command during World War II extended from Miami to China

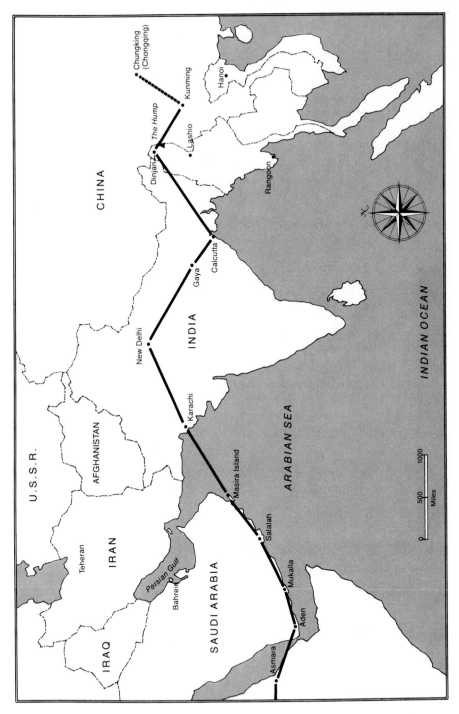

across the waist of Africa and the Middle East. Planes navigated the South Atlantic from the bulge of Brazil to West Africa.

ABOVE Trippe was received by Generalissimo Chiang Kai-shek at Nanking during a tour that marked the beginning of round-the-world service for Pan American in 1947.

BELOW James M. Landis, chairman of the Civil Aeronautics Board in 1947, opposed Trippe's chosen instrument ambition. Truman fired him because he appeared to be a political liability.

ABOVE LEFT Howard Hughes, the eccentric billionaire, thwarted Trippe's aim of acquiring T.W.A.

ABOVE RIGHT Hughes also helped discredit Senator Owen Brewster, Republican of Maine, a zealous supporter of Pan Am, during Senate hearings in 1947.

BELOW Stewards making up sleeping berths on the double-deck Stratocruiser, a commercial derivative of the B-29 Super Fortress bomber. It went into service in 1949.

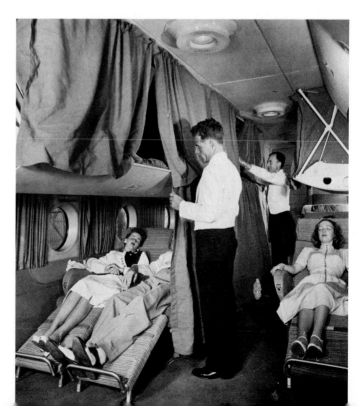

ABOVE LEFT   Evita Peron, First Lady of Argentina (second woman from right), christened a Pan American Stratocruiser in Buenos Aires in July 1950. At a reception afterward were (left to right) Wilbur Morrison, vice president of the Latin American division, Juan and Betty Trippe, and President Juan Peron. Fleur Cowles, a magazine editor, is at far right.

ABOVE RIGHT   Vice President Richard M. Nixon congratulated Trippe at a banquet in October 1955 on his speech inviting the Soviet state airline to join the International Air Transport Association. William Hildred, director general of I.A.T.A., is at right.

BELOW   President Dwight D. Eisenhower's wife, Mamie, christened Pan Am's first Boeing 707 jet in the fall of 1958. Juan Trippe was at her side, Betty Trippe at far left.

ABOVE May 1968. Trippe retired, leaving Harold E. Gray (left) to run
Pan Am as chairman and chief executive officer with Najeeb E. Halaby as
president.
BELOW The Boeing 747, the safest, most efficient jet transport of the
seventies; all major airlines were forced to follow Trippe's lead in purchasing
the jumbo plane.

ABOVE One of Trippe's most impressive financial coups was to insist that the airline have an equity interest in the Pan Am Building.
BELOW After Trippe's death in April 1981, a 747 was rechristened in his honor.

He was eternally grateful to Juan for standing by him.

Trippe had strong feelings about loyalty and betrayal too, and gradually he settled scores for the Whitney affair. George Rihl was a prime victim. Juan sent him roaming throughout Latin America on tedious assignments for a few years, then based him in Rio de Janeiro. Out of sight, out of mind.

28

The Matter of
American Export Airlines

During Trippe's nine-month ordeal as a deposed chief executive, war broke out in Europe. The President proclaimed France, England and Ireland combat areas under the Neutrality Act of 1939. Pan American was obliged to withdraw from Southampton, Marseille and Foynes and to make Lisbon, the capital of neutral Portugal, the terminating point for its transatlantic service.

Also in this period, American Export Airlines reemerged as an enemy. In April, the C.A.A. had invalidated Trippe's agreement with John Slater, and American Export applied for permission to operate parallel to Pan American on the Atlantic routes. For Juan, this was tantamount to a declaration of war.

As soon as he regained his power, he took command of the fighting. There was to be no vacillating; no defensive action as in the SCADTA affair, simultaneously unfolding. This was to be an all-out offensive to annihilate the foe.

On the surface, American Export Airlines looked like a puny adversary. It had a skeleton staff and half a million dollars in assets, which included the one twin-engine Consolidated flying boat used to survey the routes that summer. But it had assurances of financing from Lehman Brothers and a formidable ally, the President of the United States.

The American Export Airlines case before the C.A.A.* presented the first test of the Civil Aeronautics Act and the regulatory agency vis-

* The agency was reorganized in July 1940. Economic functions were housed in a Civil Aeronautics Board; safety and technical matters were entrusted to a Civil Aeronautics Administration under the Commerce Department.

à-vis foreign air commerce, and the first challenge under the new law to Pan American's monopoly of the international routes.

The issue went to the fundamental policy expressed in the act: to what extent was it necessary to promote competition by placing a second carrier on the Atlantic?

Juan chose Henry Friendly as his legal tactician. The red-haired, mild-mannered associate at Root, Clark, Buckner, Howland & Ballantine had been advanced to junior partner, a rare position for someone of Jewish faith to occupy in a distinguished Wall Street law firm. Friendly was a lawyer of legendary intellect, a summa cum laude graduate of Harvard College and Harvard Law School, a former clerk of Supreme Court Justice Louis D. Brandeis. "Don't you ever send me another man like Friendly," Justice Brandeis had said to Professor Felix Frankfurter, who had recommended his student for the job. "If you do, I'll have nothing left to do."

After a year on that hallowed training ground, Friendly repaired to corporate practice at the Root firm, where he immersed himself in the specialities of railroad and utility rates and in the developing field of aviation finance. Now there was a new body of regulatory law to be constructed for the airlines. Congress had provided the legislation, with more than a little guidance from Friendly; the rest would be shaped by the quasi-judicial agency it had created, and by the courts.

Friendly counseled his client, as intervenor in the American Export Case, not to dispute the need for additional air service, due to the disruption of ocean shipping. Mail loads were almost twice what the Post Office and Pan American had anticipated when the C.A.A. granted permission for two trips a week in April 1939. Thousands of American expatriates and refugees from Hitler's persecutions were crowding into Lisbon in hopes of fleeing Europe. Waiting lists for Clipper flights ran to a hundred names or more. Instead, Pan American applied for expanded authority, and Trippe took to the banquet circuit to announce, "Within a year, as soon as our six new Boeing super-Clippers, now well under construction, can be delivered, we plan to add a fourth, fifth and sixth schedule. Then American businessmen will have a Clipper departure for Europe every business day in the week."

Juan maintained that competition would be wasteful, because the second carrier would be offering a duplicate service. Pan American could provide all that was required and do it better and for less cost than American Export.

He cited basic airline economics. Once the capital outlay for equipment has been made, the cost of each trip decreases with greater utilization of the aircraft. He implied that the need for subsidy—the burden on the taxpayer—should diminish too. The Post Office, which was backing American Export's application, conceded it would have to spend $1,388,400 a year more to support a second carrier than if Pan American were allowed to transport the same amount of mail by increasing its flights.

Juan disparaged his opponent's equipment. American Export had taken an option on three Vought-Sikorsky S-44 flying boats, a four-engine adaptation of a Navy patrol boat. Navy officials vouched that a second carrier would be a valuable source of research and experimentation with varied types of aircraft, since a single operator tended to buy from one manufacturer. "The S-44 was out of date in 1936 when Mr. Sikorsky submitted a later design, the S-45, to Pan American, and we turned it down for the B-314," Trippe said. "So American Export will be placing in transatlantic operation in 1941 and 1942 an airplane which was designed in 1935." He went on to list the land planes Pan American had ordered since then, neglecting to mention that they lacked transatlantic range and would be used in Latin America and Alaska.

During the hearings, Pan American asked manufacturers to submit designs for an aircraft with a payload capacity of not less than 17,500 pounds and sleeping accommodations for at least 50 passengers, capable of flying 5,000 miles at maximum altitudes of 25,200 feet. In short, a plane that could make Rome nonstop.

On July 12, 1940, the C.A.B. issued its decision. The members acted cautiously—novice swimmers splashing in the surf rather than plunging into the turbulent sea of competition. The board dismissed American Export's applications to serve Southampton, Marseille and Rome (after Italy declared war on England and France on June 10, its capital was out of bounds as a terminal point under the neutrality law), but granted a temporary certificate to serve Lisbon via Bermuda and the Azores.

Since its mandate to provide competition was contained in virgin legislation, the board looked to the experience of other regulated industries. It said:

> We are unable to find that the continued maintenance of an exclusive monopoly of trans-Atlantic American flag air transportation is in the public interest, particularly since there is no such public control over the passenger or express rates to be charged or over the standards of service to be rendered as is customarily provided in the case of a publicly protected monopoly.

American Export had also asked for endorsement of its status as a subsidiary of a shipping company. Section 408 of the Civil Aeronautics Act made it unlawful, unless approved by the board,

(5) For any air carrier or person controlling an air carrier, or any other common carrier, or any person engaged in any other phase of aeronautics, to acquire control of any air carrier in any manner whatsoever.

The C.A.B. shirked the opportunity to pry the airline apart from its steamship parent. Using an *Alice in Wonderland* reasoning, it ruled that Section 408 was inapplicable because American Export Airlines was not an air carrier when it asked for a certificate. Until it had a certificate, the airline could not carry anything.

The decision was sent to the White House and speedily approved by the President. Friendly petitioned the U.S. Circuit Court of Appeals for the Second Circuit to set aside the board's order. The judges declined to pass on the route award: the President was the "ultimate arbiter" of overseas air transportation and his decisions were not subject to judicial review. Colonel Johnson's prediction that Trippe would regret his insistence on Presidential prerogative was fulfilled sooner than expected.

But there was some comfort for Pan American in the appellate ruling. The court directed the C.A.B. to make up its mind about the matter of control under Section 408, and hinted broadly what the decision ought to be. A year later, the C.A.B. ordered the separation of American Export Airlines and American Export Lines, forcing the airline to scrounge for new capital.

The main campaign in Trippe's private war against American Export Airlines was fought in the corridors of Congress, assuming the dimensions of a public confrontation between the president of Pan American Airways and the Roosevelt Administration. The President was dead set on introducing competition to the international air routes, and Juan was just as committed to foiling his objective.

Though Bob Thach was no longer Pan American's chief lobbyist, Juan relied on the support he had built among the Southern Democrats who were by now estranged from Roosevelt. Conservatives like Senators Walter George of Georgia, Millard E. Tydings of Maryland and Josiah Bailey of North Carolina turned against the New Deal in the second term.

The C.A.B. had exercised its authority to certify a competitor for Pan American and to fix mail rates for the Atlantic routes, but the money for payments still had to be voted by Congressional committees for the budget of the Post Office. In September 1940, American Export petitioned Congress for $1.5 million to finance its preliminary transatlantic flights. The request was slipped into deficiency bills.

"Pan American has been moving high heaven to block the item," noted Assistant Secretary of State Adolph A. Berle, Jr. He had developed an antipathy to Juan Trippe as a result of the SCADTA affair. Spruille Braden had persuaded him that Pan American was helping train German pilots to bomb the Panama Canal.

The appropriations committees of both houses denied the subsidy without explanation. By the sometimes quirky process of democracy, a policy question as important as whether or not to have a monopoly could be disposed of in a minor appropriations bill.

A plain-paper memorandum reached the President's desk, conveyed by Basil O'Connor. It stated that "the present emergency has revealed more clearly than ever before the importance of the foreign air transport service of the U.S. as an instrument for the furtherance of the national interest and the national defense," and proposed that the United States adopt by law a permanent policy of monopoly in the conduct of international air transportation. The only company equipped to fill the role of the single foreign carrier was Pan American Airways, it said.

"Give me your opinion on this," Roosevelt asked Nelson Rockefeller, Coordinator of the Office of Inter-American Affairs. Rockefeller thought it presented a strong case for monopoly; but, he said, "I feel that competition is in the American tradition and that some of its advantages can well be retained without loss of prestige or sacrifice of efficiency of service."

In January 1941, the President inserted a request for $1,220,736 into his next budget to subsidize a weekly airmail service to Lisbon by American Export Airlines. Hearings were scheduled by the House Appropriations Committee. Berle was assigned by the President to line up support for the subsidy from the Navy and Army as well as the State Department.

"Juan Trippe came in today and made an impassioned plea of the principle of monopoly—even if government owned—meaning thereby that he does not want American Export permitted to do business at all," Berle recorded in his diary.

The committee eliminated the amount, this time giving reasons why in a report that adopted the Pan American position:

> Distasteful as monopoly may be under ordinary conditions, the fact remains that our foreign air operation is a monopoly, instituted, grown up and encouraged by government with that knowledge, and developed into a successful and useful arm of our foreign trade.

There was no justification for spending money just to provide competition between American-flag carriers when Pan American could provide additional service at less cost, the committee concluded.

Egged on by the Administration, American Export renewed its request for subsidy to the Senate Appropriations Committee. Senator Kenneth McKellar offered the bid in an amendment to the Treasury–Post Office appropriations bill. The parade of witnesses who had testified in the House trooped before his subcommittee.

"Do you insist on having a monopoly of the foreign air service?" Senator Bailey asked.

"No," Juan replied. "This is a matter for you gentlemen to decide; but I will add this. Wherever other countries have had experience in the matter of foreign air transportation, they have always come down to one company." How could the United States compete with foreign monopolies if American companies competed against one another for the transatlantic business? he went on. "We will meet after the war the German Lufthansa in the transatlantic trade, in South America and the Orient. We will meet in all these areas the British Imperial Airways. We will meet the great Dutch company, KLM."

And if memory served him correctly, U.S. maritime law prohibited subsidies to more than one company on each route. The American Export Line was the only steamship company on the ocean route to Lisbon, was it not?

"He is the most brilliant witness I have ever heard," said Senator McKellar.

John Slater testified that American Export had already spent $3 million in preparation for the Atlantic service. Harllee Branch of the C.A.B. warned that an investment of such magnitude might never again be put to the cause of free competition. "If this attempt to create another international air company fails, it will be a very long time before anyone tackles it again," said Berle. He pleaded with the Senators to vote the appropriation on its merits—"We do need the service," he said—and also to keep the matter of competitive policy alive for a full-dress determination.

On March 24, the subcommittee approved the McKellar amendment by a vote of 6 to 4. Senator Tydings submitted an opposing amendment to the full committee on March 26. In the pandemonium that attended the voting on his motion, Tydings thought it had carried by a majority of 1. He dashed from the committee room to spread the word. After he left, Senator James J. Davis, an elderly Republican from Pennsylvania, asked the chairman how his vote was recorded. As a yea, he was informed. "I voted under a misapprehension," the flustered Davis said. "I desire to be recorded against the motion of the Senator from Maryland." His change of vote tipped the balance, 13 to 12, in favor of subsidy for American Export Airlines.

Trippe was apprised of the reversal in his room at the Mayflower

Hotel, where he was conferring with John Cooper. Toward midnight, the telephone rang again. It was Postmaster General Frank C. Walker, the successor to Jim Farley, who had broken with Roosevelt over his decision to seek a third term. Walker was calling to relay a message. "The President has asked me to tell you that we hope there will be no more dirty business about American Export," he said. The Postmaster General added, "If there is any further discussion in the Senate, all your officers and directors will be indicted."

Cooper was immeasurably distressed. Antitrust prosecution was beyond his ken, criminal charges a shame he had never contemplated. Juan tried to soothe his anxious lawyer, who had taken to pacing the carpet between the twin beds, his Phi Beta Kappa key trembling on his vest. "You can resign if you want to tonight, but I'm going down in the morning to tell him we had nothing to do with the vote in the Senate."

On May 5, the Senate took up debate on the McKellar amendment, which had been modified into an $800,000 subsidy for one round trip a week by American Export and $416,000 for one additional flight by Pan American.

The lobbyists charged upon the Hill. A Senator from the Midwest said he could not recall when so many public and private persons had concerned themselves with an amendment to a bill. He was flattered by the attention, he admitted, for normally hardly anyone knocked on his office door.

American Export rallied Tommy Hitchcock, the prince of high-goal polo players and a partner in Lehman Brothers. Hitchcock called on Senators and graced a dinner American Export gave for the press. If Tommy visited a Senator once, Juan paid his respects twice.

The debate lasted for three days. Tydings was captain of the Pan American team, assisted by Bailey, a flowery orator of the old South. Senator Pat McCarran lent the prestige of his authorship of the Civil Aeronautics Act. Like Bailey, he believed the subsidy for American Export would be a boondoggle for Roosevelt's friends.

Juan Trippe hovered over the debate, a presence unseen but on everyone's mind. Even his opponents paid him compliments. Senator Carl Hayden of Arizona, leader of the Administration forces, said:

> If there is to be a monopoly, I want to see Juan Terry Trippe at the head of it. He is a very remarkable man.

He recited Trippe's *curriculum vitae*:

> He talked people out of money. He talked governments out of concessions . . . He is a very able man; and if we are to have a

monopoly, he ought to be at the head of it. But that is the whole question: Do we want, by this indirect method, by denying an appropriation, to establish a monopoly?

Hayden was spelled by Senator Joseph C. O'Mahoney of Wyoming, a former Assistant Postmaster General. He appealed to his colleagues "to place the stamp of approval on free competition."

Repeatedly, the pot called the kettle black. O'Mahoney, chairman of a committee investigating monopoly, accused Pan American of "an artful attempt . . . to secure complete and permanent domination of the airways of the world." He noted that the airline had collected $90 million in mail subsidy over the years to fatten its assets and benefit its stockholders.

How extraordinary it was, he said, "that a great organization which has been the beneficiary of the largess of the United States Government should be attempting to prevent the government from extending a subsidy to another line."

Tydings reminded his peers that American Export Lines carried 70 percent of the mail between the United States and Lisbon, and if it were to share Pan American's 30 percent, would end up with 85 percent. Is that any way to get rid of monopoly? he asked. Tydings trotted out figures indicating that the shipping company had received subsidy of $4 million during the past three years and had earned $6 million in the first nine months of the current fiscal year. Not a bad return for the Lehman bankers, who had put up $600 to take the company off the junk heap, he said.

The next-to-the-last word on the subject, and perhaps the most persuasive, was uttered by a Coloradan with a reputation for fiscal conservatism. Senator Alva B. Adams said he found it difficult to differentiate between the two private enterprises. "I think each of them is trying to get the most it can out of the Government, and I am in favor of dealing with the one from which we can get the most for the least money."

That company was Pan American Airways. By a vote of 44 to 35, the Senate eliminated the mail subsidy for American Export Airlines from the postal appropriation.

"The forces of good government won out at the end," said Juan, a trifle smugly.

During questioning before an examiner in another C.A.B. proceeding eight years later, he bluntly admitted his role in having American Export cut off from essential mail-subsidy support. "I don't think we have the time to act as guardian of the public interest," he said. "We are concerned with our own business, and when a company operates or attempts to operate a program which we think is either illegal or not in the public interest, we seek to protect ourselves in the best manner possible."

Was he apologizing for his actions? an adversary counsel asked. His answer was emphatic: "Not a bit."

29

Mobilizing

On the morning of May 28, 1940, as three hundred thousand Allied troops were being evacuated from Dunkirk, the President telephoned Edward R. Stettinius, Jr., chairman of the United States Steel Corporation, to ask him to take charge of industrial matériel in the mobilization for defense.

The German Blitzkrieg that began on May 10 with the invasion of the Low Countries and drove the appeaser Neville Chamberlain from 10 Downing Street crystallized for Roosevelt the absolute necessity of opposing Hitler. He sent a special message to Congress calling for a preparedness program against aggressors. The United States would rearm in self-defense, while aiding Britain and France in every manner short of entering the war. He requested production of fifty thousand military planes, a partial response to a dire shopping list from the new Prime Minister, Winston Churchill. Lindbergh ridiculed this as "hysterical chatter," dangerous meddling in the internal affairs of other countries.

Stettinius resigned from U.S. Steel and from several directorships he held with other corporations. He recommended that the Metropolitan Life Insurance Company offer his seat on its board to his brother-in-law Juan Trippe.

Stettinius was raring to serve—although, he let it be known, he was making a sacrifice in giving up a salary of $100,000 a year and additional director's fees for a strenuous, nonpaying job. "I am not wealthy," he said. The board of U.S. Steel voted him $75,000 in severance pay to cover his income-tax obligations.

Stettiniuses were chronic poor-mouthers, according to the reverse snobbery that distinguishes those with properly aged wealth from par- venus. Ed practiced economy with *cachet*. He was forever bestowing gifts on family, friends and heads of state and government, usually products of his gentleman's farm in Virginia. The President received smoked turkey for Christmas, and on his visits to London, Stettinius presented the Churchills with hams wrapped in brown paper.

Behind his back, he was nicknamed "the white-haired boy"—an allusion to his prematurely silvered hair and his rapid climb in the business world. He had the unaffected friendliness and unerring mem- ory for names of an advertising salesman. Circumstances of birth and his father's connections put him in the right places at the right times, but the warmth of his personality and his skill in getting adversaries to compromise and work together earned him respect and prevented much quibbling about his advancement.

Stettinius had been director of industrial and public relations at General Motors when he attracted the interest of Myron C. Taylor, chairman of U.S. Steel. Taylor was J. P. Morgan, Jr.'s, successor in that post; Big Steel was a Morgan creation, and the elder Stettinius had been a Morgan partner. Taylor took Ed Junior out of the auto business and groomed him to take over his job in 1938. Stettinius was 38, and the press crowned him an industrial prodigy.

Five months after he answered Roosevelt's call, he became direc- tor of priorities in the Office of Production Management. Among his responsibilities was the allocation of aircraft to the commercial sector. Stettinius disqualified himself from deliberations on Pan American Air- ways' requests, always reminding his colleagues that the president of the airline was his brother-in-law. Juan referred to their relationship at every turn, as though seeking prior absolution from guilt by association through his candor. All the posts Stettinius held during World War II, including Secretary of State, to which he was named in November 1944, impinged to some degree on the destinies of Pan American Air- ways.

Juan was a logical expediter for some of the problems that ac- cumulated on his brother-in-law's desk. When Foreign Minister T. V. Soong came to Washington in December 1940 on a begging mission for the Chinese Air Force, Stettinius sent him to Trippe, who alerted him to a hundred P-40 fighter planes that had been allocated to Sweden, and then applied pressure to have them transferred. Not long after- ward Soong was demanding planes for C.N.A.C., the airline in which Pan American was a partner of the Chinese Government.

It would have been impossible for Stettinius to divorce himself completely from his brother-in-law's business, especially since Trippe breathed, ate and slept Pan American Airways. Betty and Juan, and Ed and his wife, Virginia, were the closest of siblings and friends. They visited back and forth, corresponded regularly and concerned themselves with the minutiae of each other's existences. In the wartime transportation crunch, Stettinius availed himself of Juan's executive plane for personal junkets.

On July 25, 1940, Henry L. Stimson, Yale '88, Skull and Bones, and Secretary of War, sent for Juan T. Trippe, Yale '21S, St. Anthony and president of Pan American Airways. The meeting might have been scheduled in the tomb of a Yale secret society. The older man was going to tell the younger what he could do for his country.

Stimson was an exemplar of all that could be done "for God, for Country and for Yale." During fifty years, he had alternated a Wall Street law practice with public service in Republican Administrations —as Secretary of War under William Howard Taft, a roving diplomat for Calvin Coolidge. As Herbert Hoover's Secretary of State, he enunciated a policy of standing firm against nations that tried to break the covenant of peace: the Stimson Doctrine. At 73, he responded to a plea from a Democrat whose name was anathema to his clients and many of his friends.

Roosevelt needed a showing of nonpartisan unity for a foreign policy drifting inexorably toward participation in the European war, particularly if he were to run for a third term in November. Stimson agreed with him on aid to the Allies and accepted the War post in his Cabinet. For this, his last service to the nation, he was virtually read out of the Republican Party.

During the Battle of France in May, the War Plans Division of the War Department's General Staff had weighed plans for the defense of the Western Hemisphere. Were the French fleet to fall under Nazi control and with it the naval base at Dakar, an invasion of the Americas from a launching pad in West Africa would come within the realm of possibility. The Germans had planes with 3,000-mile range, sufficient for an aerial assault across the South Atlantic to the bulge of Brazil. Historians might later conclude that such fears were exaggerated; but after France was defeated and Dakar and the French colonies in the Caribbean pledged allegiance to the puppet regime in Vichy, the rumors of an intercontinental attack intensified.

The war planners identified as the first line of security for the hemisphere a string of airfields in Canada, the West Indies and the Caribbean accesses to the Panama Canal and on the coastal rim of

South America. Two routes for ferrying bombers and fighters to the east coast of South America were selected: one from Miami to Bahia, Brazil, via the Antilles; the other from Brownsville via Panama and Trinidad.

Since neither the United States nor its neighbors were belligerents, the War Department was inhibited from openly constructing air bases on Latin American soil. Under Secretary of State Sumner Welles advised Stimson that it was futile to try to negotiate treaties for such military purposes with twenty governments and that, moreover, it would cause fatal delay. There was only one solution, as there had been in 1935 when the Navy faced a similar dilemma in the Pacific.

Stimson asked Trippe to expand Pan American's network of landing fields and communications in Latin America to accommodate the defense program under a cloak of commercial activity. The War Department went into a huddle with Navy, State, the C.A.B. and the Bureau of the Budget to figure out a clandestine modus operandi.

A secret contract was drawn up between the War Department and Pan American Airports Corporation, a specially created subsidiary which by itself or through its associated companies in Cuba, Brazil and Mexico was to make arrangements with the governments of the various countries ostensibly to launch a major expansion program for the airline. That was what most Pan American employees thought they were working on, and Trippe did not enlighten his board of directors.

The Export-Import Bank lent Pan American the funds for construction, initially estimated at $12 million, which the War Department repaid from "the President's kitty," as Stimson referred to an emergency fund for military appropriations Congress had voted the President.

The State Department was dismayed. Thomas Burke, fresh from the struggle with Trippe over the de-Germanizing of SCADTA, practically wept on the shoulder of Assistant Secretary of State Berle. "I do not trust Pan Am any farther than I can see it," Berle said, but he acknowledged the pressing need and that it was easier to build on Pan American's facilities than to start from scratch.

The government lawyers were flabbergasted at the nitpicking proclivity of John Cooper and Henry Friendly, acting on instructions from Juan, who could never be satisfied that he had squeezed enough out of a bargain. They anticipated every possible expense and demanded that Pan American be insured against any risk of loss whatsoever. "The necessity for a situation where this company that literally exists only because of Government subsidy dictates to the Government under what terms it will undertake certain improvements for our national security is too fantastic for my credulity," exclaimed Laurence Duggan, the State Department adviser on political relations.

Trippe saw a magnificent opportunity to enhance the Pan American Airways System without expending a corporate dime, and to further entrench its monopoly. He chose sites for airports and recommended improvements on existing bases purely with an eye to commercial use. He overlooked such military requirements as emergency landing fields and extra-long runways for bombers, and had to be reminded to include the west coast of South America—Panagra territory—in his plans.

The contract between the War Department and Pan American Airways was signed in November and amended ten times during the next four years to encompass fifty-two projects for airfields, seaplane bases, radio and weather stations and gasoline storage depots in sixteen countries of the Caribbean, Central and South America, and Liberia. The final cost was four times the original estimate.

Juan would later say that Pan American performed without making a profit. He based this disingenuous claim on the fixed fee of $1, a not unusual feature of government contracts. Actually, the company derived considerable financial benefit beyond the strengthening of its facilities and the additional traffic generated by military passengers and cargo. Over the next two and a half years, Pan American received $612,000 in reimbursements from the War Department for administrative and other expenses of its executive staff, Trippe included, who were said to be lending their expertise from time to time to the Airport Development Program. A special ruling from the Internal Revenue Service exempted any revenues attributable to the program from federal income, excess-profit and war-profits taxes.

The War Department had a ninety-nine-year right to use the airfields or to keep them in operation, but vague wording made it possible to infer that Pan American had sole commercial rights. In negotiating with foreign governments, Graham Grosvenor, whom Trippe put in charge of the Airport Development Program, tried to freeze out other U.S. carriers by demanding exclusive privileges. Before allowing work to proceed on the airports in Cuba, he insisted on a decree from the government in Havana conferring authority on Pan American to permit use of the facilities by U.S. military aircraft. On paper, at least, the U.S. Government was to be placed in a subordinate position to the airline.

"Such permission [is] obviously a prerogative of sovereign Cuba, not of Emperor Juan T.," protested an exasperated official of the State Department, which had already arrived at the understanding with the

Cubans about extending the courtesy of its air facilities to Army and Navy planes.

"As brazen a piece of Pan Air effrontery as I have ever seen," Laurence Duggan fumed.

Noting that the War Department contract with Pan American was a *fait accompli*, Berle observed, "I suppose there is nothing to be done about it except await the inevitable day when we shall pay for what I fear has been a mistake." Berle was in the midst of observing Trippe's political maneuvers against American Export Airlines and was leading the Administration effort to obtain subsidy for the rival carrier.

As Postmaster General Walker had warned Trippe would happen, the American Export case sparked an investigation of Pan American by the Justice Department. Trippe got wind that an announcement by Thurman Arnold, the fiery trustbuster who headed the antitrust division, was imminent. He went to General Marshall for help. The Army Chief of Staff told the Secretary of War that it would be damaging to hemispheric defense for Pan American to be "publicly discredited," and the investigation ground to a halt.

With aircraft production absorbed in the national defense program, the Secretary of War had the ultimate authority to allocate deliveries of transport planes to the airlines. One day Trippe asked for an appointment to discuss their alma mater. The Yale Club of Montclair, New Jersey, had an annual rite honoring an alumnus as "someone who had abundantly made his Y in life." The ceremony was held in a suburban barn, where the rafters rang to "Boola-Boola" and reminiscences about Yale's victories on the football field, and the honored guest, wearing a white chef's toque, was presented with a large silver bowl. Juan Trippe had been the recipient the previous year.

Stimson noted in his diary:

> Juan Trippe came in to see me, primarily ostensibly—rather ostensibly—to urge me to go to the Plainfield [*sic*] Yale meeting where they want to give me the famous Yale Bowl for the outstanding Service-of-the-Year man during the year. But really to try to wangle some more commercial planes out of me.

Late in the fall of 1941, Robert Lovett, one of the heroes of the Yale Unit, took a leave of absence from Brown Brothers, Harriman to become Assistant Secretary of War for Air. He reviewed the airport-development contract, concluded that the War Department had been taken to the cleaners and persuaded Stimson that it should be amended.

"My contracts seem improvident," the elder statesman admitted, but he added piteously, "They were the best we could do then when we were not at war, when everybody was afraid that Congress would raise hell with us for making any such preparations."

The changes Lovett prescribed served to dilute Pan American's control over the airfields. Military and civil aircraft operating under government contracts were permitted to use them free of charge for the next ninety-nine years, and airlines certificated by the C.A.B. were given that privilege for the duration of the war.

The program got off to a limping start. Some of the private subcontractors Pan American hired were inefficient, there were widespread instances of petty graft and the bargaining for exclusive rights from the foreign governments held up construction. By September 1941, the first airport had still to be completed, and the War Department rated Pan American's performance of the contract as unsatisfactory. Stimson called Trippe to task. Juan promised to retire Grosvenor and find another overseer.

Juan had been seeing quite a bit of Sam Pryor, his Sheff classmate, now a railroad-equipment executive and his golfing companion at the Round Hill Club in Greenwich. Pryor was a pillar of the community, which was a nest for Old Blues, including Henry Luce, who, like Trippe, lived there mostly on weekends.

Sam was the same as he had been twenty years before—gregarious, restless and imbued with Theodore Roosevelt's "doctrine of the strenuous life." His father's graduation gift had been a safari to Africa, where Sam had shot big game and acquired an inordinate fondness for exotic birds and beasts. He solemnly swore to having met a martini-swilling baboon in Kenya.

After that respite, Pryor Senior sentenced him to a year of hard labor in a steel mill, an industrial baptism for sons of the very rich. Sonny Whitney had done time in a mine. Sam rather enjoyed soiling his hands by day, then washing up and going to dinner with Pittsburgh society maidens. He married a steel magnate's daughter, Mary Taylor Allerdice, a strapping lass with an angelic disposition. Mary Tay cheerfully tolerated her husband's enthusiasms for mynah birds and gibbon apes as house pets. He was particularly proud of a mynah that sat on his shoulder as he shaved, screeching, "You look great, Sam, you look great!"

He donned a white collar for his second job, as a trainee with Remington Cash Register, one of his father's companies, then became a salesman for Southern Wheel Company and was promoted to assistant to the president of its parent, American Brake Shoe & Foundry.

In 1937, he jumped into the political ring in Connecticut. In the trim fighting style of an all-American collegiate boxing champion, he trounced the state Republican machine and became national committeeman and Eastern treasurer of the G.O.P.

He was chosen Eastern campaign manager for Wendell Willkie, the rumpled-looking Hoosier who challenged Roosevelt for the Presidency in 1940. Willkie, the president of the Commonwealth and Southern Corporation, a utility holding company, represented the internationalist wing of the party and was the favorite of Luce and his editorial board. Dave Ingalls, Yale's World War I Navy ace, was manager for another Republican contender, Senator Robert Taft of Ohio, a leading isolationist. Ingalls was Taft's cousin. The Taft supporters accused Pryor of packing the galleries at the nominating convention in Philadelphia for "that utility public-relations fellow," and he and Dave had a row. Afterward, the Yale gentlemen buried the hatchet, and Ingalls became an adviser to Willkie during the campaign.

Trippe, who gravitated to power sources as a moth to a light bulb, asked Pryor to have him admitted to Willkie's hotel suite on election night, and he was present for the wake as the barefoot boy from Wall Street—in the scathing words of Secretary of the Interior Harold Ickes —went down with the largest popular vote a defeated candidate had ever amassed.

Pryor was also interested in aviation. He had learned to fly after college and recently had been invited to the board of Aviation Corporation, the holding company that owned about 10 percent of Pan American Airways stock. The Harriman-Lehman interests were ousted from Aviation Corporation in 1932 by E. L. Cord, an automobile manufacturer, and he in turn was ejected five years later by Victor Emanuel, a juggler of corporate securities and a veteran proxy warrior.

On the naive assumption that an old friend of Trippe's might be able to discover what he was doing with the airline, Emanuel designated Pryor to occupy the Aviation Corporation seat on the Pan American board. Sam held a commission in the U.S. Marine Reserve as a second lieutenant, and by the spring of 1941 was in danger of being called up. Here was a chance for Trippe to co-opt the watchdog for a major stockholder by transforming him into a faithful henchman. Moreover, he was awed by Sam's political connections and his simon-pure reputation, which could be applied to countering the ill will Juan had sowed in Washington.

Trippe told Sam he needed his help on a variety of matters, but first off on a secret project for the government. Pryor leaped at the opportunity for service more adventurous and freewheeling than active military duty. Juan appointed him vice president and assistant to the president of Pan American Airways at a salary of $22,500 plus bonus, which was more than his own compensation as chief executive.

Pryor was installed in an adjacent office, with their secretaries encamped in a neutral zone. Bob Lord, Trippe's put-upon secretary, frequently crossed into Pryor's territory to have his wounds dressed.

Sam understood Juan far better than any other business associate. He knew him away from the office as "an utterly likable companion" who loved a good martini or more, was vain about his golf score in the low 80s and yet was such a tightwad that when they had a meal together, Pryor would rush back to the table after Trippe left to add something to his tip. He could also accept him as a ruthless chief executive who was incapable of showing warmth to other human beings, because he believed Juan Trippe to be "a genuine genius." Theirs was a male bonding of master and slave. The scene from the Yale *Graphic* was to be reenacted over and over again through the years: Trippe announcing his wishes with averted eyes, and Pryor scampering off to do his bidding.

Sam concurred heart and soul with Juan's vision of Pan American as an instrument of American global leadership. It was part of a larger vision Luce enunciated in a signed editorial entitled "The American Century" published in the February 17, 1941, issue of *Life*. In a rambling statement written with the sophomoric style and philosophic arrogance of his Yale compositions, he ordained the United States as a world power, militarist and capitalist, "the dynamic leader of world trade," the Good Samaritan rewarding friends with food, technical assistance and superior political wisdom, enforcing a freedom of the seas, "the right to go with our ships and our ocean-going airplanes where we wish, when we wish and as we wish." America would follow its "manifest destiny" to spread a system of free economic enterprise through its "engineers, scientists, doctors, movie men, makers of entertainment, developers of airlines, builders of roads, teachers, educators." The missionary's son rephrased American imperialism for the day when the United States would have won the war it had entered in all but formal declaration. "We are, for a fact, *in* the war," Luce wrote approvingly.

Pryor was completely loyal to Juan and never betrayed him when he played tricks with his board of directors. Trippe was wont to submit proposals to the full board saying they had been recommended by the executive committee. Sam, who was put on the committee after a while, would exchange winks with another dumbfounded member. Both were hearing the proposal for the first time.

He learned from other executives Juan trusted, like Gledhill and Bixby, not to seek his approval before acting but to use his own judgment and assume responsibility for the consequences. Ideas for projects that required the chief executive's prior backing were planted circuitously. Pryor would mention his plan to Gledhill, who introduced it in the next conversation he had with Trippe as his idea, and pretty soon Juan would tell Sam to do what he had wanted to do in the first place.

Despite previous ignorance of the subject, Pryor attacked the airport-building assignment with gusto, and the pace of construction quickened.

Rumors of vast misappropriations of funds periodically served up in the columns of Drew Pearson, a Washington newspaperman who was Pan American's adversary for twenty years, were never substantiated. After Germany declared war on the United States and most of the South American countries broke relations with the Axis, the program was directly supervised by Army engineers. A Senate committee headed by Harry S Truman of Missouri that looked into frauds and waste in war contracts examined the airport program and issued no finding, a presumption of a clean bill of health. An Axis radio broadcast blew the cover on the program, announcing it as a prelude to a military takeover of Latin America by the United States. Officials in Brazil and Mexico, whose governments were among the most vulnerable, closed their eyes to the patent violations of their sovereignty for the sake of hemispheric defense. They realized that Pan American Airways could not possibly have afforded such large-scale construction on its own. In 1943, Under Secretary of State Welles acknowledged the truth about the bases and promised that they would be vacated after the war was over.

A consideration that weighed strongly in War Department planning for an airport-development program was the likelihood of support from local elements in the Latin American population for an Africa-based invasion spearheaded by the Luftwaffe. More than four million residents were German and Italian settlers and their offspring, an incalculable number sympathetic to Nazi and Fascist ideology. In 1938, a Fascist-inspired political party made an unsuccessful attempt to overthrow the Government of Brazil.

The most dangerous aspect of Axis influence as far as the War Department was concerned was the penetration of the Latin American air lanes. The European competition Trippe had railed against in the late Twenties had become almost entirely Germanic a decade later. About 10,000 miles, or one-fifth, of the continent's routes were operated by Lufthansa and its proxy carriers, the largest being Sindicato Condor in Brazil; another 7,600 miles by airlines like SCADTA and LAB, in Bolivia, that were managed by Germans.

The British and Dutch spheres of influence were confined to the Caribbean and Central America. The French pioneers had faded away under financial stress and takeovers of their operations in Argentina and Venezuela by native owners. Air France had entered into pooling agreements with Lufthansa on the South Atlantic service and on the Buenos Aires–Santiago route, where they had undercut Panagra's fares. Their marriage of convenience lasted until their respective governments exchanged firepower in Europe.

Beyond their transport functions, the German airlines were vehicles of propaganda and trade; technical assistance was bartered for raw materials without depleting monetary reserves. Even more worrisome to the U.S. military were Condor's capable photographic-survey department, pilot-training program, extensive radio facilities and aircraft-repair shops.

At the outbreak of the war in Europe, Lufthansa suspended transatlantic service (Air France maintained its schedule until the Nazis were goose-stepping down the Champs Élysées in June 1940), but Condor assumed its Natal-to-Santiago line with brand-new four-engine Focke-Wulfs, and continued the program of aerial penetration more earnestly than ever. German ships managed to slip through the British blockade to deliver engines and spare parts.

In December 1939, the Italian Linee Aeree Transcontinentali Italiane (LATI) inaugurated service between Rome and Rio de Janeiro by way of Seville, Spanish Morocco, the Cape Verde Islands, Natal and Recife. Mussolini's aeronautical showmanship, hitherto manifested in mass demonstration flights across the Atlantic and in bombing of barefoot Abyssinians, was at last put to practical use for the Rome–Berlin Axis. LATI transported Axis agents, mail and propaganda to South America out of reach of British censors, and took back strategic materials such as industrial diamonds, quartz crystals, tungsten and platinum. The pilots of the Savoia-Marchetti trimotors reported the movements of British and U.S. ships and planes in the Atlantic to German submarines.

The cleansing of SCADTA was only the first step in Washington's determination to rid the South American airways of the Axis influence, and Trippe had been singularly uncooperative in that effort. The initial stratagem was for Pan American to kill the other German airlines with competition—newer planes, better service—paid for by the Post Office through mail contracts.

But the U.S. Post Office could not subsidize foreign local-service airlines, and Roosevelt was reluctant to have Pan American control all the air routes of Latin America, though that was precisely what Juan was telling him had to be done. Given his obstructionist behavior in Colombia and his tendency to put Pan American interests first in the airport-development program, the President could foresee Trippe pre-empting the limited supply of U.S. aircraft.

Roosevelt decided to assign the project of "delousing" the South American airlines to the Reconstruction Finance Corporation, the loan agency created in the Depression and steadily diverted to war tasks. In April 1941, $8 million from the President's Emergency Fund was allotted to an R.F.C. subsidiary, the Defense Supplies Corporation, to establish the American Republics Aviation Division. William A. M. Burden, a young aviation analyst who was a twig from the mighty Vanderbilt oak, was named to head it. As Burden and two Wall Street acquaintances, William B. Harding, an investment banker, and Allen Dulles, a lawyer, set forth on the sensitive diplomatic assignment of negotiating with the governments concerned, Trippe warned the President that it was foolish to send greenhorns to do a job for which he possessed incomparable expertise.

Burden pried twenty-five C-47s, the military equivalent of the DC-3, from the priority lists and rounded up American civilian pilots to fly them on the internal routes, while Pan American and Panagra competed with Condor on the trunk lines. U.S. Army pilots were assigned to the flights as "observers on temporary duty."

Burden directed that the aircraft radios be operated by voice, in keeping with the practice of U.S. domestic airlines. South American aviation authorities assured him that their control-tower technicians were competent in English. Pan American radio operators still used code in South America. Trippe hurried to the White House protesting that Pan American knew best. The natives were untrustworthy, he said, taking a page from Peter Paul von Bauer's book. He predicted disasters on the scale of the Army's handling of the airmail in 1934, still a sore point with the President.

Whenever Juan lunged behind his back, Burden turned to his friend Nelson Rockefeller, who told Roosevelt that Trippe was just pulling another false alarm. Voice communication proceeded without mishap, and if anything, the backwardness of some of Pan American's practices in Latin America was exposed.

The Germans refused to give up until Nelson spoke to his father,

John D. Rockefeller, Jr., about choking off their fuel supplies. Aviation gasoline was proclaimed a munition of war under the Neutrality Act in July 1940, and therefore unexportable by domestic oil companies. After the senior Rockefeller conferred with his associates at Standard Oil and their British partners, the refineries in the Caribbean and South America cut off shipments to the Axis-affiliated airlines. Deprived of fuel, they suspended service in December 1941.

Pan American's standing with travelers to Latin America deteriorated during the war years. Passengers complained of being herded like cattle, forced to lay over in way stations because the airline flew only in daylight and routed out of bed at 4 A.M. to resume their journeys. As an American Ambassador to Brazil reported, its personnel were "arrogant and unfriendly," and passengers often resolved never to fly Pan American again if there was any alternative.

Much as it left to be desired, the service was astoundingly lucrative, especially in wartime. From September 1, 1939, to May 31, 1942, when the C.A.B. completed its review of the airline's Latin American mail pay, Pan American realized an annual rate of return of 38 percent on its investment in the region—an excessive yield in the board's opinion.

The C.A.B. detected the same accounting tricks Farley had censured in 1935: overstating expenses and loading the Latin American division with administrative costs for the entire system, thereby recouping through the Post Office the money to develop the Pacific and Atlantic operations.

Yet the C.A.B. reduced Pan American's mail rate only slightly and did not demand a refund of the immoderate profits. Rather, it decreed that they be set aside to "serve the public need" instead of being distributed to the stockholders as dividends. Pan American was to place the superfluous earnings in a special reserve fund to buy new aircraft.

The decision seemed to vindicate Trippe's management of the company. He could ignore unhappy stockholders and continue aggrandizing the airline, ordering new planes knowing the government would help pay for them. And though the C.A.B. said nothing explicitly, Trippe could now justifiably infer that Pan American Airways was indeed an instrument of national policy.

30

Aid to Britain

Lindbergh's misgivings about the flying boats were borne out in the first winter of transatlantic service, when only 56 percent of scheduled Clipper flights were completed, and many of those were delayed for days or weeks by icing conditions on the East Coast and the ferocious waters around the Azores. Passengers were taken by train or domestic airline to Baltimore, Norfolk, Charleston and, when the freeze moved southward, to Miami for departure.

The weather problems were particularly acute on the westbound trip because of the stubborn head winds which, added to the swells at Horta, caused many flights to be cancelled and others to be flown with scarcely any payload. In the summer of 1940, Trippe had Richard Long negotiate permission for Pan American to use Bolama, on the coast of Portuguese Guinea, for an alternative route during winter months. The detour via West Africa across the South Atlantic to Belém and Bermuda added 4,085 miles to the return trip from Lisbon to New York.

Pan American desperately needed a long-range land plane, a type of aircraft the domestic airlines had taken the lead in developing; but none existed that was capable of spanning oceans.

Providence, in the person of a wealthy and capricious flier named Howard Hughes, bailed Trippe out of his dependence on the flying boat. Hughes, the heir to a fortune his father had accumulated from the manufacture of an oil-drilling bit, was somewhat of a mechanical genius, and aspired to fame as a pace-setting pilot and aircraft designer.

He impulsively bought a controlling interest in T.W.A. and spurred Lockheed to build a four-engine high-altitude plane for his airline. The L-49, eventually named the Constellation, was to challenge the pressurized DC-4 Douglas was building for United and American. Since T.W.A. was strictly a domestic carrier at that time, Hughes allowed Juan Trippe to enter the Lockheed program. In June 1940, Pan American ordered twenty L-49s for its Latin American service, and ten L-149s, a long-range version with a pressurized cabin that permitted high-altitude flying above the Atlantic storms. Before the delivery date in mid-1942, Lockheed had to assign the contract to the Army, which promised to turn the Constellations back to Pan American six months after the war ended or sooner by agreement.

In the meantime, Churchill and Roosevelt made a decision compelled by military realities but with far-reaching implications for commercial rivalries after the war. The British were to concentrate on the production of fighter planes and small bombers to be put in service near their manufacturing sites, or crated in sections, shipped by boat and assembled at Takoradi, in the African colony of the Gold Coast, for deployment in the Middle East theater of war. The Americans were to construct big bombers and transport planes that could be ferried across the ocean.

None of the British flying boats had the range to overfly Lisbon en route from England to the West African colonies, which would be necessary if Portugal were to fall under Axis control. In August 1940, at the urging of Harry Hopkins, Roosevelt's special assistant, Trippe sold three of the advanced-model B-314As scheduled for delivery the following spring to the British Overseas Airways Corporation (successor to Imperial Airways). Juan simultaneously won credit for helping a needy ally and turned a profit on equipment that had outlived its usefulness. The cost of the Boeings to Pan American was $804,925 apiece; Trippe's selling price to the British, $1,035,400.

With German U-boats prowling the Atlantic in wolf packs, the Pan American Clippers became the safest, fastest means of transit between the ravaged Old World and the mobilizing New. Casual tourists were no longer listed on the manifests; every passenger was presumed to be a Very Important Person. Priorities were established from the airline's private sources of intelligence. Ann Archibald of the Washington office rolled out red carpets for admirals and generals. When Colonel William Donovan, the New York lawyer, was sent on a confidential scouting trip to London and the Mediterranean by the more fervent interventionists in the Administration to gather evidence in support of increasing overt aid to Britain, Ed Stettinius dispatched a note to Juan at East Hampton, where he was spending the weekend, to impress upon him that it was "a vitally important mission." Donovan, the future spymaster, traveled under an alias but betrayed himself to newspapermen through a classic oversight, the initials W.J.D. on his suitcase.

Government officials took precedence over businessmen and exiles, while mail had priority over travelers. Pan American was obligated to accept all the mail the Post Office delivered to its terminals, and some flights carried half a million letters and a single passenger—usually a transatlantic commuter like John M. Winant, the Ambassador to London, or a State Department courier with correspondence between the President and a Former Naval Person in his sealed pouch.

Life magazine rated the Clippers "the best international club in the world," in which the elite members might be heard conversing brilliantly in three languages. Eight thousand feet over the Atlantic, Archduke Otto, pretender to the throne of the Austro-Hungarian Empire, dined with Eve Curie, the journalist daughter of the discoverer of radium. The menu: shrimp cocktail, turtle soup, filet mignon and biscuit tortoni. Raymond Clapper, the Scripps-Howard columnist, pontificated over highballs to a Tory Member of Parliament and a Swiss economist. When a westbound crossing was delayed for a day in Bolama, Juan Trippe and Wendell Willkie went lion hunting together

The press flocked to the European theater of war on the Clippers to cover the French collapse behind the Maginot Line, the retreat to Dunkirk, the bombing of London and the Nazi invasion of Norway. Back over the Atlantic and across the United States the correspondents sped to catch the Clippers for the Pacific on their way to interview Chiang Kai-shek and his court at Chongqing. The peers of the Fourth Estate Clippered to battle toting their typewriters and fifths of bourbon.

The foot soldiers of the press staked out the Pan American base at LaGuardia Airport. "It seems as if during the past year, I've interviewed every world character except Hitler and Mussolini, and I wouldn't be surprised to see them show up at any time," gloated a wire-service man who had only to stand poised, pencil in hand and police card in hatband, to catch Harry Hopkins, Lord Halifax, Clement Attlee, Prime Minister Robert Gordon Menzies of Australia, scores of Congressmen and a delegation of New York City firemen sent by Mayor LaGuardia to study the techniques of London's bomb squads debarking from the Clippers.

After the fall of France, the Pan American base at Lisbon became a singularly valuable listening post. Its radio station was the only one on the Continent not in Axis hands. The city teemed with spies, adventurers and numerous species of displaced humanity. Jack Kelly, the Pan American traffic manager, flashed his movie-star smile and graciously spurned bribes for the few available seats on the westbound flying boats. From his counterpart in Lufthansa he took readings of Nazi intentions, transmitting them to Trippe, who gave them to G-2, the War Department's military-intelligence division.

The Clippers from America alighted on the flare paths of the Tagus River at night, 23 hours after takeoff over the velvety golf courses and manor houses of Long Island. Passengers settled in at the Hotel Aviz or the Palacio, habitats of ex-kings, diplomats and assorted intriguers, to wait for other planes to take them to their destinations.

The London-bound were driven to an airfield at Sintra to board a camouflaged DC-3 parked in the shadow of a swastika-marked Focke-Wulf bomber, scourge of Allied shipping in the Atlantic. A small sign inside the cabin of the Douglas plane boasted "KLM—STILL FLYING." As the Germans descended on Holland, KLM crews jumped into their DC-3s and flew them to England to operate, under British Airways administration, the only passenger service between the beleaguered island and the outside world.

The journeys were seldom uneventful. There was a hair-raising stop to refuel at a landing field in a forest clearing at the far northern corner of Portugal. After takeoff, the plane swung out to sea, and black screens were fitted against the cabin windows. Sometimes the pilot announced that one or more Focke-Wulfs were on his trail off the coast of France, and that though he hoped to elude them in the clouds, he had radioed ahead for protection. As the aircraft approached England, Royal Air Force bombers appeared to escort the plane to a landing field outside London.

England fought alone after the surrender of France in June 1940, and rallied by the eloquence of its new Prime Minister, endured brutal bombardment by the German Air Force during the late summer. While U-boats decimated merchant shipping in the Atlantic, the Luftwaffe attacked convoys in the central Mediterranean and rained bombs on the sentinel island of Malta and on North African airfields, severing supply lines to the British Army under Italian assault in Egypt.

In September, Roosevelt revealed he had made an agreement with Churchill to transfer fifty elderly U.S. destroyers in exchange for the right to establish naval and air bases on strategic British territory in the Atlantic and the Caribbean.

Two weeks before Christmas, Churchill sent Roosevelt a four-thousand-word message of candor, stating Britain's prospects for survival. The Prime Minister asked for weapons, particularly aircraft, and for protective measures by the United States to reduce the losses at sea, and confessed that Britain was running out of cash to buy American assistance.

The President mulled over the letter during a two-week vacation cruise in the Caribbean until he figured out a way to get around Britain's dollar shortage within the limits of his popular mandate for aid short of embroiling the United States in the war. A loophole in the law permitted the leasing of Army property not required for public use. Marketing his inspiration with the analogy of lending a hose to a neighbor whose house was on fire, Roosevelt asked Congress for authority to sell, transfer, lend or lease weapons, services and food. The Lend-Lease bill, introduced in both houses in January 1941, was exhaustively debated for two months under heavy opposition from noninterventionists.

The bill, passed by a wide margin on March 8, was implemented with a $7-billion appropriation. Because he wanted to keep tight surveillance over the program, Roosevelt appointed Harry Hopkins to act as "bookkeeper" for Lend-Lease. Chronically ailing and constantly propelled toward other assignments for the President, Hopkins shifted the responsibility six months later to Ed Stettinius, who was given the official title of Lend-Lease Administrator.

While Lend-Lease was being kneaded through Congress, a delegation of British military chiefs in mufti was conferring at the War Department about ways and means to rush aircraft and supplies to the Middle East to hurl against General Erwin Rommel's crack Afrika Korps, which had come to the aid of the Italians and was harassing the British Army through the Libyan desert. The alternative shipping route to the Mediterranean, now policed on the sea and in the air by the Germans, was around the Cape of Good Hope and into the Red Sea, a journey of weeks.

Harry Hopkins flew to England to make a firsthand assessment of the situation for Roosevelt. He reported that it was urgent to supply reinforcements for the Middle East and to release British ferry pilots for combat duty. Beginning in November 1940, the bombers bought for cash were being flown by American pilots from the factories in Southern California to Montreal, where they were transferred to a British ferrying organization.

"Get hold of some of the commercial airplane people, including particularly Trippe of the Pan American Airways Company," Secretary of War Stimson ordered an aide on March 4.

The airports Pan American was in the process of constructing under the secret contract were large enough for bomber ferries. On the African side of the Atlantic, Imperial Airways had laid down a fragmentary route five years before. It extended from Cairo south along the Nile to Khartoum, in the Anglo-Egyptian Sudan, and westward to El Fasher and El Geneina, following above ancient desert caravan routes to Maiduguri and Kano, in northern Nigeria, and then swinging down to the Atlantic ports of Lagos, Nigeria, and Accra and Takoradi on the Gold Coast. Most of the bases were situated on lakes and rivers to accommodate the Empire flying boats. A few emergency airfields were scattered through desert and jungle. None of these stations could take large military aircraft, and the British lacked the resources to start improving them.

Trippe immediately grasped the possibility of fleshing out this skeleton route into a strategic transport line across the waist of Africa. Pan American was the one U.S. carrier experienced in building airports and radio stations in primitive areas and in flying multiengine planes over the oceans.

One stretch of the route between El Fasher and Fort Lamy, in Chad, which was under Free French control and would be made available by General Charles de Gaulle to the Anglo-American forces, consisted of "nearly 700 miles of sheer nothingness," according to a British official who surveyed it.

> Brown country, streaked with dry watercourses and dotted with bush: maps absolutely useless: nothing shown on them for the most part, for two hundred miles at a stretch, and where something was shown, it was obviously incorrect. Would have hated to do it without wireless.

A typical "landlubber's" comment, observed a Pan American pilot. Airmen used to flying over the ocean were accustomed to doing without landmarks and were more expert navigators.

But this was the very period in which the lobbying before the appropriations committees over the American Export airmail subsidy was reaching fever pitch, and Trippe's standing with the Roosevelt Administration was sinking to an all-time low.

His moves to block the subsidy were discussed in a Cabinet meeting on March 15 at which the premier topic was the problem of keeping the British lifeline to the Middle East open.

Secretary of the Interior Ickes recorded in his diary:

> Trippe is an unscrupulous person who cajoles and buys his way. He has made quite an unsavory record in South American coun-

tries. He has what amounts to a worldwide monopoly, and the President is against this.

The President said he had talked personally with Trippe. He describes him as a man of all-yielding suavity, who could be depended upon to pursue his own ruthless way.

Secretary of the Navy Knox suggested that the government might take Pan American over for the duration of the emergency, and others thought that might not be a bad idea. The President mentioned something about a 50-percent interest in the airline.

In April, General Henry Arnold flew to Lisbon on the *Yankee Clipper* and caught the British Airways DC-3 for London on a mission to coordinate British and American air resources. He wired Stimson on the 19th:

> British acute need for transport Takoradi-Cairo/London-Lisbon/ Libya Abyssinia Iraq Sudan/Transport air crews returning from Lisbon and across Africa/Suitable DC-3 Lodestar DC-2/British need 50/Survey Douglas and Lockheed.

The second week in May, Robert Gross, president of Lockheed, notified the War Department that he had twenty of the requested transports, stripped of cabin furnishings and refitted with steel benches along the walls and extra fuel tanks, ready to be delivered if arrangements could be made with the British.

Gross talked to Hap Arnold and to the British air liaison officer, and there was no doubt in any of their minds that Pan American Airways was the only organization with the navigational expertise for the South Atlantic and the only means of getting the ferry pilots back to the United States. "They can't very well return on the Italian airline," Trippe pointed out to Arnold. Army Air Corps pilots would fly the aircraft from California to Miami; Pan American, through a newborn subsidiary, Atlantic Airways, would train the crews assembled by Gross to ferry them to Bathurst, in British Gambia. Most of them had never flown an ocean and had to be given cram courses in celestial navigation and radio key code. Half the planes were sent on their way to Bathurst in mid-June, the vanguard of an aerial delivery system that was to grow by the thousands during the next four years. Talks at the War Department with a British air mission focused on bolstering the African supply line. The U.S. Army Air Corps surveyed the route and found it hopelessly inadequate. There were no runways long enough to take the U.S.-made bombers, and the only radio beacon in West Africa was the Pan American unit at Bolama.

On June 17, Roosevelt wired Churchill about three landing places on the West African coast: Bathurst, Freetown and a site to be selected in Liberia. Bathurst was uncomfortably close to Dakar, one of the French bases the Vichy regime had just made available to the Nazis in an explicit protocol. The Free French controlled equatorial Africa, but had failed in a joint expedition with the British in September 1940 to seize Dakar. Lying due south of the French base on the rim of the African bulge were Bathurst, Bolama (a Portuguese enclave), Freetown, in British Sierra Leone, and Liberia, an independent country under American influence. Liberia appeared to the War Department the most desirable entry point—it was 800 miles away from Dakar—although it had no airfields.

As the President's message was being dispatched to the Prime Minister, Juan was in London preparing to address the Royal Aeronautical Society. To be invited to give the annual Wilbur Wright Memorial Lecture to the British air hierarchy was one of aviation's signal honors.

His topic was "Ocean Air Transport," which he interpreted as a history of Pan American Airways and its technical prowess. He spoke for nearly two hours in an underground room at the Air Ministry, enthralling his audience of military brass and high-level bureaucrats with explanations of the howgozit curve and the team precision of the multiple flight crew, and his optimistic prediction of daily transatlantic passenger service on 12-hour schedules within two years.

When he finished, there was a banquet, and the subject shifted to flight over land—the supply route over Africa—and how it could be laid down and by whom. Juan found himself giving a second, informal lecture. He drew a line from the West African coast, preferably at Liberia, southeast to the British supply depots on the Gold Coast, then slashing northeast through the deserts to the Sudan and Egypt. It was a 10,000-mile route from Miami to Cairo, and he intimated that Pan American could manage it by adapting the Pacific island argosy to trackless sand.

Afterward he drove to the Dorchester Hotel and, before turning in for the night, went to the roof for a breath of air. As he looked out over the battered city silent under the stars, a figure materialized in the darkness. "Sir, the Prime Minister asks you to dine with him," a voice said. It was nearly 11 P.M., and Trippe had had his dinner. He assumed he was the butt of a practical joke. The man assured him he was in earnest. A half-hour later, Juan was seated before a glowing coal fire across a table from Winston Churchill in a small dining room in the basement of 10 Downing Street.

"Trippe, my good man, I've had a report about your plan. Tell me about it," the Prime Minister greeted him. Juan expounded into the small hours of the morning, his natural inclination to overstate his case abetted by quantities of brandy and his need to convince Churchill that the project should be turned over to Pan American.

This would free the Royal Air Force and its B.O.A.C. transport arm for other service, he stressed. And who was more capable of doing the job quickly and efficiently than Pan American? Trippe was aware that there would be strong objections from B.O.A.C. and the civil-aviation group at the Air Ministry, who suspected a commercial motive in everything he did.

The Prime Minister listened attentively, weighing strategic expediency against the political risk of inviting this aggressive Yank into the African folds of the Empire. The next morning Juan left for Lisbon to catch the westbound Clipper, and when he arrived at LaGuardia two days later, a U.S. Marine plane was waiting to fly him to Washington. "We can do it under Lend-Lease. How long did you tell him it will take?" the President asked.

A week after Trippe supped with Churchill, the drafting of contracts between Pan American and the War Department and the British air mission began in Washington. General Arnold understood from what Harry Hopkins told him that the British wanted Pan American to operate the trans-African route. Churchill might have given a signal to that effect, but Hopkins, who was urging full speed ahead on the project, did not stop to reckon with the animus of the British representatives toward Trippe, who they believed was taking advantage of a military emergency to poach on their commercial preserve in the Middle East and Africa.

Actually, the friction ran deeper than that. The British wanted maximum aid with the fewest strings attached, and the War Department thought the Americans should get something in return for their money. Lovett suggested that inasmuch as the route was being paid for with U.S. funds, Pan American should be guaranteed use of the facilities for an extended period. But this was never conclusively established in the contracts, and led to further misunderstanding.

Pan American could not proceed without operating rights in the various African colonies and protectorates. The air envoys in Washington delayed, inventing one excuse after another and then saying that the rights had to be negotiated with the individual colonial administrators. "If you don't get on with this," Trippe snapped at one meeting, "by the time your emissary gets down there, you'll find a Nazi greeting him at the airport." It was one of the rare instances Henry Friendly could recall when Juan had lost his temper. Usually, he expressed anger with frigid silence.

Numerous problems had to be unknotted in the Western Hemisphere as well. Neutral Brazil was loath to allow its territory to be used as a conduit for military shipments to a belligerent. General Marshall got the Brazilians to look the other way provided the planes refueling at Belém and Natal were of U.S. registry.

Then there were the neutrality restrictions impinging on Lend-Lease. Government lawyers finally decided that Pan American could operate a route in what was indubitably a combat area as long as the government owned the aircraft. The War Department bought one of the B-314s for $900,000 and leased it back to Pan American for $1. The flying boat was to be used to transport British and American officials and spare parts across the South Atlantic. A similar procedure was applied to the DC-3s for the trans-African transport service, which were purchased from the domestic airlines and also leased to Pan American.

The War Department supplied the pilots from its pool of Army Reserve officers, releasing them from active duty to fly for Pan American, for which they received bonuses of 25 percent above military pay plus $500 at the end of their tours.

Pan American signed two contracts with the British Government, one for a ferry service from Miami to Bathurst, the other to put the trans-African route into operation. The airline was granted "full operational rights" along the route—wording that was subject to several interpretations.

Three agreements were concluded with the War Department: to deliver American-made bombers and cargo aircraft to Khartoum, as well as fighter planes from the British assembly plants at Takoradi; to transport military personnel and cargo across the South Atlantic and Africa; to return ferry pilots to the Western Hemisphere.

Payments were made on a cost-plus-fixed-fee basis from a $17.8-million allotment of Lend-Lease funds and $2.8 million from the President's Emergency Fund. "This could be awkward," said Trippe, referring to his brother-in-law who was about to take over the administration of Lend-Lease.

Pan American created two new subsidiaries: Pan American Air Ferries, an enlargement of Atlantic Airways, which Juan asked Dave Ingalls to manage, and Pan American Airways–Africa, Ltd., headed by Frank Gledhill. The Old Boy network from New Haven was in place in aviation planning, with the Pan American quartet of Trippe, Gledhill, Ingalls and Pryor (on the airport-development program), Lovett at the War Department as Assistant Secretary for Air and Di Gates, who took leave of the New York Trust Company and the Pan American board to serve as Assistant Secretary of the Navy for Air.

Secrecy was no longer possible for an undertaking of such scope; nor was it desirable, since publicity furthered Roosevelt's objective of standing up to the Axis powers. On August 18, shortly after his first rendezvous with Churchill off the coast of Newfoundland, a meeting that produced a declaration of their peace aims in the Atlantic Charter, the President announced that Pan American Airways had agreed to provide ferrying and transport services "from the arsenal of democracy to a critical point in the front against aggression. The importance of this direct line of communication between our country and strategic outposts in Africa cannot be overestimated."

The New York Times commented:

Thus for the first time a United States civilian air transport service, accustomed to difficult operations in all parts of the world, will be employed as an instrument of the government in the same manner that Germany uses the Lufthansa.

The United States was still not a belligerent, and the noninterventionists were in full voice, so the transport service was described as being available for general commercial use "providing a direct air link between New York and Africa."

Pan American applied to the C.A.B. for a temporary certificate to operate between New York and Léopoldville via San Juan, Port of Spain, Belém, Natal, Monrovia and Lagos. In June, Trippe had sent a crew to find a site in Liberia. A body of tranquil water in the northwestern part of the country—Fisherman's Lake—was selected for a flying-boat base, and a vast tract adjacent to the Firestone Rubber plantation near Monrovia for a land-plane facility.

The project was to be incorporated into the airport-development program; hence operating rights were negotiated under the same pretense as in Latin America. President Edwin Barclay of Liberia believed his country was being opened to commercial airline service, and he agreed to exclusive rights for Pan American which irked the helpless State Department and heightened the suspicions of the British.

From Liberia, Pan American moved on to the Belgian Congo and concluded an operating agreement with SABENA, the Belgian airline, as a prelude to securing a concession in Léopoldville, also with exclusivity features. The Congo port was seen as the pivot of a strategic alternative route to the Middle East and beyond, but this was not something to be flaunted in open hearings before the C.A.B. American Export and Eastern Air Lines intervened, and it looked as if another contest was in the making until the War Department asked for a temporary adjournment of the hearings and gave evidence in secret session that persuaded the board to grant the application at once.

The building of the aerial highway over the African continent dwarfed previous feats of causing bases to spring up in South American jungles and on desolate Pacific islands. This time Pan American was closely supervised, and Gledhill had to be responsive to Major General Robert Olds of the U.S. Air Forces Ferrying Command and to leading lights of the Royal Air Force, the uncooperative hosts of his mission in Africa.

Equipment for constructing fourteen bases and radio stations to be strung out at 300-mile intervals along the route was collected from airports all over the United States and stored at a pier in Staten Island. The cargoes were loaded on chartered freighters, and when some ships were sent to the bottom of the Atlantic by German submarines, the lost items were reordered and rerouted by air.

From the Chrysler Building, Pan American recruited 1,200 engineers, technicians and managers to expedite the work in a part of the world that had yet to enter the twentieth century. Seven thousand natives, many of them tribal enemies, substituted for machine power. Tractors pried the earth loose to make a runway; black men carried it away in pans balanced on their heads. To areas impenetrable by wheeled vehicles, Africans bore supplies on their backs. Drums of gasoline, too heavy for human beasts of burden, were trekked across the desert by camel.

Climate posed the severest challenge, even for veterans of the tropics. At Kano, in the Nigerian interior, temperatures rose to 140 degrees. The harmattans—blistering Sahara winds—unfurled dense layers of dust, destroying visibility and clogging airplane engines. Ant armies erected 7-foot hills on freshly laid runways; islands of vegetation sprouted in rivers to block the taxi lanes of flying boats. A third of the American construction crews discovered why the coastal region was called "the white man's grave" when they were laid low by malaria.

On October 18, sixty-one days after the President's announcement, the work was completed and the first scheduled flight of Pan American Air Ferries left Miami. A stream of warplanes—C-47 cargo transports and Martin B-26 and Consolidated B-24 bombers—began to move at the rate of one a day over the route to Egypt, joined by the British Hurricane fighters and Blenheim bombers assembled at Takoradi.

On December 5, Jim Smith departed for Cairo as Pan American's special representative to negotiate with local governments and the R.A.F. Smith was the State Department lawyer Juan hired to work with John Cooper, and later promoted to assistant manager of the Atlantic division. Juan called him in for a chat the day before he left. "We're expecting the Pacific route to be cut one of these days," he said mysteriously. "And when that happens, Africa will be the main route to Australia and the Far East."

31

Pan American Goes to War

The *Hong Kong Clipper* was held at Hong Kong for two days in mid-November 1941, disrupting the Pacific schedule, on orders from the Chrysler Building in New York. The British authorities, who were expecting a Japanese strike against one of their colonies in Southeast Asia, relented to allow a Japan Airways plane from Tokyo to land at Hong Kong so that Saburo Kurusu might catch the Pan American flying boat for Manila. Kurusu was headed for Washington with terms for avoiding a final break between Japan and the United States.

At Manila the envoy transferred to the *China Clipper*, which roared on its island-hopping course across the Pacific until an engine failed. Kurusu cooled his heels for two days at Midway while it was repaired, and the diplomatic clock stopped. At Honolulu he bustled aboard the *California Clipper*, and upon landing at San Francisco doffed his black homburg for newspapermen and exclaimed that it was "so nice" to be arriving in nine days instead of the month it would have taken by ship. He was escorted to a United Airlines terminal to make connections for a transcontinental flight to New York, where he changed planes again for Washington.

On the afternoon of December 7, Kurusu was summoned with Admiral Kichisaburo Nomura, the Japanese Ambassador to the United States, for a dressing down by Secretary of State Hull. In caustic Tennessee mountain language, Hull accused them of deceit during the past three weeks of exchanging notes.

For at 7:55 that Sunday morning, the "date," said the President, "which will live in infamy," Japanese torpedo planes and dive-bombers, released from carriers that had been gaining on Hawaii from the fogs of the northern Pacific since November 26, whirred over Oahu and dropped their cargoes. The bulk of the American fleet was shattered at its moorings in Pearl Harbor, and the pride of the Army Air Forces, clustered wing to wing at Hickam Field, was destroyed.

Juan was nursing a bad case of grippe at the house in Greenwich when the radio flash came during afternoon dinner. He drove with his family, which now included a third son, 3½-month-old Edward Stettinius Trippe, to the apartment in Gracie Square. He took a call from Secretary of the Navy Knox, and then went to spend a long night at the Chrysler Building, receiving glimmers from Washington of the fate of Pan American Airways' Pacific fleet.

None of the flying boats was docked at Pearl Harbor when the Japanese struck. Within ten minutes of the attack, Pan American ground operators radioed warnings to Pearl City, Midway, Wake, Guam, Manila, Canton, Noumea and San Francisco, and to their airborne planes. Though the conventional wisdom in Washington and London had looked toward a strike on Malaya, the Dutch East Indies or the Philippines, Pan American had an emergency plan, drafted in code for its crews, that covered all contingencies including a raid on the Pacific islands.

The *China Clipper* was safe at the Treasure Island base in San Francisco, having just completed a flight from Honolulu with Soviet Ambassador Maxim Litvinov aboard. Seventeen passengers were having breakfast in the lounge of the *Anzac Clipper*, which was due to land at Pearl Harbor in an hour, when Captain H. Lanier Turner received the message "CASE 7, CONDITION A," directing him to land at Hilo, refuel and return to San Francisco.

The *Philippine Clipper* was 10 minutes out of Wake Island bound for Guam with a cargo of tires for Chinese fighter planes. Captain John Hamilton followed instructions to dump 3,000 pounds of gasoline and head back for Wake. As the M-130 was being refueled, two Japanese bomber squadrons assaulted the base, razing the buildings and piers and tattooing the Clipper with machine-gun fire.

An hour and a half after the enemy had left, Hamilton flew the plane, still airworthy despite its injuries, to Midway and then to Pearl Harbor—an unguided journey of nearly 2,500 miles.

The Condition A flash caught the *Pacific Clipper* between Auckland and Noumea, alerting Captain Robert Ford that his path to Honolulu was blocked. He returned to New Zealand, ordered a coat of camouflage paint for the B-314A and waited a week for orders to proceed to New York "the long way round"—a 31,500-mile flight that turned out to be the first circumnavigation of the globe by a commercial plane.

The *Pacific Clipper* made eighteen stops in twelve countries on five continents, flying through several war zones and over vast expanses of water controlled by the same enemy that lurked in the air above. Ford navigated by sun and stars, with textbook maps and visual reference, guarding radio silence most of the way. He followed a course over the Timor Sea to Surabaya, across the Indian Ocean and the Bay of Bengal to Ceylon, and up the Arabian Sea to Karachi. The Cyclone engines knocked displeasure at being fed automobile gasoline instead of 100-octane aviation fuel.

He flew over the Persian Gulf to Bahrein Island, crossed the Arabian Desert and paused at British bases on the Red Sea and the Nile and at the Pan American facility opened at Léopoldville the day before the attack at Pearl Harbor. From the Congo River, he headed overland to West Africa and across the South Atlantic on the Pan American route to Brazil, the Caribbean and northward to New York.

An hour before dawn on January 6, 1942, at the Pan American Marine Terminal at LaGuardia Field, fourteen crewmen trooped out of the flying boat wrapped in berth blankets over their tropical shirts and jackets. "A routine operation," Captain Ford told reporters. "It went like clockwork every mile of the way," with one change of spark plugs in 209 hours of flying time and one delay to repair an engine in port.

The *Hong Kong Clipper*, an S-42 workhorse being readied for a flight to Manila, was reduced to a charred skeleton by Japanese dive-bombers at Hong Kong on the morning of December 8. Practically the entire fleet of C.N.A.C. was at Kai-tek Airport, and seven planes were demolished on the field. Pilots rolled the five undamaged aircraft out of the hangars and into nearby vegetable patches, camouflaging them with bamboo and mud before another wave of attackers appeared.

W. L. Bond had kept the airline operating from a base in Hong Kong after Chiang Kai-shek withdrew the government of the shrunken Republic of China to Chongqing in 1938.

C.N.A.C. maintained mail and passenger service between Hong Kong and Chongqing and between Kunming and Rangoon and, for a brief time, served Hanoi. The airline's American pilots who flew the DC-2s and DC-3s also hauled cargoes of tungsten and tin out of China to earn precious foreign exchange for the nearly bankrupt Nationalist regime, and carried medicines and Red Cross supplies on the way back. Chinese pilots flew the interior routes with rickety Commodore and Douglas Dolphin flying boats.

To foil the enemy, they flew on indefinite schedules, mostly at night and in weather that discouraged feathered birds and Japanese pursuit pilots. Passengers were never sure when they would depart, how terrified they would be after bumping for hours through soupy air, or how many emergency stops would be made before their destinations were reached.

Bond ignored the air-raid warnings on December 8 and roved the colony rounding up evacuees. He instructed them to assemble at the Peninsula Hotel, and under the benevolence of an overcast night, they were taken by bus to Kai-tek and put aboard shuttle flights to Nam-yung, 200 miles inland over the Japanese lines. Later, they were transported to Chongqing.

The C.N.A.C. pilots made sixteen trips that night and the next, to remove nearly four hundred adults and children and what remained of the airline's inventory of spare parts. Among the passengers were Madame Sun Yat-sen, widow of the founder of the Chinese Republic, and her sister, the wife of H. H. Kung, the Finance Minister.

On December 13, 1941, the President issued an executive order delegating his power to take over the airlines in a national emergency to the Secretary of War. The next day, Lovett called a meeting to plan a supply system for a war being fought on opposite sides of the globe. Transport is the stem without which the flower of victory cannot blossom, Churchill said. At that moment, the Allied stem was frail.

Assembled at the War Department were representatives of the Army Air Forces Ferrying Command, the two-day-old Naval Air Transport Service, the Office of Production Management, the C.A.B., the Air Transport Association, T.W.A. and Pan American Airways.

During the past six months, the Ferrying Command had delivered more than a thousand combat aircraft from the West Coast factories to embarkation points on the Atlantic Seaboard and Canada, where Royal Air Force pilots had taken them on to Britain. Pan American Air Ferries had begun moving planes across the South Atlantic to the Middle East. Once the Japanese severed the sea and air lanes to the Philippines and were overrunning the Allied bastions in Southeast Asia, the trans-African route assumed paramount strategic importance as a supply line for the India and China theaters of war as well.

At this critical juncture, the Army and the Navy needed long-range aircraft to haul tons of cargo over distances of 10,000 to 15,000 miles. Almost all the transport planes operated by the domestic carriers were two-engine aircraft—DC-3s and Lockheed Lodestars—incapable of making an overwater jump with heavy payloads. The nation's entire fleet of oceanworthy transports consisted of eleven B-24 bombers, convertible to military cargo use, that belonged to the Ferrying Command; Pan American's eight Boeing and two Martin flying boats; and five Boeing Stratoliners owned by T.W.A.

At the meeting it was agreed that the War Department would buy five of the Pan American B-314s and the Stratoliners, while the Navy took the *China Clipper* and the *Philippine Clipper*. The planes would be turned back to the airlines to operate under military contracts.

Supplemental contracts were written with Pan American Air Ferries and Pan American Airways–Africa extending the trans-African services to Teheran, which would become a transfer station for Lend-Lease supplies to the Russians, and to India and Singapore.

On December 18, Captain Harold Gray took off from New York in a B-314 loaded with spare tires for P-40 fighter planes. He flew eastward to Calcutta, where the cargo was transferred for shipment to the Flying Tigers, a unit of American volunteers fighting in China. A week later, another flying boat embarked on Destination X, carrying .50-caliber ammunition that would reach General MacArthur in the Philippines by submarine. Pan American Air Ferries delivered four Navy PBY flying boats to the Dutch East Indies via the same circuitous route.

It was a beginning.

Though their experience was in operating short- to medium-range transports, the chiefs of the domestic airlines were chafing to demonstrate their patriotism, and to jump on the war gravy train. The job of Colonel Edgar Gorrell, as president of the Air Transport Association, was to see that his constituents obtained juicy military contracts while preserving their commercial operations. Gorrell, a West Pointer, warned that the celebrated efficiency of the American carriers would wither under a military bureaucracy. Instead of taking the airlines over, he argued persuasively, the government could best utilize their experience in scheduling transport operations by hiring them to perform the vital services.

In the winter and spring of 1942, the War Department contracted with T.W.A. to run a shuttle service between Washington and Cairo with two of its Stratoliners, denuded of their cabin furnishings and pressurization systems, and over the North Atlantic to England with a third. Northeast and American Airlines were assigned to Greenland and Iceland with DC-3s (converted to C-53 military cargo planes) and Eastern Air Lines to a Miami–Natal run. Eleven carriers, including Pan American, were enlisted for a critical airlift of supplies to Alaska to blunt the Japanese attack on the Aleutian Islands.

Juan seethed as the gates were lifted to allow domestic trespassers on Pan American's international routes. The C.A.B. was not awarding them certificates—these were strictly military contracts—but who could tell where they might lead? At the very least, to the end of the mystique of the invincible Pan American Clipper pilots. Meanwhile, the trunk carriers were gaining long-range operating experience and notions of grandeur.

Pan American had been engaged in defense operations long before the war, as the record plainly showed. The Army pilots ferrying the first B-17s to the Philippines two months before Pearl Harbor had used the Pan American facilities at Midway and Wake. Since December, the Japanese had been in possession of Wake and Guam—the mid-Pacific route was lost—but the line to Australia was open through Canton Island and New Caledonia, and the airports in Latin America and Africa were supporting a crucial lifeline. Full mobilization only changed the numbers of men and quantities of supplies as far as Trippe was concerned; Pan American could handle it all. He told General Henry Arnold, chief of the Army Air Forces, that he was going about military transport the wrong way. It was a serious mistake, he said, to ask domestic airlines that had no experience with four-engine aircraft to undertake over-ocean flying. By awarding multiple contracts, Arnold was creating a maze of paper, stupendous accounting problems and confusion in communications.

"A single large system permits efficiency and economy in the training of personnel and the use of equipment that are impossible for smaller separate units," he lectured the General. "All air transport beyond the borders of the U.S. should be centralized in one organization."

He expanded on a master scheme he had formulated in the weeks before Pearl Harbor. It was a plan to ensure that American Export Airlines would never have a second chance at starting operations, and also to consolidate Pan American's position in the defense program.

A single company, Pan American Airways, would enter into a contract with the government to operate all overseas routes. The government would have an ownership interest in return for investing capital, but no real voice in management, although the Chief of Staff of the Army, the Chief of Naval Operations and the Under Secretary of State would be invited to attend meetings.

By this plot, Trippe could achieve a monopoly with the government's consent and participation. In presenting it to Arnold, he modified it to fit the war emergency. Components of other carriers could be welded into the organization, he said, but the dominant unit would be Pan American. Since a consensus was developing that there ought to be one, strong, capable individual at the head of the air transport organization, Trippe would accept the job—only under the conditions he outlined, however.

If this seemed the height of arrogance, that was the reputation Juan had earned for himself in Washington. As a Senator observed, "Mr. Trippe made the impression upon me of a man living under the conviction he had a divine call to operate and control American aviation in the transoceanic field." In war as well as in peace.

Even if he had wanted to, and there is no evidence that he did, Arnold could not have accepted Trippe's advice. Too many members of the Roosevelt Administration were disenchanted with the president of Pan American Airways and his overweening ambition for the airline. The President and the man closest to him led the list. "I have never liked the idea of Pan American having a world monopoly of our airlines," Harry Hopkins informed Ed Stettinius, the Lend-Lease Administrator, on December 31.

By March 1942, a plane was landing or taking off every fifteen minutes at the Accra base, operational hub of the trans-African route. But trouble was brewing over what the British construed as excessive commercial zeal on the part of the Pan American organization.

Jim Smith was caught in the anomalous situation of trying to operate a civil airline as an arms runner under authority granted for circumstances no longer prevailing. Pearl Harbor had removed the need for commercial pretense.

He was left to his own devices in Cairo, never hearing a word from Trippe and only curt, oral directives from Gledhill, who was based in the Chrysler Building and swooped through Africa every month or so. Smith's most pressing responsibility was to take the legal steps to extend the route eastward from Khartoum as directed in the supplemental contracts.

Two lines branched out from the Sudan, passing through areas under varying degrees of British control. One went through Cairo, Lydda, in Palestine, and Habbaniyeh and Basra, in Iraq, to Teheran. The other led to the Far East through Asmara, in Eritrea, around the southern end of the Arabian peninsula (Aden–Mukalla–Salalah– Masira) to Karachi. From there it would be extended across central India to connect with an aerial highway over the Himalayas into China.

Hindsight reveals that the implications of Pan American's presence in the region were more extensive than air transport alone. Oil and awakening nationalism were factors, too, in the struggle between the English-speaking Allies for domination of the postwar world, a conflict temporarily masked by unity against a common enemy.

After the R.A.F. officials obstructed Smith's efforts to obtain operating rights, he proceeded to negotiate directly with the governments of Egypt, Iraq and Iran. He opened an office in downtown Cairo, overlooking Shepheard's Hotel, to book nonmilitary passengers such as news correspondents, diplomats and civilians working in the areas, on the basis of space available after the military passengers and cargo were loaded on the planes. He scheduled a weekly service between Cairo and Teheran. "That was orderly organization and made the best use of aircraft and people," he said. B.O.A.C. thought it was underhanded competition, especially after Gledhill dropped a remark on one of his visits: "We're going to undersell B.O.A.C. by 10 percent on the route."

Smith obtained a mail contract from the Egyptian Government by offering to do it a favor in expediting communications with the United States. B.O.A.C. saw this as a postwar maneuver—which, of course, it was. In 1937, when the Atlantic service was still struggling to be born, Trippe was already thinking of a round-the-world hookup with the Pacific route through the Mediterranean. He met the director of Misr Airwork, a private Egyptian airline, when he was visiting in New York, and together they drafted a technical exchange and operating agreement. Misr was to use the pact to win an Egyptian permit for Pan American. But nothing had happened; and here in January 1942 was Smith putting Pan American into the good graces of King Farouk's regime.

Cries of foul emanated from the British Embassy, where Sir Francis Shelmerdine happened to be visiting. Sir Arthur Tedder, R.A.F. commander for the Middle East, complained to the head of the American North African military mission, who asked for clarification from the War Department.

"Our contracts express an ambition by the U.S. Government to operate primarily in the interest of national defense but with a commercial purpose," Gledhill asserted when he was called to Washington to explain. He expected the War and State Departments to support his contention, but whatever understanding there may have been during the frantic negotiations of July 1941 had been transformed by the need for a smooth working relationship with the British in the bleakest months of the war.

"The recurring resentments of the British to Pan American's expansion in the Middle East and the fact that Pan American tends to regard a military effort as a commercial operation" were among the serious disadvantages General Marshall, the Army Chief of Staff, cited in having a civilian airline operating so close to a combat area.

Pan American exercised its exclusive privileges in Liberia and refused to let B.O.A.C. use Roberts Field, the land-plane facility built under the Airport Development Program. This dispute was eventually bucked to Churchill and Roosevelt to settle at Casablanca. Roosevelt ordered B.O.A.C. admitted.

On February 15, 1942, the War Department served notice that it was going to cancel Pan American's African contracts and militarize the bases and ferrying service by the end of the year. Bixby told Lindbergh he feared the government was going to take the airline over, and reports to that effect appeared in newspapers.

Trippe called out the lobbying troops. "The British are trying to have us sell Pan American down the river," Louis Johnson, former Assistant Secretary of War, fulminated to General Marshall. Johnson's law firm, Steptoe & Johnson, was retained by Pan American as outside legal counsel.

Plain-paper memoranda drifted into the State Department with reminders that Pan American's franchises with foreign countries would lapse if it were to become a military arm of the government, and this would be particularly onerous in the cases of Ireland, Brazil and Portugal, each being a fulcrum of the Atlantic routes.

The reports of takeover turned out to be grossly exaggerated. In June, the War Department established the U.S. Air Transport Command as the major instrument of logistical support for the far-flung combat operations on the ground and in the air. The A.T.C. contracted with the major carriers for specific services, and also set priorities for their regular commercial operations. Essentially, Arnold adopted Gorrell's recommendation and rejected Trippe's.

A career Army officer, Major General Harold L. George, was placed at the head of the A.T.C., and numerous airline executives were commissioned to run it. Arnold picked C. R. Smith, president of American Airlines, to be George's deputy, or chief operating officer, with the rank of brigadier general. Harold Harris was coaxed away from Panagra and made assistant chief of planning.

The A.T.C. purchased the four-engine transports coming off the production lines and leased them to eleven carriers with contracts for overseas service. Trippe saw the fruits of his diplomatic labors—the international air routes—distributed to the domestic airlines for sampling. T.W.A. and American Airlines augmented Pan American on the North Atlantic to London, United on the Pacific to Australia and India; Eastern and Braniff were assigned to Central and South America, Northwest to Alaska. American Export Airlines, presumed to be mortally wounded after Trippe's triumph in the Senate, took nourishment from a Naval Air Transport Service contract to fly the North Atlantic.

Despite the antagonism between the Air Transport Command and the Pan American organization in Africa during the transition period, the momentum of the operation quickened. A crew was routed out of bed in Accra and sent to Lagos to pick up 15 tons of fuses for antitank shells, which they whisked to Cairo for General Bernard Montgomery's British Eighth Army at El Alamein; another shipment provided 12,000 pounds of dust filters for the tank engines. Reinforced with planes and supplies delivered along the route, Montgomery's men pushed Rommel's desert rats back across Libya into Tunisia in October, paving the way for the decisive defeat of the Axis powers in North Africa.

In December, Pan American Airways–Africa and Pan American Air Ferries disappeared from the corporate masthead. Jim Smith transferred to the Navy as a dive-bomber pilot, and Dave Ingalls went on active duty as a commander to develop the Naval Air Transport Service for the Pacific. Pan American's new Africa–Orient division undertook a contract from the A.T.C. to operate the Cannonball, an express service from Miami to Karachi. The 11,500-mile run was completed in three and a half days, with a relay of five crews flying the new C-54 cargo planes. East of Karachi, another extension of the route looped down to Calcutta and up to Assam, in northeast India, to connect with the aerial funnel into China over the hump of the Himalayas, a trail blazed by C.N.A.C. Pilots dubbed it "the skyway over hell."

Pan American resumed flying its pioneer routes on the North Atlantic to Ireland, and in the Pacific to New Zealand and Australia, under contract to the Naval Air Transport Service. Airline personnel ran the radio stations, maintenance shops, hotels and medical clinics on its South Pacific bases for the Navy. It did not sit too well with enlisted men to be told by their noncommissioned officers on arrival at Canton Island or Noumea to take orders from the Pan American manager of the base.

The Pan American Airways organization considered itself a branch of the Armed Forces. For the flight crews, the distinction between war and commerce lay mainly in the choice of uniforms. On military-contract duty, they wore Army khakis or Navy greens with gold wings on their chests connoting status in the reserves. For commercial flights to South America and the neutral ports of Foynes and Lisbon, they donned their Pan American navy blues.

They drove themselves to feats of valor. One pilot bettered his own record of twelve South Atlantic crossings in thirteen days by making two flights in twenty-four hours. Another rescued forty-eight survivors of a sinking troopship in the Pacific, landing and taking off in fifteen-foot swells.

Often the destinations were known only to the division manager and the operations manager. Pilots opened their secret orders after takeoff. A captain dispatched to Bermuda learned that he was to follow a zigzag course to Léopoldville, and from there to places for which no surveys had been made. Léopoldville–Khartoum–Mombasa–Mahé–Coëtivy–Diego Garcia–Mombasa–Khartoum–Léopoldville: he deduced that plans were being made for operations in the Indian Ocean.

On January 12, 1943, the captain of the *Dixie Clipper* was given a manifest with nine passengers identified only by number. Shortly after dawn at Port of Spain, Passenger Number One swung jauntily into the lounge of the plane on leg braces and canes, followed by Harry Hopkins and two admirals. Roosevelt was the first President of the United States to fly while in office or to leave the country in wartime.

His destination was Casablanca, where he conferred with Churchill, made the acquaintance of Charles de Gaulle and set the terms of unconditional surrender for the Axis. On the way back, the stewards broke out champagne, caviar and cake for the President's 61st-birthday dinner, and the crew presented him with an envelope containing $11 for the Infantile Paralysis Fund. The pilot and Harry Hopkins initiated Roosevelt into the "Short Snorters Club of Ocean Travelers." The membership card was a dollar bill signed by the other passengers and any Short Snorters the member encountered afterward.

While numerous airline executives spent the war years in uniform, Juan served his country as president and chief executive officer of Pan American Airways. With Whitney finally departed, his authority was unchallenged at last. The post of chairman of the board was left vacant for the next twenty-two years, a sign that Trippe was reserving all power unto himself.

In the nervous weeks following the attack on Pearl Harbor, he exercised options for 50,000 shares of stock at $12.50 a share, and during the next two years, sold them at twice his cost. The $1.5 million worth of stock remaining in his portfolio made him the largest individual stockholder in Pan American Airways.

Serving as a commercial front for a nation rearming was lucrative business for Pan American. Its route system grew from 62,305 miles in 1939 to 98,582 miles in 1941—a network two and a half times B.O.A.C.'s, and larger than all European carriers' combined. Revenues doubled, and earnings increased 76 percent. As Juan had anticipated in the exercise of his stock options, a fighting war was even more profitable. With half of the Pan American Airways system employed under military contracts, revenues during the four war years rose by 75 percent to $70 million, and net income increased 125 percent, to $7.6 million.

Trippe made more forays than ever to Washington, the battlefield for his greatest conquests in the past. Betty worried about Juan's being cooped up in a tiny room at the Mayflower and suggested moving the family to the capital for the winters. The children seldom saw their father. Betty told them he was doing something important to win the war. As crises erupted in the nursery, she learned to cope, admirably and alone.

His family stayed put among their abodes in New York and Connecticut, but as a concession to the shortage of hotel and restaurant accommodations in Washington, Trippe had Pan American rent a five-bedroom house on F Street, adjacent to the F Street Club, a hangout for official Washington. The early-nineteenth-century dwelling was furnished in period style and staffed by Negro manservants—Pan American's token minority employment. Food and drink were provisioned from the best black-market butchers and liquor dealers.

Trippe's personal niggardliness of 10-cent cigars and mingy tips did not extend to Pan American's business entertainment. Pryor's bounteous hand controlled the spigot; his openhearted nature thrived on an expense account unsurpassed in airline annals.

Pan American's corporate home away from home was a private oasis of bonhomie for public figures amid the pressure-cooker atmosphere of a government town in wartime. The parties were relatively sedate, given the weakness of some of the honored guests for grain alcohol, and wives were often present. There were no hints of sexual scandal in the rumors about what went on behind the elegant facade of the house on F Street. Newspaper columnists perceived it as an influence trading post.

The house provided a setting in which Pryor could flex his muscle as a wealthy Republican politician from Connecticut. "You've got to know important people personally, and know them well enough to understand their problems and how you can help them," he said. Sam invited the important people down from the Hill and other power centers, gave them drink, meat, a sympathetic ear and exposure to Juan Trippe at his most charming. The guests were mesmerized by this shy bear of a man, with the faintly satanic smile and luminous eyes, who spoke a businessman's language of golf and trade advantages, a Navy man's language of sailing ships and strategic lines over the sea and skies, a patriot's language of concern for America's place in the world. "Don't you see," he would say, stating an order rather than a question, and he would talk for hours, without hearing anything they had to say, and always with the same message: that only one airline should carry the American flag on foreign air routes.

One of the F Street regulars was Ralph Owen Brewster, a former Governor of Maine who had been elected to the Senate in 1940 after several terms in the House. Brewster was a member of two powerful committees: Commerce, which had a continuing interest in aviation, and a Special Committee to Investigate the National Defense Program, otherwise known as the Truman Committee, looking into war frauds and profiteering.

Another guest was the Army Chief of Staff, with whom Ed Stettinius was renewing a family friendship dating back to the First World War when his father, then an eminent industrialist serving the War Department, had taken young Major George C. Marshall under his wing. Sitting next to the great soldier at dinner in the F Street Club one evening, L. Welch Pogue, the Chairman of the C.A.B., realized that Marshall's pronouncements on postwar aviation were verbatim statements of what he had heard from Juan Trippe.

Once the United States declared war on Japan, Lindbergh was wholly committed to fighting and winning. He discovered then what unyielding enemies he had made in Washington with his stubborn stand against intervention, culminating in a speech to an America First rally in September 1941 when he named as a powerful minority of war agitators "the British, the Jewish and the Roosevelt Administration."

He refused to retract his statements as the price of regaining the Army Air Corps commission he had resigned in 1939 and looked for second best, a project in the aviation industry directly related to the war effort.

Trippe sounded eager, at first, to have him rejoin Pan American. Lindbergh thought he should ascertain whether the President objected. "Maybe I should talk to Lord Halifax too," Trippe said. Halifax was the British Ambassador to Washington. Nine days later he telephoned Lindbergh to say that "obstacles have been put in the way." Charles deduced that he was referring to the President. When Trippe got around, a week later, to seeing Lindbergh in his office, his explanation was still cryptic. Avoiding proper names, Juan said that "they" posed no objections at the War Department, but it was an entirely different story at the White House. "They" were bitter about Lindbergh and would not tolerate his being affiliated with Pan American in any way.

He stressed that "they" were very angry with him for suggesting it. "Let's keep the door open; attitudes can change," Trippe said.

Charles did not press him for further details and accepted that Juan had gone to bat for him with Roosevelt and had been bruised in the process. Many years later, Trippe acknowledged that he had not spoken to the President about Lindbergh. "I felt it was really a government matter and not a personal situation," he said.

At United Aircraft and Curtiss-Wright, Lindbergh experienced the unfamiliar sensation of being blackballed, and by the very industry that once had begged for his endorsements. Only Henry Ford, phobic about Roosevelt, was unconcerned about approval from the White House. He invited Lindbergh's help on a government contract for B-24 bombers at the Ford plant in Willow Run. There was no reaction from Washington, and subsequently Lindbergh went back to the skies, testing fighter planes for Republic Aviation and Chance-Vought. Finally, in the spring of 1944, he saw action in the Pacific as a civilian representing the aircraft manufacturers to study the performance of the planes in combat. He flew fifty missions with Marine and Army squadrons. At the age of 42, he had a taste of strafing and dive-bombing, shot down one Japanese plane and had a close call when a Zero got on his tail but was frightened away by his comrades.

Part V

THE SHAPE OF THINGS TO COME

32

The Other War

While one World War was being fought on land, on sea and in the skies by nations united against the Axis Powers, another was heating up among the military allies for control of the commercial airways in the peacetime of the future. All feared that victory would be too late to press their claims. "Unless we come to agreement, there will be a race between the Americans and ourselves to control the airlines of the world," a British Member of Parliament warned. He urged a conference "to settle which sphere of influence belongs to each country."

There was still another contest—between Pan American Airways and the other airlines, foreign and American. "Trippe's plan is monopoly or nothing," said Assistant Secretary of State Adolph A. Berle, Jr. "And he is quite able to play on either side of the belligerent line, or both sides at once."

Berle's mistrust of Trippe had snowballed, from the SCADTA affair to the American Export case and the airport-development projects, until the mention of his name or the sight of his thickset figure trudging along the second floor of the State Department on his round of calls caused the Assistant Secretary's jaw to tighten and suspicious thoughts to flash through his mind.

He was Trippe's senior by four years. A Congregational minister's son from Boston, a prodigy as an undergraduate and as a law student at Harvard, he had been recruited from a professorship at the Columbia Law School to serve with the "Brains Trust," Roosevelt's inner circle of advisers during his first term.

Berle gave counsel to the Reconstruction Finance Corporation, and helped to shape banking and securities legislation without accepting a regular post in the Administration. He was short and strong-willed, an intellectual autocrat who vented his impatience with lesser minds in sarcastic outbursts. Despite his patent shortcomings as a practitioner of the sensitive art of diplomacy, Roosevelt invited him back to Washington in 1938 and appointed him Assistant Secretary of State for Latin American Affairs. After an administrative reshuffling in February 1941, he was given cognizance of finance and aviation.

In a State Department study of the problems of the postwar world, the issues of oil and air power were pinpointed as areas of potential conflict with Britain. "Aviation will have a greater influence on American foreign interests and American foreign policy than any other nonpolitical consideration," Berle told Secretary of State Hull, and suggested it warranted a separate division or special adviser.

The job eventually went to Stokeley Morgan, returning to the State Department after eight years in the Latin American division of Pan American Airways, climaxed by a falling-out with Trippe. Berle remained the senior aviation policy coordinator.

In the fall of 1942, with the British Foreign Office pestering him to open talks, he entreated the Administration to develop a program for postwar air routes. The fuss over the African bases was one of several indications that the British were going to put up a stiff fight for commercial air supremacy despite an almost total lack of transport equipment, owing to the conversion of their aircraft factories to the manufacture of fighter planes.

There was steady conflict between the R.A.F. and the U.S. Army Air Forces over ferrying and military transport operations—"The ATC has acquired considerable experience in unsatisfactory relationships with the British throughout the world," General Arnold noted—and American pique at the dual character of the B.O.A.C. organization, which shifted back and forth from military to commercial services with Lend-Lease planes. The United States was expending hundreds of millions of dollars to develop huge air bases on such British island possessions as Bermuda, Fiji and the Solomons without knowing what its rights to these installations would be after the war. The Americans had been notified, a British Air Ministry official told the House of Commons, that "as regards routes they are now running for military purposes on lines which may have commercial values, 'all bets are off' at the end of the war."

With Hull as his intermediary, Berle secured the President's permission to reassemble an Interdepartmental Committee on International Aviation consisting of Robert Lovett from the War Department, Artemus Gates from the Navy, Under Secretary of Commerce Wayne Chatfield Tayor and Welch Pogue, chairman of the Civil Aeronautics Board. Berle was chairman of the committee.

Lovett shared Berle's sense of urgency about their assignment. He instructed General Harold George of the A.T.C. to consider the future of air transport for the United States a responsibility second only to that of fighting and winning the war.

"History and common sense support the conclusion that instead of getting gratitude from the beneficiaries [of Lend-Lease] we are more than likely to get resentment, envy, and perhaps even hate," Lovett declared in a memorandum.

"We must make the trades while we still have something to trade with and not rely on the good faith and gratitude of the recipients of American help."

While the committee struggled to produce a policy outline during the next few months, a cacophony of voices was heard on the subject. In a radio interview on New Year's Day 1943, Vice President Henry A. Wallace proposed an international air force to keep the peace, and a United Nations investment corporation to finance, among other projects, the building of airports and "a network of globe-girdling airways." When not engaged in military actions, the pilots and ground crews of the aerial police unit might operate the airways as a commercial system, he said.

A respectable sector of British opinion was advocating an internationalized air service, with the great powers in control of interlocking zones of influence. Wallace's remarks echoed the idealistic principles of the Atlantic Charter and the faith in universal peace and law upheld by collective security being advanced in the United States by distinguished figures of both parties like Adolph Berle and Wendell Willkie.

Juan Trippe dismissed such philosophical abstractions. "There will always be wars," he said.

Among the principles written into the Atlantic Charter by Churchill and Roosevelt and incorporated in the United Nations Declaration of January 1942 were freedom of the seas and equal access to trade by all states. In subsequent months a higher freedom began cropping up in speeches and magazine articles. By an apocryphal account, Churchill's crony Lord Beaverbrook, Minister of Aircraft Production in the Coalition Cabinet, was expounding a doctrine of closed versus open skies to Harry Hopkins, whereupon the President's special assistant observed, "If you want to sell anything in the United States you have to put the word 'freedom' in it."

"They all talk of freedom of the air," Trippe scoffed, "but they don't know what it means." Indeed, few who used the term bothered to define it. Did they mean that the planes of all nations should be at liberty to roam the skies, over the territory of other countries as well as over the oceans? Did they intend for planes to land at any airport, as ships could put into any port, in times of peace? What about depositing and picking up passengers and cargo, and the right of cabotage—to operate between ports inside a foreign country? Vessels that enjoyed the freedom of the seas did not have the same freedom on inland waters.

The loose talk was disturbing to Trippe, for it heralded easy access to international routes, a giveaway of the economic advantages he had obtained by personal diplomacy for Pan American Airways—and, he always added, for the United States. The babble about freedom of the air implied the destruction of Pan American Airways' monopoly.

Juan Trippe and Henry Luce, scarcely more than acquaintances at Yale, had settled into the wary and superficial friendship of men who are content only in influential company. "They were both devoured by the use of power," David Bruce said. Luce, the Bonesman and laureled "Ac" student, felt the unscholarly Trippe gaining upon him from the Sheffield boondocks. After their alma mater honored them both with advanced degrees, they panted toward a seat on the Yale Corporation, the university's governing board.

At the Cloud Club atop the Chrysler Building, headquarters for their companies, Juan and Harry frequently saw each other deep in their respective business lunches. They joked about a race between Time/Life and Pan American Airways to open foreign stations.

Time, Life and *Fortune* portrayed Juan Terry Trippe as an admirable imperialist: Luce's dogma of postwar American hegemony translated fluently into Trippe's Pax Pan Americana for the airways. Juan suggested accounting procedures to Harry to maximize the earnings of his magazines, and made sure the publisher was treated royally aboard Pan American Clippers. Juan played Cupid's assistant when Harry was in the midst of arranging a divorce from his first wife so that he could marry Clare Boothe Brokaw, a writer of exceptional blond beauty and acid wit with whom he had fallen madly in love after a few encounters. Mrs. Brokaw went off on a holiday to Havana, where Pan American's Cuban manager alerted Trippe to her presence. Juan told Harry, who hotfooted down to intensify his courtship. He and Clare were married in 1935.

In a magnetic union of overweening egotists, her talents bloomed as a playwright and a war correspondent. A new career took wing at a dinner party in Wendell Willkie's apartment early in 1942. There Sam Pryor unfurled the strategy for her to be elected to Congress from Fairfield County, Connecticut. As chatelaine of a Georgian mansion in Greenwich (as well as a pied-à-terre at the Waldorf Towers), she fulfilled the residence qualification.

Clare waged an energetic campaign against the Democratic male incumbent by attacking the Roosevelt Administration for softness in its conduct of the war and waste in its New Deal programs. She won by a comfortable margin. Assigned to the House Military Affairs Committee, she cast about for an appropriate topic for her maiden speech.

Pryor called her attention to a magazine article by Vice President Wallace, an elaboration of his United Nations aerial peacekeeping plan. Wallace raised the possibility of internationalizing the airports and subsidizing the system to keep passenger fares attractively low. He espoused freedom of the air as a postwar sequel to freedom of the seas.

Sam delivered packets of Pan American propaganda to Clare's hotel suite in Washington, and after she digested them, Trippe dropped by to tutor her.

Historically, all nations protected the sovereignty of the skies above them, he said. They either made reciprocal agreements with other nations or granted concessions to individuals and private enterprises, such as Pan American Airways, to allow their planes to enter their airspace. "If Pan American had let the State Department deal with these countries on its behalf, the U.S. would have had to grant reciprocal landing rights, and today it would be crisscrossed with foreign carriers. By doing our own negotiating, we had to offer nothing but air service. Don't you see?"

Clare Boothe Luce, always a quick study, grasped Trippe's tendentious reasoning and dressed it in her glittering prose for a thirty-minute address on "America's Destiny in the Air" which she delivered late in the afternoon of February 9, 1943, an hour when the chamber of the House was usually empty. Curiosity about the ravishing creature and her penchant for blood-pricking wisecracks was responsible for filling more than half the seats.

The gentlewoman from Connecticut began with an assertion that failure to maintain U.S. leadership of the civilian air world would lay the groundwork for World War III.

A new policy of "freedom of the air" was being advanced to challenge the "sovereignty of American skies that has stood us in excellent stead both commercially and militarily," she declared, insinuating that woolly-headed Wallace was a cat's-paw for British aviation interests.

"But much of what Mr. Wallace calls his global thinking is, no matter how you slice it, globaloney. Mr. Wallace's warp of sense and his woof of nonsense is very tricky cloth of which to cut the pattern of a postwar world."

Globaloney. With that smart-aleck word, her legislative career was indelibly stamped. No matter what other trenchant words she uttered on different issues during her two terms in the House, the whiff of globaloney lingered.

Her discourse was a garble of inconsistencies, starting with Trippe's brand of private-enterprise capitalism which demanded protection from the government against all competition. She mixed warm praise for "our British cousins" with her husband's manifesto that they had enjoyed trade supremacy for two centuries and now it was America's turn.

"We want to fly everywhere. Period." That was the air policy young Americans had chosen, she said. The statement had the ring of freedom of the skies, but it quickly faded as she painted a catastrophic picture of planes of other nations, bolstered by government subsidy and cheap labor (Trippe's well-worn themes), descending upon U.S. airports.

Shall I stand on a plain, say in the heart of the gentleman from Kansas' fair land, in the year 1949, and see at the great central terminus that may be there, the air liner Queen Elizabeth put in, the Stalin Iron Cruiser, the Wilhelmina Flying Dutchman, the Flying DeGaulle, the airships of all the nations on earth—perhaps even those of the German and the Jap. But shall I scan, like Sister Anne, the skies in vain, searching for the shape of an American Clipper against the clouds?

If airports were internationalized like seaports under freedom of the seas, America's merchant airways systems would fall into the same "sorry state" as its merchant marine, withered by competition from low-cost foreign shipping. Word for word, the logic and the prophecy were Trippe's.

Three months after Clare Luce delivered her sassy version of his message, Trippe caught everyone by surprise at a National Institute of Social Sciences dinner in New York with a conciliatory speech.

He promised that Pan American Airways was going to cater to the "Average Man" in the postwar world. "Air transportation cannot be merely a luxury service for carrying well-to-do passengers at high prices," he said. To make this possible, Pan American had ordered "giant Clippers" capable of carrying 153 passengers from New York to London in 10 hours at a fare of $100.

Then, speaking as the sportsman he fancied himself, he said, "We all share the healthy American aspiration to be the winner of a ball game or international business competition. But fair is fair. If you want to win a baseball game, you try to outhit the other fellow, but you don't take away his bat.

"I urge that when the fighting stops, British Overseas Airways be permitted to secure on equitable terms all the ocean-transport planes that are needed to restore the balance for fair competition." The same would apply to the national airline of each of the United Nations, he added.

"This world of ours, in the age of flight, should be one world," Trippe concluded, borrowing the title of Willkie's book, which had just been published. Ed Stettinius congratulated his brother-in-law for being "statesmanlike and extremely wise politically" and suggested he repeat his proposal to other audiences. "It will go a long way toward correcting an impression in certain quarters that Pan American is the 'Big Bad Wolf.'"

The proposal was neither as magnanimous as it sounded nor original with Trippe. Berle had said practically the same thing to a House Committee. The Administration wanted to allay British anxiety about the overwhelming American superiority in equipment. On the other hand, having foreign countries dependent on the United States for surplus planes and spare parts would be a tremendous boon to the aircraft industry in adjusting to the inevitable letdown that peace would bring.

By airing what was tantamount to official policy as his generous idea, Trippe was not just aiming, as Stettinius hoped, to ingratiate himself with the interdepartmental committee. "Trippe, in scratching the British back, could get his back scratched anywhere Britain has influence," *Time* speculated.

A month and a half later, Albert C. Critchley, the managing director of B.O.A.C., met Trippe during an inspection tour of its B-314 facility rented from Pan American at Baltimore. The avowed purpose of their discussion was to explore other arrangements they might make when B.O.A.C. graduated to land planes. Lord Beaverbrook had Critchley shadowed by British Intelligence. The agents reported the substance of his conversation with Trippe.

Suppose that Pan American were to take the bulk of transatlantic traffic and cede the European Continent to B.O.A.C. The British airline would acknowledge Pan American's sway in South America and mount a token operation there under its auspices. Pan American would intercede with the U.S. Government to open the Hawaiian gateway to the Pacific for B.O.A.C. or one of the Commonwealth airlines.

Having tidily arranged a goodly portion of the world aerial map,

Critchley and Trippe agreed to forget what they had discussed, since neither had the power to commit his government. After he returned to London, Critchley was called on the carpet by Beaverbrook, and subsequently, when questioned by the C.A.B., he denied that he had made a bargain with Trippe. Juan lapsed into chronic amnesia, obliterating even the fact that they had ever met.

Berle did not learn of their talk for several months, but he was aware that B.O.A.C. was dickering with several European airlines, conveniently headquartered in London with their governments-in-exile, to fashion a cartel for the Continent, and this despite an exchange of promises by Foreign Secretary Anthony Eden and Secretary of State Hull that no airline would make any discriminatory agreements before a general aviation conference was held.

Wide differences of economic views within the British coalition government had been papered over so that it might concentrate on winning the war. The Air Ministry, B.O.A.C. and the Labour Party favored one nationally owned, chosen instrument. The Tories yearned to try some of that private enterprise under regulated competition which had worked such marvels for the Americans in their domestic system.

Nevertheless, both Labour and Conservative groups were united in their fear of Britain's being swamped by U.S. might in the aviation markets and in their belief that imperial unity and industrial prestige (aircraft sales weighed more heavily in their anxiety than airline passengers) were at stake in the settlement of the postwar air routes.

The Interdepartmental Committee recognized these dichotomies in the relationship with the principal ally. Its first report to the President in April 1943 recommended a broad policy of opening the skies wide, fully expecting the British to work toward imposing restrictions. "Our principal bargaining point," said Berle, "consists in the ability to grant or deny entry into the United States."

As an exporting nation, Britain theoretically favored open skies as a corollary to the open seas on which its trade had moved for centuries —but only on the celestial lanes above the oceans. The heavens above the British Empire were to be sealed off from foreign airlines. They might be allowed to land for refueling and emergency repairs, but not to discharge or pick up passengers and cargo. Gradually, it dawned on some British officials that American tourists arriving on U.S. airlines might deposit more money than could be gained by erecting barriers to competition, and they moderated their iron resolve, but not their appetite for hard bartering, especially on rights to the bases built on their territory with Lend-Lease funds.

Berle's committee concluded that the United States had to come fairly close to accommodation with the British before attempting to make headway on a general agreement among nations exchanging entry rights for commercial planes. As if that were not a formidable enough task, they were faced with "a hot political issue" at home: namely, the question of whether to entrust international air service to a monopoly or divide it among a number of airlines. Monopoly has proved inefficient for other countries, the report noted; American foreign aviation is "too big a proposition for any single company."

"This ocean has aroused an emotion toward ocean flying. We have all flown the ocean. And it is far simpler than we thought it was. We surprise ourselves with our success."

William A. Patterson, president of United Airlines, was speaking of the domestic-airline operators who had been given passkeys to the international skies by the Air Transport Command.

The Second World War, like the first, prompted great leaps forward in aeronautical technology. Military need and government funds spurred the development of larger planes with more efficient engines. Winged boxcars like the C-54 and the C-97 counterpart of the B-29 bomber made possible the strategic airlift of supplies to opposite ends of the earth. Their civilian adaptations, the DC-4 and the Stratocruiser, effected the transition to the peaceful age of mass air travel.

The waging of war caused the world to shrink and the mystery of ocean flight (though not its romance and adventure) to evaporate. Tens of thousands of young Americans—file clerks and college students, factory workers and lawyers—were taught to fly by the Army and the Navy and to pilot four-engine military transports over the oceans as though they were trucks on state highways.

From Pearl Harbor to final victory in 1945, nearly 3 billion passenger-miles of overseas routes were flown by Pan American Airways and Panagra and—to Juan Trippe's chagrin—by American Export Airlines and eight domestic carriers.

As Patterson said, it looked so easy. The contractors for the A.T.C. were tantalized by visions of their aircraft repainted silver, fitted with smartly furnished interiors and filled with tourists and businessmen instead of men in uniform—a vast market for foreign air travel.

In July 1943, General Arnold called a meeting in Washington of the nineteen airlines that had contracts with the A.T.C.; slightly more than half operated over the oceans, the rest in the United States and elsewhere in the Western Hemisphere. He announced that the Army was going to retire from the transport business as soon as the war was over, and that it was up to the airline operators to decide what to do vis-à-vis the international routes.

The executives walked out of the War Department conference room under the impression they had been encouraged to go after foreign licenses. A few days later, they formed the Airline Committee on International Routes, otherwise known as the Committee of Seventeen Airlines—only Trippe and Patterson abstained from joining—with the objective of breaking Pan American's prewar monopoly.

Their manifesto called for free and open worldwide air competition, subject to reasonable federal regulation; private ownership and management of the airlines; federal encouragement of a worldwide air-transport system; worldwide freedom of transit in peaceful flight; and the acquisition by the United States of the civil and commercial outlets required in the national interest. This last was a euphemism for subsidy of unprofitable routes. "There can be no rational basis for permitting air transport outside the United States to be left to the withering influence of monopoly," the committee asserted.

Patterson's conduct baffled the others. A tiny, immaculately groomed, prudent man—by original calling a banker—he saw himself as the statesman of the industry and took every available opportunity to pontificate. With the airlines poised at the watershed, he issued three declarations on the West Coast and in Washington that United believed in "a chosen instrument," as the only way to survive competition from foreign carriers. If too many U.S. airlines entered the overseas market, they would lose money, go out of business or have to beg for subsidy. Juan Trippe could not have put it more succinctly. His very words flowed from Patterson's press releases: the airlines should join in forming "one strong organization, under private enterprise, to compete against government-operated monopolies." Patterson was "a stooge for Juan Trippe," the domestic airmen said indignantly.

If Trippe had seduced Patterson into his camp, and seduction was one of the milder words the committee was using, he had assistance from within the United organization. Some of Patterson's executives pointed out that its coast-to-coast network was both a natural feeder of traffic to Pan American and a connecting link from New York to San Francisco for the anticipated round-the-world service.

United's economist furnished a pessimistic forecast of the international market. Taking the year 1930 as an index, and projecting the number of first-class steamship passengers as likely customers for air service in 1948, he predicted that forty-three of the 100-passenger transport planes scheduled for delivery after the war could handle all the North Atlantic traffic. Dividing the number of planes by eight (the nations that had announced plans to operate over the Atlantic) gave six planes for each country. Patterson was thus persuaded that there would be enough business for one or two U.S. carriers, certainly not a whole flock, and that United had better not wander beyond the continental boundaries.

He called for Congress to bar the domestic airlines from international flying. The Seventeen followed up by bombarding the C.A.B. with requests for overseas authority—sixty-two applications in all, of which eleven were for the North Atlantic.

The board was already fumbling to provide competition for Pan American in Latin America. The European war had disrupted ocean shipping and greatly increased the volume of air traffic to the region. The C.A.B. gave American Airlines a temporary permit to serve Mexico, selected five foreign airlines to beef up service to the Caribbean and encouraged the domestic operators to submit bids for permanent routes throughout Latin America.

33

Onward and Upward to Chicago

A long-running feud between Cordell Hull and Under Secretary of State Sumner Welles divided the State Department into rancorous partisanships, and in the summer of 1943 the tension became intolerable. Shortly before Roosevelt was to meet Churchill at Quebec, Hull persuaded him to ask for Welles's resignation. The President appointed Edward Stettinius to succeed him. The new Under Secretary asserted his pious intention to refrain, as he had done in the Lend-Lease Administration, from matters affecting Pan American Airways. The promise was an unrealistic one for the Number Two diplomat to make, for Pan American was in the eye of the raging storm about the international air routes. The promotion of Stettinius was regarded as a net gain for Juan Trippe.

Yet it was Adolph Berle's fine hand, and not Stettinius', that showed in a joint statement issued by the State Department and the C.A.B. on October 15 "to clarify their respective interests in aviation":

> The Department of State has a primary interest in the subject from the standpoint of foreign policy and international relations, including the broad economic effects of aviation in foreign countries.

> The Department and the Board would collaborate in deciding on the advisability of new international routes. State would conduct the negotiations with foreign governments on behalf of American carriers. Foreign airlines wishing to secure landing rights in the United States were urged to submit their applications through diplomatic channels.

Juan Trippe's term as shadow foreign minister for U.S. aviation seemed to have expired.

By November, the President had studied the myriad reports on postwar international aviation and distilled a policy.

The defeated Axis Powers were to be denied their own airlines. "I don't want them to be in a position to fly anything larger than one of these toy planes that you wind up with an elastic," he declared at a meeting with Berle, Lovett, Stettinius, Hopkins and Pogue.

Americans were no longer to buy up local-service airlines in foreign countries; Allied and neutral nations should own and control their internal aviation. "I would hope they hire Americans," he said, "but not as managers. And, of course, I hope they buy American equipment."

As for American international aviation, he could not support a monopoly of the overseas air routes. "Juan Trippe cannot have it all," he affirmed.

Roosevelt was not firmly set on how to arrange the competition for Pan American, although one plan appealed to him. "I don't think that anyone other than Trippe could possibly be successful in running a worldwide system," he confided to a Senator. "So for that reason and others, I want several lines assigned to different routes and zones." One might have the west coast of South America, another the east coast, a third the North Atlantic, a fourth the Mediterranean region, and so on. He did not rule out other solutions, however. He saw no need for the government to own an interest in the overseas airlines, but he was open-minded on initial subvention for sparsely trafficked routes, assuming it was in the national interest to have them.

As for operating rights worldwide, "I want a very free interchange," the President declared. "I want arrangements whereby planes of one country can enter any other country to discharge traffic and take on foreignbound traffic, but not to carry passengers and cargo between two points inside another country. So if Canada wants a line to Jamaica with stops in the United States at Buffalo and Miami, they should be able to discharge traffic of Canadian origin at Buffalo and take on passengers for Jamaica, but they should not be allowed to carry traffic from Buffalo to Miami."

In addition, he said, planes should have the general right to land at any airfield for refueling and service without taking on or discharging traffic—what was known as the rights of free transit and technical stop. In that way, there would be no need for a United Nations authority to manage airfields. Without mentioning the Vice President's name, he disposed of Wallace's ideas.

Roosevelt was fairly certain, though, that there would have to be a United Nations organization to maintain standards for safety, communications, signals and weather reporting, and perhaps also to prevent destructive competition from breaking out over rates and subsidies.

He intended to call a general conference on aviation—but "not until the time is right to have one under United Nations auspices." Until then, there could be quiet talks with Britain and other countries.

Armed with Roosevelt's blueprint, Berle started exploratory discussions with the British, and separate conversations with the Russians and Chinese, aiming toward a conference in the summer of 1944.

Lord Beaverbrook, whom Churchill had recently named Lord Privy Seal to deal with civil-aviation problems, wanted the Dominions to join the talks. Berle preferred to have only Canada, because of its strategic corridor to the Atlantic. "The Beaver" was attempting to forge a united imperial bloc on international routes that would have made the U.S. bargaining position vulnerable. Animated by painful recollections of being blackmailed by the Italians and by several Middle Eastern potentates whose territories they had had to cross over to build the Empire air network in the Thirties, the British spoke fervently of a universal right to fly through the airspaces of all countries. But as a corollary to such freedom, they stipulated that competition must be tightly controlled. They had a cozy way of putting it: "For many years to come, the Americans and ourselves will have to rule the world to all intents and purposes to see that things are rightly done."

The State Department, meanwhile, was apprised that B.O.A.C., backed by shipping interests, was pairing off with European airlines to block U.S. carriers from the Continent and the Mediterranean, further intending to bar non-British lines from connecting service between areas in the Commonwealth. B.O.A.C. envisioned pooling agreements for Latin America, the Pacific and the vital U.S. market.

The Old World tradition of monopoly by cartel was as alive in British planning as it had been three and four hundred years ago when mercantile trading companies wangled exclusive concessions in certain areas and used political influence to extend them to larger territories, combining with other traders to cut off interlopers.

Such commercial agreements spawned colonial empires. In the nineteenth century, the principle of creating orderly markets was absorbed in the socialist ideas that took seed in the industrialization of Europe, and arranged monopoly continued to be the norm for many kinds of business activity, particularly in transportation.

Europe's honored tradition was criminal behavior in the United

States; antitrust laws forbade agreements to divide territories or traffic. Berle was almost phobic on this issue. He feared that the plague of cartelism would infect air commerce if the Americans did not strive to make competitive forces prevail. In this regard, he was a devout disciple of Hull, who had made freer trade the cornerstone of his foreign policy. The Secretary of State believed that wars were caused by economic rivalries, and that colonial and imperial systems of preference were impediments to peace.

The British were in dread of being swamped by U.S. aviation. To guard against the likelihood, they wanted to be guaranteed a percentage of the available business for their airline. They were pushing for a strong regulatory commission to fix rates and frequencies of service—an international C.A.B., with overtones of a cartel. The objective was to restrain the most efficient airline operators (American) from using the most advanced aircraft (American) to lure passengers with speed, better service and lower rates.

Which was precisely what the United States was determined to do. "We want equal opportunity in the air," said Berle, at talks with Beaverbrook and his aides in London in the spring of 1944. "It is premature to make equal allocations of the business."

Equal opportunity in the air was a mid-twentieth-century rephrasing of Hay's Open Door for China and the third of Wilson's Fourteen Points of 1918.

Equality meant the chance to sell airline services to as large a market as possible, an advantage not only for the Americans but also for the smaller, aviation-proficient nations like the Netherlands and the Scandinavian countries, for they would be free to tap wider sources of traffic than under a quota system such as the British advocated. In so doing, they would become customers for American aircraft.

Berle insisted that the international authority be confined to technical matters—a demand that puzzled the British because it seemed as though the Americans were downgrading a successful institution they had invented. "We do not believe our government can delegate regulatory powers to an international commission," Berle said. Besides, the C.A.B. never went so far as to regulate the number of flights airlines could make, or to allocate the amount of traffic designated carriers could carry on certain routes.

In August, a Soviet delegation to Washington presented its position on international aviation: completely closed skies. All flights over Soviet territory must be operated by Soviet pilots in Soviet planes. Passengers on international flights must transfer to Soviet planes to cross the U.S.S.R., and transfer to other planes to exit from the other side. The nearest changeover points were to be Stockholm and Cairo. Stalin was extending the moat around his fortress to reach the Mediterranean.

By comparison, the Chinese were sublimely cooperative. Their attitude toward granting operating privileges to U.S. airlines was one of palms outstretched—take as much as you desire, just as long as you give us a present of five hundred DC-3s and DC-4s for our internal airline, and train our people to operate them.

Knowing where the major parties stood, as Berle now did, was still insufficient basis for calling an international conference. Fundamental differences between the two principal nations were unresolved, and the autumn of a Presidential election year was hardly the most propitious time for a parley, especially when a vocal faction in Congress was disinclined to follow the Administration's dictum on an open system of competition.

However, the approaching defeat of Germany created an urgency about replacing the obsolete legal machinery for air navigation and transport. The rules promulgated at Versailles in 1919 and Havana in 1928 were composed before aircraft could cross half a dozen national boundaries in one day. By 1944, no point in the world was more than 40 hours from any other point, yet airlines were limited to flying within the borders of their homelands and over the high seas unless they engaged in nation-by-nation politicking for concessions as Trippe had done.

The round-the-world routes the United States was operating for military transport would snap apart with the advent of peace, and many skyways would be closed to its commercial planes unless the broadest traffic privileges were secured beforehand. Landing routes in dozens of countries obtained before the war and mostly earmarked for Pan American Airways left vast stretches of air unaccounted for, and in the aggregate were not enough to enable American aircraft to fly beyond the coasts of Western Europe.

B.O.A.C. was already making scheduled runs in areas where the war had receded, and Beaverbrook served notice at the end of August that he would call a meeting in London if it was "inconvenient" for the Americans to do so at once.

The role of host implies leadership, and the United States was not about to abdicate its newly acquired dominance in the air. On September 11, the State Department sent invitations to the Allied nations, their associates and the neutral countries of Europe and Asia to meet in Chicago on November 1.

The President named Berle chairman of the U.S. delegation,

which included Senator Josiah Bailey, the Democratic chairman of the Senate Commerce Committee, and Senator Owen Brewster, the "stooge for Pan American," as Berle referred to him. With Brewster's shrill support, Trippe was fomenting legislation to make Pan American the national carrier for foreign air routes—a chosen instrument patterned after the British model—and Roosevelt wanted to avoid the hue and cry the Maine Republican would provoke if he were left off the conference team.

Trippe kept his distance from the conference, relying on John Cooper, who was named an adviser to the delegation, and Sam Pryor to set up the Pan American camp at the site.

Negotiators from fifty-two nations and their support battalions, seven hundred strong, assembled at the Hotel Stevens, a convention palace on Lake Michigan. Only two of the countries declined invitations—Saudi Arabia and the Soviet Union, which accepted and then withdrew five days before the meeting.

Another last-minute change auguring conflict was the substitution of Lord Swinton for Beaverbrook as head of the British delegation. Swinton, the new Minister of Civil Aviation, was an Empire-firster and, according to reports Berle received, anti-American. Over lunch the first day, the supercilious peer and the cerebral Puritan, who talked as though British mercantilism were the curse of mankind, exposed their prejudices and hardened their respective positions. Inevitably, their mutual antipathy affected the tenor of the conference.

Berle assured the throng assembled in the flag-draped ballroom that the United States believed in each nation's inalienable sovereignty over its airspace, and that without sacrificing that right, friendly nations could exchange nondiscriminatory "privileges of intercourse" so that a provisional pattern of worldwide routes, fixed like railroad lines, could be set up for their planes to fly as soon as Germany or Japan surrendered.

Swinton asserted the British position, a demand for an international agency with absolute power to apportion air traffic by setting quotas for each nation. The North Atlantic was to be an Anglo-American lake, with traffic equally shared, although there was no disputing that four-fifths would originate in the United States. "This really comes down to a request that we assign part of our traffic to support British aviation, and that's impossible," Berle told him. "Shippers and passengers should be able to choose the airlines they wish, and the airlines should be able to put on as many planes as needed to carry the traffic."

Behind the main stumbling block of how much economic and political authority to confer on the international aviation body lay an even more complex obstacle: the scope of operating rights. The Canadians analyzed them as four "freedoms"—a misnomer, since they were highly restricted grants of privilege.

The first two, freedoms of transit and technical stop, were essentially political rights awarded by sovereign nations. The third and fourth—to carry passengers, mail and cargo from the aircraft's country of origin to another country and back to the homeland—were commercial rights to do business on foreign soil. So was the fifth freedom proposed by the United States: to carry traffic between intermediate points along the way.

Since fewer than one-third of the passengers on a long route—say, from New York to Calcutta—were usually booked for the entire haul, extended air service was uneconomical without the ability to pick up passengers and freight in London, let them off at Rome and Beirut, take on other passengers in those cities and discharge them in Karachi, and so on. Absent such intermediate traffic rights, the plane would arrive at the last destination with only a few seats occupied. The fifth freedom was therefore essential to airlines with far-flung route systems, such as B.O.A.C. and Pan American Airways, and especially to KLM which had a small homeland for originating traffic.

The British, holding the keys to their bases all over the world, intended to hoard their privileges. They might grant the first two freedoms liberally, but would only barter the third and fourth, the so-called trading privileges, in direct country-to-country negotiations as part of wider cartel agreements, or concede them in a tightly regulated international system. Berle's insistence on multilateral agreements—all nations exchanging general privileges—was seen as "an impracticable ideal which would lead to chaos," and a threat to British economic security. The fifth freedom was anathema, for it endangered their short-haul lines. Just imagine, they said to the European delegations, a U.S. airline siphoning our traffic from London to Paris, Dutch traffic from Amsterdam to Rome, and Swedish traffic from Stockholm to Madrid.

That was turning back the pages of history, Berle protested: "There is no excuse for a modern air British East India Company or Portuguese Trading Monopoly or 'Spanish Main' conception."

He was convinced that B.O.A.C. was conspiring with Pan American to perpetuate the cartel system, starting with a plan to declare the North Atlantic out of bounds for other airlines. Senator Brewster was sowing divisiveness in the U.S. delegation over Berle's statement of the American position as wanting to give "all countries equal opportunity in the air" with a multilateral agreement. Such a generalized accord left the gate wide open for competition, since it could be subscribed to at a later date by countries that did not have their own airlines (as was the case with many of those represented at Chicago), and even by nations that did not yet exist.

The Senator from Maine was committed to bilateral negotiations, the British one-on-one approach favored by Trippe, who was confident he could obtain everything he wanted by reciprocal bargaining, including the fifth freedom, while seeing to it that his competitors got nothing.

Three days before American voters went to the polls, a story appeared in the *Chicago Tribune*, the leading Roosevelt-baiting newspaper, alleging that the U.S. delegation had been on the verge of giving away more than it should when it was stopped by a courageous minority. Obviously, there was a leak in the delegation, and Berle traced it to Brewster, with Sam Pryor as the conduit to the newspaper. He reported his findings to Under Secretary of State Stettinius in irate terms that almost imputed treason to Pan American Airways.

The conference dragged on. Around the green baize-covered tables, animosities hardened. The Latin American countries, China, Sweden and the Netherlands lined up behind the United States. Britain had the unflagging support of Australia, and less zealous encouragement from France. Canada played the honest broker.

After nearly a month, the British relented in secret meetings on four of the five freedoms, and the United States gave in on the 50–50 traffic quota for the North Atlantic. Sensing agreement was near, European airlines placed orders for American aircraft. Then the mood of hopefulness was shattered on the hard rock of a complicated "escalation" formula for permitting either side to increase its share of traffic if business warranted, which the British put forth to effectively block American carriers from proceeding eastward from European gateways.

At that point, Roosevelt reached for the reins to pull the conference back on track. Though buoyed by his victory at the polls, the President was in precarious health. His strength was ebbing; his deteriorated condition alarmed those who saw him at close range. Still, he took aviation back into his own hands with a direct appeal to Churchill.

Roosevelt removed his velvet glove when he told the Prime Minister:

> We are doing our best to meet your Lend Lease needs. We will face Congress on that subject in a few weeks and it will not be in a generous mood if it and the people feel that the United Kingdom has not agreed to a generally beneficial air agreement. They will wonder about the chances of our two countries, let alone any

others, working together to keep the peace if we can not even get together on an aviation agreement.

Several days passed before Churchill replied: "Your message caused me great anxiety." He recapitulated British sensitivity over the invaluable bases they were being asked to put at the disposal of other nations—"this means primarily the United States." The war agreement to divide manufacturing responsibility had placed the United States "in incomparably better position to fill air transport needs and build up its aircraft industry," he noted.

I have never advocated competitive "bigness" in any sphere between our two countries in their present state of development. You will have the greatest Navy in the world. You will have, I hope, the greatest Air Force. You will have the greatest trade. You have all the gold. But these things do not oppress my mind with fear because I am sure the American people under your re-acclaimed leadership will not give themselves over to vainglorious ambitions, and that justice and fair play will be the lights that guide them.

Churchill blamed Berle for getting everything in a hopeless knot, and suggested a temporary adjournment.

On November 27, the conference was rocked by a radio bulletin announcing the resignation of Cordell Hull and the appointment of Edward Stettinius as Secretary of State.

Two days later, Berle received a telegram from the President offering him the ambassadorship to Brazil. His partisans and the press assumed he had been "liquidated" by Stettinius and that Juan Trippe's brother-in-law had timed his sweeping reorganization of the State Department to undermine Berle's authority at Chicago. Publicly, Berle denied this, but in his diary he noted, "Ed obviously felt a little guilty at having cut the ground out from under me at Chicago."

It is unlikely that Berle could have continued the loyal relationship with the new Secretary of State he had had with Hull; his negligible regard for Stettinius' mental prowess was ill-concealed. To be sure, even *Time*, which greeted Stettinius' advancement with hosannas (and gloated over the resignation of "gnome-like, greying Boy Prodigy" Berle), appraised the new Secretary of State as an amiable pitchman who owed his job to the luck of the draw.

During his years in Washington, Berle had attracted worshipful disciples, and also many enemies in high places, not exclusively among supporters of Pan American Airways. His eloquent bias against British imperialism put him on irritable terms with the Foreign Office and with the many Anglophiles in the State Department. Though he believed he was faithfully executing the President's directives, his handling of international air policy was a little too vigorous and independent to suit others with vested interests in aviation, such as Pogue of the C.A.B. and the Congressional nucleus in the conference delegation.

Even without accommodating Juan Trippe, Stettinius could rationalize getting rid of Adolph Berle, and there is no evidence that the President tried to dissuade him.

During the week that followed the upheaval at the State Department, the conference nearly foundered. In response to Swinton's intransigeance over the escalator clause, Berle led the American delegation to retract the concessions it had made and to retrieve his earlier plan for a multilateral agreement granting all five freedoms. "Take it or leave it," he was telling Swinton.

Roosevelt made a last-ditch plea to dissuade Churchill from adjourning the meeting:

> You say that the British Empire is being asked to put bases all over the world at the disposal of other nations. Of course it is. Would you like to see a world in which all ports were closed to all ships but their own or open to one foreign ship, perhaps two if they carried only passengers and cargo bound all the way from Liverpool to Shanghai? Where would England be if shipping were subjected to such limitations? Where would it be if aviation is? I am unable to believe that you do not want an agreement at this time. I cannot agree that the answer is to hold everyone back. It must be to go forward together.

Churchill was unmoved. A dispirited Berle was ready to close up shop when Mayor Fiorello H. LaGuardia of New York, a U.S. delegate and a political thespian nonpareil, shamed Swinton into reasonableness. Drawing himself to his full 5-foot-2-inch height, the "Little Flower" exhorted the delegates to demonstrate that the nations of the world were capable of arranging one economic facet of the peace. "I plead with you not to quit now," he said in a voice that sounded like the audio track for an animated cartoon. "Let's not go back to the old system of power politics and greed that brought on the present situation." Why not agree on some freedoms, if not all five? he asked.

Swinton could not evade this opportunity to come out of the manger with honor. He dropped a large hint that he was sympathetic to an agreement on two freedoms. The Netherlands delegate seized the cue and ran it into a formal proposal, hastily seconded by the French representative.

From then on, the conference raced to expedient compromise. A final act was drawn in skeleton form, and on it were hung five supplementary agreements containing the substantive accomplishments of five weeks of travail. The bulkiest document was the Convention on International Civil Aviation, establishing principles of air navigation carefully hedged to satisfy the most nationalistic objections. The rights to fly over other countries and stop for fuel and repairs were given to nonscheduled aircraft; commercial airlines could gain them by special permission—a device to preserve bilateral negotiations. Every nation was permitted to refuse cabotage, the right of foreign airlines to conduct internal domestic service in another country.

A permanent world body, the International Civil Aviation Organization, was created to promote the development of air transport and serve as a clearinghouse for technical and economic information. A strictly consultative agency, I.C.A.O. had no authority to award commercial rights.

A three-year period of gestation was allowed for parliaments to debate and ratify the convention. In order that air routes could be opened immediately, an interim agreement set up a provisional organization (P.I.C.A.O.) based in Montreal. Freedoms one and two (for transit and technical stop) were incorporated in an International Air Services Transit Agreement. The unrestricted multilateral accord sponsored by the Americans was contained in an International Air Transport Agreement, otherwise known as the Five Freedoms Agreement.

The last, and least controversial, appendix standardized operational practices such as traffic control, communications and airworthiness requirements for aircraft.

With everything packaged in separate protocols, as though the law of the air were an à la carte menu, nations could make choices according to their readiness for aerial trade without being ostracized for not endorsing everything. They could part company while affirming universal solidarity. Virtually all countries represented at Chicago accepted the convention and the transit, or two freedoms, agreement. Only one European country, the Netherlands, China and six small, impoverished nations joined the United States in ratifying the Five Freedoms Agreement.

Berle adjourned the conference on December 7, clutching hopefully at the symbolism of the third anniversary of Pearl Harbor. "We met in an era of diplomatic intrigue and private and monopolistic privilege. We close in an era of open covenants and equal opportunity and status."

His prose soared far above reality, for what the delegates had agreed to at Chicago could not take effect without approval from home, and in London and Washington the long knives were quickly unsheathed.

Senator Brewster made agitated proclamations, dissenting from the key agreements. He capitalized on mounting tension between the Legislative and Executive branches over the conduct of foreign affairs. In guiding the nation into war, Roosevelt had circumvented the limitations in the Presidential treaty power by using Executive agreements to make commitments to other countries without seeking the advice and consent of the Senate, most conspicuously in the swap of destroyers for bases in August 1940.

There were serious doubts within the American delegation and in Congress as to whether privileges as far-reaching as those contained in the Chicago agreements could be signed away by executive fiat alone.

Early in February 1945, the State Department announced acceptance of the interim agreement and the transit and air-transport agreements. No one disputed that the International Convention, setting up an organization in which the United States would participate, was a treaty. Roosevelt sent it to the Senate for approval in March. Brewster stirred his Republican colleagues to demand that all agreements be submitted.

Not entirely by coincidence, hearings had begun before a Senate aviation subcommittee, of which Brewster was a member, on a bill to legalize Pan American's monopoly. He commuted between that panel and the Senate Foreign Relations Committee, ringing the alarm bell on the freedoms agreements.

Echoing Clare Boothe Luce's globaloney speech, Brewster warned of a multitude of foreign-flag aircraft depositing passengers at U.S. airports without so much as a by-your-leave from the C.A.B. He maintained that the Executive agreements waived the authority Congress had given the board to license foreign airlines. He cued Trippe at the monopoly-bill hearings to characterize the Five Freedoms Agreement as a sellout of American labor: without the C.A.B. regulating the entry of foreign carriers, aviation workers would be left unprotected against low wages and "unfair practices."

It was a remarkable exhibition of the tactics of confusion, and the fulfillment of Berle's premonition that Trippe would simultaneously play on both sides. Trippe and Brewster were challenging the C.A.B.'s authority to franchise American competitors for Pan American on overseas routes while decrying any lessening of the Board's power to protect the airline against competition from abroad.

Welch Pogue and Assistant Secretary of State Dean Acheson assured the Foreign Relations Committee that nothing written at Chicago changed what Congress had willed in the Civil Aeronautics Act of 1938. The five freedoms were broadly stated; the C.A.B. could still designate the routes and set standards of operation for foreign airlines, and this implied power to limit their entry. Congress had authorized the State Department to negotiate air-service agreements with other governments as long as it consulted with the C.A.B., and the President had final approval of the actions of both agencies. In the light of these mutually reinforcing safeguards, the transit and air-transport agreements were proper exercises of executive authority.

Several events had weakened the disposition of the Senators to jettison one of the tools of the new world of economic cooperation, as Roosevelt had called the Chicago agreements a few weeks before his death on April 12. The United Nations assembled in San Francisco on April 25 to draft a governing charter. By June 8, thirty nations had ratified the interim aviation agreement—more than enough for the Provisional International Civil Aviation Organization to come into being. The Senate Foreign Relations Committee bowed to the tide of history; a majority overrode Brewster's objections.

The final verdict was still to be rendered on Chicago, but a mixed record of achievement was already apparent. At last there were uniform rules of the international skies by which similarly qualified pilots who understood a common technical language could fly their planes, adhering to the same safety precautions.

Both Utopians and cartelists were disappointed. Neither the "open charter of the skies" for which Berle had hoped nor Swinton's tightly controlled air market emerged.

The United States had won for itself and other nations the right to fly everywhere in the world except for Russian-controlled territory, and in case Stalin or his heirs changed their minds, a seat was left open for the Soviet Union in the International Civil Aviation Organization, which became a United Nations agency in 1947.

Commercial air rights still had to be bargained for in bilateral pacts; Britain had killed the dream of universal air trading privileges. The United States had thwarted the British desire for a supranational authority to allocate routes and traffic.

But with the two freedoms accepted by most nations, London's stranglehold on the Atlantic was released—and so was Washington's lock on the Pacific.

The issue of international tariffs was left in abeyance at Chicago. Before the war, the European airlines had established fares jointly through the International Air Traffic Association, which Pan American had joined in 1938 as a junior member not participating in the rate conferences. As Jim Smith, Trippe's emissary, recalled, "I had to say 'We can't possibly commit ourselves to going with your rates because what you are doing is a monopoly and monopolies are illegal in the United States.' "

On April 16, 1945, in Havana, forty-four airlines from twenty-five nations that had adhered to the International Convention at Chicago breathed life into a new organization, the International Air Transport Association. The C.A.B. reluctantly approved the articles of association, opening the door for American membership but sanctioning no more than that. The State Department had endorsed I.A.T.A. as a medium for handling traffic operating problems, and the Attorney General said the airlines could participate in rate-making agreements provided they secured permission from the C.A.B., which owed its impotence to fix international tariffs largely to Trippe's lobbying at the birth of the Civil Aeronautics Act.

To the board members, I.A.T.A.'s regional traffic conferences smacked of the cartel system the U.S. delegation had wrestled to the mat at Chicago. Each airline was entitled to one vote, and unanimity was required to establish a rate. Afterward, their governments were asked to ratify what the carriers had agreed upon.

In October, Trippe threw the first general meeting of I.A.T.A., at Montreal, into an uproar by announcing from New York that Pan American was about to inaugurate DC-4 service to London at a $275 fare. The European airlines had already agreed to set a minimum one-way fare of $572 at their forthcoming North Atlantic tariff conference.

Trippe's fare was "a sure loser," his executives acknowledged privately; but he was playing to Washington, not Montreal, hoping to disprove one of the evils ascribed to monopoly—high, fixed prices.

The British Government pricked his balloon by interjecting the fare squabble into the bilateral negotiations for an air treaty then about to begin. It served notice to the State Department that it was prepared to allow two U.S. carriers (Pan American and American Export) daily schedules to London provided they adhered to a prewar rate of $375, or whatever I.A.T.A. would set. If Pan American persisted in operating at the reduced fare, His Majesty's Government would be "reluctantly obliged" to restrict the airline to the twice-weekly schedule established in 1937.

Trippe's gambit might have succeeded if Amsterdam, Brussels or Stockholm had offered its airport as a principal gateway to the Continent, permitting Pan American to bypass London. But that was as likely as the sky falling. The Dutch, the Belgians and the Swedes said they would go along with I.A.T.A. as they always had in the past. The French, on the verge of signing their bilateral treaty with Washington, repeated the British statement practically vertabim to prevent Pan American from serving Marseille with a fare that undercut T.W.A.'s tariff to Paris by $80.

Pan American raised its fares, and the first round of the phony rate war ended in a truce.

The tariff issue and everything else left up in the air at Chicago were settled at Bermuda in February 1946 with the signing of an Anglo–American civil-aviation pact.

Both sides were primed for compromise. The war was over, and the United States was impatient to activate the international routes the C.A.B. had just awarded. Britain was enduring its cruelest winter of brutal weather and shortages of necessities while its diplomats importuned the Truman Administration for a loan. An air agreement might soften public sentiment; failure to produce one would surely antagonize Congress when it took up the President's request for a $4.4-billion credit.

Promptly getting down to business in Hamilton, the British opened their bases that had been exchanged for U.S. destroyers by Churchill and Roosevelt in wartime expediency to American commercial planes. The two countries laid down the routes over which their designated airlines would fly and made a broad exchange of privileges —the disputed freedoms three, four and five—including the right to pick up passengers at each other's gateways and carry them to third countries.

The British gained the long-sought means of circling the globe, to operate from London to New York and San Francisco, and on to Singapore and Hong Kong via the American island possessions in the Pacific, as well as options to run lines to the Caribbean and South America from New York, Miami and New Orleans. The route patterns were directly competitive with Pan American Airways.

U.S. airlines were authorized to serve London and numerous Commonwealth gateways and from there to proceed to the centers of Europe, Africa, the Middle East and the Orient.

By insisting on multiple designations—each country could name one or more of its airlines to fly the routes—the United States pointedly crushed Pan American's chance of becoming its country's chosen instrument by another nation's preference, as had happened in the past.

No quotas or restrictions were placed on capacity or on frequency of service—a victory for U.S. superiority in planes, customers and efficient managers.

In exchange for this enormous concession by the British in neither limiting nor allocating the amount of service either country's airlines could offer, the United States yielded to prevent price competition. It recognized the I.A.T.A. traffic conference as the machinery for joint rate-making by the airlines, subject to the approval of their governments.

The unanimous agreement required to establish a rate would be obtained only at levels steep enough to cover the costs of the least efficient operator. Rate control thus served as a brake on unrestrained capacity, hindering the best-equipped airline from filling seats. What good were frequent schedules between New York and Europe without low enough fares to attract passengers?

A clause was inserted in the treaty binding the Executive branch of the U.S. Government to use its best efforts to make Congress give the Board the same authority over international rates that it had in domestic transportation. Britain and most of the leading aviation countries claimed the power to determine fares charged by their own and foreign carriers operating at their airports. In practice, the governments generally prescribed the rates resolved by I.A.T.A.

Once the C.A.B. gained its missing authority, it could order a rate to go into effect even over foreign objections until the dispute was ironed out in intergovernmental consultation or by arbitration. The Board was trapped by another clause which said that until Congress enacted such rate legislation, the C.A.B. acknowledged Britain's right to prevent the entry of any U.S. airline charging unsatisfactory rates.

Welch Pogue and two of his colleagues, Harllee Branch and Oswald Ryan, anguished over a Hobson's choice—whether to exert some modest influence over the rates American carriers charged by having the Board pass on I.A.T.A. resolutions, or to resign themselves to no influence at all, if they rejected the conference method. By taking the latter course, would they not be exposing the airlines to the unilateral control of foreign governments? Was the experience of Pan American with its $275 fare the precursor of further harassment?

The three Board members were cowed into believing they would be blamed if a pact was not signed, and they were under the illusion that Congress would soon give them the power they lacked. They consoled themselves, moreover, with the precedent of the U.S. Maritime Commission, which permitted American shipping companies to join in international rate-setting conferences.

But they overlooked critical differences. The Maritime Commission could modify the conferences rates; the C.A.B. would have to approve or disapprove in toto. Furthermore, whereas tramp steamers were free to do business in any ports without limitations from local governments, to charge whatever they pleased and to abstain from shipping traffic conferences, irregular airlines had yet to be franchised for international routes.

A week after they returned to Washington from Bermuda, Pogue, Branch and Ryan voted to let the airlines participate in the I.A.T.A. traffic conferences for one year. The fourth member, Josh Lee, dissented at length. "Competition by consent is not competition," he said. Lee correctly foresaw the industry in a straitjacket, with the least efficient airlines forcing rates to the level of "all the traffic will bear," curbing the growth of the market and giving the American consumer short shrift.

In hailing the Bermuda agreement, Truman emphasized the exchange of fifth-freedom rights. What Britain had been unwilling to grant to every nation in Chicago had been tendered to the United States at Hamilton.

In July, after the President signed the appropriation for the British loan, the State Department announced that the United States was withdrawing from the International Air Transport Agreement. The Five Freedoms Agreement that State had labeled a Magna Carta twenty months before was dead—"a noble effort that didn't work," a bureaucrat said.

The Anglo–American bilateral accord became the standard for agreements between the United States and more than fifty other nations. The one-on-one approach of Bermuda subsequently led the State Department to use commercial air rights as a lever for power politics, trading entry to U.S. airports by foreign airlines for pledges of allegiance and support by their governments.

Years later, Senator Warren Magnuson was to say, "We traded more horses for rabbits in international air than any field I know." But in 1946 in Bermuda, few wanted to tell the difference. The rush was on to exploit America's competitive advantage in the skies.

34

Chosen Instrument

"The fox knows many things, but the hedgehog knows one big thing." Isaiah Berlin, a political scientist, borrowed the line from a Greek poet to classify writers and thinkers, if not all mankind. By this definition, Juan Trippe was a hedgehog and "the chosen instrument" the one big thing he knew—the principle by which he organized Pan American Airways, and the centripetal force of his life.

The term was of British coinage, widely adopted by other nations. Trippe seized the concept of a government-anointed airline monopoly and packaged it for American consumption.

In the 1930 annual report, he identified the Pan American Airways system as "a community effort on the part of the American aviation industry throughout the country to operate in the international field." "Community" was a code word of Hoover economics—various segments of an industry cooperating for the sake of efficiency and self-regulation.

Initially, the community effort was channeled into "a single company, organized to represent our national interests" in competition with Europeans for trade in South America. Pan American Airways, a private American enterprise, battled the government-directed airlines of the Old World in the Western Hemisphere. In 1935, Trippe amplified the concept for the bridging of the Pacific. Pan American was "a national air transport institution" representing not only the aviation industry but all segments of surface transportation, and industrial and commercial organizations to boot. By the time war came, he had extended the field of competition to cover the globe. As far as Juan

Trippe would ever see, America's air routes to the whole world belonged to Pan American.

With the Administration and the Civil Aeronautics Board clearly on a course to destroy Pan American's monopoly and whittle him down to size, Juan Trippe lifted his eyes to Capitol Hill, from whence help had come in the past—most recently in 1941, when the Senate denied American Export Airlines a postal subsidy.

The C.A.B. was a creature of Congress. A change in the law that defined its authority could make the regulatory agency toe Trippe's mark, and frustrate the White House and the executive policymakers. At the very least, the meandering legislative process, with its protracted hearings and debates, might discourage new candidates for foreign routes and delay the C.A.B.'s certification of competitors for Pan American Airways. The board had temporarily put aside a hundred applications for international licenses in order to concentrate on war-related transport services. Ideally, Congress could legislate a chosen instrument for international air commerce, such as Pan American had represented for fifteen years until General Arnold and the C.A.B. interfered. "There was no law conferring all American aviation on Pan Am," Adolph Berle took comfort in noting. Trippe hoped to correct that omission.

Aviation's Congressional sponsors were amenable to suggestions that foreign air policy was too important to be left to the President and his prickly deputy, Adolph Berle, and that the C.A.B. was a wobbly agency in need of guidance from the Hill.

The Senate Commerce Committee was still dominated by the Southern Democrats who had been Pan American's staunch allies, though the chairman, Josiah Bailey, had a troublesome habit of keeping an open mind. He had begun to reexamine his commitment to a single international airline.

Bailey's flexibility was counterbalanced by the addition of Patrick McCarran of Nevada to the committee. "As Britannia has ruled the waves in the past," the white-maned father of the Civil Aeronautics Act declaimed, "it is my ambition that Columbia should rule the air of the future." He agreed with Trippe that Pan American was the sole means to that end. Among the six Republicans on the committee, Owen Brewster served Pan American Airways with a curious zeal, considering that the battle over air routes was not a burning concern of his Maine constituents.

During the five-year span beginning early in 1943, nearly a dozen bills were introduced in both Houses to amend the Civil Aeronautics Act and trim the powers of the C.A.B.

The fiercest assault was made with proposals for Juan Trippe's community company. As one nettled president of a domestic carrier remarked, "It's the chosen instrument in the filmy, seductive allure of one company with all airlines participating."

Even Trippe's ally William Patterson never got the hang of saying "community company." The president of United spoke up for "the chosen instrument"—an understandable gaffe considering that Trippe himself used the term, and made such transparent alterations in his monopoly plan over the years. Regardless of terminology at any given moment, Trippe persisted in calling for the United States to pit its chosen instrument against the chosen instruments of foreign nations.

In May 1944, McCarran introduced a bill to create "The All-American Flag Line, Inc.," a private company with a billion dollars in capital, financed largely through the sale of government bonds. All U.S. airlines were to have a share in it, but Pan American owned all the voting stock.

As Berle was conducting the talks with the British that led up to the Chicago conference and the C.A.B. was preparing its design for a postwar international route system, the aviation subcommittee of the Commerce Committee scheduled hearings on the bill. Thus the curtain was raised on the first repertory performance of *The Chosen Instrument*, starring Juan T. Trippe, an annual political drama already previewed in the American Export subsidy fracas.

The protagonist was a man out of the ordinary, who had accumulated great power by his wits and courage. To some spectators he appeared as a twentieth-century incarnation of a robber baron, lumbering onstage with a profusion of charts and a disarming smile, to put forth in rambling doubletalk the proposition that what was good for Pan American Airways was good for the country. Arrayed against him were almost the entire U.S. Government—the Departments of State, War, the Navy, Commerce and Justice; the Bureau of the Budget and the C.A.B.—and the U.S. airlines, save for William Patterson of United.

Every season, the actors polished their lines and injected more acid into the dialogue. New opponents confronted him, the former supporters dropped away or crossed to the other side. The hearings became a forum for criticism of Pan American Airways and its vaunted patriotism, and for personal attacks on its president.

Trippe was an exasperating witness. He exhausted the legislators, few of whom did their homework or stayed awake after lunch. They had difficulty following the trail of his reasoning, strewn as it was with half-truths, unverified recollections and distorted statistics.

He took umbrage at the term "chosen instrument" being applied to Pan American in the press. "The position of our company has been greatly misunderstood," he said. Chairman Bailey asked him to define it.

TRIPPE: The phrase is used by certain of the foreign governments, Mr. Chairman, referring to their nominated carriers. They consider their airlines as instruments not only to carry out government trade objectives abroad, but also to be coordinated into their whole defense planning.

That was precisely how he described Pan American Airways in his confidential memoranda to Presidents, in his tête-à-têtes with officials at the house on F Street and in his annual reports to his stockholders.

"I do not think the term applicable to the American position, or appropriate to fit a community company here from the point of view of American air commerce," he told Bailey.

BAILEY: I don't know. Here is the McCarran bill which does choose one instrument.

TRIPPE: But not one carrier, though. It is a merger, as I understand it.

BAILEY: But it will be one instrument.

TRIPPE: One entity, that is right.

A thousand pages of testimony from various chosen-instrument hearings boil down to a dispute over the nature of competition in the international air lanes. Trippe maintained that it was properly a competition between nations. "We favor regulated competition in the domestic field which is protected against foreign-flag competition," he said. "We do not favor it in the international field between American carriers." The airlines owned or controlled by the governments of other countries provided all the competition necessary to keep one American-flag airline responsive to the public interest. If several U.S. carriers were to jostle for overseas business, the foreigners would play one against another, and the American public would be the loser. Rather than direct their passengers to a native competitor's international flights, the domestic airlines would route them via B.O.A.C., Air France or the Soviet national carrier. Did it not make more sense for them to support one U.S. carrier in which they all had an interest?

"It would be a case of the United States' setting up a company strong enough so that it could compete on even terms with these great aggregations, monopoly aggregations, that have been reared against us," he told a doubting Chairman Bailey. By Trippe's reasoning, emulation was the only way to score against a formidable competitor.

The examples he gave had little validity for the United States in the spring of 1945. Among the nations with chosen instruments, Germany, Italy and the Soviet Union were totalitarian states—one already defeated, another on the verge of surrendering. France and Britain had traditions of state-controlled transportation. The British had just issued a White Paper proposing to modify their chosen instrument in the light of its conspicuous shortcomings before the war. KLM, the most efficient international airline, belonged to a tiny country; the Dutch Government had a majority participation in its stock and board of directors.

The Administration depicted the single chosen instrument, in the words of Attorney General Francis Biddle, as "a virtual guarantee of all of the evils associated with monopoly," from price gouging to technical inefficiency. What yardstick for judging costs and quality of service, what incentive for improvement could there be with one operator?

The War Department and the Navy regarded the commercial airlines as military backup in peacetime, a training ground for pilots and technicians, and a market for new aircraft and communications equipment.

The State Department recalled what had happened when Pan American Airways negotiated with foreign governments. "With the advent of war," Secretary of State Hull wrote to Senator Bailey, "some of the arrangements which the company had made proved to be a deterrent to our war effort and were therefore not in the best interests of this country."

With Berle personally lobbying the Senators—in his spellbinding professorial manner he imparted the wisdom of limited competition for overseas routes—and with the Committee of Seventeen Airlines unleashing a blitz of letters and telephone calls, the McCarran bill expired with the Seventy-eighth Congress. The Senator from Nevada reintroduced it in the first session of the Seventy-ninth, minus the provision for government financing. By then, Bailey and Brewster had returned from the Chicago conference; Brewster, the self-styled leader of the "anti-Chicago bloc," was bent on stopping Senate ratification of the interim agreement for an international civil-aviation organization.

The C.A.B. had completed its plan for an international route system and was deep into the North Atlantic case, weighing the claims of eleven carriers in contention for the most desirable airways to Europe and the Middle East. An examiner recommended apportioning the routes between Pan American Airways and American Export Airlines, control of which was being acquired by American Airlines after a ruling by the board prohibiting ownership of an air carrier by a steamship company.

On March 15, 1945, Trippe retaliated by filing for domestic routes for Pan American. "We don't think it's in the public interest," he said, "but if the historical policy of separating domestic and international service is to be changed, then it is essential from a competitive point of view, and from a point of view of equity, that we should operate in the domestic field."

Ten days later, the aviation subcommittee opened public hearings on the American Flag Line bill. The lone supporters of the proposed legislation were Patterson of United and the International Brotherhood of Railway Clerks. The labor union of the airline reservations personnel was impressed by Trippe's warnings about the lower wages paid by foreign airlines.

McCarran anticipated the strongest objection to his bill. " 'Monopoly' is an unpopular word in this country," he said; 'so unpopular that a great many people will oppose anything that is tagged with the 'monopoly' handle. There is nothing inherently wrong in the word 'monopoly' anyway. The Post Office Department is a monopoly— a monopoly in the public interest." According to Trippe, the community company was a "privately owned public utility."

The C.A.B. rejected that analogy in 1940 when it gave a certificate to American Export. Since the Board lacked authority over international tariffs, there was no regulatory commission able to monitor a U.S. overseas airline as to prices and quality of service, it said then.

"Now would be the appropriate time for Congress to give the Board such authority," said Trippe, doing a 180-degree turn for the Senators. How could anyone think he was trying to subvert the Board or that his community company would overcharge the public?

He cast himself as an advocate of low fares for the average man. Pan American planned to offer a $100 ticket to Europe. "But that cannot be achieved," he said, "unless the American share of the traffic can be concentrated in one carrier, in one united company." Reduced fares were predicated on economies of scale—larger and costlier airplanes; he described 100-passenger planes, 200-passenger planes, such as only an airline in sound financial health could purchase. If more than one U.S. airline engaged in destructive competition for overseas business, none would be solvent and they would be obliged to turn to the government for "exorbitant" subsidy. The champion milker of the Post Office was alarmed about the taxpayer's being "saddled" with the subsidy burden.

Although there was nothing on paper to prevent a newcomer from establishing an international air operation, only the American Flag Line could carry the mail and have the assistance of the C.A.B. and the State Department in negotiating foreign rights.

The airlines were to subscribe to Class A voting stock, in amounts proportional to their annual revenues. Pan American was entitled to the maximum 25 percent, American Airlines 12.5 percent, United 11 percent, T.W.A. 8 percent and sixteen other airlines to driblets. Carriers with aircraft properties and franchises for overseas service were to sell them to the community company in exchange for Class B voting stock. Only three had such assets—Pan American Airways, Panagra and American Export Airlines—and Pan American would garner 90 percent of Class B shares.

Trippe also demanded that stock issued for assets be distributed to individual shareholders instead of being held by the three international airlines. Chairman Bailey perked up his ears.

"Then Pan American would be dissolved, would it not?" he asked.

"It might well be dissolved, as would also be the case with the other present international air carriers," Trippe replied.

BAILEY: If it distributed its interests.

TRIPPE: Its assets would be taken over by the community company. However, it might be decided to use one of the existing international air carriers as the new corporate vehicle.

BAILEY: If it distributes those shares of stock to the holders of stock in Pan American, then Pan American is stripped of its corporate capacity?

TRIPPE: That is correct, unless it were decided, as I say, for one reason or another, that it might be in the national interest to use Pan American as the corporate structure for the community company.

There was confirmation enough for the prevalent suspicion that Pan American Airways would control the community company, and that Juan Trippe would run it. "Juan Trippe is the only candidate," a domestic-airline executive declared.

The State Department was troubled by a provision in the bill that implied the community company could strike agreements with foreign countries and then call on the U.S. Government for help. This was a reversion to Trippe's methods that the Administration had called to a halt, and that Brewster was trying to restore. One-man commercial diplomacy might have been appropriate when other countries had no airlines to send to the United States, the State Department acknowledged, but when reciprocal rights were sought, intergovernmental negotiations were necessary for coherence and order.

The hearings were interrupted by the death of Franklin Roosevelt in his cottage at Warm Springs, Georgia, on April 12, the eighty-third day of his fourth term. Harry S Truman, the popular and industrious Senator from Missouri he had selected as the running mate likely to do him the least harm, became the thirty-third President of the United States.

Truman was exceptionally well informed on the airlines in general and Pan American Airways in particular. As the head of an interstate commerce subcommittee, he had worked with McCarran on the civil-aeronautics legislation; later, he had presided over the special committee that investigated defense contracts, and scrutinized Pan American's record in the secret airport construction. He had voted for the postal appropriation for American Export Airlines. On the record, Truman was opposed to the chosen instrument.

At the end of June, the American Flag Line bill was rejected by a vote of 7 to 2.

Any doubts about where the new President stood were resolved on July 5 when Truman approved the decision of the Civil Aeronautics Board to administer a larger dose of competition on the North Atlantic than even Trippe had feared. The board certified T.W.A. as well as American Export.

In making the awards, the C.A.B. said it was not considering whether U.S. international air transportation should be rendered by a single company or by a "chosen instrument." That policy question was settled by Congress in the Civil Aeronautics Act of 1938; the Board was proceeding to fulfill its duty. "No effective substitute for healthy competition as a stimulus to progress and efficiency can be found in monopoly," it said.

In designing a peacetime route system eastward across the Atlantic to Europe and beyond, the C.A.B. fundamentally subscribed to Roosevelt's zone concept. The Board traced three main traffic flows. Service to Northern Europe was divided between Pan American, which already had a permanent certificate for Ireland and England, and American Export, which had been operating the route for the Navy. The Board extended it to Scandinavia and Moscow. A central route from London and Brussels through the Balkans and the Levant to Calcutta was awarded to Pan American. T.W.A. was licensed for a southern route through Mediterranean Europe, North Africa and the Persian Gulf to Bombay.

In light of "changing and momentous world events," the C.A.B. said, it was futile to predict future air traffic from past history of surface transport, and so it was limiting the new certificates to seven years. That the awards were not engraved in stone was of little solace to Pan American for receiving the worst pickings. T.W.A. had a windfall of major terminals—Paris, Rome, Madrid, Athens, Cairo, Jerusalem. Pan American was left with Marseille as a French gateway and was forced to share the London, Frankfurt and Lisbon markets. Although in mid-1945 the Board may not have foreseen the descent of the Iron Curtain, Pan American was to be prohibited by the Soviets

from exercising its franchises in Eastern Europe. The grant of six terminals in the United States (New York, Boston, Philadelphia, Chicago,
Washington and Detroit) did not include permission for Pan American
to operate connecting service between any of them.

The day after Truman signed the certificates, the full Commerce
Committee took up the American Flag Line bill. Bailey and Brewster
leaned with all their might from opposite sides, and the bill failed in a
tie vote to be reported to the floor. The principle of competition, parceled out at the discretion of the C.A.B. and the President, was effectively preserved.

The Senators from Nevada and Maine roused their colleagues to
issue an interim policy report—a highly irregular procedure for legislation that had died in committee. The report was written in slanted
language to imply a recommendation for the community company, and
circulated while Bailey was at the bedside of his ailing wife in Raleigh.
"As we used to say in North Carolina, it's the same old coon with
another ring around his tail," Bailey scoffed after he read the document.

He deplored the report as a ruse to simultaneously discredit the
C.A.B. and the new President while he was out of the country attending the Potsdam Conference and attempt to influence their decisions
about the Latin American routes, which were next on the agenda. His
impression that Trippe was behind the mischievous behavior was confirmed when Brewster flew to Raleigh in the Pan American executive
plane to have another argumentative round with him.

Bailey refused to do as Brewster and McCarran asked: to call a
meeting of the Committee to adopt the report. He stayed in Raleigh
and tried to rally the members of the Committee with blistering letters.

"I know a great deal about Pan American Airways' activities," he
wrote to Senator George Radcliffe of Maryland, a champion of the
airline whom Trippe buttered up with reminders of their common
origin in the Eastern Shore, even to saluting him as "cousin."

"I thought very favorably of the one-company idea myself at one
time," Bailey observed, "but I could not resist the representations of
the several departments to which the bill was submitted, nor could I
avoid the conclusion that Mr. Trippe of the Pan American was gov-
erned very largely by his own selfish interests and that he was entirely
too active."

Bailey advised the Marylander that "the best thing Pan American
officials could do for themselves is to fall in with the established policy,
take whatever may be allotted to them" and stop trying to alter the
Board's decisions or change the law.

As far as Trippe was concerned, the so-called progress report was endowed with the force of law. In subsequent appearances as a witness, he would hold up a copy and identify it as "this new aviation policy."

Three years in a row, he composed militant statements for the annual report of Pan American Airways affirming the single company. It appeared that he was daring the C.A.B. and the President to back down and admit that Juan Trippe knew better than they what was in the national interest.

Truman showed his pique during a visit to Key West, his favorite vacation spot. The White House press corps followed him in a plane chartered from Pan American Airways. Customarily, the President posed with the crew for photographs, which he then autographed individually. On this occasion, Truman waved the photographers away, shook hands with each crewman and explained in an audible voice that he would not make the slightest agreeable gesture for a company that opposed the policies of the United States Government.

Nineteen forty-six was a year of agony for Juan Trippe, despite the homage paid him for Pan American Airways' part in winning the war. As Secretary of War Robert F. Patterson pinned the Medal for Merit to his lapel, Trippe rejoiced, unaware that Sam Pryor had been designated to receive the honor, three months before, for the airport building program. "Look here, I was just implementing Juan Trippe's brain; it was his idea," Sam informed the general who bore him the great tidings. "Why don't you hold mine and give him a medal, because he really deserves it." It took some intensive selling. The General had to persuade Patterson, who had to convince the President—no easy task.

One of Truman's first Presidential decisions was to replace Ed Stettinius as Secretary of State and put him to pasture for a year as United States Representative to the United Nations in New York. Trippe always said that having a brother-in-law in the Cabinet was harmful to Pan American because it inhibited him from talking to the Secretary of State about airline matters. Nevertheless, all signs pointed to the welcome mat for Juan Trippe being withdrawn from the White House.

The C.A.B. and the President were distributing international certificates with an open hand to the domestic carriers, and seemed to be in no hurry to award compensatory internal routes to Pan American. United Airlines was licensed to serve Hawaii from California (before statehood, gateways to territories were classified as foreign markets), cutting into the only part of Pan American's Pacific operations that showed promise of profitability. United offered a $135 fare from San Francisco to Honolulu; Pan American lowered its fare from $195 to meet United's, corroborating economics-textbook theory about the beneficial effects of competition on the consumer.

The most crushing blow was the award to Northwest Airlines of the Great Circle Route to the Orient via Seattle and Alaska. Northwest had been a military contractor in Alaska and the Aleutians, and it also had an eloquent advocate in Senator Warren Magnuson, a Democrat from the State of Washington who sided with Bailey on the Commerce Committee.

For the same reasons it placed two additional carriers in the North Atlantic, said the Board, it was rejecting Pan American's contention "that it should remain the sole United States carrier in the Pacific." The airline's permanent certificate for the central Pacific was extended from Midway to Tokyo—a small consolation prize considering that passengers would be asked to travel 1,600 miles farther to the capital of Japan than if they went by Northwest.

The C.A.B. deliberated over its Latin American applications for seventeen months before giving Caribbean routes to four of the eleven domestic contenders. Truman was displeased. He wanted competition throughout Latin America, and he sent the decision back for reconsideration, specifying his choice of airlines for each route.

Franklin Roosevelt had said Juan Trippe could not have it all; Harry Truman made sure of that.

Some of his associates thought that Juan Trippe was carrying his chosen instrument too far, deliberately provoking disfavor with the President and the C.A.B.—an imprudent strategy for a company as dependent on the government as Pan American. On the whole, they agreed with him that their airline deserved the exclusive right to foreign routes, but they had come to believe that the goal was not politically realizable.

For the second time in less than a decade, there was restiveness on the board of directors. Two members of the executive committee, Sloan Colt and Tom Morgan, were the active malcontents. They had eased Trippe's return to power after the Whitney interval and then watched him revert to his secretive, freewheeling habits, reneging on his promises to name an operating officer and to keep the directors informed.

Morgan was particularly disturbed by the scene in Washington. The president of the Sperry Corporation was a political animal—"the best-connected Southern Democrat in New York City," it was said. As a Tarheel, he was particularly compatible with Josiah Bailey.

Tom Morgan made it a point to get along with people, especially the heads of Congressional committees and military chiefs. As the head of a company that had sold more than $2 billion in navigational products to the Army and Navy during the war, he felt that Trippe was violating common business sense by getting everybody mad at him. Morgan and Colt thought something had to be done to rein him in, or make him step aside.

Colt talked to John Hanes, another member of the executive committee who represented the United States Lines and its ownership of 1.5 percent of Pan American stock. They were Yale contemporaries, and Hanes served on the board of Bankers Trust, Colt's bank.

But sparking a revolt against Juan Trippe was considerably more difficult in 1946 than it had formerly been. Though bad news was pouring in from the C.A.B., the airline was in no financial bind. And Trippe had learned from the Whitney episode to stack his board with malleable directors.

Before the crisis of 1939, the board was composed of outside directors, except for the president and the chairman. Inside directors, particularly if they are managers who do not own or represent large blocks of stock, are powerless to challenge a chief executive. Now one-third of the directors were Pan American vice presidents—Bixby, Gledhill, Pryor and Howard B. Dean, a Yale stockbroker whom Trippe had hired in 1942 to run the Latin American division. Half of the Pan American board could sing "The Whiffenpoof Song" with feeling. To his complement of outsiders, Trippe had added Old Blues like Prescott S. Bush, Class of 1917, a partner in Brown Brothers, Harriman and a Greenwich Republican. Another recruit was Admiral William S. Standley, former Chief of Naval Operations and first in a long line of admirals and generals Trippe used to decorate his board and to promote the impression that the airline was synonymous with national defense.

Two of the old-timers on the board who had figured in the 1939 uprising were Eddie McDonnell and Bobby Lehman. As investment bankers, McDonnell and Lehman were more interested in commissions for their firms from underwriting Pan American Airways securities than in contesting Trippe. And even millionaires were loath to relinquish that most alluring perquisite of the Pan American director, the annual pass signed by Juan T. Trippe. Within a year, it would be good for round-the-world travel.

Colt and Morgan knew their cause was lost when Hanes declined to join them. Trippe turned his persuasive charm on the other directors. As evidence of good intentions, he promoted Bixby, who had been holding the New York office together during the war years, to administrative vice president. Trippe numbed the directors into accepting his chosen instrument. "Juan could convince anyone black is white at those board meetings and it was all I could do not to get up and cheer," the faithful Pryor recalled. "He convinced them that something difficult and unreal was the easiest thing in the world."

At the annual shareholders' meeting in July 1946, Trippe announced that Pan American Airways would no longer have the services of two directors. Colt and Morgan were not standing for reelection. One seat remained empty; the other was filled by Henry Friendly, whom he had recently invited to become vice president and general counsel.

Trippe made an unusual arrangement with Friendly, who, after seven years of pleading Pan American's cases before the C.A.B., had become the foremost aviation regulatory lawyer. Until he was appointed to the United States Court of Appeals for the Second Circuit in 1959, Friendly simultaneously held his law partnership and his corporate position, turning over his remuneration from the airline to his firm.

Henry Friendly was close to James M. Landis, Dean of the Harvard Law School. Coevals as students, they were also members of that singular elite, the former clerks of Supreme Court Justice Louis D. Brandeis. Truman appointed Landis chairman of the C.A.B. in June 1946 to fill out the term of Welch Pogue, then retiring to private law practice after completing the three big route cases—North Atlantic, Pacific and Latin American.

Jim Landis was a craggy-faced, high-strung man whose mind was a perpetual fireworks. A missionary's son, he drank and smoked to excess and found a home for his righteous principles in the New Deal. Roosevelt had brought him to Washington in 1933 as a Federal Trade Commissioner, then transferred him to the Securities and Exchange Commission, and at Joe Kennedy's urging, made him chairman for a term after the financier left.

In government and academe, Landis had made his mark in regulatory law, and his desire to reshape the airline industry with the tools Congress had given the C.A.B. transcended professional ambition to the point of emotional need. Regulated competition was an article of his faith. But that did not preclude a supremely confident lawyer like Henry Friendly from thinking he could persuade another who sat in judgment on his client, as Jim Landis was about to do, of the justness of his position. Friendship could be irrelevant in a match between intellectual equals, where only brilliance and the cogency of one's arguments counted.

Before the new chairman had unpacked his tomes, the president of Pan American Airways paid him a visit. Landis' administrative assistant saw a portly figure cross the threshold of his office, humbly turning the brim of his chocolate-brown felt hat in his hand. "I know who you are," the visitor said. "You are Stanley Gewirtz, and I've heard a lot about you. I'm sure you don't know who I am. I am Juan Trippe." Gewirtz jumped to his feet, prepared to salute a legend. "Yes, sir," he said. "I have an appointment with Mr. Landis," Trippe continued. "I wonder if you would be good enough to go into his office and see if it would be convenient for him to see me." When Gewirtz encountered Trippe again a week later, he received a blank stare of nonrecognition. But his telephone kept ringing with dinner invitations from Ann Archibald. As a new boy in town, Gewirtz failed to recognize the importance of the doyenne of Pan American's Washington office, and he declined. The underling assigned to bid him to the queenly Ann's table rang back again and again, plaintively delivering the imperative: "Mrs. Archibald will not take no for an answer."

Pan American's imperious style of courtship violated an axiom of industry–government relations—that the goodwill of the bureaucrats is as important as that of the elected and appointed officials. The staffs of the regulatory commissions and Congressional committees conduct the research, analyze the data and prepare the reports on which the commissioners and legislators rely to make their decisions. During its first forty years, the Civil Aeronautics Board was a notably staff-run agency. With the exception of a few independent thinkers like Edward Warner, Welch Pogue and James Landis, the members of the Board leaned heavily on the staff and acquiesced in its recommendations unless political pressures stimulated their personal interests to the contrary.

Most top executives of the airlines called on the department heads of the C.A.B. regularly, hoping to create a receptive climate for their requests. "On the few occasions Trippe came around, he didn't bother with the staff, and neither, really, did Pryor," a senior bureaucrat recollected. "They went straight to Oswald Ryan's office." Ryan was a Republican named by Roosevelt at the creation of the agency, and reappointed by several Presidents.

Trippe always aimed straight at the summit of any power structure into which he wanted to connect. Pan American Airways had been built with entrées to industrial tycoons and Cabinet officers provided by his rich friends. After trotting into and out of the White House, supping with a Prime Minister and having a Secretary of State for a brother-in-law, he saw no point in wasting time on persons of inferior rank.

More perceptive businessmen recognized that effective power

might be lodged elsewhere than the pinnacle. The staff of the C.A.B. resented being consigned to oblivion by Trippe and Pryor. An attitude took hold: "If they are so powerful, why do anything to help them?" a bureaucrat described it. "All of the power Trippe accumulated in the early years seemed to work against the airline in later years."

Republicans gained control of both Houses of Congress in November 1946, for the first time in sixteen years. They occupied the chairmen's seats on the committees; the elderly Southern Democrats receded to ranking minority status. A month after the election Josiah Bailey died.

"Taft is the man you want to see," Senator Wallace White of Maine, the nominal Majority Leader, told reporters. After eight years in the Senate, with quadrennial glances toward 1600 Pennsylvania Avenue (his "old homestead"), Robert Alphonso Taft of Ohio was "Mr. Republican" of the Eightieth Congress, the Party's standard-bearer on domestic issues. He insistently raised his nasal voice against Truman's Fair Deal—a disastrous extension of Roosevelt's profligacy by his sights.

Taft's cousin and campaign manager, Dave Ingalls, had returned to Pan American from the Navy to supervise Atlantic and Pacific operations. Trippy, as he still called him, told Dave he wanted to explain his thinking about the chosen instrument to "the most important man in the United States Senate." Ingalls arranged a dinner meeting at the house on F Street. The Senator arrived at 5 P.M., and what was supposed to be a quiet meal for three Yale men escalated to a two-sided debate.

The trustbusting spirit of William Howard Taft lived on in his son; Robert Taft hated monopoly in any guise. He had voted in 1941 to deny subsidy to American Export, on the grounds of curbing wasteful spending and to express lack of confidence in the Roosevelt Administration, not to solidify Pan American's exclusive position.

Trippe assumed otherwise. He pressed the single company on his guest from the first martini to the last petit four. Bob Taft refused to accept it. "You are building up an enterprise for the Army or Navy, and the Government will find it easy to take over. This could prove to be the end of free enterprise," he said. "It will also set an example for other industries to be taken over by the Government."

The argument waxed to white-hot intensity until 11 P.M., when they called it quits and went their separate ways, convictions intact. "It was the only time Juan Trippe lost an argument to anyone," commented Ingalls, testifying to a miracle.

Failing to win over the respected leader, Trippe was more dependent than ever on Owen Brewster, a satellite of Taft's. Thoroughly disliked on both sides of the aisle for his caustic tongue and underhanded tactics, Brewster was riding high after his election to a second term. The Republican landslide had given him the chairmanship of the Senate War Investigating Committee, the highly visible post from which Harry Truman had been catapulted into the vice-presidential nomination. Brewster had a dream: perhaps he could become Taft's running mate in 1948. It was not such a farfetched dream, provided he stayed in the limelight.

35

Howard Hughes
versus Owen Brewster

Howard Hughes was the lone wolf in the pack of enemies Juan Trippe made with his chosen instrument.

The 41-year-old playboy flier controlled T.W.A., the airline that was set to compete with Pan American halfway around the world, and though his erratic attention was focused on his other business toys during the war years, he still had plenty of pride and money tied up in its future.

With the exception of the Hughes Tool Company, the legacy that fueled his miscellaneous fancies, his empire was in disarray, largely owing to his persistent meddling. Only the Tool Company had the benefit of his overwhelming neglect; he left it to be managed by Noah Dietrich, a public accountant who was also kept hopping to salvage his employer's quixotic ventures.

Hughes's contributions to winning the war were steeped in controversy. Behind the receptionist's desk in his dentist's office he discovered a pinup girl for the G.I.s: Jane Russell, a long-legged California beauty with a sulky face and ponderous breasts that defied the law of gravity. Hughes framed her meager thespian talent in a movie about Billy the Kid, directing and editing it himself. Critics ridiculed *The Outlaw*; the Catholic Legion of Decency proscribed it for lewdness. While a volcano of advance publicity ensured that Miss Russell's photographs adorned the cockpits and foxholes of the Armed Forces, Hughes never recouped the millions lavished on producing the film.

There was an element of show business in his military-aircraft program. He hired John W. Meyer, a genial press agent, to overcome the hostility of Air Corps procurement officers. Meyer's formula for winning over generals and Congressmen—caviar, wine, women and gratis plane rides—differed from Sam Pryor's in style and degree: Hollywood flash versus Old Boy elegance. The Hughes entertainment site was a twenty-room mansion in Arlington, Virginia; Pan American's, a Federal house on F Street.

Meyer introduced the President's second son to Faye Emerson, an actress, who before long became his bride. Colonel Elliott Roosevelt's strong endorsement of the XF-11, an experimental air-reconnaissance plane, resulted in a $70-million contract for Hughes Aircraft. In July 1946, long past the deadline for its usefulness in spotting Nazi troop movements, Howard Hughes tested the plane himself and, when one of its propellers malfunctioned, crashed it into a house in Beverly Hills.

Another product of Hughes Aircraft, still not assembled by the time the Japanese surrendered, was the HK-1 Hercules, a 200-ton, eight-engine flying boat made of plywood—ergo its nickname, "the Spruce Goose"—with capacity for 700 passengers. In the final tally, $50 million of Hughes money went down the drain with the project, and another $22 million in losses was borne by the government.

Nowhere on the corporate stationery of T.W.A. did the name of Howard Hughes appear, although, with 45 percent of its stock owned by the Tool Company, it was his airline for all practical purposes. Jack Frye, the president of T.W.A., was a baby-faced pioneer who had set transcontinental records flying the mail in the Thirties. With Frye running it, and Hughes putting in his many millions' worth of dollars and inventiveness, T.W.A. acquired the image of a flyboy's airline. Always in the forefront of technology, it was the first trunk carrier to outwit the weather with high-altitude flying, and at the start of the war, the only domestic airline operating four-engine transports.

In 1946, the airline was exhibiting symptoms of acute postwar decompression. Passenger and cargo loads contracted, and heavy expenses attended the inauguration of international routes. The price of the Constellations Hughes had ordered from Lockheed before the war increased sevenfold by the time construction on commercial aircraft resumed. With losses accruing at an annual rate of $13.6 million, T.W.A. stock tumbled on the Big Board from $71 to $18 a share, wiping out any chance of raising capital to pay for the planes in the equity market.

Dietrich arranged with the Equitable Life Assurance Society for a $40-million loan to be applied to equipment and other capital needs. The hemorrhage worsened, and when he discovered that Frye was using the money to stanch the red ink from operations, he convinced Hughes that he should be fired. Frye blew the whistle in Washington.

In the Administration's view, T.W.A. had proved itself a valuable military adjunct, too valuable to pass out of existence. Moreover, its demise would eliminate a competitior on the international routes. In this respect, the airline was a pawn in the running battle over the single company. "If T.W.A. goes into receivership, it will be a sad but conclusive argument in favor of the chosen instrument," Owen Brewster told James Landis, chairman of the C.A.B.

T.W.A.'s destiny was entwined with that of Lockheed, the builder of the Constellation and of the P-38 Lightning pursuit plane, the attacker of Japanese positions in the Pacific during the war. If T.W.A. did not take delivery of eighteen Constellations standing ready in the Lockheed hangars, the manufacturer might well accompany the airline into bankruptcy. The President's Air Coordinating Committee, headed by Landis, accepted responsibility for saving Lockheed.

During the last days of December, a powwow to decide the fate of T.W.A. was scheduled to be held in New York among the concerned parties—government, creditors, T.W.A.'s Frye-led management and the chronically unpunctual Howard Hughes.

On the morning of New Year's Day, Juan Trippe paid an unexpected visit to Noah Dietrich at his hotel. He drew a gloomy picture of the future of the airlines which coincided with Dietrich's prognostications, and inquired whether Hughes Tool might consider a merger between T.W.A. and Pan American Airways. If Hughes did not want to sell all of T.W.A., then how about its transatlantic operations? "We would be glad to consider any proposal you care to make," Dietrich replied. "Of course, I would have to discuss it with Mr. Hughes."

The next morning found Juan in the office of Thomas I. Parkinson, president of the Equitable, who was edgy about a possible default on the loan he had made to T.W.A. After first circling the mulberry bush delivering his canned spiel about the merits of the community company, Trippe said, "The Equitable may soon be taking additional responsibilities with respect to T.W.A.'s management, and in that event you might be interested in rearranging its overseas routes."

Parkinson's attitude was properly huffy. "The Equitable does not interfere with the management of its borrowers unless they are in default, which has not happened yet with T.W.A. It is our policy, Mr. Trippe, not to discuss with a third party what we might do in those circumstances."

"I understand," Trippe replied smoothly, as though Parkinson had not caught him in the unethical act of trying to seize control of a competitor through a back door. As a director of another major insurance company, Metropolitan Life, he was presumed to know better.

"But should the time come when you do have a greater responsibility for the management of T.W.A.," he said, "you will find me and the entire organization of Pan American Airways disposed to be very friendly. I simply want to assure you of our desire to be helpful."

Hughes arrived in Manhattan on January 7, almost a week later than expected. A marathon negotiating session, led by Landis, was concluded at the "21" Club, the former speakeasy where so many affairs of high finance and national interest have been settled. With Parkinson agreeing to subordinate part of the Equitable debt to newer transfusions of funds, Hughes put up $10 million in exchange for a note convertible into 1 million shares of T.W.A. common stock and the right to get rid of Frye and install his own management. The fresh capital stabilized T.W.A. by enabling it to obtain bank loans and special credits from aircraft manufacturers.

While the meetings to save T.W.A. were going on, Brewster was stirring the ashes of the aviation monopoly legislation. Now the Republicans were at the helm of the committees, and Brewster had on his desk a bill to consolidate and merge the international airlines that had come into being since McCarran had originally tried to cow the C.A.B.

Howard Hughes was convinced that Trippe and Brewster, whom he called "Trippe's mouthpiece," were out to cheat him. The bill set the cutoff date for ownership of international assets at October 1945—before T.W.A. had acquired its overseas interests: which meant that it could subscribe to stock allotted to domestic carriers in the community company but would not be compensated for its investment in foreign routes.

He nursed malevolent feelings toward Brewster on another count. The first week in February, he was called to Washington to answer questions from the War Investigating Committee behind closed doors, a preliminary to scheduling public hearings on his gargantuan flying boat.

When he arrived in the capital a few days before his appointment, Hughes learned that the chairman was in Kansas City on a speechmaking tour. He telephoned Brewster and said he wanted to see him while he was in Washington. "If you come back, I'll see that you get to your other engagements," Hughes promised.

At lunch in the Senator's suite at the Mayflower Hotel, they talked mostly about the seaplane. Hughes defended his pet monster, which was still sitting on the ground in California (when he finally tested it the following November, the mammoth bird rose only 70 feet into the air). Whether they also discussed the aviation bill and a Pan American–T.W.A. merger was later hotly contested. Hughes said they did, and charged that Brewster offered to call off the investigation into the flying boat if Hughes would support the community company and give up T.W.A.'s international routes. Brewster and a lawyer who was present at Dietrich's recommendation denied that any such conversation was held.

Probably those topics were raised when Hughes flew Brewster to Columbus in his plane the next day. True to his word, he also had the Senator transported to Morgantown and back in a T.W.A. executive plane.

While he was in Washington, Hughes saw Juan Trippe. Two soft-spoken, unfathomable men took each other's measure. Hughes pretended not to understand the overseas-airline business. "Why isn't there more cooperation between officials of our companies?" he asked. "And why are you pushing this unification of all the international airlines?"

Trippe explained why there was room for only one U.S.-flag carrier in the skies. They parted amicably, agreeing to meet again in a month or so when Hughes was again in the East.

On March 14, a lawyer for the War Investigating Committee went to the Hughes Aircraft plant in California and demanded to see expense-account vouchers relating to the Hercules. In New York, Trippe called on Noah Dietrich in his suite at the Waldorf-Astoria and tirelessly recited the case for the chosen instrument.

As he was getting up to leave, he mentioned Pan American's application for a transcontinental route. "We have operations in the Pacific and in the Atlantic. It is most logical for the C.A.B. to allow us to connect these services," he said. "And once we obtain that franchise, it will be an easy step into local service, transcontinentally." Dietrich inferred from Trippe's velvety statement a threat to T.W.A.'s main trunk operations.

Then Trippe brought up the Brewster bill. "It's unfair to T.W.A.," Dietrich said. Trippe replied that he could have it changed. Or so Dietrich and a lawyer for Hughes Tool who attended the meetings claimed—and Trippe denied. During all the conversations between the two sides, Hughes or Dietrich had a witness; Trippe went alone.

Howard Hughes made the next move. From there on, his actions are undisputed. For what went on in his suspicious mind, we have only the word of the accountant who served him for thirty-two years. In 1947, Hughes was eccentric but not appreciably more so than other tycoons. Sonny Whitney also changed his schedule a dozen times before keeping an appointment. Juan Trippe's associates were never sure what he was plotting. According to Dietrich, "Howard could teach a few lessons to the master of manipulation, Machiavelli himself." The master of manipulation, to those who did business with him, was Juan Trippe.

Hughes telephoned Trippe early in April. Could Trippe meet him in the West? He laid down conditions of absolute secrecy ("The press must not get wind of this"). That suited Trippe fine. In later years, Hughes's passion for privacy, his indecisiveness and his numerous phobias made him the world's most celebrated recluse, and doubts about his sanity surrounded his death in 1976, 3,000 feet over Texas in a jet plane crammed with oxygen tanks. But in 1947, he was acting no more deviously than any businessman planning a merger, certainly no more than Juan Trippe.

They fixed a date to meet on a Saturday, in Palm Springs. Trippe flew out in the B-23, taking his 12-year-old son, Charles, with him just for the ride. Since Hughes had insisted they meet alone, the pilot was to deposit Trippe and return when he was summoned. Juan checked into a small inn, and later that morning Hughes telephoned and instructed him to come to a cottage he had rented in the desert. Noah Dietrich had flown from Houston in his private plane. He had T.W.A.'s figures; Trippe had Pan American's balance sheets and income accounts. The discussion got down to merger immediately. Hughes sat quietly, his 6-foot-3-inch frame slumped in a chair. He let Dietrich draw Trippe out.

"What do you have in mind, Mr. Trippe? On what basis do you propose an exchange?" Dietrich asked.

"Well, I think the most logical manner of bringing a merger about would be on the basis of book values," Trippe said. Pan American's net worth was reported at $13.66 a share, though its stock was selling at around $12.

Dietrich asserted that Pan American and T.W.A. used different methods of accounting, and therefore an exchange on the basis of the market values of their respective securities would be the fairest method. The value of T.W.A. on its books was $4.24 a share, but the stock was then trading at around $20, far above the company's net worth, as a result of speculator activity following Hughes's decision to pump more money into the airline.

Hughes bestirred himself. He talked about selling T.W.A. lock, stock and barrel. Trippe wanted to buy only the overseas part. He figured it was worth one-fourth to one-third of a combined company.

Nonsense, said Hughes, T.W.A. international is worth almost twice what all of Pan American put together is worth. "Why, that's completely out of line," Trippe rejoined. T.W.A.'s foreign business was smaller than Pan American's Atlantic service and not yet profitable.

It should have been evident from Hughes's outlandish counterproposal that he was twitting Trippe. According to Dietrich, Hughes had no intention of merging. "He was simply buying time to plot his strategy against the Brewster-sponsored legislation to freeze T.W.A. out of the overseas market." Yet Juan could not be sure. Perhaps his adversary was merely using the tactics of the Oriental bazaar. So Trippe changed the subject.

"Why don't you gentlemen read this?" he suggested, handing them a copy of the Brewster bill and a memorandum from Pan American's public-relations department setting forth reasons to support it. He asked for their position paper, and as Dietrich reached for his briefcase, Hughes snapped, "I prefer not to give it to you, Mr. Trippe." Unless they came to an agreement on a merger, he intended to oppose the legislation. "Let me think about your offer overnight and we'll meet here again tomorrow at ten," he said, and left to keep a date in Los Angeles.

The next morning, Hughes was late, as usual, and in a grouchy mood. They went over the same ground, but it was like spinning wheels in the desert sand. Trippe suggested they adjourn and reexamine their figures. "Mr. Hughes, if we can devise a basis for a merger that will be acceptable to you, will you publicly come out in favor of the community-company bill?" he asked.

Dietrich answered, "We've taken a position with the other airlines against the bill, and I don't see how we can logically change that position without looking inconsistent."

"I agree," said Hughes.

The meeting was over. Hughes was still concerned about the press getting wind of their rendezvous, and he directed Trippe to have his plane pick him up at a deserted airport near the Mexican border, to which Hughes flew him in his plane. A week later, Trippe called on Dietrich at the Waldorf to ascertain whether he and Hughes had arrived at a conclusion. "None," said Dietrich. "I've had no further instructions from Mr. Hughes and I presume that he has no further interest."

In the spring of 1947, *The Chosen Instrument* played in both houses of the Eightieth Congress.

S. 987, a bill to amend the Civil Aeronautics Act and provide for the merger and consolidation of the nation's international air carriers, was introduced in the Senate by Owen Brewster. Companion measures were submitted in the House of Representatives by three Republicans and a Democrat from Arkansas, the home base of Pan American's lobbyist Carroll Cone.

Hearings were held concurrently from April to June, to the exasperation of most of the performers other than the star. No sooner would a witness finish in one chamber than he had to repeat his testimony in the other. With Brewster directing the Senate show as chairman of the aviation subcommittee of the Interstate and Foreign Commerce Committee and with the courtly Southerners absent, the level of civility dropped sharply from what it had been at the 1945 hearings.

Trippe appeared stouter and more contemptuous toward the C.A.B. and the unmentioned foe in the White House than he had been two years before. "Since V-E day, a new American international air policy is being tried out—a policy providing for competition between American airlines abroad, domestic as well as international," he said. "The facts are that the system is not working well, and that a year hence, the situation will become progressively worse."

The latest modifications in the bill made the community company an unmanageable Goliath. Hundreds of surface-transport companies and seventeen domestic airlines were to participate, and although a maximum 3 percent was set for each subscriber, opponents were sure that in the period of six months Pan American had to dispose of its excess stock, motivated shareholders could band together, to amass blocks of shares and install the old management at the head of the consolidated company.

Cued by Brewster, Trippe assured the Senators that this could not happen. "Pan American Airways disappears as a corporation," he said.

The bill made it "obviously impossible for Pan American to be again designated to represent the United States in overseas air transport."

The hedgehog had no instinct for quitting when he might be winning. "Perhaps three or four of our directors may be permitted to serve on the new board, but the new board will be subject to approval of the C.A.B.," he said.

Speaking for the skeptics, Croil Hunter, president of Northwest Airlines, thought he discerned two plots. In "the mess and confusion," Pan American would wind up in control of the consolidated company and/or it would sell out to the government at a good price.

Indeed, this latest model of the chosen instrument was the most attractive for Pan American stockholders, because it gave them shares in a new company whose financial success was guaranteed by Uncle Sam.

Trippe had cranked into the bill a bushel of subsidies to remove the risk from the enterprise: one to pay for construction of new aircraft, another to make it profitable to operate thinly trafficked routes "in the national interest," a third to protect the company against lower wage and other operating costs of foreign airlines and a special grant to meet the higher subsidies collected by foreign airlines.

If anything ensured rejection of the bill by a Congress bent on economizing after fourteen years of Democratic spending, it was these provisions for financial aid which would have cost the taxpayer dear in administrative expenses alone. Moreover, the domestic airlines would have been severely disadvantaged, a point Trippe himself had stressed when Grover Loening proposed an identical construction subsidy as part of his scheme to place the international air service under the jurisdiction of the Merchant Marine Administration.

Chairman Landis of the C.A.B. made the point in another way: in creating a chosen instrument, Congress would destroy individual airlines, which could not be resurrected in case the chosen instrument proved a failure. "The only way out would be a government-controlled and government-owned international air transport system—the path to socialism," he said. The issue Trippe forced Congress to reckon with was one of the few on which a New Deal liberal like Landis and a Republican conservative like Taft could wholeheartedly agree.

The hearings ended, Trippe departed on June 17 on the triumphal voyage he had been envisioning for twenty years: the inauguration of Pan American Airways' round-the-world service, the first such flight scheduled by a commercial airline.

For once the hoopla did not take place at water's edge. The flying boats had been retired; the era of the land plane had arrived forever more. Glistening in the noonday sun on a runway at LaGuardia Airport was a Lockheed Constellation with four 2,200-horsepower Wright engines, a cruising speed of 260 miles an hour and a pressurized system that permitted flight at 18,000 to 20,000 feet, above the turbulence of oceans and mountains. The Clipper *America* was to take Trippe, Ingalls and twenty publishers on a two-week journey of 22,170 miles. No spouses were invited, but Oveta Culp Hobby of the *Houston Post* and Helen Rogers Reid of the *New York Herald Tribune* kept the junket from being a stag party.

Without domestic authority, Pan American had to start its round-the-world flights on one coast and terminate them at the other. The mayors of New York and San Francisco made speeches predicting that mankind would be brought closer through air commerce, and the National Anthem was played. Althea Lister, an executive secretary from the headquarters office in the Chrysler Building, approached Trippe. "I'm so happy for you today," she said. "This is the fruition of your dream. Do you remember that Christmas party when you told us, 'We're going around the world'?" Juan nodded. "I remember," he said.

He embraced Betty and their children, who had come to see him off, and turned to board the plane. His wife tugged at his sleeve and motioned with her eyes to a small, white-haired woman. Juan went over to his mother, bent down and gave her a farewell peck on the cheek.

Lucy Trippe was 76 and infirm—"a querulous old lady who thought her life should have been better than it was," according to her granddaughter Betsy Trippe. Lucy did not lack for reasons to think otherwise. Her son—dutiful if absentminded—was distinguished, wealthy and blessed with a devoted wife. Her daughter, Louise, had married Sargent Bradlee, of a Boston Brahmin family. Lucy played bridge, said her prayers, exercised matriarchal privileges ("We were quite terrified of her," Betsy said) and finally left this vale of tears in October. She named Juan her executor and bequeathed most of her estate, valued at $500,000, to Louise Bradlee and her three children.

Trippe sustained another loss with the overwhelming rejection by the committees in both Houses of the bills to merge and consolidate the international carriers.

The avenue of destruction for Pan American's competitors through Congress was closed. And with it, Pan American's last chance to be the nation's chosen instrument by force of law.

If Trippe was disheartened, as he had every right to be, no one could have guessed it from his demeanor. Everything was business as usual. Those who knew him best understood that Juan did not acknowledge failure and that when he was ready, he would give them their next marching orders. The chosen instrument was his dream and it could not be taken away from him.

On the afternoon of August 6, 1947, Howard Hughes loped into the marble-pillared Senate Caucus Room as onto the set of a movie he was financing, directing and ballyhooing by himself. He was forty-two minutes late for his appointment with a subcommittee of the War Investigating Committee.

Photographers' bulbs flashed, newsreel cameras whirred. Reporters, wearing sunglasses against the glare of klieg lights, scribbled furiously. A clatter of applause broke out from among a thousand perspiring spectators, most of them women craning for a glimpse of the capricious millionaire whose romances with filmland's leading ladies were chronicled in the tabloids and fan magazines.

Hughes was costumed to play the honest knight come to slay a dragon in the nation's capital. He wore his black hair parted in the middle and slicked back, his brush mustache neatly trimmed. A white shirt and double-breasted gray suit overwhelmed his lean body, battered in so many plane and automobile accidents. His socks drooped.

Behind a battery of microphones, Hughes raised his hand to be sworn in as a witness. Cupping a hand to a deaf ear, he strained to catch the remarks of the subcommittee chairman, Senator Homer Ferguson of Michigan, and threw a glance of loathing at Brewster, seated on the dais 20 feet away. Then he read his opening lines.

"I charge specifically that during luncheon at the Mayflower Hotel in the week beginning February 10, 1947, in the suite of Senator Brewster, that the Senator told me in so many words that if I would agree to merge T.W.A. with Pan American and would go along with his community airline bill there would be no further hearing in this matter."

The "matter" was the investigation, then in its second week, into the military contracts for the uncompleted planes. According to Hughes, Juan Trippe had told him in Palm Springs that he would try to get the Senator to delay both the hearings on the bill and the investigation, pending a merger between the airlines.

The proceedings degenerated immediately into a political circus. Hughes and Brewster staged a sideshow in the newspapers, exchanging calumnies through press releases. Before leaving California for Washington, Hughes issued a statement: "I worked pretty hard for what money I have, and I didn't make it from airplanes. All in all, in my transactions with the Government I have made no profit whatsoever." He portrayed himself as a Texan who kept his word and told the truth, and he threatened to take his story of Brewster's attempted blackmail to the Attorney General.

Brewster counterthrust with an obscure Biblical reference. Reporters consulted their King James versions of the Old Testament to discover, in Chapter VI of the Book of Nehemiah, that the prophet did not let the mischief of his enemies deter him from completing the work of God. "I will welcome and invite the most thorough exploration of this charge by the Attorney General," he added, and sent a copy of his announcement to the Justice Department.

No evidence of fraud or corruption in the procurement of the contracts for the Hercules and the XF-11 was turned up during the hearings; but there were titillating revelations about the entertainment furnished by Johnny Meyer and another publicist for Hughes. Elliott Roosevelt challenged their expense-account notations and charged that the inquiry was a continuation of "the smear" of his father by Brewster and Ferguson in the Pearl Harbor investigation.

After Hughes finished repeating to the subcommittee his account of Brewster's menacing offer, the Senator stepped down from the dais to refute him. Fifty-nine years old and Humpty Dumpty–shaped, with darkish strands combed across his perspiring pate, Brewster stood before his peers and swore to tell the truth.

He admitted having talked to Hughes about the merger and about the aviation bill, but never with an intent to "persecute" him or misuse his investigatory authority. On the contrary, Hughes had tried to "coerce" him into dropping the investigation by sending one of his lawyers, a former chief counsel to the committee, to tell Brewster he had "a hot potato" in his hands.

"They were seeking to lay a trap for me," Brewster said in a tearful voice.

What was Homer Ferguson to do? The investigation had backfired: Republican conduct was being held up to scrutiny. The subcommittee chairman ruled that neither man could cross-examine the other; if they submitted questions in writing, he would relay them.

The next day, Hughes presented his list. Ferguson read them to his crony. Brewster alternated between defiance and obsequiousness, a Uriah Heep vouching for his integrity.

The community-company bill was not drawn to favor the stockholders of Pan American Airways, he said. "Juan Trippe is a man not interested in making money."

He professed admiration for the president of Pan American, whom he had known for four or five years, though their personal associations were "very limited." "I believe I have been his guest at dinner twice. I believe these are the only times I've ever been in his home. I think he is a very able man."

He owned up to friendship with Sam Pryor—"We have a close and very gratifying personal relationship"—but minimized the vice president's bounty. Pryor's generosity to officials was well advertised in gifts of rare bourbon whiskey, tickets to sporting events and other entertainments, and for special friends, the use of his house in Hobe Sound, a Florida retreat for Eastern Old Boys who could not abide the nouveaux riches in neighboring Palm Beach.

Brewster, a Christian Scientist and a teetotaler, admitted that he and his wife had partaken of Sam's hospitality for two Thanksgiving sojourns.

"It's a very modest, bungalow-type place—a small place of five rooms," he said. "The Pryors were not there. I paid the cook five dollars a day. I went to the grocery store and bought groceries and the Thanksgiving turkey. I left the place pretty well stocked up with canned goods, as a sort of expression of my appreciation."

Pan American's house on F Street was also "very modest," according to Brewster, who compared it with T.W.A.'s "palace" in Arlington. "It has a toilet on the first floor that is always out of order, more than any other I know." He claimed to have had no more than three breakfasts on F Street.

Brewster allowed that he had accepted a ride in the Pan American plane to see Senator Bailey in Raleigh about the community-company bill. He implicated his fellow Republican Senator John W. Bricker of Ohio as a companion on the T.W.A. courtesy flight to Columbus.

The next day, Brewster left for Maine, where he said he was "gratified at the relatively few skeletons which have been found in my closet." The hearings were put back on the track of Hughes's military contracts. After a short weekend recess, Senator Ferguson startled the standing-room audience on Monday morning by suspending the hearings until November and vanishing into a hospital to be treated for poison ivy.

Encircled by well-wishers, Hughes turned to the newsreel cameras for his farewell address. "As soon as Senator Brewster saw he was fighting a losing battle against public opinion he folded up and took a run-out powder," he said.

The attempt to stain his reputation had failed. Fair play had won out. "And for that," drawled Howard Hughes, "I want to thank the people of this country and the members of the press."

On that mawkish note, Hughes accurately proclaimed his vindication. A slightly daft tycoon with a Grade B cinematic flair was judged a more credible actor than a greedy politician. Whether Brewster and Trippe actually threatened Hughes or whether he merely reached an obvious conclusion, their plan to get rid of T.W.A. as an international competitor for Pan American was incontrovertible, and the alliance to further their respective ambitions more than a shade unholy.

At least, that was the impression engraved in public memory. The hearings, which were supposed to discredit the Democrats and enhance Brewster's chances of higher political office, confirmed a relationship until then only rumored between the Senator and Pan

American Airways. Although he had five years before his next test at the polls, Brewster's political future and Juan Trippe's chosen instrument were doomed in the Caucus Room.

Republicans felt disserved by Brewster's vendetta against Hughes. In November the hearings resumed in a much calmer environment. Eager to put the shame of the past summer behind them, the Senators allowed the War Investigating Committe a merciful death, and another committee established an investigating unit to continue the partisan digging into the war years. In April 1948, the Republican majority of the committee apportioned criticism for the Hercules and the photo-reconnaissance plane between Hughes and the Air Corps. The Democratic minority absolved Hughes of wrongdoing and condemned the purpose of the investigation.

The climate was ripe for curbing the influence of pressure groups on legislators. Congress had enacted a tame law in 1946 requiring lobbyists to register with Congress and file quarterly reports of their outlays (no one from Pan American Airways signed in). The Brewster/Hughes hearings served to whet an interest in further disclosures.

Attorney General Tom Clark appointed a special prosecutor to look into lobbying activities. He examined Pan American's books and presumably found nothing to impress a grand jury, for that was the last heard of the matter. Clark was named to the Supreme Court in 1949, and thereafter Pryor sent him rare bourbon and invitations to Hobe Sound.

In subsequent years, Brewster grabbed headlines chiefly as a red-baiter and an abettor of Senator Joseph R. McCarthy of Wisconsin in his gathering campaign of terror. Brewster hectored Truman and Secretary of State Dean Acheson for being soft on Communism and abandoning Chiang Kai-shek.

The search beam of a House investigation into tax fraud shone upon Brewster in the last year of his Senate term. As chairman of the Republican Senate Campaign Committee, he was barred from distributing funds to the 1950 primary races. He gave a $10,000 check to Henry W. (the Dutchman) Grunewald, an influence peddler, to be divided between Richard M. Nixon, a California Congressman aspiring to a Senate seat, and another candidate. Brewster had gone through "the usual procedure," he said, of borrowing the money from a bank and depositing it in the account of Grunewald, an enigmatic figure who counted Sam Pryor among his legion of friends in industry and government.

Brewster met his Waterloo at a Maine primary in June 1952. Howard Hughes pumped $60,000 into the coffers of Brewster's opponent, a moderate Republican, and assigned his public-relations agency to circulate materials vilifying his would-be nemesis. The results were interpreted by some pundits as a repudiation of the strident conservative flank of the party, heralding the choice of the benignly apolitical Dwight D. Eisenhower as the Presidential candidate.

Sam Pryor, ever loyal, always maintained that "Brewster was an able Senator, and a good friend to Pan American. It's tragic that the plan for one company never went through."

Like so many others once fallen from power, Brewster ceased to exist for Trippe. In the occult maze of Juan's mind, seeds of blame were germinating. Brewster was Pryor's friend; ergo, the wreck of the chosen-instrument legislation was Sam's fault. He allotted one shred of criticism to himself. "It was a mistake for me to go to see Howard alone," he confided to a Pan American executive years later. "I thought he would be alone too, but when I got there he had that fella, what's his name, with him."

To have tied the destiny of Pan American Airways to so blemished a character as Owen Brewster seems an anomaly for Trippe. Habitually, he surrounded himself with first-rate associates—the most skilled engineers, the smartest lawyers, the most distinguished directors. The executives he hired and the wielders of government power through whom he maneuvered were usually dignified men of impeccable reputation. Trippe was too astute, too much of a snob to have it otherwise, and besides, only honorable associates could provide the antidote to the universal mistrust he himself provoked.

If there was anything tragic, Pryor thought, it was Juan Trippe's obsession with the chosen instrument—the fatal flaw that diminished his heroic achievements and irreparably damaged his company.

Part VI

THE WORLD'S
MOST EXPERIENCED
AIRLINE

36

The Strange Case of A.O.A.

Considering Trippe's proclivity for creating a Satan's image for himself in Washington and his unholy alliance with Owen Brewster, Sam Pryor was doomed to the lot of Sisyphus. With buoyant spirit and boundless energy, he rolled Trippe's chosen instrument up Capitol Hill, and when it slid back at him, he cheerfully looked for another track on which to roll it upward. Because that was what Trippe expected of him, and he worshiped Juan.

Surely no Administration could have been more antagonistic to Pan American than Truman's, and no C.A.B. chairman more eloquently hostile than James Landis. To think it was a tall order to reverse that tide was to underestimate Pryor. He was a virtuoso of corridor-creepers in a moral climate pre–Ralph Nader, pre-Vietnam, pre-Watergate. This is the judgment of his admirers and some of his rivals, and perhaps of Sam himself, though he expressed it in other words.

"Now, Presidents are pretty smart politicians; otherwise they wouldn't get to be President," Pryor once explained to someone who asked how he accomplished his goals. "They listen to people before they make their decisions. They listen to the top leaders in the Senate and the House. They listen to the Secretary of State. You have to have all these leaders believing in what you believe in before going to the President, and then when you go to him, he has listened to them and you get something done. It is not that complicated. It is a fact of life."

To be as likable as Sam, and as ecumenical, was a big help. A highly visible Republican, he had scads of Democratic friends. An Episcopal Church vestryman, he sought out Catholic bishops and members of "the Jewish church" to be his friends too. And to have the largest expense account among airline-industry vice presidents and the largest network of "consultants" was useful also. A Pryor-retained consultant to Pan American Airways might be a lawyer in Omaha, a publicist in Los Angeles, an orchestra leader in Washington. Someone who could open doors for Sam, doors that led to the people he wanted to believe in what he and Juan Trippe believed in.

James Landis was the most forceful and controversial chairman of the C.A.B. thus far. His personal life was disorderly—the magnificent brain oiled by inordinate doses of alcohol, the gaunt face, shy manner and cerebral dazzle so attractive to women, his marriage fraying at the seams. But none of this siphoned attention from his work—the mission he perceived to bring economic harmony and justice to civil aviation.

The history of other regulated industries was uninspiring. Big corporations and financial interests invariably succeeded in weakening the backbone of watchdog agencies. The one exception was the Securities and Exchange Commission, and he could take some credit for its record of incorruptibility. Landis was determined to make the C.A.B. similarly independent, and meanwhile structure the airline industry for the second half of the twentieth century.

He raised the hackles of the domestic operators with his spacious view of the amount of competition necessary for an efficient air-transport system. Landis encouraged nonscheduled airlines to supplement the services of the trunk carriers already certificated by the C.A.B.

He resembled Adolph Berle, that other minister's son and Harvard-bred New Dealer, in imputing moral principles to the conduct of business in a free society. Landis' preachings made him all the more obnoxious and untrustworthy to the airline chieftains.

In a lone dissent disapproving the purchase by United Airlines of the Denver–Los Angeles route from Western Airlines, he termed United's actions "not only uneconomic but also immoral" because its accounting treatment of the acquisition would enable it to draw higher mail-rate subsidy.

Landis censured Pan American Airways for spending nearly $1 million on an advertising blitz timed to the hearings on its application for domestic routes. "It struck me as unethical," he wrote, "for an airline to use this kind of pressure tactics on the board." Trippe requested 14,610 miles of routes crossing the United States from east to west and north to south to connect thirteen gateway cities to its international network of more than 90,000 miles. The domestic-airline leaders, including Patterson of United, closed ranks to oppose him. They contended that one-third of the traffic between the continental borders of the United States would be drained off by Pan American, resulting in a "disastrous dissipation of traffic and unbalancing the air transportation system"—this according to American Airlines, then operating internationally through American Overseas Airlines.

Trippe pointed, as always, to the competitive advantage held by foreign carriers, noting that their international routes derived financial nourishment from connections to their countries' internal lines and offered a convenience to travelers, who could book passage from one inland city to another beyond the ocean without changing airlines— say, from Chicago to Lyon on Air France. And now this advantage belonged as well to ten U.S. carriers granted overseas franchises by the Board.

To demonstrate the purity of Trippe's intentions, however, Pan American asked for domestic authority only "for such time as the major [domestic] airlines continue to be authorized to engage in overseas and foreign air transportation."

Trippe took his case to the public, aiming over the heads of his opponents and the C.A.B. with an extravagant promotional campaign. Pan American advertisements depicted speedy marvels of aircraft—the six-engine Consolidated Vultee–37 and the Republic Rainbow which was designed to fly at 450 miles an hour—and an era of cheap fares to follow the award of the requested domestic routes. His adversaries complained that it was unethical to boast of drawing-board planes and imply that Pan American was a "transportation Messiah" (in the phrase of a lawyer for Eastern Air Lines). After all, who had spurred the development of land planes—the DC-3, the DC-4, the Constellation? Not Juan Trippe, but C. R. Smith, Bill Patterson, Jack Frye and Howard Hughes.

Long before Landis had a chance to rule on the matter, he used his Chairman's post as a pulpit to inveigh against the chosen instrument, and brought his influence to bear on President Truman's Air Coordinating Committee, of which he was cochairman with Assistant Secretary of State Garrison Norton. The committee unanimously opposed the Brewster bill in the spring of 1947, and subsequently delivered a report on aviation policy which endorsed competition in the international field as "the only means of keeping from the hands of one small management group the power to interfere in policies of great national interest."

Truman turned the report over to a citizens' group appointed to help him formulate a national aviation policy. The Air Policy Commission, headed by Thomas K. Finletter, a New York lawyer, concurred: "We do not approve the Chosen Instrument policy," it said.

Truman let Landis know privately and through Congressional channels that he intended to reappoint him chairman of the C.A.B. when his term expired at the end of 1947. He was stunned when the President called him to the White House late in December, praised him for doing "a hell of a job" and then fired him. Landis was not at fault, Truman said, but there were times, as Jim Farley had warned him, when a President has to be a son-of-a-bitch. Landis sensed that the President was speaking in political vernacular, and after an infusion of alcohol, he fathomed his meaning. In less than a year, Truman was to present himself to the electorate, and he implied that Landis was a political liability.

Landis believed that Juan Trippe had had a lot to do with his not being reappointed. "He was probably right on that," Pryor said many years later. But why should the President act to satisfy someone he disliked as much as Trippe? Because Truman was going to have a devil of a time funding his campaign, so low had his popularity sunk. Through Sam Pryor, Pan American was striving to get into his good graces.

Pryor's especially good friend was Louis Johnson, an outside counsel to Pan American Airways. Johnson, a hulking politico from West Virginia, was a former national commander of the American Legion; Under Secretary of War in Roosevelt's prewar administration; "a bull who carried his own china shop with him" according to one of his critics. He and Pryor were golfing companions at White Sulphur Springs. "He always had someone in government with him. These were excellent associations," Sam said appreciatively. And Louis Johnson stood by Harry Truman when others deserted.

The following July, Truman was nominated to be his party's candidate against Governor Thomas E. Dewey of New York. Clare Boothe Luce said the President was "a gone goose"—an estimate shared by many Democrats. Henry Wallace bolted the party from the left; Senator J. Strom Thurmond of South Carolina took flight with Southern Democrats into a States' Rights coalition against Truman's civil-rights program. No one, it seemed, wanted the hopeless task of Democratic finance chairman until Louis Johnson volunteered. He signed a personal note for $250,000, the seed money for a $1.5-million campaign chest that enabled Harry Truman to take to the rails on a whistle-stop schedule, confound the pollsters and get himself reelected. Among the angels Johnson assembled in a Truman choir were those reliable Croesuses, Averell Harriman, David Bruce and C. V. Whitney, then assistant secretary of the Air Force. Carroll Cone, Pan American's assistant vice president and registered lobbyist, served as one of Johnson's most effective deputies; he wrote out a check for $3,000, raked in $300,000 (some from Republicans and Dixiecrats) and kept his home state of Arkansas in the Democratic column. How could Truman not be grateful?

Nineteen forty-eight was the year of the airline matchmaker. The postwar economic slump caught the operators in the midst of their expansion programs, and for two years the red ink flowed over their balance sheets. Joseph J. O'Connell, Jr., Landis' successor as chairman of the C.A.B., urged them to arrange mergers.

Trippe hopped on the marital merry-go-round as though Pan American's survival depended on finding a partner. Actually, his airline was doing better than most, showing profits every year, though not as large as he would have liked. Merger was a means of obtaining domestic routes while the Board dallied about making up its mind whether Pan American should have them, and it gave him another crack at the chosen instrument by picking off his competitors one at a time.

After Bill Patterson of United rebuffed his oblique courtship, Trippe made passes at Eddie Rickenbacker of Eastern and George T. Baker of National for equipment interchanges and stock swaps, and extended a feeler to C. E. Woolman for a three-way merger—Pan American, National and Delta. And he never stopped hoping that somehow he could get T.W.A. away from Howard Hughes.

In September 1948, he sensed that C. R. Smith, the chairman of American Airlines, was in the mood to sell its overseas business. Smith was the commanding figure in domestic aviation as Juan was in international, and through American's 61.9-percent stock ownership in American Overseas Airlines they were competitors on the North Atlantic.

C. R. (for Cyrus Rowlett) Smith was the same age as Juan, but his life story came from another volume of the Great American Business Classics. A rough-hewn 6-footer with a background of small-town Texas impoverishment, he was one of the few pioneers drawn to the airlines as an auditor rather than a flier. He was vice president of American Airways during the drastic reorganization of the domestic carriers following the cancellation of the airmail contracts in 1934 and was adjudged clean because he had attended no spoils conferences and had nothing to do with bidding for routes. In the face-lifting process that turned the company into American Airlines, he was named president.

Although its coffers were empty, he embarked on a program to standardize American's motley collection of airplanes with a new fleet of Douglas DC-3s. He went to Jesse Jones, a fellow Texan at the head of the Reconstruction Finance Corporation, and declared in his Wild West bookkeeper's manner, "We have a disaster, and we hear you were set up to handle disasters." The $4.5-million loan Jones extended set the precedent for airline financing by the R.F.C. and fueled American's expansion into the lead position among the trunk carriers.

He was a cold, lonely man—married briefly and divorced—and a superb administrator. He banged out instructions to the staff on a wheezy typewriter, a cigar clenched between his teeth. "You knew exactly where you stood with him; you never did with Trippe," said an executive whom Juan hired from American.

During Smith's leave of absence to operate the Air Transport Command, Ralph S. Damon, vice president and general manager of American Airlines, negotiated the purchase of a controlling interest in American Export Airlines, which was rechristened American Overseas Airlines. C.R. disclaimed having taken part in that decision, but it was common knowledge that American executives journeyed to the capital to seek advice on major matters from General Smith.

American Overseas had an excellent reputation for service— superior to Pan American's, many thought—but it operated at a deficit that cooled C.R.'s enthusiasm, particularly after American Airlines incurred substantial losses during 1947 and 1948. Undoubtedly, the additional capital requirements for American Overseas' fleet of Strato-cruisers fed Smith's pessimism about the transatlantic market. All of a sudden he was singing Trippe's tune: "It was never good sense on the part of the government to subsidize two U.S. airlines to compete directly with each other."

Juan contrived to meet C.R. in Grand Central Station (American's offices were across the street and Pan American's a block east of the rail terminal) to obviate the danger of being recognized. In a tidal wave of homeward-bound commuters, they settled the first point in an arduous negotiation to combine. They agreed that a merger might be desirable.

Then intermediaries took over: John Hanes, a former Pan American director on a consulting retainer from Trippe to search for merger prospects, and Charles S. Cheston, an investment banker on the American Airlines board. Having third parties as matchmakers in a corporate merger is advisable to demonstrate arm's-length bargaining, especially in a situation as controversial as this one was likely to be. It took them six weeks to arrive at Trippe's bargain price: $10 million in Pan American stock.

The deal was a long way from consummation. The approval of the

C.A.B. and the President had to be obtained. The Board's decision in international cases was merely advisory; the President had the ultimate power.

Even before the directors of the two airlines voted on the agreement, Pryor mounted the Pan American campaign to convince Truman it was sound and in the national interest. He paid a visit one Saturday to Secretary of State George Marshall at his home in Leesburg, Virginia. There was no one in public life whom Harry Truman respected more than Marshall—"the great one of the age," he called the soldier-statesman. Marshall was a friend of Pan American, dating back to his relationship with the Stettiniuses.

Sam stressed national security. A.O.A. was the carrier designated to operate between West Germany and Berlin, landlocked inside East Germany. In June, the Russians had thrown up a blockade around the city. A.O.A. was the lead airline in the airlift of food and supplies to the beleaguered population. Did anything more need to be said about the urgency of A.O.A.'s not going under from financial losses? Marshall told Sam that the President was coming to lunch the next day, and promised to talk to him about the merger.

On December 17, four days after the merger agreement was signed, Louis Johnson escorted Juan to the White House for an appointment with the President. "When Louis took him in, the matter had been fixed in Truman's mind by Marshall," Pryor said. It was a month and a half after the election, and Give-'Em-Hell Harry was presumed to be feeling benevolent toward Pan American. Trippe reported that he looked with favor upon the consolidation of the two international operations. C.R. came away from meeting Truman on February 17 with the same impression. His was more reliable; Smith's standing in the Democratic Party was bedrock firm.

As far as Trippe was concerned, everything else was window dressing. Pryor could take care of the political side, Friendly the nuisance of the C.A.B. proceedings.

The *North Atlantic Route Transfer Case*, as Pan American's application to acquire American Overseas Airlines was entered, began on April 18, 1949, with a hearing before a C.A.B. examiner, Tom Wrenn. Four airlines, eight labor unions, American Export Lines and the Justice Department intervened.

A.O.A. was aviation's *Scopes* trial—on a par with the 1925 airing of Darwinism and the teaching of evolution in the public schools of Tennessee. Here, the issue being tried was perceived to be Juan Trippe's chosen instrument. As in *Scopes*, it was a battle of legal titans. In place of Clarence Darrow and William Jennings Bryan were Henry

Friendly and James Landis, once the closest of friends, now contemptuous enemies.

Landis represented A.O.A. employees fighting the takeover of their airline by Pan American. The modest fee they could pay him was irrelevant. A.O.A. was a crusade for the former chairman of the C.A.B., intensified by his hatred for Juan Trippe, who he believed had robbed him of his mission to remake the airlines.

Landis was starting to fail emotionally, and his heavy drinking and chain smoking were taking their toll. He strode back and forth like a caged animal in the narrow passage between the examiner's rostrum and the long table at which the protagonists were ranged on either side in uncomfortable proximity.

Henry Friendly was in absolute possession of his imposing faculties. He chivvied his adversary with pointed references to how far he had fallen. "Does the former Dean of the Harvard Law School know what equal ownership of stock means?" he snapped with icy disdain. Stanley Gewirtz, Landis' law partner, represented Seaboard and Western Airlines, an opponent of the merger. Gewirtz coached Landis on areas he was overlooking, and Landis did the same for him when it was his turn to cross-examine witnesses. Friendly taunted Gewirtz for being "a stooge," and Stanley threatened to punch him in the nose. For a moment it seemed as though the hearing room might be turned into a sparring ring for bespectacled intellectuals.

Trippe, of course, was the star witness. His dark hair was receding; touches of gray appeared around his ears. Thirty years later, Wrenn would recollect him turning "his beautiful brown eyes" on his inquisitors. Juan was clothed in humility, his face creased in that peculiar smile, half seraph, half Beelzebub. He made his familiar statement advocating "unification of our overseas effort," which he said would result in an American-flag carrier better able to compete against B.O.A.C. and the four other foreign airlines that operated in the areas of Western Europe served by Pan American and A.O.A. He estimated that the combined company would save the U.S. taxpayer $9 million in annual mail subsidy.

Landis queried him sharply as to the basis of his traffic projections and his evaluation of A.O.A.'s assets. Trippe was evasive. "He sends me here, he sends me there!" Landis shouted. "I go around this alley and I am blocked; I go down this alley and I can't get a simple answer."

The merger agreement was drawn to terminate on September 13 if final government approval was not obtained by that date. As the hearings droned on into the summer, Smith reconsidered the terms. Conditions had improved for the airlines. "A.O.A. can remain in business and do fairly well," he said, his anxiety of a year before to dispose of the overseas business abating.

The Texan was sitting high in his saddle. Now Trippe was the anxious one. He raised his price $7 million and agreed to pay it all in cash—$17.45 million—and assume in addition about $4.5 million in A.O.A. indebtedness. In return, he was getting a valuable franchise, a fleet of the most advanced aircraft—eight Boeing Stratocruisers, seven Constellations and five DC-4s—and eventually, almost $5 million in retroactive mail pay still due A.O.A. This was NYRBA in spades.

There was another turn of events. On the sultriest day in August, Harry Truman announced he was appointing Attorney General Fred M. Vinson to the Supreme Court and naming Senator J. Howard Mc-Grath of Rhode Island, chairman of the Democratic National Committee, to succeed him. Pryor sighted an opportunity for a switch of signals to the antitrust hounds of the Justice Department. Sam congratulated McGrath on his new position and obtained an off-the-cuff opinion that he saw no reason to oppose the purchase.

Shortly before Christmas, Wrenn recommended approval of the merger. He was swayed by the prospect of subsidy savings and the expiration of some of the transatlantic certificates in July 1952, at which time the operations of U.S.-flag carriers would be reappraised.

Two counsels for the C.A.B. charged with defending the public interest filed exceptions to Wrenn's report. "The board has before it in this case an ugly record, the ugliest record it has encountered in over a decade of regulation under the act," they said. Trippe's account of other merger overtures did not square with the recollections of Noah Dietrich, Bill Patterson, Eddie Rickenbacker and C. E. Woolman. His testimony was "false in important particulars," the counsels asserted. "The charitable view is that his memory failed him."

The next day, Pryor received a telephone call from Carlene Roberts, the lobbyist for American Airlines. A daunting blond woman, Roberts was on enviable terms with everyone in a position to help her employer at the C.A.B. and the White House. One of her friends was Matthew J. Connelly, the President's secretary. Roberts informed Pryor that the Justice Department was about to send the C.A.B. a statement of forty-seven exceptions to Wrenn's report, with a covering letter from an assistant attorney general.

"Why, that can't be!" Sam said. "Howard told me he was for the merger."

He telephoned the Justice Department and learned that McGrath was attending a meeting in San Francisco. Sam left that evening on an American Airlines flight, and upon arrival went straight to the St.

Francis Hotel. "F.B.I. San Francisco. What room is McGrath in?" he barked at the reception desk, flashing a badge his good friend J. Edgar Hoover had given him as a perquisite of his volunteer work in narcotics control.

"Howard, you told me you would approve the merger and I have it from a substantial source that it's been disapproved," Pryor reproached the Attorney General.

According to his recollection, McGrath promptly called his secretary in Washington and ordered the statement recalled. The record shows that exceptions were filed, but two weeks later the Justice Department withdrew all but one, explaining that it was going to limit its argument to the possible effect of the merger on competition. In its brief to the C.A.B. it seemed to regard the consolidation of the two companies as inevitable, and suggested that in such event, the C.A.B. should reallocate the international air routes to make sure some competition prevailed.

On May 17, 1950, the C.A.B. voted 3 to 2 to disapprove the acquisition of A.O.A. by Pan American. The majority was concerned lest the merger intensify Pan American's dominance in the U.S. international airline system so as to weaken T.W.A.'s ability to compete across the Atlantic.

Oswald Ryan, the Republican vice chairman, reputed to be Pan American's most reliable friend in the agency, dissented. He approved the merger and was joined by Josh Lee, a Democrat, who attached a condition—that the Board strengthen T.W.A.'s routes to make it a forceful competitor to Pan American.

The majority opinion and implementation order had the standing under the law of a recommendation to the President. They were sent to the White House with the dissents under a cloak of secrecy pending the President's decision. Pryor and Roberts ferreted out the unfavorable news, but no one was really troubled. Trippe and C.R. were certain that Truman would overrule the Board and bless the merger.

At the White House, another set of procedural machinery started clanking. The President's Special Counsel, Charles S. Murphy, acted as liaison with the C.A.B. He turned the case over to a lawyer on his staff to coordinate with the Bureau of the Budget, whose responsibility it was to elicit and evaluate the views of the major Departments.

The Commerce Department was the only agency in favor of the merger. The Post Office supported the C.A.B. majority; State and Defense registered no objection to it. Frederick J. Lawton, the director of the Bureau of the Budget, outlined three courses of action for the President: affirm the C.A.B. majority; affirm, but indicate he would be receptive to another merger proposal adjusting the existing route pattern; approve the merger, subject to appropriate route adjustments. Lawton recommended the second course—which would effectively kill the merger and oblige the parties to start from scratch if they were still inclined to pursue consolidation.

Lawton's report was sent to Murphy's office on Thursday morning, June 29, and was placed in a file that landed on Truman's desk before noon. The President was unusually preoccupied that day. On June 25, Communist troops of North Korea had crossed the 38th parallel into the Republic of South Korea. Truman was about to hold a press conference to tell the American people, "We are not at war." The U.S. intervention was a police action under the United Nations. After talking to the reporters, he closeted himself with the National Security Council.

When he reached for his pen before the press conference to sign the green paper on which the C.A.B. order was printed, did he recall his conversations with Marshall, Trippe and C.R. more than a year before? In the interim, Marshall had become ill and retired to private life—whereupon Juan had invited him to become a director of Pan American Airways and a member of its executive committee. Louis Johnson had been serving as Secretary of Defense since March 1949, wielding an economy ax so brutally that U.S. unpreparedness for the Korean war would shortly be laid at his door and Truman would have to fire him and coax Marshall to take his place.

But that was a couple of months away, and perhaps Harry Truman was only thinking of clearing his desk when he signed his name in the place marked for approving the decision of the majority of the C.A.B. as recommended by his Budget Director.

The papers were back in Chairman O'Connell's office at the C.A.B. in midafternoon. O'Connell directed the general counsel, E. T. Nunneley, Jr., to "register and publicize" the decision—the final procedure specified by law.

It was a humid summer day, and Woody Nunneley was an unhurried bureaucrat. Tomorrow morning would be soon enough, he thought. While he was taking his relaxed time about having copies made and drafting a press release, Carlene Roberts was telephoning Sam Pryor. "We're in trouble," she said. "They're printing the order denying the merger."

"That can't be," Pryor said, hanging up and calling the Department of Defense.

The key figure was Matt Connelly, the President's Cerberus; he decided who saw Truman and when. At 8 o'clock the following morning, Louis Johnson entered the Oval Office. At 9:20 A.M., Oswald Ryan had an appointment—unknown to C.A.B. Chairman O'Connell, who received a call from Connelly at 9:50 A.M. "Hold up on everything. I may have to discuss it with the Boss," the Presidential secretary said. O'Connell had voted disapproval. At 10:20 A.M., Connelly called back. "There's going to be a revision," he warned. Fifteen minutes later, a third call, directing O'Connell to return the entire file to the President's office.

Special Counsel Murphy and his staff were excluded from Truman's meeting with Ryan and from subsequent discussions on the A.O.A. case. John R. Steelman, the President's assistant, known to be friendly to Pan American, participated; Lawton, the Budget chief, was asked for approaches to an altered objective. Upon "further consideration," as Truman described his turnabout, he rescinded his approval of the C.A.B. majority veto and issued a letter of instructions to the Board directing it to submit a pattern of route adjustments to establish a proper competitive balance between Pan American and T.W.A. as a condition for approving the merger.

Those who saw the green document noted what a poor job of ink eradication had been done on the President's signature, which now appeared on the line for countermanding orders of the C.A.B. At no time during the hectic events of that Friday was the chairman of the C.A.B. invited to the White House. O'Connell was incensed at Ryan's surreptitious conduct and hurt that the President had taken advice from a Republican member instead of from him, a loyal Democrat. On Monday, O'Connell submitted his resignation to Truman.

Ryan, as acting chairman, drafted the plan to achieve competitive balance between the two remaining carriers. T.W.A. was certified to serve London and Frankfurt; Paris and Rome, the sugarplums Trippe always desired, were given to Pan American. "Please submit an order at once," Truman directed Ryan. On July 10, the four-member Board sent to the White House the order with the amended certificates for Pan American and T.W.A. The President signed them immediately.

Trippe was gleeful. Truman had given him more than he had asked. Despite all the Presidential rhetoric about balanced competition, Pan American was a step closer to being the single international carrier. "Sam, where are you going on your vacation?" Juan inquired. It was the only time he ever mentioned the word "vacation," and Pryor understood he was being thanked.

By the end of September, Pan American and A.O.A. were one airline. C.R. said good riddance to the international business—even though when the books were closed, American sustained a million-dollar loss on its investment in A.O.A. Pan American acquired 2,500 new route miles and seven countries to serve, and a magnificent fleet of aircraft, just as international traffic picked up. A few years later, it collected A.O.A.'s retroactive mail pay.

But even within the company, there were some who thought Trippe had made a mistake. "It was looking for trouble," said Jim Smith, "because there was no chance of getting both his chosen instrument and domestic routes." It was essential for Pan American to have domestic routes, he thought, "to pump solid dollars into the till"—a stream of revenue protected from the risks of doing business wholly abroad.

On August 1, after five years and four and a half months of regulatory foot-dragging, the C.A.B. denied Pan American any domestic routes whatsoever. And there was no running to the White House for solace; domestic route awards were not subject to Presidential review.

Equity and logic pointed to some access to the trunk lines for Pan American as long as the domestic carriers were franchised for overseas service. Moreover, the C.A.B. was embarking on a wide course of granting permits to foreign air carriers to serve U.S. cities: Air France (New York, Chicago), KLM (New York, Miami), El Al (New York via London and Paris). And in years to come, the Board would accommodate the State Department as it traded off air rights for political friendship—to shore up the Western alliance, make inroads into the Communist bloc and curry favor with the Third World. Trippe's warnings of foreign competition would at last graduate from fantasy to harsh reality.

What, then, was the Board thinking of in that summer of 1950? A subsequent chairman reconstructed the frame of mind of the members. "They looked at Pan American and saw a virtual monopoly in Latin America and the Pacific, a duopoly with United from the West Coast to Hawaii. Pan American was the only one flying to Africa. The Board looked at the balance sheets and saw traffic growing. Why should they feel sorry for Pan American when it already had the world locked up?"

And there was something else. "Pan American had such great influence with the White House," he said.

37

High Finance

Many of Juan Trippe's business associates maintained that he was uninterested in money; in the next breath they extolled his financial skill. That seems like a contradiction—unless one accepts that a penny pincher can be a high-stake gambler.

"I don't think Juan ever regarded money as important except as an instrument of power. He was absolutely immune to the seductions of money; but he was not immune to the seductions of ambition, of power," David Bruce said. "Juan was as close to a genius in business as I have ever seen. He was the most imaginative man I have ever known in business. He had an imperial vision of the world," Bruce declared.

The vision and the obsession that grew out of it compromised his financial judgment. "If he had been purely profit-minded," Jim Smith believed, "he would have given up the chosen instrument and gone for the domestic route."

Trippe gave the impression that he was proudest of his financial coups. To be sure, he preened over the planes he brought and the routes he won, but he hastened to point out that he lined up the money to pay for them well in advance.

He did this with considerable ingenuity from the mid-Forties on. Pan American's financial history in its first ten years was largely one of raising capital by selling stock to speculators, buying franchises with its inflated paper and mortgaging its equipment. Although Trippe excelled at persuading others to accept the optimistic value he placed on Pan American stock, none of these approaches was particularly innovative. It was only after the company was firmly in his hands again and he was leading it into grandiose ventures that his brilliance as a financial strategist became evident.

In the fall of 1944, Trippe pondered how to get the money for Pan American to expand after the war. He planned to spend $100 million on equipment, and he figured that one-fourth of that should come from new equity capital, the rest from other sources, including mortgages on the aircraft. Twenty-five million dollars was a vast amount of equity to sell at that time, more than all the common stock marketed in 1942. Pan American's net worth was slightly less than $40 million.

Assuming the war would be over and planes released from military reserves, Trippe would be needing the funds in the second half of 1945. To avoid being caught in the predictable stampede for airline capital, he tried to nail down an advance commitment from an investment banker for an underwriting. Juan broached the topic to Robert Lehman, Pan American's banker and longtime director, but there were so many imponderables concerning the condition of the stock market a half year down the road that Lehman awaited further developments before making a concrete proposal.

In November 1944, Floyd B. Odlum, head of the Atlas Corporation, telephoned Juan to suggest he might be helpful. If Trippe was an empire builder venturing on uncharted skies, Odlum was one of the scavengers who pick at the wreckages of other men's enterprise and speculate on the opportunity for restoration. In 1923, then a young lawyer specializing in the reorganization and merger of utility companies, Odlum had established Atlas as a private investment trust with $40,000 of his own and a friend's money. It was to be a "financial hobby" for a man who worked single-mindedly at the accumulation of wealth. By 1929, Atlas was worth $6 million. Four months before the crash, he converted half its holdings to cash and sold new Atlas stock for several million dollars more, which he kept in liquid assets. In 1930 he stalked the ruins of Wall Street with a $14-million bundle, buying up controlling blocks of stock in twenty-two supine investment companies for 50 cents on the dollar or less. By 1935, Atlas had assets of $100 million.

Some of the acquired investment portfolios contained properties too weak for prompt liquidation. Among the businesses Atlas ended up managing were the Greyhound Bus Lines, the Bonwit Teller specialty store on New York's Fifth Avenue (which he turned over to his first wife, Hortense, to revivify), a Mississippi barge line and California fruit farms. Through Atlas' ownership of 50 percent of the common stock of R.K.O., Odlum exercised a decisive voice in the movie company's management.

During the Thirties, Odlum had a major stake in Curtiss-Wright, the scavenger's delight among aircraft companies, and he was further identified with aviation after his second marriage, in 1936, to Jacqueline Cochran, a onetime beauty-parlor operator whom he encouraged to turn aviatrix. Cochran set more records for speed, distance and altitude than any pilot who lived to display a roomful of trophies, and organized the Women's Air Force Service Pilots (WASPs) to ferry aircraft during the war.

As the stock market perked up in 1942, Odlum started unloading stocks from the Atlas portfolio, and by the time Trippe was looking for a banker, he was swimming in cash and on the alert for new speculative opportunities. They were nodding acquaintances. Odlum flaunted his humble background—the son of a Methodist minister from Michigan, he had worked his way through the state university college and law school in Colorado—and preserved his small-town manners. He abstained from alcohol and red meat (less on moral principles than to placate his digestive troubles), was a duffer on the golf course and consorted with film folk and other scavengers like Victor Emanuel of AVCO. Howard Hughes trusted him. Juan Trippe did not.

Yet Odlum and Trippe had much in common. Both were sharp traders, deceptively soft-spoken, inscrutable (Odlum hid behind horn-rimmed glasses) and stealthy. "You know, three times I have had the pleasure of getting control of a company before the directors had any idea I was doing it," he boasted.

Given his anxiety about securing a timely financing, Juan felt he had to listen to Odlum's proposition. Odlum offered to guarantee Pan American a minimum $25 million by underwriting a combination rights and warrants offering to shareholders. The approach was conventional enough: the right to buy stock at a discount from prevailing market prices would practically force Pan American stockholders to subscribe in order to protect their investments from dilution by the new shares. The warrants were an extra enticement, providing the holders with a call to buy still more stock at a stipulated price during a stated period of time.

To prepare the market for the offering, Pan American stock would be split beforehand 2 for 1, broadening ownership of the shares and creating more buyers for the new equity. Following the split, which would increase the total outstanding stock to about 4 million shares, stockholders would be given the right to purchase 1 new share for every 2 shares owned, at a price to be set at the time of the offering, which was tentatively scheduled for June 1945.

The Wall Street recipe for "sweeteners" usually called for 1 warrant for every 4 or 5 shares subscribed. Odlum emptied the sugar bowl. "I'll give one for one," he said. Attached to every right was a warrant entitling the holder to buy a second share for $18 at any time before December 30, 1947.

The warrants were attractively priced. In the fall of 1944, Pan American stock commanded a market price around $34 a share— equivalent to $17 a share after the proposed stock split. Odlum was counting on an end-of-the-war bull market to boost the stock, letting the warrant holders in for handsome profits. Pan American could reap as much as $36 million in additional equity capital as the 2 million warrants were exercised, creating a like number of new shares sold at $18 a share. If one took the bearish view, the price of the common stock could trade below $18 as the warrants approached the expiration date, in which case the warrants would become worthless.

But Odlum's speculative instinct was so positive about the future of airline shares that he was willing to hand Trippe an enormous bonbon. In lieu of the usual cash underwriting fee (about $1 million for a financing of that size), Atlas Corporation would take its compensation in warrants. Trippe warmed to the idea of paying with paper that cost him nothing. What difference did it make to him if Odlum wanted to gamble all the way?

Actually, Odlum was exposing himself to little genuine risk, and that was for a brief period between the time the price was set for the units and the close of the offering a few weeks later. As an underwriter, Atlas was committed to buy any stock not taken up by the shareholders. Odlum was surely astute enough about pricing, and he had two and a half years for a run with the warrants.

Once the grand design of the deal was drawn, Trippe wrestled with Odlum to fix the number of warrants Pan American should issue to Atlas and at what exercise price. This Olympic match took place for almost a month over the telephone and in their respective habitats of office and home. There were no spectators. They met alone and kept the records of their conversations in their heads. Odlum was famous for a technique of keeping opponents in a state of suspension for weeks on end until they weakened and snapped at his absolute, nonnegotiable offer. One can visualize him leaning back, thumbs in galluses, feet on the desk, scratching his freckled bald spot and chirping his figures in a flat plainsman's staccato.

One can imagine Juan, haughty in shirt sleeves and puffing a plebeian cigar that tore at Odlum's nervous innards. He was in no apparent hurry to consummate Odlum's deal; that was Trippe's notorious method of wearing out adversaries.

Finally, they came to these terms: Atlas Corp. would receive warrants for 500,000 shares exercisable at $18 a share, to be adjusted to 400,000 shares if the offering price to the public was more than $18 a unit, and to 600,000 shares if the unit offering price was less than $14.

Atlas Corp. was thus positioned to emerge as Pan American's largest stockholder. Chilled by the memory of one overpowering stockholder, Sonny Whitney, Juan insisted that Odlum limit Atlas Corp.'s holdings to 200,000 shares, or 3 percent of Pan American stock. The rest would be disposed of through a distribution to Atlas stockholders or sold in a secondary offering.

Juan had to have an escape hatch. So much could happen in the next half-year, which was certain to be a volatile period in the market. Odlum demanded a stiff price for the privilege of cancellation. If Pan American elected to pull out, Atlas would be paid cash equal to one-third of 1 percent of the maximum amount of the underwriting commitment for each month the agreement was in effect prior to cancellation—namely, $83,333 a month, or as much as $583,000 should Trippe wait until the day before the underwriting to revoke.

Just as Odlum gave in to Trippe's dread of losing his company, Trippe had to cater to Odlum's speculative fever. Odlum demanded the option to collect the penalty in stock rather than cash. Pan Am could be required to sell Atlas Corp. 25,000 shares at $16 a share for each month prior to cancellation. Trippe blanched, but relented after Odlum agreed to place a lid at 100,000 shares.

On December 5, 1944, they signed an agreement, each convinced he had outsmarted the other.

When Trippe presented the agreement to the Pan American board for approval prior to the announcement, Bobby Lehman raised a princely eyebrow. To speak out in the boardroom would have sounded like sour grapes, and besides, that was not his style. Bobby was exquisitely mannered, his courtesy disconcerting; he was a banker who helped clerks on with their overcoats.

He took Trippe aside after the board meeting and informed him that the financing was inappropriate for a blue-chip corporation. It had all the earmarks of a marginal situation, beyond the pale for an honorable investment-banking firm. There were too many gimmicks, too many sweeteners. According to Robert Lehman of Lehman Brothers, the deal lacked class and was not in the best interests of the company or the investors.

The day of the signing, Pan American stock closed at 33⅞ a share —equivalent to almost $17 a share under the projected split. When the shareholders approved the stock split and the financial agreement at a special meeting called for that purpose on February 23, 1945, the stock had declined to 25¾, or less than $13 a split share.

Spring brought intimations of German collapse; the Japanese reeled back from the Pacific islands and the stock market rallied with particular jubilance for airline shares after the domestic carriers reported an aggregate 75-percent increase in profits for the first quarter. Pan American stock shot up to $28 a share in early June—equal to $56 before the split.

Luck was in Odlum's corner. If Pan Am stock were to maintain its price level during the forthcoming rights offering, Atlas Corp., holding warrants for 400,000 shares at $18 a share, would show an immediate paper profit close to $4 million. Trippe was acutely embarrassed. His publicized stroke of genius in securing an underwriting commitment at minimal cost appeared as gullible consent to an exorbitant fee, the gratuitous enrichment of Odlum's investment company by the president of Pan American Airways.

He asked Odlum to renegotiate. The radical change in market conditions justified a reduction in the number of warrants, he said. "I expect you to honor the terms of the agreement," Odlum replied without a trace of Midwestern friendliness.

The financing was practically all set to go; the registration statement was filed with the S.E.C. on June 11 for an offering in early July. To cancel, pay the penalty and wait for other financing would inflict wounds on the company's credibility and its standing in the market. Moreover, Juan would soon be needing the equity money to pay for planes. He dashed to his escape hatch, hoping to find another underwriter on incredibly short notice.

"Won't you take it over?" he asked Lehman. There would be two modifications. The underwriting fee would be paid in cash "up front," as was customary. With Pan American stock in the high 20s, the market would now support a larger underwriting. Trippe wanted something on the order of $42 million.

The passage of seven months had not improved the deal in Lehman's opinion. "We take a broader view of these financings," Bobby said, "and we feel that this one is not well conceived for the company and will not be constructive for the investors."

On June 25, Trippe unburdened himself to the executive committee of his board—Tom Morgan, Sloan Colt and Mark McKee, the trio who had escorted him out of the crisis with Whitney; John Hanes of the United States Lines; and his loyal insiders, Harold Bixby and Sam Pryor. "Try Odlum again," they said. Juan made the telephone call from his office. Unless Odlum took his fee in part cash and fewer warrants than they had agreed to, Trippe was going to cancel. Odlum was unbending.

Trippe had one arrow left in his quiver. He called Elisha Walker, managing partner of Kuhn, Loeb & Company. Walker was an Old Blue of the generation preceding Trippe's, Yale '00; a Gentile star in the constellation of German-Jewish investment banking firms and a competitor of Bobby Lehman's. Kuhn, Loeb had been the leading financier of the nation's railroads when the Lehmans were looked upon as upstart commodity brokers from Alabama. J. P. Morgan had acknowledged Kuhn's son-in-law Jacob Schiff as his peer; the Warburg partners in the firm were the Brahmins of American Jewry.

Early in the century, Bobby's father and uncles had ventured into investment banking by selling securities for minnow industries like retail stores and the Sears, Roebuck mail-order house which were snubbed by bankers with clients in railroads and steel. After Bobby took the reins in 1925, Lehman Brothers had become the major banker for the young airline and broadcasting businesses. With his art collection worthy of a Medici, his polo ponies, his racing stable and his blue-blooded friends, Bobby Lehman had caught up with the older crowd of patrician bankers.

Walker was familiar with the Odlum financing from reading the public registration statement and reports in the press. Tradition being what it was, he knew that Lehman must have turned it down. Why else would Juan be calling him and pressing for an immediate answer as to whether Kuhn, Loeb would assume the deal?

Walker was one of the canniest of the gentleman bankers, a financier of the oil industry and a veteran proxy warrior. He perceived the airlines superseding the railroads as the transportation of the second half of the twentieth century, and he wanted to edge Kuhn, Loeb into Lehman's territory. Walker told Trippe to expect him at the Chrysler Building within an hour.

At 5:30 P.M. he was there, to make a cursory review of the legal documents, ask a few questions and say at last, "I am prepared to recommend to my partners that Kuhn, Loeb handle this underwriting —provided, of course, that you cancel your agreement with Odlum." After a round of gentlemanly handshakes he was gone, and Trippe telephoned Odlum to inform him that he was no longer Pan American's underwriter. There was contempt in his voice—no velvet, only steel. Odlum was flabbergasted. He offered to hurry over for a talk, to straighten things out. It was too late, Juan said.

On July 2, Kuhn, Loeb priced the offering, at $21.50 for a unit consisting of 1 share and 1 warrant. With Pan American shares selling at $25.75 on the New York Stock Exchange, the sale "went out the window," in broker's jargon. Ninety-four percent of the subscription was taken by the stockholders, the remaining 6 percent readily absorbed by the underwriters and distributed in the market, making it the largest sale of common stock on record in recent years. Pan American collected $43 million in new equity capital after underwriting fees and expenses of $1.9 million were deducted.

Odlum acted on June 30 to trigger his option to purchase 100,000 shares at $16 a share. This entitled him to participate in the July rights offering, and to acquire 50,000 units at $21.50 each, yielding a quick paper profit of $1.3 million. Afterward, Pan Am stock fell prey to steady erosion in the market, and Atlas Corp. salvaged its profits by selling its holdings in the airline. By December 1947, the stock was trading below $18, and stockholders who held warrants to the end could use them as wallpaper. With the sweetener gone sour, Pan American could not realize the millions of dollars in additional equity anticipated upon the exercise of the warrants. Lehman's assessment of the Odlum-structured financing as a speculative deal that would leave unhappy investors in its wake was partially borne out.

Nevertheless, the episode gave Trippe a reputation as a canny financial opportunist, and rightfully so. His timing was perfect; he obtained the money when he needed it and before he was crowded out by other airline operators. True, he was hooked by a shark, but he coolly wriggled free and strode to market on the arm of a distinguished investment banker.

Next, Juan turned to commercial bankers for additional help in facilitating his purchases of aircraft. In October 1946, he arranged for a standby credit of $40 million with a group of twenty-eight banks in twelve cities headed by the National City Bank in New York. He paid 1½-percent interest a year on the borrowed funds and a standby charge of one-fourth of 1 percent on the unused portion. The credit was converted eight months later into a four-year loan at 1¾-percent annual interest.

In February 1949, Trippe negotiated a new agreement with the same bankers extending credit up to $50 million, of which $10 million was earmarked for buying American Overseas. The interest rate was adjusted to 3 percent, the same as for blue-chip borrowers. As Pan American's operations broadened and Juan kept ordering vaster quantities of advanced equipment, the credit agreement was rolled over again and again until permissible borrowings in the hundreds of millions of dollars were structured on the original $40-million deal.

Given the volatile nature of airline operations, Juan's most striking accomplishment was in obtaining the same credit terms for Pan American as were extended to the most stable industrial corporations.

Whether he was borrowing privately from banks and insurance companies or going public with debenture offerings, he insisted on the lowest interest rates, the fewest restrictions and the most comfortable repayment schedules. After Trippe decided on the terms, he sent Robert G. Ferguson, the treasurer of Pan American, to secure them. When the lenders rebuffed his demands, he was castigated by Trippe, usually on the phone, for hours on end, until he promised to try again the next morning.

John Woodbridge, the comptroller, was in charge of internal finance. It was his job to prepare the figures for the annual report according to Trippe's grand directive. Willis Player, Van Dusen's successor as public-relations director, had the thorny task of interpreting Trippe's message. Juan was as much the compulsive editor of the Pan American annual report as he had been of the Yale *Graphic,* and the numbers and text always combined to state a case for the chosen instrument.

38

Managing
in the Fifties

As soon as the war was over, Trippe completed the corporate housecleaning he had begun after getting his company back from Whitney.

Leuteritz and Priester sensed peril in a staff meeting Juan called to announce he was reorganizing Pan American. Looking sideways at a piece of paper twice the size of a postage stamp, he said, "This is what I want to do." He was transferring the engineering department to Gledhill's domain for coordination and budgetary control and giving the vice presidents of the three operating divisions—Latin America, Atlantic and Pacific-Alaska—authority over all facets of operations.

"What does this mean, Juan?" Hugo asked after the meeting was over. Leuteritz as chief communications engineer and Priester as vice president and chief engineer had always enjoyed company-wide authority, signifying the sacredness of technical operations.

"You will have to write a letter to the vice president of the division if you want to do something in that division," Trippe said, staring at the ceiling.

"Suppose I want a check?"

"First you will get permission from a vice president. He will draw up a budget for the division. He will submit your request to New York and have me okay it."

"Suppose I see something I don't like?"

"Ask the vice president."

Later that day Priester appeared in Leuteritz' office. Trippe had given him the same explanation. "What is happening with Pan American, Hugo?" he asked. "Juan told me, 'You think of ideas and send them to me.' I think all he wants is to retire us."

Leuteritz soon found himself trapped in petty disputes between the comptroller and the division heads. His hiring recommendations for radio operators were overruled. He was vocal in his discontent, and after a few months, Gledhill said, "Hugo, it's okay with Mr. Trippe if you want to leave." Leuteritz resigned to organize an aviation electronics company.

Priester stayed on, pretending that nothing had changed when it had, and not only in Trippe's mind. "Old André's a little old-fashioned for my thinking," a younger vice president of a division said. Priester was supercautious about pushing new engines to the performance levels guaranteed by the manufacturer. His goal of maintaining Pan American's precious reputation for safety was admirable, everyone said, but the innumerable delays that resulted were costly and publicized. Lindbergh reported that a banker's wife was telling all Paris how she had been held up for a solid week in Ireland by an engine repair.

If not Priester, who else? That had been the attitude in the early days when the engineer appointed himself safety watchdog for Pan American. But after the forced strides in military-aircraft development during the war, planes were more reliable, and the government set standards for manufacturers. Trippe thought it unnecessary and economic folly for Pan American to go the Civil Aeronautics Authority one better.

Leuteritz paid Priester a visit now and then in his office on the fifty-ninth floor of the Chrysler Building—one floor above Trippe, but it might have been in another universe. "All I do is sit here crying," André said. "Hugo, do you remember when Pan American was one happy family?"

Trippe took advantage of illness to get rid of some executives. He stopped speaking to Bill Van Dusen, whom he considered a Whitney collaborator, and refused to let him cross his threshold. While recuperating from major surgery, Van Dusen learned he no longer had a job at Pan American.

But then there was John Leslie, stricken with a hideously incapacitating form of polio just after Trippe promoted him to administrative vice president and gave him a seat on the board of directors in May 1950. Leslie was 45, a graduate of Exeter, Princeton and M.I.T., and a Priester-trained engineer. He had acquitted himself well as an administrator in the Pacific and Atlantic divisions and as an impassioned witness in the domestic-route hearings.

In public as well as on the fifty-eighth floor of the Chrysler Building, he was Trippe's sycophant. "My president is very modest," he told a House subcommittee, and insisted on reading into the record the citation for Trippe's Medal for Merit.

During the anguished months of convalescence, as he realized he would need assistance to perform the simplest bodily functions for the rest of his life, it also became apparent that Trippe was keeping his job open for him. Leslie was touched when Juan invited him to attend the January 1951 board meeting and sent him the text of the annual report to work on at home. For nearly twenty years, he represented Pan American at I.A.T.A. meetings and industry gatherings all over the world and in government proceedings, a white-haired man with a steely gaze pushed in a wheelchair by a black attendant, his wife, Jean, by his side. To the consensus that Trippe was cold and lacked compassion, two exceptions were always interposed: John Leslie, whom he had saved from professional destruction by insidious disease, and Erwin Balluder, whom he had rescued from accusations of Nazi sympathy.

In recruiting outside the company for executives and directors, Trippe was a big-game hunter. He stationed himself at the revolving door between government and industry and aimed at members of the C.A.B., subcabinet officers and highest-ranking military men. In 1949, retired General of the Army George Marshall and former Chief of Naval Operations Admiral William Standley simultaneously adorned his board. Later, he bagged General Alfred M. Gruenther, onetime Supreme Allied Commander in Europe.

In the spring of 1955, at a meeting of airline presidents and Air Force officials at the Pentagon, Juan was taken with the cool wit and intellectual breadth of Roger Lewis, Assistant Secretary of the Air Force for Procurement. A rangy Californian in his early 40s, Lewis was a Stanford graduate and had previously held high-level positions at Lockheed and Curtiss-Wright.

Lewis had participated in negotiations for a contract, awarded to Pan American in 1953, to operate a guided-missile range at Patrick Air Force Base in Florida. The evaluation study that winnowed the competitive bidders from six to two, Pan American and R.C.A., had been made before he was confirmed in his post, and he had directed that certain provisions in the final contract be tightened to protect the government. The contract was renewed twice with his approval, the second time just before he announced he was resigning to return to private industry.

Juan immediately began his courtship and won out over several more generous suitors. In a rare moment of candor, he said to Lewis, "A man can be born rich, he can be born brilliant. He can be lucky or he can be persistent. Roger, the most important thing is to be persistent."

He gave Lewis the title of executive vice president—development and defense projects, with five areas of responsibility, including supervision of the guided-missile-range division "with the exception of matters having to do with the amendment or renewal of contracts with the United States Government," which Gledhill was to continue to handle as before. The line separating Lewis from conflict of interest was perceptibly thin.

When the others on the fifty-eighth floor learned the size of his salary and stock options and Trippe named him to the board at the first opportunity, they were sure that Lewis was the new favorite.

As bespoke his exalted position, Lewis occupied the balconied office in the northeast corner of the fifty-eighth floor, strategically located near the men's room. At least once a day, Trippe trudged out of his balconied office in the southeast corner to answer Nature's call, and on the way out, he stopped to chat. This daily encounter gave rise to the conviction on the part of those who dwelt in limbo along the corridor that Lewis was privy to Juan's innermost thoughts, and they came streaming into his office to ask, "What does he mean by this?" "What should I do?" Roger advised them to do what they thought best because otherwise Trippe would take advantage of their insecurity to beat them down.

Lewis figured out almost immediately that Trippe expected him to make decisions and did not want to be caught endorsing them. "He would never, never approve anything," Roger said. "When you went to him and asked, 'Shall I do this?' he would back off. Ninety percent of the time you would go ahead, but with the feeling he would jump you if it didn't turn out right. The airline ran because guys like me knew the right thing to do."

Pan American in the Fifties was an organization of eighteen thousand employees grossing several hundred million dollars in revenues, and Juan was steering it in the same intuitive manner that had helped bring on the crisis in 1939 when it was a fraction of the size. By no stretch of modern business philosophy could the company be said to be managed by Trippe. It was more like an Oriental empire kept running day by day by the Mandarins while the Emperor plotted grand strategies.

The saving grace, as Lewis noted, was Juan's ability to attract enough strong, capable men who thrived in an environment of ambiguous independence. Those he trusted he let alone. "I didn't receive two memos from Juan in twenty years," said Willis Lipscomb, vice president—traffic and sales. "I never heard from him at the I.A.T.A. conferences." Lipscomb's modus operandi was to listen to Juan pontificate, deduce his meaning and try to carry it out. Some executives made the mistake of laying out their problems to Trippe, hoping he would tell them the solution he preferred, said Lipscomb. "He couldn't do that. He just didn't want to be forced to make decisions."

Was Juan Trippe an indecisive man, as Lipscomb and Lewis maintained, citing as further evidence his unpunctuality, his protracted crossing of the *t*s and dotting of the *i*s? Or was this simply a style of devious leadership, like that of Franklin Roosevelt, who vacillated and twisted toward a set goal? Paradoxically, Trippe could not have defined his long-term objective more clearly, nor been more decisive about the most daring steps to achieve it—such as flying the oceans so many doubted could be flown, committing huge sums to the purchase of the newest equipment, buying up competitors. He merely hesitated over the intermediate steps.

The senior executives were grateful for the single-focus lens of Trippe's mind. Unable to concentrate on more than one topic at a time, he would operate by subjecting one executive to a high-intensity grilling. He called meetings to test new ideas. An executive put forth a plan and his supporters argued for it. Juan demolished it. But no one knew what that meant. He went around the room soliciting opinions, but never expressed his own.

The end of the war marked the beginning of a slow process of rehabilitation for the battered legend of Charles Lindbergh. He refrained from political activity, and the press abetted his passion for privacy; the Lone Eagle/America Firster was a relic of an era too recent to be interesting.

But in air-power circles his reputation was more lustrous than ever, thanks to his service during the war. The Air Force sought his advice on rockets and space exploration. In April 1954, President Dwight D. Eisenhower restored his commission, and he was sworn in as a brigadier general in the Reserve.

Trippe wanted him back at Pan American, but Charles was reluctant to commit himself. He made several extensive journeys to inspect the system and report on equipment, maintenance and flight service for the nominal compensation of $1 plus traveling and living expenses, but neglected to turn in an accounting.

"You know my opinion as to the impropriety of the financial terms of your consulting arrangement with the company," Juan wrote him, feeling frustration at getting something priceless for nothing.

In September 1953, Lindbergh rejoined the technical committee and traveled to aircraft plants in California and England. In November, Trippe asserted the prerogative of a chief executive. In a "Dear Colonel Lindbergh" letter, he notified him that he was instructing the comptroller to send him $500 a month—a "completely inadequate" retainer—plus expenses.

Lindbergh continued to issue mild protests now and then. "As far as salary is concerned," he wrote Trippe, "as I have said before, the less the better from my standpoint. I don't like to live elaborately, and I have all the income I need from my writing and investments."

Charles warned Juan about poor employee morale, a condition traceable through the arteries of the worldwide system to the fifty-eighth floor. "I am under the impression that our most serious problem lies with personnel," he said. "Probably the major cause is lack of close contact with management."

The pilots idolized Lindbergh, and he encouraged them, at stag dinners in faraway bases, to offer their criticisms and suggestions for improving operations. Middle managers and supervisors were not "human-relations conscious," he was told. They did not know how to "handle people." "You can do the finest job in the world and rarely will there be an acknowledgment of it," a copilot based in Berlin complained, echoing the woes of those closest to Trippe.

Nothing was explained to the employees in the field, not even the reasons for policies, Lindbergh reported. With supreme tact, he avoided saying that he heard senior executives bemoaning their inability to make contact with Trippe, to know what he was planning, what he thought of them.

He advised that "the world's most experienced airline" (the slogan created by the J. Walter Thompson advertising agency to brag about Pan American's safety record) could no longer get by on its technical reputation alone. "We must realize that the area of competition is moving from the flying field into the passenger station, and from the cockpit back to the cabin," he said, disturbed that Pan American was slipping behind the European airlines in the quality of its service.

No one was better qualified to make such observations than the nomadic Lindbergh, constantly traveling on commercial airlines, alone and pseudonymously, his one piece of luggage, a dispatch case, stowed under his seat, his underwear and shaving articles packed into pouchy pockets sewn into the lining of his raincoat.

He appraised airline cuisine as diligently as an inspector for the *Michelin Guide*. P.A.A.: "tasteless" beef, "poor" sliced potatoes, "fair" lima beans. Almost everything Air France put before him was "excellent." As for the liquor, "I'm no judge of this. Sorry," he apologized.

Trippe's infamously poor memory worsened in its variant forms. Unless they were attached to heads of state and government, industrial czars and other power wielders, names dropped into the dead file of his mental computer.

He took his 19-year-old daughter, Betsy, and her fiancé, William Duke, to dinner at "21" to celebrate their forthcoming nuptials. Duke, a socially credentialed Dartmouth graduate, had been "hanging around the house for a couple of years," as Betsy said, and was no stranger to her father. When a business acquaintance stopped by their table, Trippe stumbled over the introductions. "This is the young man who is going to become my son-in-law," he began briskly. "This is—er—this is—er . . ." A puzzled look crossed his face, followed by a frown, and then the radiant smile. "This is Mr. King," he said. Recounting the story later, Betsy said appreciatively, "He was close. It could have been Mr. Prince, too." Juan lost track of Betsy at times. "Now, son, that's pretty nice," he would say, clapping her on the back.

Juan remembered the name of Marcia Egan, Pan American's golden girl, the stewardess assigned to inaugural and press flights and photographed for the cover of *Life*. On a junket to the Moscow World's Fair, Trippe was seated next to William Randolph Hearst, Jr., the newspaper publisher, who flirted extravagantly with Egan. Juan overheard her mention that her father and brother had attended Harvard. "Are you related to Ed Eagan?" Trippe interrupted. Eagan, his Sheff classmate, was then New York State Boxing Commissioner, and they were not related. The next day at the fair, Hearst accosted the blond stewardess and playfully swept her off her feet. "Marcia Egan is my favorite stewardess," Trippe announced to everyone's astonishment, for he was notoriously blind to female pulchritude. What programming formula had retrieved her name? Harvard/Yale/Hearst/ /Pedigree/ Power, Marcia was sure. "He was impressed because his friend was impressed, and he was letting him know he was responsible for my being there," she said.

Gerry O'Donnell, Pan American's man in Hong Kong, arranged for a prominent businessman to give a luncheon in Trippe's honor. The local mogul picked up the thousand-dollar tab. Juan came through Hong Kong a year later. "Nice to see you again, Mr. Trippe," said the businessman, reintroducing himself at a reception. "We've never met,"

Juan said. The man reminded him of the luncheon. "You and I have never met," Trippe said adamantly.

How much worse it was for one of his executives to be reduced to a nonentity by Juan. What made him such a frightening figure to the employees within his periphery, considering that he never barked or upbraided them in coarse language like other chief executives, was the possibility that he might deny their existence.

As they struggled to ascertain the meaning of his words, they also grasped for signals of his favor or wrath. Since he did not utter thanks for jobs well done or give credit to others for their contributions to the company's success, approval was inferred from his lack of comment about a project.

When he was vexed, he shook his head from side to side, exasperated but always a gentleman. The angrier he was, the lower the decibel count. Prolonged silence was ominous. "If he is displeased, he may not speak to you for three days. The quieter he gets, the more you must watch out," his daughter, Betsy, remarked. "I can just imagine what it must have been like to have displeased him at work."

It was Antarctic hell. The ice of Juan's silence. His secretary gave out no appointments to see him. The offender's memoranda went unanswered. "Juan just cut off his oxygen," Lewis said.

As Western journalists scrutinized the Communist Party lineup in the Kremlin on May Day, Pan American executives looked to the corporate masthead in the annual report to ascertain their standing.

André Priester's name was missing from the 1953 annual report, and Sanford B. Kauffman, one of his engineers, appeared for the first time as an assistant vice president. This was how Trippe announced that he had taken Priester's vice presidency away, that André was a nonperson. The engineering department had been moved to new operations quarters in Long Island City, but Priester was not invited to go along. He stayed behind in the Chrysler Building and wept. He was 62 years old, just a few years from retirement, and of all corporate bloodlettings, this seemed gratuitously savage.

The repercussions on the outside were too loud for Trippe to ignore. Priester was a sainted figure in the industry. He managed to break through the secretarial barrier and corner Juan in his office to ask why he had done this to him. Under Priester's reproachful gaze, Juan stammered a promise to restore his title. And he was still head of the technical committee. He could make the rounds of the aircraft manufacturers, and attend I.A.T.A. meetings. In the next annual report, André A. Priester was back in the executive officers' lineup as vice president, no function described.

Absentmindedness was Trippe's defensive weapon when the government attacked. Years before the Watergate episode popularized the term, Juan was expert at stonewalling before Congressional committees and in C.A.B. proceedings. He had two styles for being an infuriating witness—amnesiac and verbose—which contributed to a reputation for being careless with the truth. And his recollections were often at odds with those of other witnesses to the same conversation or event.

Was Juan Trippe a liar, as the public counsels in the A.O.A. case came just short of calling him? "You have to ask whether he lies or whether he imagines it and makes it his reality," said one of his closest associates.

"It's his filtering system," said another who frequently accompanied him on visits to government officials. Hearing his version "afterwards, I couldn't believe we had listened to the same conversation," the man said. "Juan only heard what he wanted to hear."

In his 50s, he was still absolutely tireless. He could work from dawn until past midnight and expected his executives to do the same, without regard for personal considerations. "Is he there?" he asked at 7:15 A.M. without identifying his quarry or acknowledging the wife who answered the telephone.

"Let me just take a minute," he said to his victim, and took forty-five.

Lacking a sense of time, Trippe scheduled meetings for 10 A.M., called at 11:15 A.M. to say he was on the way, and adjourned them to the Cloud Club for lunch. Afternoon meetings ran into the evenings. Wives of Pan American executives could seldom plan the dinner hour.

The men learned not to tell him they were going on vacation because he would invent a reason for them to stay. The trick was to concoct a cover story of crisis in a distant outpost that required their attention.

Pan American employees grumbled about low pay. The pilots were the exception because they joined a powerful union, ALPA (the Airline Pilots Association), and after the war, the clerical employees affiliated with the Brotherhood of Railway Clerks.

Trippe's method of keeping the lid on executive protest was to draw the lowest salary of the top group—$20,000 without bonus throughout the Forties and most of the Fifties. At one point, Pryor was collecting twice as much and Lipscomb almost three times. To attract stellar talent, he had to loosen the purse strings, and after a while there were stock-option plans. He, of course, had made his fortune in entrepreneur's stock.

Although he reserved the right to pass on the expense accounts of all vice presidents, he had an aversion to approving them. Accountings piled up on his desk awaiting his initials. Once a year, the comptroller removed them and put the books in order without his signatures. In the meantime, executives put in for advances, which Trippe authorized permissively. "It could truthfully be said," an executive chuckled, "that he never questioned anyone's expense accounts."

Whenever Pan American executives got together, they crabbed about the working conditions and deplored Trippe's inhumanity. "And they never wanted to leave," Roger Lewis noted. It was sometimes said he had them by their annual passes—the same perk that kept the directors docile. Its value was incalculable during the quarter-century after World War II when the U.S. dollar was almighty, for it conferred a style of living way above the employee's station in the economy: first-class travel; bargains in foreign fashion, furniture, real estate and children's education—living like a millionaire on a military officer's salary. If the executive stayed until retirement, the pass was his until he died.

"Pan American was a kind of government service," Willis Player said. "The company appealed to those who had a feeling for public service. They were attracted by the glamour of the business, and they believed they were building and serving." They were imbued with Trippe's vision of the partnership between the company and the national interest, and it created an esprit de corps.

"There were those of us who cared more about P.A.A. and the U.S.A. than about J.T.T.," Leuteritz said.

"We loved the company," said Gerry Lister, the secretary who used to chug beside Trippe as he made for the overnight train to Washington. "We gave what we had to build the biggest and best airline. We did not work for an individual."

From Roger Lewis' perspective, the organization was stable and unified because of that very eccentric, unlovable individual. "Because of his clear, personal commitment, no one ever felt like tilting with him. In effect he was acting like an owner. There was no question he was the boss. Everybody knew he would be in charge forever."

However much of an enigma he was to those who worked for him, Trippe matched the psychological portrait of the American corporate giant. In a study of big-business leaders conducted in the Fifties by W. Lloyd Warner and James Abegglen, those individuals who had risen to the top of the pyramid were characterized as "mobile" men.

The mobile man must be able to depart; that is, he must maintain a substantial emotional distance from people, and not become deeply involved with them or committed to them; and he must be an energetic person and one who can focus his energy on a single goal. There has probably been in his life a basic and deep experience of separation and loss, that sets this system in motion in terms of his family or birth and his feelings toward his primary love objects, his parents. He must be ready to detach himself, and in moving have no continuing concern for the past.

The absence of guilt is noted in the makeup of the upward striver. He is not distracted by consideration for others; he does not weigh the damage a calculated move might wreak on others.

All of these mobile men, as a necessary part of the equipment that makes it possible for them to be mobile and leave people behind without fear or regret, have difficulty in easily relating themselves to others over a period of time. They have difficulty in accepting and imposing the kinds of reciprocal obligations that close friendships and intimate social contacts imply. They typically are isolated men.

Yale was the alma mater of the largest number of leaders in the study. Dink Stover, coming to New Haven from the outside and advised to make his mark through the group, ends up alone at the top.

The Christmas party was Trippe's one pretense at sociability with his managers during the year, an event that was gossiped and speculated about weeks beforehand and rehashed by the guests afterward. A week before the holiday, 140 executives, from department heads and assistant vice presidents to the most senior officers, and their wives were invited for cocktails from 5:30 P.M. to 7:30 P.M. at 10 Gracie Square. Forty found a handwritten note from Betty tucked into the printed invitation: "Hope so much you can come and stay on for supper with us afterwards."

Juan was completely dependent on her to identify the guests, and she relied on coaching from Balluder or another old hand. As 7:30 approached, an air of expectant curiosity such as precedes the tapping hour for a college secret society hung over the party. Guests appraised who was leaving and who had attained the status of remaining. Stragglers had to be coaxed to the door.

Betty murmured to certain wives that they might want to powder their noses. In a sitting room in the sleeping wing of the apartment, the fortunate women waited for about forty-five minutes until Betty appeared announcing that supper was served, and they filed out to find their place cards at tables set up in the living and dining rooms.

The Trippes were unaware of the awkwardness fostered by the two-tier invitations. "It was just like a big family," Betty said. "It gave the wife of a department head a chance to meet the wife of her husband's boss."

The wife of a senior executive thought otherwise. "It was a psychological misjudgment to think they could make the middle-management people feel wanted once a year."

The Trippes entertained rarely, and what they did was related to Juan's business. "We never had a social life," Betty said. "We never gave big cocktail parties. Juan never said, 'Let's have so-and-so over to dinner.' We saw people and did things we were interested in. But we never had a social life. You have to choose."

She spoke without regret or a sense of being put down. Juan's choices were hers. She bloomed in his reflected radiance, the empress of Pan American Airways, waiting for hours on end in parked automobiles for her absentminded husband to appear. According to Warner and Abegglen, it was necessary to the success of the mobile business leader that his wife not make demands on his time or his interest.

Betty supplied the glue to hold the family together, to compensate for the absence and remoteness of the paterfamilias. Betsy was the most intelligent of their children. A vivacious brunette, she was raised in her mother's pattern of debutante, wife and mother. Two of her three marriages, all ending in divorce, were to Yale men. Charles was the blustering dauphin—a chip off the old block, it was said, minus his father's suavity. John, a moody boy, never quite kept up with the others. Edward Stettinius Trippe had the sunny nature of the uncle after whom he was named.

Trippe sent his sons to Exeter and Yale. Charles and Edward went on to the Harvard Business School before starting their careers at Pan American in the Inter-Continental Hotels subsidiary. Juan encouraged George Hambleton, a Princeton graduate, to join the company. George resembled the father who had died before he was born, and had his winning manner. Upon meeting him, the old-timers asked themselves a rhetorical question: "What would Pan American have been like if John Hambleton had lived?"

39

The Jet Age

André Priester's Christmas card for 1952 showed a drawing of the Old North Church in Boston hung with three lights. The message took liberties with Henry Wadsworth Longfellow: "The British are coming! One if by land, two if by sea, three if by air."

B.O.A.C. was operating jet aircraft on its routes to the Mideast and South Africa. In May, the first De Havilland Comet to carry paying passengers had streaked from London to Johannesburg in 23½ hours. The press hailed a new era in air transportation. "Never before had travelers come so close to the silent, effortless flight of birds," an aviation writer proclaimed.

Though Lindbergh advised Trippe that the British jet was too small for Pan American's needs, Trippe placed an order for the Comet III—three planes scheduled for delivery in 1956. It was purely a protective move, for even this improved model had capacity for fewer than 60 passengers and could not fly the Atlantic nonstop. But at least Pan American could boast of being the only U.S. airline with jet aircraft on order. None of the American manufacturers was anywhere near producing one.

Trippe had started shopping for a jetliner in the summer of 1945, shortly after Lindbergh returned from a survey in Germany with a naval technical mission and confirmed the sophistication of Nazi weaponry. In the last months of the war in Europe, Messerschmitt ME-262 fighters, powered by twin jet engines to a speed of 540 miles an hour, had intercepted Allied bombers. How long was it going to take, Juan wondered, for the technical capability of the defeated enemy to be translated into commercial transports for U.S. airlines?

467

Actually, the British had a longer lead on the development of the jet engine. In 1929, Frank Whittle, a student at the Royal Air Force College, wrote a thesis on the gas-turbine engine for jet-propelled flight. Adapting Newton's third law of motion—every action produces a reaction equal in force and opposite in direction—he designed a power plant for an aircraft without a propeller. Whittle used a centrifugal-flow compressor to suck air from the outside through a frontal duct and force it into a combustion chamber, where it was sprayed with fuel and converted to hot gases. The heated air was expelled past a turbine through a nozzle at the rear to create an explosive thrust for moving the plane forward. Whittle took out patents on his design and raised private capital to form Power Jets, Limited, which built a working model of the engine in the late Thirties. It was successfully tried out in a British Gloster fighter plane in 1941. General Hap Arnold acquired a set of the blueprints during his visit to England that spring and gave them to the General Electric Company to produce a derivative for the U.S. Army Air Forces.

The British aircraft industry, determined to make up for its lost generation of transport planes, skipped immediately to the production of jet-powered airliners—the De Havilland Comet and a Vickers model that utilized gas-turbine engines activated by propellers. It appeared that U.S. manufacturers might let the jet-transport market go by default.

The U.S. airlines were saddled with debt from their postwar equipment programs, and moreover, jet engines appeared troublesome. They required frequent overhaul and consumed twice as much fuel as piston engines, and although the kerosene they drank was cheaper than aviation gasoline, it still netted 25-percent-higher fuel bills. With the price of jet-powered transports expected to be double that of the most advanced piston aircraft, the planes would have to be significantly more capacious and have far greater range to be economically viable. In the postwar slump, the thought of having to scout for higher payloads appalled the domestic-airline operators.

But not Trippe. From everything he could glean, the jet engine was particularly suited to Pan American's long-haul route system. The higher it flew, the more efficiently it performed; in the thicker air of lower altitudes it consumed more fuel, and its speed advantage was dissipated in frequent landings. If only he could persuade a manufacturer to design a jet transport specifically for Pan American.

Boeing was the most likely one. The Seattle manufacturer was acutely sensitive to its inferior position in commercial aviation. Over half the airliners flying bore the mark of the Douglas DC series. Lockheed had full order books for its Constellations.

Boeing stood for big bombers: the B-17 Flying Fortress had introduced high-altitude daylight bombing to German cities; the B-29
Superfortress dropped the first atomic bomb on Hiroshima and a second on Nagasaki. The company had lost money on its famous prewar
transports, the B-314 flying boat sold to a single customer, Pan American Airways, and the B-307 Stratoliner purchased by Pan American
and T.W.A. It had offset losses on the popular B-377 Stratocruiser,
commercial derivative of the B-29, with substantial sales of the C-97
military cargo version.

In April 1946, Boeing landed the contract to build the first American jet bomber. The B-47 looked as though it had been taken from a
science-fiction drawing. It had a skinny fuselage and drooping wings
swept back to produce less drag. Four propellerless engines were suspended in pods underneath and forward of the wings, far enough removed so as not to wreak structural damage to the plane if they caught
fire or disintegrated in midair.

The cost of building a commercial prototype was estimated at
more than $10 million, and Boeing led a fruitless campaign by the
aircraft industry for government financing. Then the Korean war, coming after the explosion of the first Russian atomic bomb, strengthened
the muscle of the air-power proponents in the Department of Defense
and Congress, and the quest was on for a new intercontinental bomber.
Boeing won the contract to build the B-52 for the Strategic Air Command's arsenal of atomic deterrents. It was to be fitted with eight Pratt
& Whitney J-57 engines—the most advanced on the market, with
10,000 pounds of thrust, and the least fuel-thirsty.

Boeing proposed to develop a jet tanker for refueling the bomber
in flight, intending the military plane to support a commercial derivative; but under budgetary constraints, the Air Force rejected the program. In April 1952, William M. Allen, president of Boeing, decided
that its financial position was strong enough, by virtue of its military
contracts, to undertake construction of a jet tanker/transport prototype
without government assistance. It was assigned the model number 707;
the Boeing technicians referred to the prototype as the Dash Eighty,
after its military model number, 367-80.

The British Comet proved to be an unlucky plane. After two
crashes in India in the spring of 1953 and two mysterious plummetings
into the Mediterranean, eventually traced to metal fatigue, the plane
was taken out of service.

In July 1953, Boeing released specifications for the 707 jet transport: cruising speed of 500 miles an hour, capacity for 60 to 120 passengers, a third more payload than the Stratocruiser. The domestic
operators clicked their slide rules and looked away. "We are all of us

still intrigued by the glamour of the jet airplane, but neither we nor you, the consumer, can now afford it," C. R. Smith declared in a publicized speech. He recited a laundry list of drawbacks. Besides the inordinate fuel consumption, the engine made a racket—the sound at takeoff was often compared to the wail of a thousand banshees—and consequently aroused hostility among residents in the vicinity of airports. Finally, there was the intimidating price—estimated at $4 million a plane.

"We can't go backward to the jet," Smith said. "I'm interested in cheap transportation and a more efficient machine, not in more expensive machines." C.R. was considering an interim step forward: the turboprop engine, in which jet power was harnessed to a propeller—less costly to operate than the pure jet. A propjet aircraft could circle an airport for hours in a holding pattern without consuming the profits of the flight.

From Trippe's perspective as an international operator, the view was infinitely brighter. After tourist fares went into effect in the spring of 1952, traffic boomed on the North Atlantic. In 1948, 775,000 individuals crossed the ocean, one-third in airplanes. By 1954, the number of airline passengers reached the half-million mark and flying had become the principal mode of foreign travel. In May of that year, Lipscomb introduced installment credit to the industry with the "Pan Am Pay Later Plan"—a small deposit and twenty months to pay for a glorious vacation. Air traffic to Europe increased by another 100,000 passengers; 70 percent went tourist class. "These days if a person has a car and a washing machine, he has to have a trip to Europe," a travel agent rejoiced.

Trippe envisioned the jet advancing the cycle of economies of scale: faster planes; lower fares; masses of Americans blessed with rising standards of living and greater amounts of disposable income to spend on such bargains as $5 hotel rooms in Rome and $2 dinners, including wine and cognac, in Madrid. Yankee legions in wash-and-wear garments and rubber-soled footwear could easily be recruited to invade the Old World, Juan believed. But the jet armadas had to be large enough or the red ink would flow. Reports on his desk recommended configurations of 180 tourist passengers seated 6 abreast.

In July 1954, Boeing tested the Dash Eighty prototype in flight. Although he had just announced a design competition for an aerial tanker, Secretary of the Air Force Harold Talbott placed a preliminary order for twenty-nine of the KC-135, the tanker version.

Frank Gledhill and Sandy Kauffman went for a ride in the Dash Eighty. Gledhill reported to Trippe that it was unlike any previous experience of flying. Powered by four J-57 engines, the plane soared to 30,000 feet and cruised at nearly 600 miles an hour. Although the prototype was without soundproofing, it was quieter inside than a piston aircraft and almost free of vibration.

Gledhill enumerated the negative factors—the problem of exterior noise, the earsplitting whine on takeoff, was still unsolved, as was the inability to cut the speed sufficiently on landing—but he told Trippe he thought this was the next step they always looked for in buying equipment, something to radically change the public perception of air travel. Why bother, then, with an intermediate step to turboprop aircraft?

Trippe fervently wanted Pan American to be the first to operate jets on the North Atlantic, the most contested market. Knowing how hollow the glory of pioneering could be without financial success, he set out to compel someone to build him a jet money-maker.

Robert Gross of Lockheed was not interested. He was placing his chips on his new Electra, designed around the Allison turboprop engine of 3,750 horsepower, well suited for medium-length domestic routes.

The Douglas plants were humming with orders for the DC-7 series, including a stretched DC-7C instigated by Trippe to outperform all other aircraft, able to cross the Atlantic without a refueling stop carrying 104 passengers. Donald Douglas, a dour Brooklyn-born Scot who slept with an adding machine on his bedside table and played the bagpipes as a pastime, was wary of being carried away with success, of expanding recklessly in good times and having to retrench painfully later on.

Now that Douglas and Lockheed were competing against Boeing for the Air Force tanker project, his engineers were anxious to resume work on a jet transport design, designated the DC-8, which he had made them put aside when customers failed to appear. Douglas swallowed his pessimism about the economics of a jet airliner and ordered them back to their drawing boards.

So now Trippe had two manufacturers to play against each other: Donald Douglas, the cautious engineer, and Bill Allen, the lawyer who hid a gambler's instinct for business under a churchwarden facade. That was the way Juan liked to do business—"Make them compete and have the showdown on price and performance," he said.

Doing business with Trippe was not the same as doing business with other airline chieftains, as both manufacturers knew. "C. R. Smith laid it out in small-syllable words, and that was it," Allen once said. "Juan did not state his position directly. He didn't lay it right out. He talked sort of indirectly on the problem, but he made his point finally by this indirection. Some people translated this as being devious. It was his around-the-barn approach, that's all."

Juan sent Gledhill to negotiate for Pan American. Frank was straightforward, tough, matter-of-fact. Kauffman and his engineers checked in at the aircraft factories and reported back to Gledhill, who reported to Trippe. Every now and then, Lindbergh appeared in Seattle to take a ride in the Dash Eighty and hang around talking to the technicians. Just as abruptly, he left without telling anyone he was going.

The next voice Allen heard was Juan's on the telephone. The point Trippe was making was that Pan American needed an intercontinental plane with more payload, range and earning potential than the DC-7C, more than the Boeing 707 promised.

He was so sure that he was going to get what he wanted that he started looking for money to pay for it. On May 10, 1955, he clinched a $60-million credit with a group of eighteen life-insurance companies led by the Metropolitan and the Prudential. The interest rate was 3¾ percent a year, and the first repayment was scheduled for ten years later. Trippe was a member of the investment committee of the Metropolitan board—undoubtedly a help in persuading the staid insurance men that they could regard the jets as earning assets with a long life ahead.

In June 1955, Douglas presented a design for the DC-8, remarkably similar to the Boeing 707 in its frame and four J-57 engines. Donald Douglas announced he was building a prototype without commitments from the airlines or a military contract to cushion his financial exposure. Boeing was the winner of the design competition for the aerial tanker, and at first the Secretary of the Air Force refused Allen's request to lease tools and factory space from the government project for a 707 program. As soon as Douglas declared himself, Allen renewed his plea and Talbott relented. That summer, the race to build an American jet transport was on in earnest.

The domestic airlines would not nibble. American placed a $64-million order for thirty-five Lockheed Electras. Eddie Rickenbacker topped it with a $100-million order for Eastern. The only potential customer Boeing and Douglas sighted for their jets was Pan American, and Juan Trippe said neither plane was big enough. The stumbling block was the J-57 engine. It was too weak to lift a planeload of all the tourists Trippe wanted to pack in, and to climb swiftly into the sonic barrier above 30,000 feet to hitch into the current of winds known as the jet stream.

"There isn't enough power in your engine," he complained on the telephone to Allen and to Douglas. "Don't you realize what it means to go to altitude quickly?" Pratt & Whitney devised a remedy of injecting water during takeoff to boost the thrust. The added weight of 4,000 pounds of liquid to an already underpowered aircraft necessitated a reduction in payload or a redesign of the airframe.

Boeing had spent more than $16 million on the Dash Eighty, and a major alteration of the prototype would mean money down the drain and the loss of lead time over Douglas. Allen was obdurate. He had his Air Force contract, and the 707 could fly coast to coast nonstop with a satisfactory payload. He was counting on the domestic airlines' coming around to buy.

But Trippe was equally unyielding, and what made his persistence so deadly was his sweet unreasonableness. "Hey, mister," he said, casually opening a telephone call to Allen. "Why don't you use the J-75?"

The existence of the J-75 was one of those industrial secrets bruited about in the trade press, the specifications restricted for military eyes only, which included the engineers at Boeing. The engine was in the experimental stage of development by Pratt & Whitney for an Air Force fighter plane; it reportedly had an initial thrust of 15,000 pounds. How many years of rigorous testing and compiling of a record of experience would it take before it was certified for commercial use? As many as five, perhaps. "I'm sure I can get it taken off the secret list," Juan said. "It wouldn't make any difference," Allen shot back.

Trippe flew to Santa Monica with his engineers. Donald Douglas leaned back in his chair, sucking on his pipe and contemplating the Douglas coat of arms on his desk with its motto "JAMAIS ARRIÈRE" (never behind). He listened to Trippe invite him to design a new plane around the J-75, a truly intercontinental jet airliner. That was farther out front than Douglas cared to go.

Trippe flew to East Hartford to see Fred Rentschler. The 67-year-old Jupiter reigned over United Aircraft, but the Pratt & Whitney division was his creation, the preeminent engine manufacturer, and it stayed under his iron thumb. Any decision to accelerate the release of the J-75 would ultimately be made by Rentschler.

"Let's have your big engine, mister," Juan wheedled. Rentschler looked to William Gwinn, the president of Pratt & Whitney, and his technical staff for their reaction. "The J-75 is a big animal," said Gwinn, "and we haven't flown it yet. We just don't know how good it's going to be."

The engine was mounted on a test bed in an insulated room, roaring day and night. It would run for thousands of hours under every conceivable simulated condition of flight, checked and monitored like an incubator baby. How long would it run before breaking down? How did it withstand heat—the standard runway temperature of 59 degrees at takeoff; the 100-degree temperatures of a field in the tropics?

The technical staff was chary about committing this new engine to commercial service. A major engine failure in a passenger transport could be catastrophic. Jet engines were notoriously short-lived. "We can make them reliable, but we don't know for how long," Gwinn said.

"You're being too conservative," Trippe said. "Look at what a wonderful job the J-57 is doing."

He left East Hartford empty-handed, then badgered Rentschler by telephone from New York: "Come on, mister, let's have your big engine." He invited Rentschler and Gwinn to lunch at the Cloud Club. They went over the same ground and parted. Word filtered back to East Hartford that Trippe was talking to Rolls-Royce about its new Conway engine. Rentschler put his technical people through their paces. "Are you sure we can't do it?" he asked. They acknowledged that the J-57s were proving astonishingly durable in the B-52 bombers, and that the J-75 was basically a bigger animal of the J-57 genus.

Trippe had lunch again with Rentschler and Gwinn at the Cloud Club. "Pan American will be needing a hundred and twenty J-75s. How soon can we have them?" Juan asked. He named a price: $250,000 apiece—a $40-million order, counting spare parts. He was offering to buy the engines for Pan American's account, even without planes into which to fit them. That was not the way aviation business was conducted. Aircraft manufacture started with the design of the frame, which was probably why there was always so much disappointment with underpowered planes. Trippe was proposing to reverse the process, to make someone design a plane for his engines.

Rentschler made up his mind to sell him the engines for delivery in the summer of 1959. It was his last major decision; six months later, he was dead.

Trippe broke the news of his purchase to Allen in Seattle first. "If you won't design a plane for the engines, then I will find someone who will," he said. Allen was hostage to the millions invested in the Dash Eighty; he would not budge.

The DC-8 was still in blueprint. "All Douglas had to do was crash it in a wastebasket," someone observed. He decided to adapt it to either engine: a model for domestic carriers fitted with the J-57, an intercontinental version with the J-75 for Pan American and the foreign customers sure to follow.

"I'll take twenty-five," Trippe said, "but let's hold up the announcement for a while."

He returned to Seattle and ordered twenty of the Model 707, the one with the J-57 engine he had rejected as inadequate a few days before. The lawyers could start drafting the contract with a delivery date for the fall of 1958.

Trippe signed the Douglas and Boeing contracts in New York on the same day. Both manufacturers prepared press releases for October 13, 1955, each under the impression it had captured the first customer for an American-made jet transport.

On the afternoon of the 13th, Trippe welcomed the executive committee of I.A.T.A. to a cocktail party at 10 Gracie Square. Instead of the usual small talk, he served a chunk of dynamite. The foreign airline executives gulped the import of his buying spree—forty-five jet planes, a $269-million order, the largest ever placed by a single airline—realizing they would have to buy jets immediately, and to buy American.

Bill Allen and Donald Douglas learned the full story in the next morning's edition of *The Wall Street Journal*. Allen felt like an earthquake victim. Although the DC-8 would not be delivered until a year after the Boeing 707, the Douglas fitted with the J-75 was the intercontinental plane. Messages were coming in from Boeing salesmen overseas. The European airlines were interested only in a jet with a more-than-4,000-mile range and the J-75 engine.

Allen surrendered to Trippe in a telephone call. If Boeing were to build an intercontinental 707, Pan American could exchange part of its order for the bigger plane with the more powerful engine. He was on his way to New York to renegotiate the contract.

Another round of meetings followed at the Chrysler Building—long days of meetings, with dinner breaks at 9 P.M. Pan American would take six basic 707s in the fall of 1958 to beat its competitors across the North Atlantic, even if it meant stopping in Gander to refuel. Trippe hung his bag of oats on the contract: a $250,000 premium for each plane in the first batch delivered three months ahead of schedule. The following year, Pan American would have fifteen 707/320s, a plane that could fly from New York to Rome nonstop with 160 passengers.

"This is the most important aviation development since Lindbergh's flight," said Trippe with all due modesty. "In one fell swoop we have shrunken the earth." The jets halved the flying time between cities: New York to Paris from 11 hours by the fastest piston plane to 6 hours 35 minutes; San Francisco to Tokyo from 25 hours to 12 hours 45 minutes. New York and Chicago became neighboring metropolises, 1½ hours apart. In keeping with the snappier pace of life, Pan American shortened its name to Pan Am.

Trippe precipitated the advent of the jet age. Once Pan Am was operating jets, what airline could afford not to do the same? The stampede was on, with C.R. leading the domestic operators to Seattle, followed by Howard Hughes for T.W.A., then B.O.A.C. and SABENA. KLM, S.A.S. and United Airlines chose the DC-8. Two and a half billion dollars' worth of American jets were sold before Mamie Eisenhower christened the Pan Am jet *Clipper America* on October 16, 1958, and Trippe escorted his newspaper moguls on a preview flight to Brussels.

The jets ushered in an era of prosperity for the international airlines—particularly for the U.S. carriers, which thrived despite loss of subsidy support. From Caribbean mail deliverer to circumnavigator of the globe, Pan American's growth was nourished by subsidy concealed in the revenues collected from the U.S. Post Office. As late as 1950, almost one-fourth of the company's total operating revenues represented mail payments. In 1954, the C.A.B. ordered separate reporting of subsidy and compensation for carrying the mail, and in 1956 the Board took Pan American completely off subsidy. The airline never drew another cent of direct subvention, in good times or bad.

lines, mostly small carriers in Asia and Africa, either to prevent them from falling into Communist Chinese hands or mainly as a front for Agency activities in the Third World. George Doole, a former operations manager for Pan Am in the Middle East, ran three airlines based in Taiwan under the umbrella of the Pacific Corporation. One of the carriers, Civil Air Transport (CAT), had acquired Pan Am's stock in C.N.A.C., which Trippe had reluctantly sold to the Nationalists in the last days of 1949 after the United States decided to withhold recognition from Mao Zedong's People's Republic of China. He would have liked to continue operating to the mainland from a base in Hong Kong.

Another Pan Am alumnus, Richard Deichler, a former head of its hotel subsidiary, was president of Foreign Air Transport Development, a proprietary that set up a contract to manage Iran Air. In 1953, the C.I.A. engineered a coup to remove the unfriendly government of Premier Mohammed Mossadegh and restore Shah Mohammed Reza Pahlevi to the Peacock Throne.

Pan Am had no connections as such with these front operations, but when the proprietary Southern Air Transport, a Miami-based cargo carrier certificated by the C.A.B. to serve the Caribbean and South America, began to deviate into Pan Am markets, the C.I.A. sought Trippe's permission, and it was granted.

Trippe looked to the State Department and the White House for an expression of "national interest" before pulling out of China and, in that same year, before putting down stakes in the Middle East. A group of prominent Lebanese asked George Doole, while he was still with Pan Am, to organize a regional carrier, Middle East Airlines. Pan Am contributed three reconditioned DC-3s in return for 46 percent of M.E.A. stock. It appeared to be one of Trippe's cannier trades, inasmuch as the two-engine aircraft was outmoded for a major international carrier.

Washington approved of the deal. The United States wanted an American presence in the sphere of waning British influence, and American aviation technology was seen as a means of warding off Communist intrusion. Moreover, the opportunities for overt intelligence-gathering by an airline that served Syria, Iraq and Egypt were boundless.

But Trippe met his match in the mentality of the Oriental bazaar. A few years later, when he offered to sell M.E.A. some of Pan Am's surplus DC-6s, the majority owners preferred to buy British Viscounts and demanded that Pan Am put up its proportionate share of the cash, to be repaid out of earnings. Seeing that the U.S. Government was not going to back up its hearty enthusiasm with financial aid, he sold Pan Am's interest in M.E.A. to the Intra Bank of Beirut at a small loss.

After the British withdrew from India in the late Forties, Afghanistan turned to the United States for protection against Soviet expansionism. The government in Kabul asked the State Department for an American international airline to serve the capital, and assistance in establishing a national carrier for internal transportation.

The State Department kept relaying such requests to Pan Am, which stood to gain little in the way of long-haul traffic from such an affiliation. "There are certain things you have to do," Trippe said, but in this instance he waited for concrete evidence that the U.S. Government found it in the national interest for Pan Am to be involved. In 1956, the governments of Afghanistan and the United States signed an Air Transport Development Project Agreement to develop an airline system for the country. To implement the pact, Pan Am acquired a 49-percent interest in Ariana Afghan Airlines and was awarded a management and technical-assistance contract funded by the International Cooperation Administration. The Export-Import Bank lent the money to buy two aircraft, one a DC-6 from Pan American's Latin American routes. The C.I.A. interceded with the C.A.B. to award Pan Am a certificate for Kabul.

The development of the U-2 plane lessened the importance of aerial surveillance by a commercial airliner straying off course into Soviet territory, but the radio communication systems and the presence of American technicians in the national airlines formed part of the electronic shield erected by the United States in the Middle East and Southeast Asia. Pan Am took on technical-assistance contracts, financed by the Agency for International Development, with Turkish Airlines, Thai Airlines, Pakistan International Airlines, Alia Jordan, Air Guinée and Air Zaïre. After the C.I.A. got out of the airline business, Pan Am assumed the Iran Air contract under the AID program.

Trippe was one of the first to receive a harbinger of the Khrushchev thaw in East–West relations when, early in 1956, the Soviet Government invited Pan American to discuss ways and means of establishing direct air service between the United States and Moscow. Three times in the 1930s Juan's negotiations with the Russians had been aborted by politics. In 1945 the C.A.B. had awarded American Export Airlines authority to serve Moscow by extension from Helsinki —authority that Pan American had inherited through the A.O.A. merger; but the right had lain dormant during the Cold War.

Juan promptly notified the State Department and was told to proceed—in effect to revert to his old-style diplomacy—even though the opening of the route would have to be the subject of a bilateral treaty between the United States and the Soviet Union. The prospect of Trippe's bargaining with the Russians was regarded as something of an Olympic contest. "If he had been Secretary of State, we would have been running the Soviet Union and the Russians wouldn't have known what happened to them," said one diplomat. "He's the smoothest operator we've ever seen."

Juan bustled off to Washington to begin a round of discussions with a Soviet delegation headed by Yevgeny F. Loginov, the Minister of Civil Aviation and director of Aeroflot. Perceiving Trippe as the embodiment of capitalist power, Loginov accorded him rare deference.

The talks focused at the start on technical matters such as maintenance facilities, radio navigation, fuel storage and baggage handling. Roger Lewis and Russell Adams, Pan Am's chief Washington representative, accompanied Trippe to one meeting at the Soviet Embassy. They were ushered up a staircase and into a dimly lit, shabbily furnished room. The apple-cheeked Loginov was seated at a conference table, beckoning Trippe and Lewis to join him. Adams was motioned to a curved sofa occupied by three glum men in ill-fitting navy-blue suits whom he took to be K.G.B. agents. He squeezed in beside them.

Loginov opened the conversation by remarking that the Aeroflot plane in which he had arrived was at Idlewild Airport, parked in New York and its crew restricted from moving beyond the city. "I am afraid my boys will become difficult unless we find something for them to do," Loginov said. "It would be nice if we could just have a look at your machine shops," he added.

"I could not be more honored and delighted to receive such a request from the director of an airline as highly respected as Aeroflot," Trippe replied, fixing his brown eyes on Loginov. "Nothing would please me more than to be able to comply with the wishes of my good friend from the Soviet Union." A tone of regret crept into his voice. "However, I am only an employee of Pan American Airways; I don't have the power to comply with the request of my good Soviet friend. I would have to discuss this first with the Civil Aeronautics Board, the Department of Defense and the State Department."

Juan leaned forward, extending his hands across the table to Loginov, palms outstretched. "I want to be perfectly open and honest with you, don't you see; I want everything above the table." At that moment, a thud was heard as Adams fell to the floor from his perch.

To no one's surprise, the negotiations were protracted. Trippe visited Moscow, where the first item on the agenda was to give the Pan Am delegation a tour of the city. As the group was being shown a huge sports stadium, Trippe darted away from the group and took Loginov by the arm to a bench halfway down the steep-sided arena for a discussion of the kind he preferred—one-to-one, with no eavesdroppers.

As an agreement was readied for signing in the summer of 1961, tensions mounted over the Berlin Wall crisis, and the New York–Moscow route went into a deep freeze; it remained there until August 1966, when Lyndon Johnson called for "a series of small steps toward understanding" and the Russians signaled willingness to conclude a bilateral air treaty.

With the President pushing hard for results, the treaty and an operating agreement providing for one round trip a week each for Pan Am and Aeroflot were signed in November.

"Pan Am does what's best for the country," Trippe said with resignation. Inasmuch as the Russians prohibited the airline from drumming up business in the Soviet Union, the service was a guaranteed money-loser. And though it may have been in the national interest for an American-flag carrier to fly to Moscow, there was no subsidy forthcoming from Washington.

41

In the Money

Trippe had a holier-than-thou attitude about salary. Since 1941, he had kept his compensation at an unvarying $20,000. He made the directors rescind a raise voted him in 1950 to $57,500, the level prevailing in the industry for chief executives. "It would be coming out of the taxpayers' pockets," he said piously, in a strained interpretation of the accounting practices for carriers drawing mail subsidy. Other airlines did not claim full reimbursement from the government for their executive salaries.

In 1958, Trippe decided he wanted more fitting compensation after all. Typically, he went around the barn to get it. He told Bobby Lehman, in confidence, of generous offers to be chief executive that he had received from the Bank of America and several other major companies. Out of loyalty to Pan American, he had declined.

Lehman and a member of the executive committee, Edward Mc-Donnell, a partner in Hornblower & Weeks, joint underwriters with Lehman Brothers of Pan American securities, took the initiative in persuading the board to increase Juan's salary to $100,000. Trippe bowed to his directors' wishes, saying that since Pan Am was now off subsidy entirely, and its stock was performing well in the market, he felt he could appropriately accept their decision.

Around the same time, he sold 35,000 shares of Pan American stock worth about $875,000, slightly more than half his holdings. After periodic profit-taking in stock gained from warrants and options, he took the money earned in the skies and put it into the ground.

His residential properties in East Hampton appreciated enormously as the conservative village became a colony of successful modern artists and new millionaires. He also bought property in Bermuda, principally an interest in the Castle Harbour Hotel.

Trippe plunged into speculative ventures of a long-term developmental nature. After Edward Stettinius died in 1949, he became president of the Liberian Development Corporation, organized by his brother-in-law to make land and resource investments in the African country, which had the benefit of the splendid airport facility built by Pan American for the War Department.

In 1958, Juan formed a syndicate to acquire a bankrupt property from Arthur Vining Davis, the Pittsburgh aluminum king, on the southern end of Eleuthera, one of the loveliest untouched islands in the British Bahamas. His concept was visionary: to capitalize on the convenience and economics of jet aircraft in establishing a major tourist industry off the east coast of the United States.

An exclusive enclave was created in the Cotton Bay Club, consisting of villas built around a golf course designed by Robert Trent Jones. The emperor of Pan Am chose the notables he wanted to surround him on his island retreat. He personally solicited buyers from among old friends like Dave Ingalls, and powerful acquaintances made through the Business Council, like George Love of Consolidation Coal of Pittsburgh and John A. McCone, head of a California engineering company, whom Kennedy appointed director of the Central Intelligence Agency.

In diversifying Pan American's business away from strictly airline operations, he selected related markets such as hotels, corporate jet aircraft and support services for the U.S. space program, and these were generally profitable. His greatest financial coup for Pan Am was, however, a real-estate transaction.

In the late 1950s, Erwin S. Wolfson, a New York builder and real-estate promoter, laid plans to erect a skyscraper adjacent to Grand Central Station. He secured a long-term lease from the New York Central and New Haven Railroads on a 3½-acre site north of the railroad depot occupied by a modest office building. A demolition crew started to tear it down in June 1960 before Wolfson had corralled a prominent tenant for a major block of space. Without such a bellwether to attract other tenants to his huge and costly fold, financing could not be completed. Wolfson had been turned down by a half-dozen candidates including General Motors and I.B.M. when an associate learned that Pan Am's thirty-year lease in the Chrysler Building was due to expire around the time his building was scheduled to be finished, and that it had long since outgrown the space.

Pan American was run by one man, Wolfson was informed, and getting past his secretarial barbed wire was well nigh impossible. Senior executives of the airline, some of whom were friendly with members of the Wolfson organization, were unable to provide an Open-Sesame; they had their own troubles arranging appointments to see Juan Trippe. He was a sovereign, unapproachable except by other heads of state.

Finally, one of Wolfson's directors found a banker who knew Trippe and consented to write him a letter outlining the project. Juan's interest was piqued. He treated the discussions like any other clandestine activity. His first meeting with Wolfson was held on a July evening in the empty grillroom of the Cloud Club; the second, on the following night, in the builder's office. The ensuing negotiations went by the code name Project X; Pan Am was "Prince Albert" and Trippe "The Traveler."

Juan was impressed that Wolfson had British partners in the project. He liked doing business with Englishmen. His forebears had been English, he said with pride, and it was only fitting for an international airline to have its headquarters in a building supported by London capital. Someone assured him that Pan Am's name and logo in lights on a midtown tower would be worth at least $1 million in publicity.

The size of the signs was one of the troublesome details that stretched the bargaining by the respective teams of lawyers and consultants over two months. Trippe held out for lettering 30 feet high and eventually came down halfway. He extracted a promise from Wolfson to crown the building with a landing field for helicopters.

His most significant demand was for an equity participation in what turned out to be one of the choicest real-estate properties in the country. He wangled 10 percent of the stock for $1 million, with an option to increase Pan Am's ownership interest; the British investors received 45 percent for $4.5 million, and Wolfson took the balance, largely in return for his promotional efforts. Wolfson's Diesel Construction Company was the general contractor for the building, which took nearly three years to put up, at an ultimate cost of $115 million.

Pan American leased nine full floors and a sales office on the street level for approximately thirty years, with renewal options for further ten-year periods. At a total rental of $115.5 million, it was the largest commercial lease ever taken on a Manhattan property; the terms were spelled out in a hundred-page document signed on September 28, 1960.

Wolfson commissioned Walter Gropius, the apostle of Bauhaus and former dean of architecture at Harvard, and Pietro Belluschi of M.I.T. as consultants on the design of the fifty-nine-story edifice that was billed as the world's largest commercial office building, secured by the fattest mortgage ($70 million) to encumber a single business property in New York.

At the dedication ceremonies in March 1963, Governor Nelson Rockefeller hailed it as "a symbol of the genius and creativity of the free-enterprise system." Assessments by urban-design critics, scholars of architecture and citizens who cared passionately about the city were scathing.

They characterized the Pan Am Building as a "monument to greed and irresponsibility," "a precast-concrete monster," a "Gropius fiasco" and just plain ugly. Protests against the octagonal, glass-pocked slab were couched in the very terms that had been applied through the years to the airline and its founder. The "arrogant, oversize intruder" sat astride Park Avenue blocking the north–south vista, a barrier to others' vision, monopolizing the sky at the center of the island. The skyscraper jutted between the elegantly proportioned New York Central Building and the Beaux Arts temple that enclosed Grand Central Station—a rude reminder that the airlines had dwarfed the railroads. Its main entrance opened on Vanderbilt Avenue at Forty-fifth Street, directly across from the Yale Club.

The Sky Club on the fifty-seventh floor soon eclipsed the Cloud Club as a bastion for male corporation executives. Sam Pryor supervised the interior decoration; the style was affluent Connecticut Yankee, a blend of Oriental rugs, reproductions of eighteenth-century American furniture and a 500-foot mural depicting the ports of call of old clipper ships.

Sam hung a gilded bas relief from Thailand in the reception hall. The tableau, representing scenes from the Hindu epic Ramayana, was carved in sections, each packed with minute figures engaged in intrigue and mischief. "That's the Pan Am table of organization," the airline's executives gibed.

Trippe's new office on the forty-sixth floor was as utilitarian as the old. He sat at a massive presidential desk—the rolltop was sent to storage to join his globe and other artifacts—flanked by brown leather-upholstered chairs that were seldom occupied. He received fewer and fewer visitors, and when persuaded to call a meeting, he held it in an adjoining conference room.

42

The Succession

At the end of 1961, Trippe learned that Henry Crown, the Chicago financier and controlling stockholder of General Dynamics Corp., was planning to ease out Juan's Greenwich neighbor and golfing companion Frank Pace, Jr., as chief executive and replace him with Roger Lewis. Because of his Number Two listing on Pan American's corporate masthead, his place on the executive committee and the respect Trippe showed him, Lewis was conjectured to be his heir apparent. Juan was past 62, an age when most heads of large business organizations contemplate retirement, if not with pleasure then with a sense of obligation to prepare for a successor—unless they are entrepreneurial founders, in which case the rule may be breached. Trippe gave no hint that he ever considered surrendering his power.

Roger submitted his resignation one morning, whereupon Juan invited him to lunch at the Cloud Club. He talked through most of the meal, and while the waiters cleared the table, and until the cocktail crowd arrived at 5. He talked through dinner, trying to deter Roger from leaving, and while the waiters cleared the table again. When they dimmed the lights at 10, he offered him a taxi ride uptown. At 2 A.M., he telephoned. "I've been talking to Betty and she thinks it's just terrible for you to resign. Won't you come over here so we can talk about it?" he pleaded.

Roger dressed and went to 10 Gracie Square for more conversation. They resumed talking at the office and continued through most of the afternoon and part of the next day. Lewis calculated it had taken him fifty hours to resign from Pan Am and said that during Trippe's marathon effort at dissuasion, he had never promised, "I'll make you president." Roger marveled at his skillful use of language, implying he would designate him to run the company, making it sound definite and constitutional, but never actually saying so.

Lewis held firm, steeling himself to take the advice he had given others: "Trippe will roll his big brown eyes and pour on the charm, but don't let him talk you out of leaving, because after he does he will have no use for you and you'll be looking for another job, having lost the one he talked you out of."

Roger accepted Crown's bid because he saw a challenge to rescue a troubled aircraft-manufacturing company, a field in which he had expertise. He got along well with Trippe, whom he regarded as "the politest and least compassionate man I have ever known," and was respected by his colleagues at Pan Am. But despite the healthy black ink on its balance sheets, Lewis was less sanguine about the future of the company than he had once been. The continuous political maneuvering had failed to halt the erosion of Pan Am's relative position.

He detected evidence that Trippe's obsession had poisoned the Washington wellhead. Early in his tenure at Pan American, in a discussion with William P. Rogers, Eisenhower's Attorney General, Lewis had referred to "the chosen instrument." Rogers scolded him, "Don't you ever use that phrase again."

Like several mandarins who had left the company, Lewis believed Juan made a major miscalculation in foreclosing a domestic artery for the international system. Jim Smith was one; Henry Friendly (who was elevated to the federal bench in 1959) was another. Friendly identified the critical error as Trippe's decision not to bid for the New York–Miami route in 1944 when the C.A.B. was casting about for a competitor for Eastern, the sole operator. To have done so would have killed his case for a single international carrier separate from the domestic system.

Lewis thought Trippe should have made a deal with American or Northwest for a transcontinental linkup instead of buying A.O.A. Pan Am did not receive one important route after A.O.A., and its remaining monopoly in the Central and South Pacific was jeopardized by a pack of domestic carriers clamoring to provide aggressive competition. The C.A.B. was receptive, and after extensive hearings in the late Fifties, awarded new Pacific routes to several applicants, subject, of course, to the President's approval.

Sam oiled his magnificent lobbying machine and saved the day. As a government bureaucrat observed, "When you close the door to Pan Am it comes in the window. And when you close the window there they are, coming right through the wall." Pryor had had the foresight to cultivate Dwight Eisenhower before 1952—he cherished a handwritten note from the General thanking him and Juan profusely for the use of the B-23—and on the eve of John Kennedy's inauguration, the retiring Republican President sent the Pacific case back to the C.A.B. for reconsideration. Pryor had gained a seven-year breather for Pan Am; but how long could he keep delivering rearguard miracles?

Pryor drove the Pan Am wagon into the New Frontier, staking a tent in the office of Myer Feldman, assistant special counsel to the President in charge of transportation. Although John Kennedy was heard alluding to Trippe as a pirate, he and his brother Robert were persuaded he could be useful. "Trippe had better access to the White House than I did," said Alan S. Boyd, Kennedy's appointee as chairman of the C.A.B.

Boyd was a forceful young lawyer from Florida whom Eisenhower had named to fill a Democratic seat on the Board in November 1959. He had been on the job a week when Trippe called for an appointment. Juan plodded into Boyd's office and instead of taking one of the leather armchairs for visitors, he made a beeline for the side chair closer to the desk, which the secretary used when taking dictation. He sat down, placed his briefcase on his knees and his brown hat atop the briefcase and said, smiling sweetly, "Mr. Boyd, I just wanted to meet my new boss."

Boyd recalled thinking, Boyd, you'd better zip your pockets.

After Boyd became chairman, Trippe talked to him in a different manner. Juan's most valuable affiliation was his membership on the Business Advisory Council, originally a quasi-official group of big-business leaders created in the Roosevelt era as a liaison between government and industry. The council was invited to the White House a few times a year. As head of the transportation committee, Trippe asked Boyd to make presentations at the council's powwows in Washington and at the luxurious Homestead resort at Hot Springs, Virginia. "It was a lot of fun for a Florida boy getting to rub elbows with the effete Easterners and the mighty of the commercial world," Boyd said. Concurrently, Juan flaunted his ability to get into the White House. "It was an 'I can trump your ace' sort of thing," the chairman of the C.A.B. said.

Boyd crusaded for lower international fares, on the theory that the efficiencies of the jets should be passed on to the 2.3 million travelers, the majority Americans, crossing the Atlantic by air. He suspected Trippe of "being all things to all men," advocating lower fares and then siding with I.A.T.A. when its members refused to go along, and he knew that Juan worked through the Air Transport Association to kill the C.A.B.'s every attempt to win international rate authority from Congress.

The chairman was flabbergasted when Charles C. Tillinghast, Jr., the president of T.W.A., came to see him in December 1962 to announce a merger agreement with Pan American. Tillinghast, a lawyer who had been installed by the trustees of a voting trust imposed by the banks to wrest control of the airline from Howard Hughes, had been shopping for a merger partner to stanch T.W.A.'s hemorrhage of red ink.

Boyd thought he was naive. The complex holding company devised by Tillinghast and Trippe would have placed Pan American in control of T.W.A. and prevented Hughes from ever regaining his airline. The chairman was positive that Trippe's game was to create chaos in the T.W.A. organization and have the last laugh when the C.A.B. disapproved the merger. "In short, it was another way to the chosen instrument," Boyd said.

The C.A.B. chairman and Najeeb E. Halaby, the Federal Aviation Administrator, were the principal figures behind the Kennedy Administration's statement of aviation policy that was released early in 1963, rejecting the chosen instrument. By the end of the year, Tillinghast, buoyed by an improvement in T.W.A.'s earnings, called the merger off.

When the final tally was made, Trippe's shenanigans proved in vain; he had been spinning wheels and reinforcing the impression embedded in official Washington over a quarter-century that Pan Am was the world's most arrogant and greediest airline.

The chosen instrument might have been smashed to pieces, but Pan Am still had to fend off attacks from trustbusters. In 1956, a subcommittee of the House Judiciary Committee conducted three and a half months of hearings on antitrust and monopoly problems in regulated industries. The testimony consumed 3,100 pages, of which one-fifth was devoted to Pan American. Emanuel Celler, the chairman, a Brooklyn Democrat, was keenly aware of the political gold Hugo Black had sifted from the aviation source twenty-two years before. Fresh impetus for turning the spotlight on the airlines came from the supplemental carriers chafing under the stringent restrictions imposed on their operations by the C.A.B., particularly in the international field, where they were permitted to carry passengers only on charter flights.

Despite Trippe's putting his worst foot forward as a forgetful, condescending witness, the committee paid him tribute in its final report:

The committee believes that Pan American's dominance of United States flag foreign and overseas air transportation is due in considerable measure to the vision and acumen of its president, Juan Terry Trippe, and of the able men with whom he has surrounded himself through the years of the company's development . . . Mr. . Trippe had the foresight to secure for Pan American a foothold in the new industry and the ability to keep it.

Compliments notwithstanding, a majority of the committee accused Pan American of "excessive competitive aggressiveness," "sharp business practices" and bringing undue influence to bear on governments at home and abroad. It noted that Pan American spent nearly $700,000 a year in fees and expenses to public-relations and legal consultants in fifty-four foreign countries and sixteen U.S. cities. The Democrats on the committee recommended a sweeping investigation of the airline by the C.A.B. to determine whether it violated federal antitrust policy. The Board was content to leave that inquiry to the Justice Department. For years, Pan American was threatened with the possibility of criminal indictment for monopolizing international air routes.

The case finally brought by the Attorney General was narrowly drawn to the scope of Pan American's peculiar partnership in Latin America. In January 1954, an action was filed under the Sherman Act against Pan American and W. R. Grace, charging them with a conspiracy to divide the U.S.–Latin American air-transportation markets and seeking to compel the divestiture of their stockholdings in Panagra. The Justice Department alleged that Pan American prevented Panagra from competing with it through an extension of its routes, and that Grace blocked Panagra whenever it threatened the parallel shipping routes of the Grace Line.

The unworkable 50–50 partnership had festered into a gangrenous feud after J. Peter Grace, Joseph Grace's son, took the reins at W. R. Grace in 1945. The younger Grace was determined not to be pushed around by Trippe.

Once planes had the range to fly between the continents without intermediate stops, the Grace directors tried to change the original agreement limiting Panagra to accepting traffic as handed over by Pan American at the Canal Zone, and sought authority to operate to the U.S. mainland. Trippe forbade the Pan American directors to attend the meetings at which such matters were scheduled for discussion, and for lack of a quorum Panagra was prevented from making an application to the C.A.B.

Peter Grace and Juan Trippe were barely on speaking terms. Their executives exchanged sulfurous letters and snubbed each other on the golf links and at luncheon clubs. The wretched marriage continued until a federal district court in New York, hearing the antitrust case in March 1961, dismissed the charges against Grace, found Pan American guilty of Sherman Act violations through its blocking tactics on the Panagra board, and ordered it to sell its stock.

Pan American appealed to the Supreme Court. Early in 1963, the High Court dismissed the government suit on the ground that the C.A.B. and not the courts had jurisdiction over airline antitrust matters.

Trippe offered Grace $10.6 million in cash or Pan American stock for his share of Panagra, and Grace accepted, content to take a capital gain on a thirty-five-year-old investment of $500,000. The C.A.B. vetoed the plan, preferring to have Panagra acquired by Braniff rather than give Trippe the west coast of South America.

After Roger Lewis left, Juan rearranged the corporate masthead to place Wilbur Morrison, executive vice president of the Latin American division, in the number two position. Morrison was two years Juan's junior and was based in Miami.

Several other mandarins were also approaching retirement age, and Trippe was unceremoniously pushing them to the exit door. What sin Gledhill had committed to deserve the cruel treatment Juan meted out to him, no one could fathom. In a strange exception to his habit of silent punishment, he heaped verbal abuse on Frank in the presence of others.

Trippe humiliated Sam Pryor by not speaking to him for months on end—a disconcerting state of affairs for the public-relations and Washington executives who reported to him. Having a leader deprived of oxygen left the junior officers baffled as to the direction in which they were supposed to proceed. Sam carried on, spunky and amiable as ever, a Damon still worshiping his distant Pythias. "Juan lacks human warmth," Sam said, "but he is a genius. No one has his vision."

Similar uncertainty gripped other areas of the company. Tom Flanagan, vice president—Far East Operations, based in Hong Kong, negotiated the sale of two Boeing 727s to Air Vietnam at a good price, all cash on the barrelhead, and had government approval for the deal. Flanagan flew to New York to get the letter of agreement signed. He waited a week and then headed back for Saigon, empty-handed. He was intercepted at San Francisco by a message that Trippe liked the agreement. He stayed overnight—and as he was boarding the plane, was handed another message instructing him to scrap the plan; Trippe had reread the document in Bermuda and changed his mind.

Slow paralysis was setting in at the highest levels of an organization with twenty-five thousand employees and revenues past the half-billion-dollar mark, ruled by one increasingly capricious and absent-minded man.

Juan was isolated in his office on the forty-sixth floor of the Pan Am Building mulling over grander and grander schemes. He dreamed of a metropolitan transport system in which the heliport on the roof was the linchpin for a shuttle between the airports and the center of Manhattan and a helicopter and STOL-aircraft service to Philadelphia and Washington—a vast ingathering of regional traffic to feed Pan Am's international network. Except for the helicopter shuttle to Kennedy International Airport which started at the end of 1965, it remained a dream. He asked Will Player to reduce it to writing and, after this was done, abandoned the scheme.

The more aloof he became within the Pan Am organization, the more gregarious he was on the outside. He gloried in acting the part of an Establishment mover and shaker. Aside from the Business Council, his proudest affiliation was the Yale Corporation. Trippe was one of 10 successor trustees who ran it. They met in New Haven ten times a year for two-day sessions. On Friday evenings, they repaired to Mory's to dine on shellfish and steak and to listen to Juan Trippe spin yarns about the presidents and prime ministers he had known. The trustees enjoyed his versions of Washington power brokerage, and his insights into the university's financial problems. He perceived that the administrative overhead collected on federal research grants was akin to the overhead Pan Am charged on military contracts and showed them how to get the payments increased.

In 1963, Juan led a contingent of trustees to Washington in the Pan Am executive plane to ask McGeorge Bundy, special assistant to President Kennedy, to accept the presidency of Yale, and when Bundy declined, Trippe and two other trustees, Irwin Miller of the Cummins Engine Company and Harold Howe of the Ford Foundation, got behind Kingman Brewster, the Yale Provost, and sold him to the other trustees.

If Yale and the Business Council were his most prestigious extra-curricular activities, the honor he boasted about was the Gold Medal Award of the National Football Foundation, which entered him in the Football Hall of Fame in the company of Presidents Hoover, Eisenhower and Kennedy (and later, Gerald Ford). The citation referred to Trippe as "one who carried into professional life the lessons of team work and competition in spirit taught on the football field."

The Pan Am board of directors exempted the founder from the mandatory retirement age of 65 for officers and inside directors. But the board was concerned about his failure to arrange an orderly succession. "It was hard for us to tell anything about the organization because Trippe ran every detail of the company and never took any advice from the directors. He was so devious," said Dave Ingalls, a member of the executive committee and an outside director since 1949, when he had resigned from management to run Bob Taft's Senate-reelection campaign.

As his 65th birthday drew near, Juan suddenly made his choice. Harold Gray, executive vice president for the overseas division (the consolidated east–west services), was to be president of Pan Am; Trippe would assume the title of chairman and chief executive officer, last used by Sonny Whitney in 1939.

Gray was 58, the youngest of the pioneer generation of Pan Am executives. A pilot and a scientist who tinkered in his spare time in the cellar workshop of his home in Greenwich and had several patents on devices for instrument flying, he also had proven ability as a business manager. He made the Pacific division show a profit independent of subsidy and put in cost controls that turned the Atlantic division into a money machine. Gray evoked loyalty from his subordinates. He called them into his office after the announcement and said, "I want you all to know that I couldn't have gotten this job without you."

Gray was a political innocent; he had contempt for the Washington scene. He subscribed to the better-mousetrap theory. If you run a good company—safe, efficient, honorably behaved toward the public and the employees—the word will get out; the passengers will beat a path to your boarding gates. Though he trusted Will Player, vice president—public relations, a man of intellect and probity, he told him that if he had his way he would do away with that department.

Juan decided he needed a political offset for Harold's naiveté. He had asked Roger Lewis, while he was still at Pan Am, for an introduction to Najeeb Halaby, the Federal Aviation Administrator. Halaby was a New Frontier glamour boy, quick-witted, photogenic and possessed of intriguing credentials. The son of a Syrian father and a native-Texan mother, he was a graduate of Stanford and the Yale Law School, had been a Navy test pilot during the war and had held several government jobs, including Deputy Assistant Secretary of Defense for International Security Affairs. He had been an apprentice venture capitalist on the staff of Laurance Rockefeller, the largest stockholder in Eastern Air Lines. Kennedy's recruiters had spotted him for the F.A.A. post when he was practicing law in California and dabbling in Democratic politics.

Congress had created the independent agency in 1958 to supersede the Civil Aeronautics Administration as safety regulator of the nation's airspace. Halaby was an activist chairman. He decentralized the F.A.A. bureaucracy, and tackled long-simmering controversies with obsolescent flight engineers and militant air controllers. Wherever Jeeb Halaby went—dashing to plane crashes while embers still smoldered; skydiving over Massachusetts to ascertain whether the sport needed regulation; climbing into cockpits to personally test new aircraft models before granting certification—photographers and reporters were at his heels.

He tangled with Trippe over the order Juan placed for the Anglo–French Concorde after he asked him to hold off until the President decided whether to go ahead with an American S.S.T. program.

Halaby came to the Pan Am Building to relay Kennedy's wrath. He spoke to the Oval Office on Juan's telephone and repeated the message "You tell Mr. Trippe we will not forget this." Standing at his desk with the President's voice crackling over the wire, the 47-year-old Halaby struck Juan as power incarnate.

Early in 1965, Trippe heard that he was thinking of leaving the F.A.A. for a better-paying career in private industry. Juan began to court Halaby on the telephone and over breakfasts and lunches in Suite 1040 at the Washington Statler-Hilton, the Pan Am retreat since the sale of the house on F Street. Throwing propriety to the winds, the head of a regulated airline waltzed one of its regulators around the topic of a job, never quite making an offer but letting him know how much he cared. "If you ever leave the government . . ." Trippe said.

Halaby was properly noncommittal before he tendered his resignation to Lyndon Johnson under less-than-cordial circumstances. Rumors that the F.A.A. administrator was quitting to become an executive vice president of Pan Am were aired in the Washington press, and the President was angered to learn in that manner of the departure of still another Kennedy holdover.

Trippe's mental filter was working overtime to convince him that Jeeb Halaby had the influence in Washington Pan Am desperately needed. The day the new F.A.A. administrator was sworn in, he telephoned Halaby at his home to say he was mailing him an offer of a senior executive position with Pan Am.

"I'd be interested only if I was assured of shortly becoming chief executive," Halaby stated at the start of negotiations that extended from a weekend in early July at East Hampton through the summer. Trippe would not be pinned down to promising him the Number One position in the company. After so many years of distinguished service, Harold Gray was entitled to at least a fair chance, he said. The most Halaby could draw from him was a vague assertion that he would have an equal chance at the top job. Juan confided what he had told no one else, that he was going to retire within two years and was going to devote the next months to training a successor.

Halaby finally said yes to an annual salary of $87,000 plus incentive compensation (which amounted to $50,000 the first year), the third-highest executive remuneration after Trippe and Gray, and options for 25,000 shares of stock at $71 a share. He would have the title of senior vice president and a seat on the board and would serve on the executive committee.

Juan invited him and his wife, Doris, to spend the Labor Day weekend at East Hampton with the Trippes and Harold and ExaBell Gray. Harold was given to believe that Halaby would be taking orders from him.

The other Pan Am executives read about their new colleague in a newspaper story that identified him as the new heir apparent. Halaby was given a frigid reception when Trippe introduced him at the Monday executives' luncheon at the Sky Club. They sized him up as just another of the ministers without portfolio Trippe hired impulsively, usually because they were sons of Eli or bemedaled military officers, and with whom he soon became disenchanted.

Indeed, Halaby ruefully observed later on, his title should have been senior vice president—miscellaneous. Trippe gave him responsibility for the guided-missile range, business jets, helicopter service and all nonairline businesses except hotels, which were left with John B. Gates, Jr., Yale '31, Yale Law School '34, National Chairman of the Yale Alumni Fund and a member of Juan's Greenwich golfing foursome. "It was a kind of public service at private profit," Halaby said, and not at all the training he expected for chief executive, which was what he told Will Player he was going to be.

When Player repeated this to Juan, he laughed and said, "All I told him was that he could have a chance."

Trippe told his directors something slightly different. "We thought Halaby had a delightful personality, was a good speaker, understood problems quickly and that he was going to look after Washington while Gray ran the company," Ingalls recalled. If he was giving confusing signals about Halaby, Juan's intentions in regard to two other appointments could not have been plainer. In December he promoted Ferguson, the treasurer, to senior vice president—finance and created a new post of vice president and treasurer for 31-year-old Charles W. Trippe.

Charlie's abrasive manner had not made him popular with his colleagues in the hotel subsidiary. "He was smart, but he didn't have

Daddy's charm and tact," said his sister, Betsy. She disapproved of her brother's going to work at Pan Am.

Even his detractors acknowledged that Charlie had a keen analytical mind—he dug into problems with the tenacity of a Yale bulldog and never let go. Said an older executive, "Whereas with his father, the great steel trap of a mind finally closed on a decision, this never happened with Charlie."

Placing him in the key position of a financial officer, his father's area of special interest, could be regarded as unadulterated nepotism such as violated the rules of professional management in publicly held companies. What additional proof was needed that Trippe considered Pan Am his private empire and intended to keep it that way?

43

The 747

In the mid-1960s, the airlines seemed to be operating in Utopia. The jet fleets were fulfilling the rosiest prophecies, particularly on international routes, where Trippe's dire predictions as to what would happen if the United States were to have more than one carrier sounded like cries of the Big Bad Wolf. Traffic was growing by about 15 percent a year, profits were rolling in, airline shares were favorites in the stock market and there appeared to be no end in sight to the era of plenty.

The bonanza created one problem. Skies and airports were congested with planes—military planes, corporate and private planes, and scheduled airliners. At 33,000 feet above the North Atlantic, the airways were clogged with jet traffic. Forecasters sighted a 200-percent increase in the number of air passengers by 1980, and a proportionately larger volume of freight. A corresponding proliferation of planes was untenable. There simply had to be a new generation of more efficient aircraft—bigger, faster and less expensive to operate. It was time for the next step—probably two steps, along different skyways, as Lindbergh had predicted twenty years before when he said that very high speed and low cost would have to be offered to different classes of passengers.

The technical feasibility of supersonic flight was proved; the economics was another matter. In January 1963, President Charles de Gaulle consented to a joint construction program for a commercial S.S.T. plane by Sud Aviation and the British Aircraft Corporation. The Concorde, designed to fly at Mach 2.2, or 1,450 miles an hour, with 110 passengers—fewer than the Boeing 707—was to be the carrier for an affluent minority.

Trippe sent Lindbergh to Europe to inspect the Concorde prototype, and then to the West Coast to visit the manufacturers who would be competing for the U.S. contract if one was authorized. "It looks hopeful but still to be demonstrated" was his initial comment about supersonic development. Pretty soon his guarded outlook turned to skepticism. He suspected there were hidden costs in the S.S.T., and he worried about the effects of sonic boom on man and the environment. "I am disturbed about the effect I think ultrahigh speeds will have on American people and on Western civilization," he told Juan. "I wish we had been able to use our excess energy expanding the world in space instead of contracting it in time so greatly."

Charles was undergoing a spiritual transformation that shook his lifelong confidence in science and technology, and caused him to deplore the rapid progress in communications he had played a part in bringing about. "I realized that if I had to choose, I would rather have birds than airplanes," he declared.

He recalled what it had been like when he surveyed air routes for Pan American in the early days. Then every place he landed had had a distinctive character and beauty. Now the world was homogenized, and the airplane was much to blame. Lindbergh, the most footloose of men, fretted that jet travel brought about an aimless rushing about by masses of people. "The environment of life has changed too greatly, too quickly; too many elements are in flux."

Trippe had enormous respect for Charles's technical judgment, but he discounted his philosophical turnings as he had once overlooked his political involvement. In May 1963, Juan went to England and France to make his own determination about the Concorde, and took an option on eight planes. Pan American thus became the first airline other than Air France and B.O.A.C. to order a supersonic airliner. Shortly thereafter, President Kennedy gave the signal for a commercial supersonic program to proceed, and Trippe signed up for fifteen American-brand S.S.T.s designed to fly at 1,800 miles an hour with capacity for 200 passengers. Neither the European nor the American S.S.T., however, was due to fly until the early Seventies.

Meanwhile, the problem of the traveling hordes anticipated for the next decade remained unsolved. Concurrently, therefore, Trippe pestered American manufacturers about their subsonic plans: "What is your next step?" he asked. An improvement in the jet engine cleared the way for dramatic increases in the size of transport planes. Large blades placed inside the engine cowling at the front to act as a propeller augmented the volume and force of the exhaust. With the added power in Pratt & Whitney's JT3D fan-jet engine, Boeing was able to produce the 707/321 model with 10 feet in additional length, capacity for 189 passengers and New York–to–Rome nonstop range. Aircraft for 200 to 300 passengers appeared to be the next step for Boeing, Douglas and Lockheed.

In 1964, the Air Force, influenced by the logistics of long supply lines to Southeast Asia, opened a competition for a huge military cargo plane to operate from short airfields. The three manufacturers were in the running to construct the airframe for the C-5A; General Electric and Pratt & Whitney contended to build the engine.

In the past, government-paid research and development for military aircraft had yielded dividends in commercial derivatives. In September 1965, the contract was awarded to Lockheed, with G.E. designated as the engine maker. As soon as the news came out of Washington, Trippe placed a call to Courtlandt S. Gross, the president of Lockheed. "Congratulations," he said. "Shall we talk about a commercial ship?"

"We're going to have our hands full with the military contract for a while. We'll get back to you when we're ready to talk," Gross said. As it turned out, Lockheed had underpriced its bid, and the cost delays and overruns during the next five years earned for the cargo plane a dubious distinction as one of the most notorious production fiascos in aerospace history.

Donald Douglas, the next person Juan called, was committed to stretching his DC-8 to match Boeing's elongated 707. Trippe turned to Bill Allen at Boeing. In the face of losing the C-5A contract and expecting other military programs to be phased out, the Seattle manufacturer needed a new commercial success to provide stability for the next decade. Allen's major problem was determining how big a supersize plane the airlines really wanted. In Trippe's view, the next step had to be a giant leap forward, a totally new concept of air transport to dazzle the traveling public.

Pratt & Whitney was anxious to find a customer for the 41,000-pound-thrust engine developed for the C-5A competition it had lost to G.E. During the rest of 1965, the engineering staffs of Pan American, Boeing and Pratt & Whitney met repeatedly in Seattle, New York and Hartford.

Cargo was as important a factor in their planning as passengers. All-cargo companies such as Flying Tigers and Seaboard World Airways were posing fierce competition for scheduled carriers in the lucrative business of air freight. The latest trend in the international shipment of goods was by a combination of surface and air transportation using standardized containers that measured 8 feet long by 8 feet wide. The requirement of loading them straight into the aircraft from a truck and stacking them two abreast dictated the wide body design of the plane, which was to be convertible from passenger/cargo to all-cargo configuration.

On December 22, 1965, Trippe and Allen signed a letter of intent for the Boeing Model 747. The specifications for the plane: gross weight of 550,000 pounds, capacity for 350 to 400 passengers, 5,100-mile range with full passenger payload, initial cruise altitude of 35,000 feet, flying at Mach .9, or just below the speed of sound. The plane had to operate from airports that accepted jet aircraft, but at lower noise levels. Estimated price: between $15 million and $18 million.

Boeing estimated that it had to sell at least fifty planes to cover initial tooling costs, and that half would have to be ordered by one customer to whet demand from other airlines. Trippe agreed to buy a minimum of twenty-five planes, provided they were delivered to Pan Am before any other airline, between September 1969 and May 1970. Juan was a niggard in small matters—breakfasting with a Pan American executive in a hotel coffee shop, he would insist on splitting the $3.80 check—but without blinking an eyelash, he committed Pan Am to an outlay of more than $500 million, including spare parts: a sum equal to its total passenger and cargo revenues for the previous year.

The 747 was such an expensive project for Boeing to undertake without help from the government that Allen demanded a stringent schedule of progress payments: a 2.5-percent deposit upon signing the contract, and half the entire amount, paid in quarterly installments, six months before delivery of the first plane. Even before the F.A.A. certified the 747 as airworthy and safe for passengers, Pan Am was to shell out a quarter of a billion dollars, not counting the interest it would be paying on the money borrowed. Past experience had taught Trippe that airframe manufacturers passed blame for disappointing performance to engine manufacturers. He insisted that Boeing assume full responsibility for the performance of the 747; it could pick the engine maker and bear the liability for its choice.

It was a spectacular gamble for a 66-year-old businessman, placing his company, its employees and its shareholders at enormous risk. If he judged correctly and was lucky to boot, Pan Am's leadership would be maintained. If he was wrong or fate was cruel, the airline might well go bankrupt. Trippe's career had begun in the wake of bankruptcy. He had staked the residue salvaged from Trippe & Company on a new industry—some thought it was folly at the time—and won the pot of gold. He had wagered again and again—on the Pacific crossing; on the purchase of the jets. This was his most audacious bet in financial terms, though not so much for him personally. Trippe owned 19,500 shares of Pan Am stock, then valued in the market at around $800,000—fewer than held by Pryor, Balluder, Morrison and Dave Ingalls. He had taken profits on most of his Pan Am holdings and invested them elsewhere. What he was subjecting to jeopardy this time was his place in the pantheon of aviation pioneers.

Between the signing of the letter and the closing of the definitive contract four months later, the 747 put on weight: 130,000 additional pounds. The jumbo extended three-fourths the length of a football field, its tail poised above the ground at the height of a five-story building. The cabin was 20 feet wide, affording passengers an opportunity to stroll along double aisles under 8-foot ceilings. Suddenly Trippe was asking to seat 490 passengers in thrift class, or 375 mixed first and economy classes. To protect the crew from 100 tons of lurching cargo in the event of an accident, the cockpit was situated on an upper deck rather than in the nose of the aircraft. Early in March 1966, seeing a plywood mock-up of the 747, Trippe recalled the evergreen popularity of the Stratocruiser. "Why can't we have a cocktail lounge on top, and a spiral staircase?" he asked. The suggestion added 4,420 pounds to the weight and $200,000 to the price tag. "Perhaps we should have a few staterooms on the second deck," Trippe said.

Out of the blue, as the corporate lawyers for Pan Am and Boeing were laboring overtime to draw the final contract, the project was endangered.

The President invited the Business Council to dinner at the White House on March 30. "The greatest group of businessmen in the world," said Lyndon Johnson, pouring on the blandishments to win them to his side. He regularly had them to dinner and to briefing sessions, exposed them to his Cabinet officers and to his overbearing self. If you have problems, he said, call the White House. Sometimes he answered the phone when they called.

Trippe's persistent calls were unanswered, however. For the first time in thirty-eight years, Juan was unable to secure a personal interview with the President of the United States. He noted that Texans had Johnson's ear—C. R. Smith of American Airlines, and Harding Lawrence of Braniff—while he had to settle for sharing a Presidential audience with a hundred other captains of industry.

At the dinner, Johnson appealed to their patriotism. The economy was becoming dangerously overheated, he said—without dwelling on the root cause, the war in Southeast Asia. Inflation was menacing the country; he was going to tell the American people that it was the crucial domestic issue of the day. But first, he was asking the industrial leaders to exercise restraint in capital spending, to curb expansion and let the economy cool down a bit. If you have plans to build new plants, he said, put the plans on the back burner for a while.

Juan and Bill Allen, seated apart at the dinner, were jolted by the President's plea. Boeing was planning to construct a manufacturing and assembly plant for the mammoth 747—a forest adjacent to an airfield near Everett, Washington, had been selected for the site—and a 35-mile railroad spur to haul building materials from Seattle and later, components for assembly at the facility.

If Pan Am were to announce a half-billion-dollar investment in new planes, and Boeing were to proceed with the $250-million project at Everett, it might be viewed as a mockery of the President's program of restraint. Johnson's vindictive streak was too well advertised for military contractors like Boeing and Pan Am to chance provoking it.

When the President signaled that the meeting was over, Allen drifted toward the door with the other guests, unaware that Juan was sidling toward Johnson. The President was in agitated conversation with a steel executive. William McChesney Martin, chairman of the Federal Reserve Board, stood a few feet away, in a waiting posture that indicated the President expected to talk to him next. Trippe knew Martin as a fellow trustee of the Yale Corporation. "I must speak to the President. It's a matter of vital interest to the country," he said to Martin, and brazenly elbowed himself into an audience with L.B.J.

One of the baffling complexities of Juan Trippe, a notably digressive mumbler, was his ability in moments of crisis to get to the point. Adrenaline pounded his thoughts to conciseness. Under Johnson's sullen glare, figures rat-tat-tatted from Juan's lips, synthesizing the wonders the 747 would accomplish for the aerospace industry and for the economy as a whole. The site for the plant had to be cleared immediately, but production and subassembly of components would not begin for another year, and the impact of the program would be felt in 1968 at the earliest. By then, Juan said, the country would be experiencing a postwar downturn and new investment would be just what the President would be prescribing. Trippe was discreet enough not to add: in an election year.

The jobs generated by the program would have the effect of a massive vitamin dose for several states. Probably 40 percent of the planes would be bought by foreign airlines. Eighty planes sold abroad by December 1972 would yield $1.6 billion to tip the balance of payments in America's favor. "If the United States does not build such a plane, Mr. President, the British or the French will build one, and then what will happen to the balance of payments?" Trippe asked.

He pressed on. Fleets of 747s operated by U.S. airlines would provide a reserve airlift capability for military passengers and cargo in the event of national emergency. One plane will carry 214,000 pounds of freight, compared with a maximum 90,000 pounds in present aircraft, he said.

"Does anyone else know about this?" the President asked. "No one but you, Mr. President," Trippe replied, stretching fact. Johnson brooded for a moment and then said, "I want you to see someone tomorrow morning. Be here at ten A.M."

The next day, Trippe was chauffeured from the White House to the Pentagon and ushered into the office of Secretary of Defense Robert S. McNamara. "Why can't you wait for Lockheed to make a commercial derivative of the C-5A?" McNamara wondered. Trippe rattled on about airport congestion, and the differences between military need and F.A.A.-mandated requirements for passenger safety. It was impossible to modify a plane such as the C-5A, designed to lift off short, soft fields with a load of tanks and armored vehicles, into a passenger plane for long, smooth runways without paying a horrendous penalty in operating costs.

"We're going to the White House to see the President," said the Secretary of Defense. Johnson had more questions to ask, mostly about jobs and the states where the subcontractors' plants were located. After a half-hour, he said to McNamara, "Get someone from Boeing down here and work it out."

During the following week, Juan and Bill Allen met with White House subordinates and with McNamara's aides at the Pentagon. Then both men went through the ritual of seeking approval from their directors.

The directors of Pan Am gathered in the walnut-paneled boardroom on the forty-sixth floor. A dozen stories above, the helicopters of New York Airways clattered in landings and takeoffs on the rooftop. The court of Emperor Juan sat ready to receive his momentous decree. The 747 had been analyzed to a fare-thee-well by the Pan Am engineering, marketing and financial staffs and at the Monday-morning operations meetings. The insider directors, as active officers of the company, were acquainted with the superjet project and were excited about the Pan Am plane for the Seventies. The only thing they were unsure of as they entered the boardroom was what Trippe was going to do about it; he took none of them into his confidence. As usual, the outside directors had the sketchiest information on which to base their approval of Juan's *fait accompli*.

Trippe reviewed the figures—the ecstatic traffic projections, the gloom and doom about running out of air and landing space, the dimensions of the plane. One 747 would replace two and a half 707s, fly a mile higher and 10 percent faster, shaving 25 minutes from the New York–London schedule. The operating costs per seat-mile would be 30 percent less. That was the businessman's clincher.

President Johnson approved; that convinced the outside directors. To a man, they were advocates of air power, both military and commercial, to perpetuate U.S. leadership of the free world. Who were they to say no after the President said yes? Not Dave Ingalls; not General Alfred Gruenther; not Mark McKee, who had difficulty staying wide awake at board meetings. And in April 1966, who among them was to ask, "What if?" An option for ten additional planes was authorized for incorporation into the contract, the largest single order for a single aircraft model in the history of commercial aviation.

As a decade before, the airlines had followed Trippe into the jet age, now they had no choice but to rush after him into what the Pan Am press releases called "the spacious age" of air travel. By August, Boeing had orders for fifty-six jumbos, and every week brought more.

Adding the 747 program to a previous order for the advanced 707 and other Boeing jets, Trippe had committed Pan Am to nearly $1 billion for new aircraft.

Juan lost no sleep over the mind-boggling sum of money involved; as usual, he had prepared the ground for financing. A year and a half before, he had renegotiated loan agreements for $140 million with a group of insurance companies and obtained a revolving credit of $100 million from banks at the lowest interest rates—a tribute to his acumen and the company's credit standing. Lenders were fairly thrusting money at Pan Am because, from 1960 on, the airline was producing record profits every year. And the prognosis for 1966 was that earnings would surpass previous peaks.

Pan Am stock was trading at levels not seen since the aviation fervor of 1928–29. Juan took advantage of the booming environment to float a $175-million issue of convertible debentures—a sellout, with 250 investment firms across the country, led by Lehman Brothers, participating in the underwriting.

Still, these amounts fell far short of the total needed to pay for the 747s. The rest was to come from profits derived from passenger and cargo revenues and from cash generated through accounting charges and tax credits that would be applied only in the event of substantial earnings. In short, everything depended on continuing profits and on underlying assumptions about cost reductions and traffic growth.

Trippe cut a magnificent financial pattern to fit his jumbo purchase, but he left no margin for pessimism or the unexpected.

44

The Last Word

The 1966 annual report was Trippe's pride and joy: a testimonial to one man's vision; a celebration of the world's largest international airline. In its thirty-ninth year, Pan Am showed an $83.7-million profit (up 60.7 percent from the year before) on operating revenues of $841 million (up 25.7 percent). The earnings of $5.37 per share, the figure scrutinized by Wall Street's go-go security analysts, represented a 48.8-percent increase. All this was a tribute to private enterprise. More than two-thirds of the revenues were derived from carrying passengers over a 77,818-mile route system, the rest from cargo and mail. Not a cent was culled from government subsidy.

"Maybe it's time for me to retire," Trippe mumbled to Will Player now and then during the spring of 1967. "The succession is set," he said. Not for a moment did Will or any of Pan Am's senior executives believe he would retire. "He'll stay until he's a hundred and ten," they said. "He'll have to be carried out in a coffin."

If the example of the other pioneers meant anything, it was time for Trippe to go. Eddie Rickenbacker had retired from Eastern Air Lines a few years back at 73, leaving an airline scarred by his autocratic rule. William Patterson, born the same year as Juan, withdrew from United on the dot of his 67th birthday. C. R. Smith, three months younger than Trippe, was due to pack it in at American at the end of 1967, soon to become Lyndon Johnson's Secretary of Commerce. Juan was the last airline founder still in office.

"I want to do the right thing," he told Betty.

relegated by Trippe to deepest Siberia but whose name began with A. Charles Trippe was second from the bottom.

What was the meaning of this? Was Juan trying to throw succession sleuths off the trail or heighten a dramatic surprise? During the first weekend in May, he telephoned his directors and swore them to secrecy. He told them that he had decided to retire and that after the annual shareholders' meeting on Tuesday, he was going to nominate Harold Gray to succeed him as chairman and chief executive officer and Najeeb Halaby as president. The board had mixed feelings about this latest *fait accompli* Trippe was dumping in its lap. Halaby seemed such a personable fellow, but what did he know about operating an airline? Maybe with Trippe gone, he would learn. Ignorant of Gray's sickness, the directors calculated that he had about five years to train Halaby before he retired.

A former director, on being informed, questioned Gray about the decision. Knowing there were signs of antipathy between him and Halaby, he wondered what kind of management team they would make. "What difference does it make?" Harold answered wearily. "There isn't anybody else."

He was right. There was no second tier of executives qualified to lead a billion-dollar company with forty-four thousand employees. Behind Halaby were veterans preparing to draw their pensions and younger men with only specialized experience, among them the 33-year-old vice president and treasurer, Charles Trippe. Later, Betty Trippe would say, "If only John Leslie hadn't gotten sick; if only Roger Lewis hadn't been so impatient."

Halaby was crestfallen when Juan gave him the news on Monday morning; but before he could voice his disappointment at not being named chief executive, Trippe said, "Harold has cancer, but it seems to be under control. He has been taking these treatments."

On Tuesday morning, Trippe told his secretary that he was retiring later in the day, and that Harold Gray was taking over. He spent the next few hours hunched over the statement he planned to make to the shareholders, laboring over every comma, changing his mind at every sentence.

Around noon, he buzzed for Will Player. "What time is the meeting?" he asked.

"Two fifteen," Will said. Trippe went back to his writing.

At 1:30 P.M., Player appeared. "It's time to go, Juan." Trippe sighed, "I guess I'll have to give it this way" and stuffed the papers into his briefcase.

At the bank of elevators, Will realized he had left the folder con-

The signing of a contract involving new technology often marks the opening round of further negotiations in which the design may be changed and standards of performance revised. A game of trade-offs ensues to determine which party will bear the cost of the modifications.

If anyone was well rehearsed in contractual bargaining with Juan Trippe—the subversive feints, the surprise thrusts, the endless delays— it was Bill Allen of Boeing. The supporting cast of characters in the 747 drama had changed, however. In the place of Frank Gledhill was Laurence S. Kuter, a former Air Force general. Since joining Pan Am in 1962, Kuter had been learning the vagaries of Juan's style of management by concealment. In his memoir of the 747 saga, he described Trippe's bargaining technique:

> His own negotiations were never written, always oral, and under circumstances where there were no observers or staff members to make notes or to report. His ability to disclaim in private what his staff had proposed in conferences was a negotiating weapon he cherished. He reserved the right, and frequently exercised it, to redirect the subjects under discussion into new and unexpected directions.

Several of the Boeing team were also newly promoted from the ranks. Consequently, the trading back and forth advanced on two levels —one for the semi-inexperienced staffs, the other between Allen and Trippe. The technical men were never sure of what their chief executives had said to each other or whether they were having further discussions.

The contract for the 747 specified Boeing's choice of the Pratt & Whitney JT9D-1 engine to deliver, initially, 41,000 pounds of thrust (more than double the engine power of the long-range 707), which was to be stepped up by the end of six years to a maximum 47,000 pounds. Pratt & Whitney normally developed new engines in three-year cycles.

As a year elapsed, the aircraft kept gaining structural weight to accommodate Pan Am's requests for more passenger and cargo capacity, and to meet unexpected requirements such as the new restrictions on noise imposed by the London Airport Authority which entailed additional silencing materials. By the summer of 1967, it was evident that the engine was underpowered for a machine that weighed 710,000 pounds fully loaded on takeoff for intercontinental routes. At that point, the 747 would be capable of carrying a full load of passengers without cargo or mail from New York to Paris. Rome nonstop was beyond its range. Having forked over $24 million in installment payments, Pan Am was presented with an ideal plane for its competitors to operate on their high-density, short- to medium-range domestic routes. Instead of a great leap forward, the 747 represented for Pan Am an economic step backward; its performance level was inferior to that of the 707-321B.

Boeing's solution was to put the plane on a weight-reduction regimen without making expensive changes—a diet that meant fewer passengers and lost profits for Pan Am.

What was Pan Am to do? Sue Boeing for nonperformance and possibly throw the manufacturer into bankruptcy? The airline would still be without its plane for the Seventies. Accept postponement on delivery until the engine thrust could be advanced? Delays would be costly for both Boeing and Pan Am in terms of lost revenues, and the meter would be running at the rate of almost $2 million a month on interest charges for the prepayments. Accept the aircraft with JT9D-1 engines? That would negate the premise for entering the contract in the first place. The fourth alternative was to negotiate a trade-in of the substandard plane for an improved model.

After the signing of the contract, Trippe had receded from the scene, leaving Kuter and the Pan Am engineers at the front lines in Seattle. They reported by telephone and telex to Harold Gray in New York. Kuter begged Gray to draw Juan back into the fray.

Trippe began by telephoning William Gwinn, president of United Aircraft, in East Hartford. "We must have the JT9D-7," he said, referring to the model planned for introduction in 1973 to power a second generation of 747s. Gwinn pointed out that the larger fan and packaging for this biggest of engines necessitated a major design of the wing, engine mounting and landing gear.

Bill Allen resisted such costly and delaying changes; but Trippe hounded him by telephone and during a fishing trip in Alaskan waters. With the fate of the basic plane in doubt, he was setting specifications for the later-model 747-B: "Now you'll give us five hundred economy passengers and twenty tons of cargo for Pan Am's longest routes, an initial cruise altitude of thirty-seven thousand feet and pressurizing to fly at forty-five thousand feet, above all other traffic."

He dispatched Kuter to East Hartford to "build a fire" under Pratt & Whitney to produce a 50,000-pound- to 60,000-pound-thrust engine in a year and nine months. Trippe was demanding a plane quite different from the one he had contracted to buy, and he expected the manufacturers to absorb the higher cost of giving it to him.

In November, Gray and Lindbergh, who was now a director of Pan Am as well as a technical adviser, made the trek to Seattle to

investigate Boeing's excuses for not being able to meet Trippe's a celerated timetable. When they returned, they tried to make Jua understand that it was impossible to satisfy his demands before la 1972 or early 1973.

Trippe had never believed in the impossible. He had alway driven engineers, his own and the manufacturer's, to give him what h wanted, impervious to how they managed it. Somehow, they alway did. But not this time. "Do the best you can," he said, finally.

Just before Christmas, Pratt & Whitney's engineers said they could beef up the JT9D-3 engine to 45,000 pounds of thrust by injecting distilled water into the combustion chambers during takeoff. It was to add $100,000 a year to the cost of operating each plane.

In March 1968, Juan invited the Allens to Eleuthera for a long weekend. It was to be a working vacation for the men. For the first time, he asked Harold Gray to join the sessions with Allen. They went over the contract with a fine-tooth comb, reviewing the performance guarantees, tabulating the shortcomings and haggling over the amounts Boeing owed Pan Am for failing to meet specifications. At stake were millions of dollars in added operating costs for Pan Am.

Nothing was resolved then, or during the spate of telephone conversations between New York and Seattle immediately afterward.

Four months before, Harold Gray had confided a secret to Trippe. He was suffering from cancer of the lymph glands. The prognosis was encouraging, he said. His doctors advised him the disease could probably be arrested by treatment and that he could handle his job as well as ever.

Harold told one other person. "No one knows except Juan," he said to Will Player, "but I want you to know because if I disappear for a day or two, it's because I'm going to take cobalt treatments."

Gray was a disciplined man with tremendous self-control. He bore the ordeal of cancer without flinching. Player marveled at "this bull of a man with those needles in his leg veins, withstanding tremendous pain and not showing it."

And Trippe, by now as accessible as the Dalai Lama, was giving no clues as to his plans. The annual report for 1967, published early in 1968, contributed a mystifying note. For the first time, the corporate officers below the chairman and president were listed in alphabetical order. Halaby, formerly in third place, was wedged in a grouping of senior officers between Ferguson and John T. Shannon, senior vice president—operations, a NYRBA veteran who was due to retire. There followed an army of thirty-four vice presidents, led by a Yale man

taining the questions expected to be asked at the meeting and the chairman's answers on his desk. "Please wait a minute; I'll be right back," he said. Glancing over his shoulder as he ran, he saw Juan moving like a sleepwalker into an elevator.

Trippe had inhabited his imperial cocoon for so long—protected by secretaries; served by chauffeurs, pilots, ground crewmen and assorted lackeys; waited on hand and foot by his wife; growing vaguer with each passing year—that his executives assumed he would misplace himself if left to his own devices. He won't remember where the meeting is to be held, Player said to himself in panic.

Will reclaimed the folder and descended in a high-speed elevator in twenty-three seconds flat. He found Juan at the foot of a staircase in the main lobby staring at the wing tips of his shoes. "Will we be on time, do you think?" he asked.

They took the escalator into Grand Central Station, then shouldered their way through the lunch-hour crowd and into the underground corridor to the Commodore Hotel. In the Windsor Ballroom, Pan Am stewardesses in blue gabardines and winsome smiles stood ready to assist the 800 of the company's 112,975 stockholders present.

Trippe called his fortieth stockholders' meeting to order. He was always meticulous about parliamentary procedure. Peering through pale-rimmed bifocals, he recited the disappointing results of the first quarter: revenues up 15.6 percent, operating expenses up 22.6 percent, a loss of 4 cents a share compared with a 15-cent net profit for the same period a year before.

Nineteen sixty-seven had been a good year, but the earnings of $65.7 million on revenues of $950 million showed up as a 21.5-percent decrease from the glorious year of 1966. There was another disquieting note: load factors on the long-range routes to Europe and Asia were shrinking—the big jets were flying more than half empty; and in a year and a half, Pan Am would have a fleet of jumbos to fill. More than 50 percent of the Americans traveling abroad flew on foreign-flag airlines.

Trippe spoke in a New York patrician monotone, lulling his audience to the verge of boredom. Turning to the business of the election of directors, he announced that the new board was going to meet after the stockholders' meeting was adjourned. "It is my intention to retire," he said. "At the meeting of the board I plan to nominate President Harold Gray to succeed me as chairman and chief executive officer of our company."

There was no immediate response from his inattentive listeners. Then someone in the back of the ballroom began to clap, and others hesitantly picked up the cue. A reporter dashed for a telephone to alert an editor that the last of the aviation pioneers was bowing out. Harold Gray bent forward to grasp the microphone and pay tribute to the founder. "As chairman of this meeting, I rule your remarks out of order," Trippe said. Gray shrugged. "I seldom defy the boss," he said.

An hour later, in the Pan Am boardroom, Juan Trippe, still the chairman and chief executive officer, asked Robert Lehman, 76 and feeble, to act as temporary chairman of the directors' meeting. Trippe then nominated Harold Gray for the post of chairman and Najeeb Halaby for president. The vote was unanimous. Lehman turned the meeting over to Gray to chair.

Power had passed, by prosaic routine. "It's done all the time," Trippe said.

Charles Lindbergh nominated Juan Trippe to be honorary chairman. A unanimous vote.

When the meeting was over, Juan walked back to his office with Harold Gray. "It's yours," he said. "You don't have to change a thing. You can have my desk." He would be moving down the hall to a smaller office.

"I'll be in in the morning," he promised.

The next day, Harold Gray rearranged his office. He shoved the furniture around himself after ordering Trippe's desk removed.

The signing of a contract involving new technology often marks the opening round of further negotiations in which the design may be changed and standards of performance revised. A game of trade-offs ensues to determine which party will bear the cost of the modifications.

If anyone was well rehearsed in contractual bargaining with Juan Trippe—the subversive feints, the surprise thrusts, the endless delays—it was Bill Allen of Boeing. The supporting cast of characters in the 747 drama had changed, however. In the place of Frank Gledhill was Laurence S. Kuter, a former Air Force general. Since joining Pan Am in 1962, Kuter had been learning the vagaries of Juan's style of management by concealment. In his memoir of the 747 saga, he described Trippe's bargaining technique:

> His own negotiations were never written, always oral, and under circumstances where there were no observers or staff members to make notes or to report. His ability to disclaim in private what his staff had proposed in conferences was a negotiating weapon he cherished. He reserved the right, and frequently exercised it, to redirect the subjects under discussion into new and unexpected directions.

Several of the Boeing team were also newly promoted from the ranks. Consequently, the trading back and forth advanced on two levels —one for the semi-inexperienced staffs, the other between Allen and Trippe. The technical men were never sure of what their chief executives had said to each other or whether they were having further discussions.

The contract for the 747 specified Boeing's choice of the Pratt & Whitney JT9D-1 engine to deliver, initially, 41,000 pounds of thrust (more than double the engine power of the long-range 707), which was to be stepped up by the end of six years to a maximum 47,000 pounds. Pratt & Whitney normally developed new engines in three-year cycles.

As a year elapsed, the aircraft kept gaining structural weight to accommodate Pan Am's requests for more passenger and cargo capacity, and to meet unexpected requirements such as the new restrictions on noise imposed by the London Airport Authority which entailed additional silencing materials. By the summer of 1967, it was evident that the engine was underpowered for a machine that weighed 710,000 pounds fully loaded on takeoff for intercontinental routes. At that point, the 747 would be capable of carrying a full load of passengers without cargo or mail from New York to Paris. Rome nonstop was beyond its range. Having forked over $24 million in installment payments, Pan Am was presented with an ideal plane for its competitors to operate on their high-density, short- to medium-range domestic routes. Instead of a great leap forward, the 747 represented for Pan Am an economic step backward; its performance level was inferior to that of the 707-321B.

Boeing's solution was to put the plane on a weight-reduction regimen without making expensive changes—a diet that meant fewer passengers and lost profits for Pan Am.

What was Pan Am to do? Sue Boeing for nonperformance and possibly throw the manufacturer into bankruptcy? The airline would still be without its plane for the Seventies. Accept postponement on delivery until the engine thrust could be advanced? Delays would be costly for both Boeing and Pan Am in terms of lost revenues, and the meter would be running at the rate of almost $2 million a month on interest charges for the prepayments. Accept the aircraft with JT9D-1 engines? That would negate the premise for entering the contract in the first place. The fourth alternative was to negotiate a trade-in of the substandard plane for an improved model.

After the signing of the contract, Trippe had receded from the scene, leaving Kuter and the Pan Am engineers at the front lines in Seattle. They reported by telephone and telex to Harold Gray in New York. Kuter begged Gray to draw Juan back into the fray.

Trippe began by telephoning William Gwinn, president of United Aircraft, in East Hartford. "We must have the JT9D-7," he said, referring to the model planned for introduction in 1973 to power a second generation of 747s. Gwinn pointed out that the larger fan and packaging for this biggest of engines necessitated a major design of the wing, engine mounting and landing gear.

Bill Allen resisted such costly and delaying changes; but Trippe hounded him by telephone and during a fishing trip in Alaskan waters. With the fate of the basic plane in doubt, he was setting specifications for the later-model 747-B: "Now you'll give us five hundred economy passengers and twenty tons of cargo for Pan Am's longest routes, an initial cruise altitude of thirty-seven thousand feet and pressurizing to fly at forty-five thousand feet, above all other traffic."

He dispatched Kuter to East Hartford to "build a fire" under Pratt & Whitney to produce a 50,000-pound- to 60,000-pound-thrust engine in a year and nine months. Trippe was demanding a plane quite different from the one he had contracted to buy, and he expected the manufacturers to absorb the higher cost of giving it to him.

In November, Gray and Lindbergh, who was now a director of Pan Am as well as a technical adviser, made the trek to Seattle to investigate Boeing's excuses for not being able to meet Trippe's accelerated timetable. When they returned, they tried to make Juan understand that it was impossible to satisfy his demands before late 1972 or early 1973.

Trippe had never believed in the impossible. He had always driven engineers, his own and the manufacturer's, to give him what he wanted, impervious to how they managed it. Somehow, they always did. But not this time. "Do the best you can," he said, finally.

Just before Christmas, Pratt & Whitney's engineers said they could beef up the JT9D-3 engine to 45,000 pounds of thrust by injecting distilled water into the combustion chambers during takeoff. It was to add $100,000 a year to the cost of operating each plane.

In March 1968, Juan invited the Allens to Eleuthera for a long weekend. It was to be a working vacation for the men. For the first time, he asked Harold Gray to join the sessions with Allen. They went over the contract with a fine-tooth comb, reviewing the performance guarantees, tabulating the shortcomings and haggling over the amounts Boeing owed Pan Am for failing to meet specifications. At stake were millions of dollars in added operating costs for Pan Am.

Nothing was resolved then, or during the spate of telephone conversations between New York and Seattle immediately afterward.

Four months before, Harold Gray had confided a secret to Trippe. He was suffering from cancer of the lymph glands. The prognosis was encouraging, he said. His doctors advised him the disease could probably be arrested by treatment and that he could handle his job as well as ever.

Harold told one other person. "No one knows except Juan," he said to Will Player, "but I want you to know because if I disappear for a day or two, it's because I'm going to take cobalt treatments."

Gray was a disciplined man with tremendous self-control. He bore the ordeal of cancer without flinching. Player marveled at "this bull of a man with those needles in his leg veins, withstanding tremendous pain and not showing it."

And Trippe, by now as accessible as the Dalai Lama, was giving no clues as to his plans. The annual report for 1967, published early in 1968, contributed a mystifying note. For the first time, the corporate officers below the chairman and president were listed in alphabetical order. Halaby, formerly in third place, was wedged in a grouping of senior officers between Ferguson and John T. Shannon, senior vice president—operations, a NYRBA veteran who was due to retire. There followed an army of thirty-four vice presidents, led by a Yale man relegated by Trippe to deepest Siberia but whose name began with A. Charles Trippe was second from the bottom.

What was the meaning of this? Was Juan trying to throw succession sleuths off the trail or heighten a dramatic surprise? During the first weekend in May, he telephoned his directors and swore them to secrecy. He told them that he had decided to retire and that after the annual shareholders' meeting on Tuesday, he was going to nominate Harold Gray to succeed him as chairman and chief executive officer and Najeeb Halaby as president. The board had mixed feelings about this latest *fait accompli* Trippe was dumping in its lap. Halaby seemed such a personable fellow, but what did he know about operating an airline? Maybe with Trippe gone, he would learn. Ignorant of Gray's sickness, the directors calculated that he had about five years to train Halaby before he retired.

A former director, on being informed, questioned Gray about the decision. Knowing there were signs of antipathy between him and Halaby, he wondered what kind of management team they would make. "What difference does it make?" Harold answered wearily. "There isn't anybody else."

He was right. There was no second tier of executives qualified to lead a billion-dollar company with forty-four thousand employees. Behind Halaby were veterans preparing to draw their pensions and younger men with only specialized experience, among them the 33-year-old vice president and treasurer, Charles Trippe. Later, Betty Trippe would say, "If only John Leslie hadn't gotten sick; if only Roger Lewis hadn't been so impatient."

Halaby was crestfallen when Juan gave him the news on Monday morning; but before he could voice his disappointment at not being named chief executive, Trippe said, "Harold has cancer, but it seems to be under control. He has been taking these treatments."

On Tuesday morning, Trippe told his secretary that he was retiring later in the day, and that Harold Gray was taking over. He spent the next few hours hunched over the statement he planned to make to the shareholders, laboring over every comma, changing his mind at every sentence.

Around noon, he buzzed for Will Player. "What time is the meeting?" he asked.

"Two fifteen," Will said. Trippe went back to his writing.

At 1:30 P.M., Player appeared. "It's time to go, Juan." Trippe sighed, "I guess I'll have to give it this way" and stuffed the papers into his briefcase.

At the bank of elevators, Will realized he had left the folder con-

Epilogue

Upon taking over as chief executive, Gray acknowledged that the 747 contract was "a mess." During the summer, the wrangling continued over which company was to bear the cost of increasing the engine power. A compromise was reached just before the rollout ceremonies for the jumbo jet in September. The 747 had yet to make its first test flight when the date loomed for the exercise of the option on eight additional planes for $175 million, to be delivered in the spring of 1971. Relying on the advice of Laurence Kuter and his chief engineer, John Borger, and with Halaby's acquiescence, Gray decided in January 1969 to go ahead. He commissioned new maintenance facilities and a terminal at Kennedy International Airport to the tune of $200 million. Pan American was now committed well past the billion-dollar mark for the superjets.

The figures for 1968 were disappointing: an 18.7-percent decrease in earnings over the year before. Pan Am's stock fell one-third below the $39 a share reached in the golden year of 1966.

The decline attracted a corporate raider. Charles Bluhdorn of Gulf & Western Industries began buying Pan Am shares on the open market until he amassed 6 percent of the company's equity, to become the largest individual stockholder. He made the standard disclaimer that he was buying for investment purposes only, but some of his investments in the past had ripened into takeovers.

Trippe was appalled, and so was Halaby, who counseled opposition to "the pirate." Gray, politically naive, delayed mounting a counterattack. Early in 1969, reports reached the forty-sixth floor that

Bluhdorn had offered to sell his stock to another conglomerator, James Crosby, chairman of Resorts International, a complex of hotels and gambling casinos in the Bahamas, and that the head of the trust department of the Chase Manhattan Bank, which controlled 1.5 million shares, was abetting a plan for Crosby to gain control of Pan Am.

Trippe flew straight as a homing pigeon to the Nixon White House. Halaby zeroed in on the House and Senate Commerce Committees, which, after receiving calls from 1600 Pennsylvania Avenue, reacted favorably to bills to prevent an outside company from acquiring more than 5 percent of an airline's stock without the approval of the C.A.B. The legislation was passed and the raid blocked.

The outcome of the transpacific case, after more than a decade of political maneuvering by Pan Am to keep its semimonopoly, and by a slew of domestic carriers to make inroads, was a devastating blow. In one of the closing acts of his Administration, Lyndon Johnson distributed routes in tall Texas order. Though Nixon reviewed the case and modified the cast of winners, the net result was the same: five additional carriers on the California–Hawaii route Pan Am had shared with United; two to serve the Orient, formerly divided between Pan Am and Northwest, and one to operate to the South Pacific, where Pan Am already battled Qantas and Air New Zealand.

On every sector of its route system, Pan Am was crowded by competition from foreign and U.S. carriers, and without compensatory rights to draw traffic from America's inland cities. Pan Am, said Jeeb Halaby, was "an airline without a country."

In the first six months of 1969, Pan Am reported a loss of $12.7 million, which would double by the end of the year. The board voted to omit the dividend for the second quarter—a lugubrious step last taken in 1939 prior to the Whitney takeover.

Harold Gray's strength was ebbing. By the cruelest coincidence, he was waging a valiant struggle against cancer as the company was beginning to hemorrhage. "I want to get the company profitable again before I leave," he said to Will Player. "Then I'll go back to my cellar and finish my inventions."

Player answered, "Harold, you have to ask yourself whether by staying you can best serve the company and yourself." Gray was silent.

He grudgingly allowed certain functions to report to Halaby, who showed his impatience to be rid of Gray. "I don't think Jeeb's competent yet. I haven't trained him enough," Harold said when Player pressed him to transfer power.

On November 18, Gray informed the directors he planned to retire in May and proposed to relinquish the functions of chief executive officer to Halaby at once. He was 63 and had three years to live.

With a display of grim vitality, Halaby seized the job he had coveted for so long. He described Pan Am as being "locked in a shrinking box, with the top, bottom, and sides all closing in at once."

Everyone agreed with his diagnosis of the ailment. The symptoms were manifest: a reputation for arrogance, ascribed to poor service aboard the aircraft and to a political legend that reaped vengeance from the C.A.B. and the White House in the form of a surfeit of competition for Pan Am. Its 81,430-mile route system was over-extended—the product of one man's vision of the airline as the carrier of national interest abroad. To believe that Pan Am had to serve Moscow and Pago Pago because it was Pan Am was an illusion of grandeur that could not be sustained without government subsidy or a monopoly of lucrative markets to compensate for the losses on these lines.

The heaviest burden Halaby had to bear was the 747. The first jumbo was delivered on schedule in mid-December, christened by Mrs. Richard Nixon on January 15, 1970, and dispatched on an inaugural flight to London a week later.

The second phase of the jet age, the truly mass airlift precipitated by Juan Trippe, was ushered in during a recession he could not have foreseen. For Pan Am, in possession of twenty-five wide-body planes by the summer of 1970, the economic slump was translated into acres of empty seats.

All the assumptions on which Trippe had made his last grandiose decision were turned upside down. Instead of a 17-percent growth in traffic, the rate of increase slipped to 4.6 percent, while Pan Am had 15.8 percent more seats to fill. The vaunted productivity gains of the 747 were predicated on expanding loads. Unanticipated rises in labor and maintenance expenses and the end of the era of cheap energy caused the direct operating costs of the superjets to soar rather than plummet. The price of jet fuel became a nightmare for airline managers when the Arab oil producers quadrupled their prices in the winter of 1973–74. Several countries engaged in a form of extortion against operators of the U.S.-made jumbo by raising the fees for the use of their airports.

The 747 spelled catastrophe for most of the major airlines of the world. Impelled to follow Trippe's lead in ordering the plane, they were suddenly endowed with Noah's Arks at a point when they were barely able to fill the capacity of prewar flying boats. As its members thrashed about for ways to fill their empty aircraft and also stem competition from the supplemental carriers which were siphoning more than half the international traffic, I.A.T.A. finally agreed to cutting fares. Instead of making straightforward reductions, the cartel instituted so many confusing promotional gimmicks that yields from passenger revenues shrank.

The airlines were not alone in suffering misfortune from the 747. Boeing laid off so many workers, as orders for the plane dried up, that Seattle was designated an economic disaster area. Pratt & Whitney lost $137 million on its accelerated development of the JT9D engine, which was still too weak to power the 747 satisfactorily during the first two years.

Trippe was nominated the culprit for the aviation industry's troubles in the early Seventies. He endured the criticism stoically. "It was the logical next step, don't you see," he said, trotting out figures to bolster his confidence that his judgment would be vindicated in time.

Meanwhile, Pan Am was paying $10 million a month in financing charges for its 747 fleet and supporting facilities. In 1970, the airline lost $47.9 million.

Halaby was unequipped by temperament or prior training to cope with the avalanche of woes cascading upon the company. His response to problems he had had no part in creating was to institute a purge. Three dozen upper-level managers departed in the first two years of the Halaby administration, aggravating the weakness in the executive structure Trippe had bequeathed. Guided by management consultants, he replaced them with outsiders, mostly from other industries. Halaby transferred Charlie Trippe out of the key financial post of treasurer and assigned him to the stylish new function of planning—something that had been contained in his father's head for forty years. He nudged Juan to get off the executive committee of the board and to vacate his office on the forty-sixth floor. Trippe had his papers packed and moved with his secretary to a room on the twenty-third floor.

Under Juan Trippe, Pan Am had been an imperial dictatorship, operated with a token nod to twentieth-century principles of management. Halaby latched on to every current of wind whistling out of the business schools and the manuals of the American Management Association. He gave pep talks to the thirty-nine thousand employees, tape-recorded messages of six minutes' length which they could hear by dialing a special number: "Fellow Pan Americans, this is Jeeb Halaby on the Pan Am line. Don't look upon youth-fare passengers as problems. Look upon them as prospects and love them. We need them."

Applied psychology was then a raging fad in American business. Halaby embraced it as a remedy for Pan Am's manifold ills—which was as effective as rushing a psychiatrist instead of a blood-plasma unit to the stretcher of a soldier whose limbs had just been blown off by a land mine. He hired one psychologist to sit in on top-management meetings and advise him on restructuring the airline. Other psychologists established a company-wide sensitivity-training program that set new benchmarks for ineptitude. A therapist told James Montgomery, vice president—sales, "The people who work for you hate you." Montgomery shot back, "I know that isn't so."

Even with the help of an executive recruiter, Halaby was unable to find a Number Two man to run the company while he dashed to Washington trying to make friends in the Nixon Administration, and desperately looked for a merger partner to give Pan Am the domestic routes it needed more than ever. A trendy device for chief executives reluctant to share power was the Office of the President which Halaby created, parceling operational responsibility among four group vice presidents—all newcomers to Pan Am, and only one an airline veteran. Soon they were at one another's throats competing for promotion.

Pan Am's directors began hearing horror stories about the Halaby administration: the psychology treatment ostensibly embarked upon to lift morale seemed to be inducing a company-wide depression. The gravity of Pan Am's condition was accentuated by the collapse of merger talks Halaby was having with Charles Tillinghast of T.W.A. By every measure, Pan Am's costs and efficiency suffered by comparison with those of T.W.A., which was also a faltering carrier until its domestic business picked up and Tillinghast terminated the discussions.

In September 1971, the directors ordered Halaby to find a president and chief operating officer. On the recommendation of still another management consultant, he chose William T. Seawell, president of Rolls-Royce Aero, Inc., the North American subsidiary of the British engine manufacturer.

Seawell was 53, tall, wavy-haired and just good-looking enough to meet the Pan Am tradition of photogenic executives. His record was a headhunter's dream: a graduate of West Point and the Harvard Law School, commandant of the Air Force Academy, and senior vice president—operations American Airlines before going to Rolls-Royce.

Trippe, kept at a distance of twenty-three floors but still able to work the telephone and attend board meetings, was in anguish at the deterioration of the company. "I made a mistake in hiring Halaby," he told Will Player and the directors he had named to the board.

Pan Am reported a $45.5-million loss for 1971, and an accumulated deficit of $120.3 million for the past three years. One billion dollars in debt was hanging over the company, and the $270-million revolving credit Juan had secured in 1965 had to be renegotiated with the thirty-eight banks by March 31, 1972, or else the outstanding balance became a one-year term loan. The bankruptcy of the Penn Central made bank-

ers and corporate directors nervously aware of their fiduciary responsibilities to stockholders and the personal liabilities they could incur for
inattention.

Ironically, it was one of the directors Halaby had picked—Donald
M. Kendall, chief executive officer of PepsiCo and friend of Richard
Nixon—who led the campaign to dump him. At a special meeting of
the board called on March 22, 1972, the directors declined to give
Halaby a vote of confidence and accepted his resignation.

Capitalizing on his Syrian ancestry, Halaby set up a venture-
capital firm to provide aviation support services in the Middle East.
One of the clients he attracted was Alia, the Jordanian airline. There
his daughter Lisa found employment and caught the attention of King
Hussein. After a whirlwind courtship, the monarch and the Princeton
graduate were married, making the ousted chairman of Pan Am the
father-in-law of the ruler of Jordan.

Bill Seawell took up the struggle to save Pan Am. The airline
hemorrhaged for another five years, accumulating losses of $364 mil-
lion from 1969 through 1976.

A deathwatch was posted in 1974. In addition to its several mala-
dies, Pan Am was especially vulnerable to the oil price hikes posted by
the Organization of Petroleum Exporting Countries, since only 6 percent of the fuel consumed by its jets came from price-controlled domestic sources. Pan Am's fuel costs increased by more than 100 percent
that year. In April 1974, Pan Am applied to the C.A.B. for subsidy
relief while it digested the fuel increase and made certain financial
adjustments. The C.A.B. sat on the request and then denied a second,
urgent plea in August. The new Ford Administration reviewed international air policy and came out in opposition to airline subsidies.
Moreover, it was disinclined to guarantee loans for Pan Am, as the
Nixon Administration had encouraged Congress to do for Lockheed to
save the aircraft builder from bankruptcy.

Seawell was grasping at any straw. In late summer, Pan Am's
manager in Teheran relayed the message that officials of Iran Air were
interested in being helpful. A month later, Seawell encountered General Ali M. Khademi, managing director of Iran Air, at the annual
meeting of I.A.T.A. in Montreal.

Khademi said he was puzzled by the apparent failure of the U.S.
Government to recognize how important Pan Am was to the national
interest. Seawell nodded. "Do I have your permission to speak to the
Shah about helping you?" the General asked. Seawell nodded again. A
few days later, Khademi called him from Australia, where he was trav-

eling with the Shah, and said that His Majesty was favorably disposed to an infusion of cash.

Seawell dispatched Player to Teheran for an exploratory talk, the substance of which Will reported to Ambassador Richard Helms, who listened without comment. A few days later in New York, Player received a telephone call from Washington. "How can you be entertaining such a proposal?" an assistant secretary of state upbraided him. "Don't you know that Pan Am is vested with the national interest?"

"We've been waiting a year for someone to acknowledge this," Will replied acidly. That ended the conversation as well as any move by Washington to call a halt to the negotiations.

Pan Am executives shuttled back and forth between New York and Teheran for months until the broad outlines of a plan emerged. The Government of Iran would extend to the airline a ten-year loan of $245 million for capital restructuring through the repurchase, at a substantial discount, of Pan Am notes held by U.S. insurance companies. Iran would also acquire a 55-percent interest in its Inter-Continental Hotels Corp. subsidiary for $55 million, and receive warrants to buy 6 million shares of Pan Am stock at $2.50 a share. The warrants represented a call on about 13 percent of Pan Am stock. A government representative, presumably Khademi, would take a seat on the Pan Am board of directors.

The agreement was concluded in mid-May 1975 subject to the approval of the Shah, which Seawell was led to believe was imminent. After a series of bewildering reports from the Iranian capital during the summer, Seawell realized that the deal was moribund. Why, he would never really know. According to one theory, the monarchy was overcommitted to defense and industrial projects, and as the country's oil revenues slumped, cutbacks were made in expenditures across the board.

Less than four years later, the Shah was overthrown. Macabre speculation followed as to what might have happened if the agreement had been consummated and the U.S. Government ultimately had to contend with Ayatollah Khomeini as part owner of Pan Am.

Denied fresh capital from an Iranian source, Seawell instituted further belt-tightening measures at Pan Am and set about renegotiating loans. In October, a group of executives met secretly to lay contingency plans for bankruptcy. The plans were never activated. After Pan Am put up additional aircraft as collateral, the banks provided credits to keep the company going another year.

Hoping to shrink the airline to more efficient size, Seawell performed drastic surgery on the route system. Pan Am withdrew from

Paris, Vienna, Moscow and most of the Caribbean. Money-losing services, which amounted to one-fourth of the system, were cut off. He reduced the personnel by one-third. In an outpouring of pride and loyalty, the remaining employees rallied and formed AWARE, a self-improvement and political-action group which raised money to publicize the airline's plight in newspaper advertisements and lobby its cause in Washington.

It was there in the nation's capital that Trippe's legacy was hardest to erase. The government bureaucracy and the legislators on the Hill had long memories about Pan Am, the imperial airline.

How long was Pan Am to do penance for the chosen instrument? If it was to survive, it had to secure the domestic connection Trippe had foreclosed with his hedgehog fixation on an international monopoly. Was it necessary for Pan Am to repudiate its founding father?

Seawell believed it was not. He tried to be considerate of Trippe. "He's one of the great pioneers," he said. When Juan retired from the board in 1975, Bill invited him to keep attending the meetings and to go on the directors' junkets abroad.

Lindbergh left the Pan Am board at the mandatory age of 72 in the spring of 1974. He was weary from a lingering malaise diagnosed a few months later as terminal cancer of the lymphatic system.

"Don't you want to talk to Juan?" Sam Pryor asked Charles as he lay for almost a month at Columbia Presbyterian Hospital in New York. "No," he said. "He would talk too long."

Charles wanted to die in the house he and Anne had built on a cliff overlooking the sea at Maui, one of the smaller Hawaiian islands, which Sam had staked out as a base for himself and Mary Tay and his menagerie. Lindbergh, a naturalist, took exception to the three gibbon apes Sam indulged as grandchildren, giving them the run of his house and feeding them from his plate at the dinner table. "Those goddamn apes," Charles said, using rare profanity about his neighbors; Sam had sold 5 acres from his Kipahulu Ranch to the Lindberghs for their retreat.

On a Friday evening in August, Charles called Sam from his hospital bed and asked him to make arrangements for him to go to Hawaii the next day. Pryor was unable to raise anyone at the Pan Am offices or to reach the executives at home. His day had passed at Pan Am.

He had better luck with United Airlines. The New York manager had a berth installed on a 747 bound for Honolulu for the Lone Eagle to make his last, anonymous flight, accompanied by Anne and their son Land.

During the next nine days at Maui, Charles slipped toward death, making detailed preparations for a simple funeral service. On the morning of August 26, he drew his last breath. Three hours later, he was buried in a plain coffin of eucalyptus wood in a nearby church- yard. The plot, a gift from Sam, adjoined the final resting place of one of Pryor's beloved apes.

As if the agony of watching the upheaval in the company that had been his lifeblood and knowing others thought he was to blame were not enough, Trippe's other dreams were crumbling too.

The Eleuthera Island paradise into which he poured some of his airline profits came near to debacle. Here too, the causes were unpre- dictable—economic recessions and political upheaval in the Bahamas. Stock in South Eleuthera Properties which had originally commanded a market price of $4 to $6 was quoted at 20 cents.

Juan completely dominated the management of the venture from the beginning, and as conditions went from bad to worse, the "dicta- tor," as he had laughingly been called in better days, imposed his solutions to problems. "Trippe can't be in a situation unless he runs everything one hundred percent," said Dave Ingalls, one of the un- happy investors, speaking from experience. Juan had settled his island with powerful men who were also accustomed to running things, and when they stood to lose money they rose up in indignation and de- posed him, as the directors of Pan Am had done in a time of financial stress. They left him with the title of chairman of the board, shorn of power, while others set about rehabilitating the enterprise.

He behaved honorably. Instead of cutting his losses and walking away from the venture, Trippe made personal contributions to keep it going and remained the largest investor, though a passive observer of the management.

"It's horrible to watch someone lose power," his daughter, Betsy, said.

His son Charles hung on uncomfortably at Pan Am. Juan wanted him there; he was his pipeline into the company. But finally, James H. Maloon, the executive vice president for finance and development, called on Juan and told him that Charlie had to leave. Trippe accepted it, silently.

In June 1977, a New York Airways helicopter ferrying passengers from Kennedy Airport had a freak accident landing on the roof of the Pan Am Building. One of its propeller blades was flung loose and plummeted sixty stories into the home-going traffic, killing a passerby. The prophecy of the environmentalists who had blocked the service for years was fulfilled, and the operation was permanently suspended.

Trippe turned 80. His stooped, pear-shaped figure was seen regularly at the Sky Club and at Business Council meetings. He was honored at Wings Club banquets as a visionary among a dwindling band of pioneers like C. R. Smith of American Airlines and Bill Allen of Boeing—whose company was thriving on sales of the 747, the safest and most efficient transport plane of the century.

Betty was at Juan's side, sapphire eyes blazing, to supply the cues as she had done for fifty-one years. Trippe's peculiar memory was occupied mostly by giants—Churchill, Roosevelt, Marshall—and in his stirring versions of history, he met them as an equal. An audience with Juan Trippe was more than ever like a Pirandello play: what was illusion, what was reality? the listener wondered.

Trippe had had the foresight to demand an equity stake with his rental in the Pan Am Building. In 1969 and 1978, Pan Am exercised its options to increase its ownership interest and bought out the British investors for $15 million, and the remainder from the estate of Erwin Wolfson for $8.6 million. Then it purchased the land under the building from the Penn Central Corporation for $25 million and in July 1980 sold the entire real-estate package, land and building, to the Metropolitan Life Insurance Company for $400 million—the highest price ever paid for a single office building in Manhattan. Pan Am turned a profit on the transaction of more than $294 million. Trippe had been right to favor land over sky for moneymaking purposes over the long term.

In reality, there was to be continuing doubt about Pan Am's viability as an airline.

Shortly before Christmas 1979, President Jimmy Carter approved Pan Am's acquisition of National Airlines, a carrier serving the East Coast from New York to Florida and the West Coast by a Southern transcontinental route. Pan Am entered the Eighties with a domestic artery at last, to pump traffic into its international system; but the prize was too late in coming.

Under a new policy contained in the Airline Deregulation Act of 1978, Pan Am would face more competition than even Trippe had predicted at his most alarmist. Congress ordained that the government cease regulating the airlines. Domestic carriers could be permitted to fly directly from any point in the United States to anywhere in the world. Foreign carriers could have more access to the U.S. interior. The State Department and the C.A.B.—as it prepared to pass out of existence—encouraged them to serve a multitude of inland cities directly, in exchange for promises by their governments to permit competitive pricing. I.A.T.A.'s fare-setting grip was broken.

For Juan Trippe ever to have thought that Pan Am could have it all—that was the illusion.

In September 1980, he was stricken with a massive cerebral hemorrhage and his passing was assumed imminent. Characteristically, he defied probability and kept death waiting for seven months.

His funeral was held at St. James Episcopal Church on an April morning ablaze with sunshine, a perfect day for flying. The service was a pageant for a momentous inaugural journey, from the singing of the Mariner's Hymn to the Apocryphal reading from Ecclesiasticus: "Let us now praise famous men . . . The Lord hath wrought great glory by them through his great power from the beginning . . . men renowned for their power, giving counsel by their understanding, and declaring prophecies . . ."

With the ethereal beauty of love transcendent, Betty walked behind the seven grandsons who bore Trippe's coffin blanketed in the Stars and Stripes.

Acknowledgments

The authors, who happen to be husband and wife, had long been wanting to undertake a collaborative literary effort when the subject of Juan Trippe and Pan Am occurred to them. Marylin Bender, then a business news editor for *The New York Times*, had acquired her passion for flying during her college years from the writings of Antoine de Saint-Exupéry. Selig Altschul, who had served as a chief economic analyst for the Civil Aeronautics Board and in his subsequent career as an independent aviation consultant to industry and government, had become acquainted with most of the titans of the airlines and aircraft manufacturing.

We were both initially intrigued by Pan Am's equivocal nature— a private enterprise with a peculiarly intimate relationship to the United States Government. Most observers, and its own employees, regarded the airline as a quasi-governmental institution, a business wrapped in the American flag. Certainly, Juan Trippe always strove to foster that impression at home and abroad.

An uncommonly secretive man who abhorred personal publicity unless he could control it, he had for years thwarted the writing of an official history of Pan Am. He detested Matthew Josephson's *Empire of the Air*, an unauthorized biography that grew out of a series of articles written for *The Saturday Evening Post* in 1943. Josephson treated Trippe respectfully, although he saw him as a successor, on an international scale, to the nineteenth-century American capitalists whom he had portrayed in an earlier book, *The Robber Barons*. Josephson's view was essentially valid at that stage, and was not seriously impaired by a number of minor factual errors.

Starting in the 1950s, Pan Am, with the encouragement of Charles A. Lindbergh, its technical adviser and later a director, initiated an official-history project. Several writers engaged for this purpose fell by the wayside—one after ten years of research for which the airline expended $265,000. Trippe's lack of cooperation was always the stumbling block.

Following his retirement from the company in 1970, John C. Leslie, vice president—international affairs, devoted five years to the project. In 1976, shortly after we embarked on our independent inquiry, we learned that Trippe had at last consented to an authorized biography. Influenced by his wife's concern about his place in history, he created the Pan American Foundation as a repository for corporate records and a vehicle for reimbursing Leslie and retaining a professional writer. In exchange for the promise of complete access to the records (including the work of previous writers) and to Juan Trippe's memories, Robert Daley agreed to turn over to the foundation a percentage of any royalties resulting from *An American Saga: Juan Trippe and His Pan Am Empire*, which was published in 1980.

While he was cooperating with his chosen biographer, Trippe agreed to be interviewed by the authors of this book, even though he knew he would never be shown a word of their writing in advance of publication. He and his wife, Elizabeth Stettinius Trippe, met us seven times for extensive conversations. Mrs. Trippe granted Marylin Bender three separate interviews (two on the telephone) and lent her several personal scrapbooks. Marylin Bender met once with their daughter, Betsy Trippe Wainwright, and had two interviews on the telephone with Trippe's sister, Louise Trippe Bradlee.

No historians can possibly shun opportunities for contact with the central figure of their study, and the authors appreciate Juan and Betty Trippe's gift of their time. But the meetings proved to be frustrating experiences in that they led to repeated chases down blind alleys. Juan Trippe was volubly responsive to questioning, and his accounts of pivotal events matched what he told Robert Daley. Unfortunately, in several instances they were contradicted by official documents (including his own written statement to a Senate committee) and the testimony of other witnesses to the same events. Such are the pitfalls of oral history.

The authors relied on a variety of sources both printed and oral. The nucleus of interest for this project was an unclassified report in Selig Altschul's files from his C.A.B. days. *Financial History and Organization of Pan American Airways System*, dated March 14, 1934, was compiled for a Senate investigation of airmail contracts and is an unvarnished record of the company's growth during its first half-dozen years.

Also basic to this endeavor were the vast diplomatic and military records of the United States Government pertaining to Pan Am in the National Archives and the official and personal papers of President Franklin D. Roosevelt at Hyde Park, New York, and of General

Henry H. Arnold in the Library of Congress. The private papers of Charles A. Lindbergh in the Yale University Library shed light on Juan Trippe's behavior toward his associates, many of whom confided in Lindbergh, as well as the impressive advice he received from the controversial flier who has been called America's last hero. We are deeply grateful to Anne Morrow Lindbergh for granting us access to her husband's papers and for permission to quote from them.

In July 1979, just when we believed we had exhausted the available founts of research, Juan Trippe suddenly donated his personal papers to the National Air and Space Museum of the Smithsonian Institution. We are thankful to Donald S. Lopez, assistant director of aeronautics, for allowing us to examine them in their packing boxes—an adventure akin to panning gold.

A year later, following the publication of *An American Saga*, steps were taken to dissolve the Pan American Foundation and return the files to the corporate library at Pan Am, where we were permitted to study them. They confirmed and, in regard to a few matters, amplified our independent research. Until then, requests for information contained in corporate records, such as the minutes of significant meetings of the board of directors of Pan Am, were submitted to J. Howard Hamstra, vice president and general counsel, who gave us the information in digest form.

Together and separately, we interviewed more than two dozen Pan Am employees, directors and other associates of Juan Trippe, some of whom have since died. We particularly value our lengthy meeting with the late David K. E. Bruce, diplomat and distinguished public servant, in October 1977.

We are indebted to Willis Player, senior vice president and assistant to the chairman of Pan Am, who afforded our introduction to Juan and Betty Trippe and provided personal insights into the company and the man. Samuel F. Pryor, Trippe's classmate and later his chief lobbyist, Erwin Balluder and Hugo Leuteritz, two authentic pioneers from Pan Am's infancy, and three of later vintage, James H. Smith, Jr., Roger Lewis and Willis Lipscomb, were especially helpful. George B. E. Hambleton furnished precious material about his father, John A. Hambleton. The third member of the founding triumvirate, Cornelius Vanderbilt Whitney, was also most obliging.

Special appreciation is due Althea Lister, retired curator of Pan Am history, and to her successor, Ann Whyte.

The help of several archivists and scholars outside Pan Am was crucial to this book. We could not have gone as far as we did without the guidance of Judith A. Schiff, chief research archivist in the Manuscripts and Archives Section of the Yale University Library; of Milton O. Gustaffson, chief of the Diplomatic Section of the National Archives; of William H. Cunliffe, assistant chief of the Modern Military Branch, Military Archives Division; and of Richard K. Smith, an aviation historian who generously shared the fruits of his research.

We are thankful to Edmund Berkeley, Jr., curator of manuscripts at the Alderman Library of the University of Virginia Library, for arranging permission to quote from the papers of Edward R. Stettinius, Jr., and to Catherine B. Barrett for making the unpublished memoir of her father, Harold M. Bixby, available to us and giving us permission to quote from his letters.

Two mentors and friends emerged from Marylin Bender's past to lend support. Mina Curtiss, in whose memorable writing course at Smith College the seeds of hope and confidence were planted, supplied infusions of courage at several crisis points. Leads for the first chapter were provided by James D. Horan, historian of American outlaws and their police nemeses, who taught Marylin Bender the rudiments of investigative journalism when he was special events editor of the *New York Journal-American* and she a novice reporter.

Valuable legwork was done by Bill Abrams at the Missouri Historical Society, by Jean Christensen at the Harry S Truman Library and by our son, James Altschul, a Harvard undergraduate, in the newspaper and periodical files of the New York Public Library and the New York Society Library and at the Library of Congress. Ruth E. Erlichman, chief of the docket section of the C.A.B., facilitated research into the voluminous cases before that regulatory agency.

Various kinds of assistance must be acknowledged from Michael Altschul, Richard Barkle, Kingman Brewster, William A. M. Burden, Lewis B. Calisch, Joan Cook, Endicott P. Davison, George Dessart, Thomas Flanagan, Stanley Gewirtz, Charles Gordon, Charles Hawkins, Maury Hanson, Margaret Hennig, Seymour Hersh, Anne Jardim, Marilyn Machlowitz, John Marks, Henry Marx, William J. McEvoy, the late Samuel W. Meek, James Montgomery, Carla Jean Montori, Richard E. Mooney, Marvin Parks, Rita Reif, G. Erskine Rice, Arnold Rogow, Irving Roth, Elihu Schott, Robert J. Smith, Robert J. Smith, Jr., Frank Wangeman, Charles C. Watson, Donald West and Joan Whitman.

As always, Ann Elmo was a pillar of strength in addition to acting as literary agent. Vera Klippel transformed the early drafts into legible form, and Lorraine Farrell typed the final manuscript with dispatch and unfailing good cheer.

Bibliography

Acheson, Dean, *Present at the Creation*, W. W. Norton & Company, New York, 1969.

Arnold, H. H., *Global Mission*, Harper & Brothers, New York, 1949.

Baltzell, E. Digby, *The Protestant Establishment*, Random House, New York, 1964.

Beaty, David, *Water Jump*, Harper & Row, New York, 1976.

Berle, Adolph A., Jr., *Navigating the Rapids*, from the papers of Adolph A. Berle, Jr., edited by Beatrice Berle and Travis Beal Jacobs, Harcourt Brace Jovanovich, New York, 1973.

Berlin, Isaiah, *The Hedgehog and the Fox*, Simon and Schuster, New York, 1953.

Bixby, Harold M., *Topside Ricksha*, unpublished memoir, privately printed, 1938.

Borg, Dorothy, *The United States and the Far Eastern Crisis of 1933–38*, Harvard University Press, Cambridge, Mass., 1964.

Braden, Spruille, *Diplomats and Demagogues*, Arlington House, New Rochelle, N.Y., 1971.

Burden, William A. M., *The Struggle for Airways in Latin America*, Council on Foreign Relations, New York, 1943.

Burner, David, *Herbert Hoover*, Alfred A. Knopf, New York, 1979.

Byrnes, Thomas, *Professional Criminals of America*, Casell & Company Ltd., New York, 1886.

Canby, Henry Seidel, *Alma Mater: The Gothic Age of the American College*, Farrar & Rinehart, New York, 1936.

Chittenden, Russell Henry, *History of the Sheffield Scientific School of Yale University*, Yale University Press, New Haven, 1928.

Churchill, Winston, *Their Finest Hour*, Houghton Mifflin Company, Boston, 1949.

———, *The Grand Alliance*, Houghton Mifflin Company, Boston, 1950.

Cole, Wayne S., *Charles A. Lindbergh and the Battle Against American Intervention in World War II*, Harcourt Brace Jovanovich, New York, 1974.

Craven, Wesley Frank, and Cate, James Lea, *The Army Air Forces in World War II, Vol. I, Plans and Early Operations*, The University of Chicago Press, Chicago, 1948; *Vol. VII, Services Around the World*, 1958.

Daley, Robert, *An American Saga: Juan Trippe and His Pan Am Empire*, Random House, New York, 1980.

Dallek, Robert, *Franklin D. Roosevelt and American Foreign Policy, 1932–45*, Oxford University Press, New York, 1979.

Dau, Frederick W., *Dau's New York Blue Book*, 1913, 1926.

Davies, R. E. G., *A History of the World's Airlines*, Oxford University Press, London, 1964.

De Gaulle, Charles, *War Memoirs, Vol. I, The Call to Honour, 1940–42*, Collins, London, 1955.

Delear, Frank J., *Igor Sikorsky*, Dodd, Mead & Company, New York, 1969.

Dessart, George, *Fifty Years After*, film on the Yale Unit made for WCBS-TV, New York, Channel 2, *Eye on New York*, 1966.

Dietrich, Noah, *Howard: The Amazing Mr. Hughes*, Fawcett Publications, Greenwich, Conn., 1972.

Donovan, Robert J., *Conflict and Crisis*, W. W. Norton & Company, Inc., New York, 1977.

Earnest, Ernest, *Academic Procession*, The Bobbs-Merrill Company, Inc., New York, 1953.

Farley, James A., *Jim Farley's Story*, Whittlesey House, McGraw-Hill Book Company, Inc., New York, 1948.

———, *Behind the Ballots*, Harcourt, Brace and Company, New York, 1938.

Fitzgerald, F. Scott, *This Side of Paradise*, Charles Scribner's Sons, New York, 1920.

Fokker, Anthony H. G., and Gould, Bruce, *Flying Dutchman*, Henry Holt and Company, New York, 1931.

Freud, Sigmund, *Standard Edition of the Complete Psychological Works of Sigmund Freud, Vol. XI*, The Hogarth Press, London, 1963.

Freudenthal, Elsbeth E., *The Aviation Business from Kitty Hawk to Wall Street*, The Vanguard Press, New York, 1940.

Friedman, B. H., *Gertrude Vanderbilt Whitney*, Doubleday & Company, Inc., Garden City, N.Y., 1978.

Goerner, Fred, *The Search for Amelia Earhart*, Doubleday & Company, Garden City, N.Y., 1966.

Goldberger, Paul, *The City Observed: New York*, Vintage Books, New York, 1979.

Grew, Joseph C., *Turbulent Era: A Diplomatic Record of 40 Years*, Houghton Mifflin Company, Boston, 1952.

Grooch, William S., *Skyway to Asia*, Longmans, Green and Company, New York, 1936.

———, *Winged Highway*, Longmans, Green and Company, New York, 1938.

———, *From Crate to Clipper*, Longmans, Green and Company, New York, 1939.

Halaby, Najeeb E., *Crosswinds: An Airman's Memoir*, Doubleday & Company, Inc., Garden City, N.Y., 1978.

Hambleton, George B. E., *The Chosen Instrument*, a senior thesis submitted to the Woodrow Wilson School of Public and International Affairs in partial fulfillment of the requirements for the degree of Bachelor of Arts, Princeton University, April 21, 1952.

Havemeyer, Loomis, *Sheff Days and Ways: Undergraduate Activities in the Sheffield Scientific School*, privately published, 1958.

————, *Go to Your Room*, Yale University, privately published, 1960.

Heckscher, August, with Robinson, Phyllis, *When LaGuardia Was Mayor*, W. W. Norton & Company, New York, 1978.

Hersh, Burton, *The Mellon Family*, William Morrow and Company, New York, 1978.

Holbrook, Francis X., *United States National Defense and Trans-Pacific Commercial Air Routes, 1933–41*, dissertation in partial fulfillment of the requirements for the degree of Doctor of Philosophy in the Department of History at Fordham University, New York, 1969.

Holden, Reuben, *Yale: A Pictorial History*, Yale University Press, New Haven, 1967.

Hoover, Herbert, *Memoirs of Herbert Hoover, Vol. II*, The Macmillan Company, New York, 1952.

Horan, James D., *The Pinkertons*, Crown Publishers, Inc., New York, 1967.

Hull, Cordell, *The Memoirs of Cordell Hull* (2 vol.), The Macmillan Company, New York, 1948.

Ickes, Harold L., *The Secret Diary of Harold L. Ickes, Vol. III, The Lowering Clouds, 1939–41*, Simon and Schuster, New York, 1954.

Ingells, Douglas J., *747: The Story of the Boeing Super Jet*, Aero Publishers, Fallbrook, Calif., 1970.

James, Henry, *The Portrait of a Lady*, Oxford University Press, London, 1947.

Johnson, Owen, *Stover at Yale*, Frederick A. Stokes Company, New York, 1912.

Josephson, Matthew, *The Robber Barons*, Harcourt, Brace and Company, New York, 1934.

————, *Empire of the Air*, Harcourt, Brace and Company, New York, 1944.

Kelly, Charles J., Jr., *The Sky's the Limit*, Coward-McCann, New York, 1963.

Kirkpatrick, Lyman B., Jr., *The Real CIA*, The Macmillan Company, New York, 1968.

Kuter, Laurence S., *The Great Gamble: The Boeing 747*, The University of Alabama Press, University, Ala., 1973.

LaFarge, Oliver, *The Eagle in the Egg*, Houghton Mifflin Company, Boston, 1949.

Lanier, Henry Wysham, *The Far Horizon*, Alfred A. Knopf, New York, 1933.

Lash, Joseph P., *Roosevelt and Churchill, 1939–41*, W. W. Norton & Company, Inc., New York, 1976.

Leary, William M., Jr., *The Dragon's Wings*, The University of Georgia Press, Athens, 1976.

Lindbergh, Anne Morrow, *North to the Orient*, Harcourt, Brace & World, Inc., New York, 1935.

————, *Hour of Gold, Hour of Lead: Diaries and Letters, 1929–1932*, Harcourt Brace Jovanovich, New York, 1973.

————, *Locked Rooms and Open Doors: Diaries and Letters, 1933–1935*, Harcourt Brace Jovanovich, New York, 1974.

————, *The Flower and the Nettle: Diaries and Letters, 1936–1939*, Harcourt Brace Jovanovich, New York, 1976.

————, *War Within and Without: Diaries and Letters, 1939–1944*, Harcourt Brace Jovanovich, New York, 1980.

Lindbergh, Charles A., *The Spirit of St. Louis*, Charles Scribner's Sons, New York, 1953.

————, *The Wartime Journals of Charles A. Lindbergh*, Harcourt Brace Jovanovich, New York, 1970.

————, *Autobiography of Values*, Harcourt Brace Jovanovich, New York, 1977.

Lissitzyn, Oliver James, *International Air Transport and National Policy*, Council on Foreign Relations, New York, 1942.

Loening, Grover, *Our Wings Grow Faster*, Doubleday, Doran & Company, Garden City, N.Y., 1935.

————, *Takeoff into Greatness*, G. P. Putnam's Sons, New York, 1968.

Mansfield, Harold, *Vision*, Duell, Sloan and Pearce, New York, 1956.

Miller, John Andrew, *Air Diplomacy: The Chicago Civil Aviation Conference of 1944 in Anglo-American Wartime Relations and Post-War Planning*, a dissertation to the faculty of the graduate school of Yale University for the degree of Doctor of Philosophy, 1971.

Mitchell, William, *Memoirs of World War I*, Random House, New York, 1960.

Mosley, Leonard, *Lindbergh*, Doubleday & Company, Garden City, N.Y., 1976.

Munro, Dana Gardner, *The Latin American Republics*, D. Appleton–Century Company, New York, 1942.

Nettleton, George Henry, *Yale in the World War*, edited by George Henry Nettleton, Yale University, New Haven, 1925.

Newton, Wesley Phillips, *The Perilous Sky*, University of Miami Press, Coral Gables, 1978.

New York Social Register, Social Register Association, New York, annual editions 1908 through 1979.

O'Neill, Ralph A., with Hood, Joseph F., *A Dream of Eagles*, Houghton Mifflin Company, Boston, 1973.

Paine, Ralph D., *The First Yale Unit: A Story of Naval Aviation* (2 vol.), The Riverside Press, Cambridge, 1925.

Patterson, James T., *Mr. Republican*, Houghton Mifflin Company, Boston, 1972.

Phelps, William Lyon, *Autobiography with Letters*, Oxford University Press, New York, 1939.

Pierson, George W., *Yale: College and University, 1871–1937, Vol. I*, Yale University Press, New Haven, 1952.

Pogue, Forrest C., *George C. Marshall: Ordeal and Hope*, The Viking Press, New York, 1965.

Pudney, John, *The Seven Skies*, Putnam, London, 1959.

Quezon, Manuel Luis, *The Good Fight*, D. Appleton–Century Company, New York, 1946.

Ray, Deborah W., *Pan American Airways and the Trans-African Air Base Program of World War II*, dissertation for the Doctor of Philosophy degree, New York University, January, 1973.

Rickenbacker, Edward V., *Rickenbacker*, Prentice-Hall, Inc., Englewood Cliffs, N.J., 1967.

Roseberry, C. R., *The Challenging Skies*, Doubleday & Company, Garden City, N.Y., 1966.

Ross, Walter S., *The Last Hero*, Harper & Row, New York, 1964.

Rowe, Basil, *Under My Wings*, The Bobbs-Merrill Company, Inc., New York, 1956.

Saint-Exupéry, Antoine de, *Vol de Nuit*, Librairie Gallimard, Paris, 1931.

Schlesinger, Arthur M., *Political and Social Growth of the American People*, The Macmillan Company, New York, 1941.

Schlesinger, Arthur M., Jr., *The Age of Roosevelt: Vol. II, The Coming of the New Deal*, Houghton Mifflin Company, Boston, 1958.

Sherwood, Robert E., *Roosevelt and Hopkins*, Harper & Brothers, New York, 1948.

Sikorsky, Igor, *The Story of the Winged S*, Dodd, Mead & Company, New York, 1967.

Smith, Henry Ladd, *Airways*, Alfred A. Knopf, New York, 1942.

————, *Airways Abroad*, The University of Wisconsin Press, Madison, 1950.

Stettinius, Edward R., Jr., *Lend-Lease, Weapon for Victory*, The Macmillan Company, New York, 1944.

Swanberg, W. A., *Luce and His Empire*, Charles Scribner's Sons, New York, 1972.

Taylor, Frank J., *High Horizons*, McGraw-Hill Book Company, New York, 1951.

Thayer, Frederick C., Jr., *Air Transport Policy and National Security*, University of North Carolina Press, Chapel Hill, 1965.

Trippe, J. T., *Ocean Air Transport*, 29th Wilbur Wright Memorial Lecture delivered before the Royal Aeronautical Society, London, June 17, 1941.

Truman, Harry S, *Memoirs: Vol. I, Year of Decisions*, Doubleday & Company, Inc., Garden City, N.Y., 1955.

Turner, P. St. John, *Pictorial History of Pan American World Airways*, Ian Allen, London, 1973.

Warner, Edward Pearson, *The Early History of Air Transportation*, a lecture at Norwich University, November 21, 1937.

Warner, W. Lloyd, and Abegglen, James, *Big Business Leaders in America*, Harper & Brothers, New York, 1955.

Wassenbergh, H. A., *Post-War International Civil Aviation Policy and the Law of the Air*, 2nd edition, Martinus Nijhoff, The Hague, 1962.

Weber, Max, *The Protestant Ethic and the Spirit of Capitalism*, translated by Talcott Parsons, Charles Scribner's Sons, New York, 1958.

Werth, Léon, *La Vie de Saint-Exupéry*, Éditions du Seuill, Paris, 1948.

White, William Allen, *Calvin Coolidge*, The Macmillan Company, New York, 1925.

Whitney, C. V., *High Peaks*, The University Press of Kentucky, Lexington, 1977.

Willkie, Wendell L., *One World*, Simon and Schuster, New York, 1943.

Young, Arthur N., *China and the Helping Hand*, Harvard University Press, Cambridge, 1963.

CONGRESSIONAL HEARINGS AND REPORTS

Black Hearings
U.S. Senate Special Committee on Investigation of Air Mail and Ocean Mail Contracts, 73rd Congress, 2d Session, 1934.

C.A.A. Hearings
U.S. House of Representatives Committee on Interstate and Foreign Commerce, 75th Congress, 3d Session, 1938, "To Create a Civil Aeronautics Authority."

C.A.A. Report
U.S. House of Representatives, 75th Congress, 3d Session, Conference Report, June 7, 1938, including Civil Aeronautics Act of 1938.

Celler Hearings
U.S. House of Representatives Antitrust Subcommittee of the Com-

mittee on the Judiciary, 84th Congress, 2d Session, 1956, "Monopoly Problems in Regulated Industries."

Celler Report
U.S. House of Representatives Antitrust Subcommittee of the Committee on the Judiciary, 85th Congress, 1st Session, Report on Airlines, April 5, 1957.

Chosen Instrument Hearings
U.S. Senate Subcommittee on Aviation of the Committee on Interstate and Foreign Commerce, 80th Congress, 1st Session, 1947, "Consolidation of International Air Carriers."

Church Report
U.S. Senate Select Committee to Study Governmental Operations with Respect to Intelligence Activities, 94th Congress, 2d Session, Final Report, April 14, 1976.

Crane Report
U.S. House of Representatives Committee on Post Offices and Post Roads, 72nd Congress, 2d Session, 1933, Report 2087.

Farley Report
U.S. Senate Special Committee on Investigation of Air Mail and Ocean Mail Contracts, 74th Congress, 1st Session, Postmaster General's Report to the President, 1935.

McCarran Hearings
U.S. Senate Subcommittee on Aviation of the Committee on Commerce, 79th Congress, 1st Session, 1945, "To Create the All-American Flag Line, Inc."

McKellar Hearings
U.S. Senate Committee on Post Office and Post Roads, 73rd Congress, 2d Session, 1934.

Magnuson Hearings
U.S. Senate Committee on Commerce, 88th Congress, 1st Session, 1963, "International Air Transportation Rates."

Post Office Hearings
U.S. House of Representatives Committee on Post Offices and Post Roads, 70th Congress, 1st Session, 1928.

Harris Hearings
U.S. House of Representatives Subcommittee on Transportation and Aeronautics of the Committee on Interstate and Foreign Commerce, 89th Congress, 1st Session, 1965.

PUBLIC RECORDS AND PRIVATE PAPERS
(with abbreviations cited in the source notes)

National Archives and Records Service, Washington, D.C.

Diplomatic Branch: U.S. State Department Records	US/SD
Military Archives Division:	
Modern Military Records	US/MM
Navy Department	US/MM/A21-5
Army Air Forces	US/MM/AAF
Secretary of War	US/MM/SW
Adjutant General	US/MM/AG
Lend-Lease Administration	US/LLA

Franklin D. Roosevelt Library, Hyde Park, N.Y.
    Franklin D. Roosevelt Papers:
        Official File   FDR/OF
        President's Personal File   FDR/PPF
Harry S Truman Library, Independence, Mo.
    Papers of Harry S Truman: Official File   HST/OF
Library of Congress, Washington, D.C.
    Papers of Henry H. Arnold   HHA
    Papers of Grover Loening   GL
National Air and Space Museum, Smithsonian Institution, Washington, D.C.
    Papers of Juan Terry Trippe   JTT/NASM

Charles A. Lindbergh Papers, Yale University Library, New Haven, Conn.   CAL/YUL
Charles A. Lindbergh Papers, Missouri Historical Society, St. Louis, Mo.   CAL/MHS
Henry L. Stimson Papers, Yale University   HLS/YUL
Edward R. Stettinius, Jr., Papers (#2723), Manuscripts Department, University of Virginia Library, Charlottesville, Va.   ERS
Financial History and Organization of Pan American Airways System, March 14, 1934, unsigned report based on information supplied to the Special Senate Committee on Investigation of Air Mail and Ocean Mail Contracts—from the Selig Altschul Aviation Collection, Transportation History Foundation, University of Wyoming at Laramie   SA/UW
Foreign Relations of the United States, Diplomatic Papers: Department of State memoranda, telegrams and reports of conversations (cited by year and volume)   FR/US
Materials from the files of Pan American World Airways, usually cited with the corporate library file number. The company magazine, *Pan American Air Ways*, was later renamed *New Horizons*.   PAWA

Other abbreviations:

New York Times	NYT
New York Herald Tribune	NYHT
Wall Street Journal	WSJ
Business Week	BW
Newsweek	NW
Pan American Airways	PAA
Juan Terry Trippe	JTT
Betty Trippe	BT
Charles A. Lindbergh	CAL
Samuel F. Pryor	SP
Cornelius V. Whitney	CVW

Interviews with Selig Altschul are cited as SA; with Marylin Bender as MB.

CIVIL AERONAUTICS BOARD CASES

Transatlantic Case
    Pan American Airways Company (of Delaware) Certificate of Public
    Convenience and Necessity, decided 5/17/39, Docket 163, 1 CAA 118.
Bermuda Mail Rate Case
    Pan American Airways Company (of Delaware) Mail Rates, decided
    2/28/40, Docket 37-406 (A)-1, 1 CAA 529.
American Export Case
    American Export Airlines, Inc., Certificate of Public Convenience and
    Necessity, decided 7/12/40, Docket 238, 2 CAB 16.
Matson Case
    Pan American Airways, Inc., et al., Pan American–Matson–Inter-Island
    Contract, decided 7/29/42, Docket 544, 3 CAB 540.
Latin American Rate Case
    Pan American Airways, Inc., et al., Latin American Rate Case, decided
    8/28/42, Docket 298, 3 CAB 657.
Panagra Terminal Case
    Panagra Terminal Investigation, decided 5/24/44, Docket 779, 4 CAB
    670.
CNAC Case
    Acquisition of China National Aviation Corporation by Pan American
    Airways Corporation, decided 9/29/44, Docket 1351, 6 CAB 143.
North Atlantic Route Case
    Northeast Airlines, Inc., et al., North Atlantic Route Case, decided
    6/1/45, Docket 855, 6 CAB 319.
American Airlines Control Case
    American Airlines, Inc., Control of American Export Airlines, Inc.,
    decided 6/1/45, Docket 1346, 6 CAB 371.
Hawaiian Case
    Hawaiian Airlines, Ltd., et al., Hawaiian Case, decided 5/17/46,
    Docket 851, 7 CAB 83.
Added Latin American Case
    Additional Service to Latin America, decided 5/17/46, Docket 525, 6
    CAB 857.
Pacific Case
    Northwest Airlines, Inc., et al., Pacific Case, decided 6/20/46, Docket
    547, 7 CAB 209.
Alaska Mail Rate Case
    Pan American Airways, Inc., Alaska Mail Rates, decided 7/9/47, Docket
    1499, 8 CAB 244.
U.S. Lines Case
    Pan American Airways, Inc., and John W. Hanes, Interlocking Rela-
    tionship, decided 10/20/47, Docket 2114, 8 CAB 617.
North Atlantic Route Transfer Case
    North Atlantic Route Transfer Case, decided 7/10/50, Docket 3589,
    11 CAB 676.
Domestic Route Case
    Pan American Airways, Inc., Domestic Route Case, decided 8/1/50,
    Docket 1803, 11 CAB 851.
Hughes Tool Case
    Trans World Airlines, Inc., Further Control by Hughes Tool Company,
    decided 10/6/50, Docket 2796, 12 CAB 192.

Notes

PROLOGUE *(pages 9–16)*

Principal source is "Memorandum of Conversation by the Assistant Secretary of State (Berle), November 11, 1943," alluding to meeting held the previous day. (FR/US 1944, Vol. 2.) Welch Pogue told what transpired when Stettinius left the room to SA in interviews 12/15/76 and 1/19/79.

10   "almost as much of a war as the European war": Adolph A. Berle, *Navigating the Rapids*, entry 9/30/40.

12   Hull claustrophobic: *The Memoirs of Cordell Hull, Vol. II.*

13   "Big Bad Wolf": Stettinius letter to JTT 5/20/43 (ERS).

13   "Yale gangster": Benjamin Sonnenberg to authors, 7/26/77; "American Century": editorial *Life* 2/17/41; "globaloney": speech reported in *Congressional Record,* House of Representatives 2/9/43.

14   "I do not trust Pan American": Berle, *op. cit.,* 9/26/40; "Trippe is unscrupulous": *The Secret Diary of Harold L. Ickes: Vol. III, The Lowering Clouds;* "heaven and earth": Berle, *op. cit.,* 9/30/40.

15   "if the front door was open": William A. Patterson, retired chairman of United Airlines, to SA 4/27/76.

15   Lovett on airport-development program: Stimson diaries 4/22/42 (HLS/YUL), Lovett memorandum for Stimson, 7/29/44 (US/MM/ SW); Trippe's machinations: Robert E. Sherwood, *Roosevelt and Hopkins;* Hopkins to Stettinius: 12/31/41 (US/LLA).

PART I: INCORPORATING A DREAM

1: *A RESPECTABLE BEGINNING (pages 19–32)*

The exploits of Bullard and Worth are documented in Thomas Byrnes, *Professional Criminals of America*, and James D. Horan, *The Pinkertons*. Charley's life with Catherine Flynn was reported in NYT 3/22/94, *New York World* 3/21/94, 3/24/94, and *New York Herald* 8/25/97. The *Annuaire Almanach du Commerce*, Didot-Bottin 1871–72, 1873, 1875 (filed at the Paris Police Prefect), lists C. H. Wells, Bar Américain, Scribe 2; the 1874 edition also lists Raymond at the same address.

Copies of birth, death and matrimonial records were obtained from the Municipal Archives of the City of New York, New Jersey Registry of Vital Statistics in Trenton, General Register Office in London; wills from the New York County Surrogate's Court; Lucy and Charles Trippe's wedding is in the matrimonial register of the Church of the Heavenly Rest; Juan's baptismal certificate at Holy Trinity Church, where Monsignor George Murphy spoke of "putting on airs and graces" to MB, 9/5/78.

In a biographical fact sheet JTT gave the authors, his mother's father is listed as J. D. Terry (France), his maternal grandmother as Catherine Louise Flynn (England). BT talked to MB about Juan Terry and his family's Cuban sugar plantations on 11/8/76 and 6/7/77, and JTT's sister, Louise Bradlee, discussed the Terry origins and the railroad-crossing accident on the telephone with MB on 11/22/77.

Kate Terry's whims: NYT 6/10/83, 6/16/83, 5/7/91; Tomaso and Juan Terry's wills: NYT 11/16/86, 11/21/86; *Genealogy of the Trippe Family*, presented by Lucy Trippe to New York Public Library in 1944; *Colonial Families of the United States of America*, edited by George Norbury Mackenzie, Vol. VI, The Seaforth Press, Baltimore, 1917, New York Genealogical Society Library; Frederick Trippe's death: NYT 8/23/91, 8/24/91, 8/26/91; also Louise Bradlee to MB 9/8/78.

Railroad-crossing accident: *New York Herald* 8/24/99, 8/25/99, 8/26/99, 8/27/99, 8/29/99; burial of victims, *New York World* 9/1/99.

Lucy Trippe's right to share in half-sister's estate: *Laws of the State of New York*, 119th Session of the Legislature, 1896, Albany, James B. Lyon, Printer, Vol. I; *Revised Statutes, Codes and General Laws of the State of New York*, 2d edition, by Clarence F. Birdseye, Vol. I, Section 95, para. 13, Baker, Voorhis & Company, New York, 1896.

Louise Bradlee spoke of JTT's childhood and of their parents to MB; the Bovée School is described by C. V. Whitney in *High Peaks*.

30 Hubert Latham: NYT 7/20/09, 7/17/12; Juan's model plane: BT to MB 11/8/76; Governor's Island race: BT *ibid.*, NYT 9/30/09, 10/4/09, 10/5/09; Grover Loening, *Our Wings Grow Faster*.

31 *The Dial 1917*, The Hill School; Charles Trippe's application for Juan's admission to Hill: 3/24/13; character of school: Charles C. Watson, headmaster, to MB 3/7/77, JTT to authors, 7/15/76.

32 *Fifty Years of the Maidstone Club, 1891–1941*, The Maidstone Club, East Hampton, Long Island.

2: THOSE BRIGHT COLLEGE YEARS
(pages 33–51)

Principal sources are the histories of each Yale class, published at graduation and brought up to date at major reunions; *The Banner and Pot Pourri*, 1921–22, a directory of extracurricular activities; the *Yale Daily News* and the *Graphic*, 1919 to 1921.

For Yale tradition and environment before and during World War I: Reuben Holden, *Yale: A Pictorial History*; George W. Pierson, *Yale: College and University, 1871–1937*; Ernest Earnest, *Academic Procession*; William Lyon Phelps, *Autobiography with Letters*; E. Digby Baltzell, *The Protestant Establishment*; Henry Seidel Canby, *Alma Mater: The Gothic Age of the American College*; Russell Henry Chittenden, *History of the Sheffield Scientific School of Yale University*; Loomis Havemeyer, *Sheff Days and Ways, Go to Your Room*; George Henry Nettleton, *Yale in the World War*, Vol. II.

33 "Bright College Years," *History of the Class of 1920S*.

34 "Whiffenpoof Song" is a play on "Gentlemen Rankers," Rudyard Kipling, *Departmental Ditties and Ballads and Barrack Room Ballads*, Doubleday, Page & Company, Garden City, N.Y., 1913.

35 Nickname Wang: JTT to authors, 7/15/76; "Cuban connections": Marshall Root, Jr., to MB 8/7/78.

39 Yale Naval Aviation Unit: Endicott Davison to authors, 4/22/76; *Fifty Years After*, WCBS-TV, 1966; Ralph D. Paine, *The First Yale Unit, a Story of Naval Aviation*.

42 Horseplay of Di and Dave: Ingalls told SA, 9/29/76.

43 On 9/22/76 JTT told authors of failing physical exam and said F.D.R. was his cousin—a statement he amended on 6/7/77 to a kinship between Woolsey and Roosevelt. He described his enlistment and naval career on 7/15/76.

44 Luce and Hadden: W. A. Swanberg, *Luce and His Empire*.

45 SP to authors, 8/9/76.

46 "You hardly spoke to people at Sheff": CVW to MB, 5/24/76; fails color test: Whitney, *op. cit.*

47 Whitney's mother follows him: B. H. Friedman, *Gertrude Vanderbilt Whitney*; "fatal blue eyes": *ibid.*; accident: NYT 11/25/19.

47 Breach-of-promise suit: NYT 3/6/21, 1/9/23, 6/28/25, 1/19/23, 4/18/29, 5/30/29; Friedman, *op. cit.*; "Wang wasn't very talkative": Root to MB 8/7/78; Bradlee to MB 11/22/77.

50 Charles Trippe's death: NYT 7/24/20, 7/26/20, BT to MB, 9/22/76, Bradlee to MB 11/22/77; Trippe & Company bankruptcy: NYT 8/25/21; Lucy in mourning: Bradlee to MB 9/8/78.

50 JTT spoke proudly of his football and crew activities to the authors, 7/15/76, and of the *Graphic's* financial success.

51 Santayana: Pierson, *op. cit.*; to Lee, Higginson: JTT to authors, 7/15/76.

3: *WAS THERE AN AVIATION BUSINESS?*
(*pages 52–64*)

A principal source is Edward P. Warner, *The Early History of Air Transportation.*

52 "Thus aviation, too, which in our day is at last achieving its aim, has its infantile erotic roots." *Standard Edition of the Complete Psychological Works of Sigmund Freud*, Vol. XI.

54 Gun mounts at Le Bourget: Loening, *op. cit.*

55 Léon Werth, *La Vie de Saint-Exupéry*; Oliver James Lissitzyn, *International Air Transport and National Policy.*

57 "We were born to the air": CVW to MB 5/24/76.

57 CVW to MB, *ibid.*; "Juan Trippe didn't have any money," David K. E. Bruce told the authors on 10/1/77 during a long interview that is the source for further attributions in the book.

58 John Hambleton was described by Bruce, *ibid.*; by JTT to authors, 7/15/76, 5/25/78; by BT to MB 1/13/78; by George Carey to MB, 11/18/77, 5/2/78.

58 Hambleton's war record: NYT 5/31/18; letter to the editor of the Baltimore *Sun* by William Mitchell, 6/12/29; letter from Merian C. Cooper to Wolfgang Langewiesche, 5/31/61 (given to authors by George B. E. Hambleton).

59 Founding of *Time*: Swanberg, *op. cit.*

60 Details of the Long Island Airways venture are taken from correspondence in JTT/NASM, and from a letter Trippe wrote on March 10, 1934, to an investigator for the Black Committee; also in JTT/NASM. Robins' father irate: JTT to authors 5/25/78.

60 Stunt fliers: NYT 7/13/24, 7/24/24, 7/25/24; rumrunners: NYT 5/11/24; JTT's Pierce Arrow: BT to MB 1/13/78.

61 JTT to authors 5/25/78.

62 J. Terry Trippe testifies: NYT 1/18/25.

62 Odell and Spencer: JTT to authors, 5/25/78; undated subscription agreement for Eastern Air Transport (JTT/NASM); Anthony H. G. Fokker and Bruce Gould, *Flying Dutchman.*

63 Profile of Edward R. Stettinius, Jr.: *Time* 12/11/44, obituary NYT 11/1/49; biographical data on the elder Stettinius: ERS.

64 JTT meets Elizabeth Stettinius: BT to MB, 7/15/76, 6/7/77.

64 Betty's trust fund: ERS; "until Juan has a business": BT to MB 7/15/76; Long Island Airways account in the Bank of New York in 1933 (JTT/NASM).

4: MAIL CARRIER (pages 65–77)

65   Warner, *op. cit.*

65   JTT bombards Kelly: JTT to authors, 6/7/77; "U.S. Aviation and the
Air Mail," *Fortune* May 1934; Clement M. Keys: obituary NYT
1/13/52 and in William M. Leary, Jr., *The Dragon's Wings.*

66   Unsigned memo dated 4/9/25 proposing organization of air-transport company to obtain contract under the Kelly Act (JTT/NASM).

67   Letter from JTT to Spencer with draft of subscription agreement for
Eastern Air Transport, Inc., 7/28/25; memo of agreement regarding
participation in Eastern Air Transport alludes to purchase of stock
of Colonial Airlines, 8/26/25 (JTT/NASM); incorporation of
Eastern Air Transport 9/12/25, name changed to Colonial Air Transport 10/5/25 (PAWA, 20.04.00); merger announcement: NYT 12/
15/25; award of airmail.routes: *Fortune, loc. cit.*

67   Billy Mitchell's career: H. H. Arnold, *Global Mission,* and in Wesley
Frank Craven and James Lea Cate, *The Army Air Forces in World
War II,* Vol. I.

68   Morrow Board findings: NYT 12/3/25, and in *C.A.A. Hearings.*

68   Warner, *op. cit.*

68   Juan attracts subscribers: JTT to authors, 5/25/78; Whitney marriage: *New York World* 3/5/23; Whitney enters business: CVW to
MB 5/24/76.

69   JTT's salary: letter to Black Committee investigator, *op. cit.*

70   JTT told authors about Colonial Air Transport and the voting trust
on 11/8/76 and 5/25/78.

70   JTT instructs Bruno: Matthew Josephson, *Empire of the Air.*

70   Havana trip related to authors by JTT 5/25/78 and by BT to MB
4/26/78; also described in 4/15/44 memo by George Dacy to the
P.A.A. public-relations department, and in notes by the Wright mechanic Kenneth Boedecker in July 1967 (PAWA 10.06.00).

71   "where people pay four hundred dollars": Josephson, *op. cit.*; Alaska
venture: JTT to authors, 5/25/78.

72   JTT recounted to authors on 5/25/78 the friction between the New
York and New England factions.

72   Single-engine mail planes versus trimotor passenger planes: testimony
of Frederick Rentschler, *Black Hearings,* Part 4, p. 1811.

72   JTT reported meeting with Glover in letter to Hambleton, 6/19/26
(PAWA 20.07.00).

73   Press release announcing start of service 7/1/26 (JTT/NASM); JTT
sends Betty first-day cover: BT to MB 9/22/76; problems mount:
Hartford Times 11/6/26, 11/17/26.

74   JTT and O'Ryan: Josephson, *op. cit.*; O'Ryan appointment, NYT 9/20/26; JTT letter to Hambleton 8/9/26 (PAWA 50.08.03).

74   JTT memoranda on Buffalo survey, 9/14/26, 11/11/26 (PAWA 20.12.00); competition for Chicago bid: NYT 1/14/27, 1/24/27; additional resources: NYT 11/18/26, 11/24/26; new subscribers: JTT letter to Robert Ramsdell of Buffalo, 3/4/27 (PAWA 20.12.00); JTT put in all he had from father's estate: BT to MB 1/13/78; O'Ryan letter to JTT 12/20/26 treating him as lackey: JTT to Irving Bullard, 1/18/27.

75   JTT whistling in dark: JTT letter to Hambleton 12/2/26 (PAWA 50.08.03).

75   "We are running in the hole": JTT to Howard Coonley 3/9/27; feuding over the bidding reviewed by JTT in letter to Reginald Taylor 5/2/27 (PAWA 20.12.00); recourse to the voting trust: JTT to authors 6/7/77, 5/25/78.

77   JTT told authors on 5/25/78 that Trumbull agreed to buy him and his investors out and that "we made four times what we put in." Not only is this unlikely considering Colonial's straitened condition, but in his statement to the Black Committee he wrote, "My second venture in air transport in connection with Colonial Air Transport, Inc. in 1926 ended in a loss of more than $24,000."

77   Juan and Betty walk on Park Avenue: BT to MB 9/22/76.

5: *WHAT EVERYONE WAS WAITING FOR*
(pages 78–88)

79   JTT told authors on 8/11/76 that he observed Lindbergh's takeoff, and later that of Richard Byrd, and described the Lindbergh event in a speech to the Wings Club on May 20, 1977, the fiftieth anniversary of the flight. Lindbergh's account is in *The Spirit of St. Louis*; the circumstances surrounding the event are chronicled by Walter S. Ross, *The Last Hero*, and Leonard Mosley, *Lindbergh*.

79   JTT accepts invitation to Brevoort, 6/15/27 (CAL/YUL); millionaire friends to guard him: letter from Harry Davison to CAL 11/4/27 (CAL/MHS).

80   "We've got to get to him": CVW to MB 5/24/76; "orgy of airmindedness," Warner, *op. cit.*; stock-market boom, Elsbeth Freudenthal, *The Aviation Business from Kitty Hawk to Wall Street*.

81   Loening, *op. cit.*; incestuous relationships documented in the *McKellar Hearings*, p. 76 ff.

81   Richard F. Hoyt: obituary NYT 3/8/35.

81   Hoyt as womanizer: Harold R. Harris to authors 12/7/77; "straighten out Colonial mess": JTT to Hambleton 8/16/27 (JTT/NASM); O'Ryan willing to sell: NYT 8/3/27.

81   Organizing another company: JTT letter and memo to Buffalo investors 6/21/27, 7/5/27, minutes of Aviation Corporation of America board meeting 7/9/27 (PAWA 20.02.00); JTT letter to William

82   Beckers 3/6/28 (JTT/NASM); "we had great faith": CVW to MB 5/24/76.

82   Hambleton with JTT and friend: Cooper letter, *op. cit.*

84   Genesis of Pan American Airways is related in Arnold, *op. cit.*, and in HHA.

84   Florida Airways: Edward V. Rickenbacker, *Rickenbacker.*

85   Details of the coming together of the different groups is in *Financial History and Organization of Pan American Airways System*, March 14, 1934 (SA/UW).

85   Bevier on Hoyt's yacht: Ralph A. O'Neill, *A Dream of Eagles*; 40½¢ bid: *Farley Report*; Whitney's contribution: CVW's press releases 8/18/40 and 6/2/41 (NYT Morgue); recollections about André Priester (PAWA 50.06.02).

86   Montgomery to Arnold: 6/18/27, 7/19/27, 7/27/27, retrospective account 1/22/29; Bevier wrote Arnold 7/22/27 that they were "faced with a proposition of making substantial concessions to rival Air Lines in order to obtain the Government contract from Washington" (HHA).

86   Hoyt misgivings about JTT: Harris to authors 11/19/77; also William Van Dusen interview with John Leslie 10/24/72 (PAWA 50.22.01), Althea Lister to MB 10/26/78; file on Atlantic, Gulf & Caribbean Airways board meeting (PAWA 20.01.01).

87   "Story of PAA's First Flight" by George Dacy (PAWA 10.06.00), also recounted by Josephson, *op. cit.*, and Robert Daley, *An American Saga: Juan Trippe and His Pan Am Empire.*

88   JTT cables Betty: BT to MB 9/22/76.

PART II: LATIN AMERICA

6: *BEHIND THE SCENES (pages 91–106)*

91   Keys: NYT 10/31/48.

91   William Allen White, *Calvin Coolidge*; David Burner, *Herbert Hoover.*

93   Interdepartmental committee report: Wesley Phillips Newton, *The Perilous Sky.*

93   Hambleton's meeting with Mellon recounted in his letter to JTT 12/2/27 (JTT/NASM).

95   "Mr. Trippe, of course, was a friend of Mr. Glover's": testimony of R. L. Johns, *Black Hearings*, Part 4; Glover obituary, NYT 5/1/56.

95   "giving the government a chance to make money": JTT to authors, 5/25/78; testimony of Glover (*Post Office Hearings*).

96   Preparing for bidding on Latin American routes: JTT memo 2/1/28 (PAWA 20.01.01); JTT letter to Beckers, 3/16/28 (JTT/NASM).

96   Beckers to JTT 3/21/28 (JTT/NASM); P.A.A. to Havana: NYT 1/17/28.

97   Lindbergh's Central American flight extensively reported in NYT from 12/29/27 to 2/13/28 with dispatches by CAL; he described flight conditions in letter to Wolfgang Langewiesche, 11/19/67 (CAL/YUL).

98   Hambleton to CAL 2/20/29 (CAL/YUL).

98   The awarding of all the foreign airmail routes is documented in the *Farley Report.*

99   West Indian Aerial Express (PAWA 20.09.00) and Basil Rowe: *Under My Wings.*

99   On 7/11/28, JTT described his meeting with Glover in telegrams to Hoyt, CVW and George Mixter of Stone and Webster, assuring them the Puerto Rican contract would be obtained (JTT/NASM).

100   Acquisition of West Indian Aerial Express: *Financial History, etc., op. cit.*

100   "Dear Slim" letter undated except for "Saturday afternoon" (CAL/YUL); CAL letter to Kelly: NYT 2/19/29; Kelly Act amendment: P.A.A. collected $426,142 in illegal payments for return trips before it was passed (*Farley Report*).

101   "Too often, I'm afraid, we wrote not to reveal but to conceal," Van Dusen told Leslie 10/72 (PAWA 50.22.01); "The Story of Pan-American, America's International Air System," a glowing account by W. I. Van Dusen, *Air Transportation* 1/5/29.

102   Engagement announcement: NYT 1/26/28; "so serious and full of zeal": BT to MB, 1/13/78; "it's not who your ancestors were": BT to MB, 8/11/76.

102   The wedding, NYT 6/17/28, described by BT to MB, 11/8/76, 1/13/78.

103   JTT and the office were described to MB by Althea Lister 9/26/78, 10/26/78, 7/1/80; by Basque freight man, Antonio de Zalduondo, to MB, 9/24/78.

104   JTT's salary: letter to Black Committee investigator, *op. cit.*

105   Creation of Aviation Corporation of the Americas: *Financial History, op. cit.,* memo 6/15/28 (PAWA 20.01.01), JTT to Beckers, *op. cit.*; Hoyt's list: JTT letter to Herbert Hoover, Jr., 3/30/55 (PAWA 30.04.01).

105   Letting friends "in on the good thing": JTT to authors 11/8/76; *Financial History, op. cit.*

106   First annual report of Aviation Corporation of the Americas, issued in June 1929 and covering operations for calendar year 1928, reports income from operations as $298,968 with a net deficit of $29,659; JTT refers to operating loss of $300,000 in his statement to the Black Committee, *op. cit.*

7: THE MEXICAN COMPANY (pages 107–115)

107   William A. M. Burden, *The Struggle for Airways in Latin America.*

108   "engine of foreign trade conquest": Burner, *op. cit.*

109   British prestige: Oliver Lissitzyn, *International Air Transport and National Policy*; Goering statement: Rickenbacker, *op. cit.*

110   Morrow Board export recommendation: Frederick C. Thayer, Jr., *Air Transport Policy and National Policy.*

111   "I have entrée": CVW to MB 5/24/76; Whitney, *High Peaks*; Whitney profile, "The Man Who Is Not His Cousin," by Geoffrey T. Hellman, *The New Yorker* 6/21/41.

111   History of Compañía Mexicana related to authors by Erwin Balluder, 11/27/76, 11/21/77.

112   Glover's assistant told reporters the award would probably go to P.A.A., NYT 2/9/29; JTT testimony, *Celler Hearings.*

113   Hoyt told officers of W. R. Grace he had option on CAL's services to survey Latin American routes: Patchin memo to Iglehart 5/23/28, *Panagra Terminal Case.*

113   CAL told Senators in 1934, "I felt more interest in aviation than in any other field" (*McKellar Hearings*); his agreement with T.A.T. is in letters from C. M. Keys, president, 5/23/28, 6/6/28, 6/14/28 (CAL/MHS).

114   CAL visits JTT: related by JTT to authors, 8/11/76; Breckinridge to JTT, 1/7/29, agreement between CAL and Aviation Corporation of the Americas in letter from JTT, 1/7/29 (CAL/MHS); warrants to CAL: *Financial History, op. cit.*; *McKellar Hearings.*

115   Hambleton prepares for flight: *Junior League Magazine* 2/30; Miamians clog roads: NYHT 2/4/29; memo from consul Taggart in Belize about arrival of CAL and Hambleton, 2/4/29: US/SD 810.796.

8: GOING 50–50 (pages 116–122)

116   Harold Harris to authors, 11/19/77.

117   Keys to Hoyt: NYT 10/31/48.

117   Patchin memo 5/23/28: *Panagra Terminal Case*; "W. R. Grace and the Enterprises He Created," speech by J. Peter Grace, Jr., to the Newcomen Society, 11/19/53, and "Casa Grace," *Fortune* 12/35.

118   Step into partnership: *Financial History, op. cit.*

118   Harry New: NYT 2/1/29, 3/3/29, obituary NYT 5/10/37.

119   Glover to JTT: *Farley Report*; Hoover discusses aviation rights: "these conversations furnished the foundation for the establishment

119　of Pan American Airways," he wrote in *Memoirs of Herbert Hoover,* Vol. II; "go right ahead with your plans": Harris to authors 11/19/77.

119　New's reasons for the award: NYT 3/3/29, *Farley Report.*

120　New becomes director of Aviation Corporation of Delaware: Elsbeth Freudenthal, *The Aviation Business from Kitty Hawk to Wall Street;* Henry Ladd Smith, *Airways.*

120　"no profits for a long time": Harris to authors, 12/7/77; "Grace would attend to the business on the Coast": letter from Harold Roig to D. S. Iglehart 3/4/30 shows friction between Grace and P.A.A., and particularly the animosity toward JTT; *Panagra Terminal Case.*

121　Patchin testimony, *ibid.*

122　Flight over the Andes: Harris speech to Connecticut Aeronautical Historical Association 10/12/74, pilot Marvin Parks to MB 12/26/78.

9:　IMPERIAL DIPLOMACY *(pages 123–134)*

Unless otherwise cited, letters, telegrams, dispatches and memoranda are from US/SD 810.796.

123　P.A.A.'s special relationship with the State Department: memo by Joseph W. Stinson, Division of Latin American Affairs, 3/7/31.

123　Legal framework: Lissitzyn, *op. cit.*

124　Stinson memo, *op. cit.*

124　JTT letter to Francis White, 4/23/28; White to Curtis, Havana, 7/12/28.

125　About White: obituary NYT 2/24/61; Newton, *op. cit.;* exchange of telegrams between Washington and Central American legations, January and February 1928; "moving heaven and earth": Morgan memo 1/14/29; sixty messages: Stinson memo, *op. cit.*

126　Memo from Arthur Geissler, Minister to Guatemala, about contract, 4/14/28; memo from Charles C. Eberhardt, Minister to Nicaragua, 6/23/28; Nicaragua contract: NYT 6/22/28; Cuban concession: NYT 7/1/28.

126　Ecuador operating permit granted to H. R. Harris, 2/22/29; "That put him on the right side": Harris to authors, 11/19/77; memo from Solicitor of the State Dept., 7/24/28.

127　Balluder to authors, 11/27/76.

128　Eberhardt in Managua, forwarding MacGregor message to P.A.A. 6/6/28, suggests contacting president of United Fruit to relinquish Nicaraguan rights to P.A.A.; Nicaragua assented: Eberhardt message 11/13/28.

128   Hambleton phone call to White, telegram to Amlegation Tegucigalpa, 7/5/28; JTT authorized by board of directors to consummate contract with United Fruit, 9/17/28 (PAWA 50.08.03); "The Fruit people were very helpful," JTT to Ann Crittenden, "Juan Trippe's Pan Am," NYT 7/3/77; White telegram, 7/11/28; NYT 7/1/28; Summerlin dispatches, 7/2/28, 7/14/28, 7/20/28.

129   Geissler dispatch including copy of MacGregor memo and details of Guatemala contract, 4/12/28, 4/14/28; dispatch reporting delay, 4/24/28; terms unacceptable to Guatemala Government: dispatch 4/26/28.

129   Geissler dispatch informing of MacGregor departure, 5/2/28; JTT letter to Morgan, 5/1/28, asking him to forward message to MacGregor.

130   Memo by legation secretary Hawks in Guatemala City on Rihl activities, 5/25/29, 5/28/29; by Geissler, 5/27/29, 5/29/29.

131   Letters from Stimson to Brown, 6/21/29, Brown to Stimson, 6/25/29, US/SD 810.712; Walter Brown obituary, NYT 1/26/61.

132   Brown testimony, *Black Hearings*, Part 6.

132   Morrison's turn: Geissler dispatches 8/20/29, 8/21/29.

133   Geissler, 8/20/29; change of orders: Geissler dispatch 8/30/29.

134   Geissler dispatches 8/30/29, 9/4/29; provisional license reported by Benjamin Thaw, Division of Latin American Affairs, 9/20/29.

134   Stimson to Richey, 8/21/29.

10: TOUR DE FORCE *(pages 135–146)*

Unless otherwise noted, State Department documents are from US/SD 810.796.

135   Allegations that Juan changed his name: BT to MB 8/11/76.

136   Coverage of the trip, NYT 9/21/29 to 10/4/29; Anne Lindbergh's diary, *Hour of Gold, Hour of Lead*.

138   CAL's and JTT's activities reported in Engert dispatch from Caracas, 9/29/29.

138   BT recalled the forced landing to MB, 7/15/76.

139   Geissler dispatch on meeting CAL and JTT, 10/4/29.

140   Windup of P.A.A. in Guatemala, Thaw memo 10/19/29, Hawks report 11/14/29; Evan Young of P.A.A. to White asking permission to operate Compañía Mexicana planes, 3/27/30; White's reply, 4/1/30; Pickwick withdraws: Hawks report, 3/30/30; expected ratification of contract: Sheldon Whitehouse dispatch, 5/1/30; "vigorously opposing": Stinson memo, *op. cit.*

141   Newton, *op. cit.*, has comprehensive account of Peter Paul von Bauer's efforts to expand SCADTA; also White memo to Secretary of State, 4/25/29.

142   Von Bauer a charmer: BT to MB, 4/26/78; White to Poole, chargé d'affaires Berlin, 10/2/28; US/SD 821.796; new airline organized: Jefferson Caffery, Minister in Bogotá, dispatch 2/5/29, US/SD 810.796.

142   JTT letter to White with memo, 12/14/28, *ibid.*; "Columbia controls our extension to the south . . .": White memo 4/25/29.

143   JTT to White, 2/8/29; exchange of notes between Enrique Olaya and Frank B. Kellogg, 2/23/29, US/SD 821.796, NYT 2/24/29.

144   Negotiations to acquire SCADTA: Newton, *op. cit.*; Willcox complains: Caffery dispatch, 7/18/29, US/SD 810.796.

144   Henry Friendly's account to Oral History Project at Columbia University, July 1960 (PAWA 50.06.02); *Financial History, op. cit.*

145   In conversation with Laurence Duggan, chief of the Division of the American Republics, 3/17/39, JTT revealed Lufthansa acceptance of the deal, which was maintained "in the very greatest secrecy." Clauses provided that SCADTA not engage in international communications and that von Bauer remain as operative manager; letters from von Bauer to JTT, 9/16/33 and 11/6/33, disclose German character of SCADTA management and prevailing secrecy (JTT/NASM); memo of H. F. Matthews, Latin American Division, to Thurston, 5/26/31, initialed by White, says "Pan American has bought out SCADTA but is getting their Colombian contracts in the first instance through the Scadta company. In a year or so the Scadta company will be completely Americanized" US/SD 821.796; Balluder to authors, 11/27/76; P.A.A. Executive System Memorandum No. 9, 4/18/31, announces a "general working agreement and reciprocal exchange," with P.A.A. having acquired "a financial interest" in SCADTA, and a press release to be issued 4/27/31; PAWA; according to NYHT 4/30/31, JTT announced a reciprocal operation agreement, no financial details mentioned. He said the agreement was "in pursuance of the program sponsored by President Hoover, that American enterprises in South America should expand with successful business enterprises already operating there" (P.A.A. Annual Report 1931); Colombian press accounts cited in dispatches from Fletcher Warren, consul in Barranquilla, 4/23/31, and from Minister Caffery, 4/30/31, US/SD 821.796.

146   Grace, in the dark, considered SCADTA a breach of its agreement with P.A.A.: letter from Roig to MacGregor, 9/23/36; testimony of Roig, "the extent of the investment was a mystery . . ."; "a very long and metaphysical discussion": *Panagra Terminal Case.*

11:   *FIGHT FOR CONTROL (pages 147–152)*

147   Aviation Corporation of Delaware: *Aviation* 3/16/29; within a year it comprised 80 manufacturing and transport companies including Colonial Air Transport.

148   Hoyt's plight is gleaned from *Financial History, op. cit.*, and from the testimony of William Boeing, *Black Hearings*, Part 5. In his statement to the Black Committee investigator, *op. cit.*, JTT alluded

148   to March 1929 "during the stock market boom, and a time when others were seeking to purchase control of the company in the stock market . . ."

149   Daniel Drew: Matthew Josephson, *The Robber Barons*.

149   Rentschler testified as to the formation of United Aircraft & Transport Corporation, *Black Hearings*, Part 4; Hoyt's proposal, Boeing's testimony, *Black Hearings*, Part 5.

149   *Financial History, op. cit.*

150   Curtiss-Wright: NYT 6/27/29, 6/29/29; Aviation Corporation of the Americas Annual Report 1930 (PAWA); Fairchild's attitude toward JTT: Henry Friendly interview with John Leslie, 6/8/73, PAWA 50.06.02.

150   "community effort": Aviation Corporation of the Americas Annual Report 1930; P.A.A. was Juan's to run: CVW to MB, 5/24/76; JTT in awe of Hambleton: Althea Lister to MB, 10/26/78; Al Capone incident: George Hambleton to MB, 11/17/77.

151   CVW supporting JTT: Van Dusen to Leslie, 10/24/72, PAWA 50.22.01; "our paths didn't cross": CVW to MB, 5/24/76; "Oh, gosh": *Life*, 10/24/41; BT spoke to MB, 9/22/76, about CVW's carryings-on; "my father died from overwork": BT to MB, 1/13/78.

152   Hambleton's death: NYT 6/9/29; Billy Mitchell letter to the editor of the Baltimore *Sun*, 6/12/29; CVW in *The Sportsman Pilot*, July 1929.

12: *THE SCIENCE OF ADVENTURE*
(pages 153–165)

153   The meeting in Havana: *Life* 10/20/41; arrangement with Atlantic Coast Line R.R.: George Hambleton to MB, 11/17/77.

153   Chenea was recalled in a memorandum of June 1957, Employees' Memories File (PAWA 30.10.08).

154   "Trippe visualized success": James H. Smith, Jr., to authors, 6/6/80.

155   André Priester obituary, NYT 11/29/55, memoranda recalling Priester, PAWA 50.02.05, 50.16.02.

155   Priester and safety: JTT to authors 11/8/76; Priester's manual, 1st edition 11/29, 2d edition 3/31, PAWA.

156   Priester and a seductive image: George Hambleton to MB, 11/17/77; at the airport in Brazil: Balluder to authors, 11/27/76.

157   PAA Executive System Memorandum No. 1, 12/29/30 (PAWA); Priester's Christmas cards: PAWA 50.16.02.

158   Priester against smoking and drinking: *Fortune* April 1936; "always be fair": Daley, *op. cit.*

158   Lindbergh flying without a radio: CAL letter to Langewiesche, 11/19/69 (CAL/YUL).

159   Leuteritz to authors, 6/8/78.

163   Jimmy Doolittle and blind flying: NYT 9/25/79.

164   Pilots in Central America: Basil Rowe, *op. cit.*

164   Building airports: *The American Magazine* April 1939; airport in Bolivia: Harold Harris speech to Connecticut Aeronautical Historical Association, 10/12/74.

13: *CLOSING THE LOOP* (pages 166–176)

All State Department documents are from file US/SD 810.796.

166   Profile of Ralph A. O'Neill: *NY Mirror* 6/13/39; O'Neill's autobiography, *A Dream of Eagles.*

167   "a grudge fight from the start": William S. Grooch, *Winged Highway.*

167   "Competitive bidding . . . is more or less of a myth": Walter Brown, *Black Hearings*, Part 6.

168   Culbertson dispatch on Trimotor and Latécoère, 4/16/29; White's telegrams to Caracas, Buenos Aires, Santiago, 5/13/29, 5/16/29; White in Buenos Aires reports negotiations to cooperate, 5/20/29; "what policy is to be adopted toward NYRBA": handwritten memo from Thaw to Munro, 5/21/29; memo from Munro to White on conversation with Montgomery, 5/24/29; Munro to White, 5/24/29.

169   White to Norman Armour, chargé d'affaires Paris, 9/26/28; White to Harold Williamson in Paris, 10/21/29.

169   "muddying the water": letter from Glover to White, 8/1/29, forwarded by White to Secretary of State 8/2/29; competition between P.A.A. and NYRBA: *Time* 7/22/29.

170   O'Neill's strategy: letter from O'Neill to MB, 6/23/79.

170   JTT's strategy of keeping route from being advertised: letter from George Rihl to JTT 1/14/30 (JTT/NASM); letter from Glover to White, 8/7/29, enclosing memo from James Summers to JTT, 7/15/29; Munro memo 8/9/29 on discussion with Donovan about O'Neill's allegation; O'Neill gets affidavit from Brazilian: *A Dream of Eagles*; Bliss telegram from Buenos Aires, 8/24/29.

171   Donovan and Hoover: O'Neill *op. cit.*; Hoover says NYRBA ought to have a chance: Newton *op. cit.*; JTT's politicking on extension of FAM 6: Friendly interview with Leslie 6/8/73 (PAWA 50.06.02).

172   JTT announces Lindbergh inspection tour: NYT 12/16/29.

172   O'Neill's cable to the employees: Henry W. Lanier, *The Far Horizon*; Rihl to JTT 1/14/20 (JTT/NASM).

172   O'Neill to MB 6/23/79; O'Neill's miscalculation: *New York Sun* 7/17/30; anonymous memorandum 6/5/30 (CAL/YUL); *Farley Report.*

173   Brown's testimony, *Black Hearings, op. cit.*; O'Neill to MB, *op. cit.*

173   *A Dream of Eagles*; NYT 7/21/30 reported tangible signs of merger between NYRBA and P.A.A. and meetings between JTT and Mac-Cracken.

175   JTT on Pierson's yacht: Friendly to Leslie, *op. cit.*; purchase of NYRBA: *Financial History, op. cit.*; "you can steal my house": O'Neill in a speech to the Clipper Pioneers 10/71, PAWA 40.04.00.

175   "They were nice young men": Josephson, *Empire of the Air*; NYRBA asks to cancel Argentine contracts: NYT 8/22/30; *Farley Report*; PAA Annual Report 1931; *Time* 7/31/33.

14: *THE AUTOCRAT (pages 177–181)*

177   Plight of P.A.A.: JTT letter to the Black Committee, *op. cit.*; JTT's warrants: *Financial History, op. cit.*

178   PAA Executive System Memorandum No. 1 (PAWA).

178   Balluder to authors, 11/27/76.

178   Wyman the butt of others' frustrations: Wilbur Morrison to SA, 11/3/77.

179   Whitney, *op. cit., The New Yorker* 6/21/41; Marie Whitney marries W. A. Harriman: NYT 2/22/30.

180   Whitney wedding: NYT 9/30/31.

180   Hoyt obituary 3/8/35; his tangled affairs are revealed in the accounting of his estate, New York County Surrogate's Court; JTT on naming his daughter: BT to MB 9/22/76; forsakes Catholicism: BT to MB 1/13/78.

181   JTT elbowing his way into photographs: Willis Player to authors, 1/10/79.

15: *TO BUILD THE BETTER MACHINE*
(pages 182–191)

182   Pilots' fears: CAL to Langewiesche, 4/27/61, 11/19/67.

183   Debate over sea versus land planes: CAL to Cooper 12/3/36, André Priester to CAL 12/8/36, 8/3/37, CAL to Priester 8/19/37 (CAL/YUL).

183   Correspondence between Dornier and JTT 11/17/28 (JTT/NASM); development of flying boats is recounted in Igor Sikorsky, *The Story of the Winged-S*, Frank J. Delear, *Igor Sikorsky*, and "The Winged-S" by Geoffrey T. Hellman, *The New Yorker* 8/10/40, 8/17/40.

185   Scene in JTT's office described to authors by Leuteritz, 6/8/78, and by CAL to Langewiesche, 4/27/61, *op. cit.*

186   CAL recommending purchase of Sikorsky amphibians: letter to JTT 11/12/29, 11/21/29 (CAL/MHS).

187 Christening of the S-40: NYT 10/13/31.

188 Pilots' uniforms and training: *Fortune* April 1936, PAA System News Bulletin—Dear Señor Letter July 1937 (PAWA).

188 Pilots' complaint: Rowe, *op. cit.*

189 Stewards: Leuteritz to authors, 6/8/78; Jupiter Rex ceremony: *New Horizons* January 1943; Bebe Rebozo: *Life* 7/31/70.

190 Cuban coup d'état: William S. Grooch, *From Crate to Clipper.*

190 *Time* 7/31/33; *Farley Report.*

190 Brown's spoils conferences: *Fortune* May 1934, *op. cit.*; Brown's testimony, letter from Thomas B. Doe to Brown, 7/2/31, *Black Hearings*, Part 6.

191 Brown's reply to Doe, 7/7/31, *ibid.*; *Financial History, op. cit.*

PART III: THE OCEANS

16: *PREPARING TO CROSS AN OCEAN*
(pages 195–203)

195 European airlines "follow the flag": Lissitzyn, *op. cit.*

196 Floating islands: NYT 10/31/33; JTT discourages the project: memo of conversation between Under Secretary William Phillips and JTT, 12/12/33, US/SD 811.796.

197 International Zeppelin Transport Company: NYT 10/21/29, 10/23/29, 10/29/29; McNary-Parker Airship Act: NYT 6/8/30.

197 Atlantic crossing attempts: C. R. Roseberry, *The Challenging Skies*; the DO-X in New York: NYT 8/28/31.

198 JTT on honeymoon: White to Armour, 9/26/28, 10/2/28, Armour to White, 11/13/28, memo for Armour from John Jay Ide, Paris embassy, 11/15/28, US/SD 810.796.

198 Imperial Airways: David Beaty, *Water Jump*, John Pudney, *The Seven Skies.*

199 Less efficient aircraft: CAL to JTT, 10/16/33 (CAL/YUL); Eric Geddes: Pudney, *ibid.*

199 "History of the Transatlantic Air Services," an exhibit by P.A.A. in the *North Atlantic Route Case*, gives a résumé of the early negotiations; Pan American–Imperial Airways Company (Geddes was chairman, JTT president) PAWA 40.06.00.

200 Bouilloux-Lafont eager to negotiate with JTT: memorandum from Thaw in Paris 9/26/30, US/SD 810.796.

200 The tripartite conference: NYT 11/14/30, 11/15/30, 11/17/30, 11/18/30, 11/22/30; unsigned copy of the agreement among Imperial Airways Ltd., Société Générale d'Aviation and Aviation Corporation of the Americas, 11/20/30 (JTT/NASM).

200   Postmaster invites bids: NYT 12/1/30: withdraws bids: NYT 12/18/30; FAM 12: P.A.A. annual report 1931; bids for new plane: "History of the Transatlantic Air Services," *op. cit.*

201   The Lindberghs' flight is the subject of Anne Lindbergh's *North to the Orient.*

202   CAL discouraged with the route: *Autobiography of Values*; JTT's letter to the Soviet Union, 10/30/31 (JTT/NASM).

203   "History of Pan American Airways' Air Services to and Through Alaska," an exhibit in the *Pacific Case*; purchase of Alaskan Airlines, *Financial History, op. cit.*

17: BABES IN THE ORIENTAL WOODS
(pages 204–209)

The State Department documents are in US/SD 893.796.

204   The fight between Keys and Rentschler: Henry Ladd Smith, *Airways*; Thomas A. Morgan described to MB by W. L. Bond 11/30/78; Morgan obituary, NYT 10/30/67.

204   "Aviation in China," a report by Lincoln C. Reynolds, vice consul in Tientsin, 3/14/35.

205   Contract between American Exploration and China National Aviation Corp. 7/8/30, enclosed with dispatch from Nanking consul 7/9/30; Consul Edwin Cunningham to Minister J. V. A. MacMurray, 4/26/29.

206   Correspondence from JTT to Morgan, 1/26/33, Morgan to JTT, 2/1/33, JTT to Morgan, 2/7/33 (PAWA 10.05.00); P.A.A. purchase of C.N.A.C., *Financial History, op. cit.*; and *CNAC Case.*

206   Harold Bixby described by his daughters Catherine Barrett, 11/10/78, and Elizabeth Hawkins, 11/13/78 to MB; Bixby obituary, NYT 11/20/65. Bixby recalled his adventures in China with C.N.A.C. in an unpublished memoir, *Topside Ricksha.*

207   Most-favored-nation clauses: memorandum from Willys Peck, Nanking legation, to Nelson T. Johnson, Minister in Peiping, 7/26/33.

208   William S. Grooch, *Winged Highway*; Bixby to Lindbergh, 5/13/37 (CAL/YUL); the Yangtze enemy: Bond to MB 11/30/78.

209   Luce advocacy: Swanberg, *op. cit.*

18: SETBACKS (pages 210–214)

210   Air roads to Europe: "Atlantic Airways" by Edward P. Warner, *Foreign Affairs* April 1938; Iceland franchise: "History of the Transatlantic Air Services," *op. cit.*

210   JTT to Edgar A. Bowring, Jr., 3/26/32 (JTT/NASM); JTT on Winslow, to authors, 5/25/78.

211 JTT to authors, 5/25/78; mob attacks legislative building: NYT 4/6/32; British Navy restores order: NYT 4/13/32, 4/18/32; American consul's reports on Winslow's activities, 4/22/32, on Logan, 11/9/32, US/SD 843.796.

212 "Moral obligation": JTT to authors, 5/25/78, Memorandum of Pierrepont Moffat, Division of West European Affairs, on conversation with JTT, 9/12/34, US/SD 843.796; July meeting: report on commercial air transport in Newfoundland by American consul in St. John's, 6/11/34, US/SD 800.796.

212 Winslow's death: NYT 8/13/33; obituary, NYT 8/16/33; Newfoundland reverts to Crown Colony: NYT 11/29/33, 12/3/33; in letter to Woods Humphery in October 1933, JTT noted that Winslow had been about to leave for Portugal to negotiate and that word had just been received of the imminent cancellation of the French concession (PAWA 40.03.00).

212 Such a marvelous route: CAL letter to Langewiesche, 11/19/67; Anne Lindbergh, *Locked Rooms and Open Doors*; CAL letter and report to JTT, 9/15/33; report to P.A.A. from CAL, "Observations and Studies During Survey Flights over Greenland/Iceland," 5/29/34 (CAL/YUL).

213 Bermuda–Azores route most satisfactory, Lindbergh, *Autobiography of Values*.

213 Letter from CAL to JTT 12/10/31; to Priester 12/3/36 (oxygen at high altitude and refueling in air); CAL to Cooper 12/3/36 (little confidence in flying boats); Priester to CAL 12/8/36 (pro–flying boats), 8/3/37; CAL to Priester 8/19/37 (pro–land plane); CAL to JTT (about preceding debate) (CAL/YUL).

19: *A NEW DEAL (pages 215–226)*

215 A "staunch" Republican: JTT to authors, 8/11/76; "But we didn't vote for Goldwater," BT added.

216 Whitney's campaign: *The New Yorker* 6/21/41; Roosevelt note thanking CVW for his "excellent run," 11/19/32; McIntyre telegram inviting him to lunch, 9/15/36 (FDR/PPF); Basil O'Connor's retainer: memorandum from CVW to JTT, 9/29/39 (JTT/NASM); O'Connor's memoranda to FDR and JTT's messages to the President (FDR/OF).

216 Jimmy Roosevelt dropped off beside Astor's yacht: *New Horizons* February–April 1935 (PAWA); JTT's proposal for an interdepartmental committee: memorandum of conversation with JTT by Under Secretary of State William Phillips, 12/12/33, letter to Phillips from JTT, 1/27/34, memorandum of conversation with JTT by Pierrepont Moffat, 5/3/34, FDR to Secretary of State, 6/20/34, US/SD 811.796.

217 JTT addresses interdepartmental committee: memorandum 11/1/35, US/SD 811.796; recollections of Robert Thach, William J. McEvoy to SA, 6/13/77, Benjamin Sonnenberg to authors, 7/26/77, Althea

218   Lister to MB 1/28/79; recollections of Ann Archibald: SP to authors, 11/19/76, Stanley Gewirtz to authors, 11/10/77.

218   *Black Hearings*: NYT 1/8/33, 1/10/34, *Fortune* May 1934.

219   Pecora Hearings (Senate Banking and Currency Committee): Arthur M. Schlesinger, Jr., *The Age of Roosevelt: Vol. II, The Coming of the New Deal*; Brown as a witness: NYT 2/16/34, 2/20/34.

219   James A. Farley's version of the cancellation of the airmail contracts: *Behind the Ballots* and *Jim Farley's Story*.

220   Lindbergh telegram to Roosevelt, 2/11/34; Early's statement, 2/12/34 (FDR/OF).

220   New airmail legislation, S. 3170, 73rd Congress, 2d Session, Ch. 466, 6/12/34.

222   Foreign airmail under investigation: NYT 2/17/34; Pan American welcomes inquiry: NYT 2/18/34.

222   Fish charges: NYT 2/17/34; JTT and Thach meet with Black: McEvoy to SA, 6/13/77; meeting of the Cabinet on P.A.A. contracts: NYT 2/22/34.

223   "I can't see much future": JTT to authors, 5/25/78; Geddes to stockholders of Imperial: NYT 10/31/33; Empire Air Mail Scheme: Pudney, *op. cit.*

224   Press conference: NYT 12/1/32.

225   "a dangerous plane": CAL to Priester, 7/28/34 (CAL/YUL); price of aircraft: "History of the Transatlantic Air Service," *op. cit.*; meeting in JTT's office: Leuteritz to authors, 6/13/79; about the decision: JTT to authors, 5/25/78.

226   JTT's dialogue with the Japanese: letter from JTT to Stanley Hornbeck, 8/1/39 attaching draft of letter to Secretary of the Navy, US/SD 811.796.

226   Negotiations with the Soviet Union: memorandum of conversation between Hornbeck and JTT, 3/19/35 (US/SD 811.796) and *Celler Hearings*, Part I, Vol. 4.

226   Attempts to fly the Pacific: "History of the Transpacific Air Services to and Through Hawaii," P.A.A. exhibit *Hawaiian Case*.

20:   PACIFIC PARTNERS *(pages 227–243)*

227   U.S. relations in the Pacific: Dorothy Borg, *The United States and the Far Eastern Crisis of 1933–38*, Joseph C. Grew, *Turbulent Era, A Diplomatic Record of Forty Years*, Francis X. Holbrook, *United States National Defense and Trans-Pacific Commercial Air Routes, 1933–1941*.

228   Washington Naval Treaty: "An Earlier Attempt to Limit Arms," by Charles H. Fairbanks, Jr., WSJ 6/21/79.

230 Tydings-McDuffie bill: NYT 4/22/34, Manuel Luis Quezon, *The Good Fight.*

230 Memorandum of call to Historical Adviser to State Dept., 6/20/34, US/MM A21-5.

231 JTT to Secretary of the Navy, 10/3/34, US/MM A21-5.

231 Farley's reply, 10/12/34, *Hawaiian Case, op. cit.*, NYT 10/15/34; "stigma of inferiority": Borg, *op. cit.*; "if highly desirable": letter from William Phillips to the Secretary of the Navy, 12/13/34; US/MM A21-5.

232 Grew, *op. cit.*; Hornbeck memorandum: Borg, *op. cit.*; Executive Order 6935, 12/13/34, US/MM A21-5.

232 Gatty letter to Swanson on behalf of South Seas Commercial Company, 9/22/34; JTT to Swanson on Gatty proposal, 12/5/34, US/MM A21-5.

233 Memorandum from Director of Naval Communications to Chief of Naval Operations, 11/23/34; Acting Secretary of State Phillips to Swanson, 12/13/34; P.A.A. to use San Diego and Pearl Harbor, 12/31/34; revocable leases for Midway, Wake and Guam, 3/12/35 (US/MM A21-5); Japanese reaction: NYT 3/15/35, 4/26/35, NW 3/23/35.

233 Purchase of South Seas Commercial Company 5/10/35, dissolved 9/30/40 (PAWA Legal Department files).

234 Howard letter to Thacker, 4/17/35 (PAWA 10.10.00); P.A.A. agreements with Matson and Inter-Island, *Hawaiian Case.*

234 *North Haven* expedition described by Grooch in *Skyway to Asia*, NYT 6/30/35 and *Pan American Air Ways*, May–June 1935, July–August 1935.

235 Trippe kept tabs: Leuteritz to authors, 6/13/79.

235 "He understood": Leuteritz to authors, 6/8/78.

236 Long-range forecasting, exhibit *Hawaiian Case*; point of no return: "Ocean Air Transport," 29th Wilbur Wright Memorial Lecture by JTT to Royal Aeronautical Society, London, 6/17/41 (PAWA).

237 Adcock: Leuteritz to authors, 6/13/79; *Pan American Air Ways* February–March–April 1935.

238 Post Office withholding approval: telegram from Governor Merriam to President, 3/22/35, memo from James Donaldson to Farley, 3/26/35, memo from Farley to Early, 3/28/35 (FDR/OF); Commerce experiments: NYT 3/14/35; feasibility undemonstrated: NYT 4/23/35; JTT arrives: Leuteritz to authors, 6/13/79.

239 S-42 flight to Honolulu: *Pan American Air Ways, ibid.*; return flight: NYT 4/23/35, 4/24/35.

239 Fuel supply exhausted: Daley, *op. cit.*

240 P.A.A. waives its rights: Friendly to Leslie 6/73 (PAWA 59.06.02); Farley charges favoritism: NYT 6/13/35: *Farley Report.*

241 JTT worried: memorandum of conversation between Richard South-gate and JTT, 5/24/35 (US/SD 811.796).

242 Pacific airmail bids advertised: NYT 8/13/35; P.A.A. settlement: Post Office Dept. press release 9/27/35 with Postmaster General's letter to the President 9/25/35 attached (FDR/OF).

243 JTT telegram to CAL, 10/21/35 (CAL/YUL); P.A.A. bid accepted, NYT 10/25/35.

21: *CHINA CLIPPER (pages 244–257)*

244 Glenn L. Martin, "Hero for Business Reasons" by Alva Johnston, *The New Yorker* 11/24/42, 12/5/42.

245 Delivery of the *China Clipper: Pan American Air Ways*, September–October 1935; telegram CAL to JTT, 7/27/34; asks discontinue retainer: letter to JTT 6/11/35 (CAL/YUL).

245 Van Dusen's hokum: NYT 1/19/35; CAL sends check to JTT: letter 12/21/35 (CAL/YUL).

246 Musick described by Grooch in *From Crate to Clipper*, also profiles in *U.S. Air Services* November 1935, NW 4/27/35, *Time* 12/2/35 (cover story) and 2/24/36.

247 "the back stairs of aviation magic": Anne Lindbergh, *North to the Orient*; *Brazilian Clipper* flight: NYT 8/25/34.

247 JTT habituates the public: Hornbeck memo of conversation with JTT, 8/13/35 (US/SD 811.796); problem of Manila rights: Bixby, *Topside Ricksha*, NYHT 7/11/35, 7/17/35.

248 Attempted sabotage: Josephson, *op. cit.*; Loening finds fault with the M-130: letters to JTT 11/30/34, 1/5/37, to Priester 11/12/36 (GL); inaugural flight of the *China Clipper*: Grooch, *ibid.*, *Pan American Air Ways* November–December 1935, Pacific Supplement No. 2.

252 Problems for the *China Clipper*: letters from Ted Wyman to CAL, 2/14/36, 2/26/36 (CAL/YUL); problems with S-42: Wyman to CAL, 4/20/36, Priester to CAL, 9/15/36 (CAL/YUL).

252 Problems concealed: confidential memorandum to the chairman, Maritime Commission from Grover Loening, undated (FDR/OF); Van Dusen didn't disclose: "Now to China in 65 Flying Hours" by W. I. Van Dusen and Daniel Sayre, *Hearst's International Cosmopolitan*, December 1935, NYT 11/23/35.

252 "without batting an eye": Van Dusen to CAL 7/3/36 (CAL/YUL); review of *China Clipper*, NYT 8/12/36.

253 Letter from Bixby to CAL, 5/13/37 (CAL/YUL).

254 Letter from Woods Humphery to JTT, 9/11/33; letter from JTT to Woods Humphery, 10/3/33 (JTT/NASM).

254 Bixby to CAL, *ibid.*; letter from JTT to Colonial Office, London, 5/8/35 (puts out feelers); memo from Southgate, 5/24/35 (Philippine reciprocity) (US/SD 811.796).

255   Macao ploy: memos from Vice Consul Hoover, Hong Kong, 9/13/35, 1/21/36, synopsis of above by Vice Consul Gourley, 3/13/36, memo from Consul Gauss to Johnson, Peiping, 3/18/36, Gourley synopsis of Lisbon/Macao developments, 4/24/36 (US/SD 811.796).

255   JTT declines Hong Kong invitation: letter to R. Walton Moore, 12/26/35; Consul Hoover report, 6/30/36; résumé of aviation developments in Hong Kong by Consul Southard, 12/13/37 (US/SD 811.796).

256   JTT's flight to the Orient: NYT 10/16/36; other reports of trip, *South China Morning Post* 10/24/36, *Shanghai Times* 10/24/36, *Nashville Banner*, 11/15/36; JTT wire to the President, 10/23/36 (FDR/OF).

256   Trippes accompanied by Bob Lord: letter from Wyman to CAL, 11/12/36 (CAL/YUL); JTT wanted no publicity: BT to MB 1/11/79.

257   The Trippes return: NYT 12/5/36; Collier Trophy, NYT 8/7/37, *Time* 8/16/37; criticism: NYHT 8/7/37.

22: *THE ATLANTIC (pages 258–266)*

258   Memo by Stephen Latchford of the Treaty Division, May 6, 1935, FR/US 1935, Vol. 1.

259   *Times* of London 11/6/34 reporting on Geddes' remarks at annual meeting: clipping attached to Atherton memo 11/12/34 (US/SD 841.796); Empire Air Mail Scheme: John Andrew Miller, *Air Diplomacy: The Chicago Civil Aviation Conference of 1944 in Anglo-American Wartime Relations and Post-War Planning.*

260   Atlantic Company: JTT to authors, 6/7/77; "square deal": memorandum of agreement between P.A.A. and Imperial Airways, 9/12/35 (PAWA 40.03.00).

260   Delegates wish to confer: NYHT 12/1/35; JTT asks Hull, 11/30/35 (US/SD 841.796); memorandum of interdepartmental committee meeting, 12/2/35, Walton Moore Papers (FDR).

261   State Dept. press release, 12/4/35 (US/SD 841.796); "who could possibly get ready": JTT to authors, 6/7/77, 5/25/78; reports of conference: NYT 12/5/35, 12/7/35, 12/10/35, 12/12/35, 12/13/35; Imperial and P.A.A. "acceptable": "History of the Transatlantic Air Services," *op. cit.*

261   Clause H: NYHT 1/29/38; State defends itself: Southgate memo, 12/9/37 (US/SD 811.796); "electric fan": Wyman to CAL, 9/22/36 (CAL/YUL).

262   Morale at P.A.A.: Wyman to CAL, 2/14/36 (CAL/YUL); notes of conversations between JTT and Woods Humphery (PAWA 40.03.00); French and Germans accuse JTT: Wyman to CAL, 2/26/36 (CAL/YUL).

262   Contract between P.A.A. and Compagnie Générale Air France Transatlantique, 2/7/36: letter from JTT to Secretary of State 2/28/36

263   (US/SD 811.796); memoranda from French Air Mission to inter-departmental committee, 3/4/36, 3/6/36 (US/SD 851.796); German agreements, NYT 2/9/36.

263   Use of P.A.A. base: Leuteritz to authors, 6/13/79; fresh obstacles: notes of JTT conversations with Woods Humphery, *op. cit.*; JTT convinced: letter to CAL 2/4/37 (CAL/YUL); memo from Colonel Johnson to interdepartmental committee, 2/2/37 (FDR/PPF).

263   Ceremony in Roper's office: NYT 4/21/37; Gledhill letter: "History of Transatlantic," *op. cit.*; "bag of oats": JTT to authors 5/25/78.

264   "Martin didn't have the next step": JTT to authors, 5/25/78; CAL prefers Sikorsky: letter to JTT 6/28/36, Gledhill to CAL 6/20/36, Priester to CAL 7/13/36, CAL to Priester 7/19/36 (CAL/YUL).

264   JTT tries to pay CAL: letter 12/11/36; CAL's cable expenses: letter to JTT 1/12/37 (CAL/YUL); James Smith to authors, 6/6/80.

265   *Cavalier* assembled in Bermuda: Wyman to CAL 2/8/37 (CAL/YUL); survey trip: NYHT 7/7/37, 7/9/37; Gray's report for *North American Newspaper Alliance* 7/15/37.

23:   SOUTH PACIFIC (pages 267–272)

267   British–American rivalry over islands: memo from Consul Bucklin in Wellington, 10/13/36 (US/SD 811.014).

268   Memo from Acting Secretary of the Interior on history of the islands and P.A.A.'s interest, 6/15/35 (US/MM A21-5); "the little company we formed under the bridge": JTT to authors, 8/11/76.

269   Letter to Secretary of State from Ocean Nitrates, 9/24/35, signed Samuel Davis Robins; memo from State Dept. Legal Adviser saying Oceanic "entirely independent," 9/26/35 (US/SD 811.014); memo from Office of the Historical Adviser, 6/6/35 (US/SD 811.796); *Kinkajou* expedition: NYT 7/21/35; Cooper reports favorable droppings: memo from Phillips 9/18/35 (US/SD 811.014); memo from Johnson to Phillips, 11/19/35, on placing islands under Interior (US/SD 811.014).

269   Fred Goerner, *The Search for Amelia Earhart.*

270   Cooper to Secretary of State, 11/9/35, Hull telegram to Wellington consul, 11/12/35, Bucklin memo 11/13/35 (US/SD 811.796).

270   P.A.A. asks for extension: JTT to Moore, 2/15/37; Prime Minister to Gatty 3/11/37 granting extension (US/SD 811.796); Bureau of Budget memo against the reciprocal clause, 7/20/37 (FDR/OF), Moore to the President, 2/16/37, Moore to the Postmaster General, 6/15/37, Bucklin dispatch 4/1/37, British Embassy in Washington to Secretary of State, 8/6/37, Johnson to Moore, 8/7/37, Gatty to Prime Minister New Zealand, 7/30/37 (US/SD 811.796).

271   Prime Minister's Office to Gatty, 10/4/37.

271   Loss of the *Samoa Clipper*: NYHT 1/12/38, NYT 1/13/38, Navy Dept. Reports 1/13/28, 1/28/38 (US/MM A21-5).

24: *THREAT OF COMPETITION (pages 273–283)*

273 Loening an egotist: David Bruce to authors, 10/1/77; Loening criticized JTT's course in an undated memorandum on proceeding to transatlantic service (JTT/NASM).

273 "political rumpus": Loening letter to JTT, 7/9/36 (GL) referring to memo on P.A.A. (JTT/NASM); JTT's replies, 7/13/36, 1/25/37 (GL); Black ocean-mail investigation: "H.R. 8555," *Fortune* September 1937.

274 Loening report to the Maritime Commission, *op. cit.*

275 Kennedy summons Trippe: JTT to authors 6/7/77; American Export plans: *American Aviation* 8/15/37.

276 CAL to JTT 8/20/37 (CAL/YUL).

276 Gledhill solicits bids: "History of the Transatlantic," *op. cit.*, Van Dusen's Dear Señor letters, 11/29/37, 12/20/37 (PAWA); Lindbergh's "dream ship": *NY Sun* 6/23/38.

276 CAL to JTT, 1/11/38; to Van Dusen, 7/11/38 (CAL/YUL); Lindbergh's feelings about the Germans and the French were reiterated in his posthumously published *Autobiography of Values*; Anne Lindbergh's account of the visits to Germany is in *The Flower and the Nettle*.

277 CAL to Gledhill, 10/27/37 (PAWA 30.17.17).

278 State of the airline industry: "New Hope for Air Transport" by Selig Altschul, *Barron's* 7/18/38; P.A.A.'s precarious condition: Friendly to Langewiesche, 10/28/50 (PAWA 50.06.02).

278 *Bermuda Mail Rate Case*; history of creating a regulatory agency for aviation, *CAA Hearings*; JTT letter to Joseph Eastman, 7/21/37, JTT memorandum to the President, 2/23/37 (FDR/OF).

278 JTT's strategy: James Smith to authors, 6/6/80; Thach's expenses were cited in *Ben Grey v. PAA*, a lawsuit brought by a lobbyist in 1940, presented as evidence in the *North Atlantic Route Transfer Case*; copies of plain-paper memoranda on the various regulatory bills: JTT/NASM.

279 Filibuster: *American Aviation* 9/1/37.

279 Loening named technical adviser: undated memo of a conversation between JTT and Loening (JTT/NASM); "our troubles will be over": Friendly to Langewiesche, *op. cit.*; new McCarran and Lea bills: NYT 1/3/38, 5/29/38; amendments to Merchant Marine Act: NYT 3/23/38.

281 Moore asks the President to see JTT and CVW, 2/3/37 (FDR/OF); "the White House his playing field": Smith to authors, 6/6/80.

281 Johnson predicts Presidential prerogative will haunt P.A.A.: William McEvoy to SA 6/13/77.

283   JTT phones CAL, 6/3/38: Lindbergh, *Wartime Journals.*

283   "The Albatross": Anne Lindbergh, *The Flower and the Nettle.*

25: DARKENING CLOUDS *(pages 284–293)*

284   PAA annual report 1938.

285   What a pity: Bixby to CAL, 9/6/37 (CAL/YUL); Bixby withdraws
from C.N.A.C.: NYT 8/22/37; State Dept. policy: Arthur N. Young,
China and the Helping Hand.

285   W. L. Bond to MB, 11/30/78; Hornbeck memo of conversation with
JTT, 9/9/37 (US/SD 811.796).

286   Hull's sharp protest: NYT 8/27/38; Grew to Hull, 9/3/38 (US/SD
893.796); Hull telegram to consuls in Canton, Chongqing, Peiping to
advise Japanese of P.A.A. interest in C.N.A.C., 1/28/39 (US/SD
893.796).

286   Loss of *Hawaii Clipper*: NYT 7/31/38, Daley, *op. cit.*; Wyman letter
to CAL 5/27/38 (CAL/YUL); British and U.S. squabble over
Canton Island: NYT 3/5/38.

288   FDR claims Canton I.: NYT 3/6/38; motivated by commercial
aviation needs, NYT 3/8/38; Japanese suspicions, NYT 3/10/38.

288   Mistake to let foreign country use Hawaii: Johnson letter to Moore,
8/7/37 (US/SD 811.796); memo of conversations by Chief of Division of European Affairs, 4/18/38 (FR/US 1938, Vol. 2); Ickes
licenses P.A.A. for Canton: NYT 4/2/38; JTT to Secretary of the
Navy asking for help, 4/20/38 (US/MM A21-5); "our cook is
leaving": Josephson, *op. cit.*, Leuteritz to authors, 6/13/79.

288   Transatlantic mail subsidy: NYT 3/21/38; Boeing troubles: Harold
Mansfield, *Vision*; Loening makes political rumpus: NYT 1/29/38,
Loening letter to Southgate, 2/4/38 (US/SD 811.796).

289   Woods Humphery goes to bat: Beaty, *op. cit.*, Miller, *op. cit.*;
British aircraft deficiencies: NYT 3/21/38, Beaty, *ibid.*

289   Attacks on British aviation: report by Herschel V. Johnson, counselor of London embassy 11/18/37; Cadman report in Johnson
dispatches 3/10/38, 3/16/38, 3/31/38; Albatross and Mayo Composite: *Shell Aviation News* January 1960.

290   German crossing: NYT 8/12/38.

291   JTT agreement with American Export: *Celler Hearings*, Part I,
Vol. 4; JTT startles meeting: Latchford memo of conversation,
11/29/38 (US/SD 811.796).

291   Latchford memo of meeting with JTT, 12/23/38 (US/SD 811.796);
State Dept. requests French permit for P.A.A.: NYT 1/20/39; blunt
inquiry of London embassy, NYHT 2/3/39.

291   Imperial announces air service: NYHT 1/4/39; Clause H waived:
aide-mémoire of British Embassy in Washington, 2/1/39, Herschel
Johnson dispatch 2/4/39 (US/SD 811.796).

292 JTT's offer to waive Portuguese exclusivity: *Celler Hearings, op. cit.*; *Transatlantic Case.*

293 *Yankee Clipper* takeoff: NYT 5/21/39.

26: *DEPOSED (pages 294–304)*

294 *Fortune* March 1938; Yale degree: NYHT 6/24/37; *Look* 11/22/38; PAA annual report 1938.

294 "Up to the spring of 1939 . . .": Thomas Burke memo 1/9/40 (US/SD 811.796).

295 Bixby to CAL, 1/17/39 (CAL/YUL).

296 P.A.A. financial plight described in handwritten report from CVW to the President, 3/24/39 (FDR/PPF).

296 JTT told authors 6/7/77 that Edward Warner of the C.A.A. offered to use his influence to defer Pacific rights; Pan American Airways Company (of Delaware) Mail Rates, decided 6/30/39, Docket 202, 1 CAA 220; Pan American Airways Company (of Nevada) Mail Rates, decided 9/12/39, Docket 6-406 (A)-1, 1 CAA 385; PAA proxy statement 1939.

297 Minutes of the board of directors' meetings and change of bylaws, 3/14/39 (PAWA Legal Dept.); NYT 3/15/39.

297 "most qualified": CVW letter to MB, 12/8/76; "the board didn't feel": CVW to MB 5/24/76; "it didn't change anything": JTT to authors, 11/8/76.

298 Report of audit committee to board of directors, 11/14/39 (JTT/NASM); Whitney's office described to authors by Leuteritz, 6/8/78.

299 Memoranda from CVW, chairman, to JTT, president (JTT/NASM); Rihl's problem: Leuteritz to authors, 6/8/78, Althea Lister to MB, 10/26/78.

299 Lindbergh, *Wartime Journals* entry 5/23/39.

300 Letters and reports of the flight by passengers (JTT/NASM).

301 Draft of report from Chief of Naval Operations to the C.A.A., 10/6/39 (US/MM A21-5); Pacific losses reduced: PAA annual report 1939.

301 "like the deposed kings at Estoril": Benjamin Sonnenberg to authors, 7/26/77; Basil O'Connor to the President, 10/9/39, FDR memo to General Watson, 10/10/39 (FDR/PPF); report of audit committee, *op. cit.*, report of Allen R. Smart & Co., 9/5/39 (JTT/NASM).

302 PAA minutes of directors' meetings, 9/28/39, 1/9/40 (PAWA Legal Dept.); "ask Trippe": *Time* 2/5/40.

303 Press releases put out by Ted Ramsay for CVW, 10/18/40, 6/2/41 (NYT Morgue); Paley wanted to resign: William S. Paley to Donald West of *Broadcasting*, 10/18/76; "our paths don't cross": CVW to MB, 5/24/76.

PART IV: THE WAR YEARS

27: *COVER-UP (pages 307–319)*

Unless otherwise stated, State Dept. documents are from US/SD 821.796.

307   JTT ordered to replace German pilots: memorandum of conversation with JTT by Laurence Duggan, 3/17/39; JTT gives von Bauer a free hand: letters from von Bauer to JTT 9/16/33, 11/6/33 (JTT/NASM).

307   Iglehart letter to CVW, 11/29/38, and memorandum of agreement between W. R. Grace and P.A.A., 2/14/39, *Panagra Terminal Case*; JTT sells surplus planes to SCADTA: unmarked memorandum on SCADTA sent by Basil O'Connor to the President, 4/28/40 (FDR/PPF).

308   Letter with confidential information on SCADTA from JTT to Duggan, 3/30/39; von Bauer letter 11/6/33, *op. cit.*

308   Attaché's Report, Intelligence Division, Office of Chief of Naval Operations, Navy Dept., 3/29/37 (US/SD 821.796).

309   "We were suspicious": *Celler Hearings, op. cit.*; von Bauer to JTT 2/4/36 (JTT/NASM).

309   Root to FDR, 2/27/37; German pilots: James Wright memorandum of conversation with Evan Young, 7/26/39.

310   Spruille Braden, *Diplomats and Demagogues.*

311   Balluder to authors, 11/27/76; Braden dispatches 6/13/39, 6/26/39.

312   "hokus-pokus": Braden dispatch 9/12/39; Rihl memorandum on SCADTA, 10/31/39 (JTT/NASM).

313   Braden dispatch 10/27/39; Thomas Burke memorandum of conversation with JTT and CVW, 12/5/39; JTT's solution: memorandum of meeting with JTT and Rihl at the State Dept., 12/11/39.

313   "Mr. Trippe, perhaps": Braden dispatch 10/30/39; "This is most unusual": memorandum by Ellis Briggs, 12/15/39; Burke memorandum, 1/9/40.

314   F.B.I. report on Balluder, 6/12/40, sent to Assistant Secretary of State A. A. Berle, Jr. (US/SD 812.796); Duggan memo of conversation with JTT, 6/20/40, Duggan memo 7/1/40 (US/SD 810.796); Balluder to authors, 11/27/76; Ambassador waxing apoplectic: Braden, *Diplomats and Demagogues.*

315   O'Connor to FDR, 4/28/40, *op. cit.*

316   Memorandum of fact concerning the relations of P.A.A. with the Colombian airline SCADTA and its successor AVIANCA (PAWA Legal Dept.), Braden, *op. cit.*

316   Von Bauer contributes to Nazis: Duggan memo 10/1/40 (US/SD 810.796); not a Nazi: Balluder to authors, 11/27/76, BT to MB, 4/26/78.

317   Reorganization of SCADTA: "Reimbursement of PAA and Avianca for costs of the de-Germanization of AVIANCA": memorandum for the Secretary of War by Lt. Col. George A. Brownell, 6/3/42 (US/MM/SW); Duggan choleric: Duggan memo, 10/1/40, *op. cit.*; "Mr. Welles had no brief": Selden Chapin memo, 9/21/40 (US/SD 810.796).

318   Balluder transferred: PAA Executive System Memorandum No. 65, 9/15/42 (PAWA).

319   Rihl transfer: PAA Executive System Memorandum No. 79, 4/26/44 (PAWA).

28: THE MATTER OF AMERICAN EXPORT AIRLINES *(pages 320–328)*

320   *American Export Case*; Henry Friendly profile, NYT 3/10/59.

323   *Pan American Airways Co. v. Civil Aeronautics Board*, Circuit Court of Appeals, 2d Circuit, decided 7/16/41, 121 Federal Reporter 2d Series 810; *American Export Lines, Control of American Export Airlines*, decided 7/30/42, Docket 319, 3 CAB 619, rehearing decided 1/25/43.

323   Berle, *Navigating the Rapids, op. cit.*, 9/30/40.

324   Plain-paper memorandum, forwarded by President to Rockefeller 12/26/40; Rockefeller reply 12/30/40 (FDR/OF).

324   Berle, *op. cit.*, 3/5/41; NYT 2/11/41; NYT 3/12/41.

324   Hearings before the Subcommittee of the Committee on Appropriations on H.R. 3205, U.S. Senate, 77th Congress, 1st Session, March 1941.

325   NYT 3/25/41, 3/27/41; JTT to authors, 8/11/76, 5/25/78.

326   *Congressional Record*, May 5–7, 1941.

327   "The forces of good government": Josephson, *Saturday Evening Post, op. cit.*; "guardian of the public interest": *North Atlantic Route Transfer Case*.

29: MOBILIZING *(pages 329–341)*

329   Edward R. Stettinius, Jr., *Lend-Lease*.

329   The papers of Edward R. Stettinius, Jr. (ERS); "white-haired boy": *Time* 12/11/44.

330   Stettinius disqualified from P.A.A. matters: JTT to authors 8/11/76; ERS, Jr., memorandum to Arthur Whiteside, chairman Commercial Aircraft Priority Committee, 1/24/41; letter from JTT to ERS, Jr., 12/19/40 on T. V. Soong (ERS).

331   Stettinius and executive plane: letters to JTT 9/22/42, 6/16/43, 6/24/43 (ERS); Diaries of Henry L. Stimson, 7/25/40 (HLS/YUL).

331   FR/US 1946 Vol. 11, Provision of Military Assistance; historians might conclude: Forrest C. Pogue, *George C. Marshall: Ordeal and Hope*; in notes by Stettinius, Marshall is quoted as saying, "Remember those air bases in the Caribbean that we did through Pan American? Of course, we went in after the fall of Dunkirk and we went in and built Bases to protect us because after England's fall that would be our first line of defense. Now it is money down the sewer and we may be criticized for it." (Random notes on book, title *Lend-Lease*, ERS.)

331   War planners: memorandum for the Secretary of War from Robert A. Lovett, Assistant Secretary of War for Air, 7/29/44 (US/MM/SW); numerous entries in the Stimson diaries from September through November 1940 pertain to the secret contract (HLS/YUL); copies of the contract, amended contracts and numerous reports on same in US/MM/AG, US/MM/AAF, US/MM/SW and US/SD 810.796.

332   P.A.A. directors uninformed: JTT to authors 11/8/76; Berle, *op. cit.* 9/26/40; Burke memorandum to Welles and Duggan, 9/19/40 (US/SD 810.796).

332   Duggan memo to Berle and Welles, 12/27/40, "Panagra territory"; memo from Duggan to Welles, 6/20/40 (US/SD 810.796).

333   Tax indemnity: letter from Secretary of the Treasury to the Secretary of War, 11/25/41 (US/MM/AAF); "Emperor Juan T.": memorandum by W. N. Walmsley, Jr., Division of the American Republics, 9/22/41 (US/SD 810.796).

334   "Pan Air effrontery": Duggan memo 12/27/40; "nothing to be done": Berle memo 12/28/40 (US/SD 810.796).

334   Stimson diaries 10/15/41, 4/22/42 (HLS/YUL); Lovett memo, 7/29/44 *op. cit.*

335   JTT called to task: Secretary of War to JTT, 9/19/41 (US/MM/SW).

335   Authors' interviews with SP, 8/9/76, 10/18/76; "that utility public-relations fellow": Ingalls to SA, 9/29/76.

338   Cleansing the Latin American airways of the Axis presence: William A. M. Burden, *The Struggle for Airways in Latin America*; interview with Burden 7/12/76; *Celler Hearings*, Part I, Vol. 4; US/MM/AG; L. Welch Pogue letter to the Secretary of State 1/27/42 (US/SD 810.796).

341   P.A.A. "arrogant and unfriendly": Ambassador to Brazil William D. Pawley to Acting Secretary of State William L. Clayton, 9/10/46 (US/SD 711.322); *Latin American Rate Case*.

30: *AID TO BRITAIN (pages 342–354)*

342 "History of the Transatlantic": *op. cit.*

343 Sale of Boeings at Harry Hopkins' urging: notes dictated by E. R. Stettinius 8/11/43 (ERS); sale price, PAWA 40.03.00.

344 "vitally important mission": Stettinius to JTT, 7/13/40 (ERS); "Life Flies the Atlantic," *Life* 6/3/40.

344 The press flies the Clippers: *New Horizons* December 1941.

345 Kelly spurns bribes: David Bruce to authors, 10/1/77; readings of Nazi intentions: memo from Brigadier General Sherman Miles, 8/8/40 (US/MM/SW); from Lisbon to London: *New Horizons* November 1941, also JTT to authors, 8/11/76; and the diary of H. H. Arnold (HHA).

345 50 destroyers, Churchill's message of candor: Winston S. Churchill, *Their Finest Hour.*

346 Hopkins as "bookkeeper": Robert E. Sherwood, *op. cit.*, Stettinius, *op. cit.*; military chiefs in mufti: Deborah W. Ray, *Pan American Airways and the Trans-African Air Base Program of World War II.*

346 Hopkins assessment: Arnold, *Global Mission*; Stimson diaries, 3/4/41 (HLS/YUL); fragmentary route in Africa: Wesley Frank Craven and James Lea Cate, *The Army Air Forces in World War II, Vol. I, Plans and Early Operations.*

347 "700 miles of sheer nothingness": Air Marshal Sir Arthur Tedder quoted in Ray, *op. cit.*

347 *The Secret Diary of Harold L. Ickes, Vol. III, The Lowering Clouds*; Arnold to Stimson, 4/19/41, Lovett memoranda to Marshall 4/18/41, 4/26/41 about urgency of providing transport for British and U.S. officials, memoranda from Gross to Arnold, 5/10/41, Arnold to British liaison officer Tomlinson, 5/13/41, of phone conversation between Tomlinson and Gross, 5/16/41, of conversation between Tomlinson and Arnold, 5/15/41, of conversation between Tomlinson and Bixby, 5/16/41 asking to borrow P.A.A. crews to ferry 20 transports from Natal to Africa (HHA).

348 "can't return on the Italian airline": JTT memo to Arnold 5/16/41 (HHA); "motley group of airmen": *New Horizons* December 1942; June developments, Ray, *op. cit.*

349 According to Daley's account of JTT's meeting with Churchill, which was essentially the story Trippe told the authors on 8/11/76, he traveled to London with Arnold and watched the bombs falling on the city from the Dorchester Hotel roof. JTT said that British military chiefs attending his lecture asked him to solve the Middle East supply problem, that he told them the solution and later explained it to Churchill. BT and SP repeated parts of the same story to the authors, but nevertheless, it is flawed. According to Arnold's detailed diary and memoranda (HHA), the general was in London in April

349 during the second phase of the blitz (which had stopped by June) unaccompanied by JTT. Arnold did not attend the Wright lecture two months later. Moreover, a memorandum of 6/17/41, the day of the lecture, from Brigadier General Carl Spaatz for the Under Secretary of War, describes "contracts now under consideration between the British, the War Dept. and PAA" for a South Atlantic–trans-African transport and ferrying service. From other references in HHA, Ray, and Craven and Cate, it is clear that the supply program had been worked out by the British and U.S. Governments before JTT left for London. If he did see Churchill (as he told BT and SP as soon as he returned), it was to provide him with details of the plan and try to overcome the opposition from British quarters to P.A.A. encroachment on B.O.A.C.'s sphere of influence.

350 Memorandum of contracts drafted with P.A.A. under Lend-Lease and the President's Emergency Fund, 6/24/41, notes that P.A.A. could not sign until it obtained franchises from the British protectorates in Africa (HHA); memo for Arnold of minutes of meeting at War Dept. with British Mission and P.A.A., 6/26/41 (JS/MM/AAF); British–American friction: Ray, *op. cit.*

350 JTT loses his temper: Friendly to Oral History Project at Columbia University, 7/60 (PAWA 50.06.02); Marshall and Brazil, Arnold, *Global Mission* and Marshall memo, 3/6/41 (US/MM/SW); neutrality restrictions: Ray, *op. cit.*

351 Memorandum on contract with P.A.A., 10/8/41, from Lovett to the President on payments, 7/17/41 (US/MM/AAF); "this could be awkward": JTT to authors, 8/11/76; P.A.A. subsidiaries: Executive System Memoranda No. 58, 7/15/41, No. 59, 7/31/41 (PAWA).

352 NYT 8/19/41; *Pan American Airways, Inc. Acquisition of PAA-Africa Ltd.*, decided 8/28/41, Docket 640, 3 CAB 32; *Pan American Airways Company—Temporary Certificate of Public Convenience and Necessity, US–Africa Service*, decided 9/9/41, Docket 442, 3 CAB 47.

352 President Barclay believed: memorandum 12/31/41, "The Protection of Liberia" (US/MM/AG); Docket 442, *op. cit.*

353 Trans-African project: *New Horizons* January, March and May 1942, also Ray, *op. cit.*

354 JTT chats with Smith: James Smith to authors, 4/29/80.

31: *PAN AMERICAN GOES TO WAR*
(pages 355–368)

355 Kurusu's flight: *New Horizons* December 1941.

356 JTT on December 7, BT to MB 1/11/79; fate of the Clippers: *New Horizons* January 1942.

357 Bond and C.N.A.C.: *New Horizons* February 1942, Leary, *op. cit.*

358 Executive Order 8974, 12/13/41; letter from Stimson to Secretary of the Navy, 12/14/41, waiving power under executive order to take

358 over P.A.A.'s and American Export's flying boats except by mutual consent of Army and Navy (HHA); meeting at War Dept.: Craven and Cate, *op. cit.*

359 Gray's flight: Employees' Memories File (PAWA 30.10.08).

359 Craven and Cate, *op. cit.*

360 JTT's plan: undated memo believed written in 1941, for a single company handling air transport beyond the U.S. (PAWA 30.04.02), also undated memo (PAWA 50.20.02).

360 Draft of plan 11/17/41 for P.A.A. to sell $25 million preferred stock to government called for 15-year contract to operate overseas service, swallowing assets of American Export Airlines, and three government officials on board of directors (PAWA 30.04.02); Trippe's "divine call": Senator Josiah Bailey letter to Senator George Radcliffe, 7/24/45, *American Flag Hearings.*

361 Hopkins to Stettinius, 12/31/41 (US/LLA); Smith to authors, 4/28/80.

362 Misr pact: "History of the Transatlantic," *op. cit.*; Gledhill's assertion: Radiograms 763 and 764 from Cairo to Adjutant General, 2/4/42 (US/MM/AG).

362 Marshall letter to Louis Johnson, 7/8/42 (US/MM/AG); Liberia dispute: FR/US 1943, Vol. 4; Bixby's fear: Wartime Journals, 3/10/42; Johnson to Marshall, 6/9/42 (US/MM/AG).

363 Daley accepted JTT's word that Arnold had asked him to head the A.T.C., but the story is unverifiable and, in the opinion of the authors and sources like Harold Harris and James Smith, unlikely. In *Administrative History of the Ferrying Command, 29 May 1941– 30 June 1942,* Army Air Forces Historical Studies, No. 33, candidates for the top assignments are listed without any mention of JTT; details of A.T.C. contracts in memo from Arnold to Colonel George, 3/24/42, and "Report on Utilization of Transport Facilities of the Domestic Air Carriers by the Army Air Forces and Recommendation with Regard to Present Policy," 1/25/44 (HHA), also Craven and Cate, *op. cit.*, Vol. 1.

364 Ray, *op. cit.*; Smith to authors, 4/29/80; Executive System Memorandum No. 66, 10/21/42 (PAWA); C.N.A.C.'s exploits: Craven and Cate, *op. cit.*, Vol. VII, *Services Around the World.*

365 FDR flies to Casablanca: *New Horizons* January 1943.

365 PAA proxy statements and annual reports 1939 through 1945; BT letter to Stettinius, 3/16/42 (ERS).

366 BT tells children: Betsy Trippe Wainwright to author MB, 10/25/78; the house on F Street: SP to authors, 10/18/76, William McEvoy to SA, 6/13/77.

367 Pogue to SA, 12/15/76; Lindbergh Des Moines speech, 9/11/41; attempts to serve: 1/13/42, 1/15/42, 1/16/42, 1/17/42, 1/26/42, 2/1/42, 2/3/42; *Wartime Journals*; Stimson diaries 1/12/42 (HLS/ YUL).

368 "a government matter": JTT to SA, 6/7/77.

PART V: THE SHAPE OF THINGS TO COME

32: *THE OTHER WAR (pages 371–381)*

371   Remarks of Mr. Perkins in House of Commons debate 12/17/42, cited in extension of remarks of Clare Boothe Luce, 2/9/43 in the House of Representatives, *Congressional Record*; Berle, *Navigating the Rapids*, 9/29/40.

372   Arnold memo to General C. R. Smith, "Air Transport and Allied Problems," 1/18/43 (HHA); Captain Harold Balfour, House of Commons debate, *op. cit.*; Berle, *ibid.*

373   Lovett to George, 1/18/43 (US/MM/ASWA); Henry Wallace, "What We Will Get out of the War," *American Magazine*, March 1943; British opinion for internationalized air service, House of Commons debate, *ibid.*, Winant telegram 2/28/44 (FR/US 1944, Vol. 2); "there will always be wars": Josephson, *Empire of the Air.*

373   "They all talk of freedom of the air": *ibid.*

374   Race between Luce and JTT: Clare Luce to MB, 4/29/77; royal treatment: Clare Luce to MB, 10/19/77.

375   Dinner at Willkie's: SP to authors, 8/9/76.

375   Clare Luce to MB, 4/29/77; her Congressional debut: NYT 2/10/43, *Congressional Record*, House of Representatives, 2/9/43.

376   JTT speech: NYT 5/20/43.

377   Stettinius to JTT 5/20/43 (ERS); British anxiety: "The Future of Air Transport, A British View" by Peter Masefield, *Atlantic Monthly* January 1944; the U.S. aircraft industry was producing 85,000 planes a year compared with 3,715 units in 1939, and employing 1.6 million workers under more than $20 billion worth of government contracts: NYT 10/2/43.

377   *Time* 5/31/43; Critchley–Trippe meeting, testimony of Berle, JTT and Critchley in *North Atlantic Route Transfer Case*, reprinted in *Celler Hearings*, Part I, Vol. 4, Berle, *op. cit.*, 6/23/44.

378   Eden–Hull exchange, FR/US 1942, Vol. 4, p. 1866.

378   British planning: "Blueprint for World Civil Aviation," State Dept. Publication 2348, Conference Series 70, 1945; memo of meeting of Committee on International Aviation Policy, 4/29/43 (US/SD 800.796).

379   "This ocean has aroused": *McCarran Hearings*; overseas routes flown: *Time* 4/23/45, *American Aviation* 12/1/44.

379   Arnold meeting: *Time* 7/26/43; NYT 8/4/43.

380   Patterson's conduct: draft of letter to the C.A.B., July 1943, jointly signed by JTT and Patterson urged a "single enterprise" with which the domestic airlines were to have "the closest affiliations" (PAWA 30.04.02). No indication whether letter was sent. "a stooge for

380 Juan Trippe": Frank J. Taylor, *High Horizons*; United's forecast: NYT 10/5/43.

381 Airlines bombard C.A.B.: *Annual Report of the Civil Aeronautics Board 1943; American Airlines, Inc.—Temporary Certificate of Public Convenience and Necessity* (Mexico City Operation), decided 4/14/42, Docket 510, 3 CAB 418; *Caribbean Investigation*, decided 4/7/43, Docket 778, 4 CAB 199.

33: *ONWARD AND UPWARD TO CHICAGO*
(pages 382–398)

382 Hull–Welles feud: *Memoirs of Cordell Hull*, Vol. II, Dean Acheson, *Present at the Creation*; Stettinius appointment: *Time* 12/11/44; joint statement: *Annual Report of the CAB 1943, op. cit.*, NYT 10/16/43; memorandum of conversation (Berle) 11/11/43, FR/US 1944, Vol. 2, *op. cit.*

383 Point One: The International Civil Aviation Conference held in Chicago in November 1944 abstained from deciding whether the Axis nations should be allowed to engage in commercial aviation. Subsequently, the International Civil Aviation Organization (I.C.A.O.) established by the conference admitted ex-Axis states by four-fifths vote of its assembly and the assent of any nation attacked by the state seeking admission. (Memorandum of ICAO, the Story of the International Civil Aviation Organization, Montreal, May 1951.); account of meeting with FDR: Pogue to SA 12/15/76, 1/19/79: FDR to a senator, FDR meeting with Bennett (Champ) Clark: memorandum of conversation (Berle) 6/10/44, FR/US 1944, Vol. 2, *op. cit.*

384 Stettinius telegram to Winant, 2/17/44, memoranda of conversations (Berle) 2/3/44, 2/23/44 (FR/US 1944, Vol. 2); "for many years to come": Sir Lindsay Everard, House of Commons debate, *op. cit.*

384 Old World tradition of monopoly: Berle "Freedoms of the Air," *Harper's Magazine* March 1945; Hull a free-trader: *Memoirs of Cordell Hull*, Vol. I; British dread: Winant telegram 2/28/44 *ibid.*; Berle positions: memorandum of statement to Canadian Minister Counselor Pearson, 3/24/44, *ibid.*; Berle report on air conversations in London, 4/19/44, *ibid.*

385 Meetings with Soviet delegation: Berle to British Embassy Counselor Wright, 6/29/44, memorandum of conversation (Berle) 8/2/44; (FR/US 1944, Vol. 2).

386 Chinese cooperative: memorandum of conversation (Grew) 6/10/44, memorandum of conversation (Berle) 6/20/44, *ibid.*

386 Berle preferred to postpone: Hull telegram to Winant, 8/21/44; Beaverbrook telegram to Berle, 8/29/44; memorandum of conversation (Berle) with FDR, 9/9/44; State Dept. invitation: 9/11/44, *ibid.*

387 Soviet note: Stettinius telegram to Kennan, 10/26/44 (FR/US 1944, Vol. 2); reports on Swinton: memorandum of conversation (Berle) 10/9/44, *ibid.*; Chicago conference, NYT 1/12/44, 11/3/44.

388   Four "freedoms": memorandum by J. D. Walstrom, 4/1/44, FR/US 1944, Vol. 2; fifth freedom: W. A. Burden, "Opening the Sky: American Proposals at Chicago," *Atlantic Monthly* March 1945.

388   Winant telegram on British White Paper, 10/21/44, FR/US 1944, Vol. 2; Berle, *Navigating the Rapids*, 11/18/44.

389   British relent: NYT 11/25/44, 11/27/44, 11/28/44, Berle to FDR, 11/29/44.

389   "We are doing our best": FDR telegram to Winant with message for Churchill, 11/24/44; "great anxiety": Churchill message to FDR, 11/28/44 (FR/US 1944, Vol. II).

390   Stettinius reorganization: *Time* 12/11/44, Acheson, *op. cit.*; "Ed felt a little guilty": *Navigating the Rapids*, 12/28/44.

391   FDR to Churchill, 11/30/44, FR/US 1944, Vol. 2.

392   Berle report to President on conference, 12/7/44, *ibid.*, NYT 12/2/44, 12/3/44; *Final Act and Related Documents of the International Civil Aviation Conference, November 1 to December 7, 1944*, Dept. of State Publication 2282, Conference Series 64.

392   "We met in an era": NYT 12/8/44.

393   Doubts in Congress: NYT 12/21/44; Brewster stirred his colleagues: NYT 3/13/45; *McCarran Hearings*.

394   NYT 6/8/45.

394   H. A. Wassenbergh, *Post-War International Civil Aviation Policy and the Law of the Air.*

395   James Smith to authors, 6/6/80; *IATA Traffic Conference Resolution* approved 2/19/46, 6 CAB 639; State Dept. endorses I.A.T.A.: Clayton to Bailey, 2/22/45 (US/SD 811.796).

395   NYT 10/17/45; fare a "sure loser": Willis Lipscomb to SA, 6/5/80; "His Majesty's Government": Masefield to Morgan, 11/24/45, *Celler Hearings*, Part I, Vol. 4; French action: NYT 2/15/46.

396   Bermuda Conference: *Time* 2/11/46, FR/US 1946, Vol. 1; British loan: NYT 1/22/46.

397   C.A.B.'s missing authority over international fares: *Magnuson Hearings, Harris Hearings.*

398   Lee dissent, 6 CAB 638.

398   "a noble effort": *Time* 8/5/46; consequences of Bermuda: "A New Takeoff for International Air Transport" by Andreas F. Lowenfeld, *Foreign Affairs* October 1975; *Magnuson Hearings.*

34:   CHOSEN INSTRUMENT (pages 399–414)

399   Isaiah Berlin, *The Hedgehog and the Fox.*

400   Berle, *Navigating the Rapids*, 6/23/44; "as Britannia ruled": *McCarran Hearings.*

401   "filmy, seductive allure": C. Bedell Monro, president of Pennsylvania Central Airlines, *Time* 8/23/43. In September 1943, JTT drafted a pamphlet entitled "Plan for the Consolidation of All American-Flag Overseas and Foreign Air Transport Operations" in which he urged the United States to emulate other nations which concentrated on "chosen instrument" airlines (PAWA 30.04.02). He often referred to P.A.A. as an "instrument of U.S. policy," and the 1941 memorandum (see Chapter 33) for a single company alludes to P.A.A. services as "an instrument for the furtherance of the national interest and the national defense." Balluder told a pilot–management seminar in 1954, "Our government looked upon us as the standard bearers, as the chosen ones . . .'"

403   Letter from the Attorney General of the U.S. transmitted to the House of Representatives 2/28/45 including *Report by the Attorney General on International Air Transport Policy*; Forrestal to Bailey, 12/11/44.

403   Hull to Bailey, 8/18/44 (US/SD 811.796); Brewster bent on stopping Senate ratification: NYT 3/3/45, 3/13/45; *North Atlantic Route Case*.

404   *Domestic Route Case*; *McCarran Hearings*.

405   "Trippe the only candidate": *Time* 5/14/45.

405   State Dept. troubled: Morgan to Acheson 2/20/45 (US/SD 811.796).

407   Commerce Committee takes up bill: *Time* 7/9/45, NYT 7/7/45.

407   "same old coon": Bailey to Senator Bilbo, 7/24/45; no legislative power: Bailey to Senator Radcliffe, 7/24/45, reprinted in *Chosen Instrument Hearings*; Brewster admitted he had ridden in the P.A.A. plane in 1947 Senate hearings (NYT 8/8/47), and SP verified this to authors, 11/19/76; Senate Report 805, 79th Congress, 1st Session, together with minority reviews, reprinted in *Chosen Instrument Hearings*.

408   Truman at Key West: William McEvoy to SA, 6/13/77.

408   "implementing Trippe's brain": SP to authors, 8/9/76; Stettinius was replaced—in *Memoirs, Vol. I, Years of Decision*, Truman said he was troubled by having as Secretary of State (then the next in line to succeed him) someone who had never stood for elective office, and he replaced Stettinius with James J. Byrnes of South Carolina, who had served in both the House and the Senate; international certificates to domestic carriers: *Hawaiian Case*.

409   *Pacific Case*; *Added Latin American Case*.

409   JTT's goal not politically realizable: David Bruce to authors, 10/1/77; Sonnenberg to authors, 7/26/77; Morgan and Colt act: *Time* 7/29/46.

411   SP to authors, 11/19/76.

411   James Landis described to authors by his associate Stanley Gewirtz, 11/10/77, 8/17/78; Landis obituary, NYT 7/31/64.

412   JTT and the C.A.B.: Irving Roth to the authors, 12/13/78.

413   "Taft is the man you want to see": James T. Patterson, *Mr. Republican*; Ingalls to SA, 9/29/76.

414   Owen Brewster biography, *United Press* 12/28/50, NYT 6/22/52, obituary, NYT 12/26/61.

35: *HOWARD HUGHES VERSUS OWEN BREWSTER (pages 415–429)*

415   Noah Dietrich, *Howard: The Amazing Mr. Hughes.*

416   Hughes entertains: *Time* 8/18/47; report of Edward T. Stodolo, Examiner, *TWA–Hughes Tool Company Investigation.*

417   Brewster to Landis, memorandum from Garrison Norton to William Clayton, 1/10/47 (US/SD 811.796).

417   Norton memo, *ibid.*, testimony of JTT, Dietrich and Palmer Bradley in *North Atlantic Route Transfer Case*, and Hughes testimony before Senate investigating committee, NYT 8/7/47, 8/8/47.

421   *Chosen Instrument Hearings.*

423   Round-the-world trip: NYT 6/18/47, 7/1/47; Althea Lister to MB, 9/26/78.

424   "a querulous old lady": Betsy Wainwright to MB 10/25/78; Lucy Trippe's sole bequest to Juan was her cooperative apartment on Park Avenue, valued at $19,000; his children received contingent interests in the Bradlee trusts (New York County Surrogate's Court).

424   Hughes before the Senate: NYT 8/7/47, 8/8/47, 8/10/47, *Time* and *NW* 8/18/47, Dietrich, *op. cit.*

428   Senator Ferguson's hearings in November: NYT 11/7/47, 11/16/47, 11/23/47, 12/15/47, 2/26/48, 4/25/48, 5/18/48; Tom Clark appoints prosecutor: *NY Evening Post*, 12/3/47, *Aviation Week*, 1/26/48; SP showed the authors on 11/19/76 letters of appreciation from Clark dated 1/3/51 and 2/16/51.

428   Brewster as red-baiter: NYT 10/4/51, 12/26/61 (obituary); Grunewald story, NYT 4/19/53, *Time* 12/31/51, 3/31/52; Brewster defeated: NYT 6/18/52, 6/22/52; Hughes helps defeat him: Dietrich, *op. cit.*

429   SP to authors, 8/9/76. On 11/19/76, SP told the authors he blamed JTT for sending Brewster in the B-23 to see Bailey about the community-company bill. "I always chartered a separate plane," he said. "I would never send a Senator in a company plane." Albert Ueltschi, the pilot, 12/9/76, and William McEvoy, 6/13/77, assistant vice president of P.A.A. in Washington in those years, confirmed that Brewster was a frequent passenger in the B-23. Willis Player told the authors on 8/7/80 that JTT said it was a mistake for him to have seen Hughes alone in California.

PART VI: THE WORLD'S MOST EXPERIENCED
AIRLINE

36: *THE STRANGE CASE OF A.O.A. (pages 433–445)*

Principal sources are the exhibits in the *North Atlantic Route Transfer Case*, the Official File in the Papers of Harry S Truman, and interviews with JTT (8/11/76, 11/8/76, 6/7/77), SP (8/9/76, 11/19/76, 11/21/76), C. R. Smith (2/4/77), Stanley Gewirtz (11/10/77), Charles S. Murphy (8/16/77), Tom Wrenn (12/7/78) and William Kennedy (10/27/77).

434 Landis dissent in *United Air Lines, Inc.–Western Air Lines, Inc., Acquisition of Air Carrier Property*, decided 8/25/47, Docket 2839, 8 CAB 325; Landis censures P.A.A.: NYT 1/3/48; *Domestic Route Case*.

435 President's Air Coordinating Committee Report, NYT 8/19/47; Finletter Report, NYT 1/14/48.

436 Truman fires Landis: NYT 1/1/48, 1/3/48; "a bull who carried his own china shop": Louis Johnson obituary, NYT 4/25/66.

436 "a gone goose": Robert J. Donovan, *Conflict and Crisis*.

437 Merger attempts: memorandum on acquisition of Company X, 4/22/48; Ferguson memorandum to JTT on merger with U.A.L. or T.W.A., 5/20/48 (JTT/NASM).

437 C. R. Smith profiles, American Airlines *Flagship News* 4/25/66, *Time* 11/17/58; "you knew exactly where you stood": Lipscomb to authors, 4/14/80.

441 Truman appoints McGrath, NYT 8/2/49; McGrath obituary, NYT 9/3/66.

441 Wrenn's report: *Time* 1/2/50; exceptions filed: NW 1/16/50.

445 James Smith to authors, 4/28/80.

445 *Domestic Route Case*; C.A.B.'s frame of mind: Alan Boyd to authors, 7/9/80.

37: *HIGH FINANCE* (pages 446–454)

Principal sources are "Not So Common," an article on the Odlum financing in *Fortune* October 1945, and an interview SA had with Herman Kahn, a partner in Lehman Brothers, on 3/10/80.

446 James Smith to authors, 4/28/80.

447 Capital needs in postwar aviation: NYT 11/5/44, *Time* 12/18/44.

447 Floyd Odlum profiles: *Fortune* September 1935, *The New Yorker* 8/26/33, BW 5/10/33, 5/27/44, NYT 1/28/73, obituary NYT 6/18/76.

448 The deal is set forth in the PAA Annual Report 1944.

450 Agreement signed: NYT 12/6/44; directors' meeting: undated memo of conversation between JTT and Langewiesche (PAWA 30.08.00); Lehman's background: Marylin Bender, *At the Top* (Doubleday & Company, Garden City, N.Y., 1975).

452 Elisha Walker: obituary NYT 11/10/50; agreement terminated: NYT 6/29/45.

452   New underwriting a sellout: NYT 7/25/45; Odlum explains to Atlas shareholders: NYT 8/7/45.

453   PAWA annual reports, 1946, 1949.

454   Ferguson castigated: James Montgomery to SA, 5/28/80; Willis Player to authors, 11/17/77.

38: *MANAGING IN THE FIFTIES*
(pages 455–466)

Principal sources were interviews with Hugo Leuteritz (7/8/78), Roger Lewis (5/10/76, 11/17/76, 5/25/78, 6/19/78), Willis Player (11/15/76, 4/13/78, 7/1/80), Willis Lipscomb (9/7/77, 4/14/80), Erwin Balluder (11/27/76) and Samuel Pryor (11/19/76).

455   PAA Executive System Memorandum No. 86, 9/28/45 (PAWA).

456   John Leslie, testimony in *Celler Hearings*; Leslie told SA 12/7/77 how JTT treated him during his illness.

457   JTT recruits Lewis, *Celler Hearings*.

460   Letters from JTT to CAL, 12/5/47, 4/9/53, 11/2/53; CAL to JTT, 6/17/53; R. J. Forhan to CAL, 6/26/53, Edwin Sippel to CAL, 6/30/53; CAL to Gray, 9/11/56 (CAL/YUL).

460   Lindbergh a nomad: Willis Player memoir in *Clipper* May 1977.

461   Betsy Wainwright to MB, 10/25/78; Marcia E. Miller to MB, 6/24/80.

461   Gerry O'Donnell to authors, 9/22/79.

462   Interview with Ona Cooper, Priester's secretary (PAWA 50.16.02); PAWA organization chart, September 1954, *Celler Hearings*; Priester died 11/28/55 in Paris while attending a meeting of the I.A.T.A. technical committee.

463   JTT testimony, *Celler Hearings*.

463   "Is he there?": Doris Player to authors, 11/15/76; taking 45: Ingalls to SA, 9/29/76; Elly Lewis to authors, 11/17/76.

463   Executive pay, comparative listing of salaries of JTT, SP and Lipscomb from 1927 to 1965 (JTT/NASM); stock options for 1953 (*Celler Hearings*).

464   W. Lloyd Warner and James Abegglen, *Big Business Leaders in America.*

465   BT to MB, 6/7/77.

466   BT to MB, 1/13/78.

39: *THE JET AGE (pages 467–476)*

Major sources are the files on jet procurement (PAWA 30.07.18, 50.20.07); Douglas J. Ingells, *747: The Story of the Boeing Super Jet;*

"The Selling of the 707," *Fortune* October 1957; SA's interviews with William Allen, 4/29/76 and with JTT, 8/11/76 and 5/25/78.

467   JTT orders Comets: *Time* 10/27/52; *Life* 1/25/54.

468   British jet developments: Arnold, *Global Mission*.

469   Unlucky Comet: *Time* 5/10/54; "Jet Transports: Why U.S. Holds Back," BW 4/18/53; Boeing specifications: *Time* 7/6/53; C. R. Smith: NYT 4/30/53.

471   Donald Douglas profiles, *Time* 11/22/43, NW 3/5/76.

472   PAWA Annual Report 1955; Talbott relented: Boeing Airplane Company press release, 7/13/55; American orders Electras: NYT 6/9/55.

473   J-75 a secret: NW 3/8/54.

473   Rentschler profiles, *Time* 5/28/51, obituary NYT 4/26/56, William Gwinn to SA, 4/17/78.

475   WSJ 10/14/55.

476   Advent of the jet age: NW 3/5/56; subsidy removed: PAWA Annual Report 1956.

40: *INTELLIGENCE* (pages 477–484)

This chapter is based on material in the *Church Report, Book I*; Lyman Kirkpatrick, Jr., *The Real CIA*; "The CIA's Corporate Shell Game" by John Marks in *The Washington Post*, 7/11/76, and on interviews with SP (11/19/76); G. Erskine Rice, a PAWA vice president in charge of technical assistance programs (11/3/77); Lawrence R. Houston, former general counsel of the C.I.A. (6/16/80) and George Doole (6/17/80). A retired C.I.A. operative, formerly based in Panama, requested anonymity.

478   Boyd to authors, 7/9/80; Gerry O'Donnell to authors, 9/22/79.

478   Telegram about Trujillo mistress, 2/21/49 (US/SD 810.796).

479   Whitney and Meek; NYT 12/26/77.

481   JTT sells M.E.A.: Balluder to authors, 11/21/77; American airline for Afghanistan: memorandum of conversations (Division of Middle Eastern Affairs) with George Doole 2/20/46, US/SD 812.796; memorandum from L. W. Henderson to Armour, 11/10/47, Allen telegram on airline running through Ankara, Teheran and Kabul, 9/19/46 (US/SD 811.796).

482   Soviets invited Pan Am: *Celler Hearings*.

483   "smoothest operator": William A. M. Burden to authors, 7/12/76; Loginov meeting: Lewis to authors, 5/10/76, 4/14/80.

483   JTT in Moscow: Player to authors, 8/7/80.

484   Agreement signed: NYT 11/5/66.

41: *IN THE MONEY* *(pages 485–488)*

485 McDonnell's and Lehman's statement to the board of directors, undated and unsigned (JTT/NASM).

486 Eleuthera investment: *The Nutmegger* July 1968 (a magazine published in Greenwich, Connecticut), Ingalls to SA 9/29/76, William W. Wolbach letter to MB 7/30/79 and interview with SA 9/12/79.

486 "Sky-High Deal for a Skyscraper," *Fortune* December 1960.

487 Lease terms: prospectus 1/8/60 PAWA Inc. 4⅝% convertible subordinated debentures.

488 Critics: *Time* 3/15/63, *NYT* 4/7/63.

42: *THE SUCCESSION* *(pages 489–499)*

489 Lewis recounted his resignation to authors, 12/7/77, 5/25/78.

490 Rogers on chosen instrument: Lewis to authors, 11/17/76; Friendly to Leslie 6/8/73 (PAWA 50.06.02); Lewis to SA 5/10/76.

490 "coming right through the wall": *Time* 3/28/49; Boyd to authors, 7/9/80.

492 Kennedy aviation policy: *Aviation Week* 2/11/63; Pan Am's arrogance: WSJ 1/10/79, Player to authors 1/10/79.

492 *Celler Hearings*; *Celler Report*.

493 *U.S. v. Pan American World Airways, Inc., W. R. Grace and Company, and Pan American–Grace Airways, Inc.*, Civ. 90-259, *Aviation Week* 1/25/54.

493 JTT forbade P.A.A. directors: Roig memorandum to Rihl 7/3/41 (JTT/NASM); *Panagra Terminal Case*; BW 3/30/57; *Pan American World Airways, Inc. v. United States*, 371 U.S. 296.

494 JTT offered Grace $10.6 million: WSJ 4/19/63; C.A.B. press release, 7/17/63; in 1966, JTT and Grace sold Panagra to Braniff for $30 million, reaping for Pan Am a net profit of $11.8 million on its 50% stock investment (PAWA Annual Report 1966); cruelty to Gledhill: Lewis to authors 11/17/76; SP to authors, 8/9/76.

494 Thomas Flanagan to authors, 4/17/78; Player to authors, 4/13/78.

495 Yale Corporation meetings: Harold Howe to authors, 10/18/78; Reuben Holden to MB, 11/28/78.

495 Football Hall of Fame, NYT 9/14/65, JTT to authors, 9/22/76; "so devious": Ingalls to SA 9/29/76.

496 Gray tinkering: ExaBell Gray to authors, 11/11/77; Player to authors about Gray, 11/15/76, 7/20/77, 11/17/77; introduction to Halaby:

496   Lewis to SA, 8/15/79; Najeeb E. Halaby, *Crosswinds: An Airman's Memoir.*

498   PAWA proxy statements 1966, 1967.

498   "he could have a chance": Player to authors 7/20/77; Ingalls to SA, 9/29/76; Betsy Wainwright to MB, 10/25/78.

43:   THE 747 *(pages 500–507)*

Primary sources were Laurence S. Kuter, *The Great Gamble: The Boeing 747*, Ingells, *op. cit.*, Halaby, *op. cit.* and SA interviews with William Allen, 4/29/76, and JTT 7/15/76.

500   Utopia: unsent letter from CAL to JTT, 7/3/65 (CAL/YUL).

501   "It looks hopeful": CAL to JTT, 1/17/62; "disturbed": CAL to JTT, 5/12/63 (CAL/YUL); "if I had to choose": CAL, "Is Civilization Progress?" *Reader's Digest* July 1964.

501   "too many elements in flux": CAL to JTT, 12/10/65 (CAL/YUL).

503   Letter of intent: 12/22/65 (CAL/YUL).

503   A niggard at breakfast: William McEvoy to SA, 6/13/77.

504   PAWA proxy statement 1966.

505   Balance of payments: PAWA press release 4/13/66; NYT 10/21/66.

507   Financing: PAWA Annual Report 1966, prospectus 8/10/66 PAWA, Inc., $175 million 4½% convertible subordinated debentures.

44:   THE LAST WORD *(pages 508–514)*

508   Player to authors, 11/17/77.

508   "do the right thing": BT to MB, 1/13/78; Kuter, *op. cit.*

511   Gray's secret: Player to authors, 7/20/77, 7/17/80.

512   The board's view of Halaby: Ingalls to SA, 9/29/76; "What difference does it make?": Lipscomb to authors, 9/7/77; BT to MB 9/22/76, 6/7/77; Halaby, *op. cit.*

512   JTT and the annual meeting: Player to authors, 7/20/77, 5/7/78, 1/10/79, 7/17/80.

513   Annual meeting: NYT 5/8/68, *Time* 5/17/68, PAWA report of the 40th annual meeting; PAWA Annual Report 1967.

513   Agenda for the board meeting (CAL/YUL); "You can have my desk": Daley, *op. cit.*; Gray removes desk: NYT 5/19/68.

EPILOGUE (pages 515–525)

515   Gray, as chairman and chief executive officer, announced the exercise of the option (PAWA press release 12/3/69). In *Crosswinds*, Halaby wrote, "He [Gray] asked his brand-new president for his concurrence, and I gave it," but on 3/25/80 he told SA that Gray casually mentioned his impending decision when they met in an office corridor; Bluhdorn-Crosby buying: *Forbes* 12/1/68, *Time* 3/21/69.

516   "Pan Am Finds the Going's Not Great," BW 10/11/69; Gray struggles: Player to authors, 7/20/77, 11/17/77; "shrinking box": *Fortune* January 1970.

517   Halaby, *op. cit.*; 747 in recession: NYT 4/9/72.

518   United Aircraft Annual Report 1970; JTT to MB in interview for NYT article, *ibid.*

518   Halaby acts: *Aviation Week* 6/1/71, WSJ 10/5/71, *Fortune* January 1972.

518   Use of psychologists: NYT 4/3/77, Montgomery to authors, 10/24/78.

519   "I made a mistake": Player to authors, 7/20/77.

520   Pan Am and Iran: Player to authors, 1/10/79, Selig Altschul "Freewheeling Carrier," *Barrons* 8/23/76.

521   Contingency plans for bankruptcy: Player to authors, 8/7/80.

522   "talk to Juan": SP to authors, 11/19/76; "goddamn apes": Player to authors, 12/20/77.

523   CAL's death, NYT 8/27/74; burial plot: SP to authors, 8/9/76; Eleuthera project: Ingalls to SA, 9/29/76.

523   Rehabilitation of Eleuthera: William Wolbach to SA, 9/12/79.

524   Sale of Pan Am Building: NYT 7/29/80; PAWA Annual Report 1980.

525   The authors attended the funeral.

Index